Information Systems Concepts for Management

McGraw-Hill Series in Management Information Systems

Gordon B. Davis, *Consulting Editor*

Davis: Management Information Systems: Conceptual Foundations, Structure, and Development
Davis and Everest: Readings in Management Information Systems
Lucas: The Analysis, Design, and Implementation of Information Systems
Lucas: Information Systems Concepts for Management
Lucas and Gibson: A Casebook for Management Information Systems
Weber: EDP Auditing: Conceptual Foundations and Practice

Information Systems Concepts for Management

Second Edition

Henry C. Lucas, Jr.
Schools of Business
New York University

McGraw-Hill Book Company
New York St. Louis San Francisco Auckland Bogotá
Hamburg Johannesburg London Madrid Mexico Montreal New Delhi
Panama Paris São Paulo Singapore Sydney Tokyo Toronto

This book was set in Times Roman by The Total Book (ECU/BD).
The editor was James E. Vastyan;
the production supervisor was Diane Renda.

INFORMATION SYSTEMS CONCEPTS FOR MANAGEMENT

234567890 HDHD 898765432

ISBN 0-07-038924-1

See Acknowledgments on pp. xi–xii. Copyrights included on this page by reference.

Library of Congress Cataloging in Publication Data

Lucas, Henry C.
    Information systems concepts for management.

    (McGraw-Hill series in management infor-
mation systems)
    Includes index.
    1. Management information systems.
I. Title. II. Series.
T58.6.L815 1982   658.4'0388   81-8233
ISBN 0-07-038924-1   AACR2

To Jonathan

Contents

Preface   ix
Acknowledgments   xi

PART 1 MANAGERS AND INFORMATION

1 The Information Systems Field   3
2 The Nature of Information and Decision Making   19
3 Frameworks for Information Systems   39
4 An Overview of Computer-Based Information Systems   53

PART 2 ORGANIZATIONAL ISSUES

5 The Impact of Information Systems on the Organization   65
6 Top Management and Information Systems   83

PART 3 COMPUTER TECHNOLOGY

7 Fundamentals of Computer Equipment   109
8 Computer Software   155
9 Computer Files, Data Structures, and Data Bases   203
10 Future Trends   241
11 System Alternatives and Acquisition   265

PART 4 SYSTEMS ANALYSIS AND DESIGN

12 Introduction and Overview   289
13 Inception through Specifications   325
14 Programming through Installation   359
15 Project Management   375
16 Successful Implementation   385

PART 5 EXAMPLES OF INFORMATION SYSTEMS

17 General Information Systems   403
18 Decision Support Systems   441

PART 6 SPECIAL MANAGEMENT CONCERNS

19 Information Systems Issues for Management   461
20 Societal Implications   479

Glossary   494
Index   509

Preface

The purpose of this book is to help students of management learn the concepts of computer-based information systems. Managers allocate resources to the development and operation of computer-based systems and often use systems themselves. Managers make critical decisions about information systems: What applications areas are to be emphasized? What should a plan for information processing in the organization contain? Which specific alternative for a proposed system will be implemented? What equipment should the organization acquire? How should one charge for and monitor information processing?

Many managers are users of information systems and work directly with computer input and/or output: they may also supervise people who work with information systems. These individuals also come in contact with colleagues in the computer department, and the information services department reports to a manager in the organization.

Thus, the modern manager is confronted with many information-systems-related decisions and must understand issues in the management of information systems. This text is written from the perspective of the student who will be a user of information systems: It is not intended for the student who specializes in computer-based systems.

The text has been developed from M.B.A. courses at Stanford and New York University. The students viewed these courses as their only exposure to computer-based information systems. One of the main goals of the book, therefore, is to help students majoring in such functional areas as finance, accounting, or marketing learn to make intelligent decisions about information systems and computers. No background on the part of the student is assumed, though it would be helpful to have written at least one program in a language such as BASIC or FORTRAN. In most instances, the student can function with no further technical knowledge than that contained in the text and its recommended readings; however, the student should also learn from the text when additional expertise is required.

Cases can be used to supplement the text and to show how to apply the reading material. We have also used videotapes and computer demonstrations in class to illustrate the points raised in cases and the text.

Specific questions and problems may be found at the end of each chapter along with key words and recommended readings. Throughout the chapters themselves there is a series of management problems. These problems describe a situation in brief and ask the reader to suggest a solution. The management problems attempt to illustrate how the material in each chapter relates to a managerially oriented decision. The problems should help the student appreciate that a manager needs to have some grasp of technical issues in order to make decisions about information systems.

This edition also contains a series of brief applications descriptions. These examples show the variety of ways computer-based systems have been used to support decisions, control the organization, and process transactions. The applications are intended to help the student become more creative in using information systems for problem solving.

The ultimate goal of the book, then, is to help the reader use information technology to become a more effective manager and decisionmaker.

I am indebted to my students and colleagues whose suggestions have helped shape the contents of the book, in particular to Nicholas Markoff and Jack Baroudi who conducted some of the research required to revise the original edition. Professor Jon Turner provided a number of useful suggestions from his experience using the text. Most important, I acknowledge the invaluable support of my wife, Ellen. She continues to provide insightful editorial advice on the manuscript while creating an environment which makes the development of the text possible.

Henry C. Lucas, Jr.

Acknowledgments

I acknowledge the permission of the following publishers to include the material described below in the text:

Columbia University Press for Figure 2-1 from H. C. Lucas, Jr., *Why Information Systems Fail,* 1975.

The editors of *INFOR* for Tables 1, 2, and 3 from H. C. Lucas, Jr. and J. R. Moore, "A Multiple-Criterion Scoring Approach to Information System Project Selection," February 1976.

The Institute of Management Sciences for Figure 1 from W. F. Hamilton and M. A. Moses, "A Computer-based Corporate Planning System," *Management Science,* October 1974.

The editors of the *IBM Systems Journal* for Figure 3 and Table 1 from J. H. Wimbrow, "A Large-Scale Interactive Administrative System," 1971.

Osborne/McGraw-Hill for Figure 7-6 from An Introduction to *Micro Computers* vol. 1, 2d. ed., A. Osborne.

Scientific American for Figure 7-3 from "Microelectronic Memories" by O. Hodges, September, 1977.

McGraw-Hill for Figure 7-7 from T. C. Bartee, *Digital Computer Fundamentals,* 4th ed., 1977; Figure 3-17 from R. W. Watson, *Timesharing System Design Concepts,* 1970; Figure 11-5 from G. Davis, *Computer Data Processing,*

2d ed., 1973; Figure 18-12 from G. Davis, *Introduction to Computers*, 3d ed., 1977; Figures 20-1 and 20-4 from N. Nie et al., *Statistical Package for the Social Sciences*, 2d ed., 1975; Figure 8.3-1 from W. Cole, *Introduction to Computing*, 1969; Figure 8-3 from G. Bell and A. Newell, *Computer Structures: Readings and Examples*, 1971; and Figure 2-11.1 from H. Hellerman and I. Smith, *APL 360: Programming and Applications*, 1976.

Some of the material on managerial activities, computer files, vendor selection, systems analysis and design, project management, conversion and installation of systems, social issues, and the Hardserve example is taken from my earlier McGraw-Hill book, *The Analysis, Design, and Implementation of Information Systems* (2d ed.). Interested readers should consult this text for more details.

Part One

Managers and Information

In the first part of the text, we introduce the concept of information and define an information system. What is the nature of information? How are data interpreted by each individual and organization to become information? We examine decision making in some detail because one objective of an information system is to provide information to support decision making. Emphasis is placed on distinguishing among different types of decisions and their information requirements. With this background, we can examine frameworks for information systems—frameworks that provide a conceptual model to aid in the design of systems. Part One concludes with a scenario showing the wide variety of computer-based information systems existing today.

OVERVIEW
THE HISTORICAL EVOLUTION OF COMPUTERS
INFORMATION SYSTEMS
THE ORGANIZATION AS AN INFORMATION PROCESSING
ENTITY
THE INTERDISCIPLINARY NATURE OF THE FIELD
PREVIEW
KEY WORDS
RECOMMENDED READINGS
DISCUSSION QUESTIONS

Chapter 1

The Information Systems Field

CHAPTER ISSUES

- What information is critical for the organization?
- What are the key decision areas for users and management involvement in information systems activities?

During the past two decades, the number of computer-based information systems in private- and public-sector organizations has grown exponentially. A new computer products and services industry has developed to supply the tools necessary to build computer-based information systems. A substantial number of individuals who design, build, and operate computer-based information systems now classify themselves as computer professionals.

Although a large number of people are employed to design and operate information systems, many more individuals are involved as users or "consumers" of information systems. Users include individuals from a broad spectrum of occupations, ranging from workers in a factory to the top management of a corporation. Use of an information system includes the receipt of a report, the submission of input for a system, and the operation of a terminal or a similar activity. In addition to work experiences with computer-based information systems, most individuals encounter these systems in other activities. Credit card users, travelers making reservations, social security recipients, and many others confront computer-based systems directly or indirectly.

In today's complex society, a knowledge of computer-based information systems is vital for an educated individual, particularly for the professional manager. It has been estimated that one-third to one-half of the current gross national product of the United States is currently attributable to the production and distribution of information. This trend is a departure from a traditional economy based on the production and distribution of tangible goods; the United States is entering an "Information Age." For most organizations—in the future, if not already—the determining factor in competition will be the processing and analysis of information.

OVERVIEW

The purpose of this book is to present the concepts and issues necessary for the reader to understand and work successfully with computer-based information systems. The goal of the text is to help the reader develop sufficient knowledge to make intelligent decisions about these systems. Our perspective is that of the manager and user of information systems, not that of the computer professional. However, we shall discuss some topics of interest to computer professionals to gain an understanding of crucial issues in the field.

Table 1-1 contains the key areas for management attention to information processing activities in an organization. There are three main groups to consider in reviewing these activities: managers, users, and the staff of the information services department. It is difficult to distinguish between managers and users since the groups overlap. For our purposes, managers are those executives in the firm who make key decisions and allocate resources. Users, on the other hand, have daily contact with information systems and work with input, output, and/or the design of systems. Managers may also be users of systems. However, it will be helpful in a number of later discussions to distinguish between managers when they make decisions about information processing activities and when they act as users in the firm. Users work with systems but have more limited responsibilities for key decisions about information processing in general.

The third relevant group is the information services department staff. These individuals are charged with the responsibility for the design and operation of computer-based information systems. The staff consists of computer professionals who possess a number of technological skills. In later chapters, we shall discuss further the typical activities involved in operating the information services department. For now, these individuals represent some of the resources available to us in developing and operating computer-based systems.

Table 1-1 summarizes how the three groups are involved in the key

Table 1-1 Areas and Roles in Managing Information Processing

Management area	Chapters	Management	Users	Information services department
Policy	6	Establish, monitor	Influence, execute	Participate, execute
Planning	5, 6	Formulate, influence	Recommend, influence, execute	Formulate alternatives, evaluate, consult on technology
Organizational structure (pattern of processing)	7–11	Specify, select, provide resources	Delineate alternatives, develop criteria, evaluate, recommend, implement	Delineate alternatives, influence criteria, evaluate, implement
Applications	1–4, 17, 18	Select areas, set objectives, participate in development	Recommend areas, establish criteria, delineate and evaluate alternatives	Influence areas, criteria, evaluate
Systems analysis and design	12–16	Set objectives, provide resources, participate in design	Choose alternatives, control and influence design, implement	Evaluate alternatives, serve as expert consultant, furnish technological leadership, work on joint design/implementation effort
Operations	19	Provide resources, evaluate	Establish performance criteria, evaluate	Influence criteria, monitor, report
Selection of equipment/services	11	Choose	Establish criteria, evaluate, recommend	Influence criteria, evaluate, recommend, execute decision
Charging	19	Establish policy, monitor	Recommend policy, monitor	Recommend, implement, execute
Control	6, 19	Evaluate, monitor	Report, monitor	Report

management areas for information processing. One role of top management is to establish and monitor *policy* for information systems. Users try to influence the formation of policy and must execute policy once it is established. The information services staff desires to participate in the development of policy and its execution. All three groups are involved in *planning* for information systems. Top management must lead the planning effort, formulate plans, and influence others in the organization. Users make recommendations to influence the planning process and execute the plan. The information services staff must help formulate various alternatives and evaluate them, particularly where questions about technology are involved.

As we shall see in Chapter 6, a number of activities are subsumed under the planning process. The first of these is determining the *organizational structure* for information processing. Top management specifies the structure desired, selects alternatives, and provides resources to produce the agreed on information processing environment. Users help delineate alternatives and develop the criteria to evaluate them. They make recommendations and assist in implementing the organizational structure chosen. The information services staff helps develop alternatives and decision criteria and evaluates the alternatives. The staff also implements the chosen structure for processing.

The selection of *applications* areas and specific alternatives for applications is a critical task. Top management through the planning process selects areas for applications, sets the objectives of each application, and ideally participates in design activities. Users recommend areas for applications, establish criteria for selecting alternatives, and delineate various alternatives for a particular application. The information services staff serves as a resource to help establish criteria and evaluate alternatives.

During *systems analysis and design* top management must set the overall objectives, provide resources, and participate in key design decisions. Users choose the processing alternative and should have a major role in controlling the design and implementation of a new application. The information services department serves among other things as an expert consultant to evaluate alternatives, guide the project, and suggest tradeoffs and how to evaluate them during design.

The *operations* function is responsible for providing service to users of already developed information systems. After applications have been installed, they become operational; systems are executed on a routine basis. The interface among managers, users, and the information services department is often centered on the type of operational service provided. Top management must provide adequate resources for achieving satisfactory levels of operations and must evaluate the success of the information services staff in providing service to users. Users also want to help establish performance criteria and evaluate the quality of service. Finally, the information services staff must monitor service levels and report to management and users.

The development of a plan for information systems often results in the need to *select equipment or services*. Top management ultimately must approve the acquisition and help choose an alternative. Users establish criteria and evaluate alternatives before making a recommendation to management. The information services staff wants to influence evaluation criteria and also participate in the evaluation. Of course, the staff is also responsible for working with the results of the decision.

A critical decision for top management is whether and how to *charge* for information processing services, a topic we shall discuss in more detail later in the text. This topic is also important to users who want to be involved in setting a charging policy and monitoring its execution. The implementation and execution of a charging policy and plan require action by the information services staff.

Given a plan for information processing activities in the organization, it is necessary to see that these activities are under control. Top management must evaluate and monitor the activities involved in information processing. Users also should be involved in this process. The information services staff must report to users and management about their progress in executing the plan and on the level of service they provide for users.

We shall explore all these topics further. Our primary focus will be that of the manager and/or the user, though occasionally we shall also discuss the role of the information services staff.

THE HISTORICAL EVOLUTION OF COMPUTERS

In the late 1800s, Herman Hollerith invented the punched card for processing the 1890 census data. Gradually, the use of mechanical tabulating equipment for processing data spread to a number of different organizations. Tabulating operations include sorting, listing, summarizing, and performing limited mathematical computations on data in punched card form. These operations were performed with electronic accounting machines (EAM) through the end of World War II. However, EAM equipment is limited to the execution of a series of fixed instructions wired into control panels. Wires are plugged in to holes in the panels or "boards" and by changing the plugs, new instruction sequences are created.

In the 1940s, Howard Aiken at Harvard developed an electromechanical computer. John Mauchly and J. P. Eckert at the Moore School of Electrical Engineering at the University of Pennsylvania constructed the first all-electronic computer, the ENIAC, in 1945. The exclusive use of electronic components made the ENIAC much faster than its predecessor EAM equipment. The electronic computer also features a stored program that can be modified dynamically according to the data being processed. (John von Neuman, a Princeton mathematician, developed many of the concepts used in the invention of electronic computers.)

In 1954, the first computer for business applications was installed. Only two decades later, there are hundreds of thousands of different computers in the United States, plus many more in other parts of the world. We have progressed through several generations of computers and their associated programs since the early days of the computer industry. In Part Three, especially Chapters 7, 8, and 9, we discuss computers and programs in much greater detail. Particular attention will be given in these chapters to the evolution of computers and to the major changes in each generation of equipment.

INFORMATION SYSTEMS

What is an information system? Of the many definitions, we shall adopt one for discussion purposes. An information system is a set of organized procedures that, when executed, provides information to support decision making and control in the organization. We define information as a tangible or intangible entity that serves to reduce uncertainty about some state or event.

The basic functions of an information system are diagramed in Figure 1-1. One of the most important parts of this figure is the user who interprets information. We shall explore the role of the user and the nature of information further in the next chapter. We should note that information is not just raw data. Rather, data are processed in some way, for example, collated and summarized, to produce output that is interpreted as information by the user–decision maker.

Since people first inhabited the earth, there have been information systems. Early systems were, of course, quite rudimentary and subject to extensive distortion and delays. Individuals, organizations, and nations have always collected and processed "intelligence." Early information systems were highly informal and involved the exchange of news, stories, and anecdotes with neighbors. As economies progressed beyond the subsistence level, information on the changing value of goods and services for barter and trade became important.

Formal organizations, from their inception, have required information systems to operate successfully. Production, accounting, financial, and external data on consumers and markets are vital to the operation of most modern businesses. As governmental bodies provide more services, they too develop

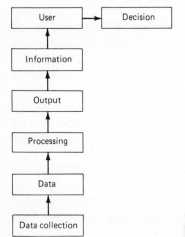

Figure 1-1 A schematic representation of an information system.

greater needs for information. In fact, the overwhelming task of tabulating the 1890 census stimulated the invention of equipment to process data represented by different patterns of holes punched in cards.

What is the role of computers in information systems? Why are we concerned with computer-based information systems? Clearly, from the discussion above, information systems existed long before the development of electronic computers. However, the explosion of information and the need to process large amounts of data to extract small amounts of information have contributed to the increasing importance of computer-based information systems. Of course, such systems are possible because of the high-speed processing capabilities of computers.

We also need to study computer-based systems because the technical aspects of computers have added a whole new set of problems to the development of information systems. Table 1-2 presents some of the differences between manual and computer-based information systems. Computers are machines of arbitrary design; they are difficult for the average user of an information system to understand. This means that the design and implementation of information systems featuring computer processing will be more difficult than the design of a manual system. An automated system has to be clearly defined in advance of conversion so that computer programs can be developed to process the data. In contrast, manual systems may never be completely documented; individuals simply make changes in their current information processing procedures. It is also usually easy to alter these manual procedures on short notice, something very difficult with a computer system.

Managing the development of a manual information system is also usually

Table 1-2 Comparison of Manual versus Computer-Based Information Systems

	Manual	Computer
Understanding the technology	Easy: usually human processing or simple tabulation operation	Difficult: arbitrary and poorly understood technology from standpoint of users
Developing specifications	Very informal and easily changed when tried	A formal process requiring great precision and detail; must be specified in advance
Managing project	Simple to institute procedures	Very difficult to complete on time and within budget
Converting and installing	Usually an easy process involving a few new procedures	Can be a major task requiring significant changes and training
Organizational impact	Often minimal	Can be significant, involving behavioral and organizational changes
Flexibility	Usually easy to change quickly	Often very difficult to modify; changes can be costly and time consuming

an easy task. It may be necessary to develop new paper forms or calculations, but there is little uncertainty in project management. In contrast, the development of computer-based information systems involves considerable uncertainty. We have had a notable lack of success in meeting systems goals and specifications on time and within original budget estimates.

The implementation of a manual information system is usually a part of its design; that is, individuals simply change or add to their present duties. Computer systems, however, involve major training and often require substantial changes for users. The organizational impact of manual information systems is usually minimal; workers are involved in making easily understood changes in procedures. Computer-based information systems may require major changes in behavior on the part of the users.

Nearly all computer systems result in new input techniques such as the use of new forms or terminals and new output such as paper reports or displays. Some computer systems are even significant enough to create changes in the structure of an organization. For example, the development of a computer system in one manufacturing firm stimulated management to create a production control department. The process of developing the system showed that a department was needed to monitor and schedule production; furthermore, the new system provided information that could be used for these activities.

The flexibility of manual information systems is high; it is easy to change simple manual procedures. For computer-based information systems, many months and great expense may be required to make an alteration. As a result, these systems tend to be much less flexible than their manual counterparts.

For the above reasons, we need to consider the special requirements of computer-based information systems and the problems they create. Because these computer-based systems are usually very expensive to develop, their failure can be quite costly to the organization. In addition to direct costs, the failure of a computer-based information system will have an adverse impact on the organization's human resources. Information system failures have created dissension in organizations and led to conflict among individuals and departments. If one system fails or is not well received by users, it will be very difficult to develop new systems in the future. As a result, the organization misses the significant benefits possible from a well-designed and operated computer-based information system.

THE ORGANIZATION AS AN INFORMATION PROCESSING ENTITY

- Product managers at Connoisseur Foods, a company discussed in Chapter 18, require reports on the sales of their products by region. If a product is not selling well, the manager can take immediate action.
- Supermarket buyers need to know how a new brand of a product is selling so that they can order supplies to replenish stocks. If the product is not selling well, then it is a candidate for removal from store shelves where space is highly competitive.

- Managers at an airline need to know load factors on various flights to plan schedules and marketing campaigns. This information is produced as a by-product of computer-based airline reservations systems.

From these examples, we can see one feature that almost all organizations have in common: they must acquire and analyze information and take action based on their interpretation of that information. Whether an organization manufactures a product or sells a service, it needs to process information. Most businesses need to know information on markets, sales, and costs. Manufacturing firms need the above information plus information on the manufacturing process itself. For example, a firm needs information about the status of inventories, orders, and basic manufacturing data for production control. Government agencies are also confronted with substantial information processing requirements. Who are the recipients of the agency's services? What is the cost of these services?

A view of the organization as an information processing entity is presented

---

MANAGEMENT PROBLEM 1-1

The president of Amalgamated Mills has recently become concerned over the firm's difficulties in processing transactions such as the receipt of orders and the preparation of invoices. Amalgamated Mills was founded shortly after World War II to manufacture women's and girls' sports clothing. The company has grown steadily; yearly sales currently exceed $15 million.

The office staff expanded to process the increasing volume of paperwork necessary to enter orders and process shipments and payments. Last year, over 40,000 invoices were written manually in the shipping department! Existing procedures have been modified only slightly to deal with the higher volume of processing necessary to support current sales levels.

The president is considering the development of a computer-based system to handle some of the processing associated with order entry and projections of raw materials requirements. The firm currently uses a service bureau for accounts-receivable processing on a monthly basis.

At one point in time, the president felt he understood all the office procedures. However, in recent years the president has grown uneasy since he is no longer familiar with all the procedures used in the office. There is one office manager who knows everything about operations; unfortunately no one else in the firm fully understands these procedures.

In contemplating a computer system, the president is worried that it might result in less control over operations. On the other hand, he feels that he personally has little control or understanding of present procedures. The president is also worried about becoming dependent on a small computer "elite" to process crucial information.

What advice would you offer the president to help in making his decision on whether to pursue computer processing?

---

in Figure 1-2. The organization collects data from a number of sources, including its own internal operations and customers. Most organizations also attempt to gather data on their competition and on other phenomena external to the organization, such as the economy. In fact, a number of firms exist to gather and sell data such as economic forecasts. Many government statistics are also used by organizations, and we classify these data as externally derived too. For example, the United States Department of Agriculture publishes detailed crop forecasts, which are very important to the food industry.

The organization must process all these data, and frequently some type of computer-based information system is used for this purpose. The output from processing may take many forms, such as tabular reports or graphic displays. It is likely that the output is interpreted and action taken on the basis of the information. For example, a firm might offer a new product or enter a new market because of the information derived from a market research study. Once the decision has been made to enter a new market, the product will be closely monitored. The firm may conduct research on how to best promote the product through advertising or free samples. The data collected on the experiment are then analyzed, and the product manager derives information from them to help in devising a marketing plan.

A great deal of interpreted information is disseminated within an organiza-

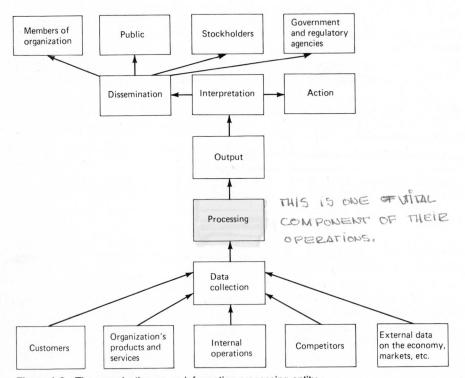

THIS IS ONE OF VITAL
COMPONENT OF THEIR
OPERATIONS.

Figure 1-2   The organization as an information processing entity.

tion for use by its members. The orders processed by a manufacturing firm using a computer provide important information for several groups in the firm. For example, the file of open orders is of interest to the sales force because it shows what products are selling well. The production scheduling department would like to see what goods must be shipped by certain dates to plan production. Customer services would like to be able to inquire about the status of individual orders when customers or sales representatives phone with a question.

Many organizations must also make information available to the public, for example, to stockholders. Publicly held firms and government agencies are faced with reporting requirements by the Securities and Exchange Commission and by legislation, respectively. Many private organizations also provide information to government agencies and regulatory bodies. Automobile firms must provide large amounts of data about tests conducted on vehicle safety and pollution. Drug companies submit extensive information to the government concerning tests of new medicines. Most firms and individuals also furnish a large amount of data to the Internal Revenue Service.

Although processing information clearly is not the ultimate goal of most organizations, we can see that it is one vital component of their operations. Individuals who are or will become members of organizations need to understand the role of information: How is it produced and analyzed, and how is it processed to contribute to the goals of the organization? In a modern organization, the processing of information contributes significantly to the success of the enterprise, and managers should be knowledgeable about information processing tools, techniques, and concepts. This book has been written for the manager who wishes to become an intelligent user or "consumer" of computer-based information systems.

THE INTERDISCIPLINARY NATURE OF THE FIELD

It is not really possible to present a theory of information systems; as in many other fields, there is no one central theory on which we can rely. This lack of unifying theory should not be alarming; there is no one theory of marketing, just as there is no one theory of accounting. Accounting is a field created by humans, and accounting theory is arbitrary when compared with the scientific theories of a field like physics.

The information systems field in general is concerned with the effective use of information technology in an organization. Figure 1-3 places the information systems field in perspective on a continuum ranging from computer science on one extreme to psychology on the other. Computer science contributes the mathematical foundation of computer systems. These results help electrical engineers develop computer devices and programs. Operations research provides a number of approaches to improve decision making and to develop solutions to complex problems. The functional areas of management, such as accounting, finance, production, and marketing furnish the specific decision setting and context for information systems.

			Continuum			
Psychology	Organizational studies	Functional areas of business	Information systems	Operations research	Electrical engineering	Computer science
			Contribution			
Decision making	Impact of information on the organization	Accounting, marketing, finance, production	Combination and synthesis of fields: effective use of information technology in organization	Problem-solving techniques	Machine design	Hardware theory
Use of information Impact of systems					Software design Management techniques File design	Software theory File structures

Figure 1-3 The nature of the information systems field.

Organizational studies help us understand how information systems affect the organization. How can we design systems to ensure successful implementation? The field of psychology also aids in understanding the decision processes of individuals and the nature of information necessary for decision making. Individual psychology is also important in planning the successful implementation of a new system.

Those who study the information systems field must extract relevant components from these many different contributing fields and combine them into a meaningful set of concepts dealing with information processing in organizations. The interdisciplinary nature of the field contributes richness but also increases the complexity of information systems. It is hoped that the student of information systems will find the lack of precise boundaries challenging and intellectually stimulating.

PREVIEW

With this introduction to the information systems field, we are prepared to explore the nature of information in greater detail. In Chapter 2 we examine the nature of decision making and managerial activities, and Chapter 3 introduces several frameworks for systems. Before concluding Part One, we survey a number of computer-based information systems to demonstrate the pervasive nature of these systems.

The second part of the book deals with the interaction of the organization and information systems. Part Three discusses computer technology: users need a basic understanding of computers, especially computer files, to make many decisions about information systems.

In Part Four, we present systems analysis and design techniques, topics of vital importance for a user. We shall advocate that users form a significant part of a design team and that a user be in charge of the design of a new system. Part

---

MANAGEMENT PROBLEM 1-2

Assume that you have just been appointed to chair the board of a medium-sized manufacturing firm that makes small consumer appliances. The company has experienced stagnant growth over the last five years, and a new board of directors was just elected by dissident stockholders.

One of your first tasks is to help top management discover why sales are constant and profits have been declining. Currently, the firm is faced with excessive inventories and problems in the acquisition of raw materials. Prices for these materials have been fluctuating widely in recent months, and the previous management seems to have been unable to cope with this problem.

How would you approach this task? What sources of information would you seek to help understand and solve problems in the company?

Five presents detailed examples of several different information systems to illustrate the material covered to this point. Finally, the last part of the book presents issues of special management concern: the relationship between user departments and the information services department and the social consequences of information systems.

KEY WORDS

Computer science	Implementation	Organizational studies
Data	Information	Output
Data collection	Intelligence	Processing
Decision making	Interdisciplinary field	Psychology
EAM	Internal information	Program
External information	Interpretation	System
Electronic computer	Operations research	Users

RECOMMENDED READINGS

Aaron, J. D.: "Information Systems in Perspective," *Computing Surveys,* vol. 1, no. 4, December 1969, pp. 213–216. (An overview of information systems and how they have developed in organizations.)

Ackoff, R. L.: "Management Misinformation Systems," *Management Science,* vol. 14, No. 4, December 1967, pp. B140–B156. (This article should be read by all students of information systems; it points out some common fallacies in the assumptions underlying many approaches to information systems.)

Blumenthal, S.: *MIS—A Framework for Planning and Development,* Prentice-Hall, Englewood Cliffs, N.J., 1969. (This somewhat complex book presents a functional approach to viewing information systems.)

Dearden, J.: "MIS is a Mirage," *Harvard Business Review,* January–February 1972, pp. 90–99. (Dearden is a consistent critic of information systems; do you agree with his contentions? Why or why not?)

Mason, R., and I. Mitroff: "A Program for Research in Management Information Systems," *Management Science,* vol. 19, no. 5, January 1973, pp. 475–487. (This article describes an information system from the perspective of an individual decision maker. While delving into the philosophical concepts underlying information systems, it presents a very appealing framework for the study of systems.)

DISCUSSION QUESTIONS

1 What is responsible for the explosion of information processing that has occurred over the past several decades?

2 What role does the manager play in the development of information systems? Does this role change in the operation of a system after it has been implemented?

3 Why does the addition of a computer to a manual information system result in complications?

4 What is the similarity between the fields of accounting and the interdisciplinary field of information systems? What are the major differences between these two fields?

5   Manufacturers of early computer devices forecasted far fewer sales than actually occurred. Why do you suspect that the sales estimates were so incorrect?

6   Can you think of other definitions of information systems than the one presented in this chapter? What are their advantages and disadvantages compared with the one we adopted?

7   How can there be more than one interpretation of information? Can you think of examples where the same information is interpreted in different ways by different individuals?

8   What is the value of information? How would you try to assess the value of information to a decision maker?

9   What different types of information exist? Develop categories for describing or classifying information, for example, timeliness and accuracy. Develop an example or two of information in each category.

10 What do you think the crucial factors are in the success of an information system from the standpoint of a manager?

11 How would you define successful implementation? How would you measure it?

12 Can you think of an example where the failure of an information system led to a major disaster? What can we learn from such a catastrophe?

13 What types of organizations are likely to have the most severe information processing problems?

14 What is the relationship between information systems and marketing?

15 How would you characterize the training of a computer scientist compared with the training of a specialist in information systems?

16 What is the role of operations research in information systems? Is an operations research model an information system?

17 How can operations research be used to design information systems? Can operations research be used in the operation of information systems?

18 Develop a list of the different information systems that you encounter during a typical week. How many of these systems are computer-based?

19 What factors would you consider if you were placed on a design team developing a new information system? What would be your major concern about the project?

20 Do you think the information systems field, while lacking a theory, will ever develop principles similar to those of accounting? Would this in your opinion be desirable? Why or why not?

DEFINITION

THE INTERPRETATION OF INFORMATION
    The Context of the User
    An Interpretational Model
    Implications for Information Systems

DECISION MAKING
    Problem Finding and Solving
    Stages in Decision Making
    Types of Decisions

CHARACTERISTICS OF INFORMATION

INDICATORS

✗ FORMAL THEORIES OF INFORMATION

KEY WORDS

RECOMMENDED READINGS

DISCUSSION QUESTIONS

Chapter 2

The Nature of Information and Decision Making

CHAPTER ISSUES

- What kind of decisions are made in the organization?
- What information should be provided for decision makers?
- What decisions are amenable to computer support?

The user of a system receives information in the form of output. In this chapter, we explore the nature of information and how it is interpreted. Too frequently the designers of an information system have considered output to be information while users have not. The decision maker, not the systems designer, defines and uses information. It is extremely important for users of information systems to be aware of different types of information and to think about how they interpret that information.

DEFINITION

In the last chapter, we defined information as some tangible or intangible entity that reduces our uncertainty about some state or event. As an example, consider a weather forecast for clear and sunny weather tomorrow; this information reduces our uncertainty about whether an event such as a baseball game will be held. Information that a bank has just made our firm a loan reduces uncertainty about whether we shall be in a state of solvency or bankruptcy next month.

Another definition for information has been suggested by Davis (1974): "Information is data that has been processed into a form that is meaningful to the recipient, and is of real perceived value in current or prospective decisions." This definition of information systems stresses the fact that data have to be processed in some way to produce information; information is more than raw data. In later chapters we shall discuss information systems that process data to produce information. In this chapter, however, we focus on information and its interpretation.

THE INTERPRETATION OF INFORMATION

The Context of the User

In a discussion of research programs for information systems, Mason and Mitroff (1973) suggested in part that an information system serves an *individual* with a certain *cognitive style* faced with a particular *decision* problem in some *organizational setting*. In addition to these variables, Lucas (1975) has suggested the importance of *personal and situational* factors in the interpretation of information. We shall examine each of these factors to see how they influence the interpretation of information. (See Figure 2-1.)

Clearly, the nature of the problem influences the interpretation of information. How serious is the decision? What are the consequences of an incorrect decision versus the gains from a correct one? A more important decision may require extra care in analyzing data compared with a minor decision. The decision by an oil company to enter the information processing field is more important than the decision to lease additional office space. In such a strategic decision to diversify, the consequences and costs involved plus the impact on the organization mean that information will be scrutinized much more closely.

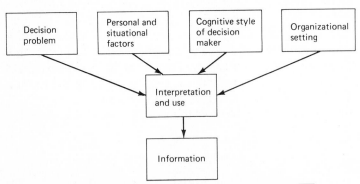

Figure 2-1 Influences on the interpretation and use of information.

The organization itself affects the interpretation of information. Studies have shown that an individual becomes socialized by the organization; that is, over time we are influenced by the organization in the way we approach problems. The attitudes of a new employee at an automobile company differ substantially in most instances from those of the chairman of the board. As the new employee associates over the years with other employees of the firm, he or she is influenced by their attitudes and the environment of the workplace. Gradually new employees begin to change their attitudes to ones more consistent with those with whom they associate—a process known as socialization.

People who have different ideas interpret information differently; many of the ideas will have been influenced by peers and by the socialization process in the particular organization for whom the individual works. Several individuals trying to influence a decision by the government to regulate prices in an industry may use the same information. However, the head of a corporation in the industry, the leader of a consumer group, and a government decision maker in a regulatory agency will probably all interpret the information differently.

Personal and situational factors also influence the interpretation of information. One study showed that given comparable information, decision makers interpreted a problem differently depending on their position. In this exercise, finance executives saw financial problems, sales executives recognized sales problems, and so forth. In all these scenarios, the information was the same—it was just interpreted differently (Dearborn and Simon, 1958).

Psychologists studying the thought patterns of individuals have developed the concept of "cognitive style" (Doktor, 1973). Although there is no agreement on exactly how to describe or measure different cognitive styles, the concept is appealing since people do seem to have different ways of approaching problems. One of the simplest distinctions is between analytic and heuristic decision makers. The analytic decision maker looks at quantitative information; engineering is a profession attractive to an analytic decision maker. The heuristic decision maker, on the other hand, is interested in broader concepts and is more intuitive.

Most researchers believe that we are not analytic or heuristic in every problem, but that we do have preferences and tend to approach the same type of problem with a consistent cognitive style. In one recent study, the author found that more quantitative individuals tended to make less use of the output from interactive computer-based planning models than did more intuitive individuals. Possibly, the more quantitatively oriented individuals had less faith in the assumptions behind the model because of their knowledge of mathematics and modeling (Lucas, 1976a).

The phenomenon of cognitive style can create considerable problems in the interpretation of information. Consider the staff member who brings a report laden with data to a heuristic decision maker. The recipient of the report says, "Don't give me all these numbers; I want to know your conclusions and recommendations." The analyst, sadder but wiser, prepares the next report without any data; instead only interpretations and conclusions are presented.

Unfortunately, the recipient of this report is an analytic decision maker who rejects it: "You haven't given me the data so that I can draw my own conclusions and compare them with yours."

An Interpretational Model

We have suggested a number of factors that influence the interpretation of information. How are all these factors combined; what is their net impact on the interpretation of information? Figure 2-2 summarizes all the variables described above. The figure portrays one representation of how a user of information systems develops a model to interpret information and how this model is constantly executed and revised.

Before discussing Figure 2-2, we should define what is meant by the term "model." A model is a representation of some physical entity or intangible quantity. An architect frequently builds a small physical model of a building from wood or cardboard before constructing the actual building.

Four types of decision models have been identified by Montgomery and Urban (1969). An intuitive model is implicit and intangible; a partially formed idea of how two variables are related is an intuitive model. A verbal model marks the next stage of model development; the decision maker feels that if a particular course of action A is followed, then B will result.

When a model becomes more concrete, it can be expressed as a logical flow model. At this stage, the relationships among variables can be diagramed to show various alternatives graphically. Logical flow diagrams are often used in scheduling to show how the tasks in a project, such as building a house, are related.

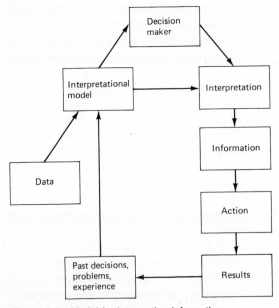

Figure 2-2   Model for interpreting information.

MANAGEMENT PROBLEM 2-1

A group of information systems designers was discussing problems in the bank where they work. One of the designers said, "No matter what I do, there seem to be some people who just will not use the branch market potential report. This report should be very valuable since it shows the potential for various types of loans and deposits, in the area served by the branch."

Another analyst commented, "I have had the same problem with some of the systems I have developed. We recently installed a system that would allow managers to inquire on a terminal about the status of the bank's commercial loan portfolio. The other day I looked at the results of a monitor which keeps track of who makes an inquiry and the nature of the request. It turns out that a group of four or five managers is using the system a lot while some fifteen people we thought would use it are not."

As a manager interested in the effective utilization of information systems, what do you think is the cause of these problems? How could they be solved?

The most explicit model is a mathematical one because it expresses the magnitudes and relationships among variables. An example of such a mathematical model is Ohm's law: $V = IR$, where V is the voltage in volts, I the current in amperes, and R the resistance in ohms. This mathematical model states that a current of 1 ampere flowing through a resistance of 1 ohm produces a voltage of 1 volt.

In our discussion of the interpretation of information, what kind of model do we expect to find? The most likely model for interpreting information is intuitive, although in many instances the decision maker is probably unaware of the existence of a model. One representation for such an interpretational model is shown in Figure 2-2. We expect this model to be formed inductively by the decision maker and to be heavily influenced by beliefs. For example, a decision maker may observe data on sales and production over time and find that these data seem to predict customer reaction to a product. The decision maker is building an interpretational model based on his or her beliefs and analysis of historical data and observations. In addition to this inductive approach, Pounds (1969) identified several other common models, for example other people's models (a superior's) or extraorganizational models (one from a competitor or the government), that might contribute to the development of an interpretational model.

After testing the interpretational model and developing confidence in it, the decision maker uses the model deductively. Data are observed and the decision maker uses the model to interpret them. Now, the decision maker perceives data on sales and production as constituting information on product acceptance; he or she may even ignore other information conveyed by these data.

After an interpretational model has been formed, further experiences are fed back to modify the model; past decisions, problems, and experiences all influence the future interpretations of information. These experiences are based on actions taken on the basis of information and the results of those actions. If changes in a new product based on sales and production data increase sales, then the interpretational model described above will be reinforced.

Implications for Information Systems

What does the existence of a model for interpreting information imply for information systems? The presence of different interpretational models creates many serious problems for the designer and user of information systems. First, the meaning of information is clearly in the mind of the recipient. What one party perceives as useful and relevant information may be meaningless to another person. Even more serious is a situation where two individuals agree on the importance of information but develop completely opposite interpretations of what the information means.

An example will help show the difficulty of designing an information system, given the diversity of interpretational models. Suppose that we have received the following information. An unfriendly country within the last 48 hours has

1 Called the U.S. ambassador for an urgent meeting tomorrow
2 Nationalized the subsidiaries of two United States firms
3 Held joint maneuvers of its Air Force and Army along its borders

A "hawk" might interpret this information to mean that the unfriendly country is planning to expropriate all U.S. investments, and call for U.S. troops to evacuate American citizens. The hawk might also suggest economic sanctions against the country.

A "dove," on the other hand, might interpret the above information to mean that the country wishes to negotiate compensation with the United States for expropriating U.S.-owned companies. The unfriendly country may also want to arrange for technicians from the United States to assist in running these firms.

A cynic might suggest that all the information is unrelated and has no significance whatsoever. The unfriendly country is so bureaucratic and has such poor communications that none of the events is really connected. The action of the United States should be to do nothing.

All three individuals agree on the information; only the interpretational models differ. In each instance, however, the differing interpretations based on different backgrounds and beliefs lead to widely varying recommendations for action. The point is that we must carefully consider how information is interpreted in thinking about information systems.

DECISION MAKING

We have suggested that, in general, information systems exist to support decision making. Before we can continue our discussion of the nature of information, we need to examine the decision-making process in more detail to see how information is used.

Problem Finding and Solving

A manager must be aware of a problem before a decision can be made. A problem exists when the decision maker's ideal situation differs from reality, for example, when sales are below expectations. This example corresponds to something we call "disturbance handling"; the manager discovers the discrepancy between an ideal model and reality and attempts to find some way to eliminate the discrepancy.

After noting the existence of a problem, the decision maker must decide what caused it. Are inventories up? Is the advertising budget too low? After determining the cause or causes, the decision maker tries to solve the problem by developing some program to remedy the situation. There is also another type of problem-finding activity undertaken by the manager who is looking for improvement projects. In this sense, the problem can be defined as "what else could we be doing at the present time?" The manager is trying to anticipate problems and plan for them.

Stages in Decision Making

In finding and solving a problem, the decision maker faces a myriad of decision cycles. What is the problem and what is the cause of the problem? What additional data are needed, and how should the solution be implemented? Each of these major steps in solving a problem involves the solution of subproblems, and many decisions have to be made.

Simon (1965) suggests a series of descriptive stages for decision making that help in understanding the decision process. The first stage is defined as

---

MANAGEMENT PROBLEM 2-2

The governor of a state is confronted with a series of conflicting recommendations from his staff. All the reports he read on current welfare problems indicated that projected payments would rise well beyond budgeted levels for the rest of the year.

The director of welfare suggested in her report that the new higher amounts for payment passed by the legislature were to blame for the problem.

The governor's advisor for economic affairs indicated that the recent decline in the state's economy had resulted in a large increase in unemployment. As unemployment benefits ran out, he said, many of the unemployed became eligible for welfare, thus accounting for the increase in expenditures.

A state senate leader felt that most of the increase resulted from cheating by many people on welfare, which resulted in abnormally high expenditures in the early part of the year. This high rate of expenditures was the basis for the projections for the rest of the year. The obvious solution was to increase the standards for obtaining welfare and investigate applicants and present recipients more closely.

Who is right? What is responsible for so many different positions? How can the governor solve these conflicting viewpoints and arrive at the cause of the problem?

Intelligence, which consists in determining that a problem exists. The decision maker must become aware of a problem and gather data about it. We described this stage as problem finding or identification.

During the Design stage, the problem solver tries to develop a set of alternative solutions. The problem solver asks what approaches are available to solve the problem and evaluates each one. In the Choice stage, the decision maker selects one of the solutions. If all the alternatives have been evaluated well, the Choice stage is usually the simplest one to execute. We should also add a stage to Simon's model called Implementation, in which we ensure that the solution is carried out.

Types of Decisions

To complete our discussion of problem solving and decision making, we relate different types of solutions to the type of problem involved. Anthony (1965) offers one view of three different types of decisions made in organizations. Clearly, these are not discrete categories, but instead they form a continuum for classifying decisions.

DECISION SUPPORT SYSTEMS

At Florida Power and Light Company a decision support system showed that centralizing the inventory distribution system could bring added efficiencies. The utilities saved $13.5 million last year in inventory carrying costs. Shaklee Corporation should be able to cut its delivery time to customers by one-third and save $850,000 through a computer system. National Airlines is saving as much as $500,000 a month in fuel costs as a result of a new system.

These companies are taking advantage of decision support systems which differ from conventional computer applications like inventory control; the primary use of the systems above is in operational planning such as helping develop complex production schedules. Other firms use decision support systems to aid strategic planning and to guide decisions, for example, on whether to enter a new market.

The heart of these systems is a computer software model describing the decision. The computer simulates a number of "what if" scenarios given different assumptions by the firm.

A good example of one of these systems is a fuel management allocation application developed at National Airlines. During the first month of operation fuel cost was cut by two cents a gallon. Since the airline used 25 million gallons that month it saved $500,000. The Airline stores data on fuel prices and availability along with storage costs and capacities at the 30 cities it serves. For each of its 56 aircraft, performance and a tentative monthly schedule are included. The computer requires only fifteen minutes to produce a list of the best fueling stations and vendors for each flight, a task that required over a month to perform manually. Now the schedule can be run two or three times a week.

Decision support systems offer the opportunity for direct cost savings in operational applications and for improving the decision making process in general.

Business Week, January 21, 1980.

The first decision area is strategic planning in which the decision maker develops objectives and allocates resources to obtain these objectives. Decisions in this category are characterized by long time periods and usually involve a substantial investment and effort. The development and introduction of a new product is an example of a strategic decision.

Decisions that are classified as managerial control in nature deal with the use of resources in the organization and often involve personnel or financial problems. For example, an accountant may try to determine the reason for a difference between actual and budgeted costs. In this case, the accountant is solving a managerial control problem.

Operational control decisions deal with the day-to-day problems that affect the operation of the firm. What should be produced today in the factory? What items should be ordered for inventory?

Who makes the preponderance of each of the three types of decisions? Anthony does not really specify what types of decisions are handled by different managers. However, from the nature of the problems, we suspect that top managers in the organization spend more time on strategic decision making than supervisors, while the reverse is probably true for operational decisions.

CHARACTERISTICS OF INFORMATION

Information can be characterized in a number of ways; some kinds of information are more suitable for a decision problem than others. We must be certain that the characteristics of information fit the decision situation and the interpretational model of the decision maker. Table 2-1 shows some of the many characteristics of information arrayed against possible uses of that information (Anthony, 1965). Depending on the particular decision problem, the entries in this table vary.

The time frame for information can be historical or predictive. Historical information can be used to design alternative problem solutions and to monitor performance. Predictive data can be used in Design and to evaluate the alternatives for the Choice stage. Predictive information is also good for Implementation and Monitoring to provide a standard for comparison.

Information may be expected or it may be unanticipated. Some information systems experts feel that information is worthless unless it is a surprise to the recipient. However, information that confirms something does reduce uncertainty. Anticipated information helps in designing and evaluating alternatives and in Implementation and Monitoring. Surprise information often alerts us to the existence of a problem; it is also important in developing and evaluating different decision alternatives. Surprise results from Implementation and Monitoring suggest that action is needed. Information may come from sources internal to the organization or from external sources such as government agencies. For the various areas described in Table 2-1, the source is determined by the requirements of a particular decision problem.

Information may be presented in summary form or in detail. Summary

Table 2-1   Possible Relationships between Information Characteristics and Uses

Characteristics	Problem finding	Problem solving			
	Intelligence	Design	Choice	Action	Implementation and monitoring
Time frame					
Historical		X			X
Predictive		X	X	X	X
Expectation					
Anticipated		X	X	X	X
Surprise	X	X	X	X	X
Source					
Internal	X	X	X	X	X
External	X	X	X	X	X
Scope					
Summary	X	X	X		X
Detailed		X	X	X	X
Frequency					
High	X			X	X
Low	X	X	X	X	X
Organization					
Loose	X	X	X		
Structured				X	X
Accuracy					
High		X	X	X	X
Low	X	X	X		

information is often sufficient for problem finding; however, both summary and detailed information may be needed for other uses. Information can be frequently updated or relatively old, and for problem identification, both types are often used. For many types of problems, Implementation and Monitoring require frequently updated information.

Information can also be loosely or highly structured. An example of highly structured information is a report with clear categories to classify all the information it contains. Loosely organized information, for example, different forms of information from multiple sources, is fine for problem finding and solving. However, for Implementation and Monitoring we probably need structured information. Information also varies in its accuracy. For Intelligence, some inaccuracies are acceptable when we are being alerted to the fact that a problem exists. Extreme accuracy is also not usually required for Design or Choice. However, for Implementation and Monitoring, accurate data are necessary.

It is also instructive to see what characteristics of information are associated with different types of decisions. (See Table 2-2.) In general, different types of decisions require different kinds of information; providing inappropriate information is one common failing of computer-based systems. In one organization, the vice president of finance receives detailed reports on the status of an inventory with 52,000 items at a remote location. The report is not used, and this executive is frustrated with the information.

Operational control decisions are characterized by historical information. Usually the results are expected, and the source of the information is the internal operations of the organization. The data—for example, production-control data, inventory status, or accounts-receivable balances—must be detailed. Because we are working with the day-to-day operations of the firm, operational control information is often required in close to real time. This information tends to be highly structured and accurate.

Information for strategic decisions, on the other hand, tends to be more predictive and long range in nature. Strategic planning may uncover many surprises. Often, external data on the economy, competition, and so forth are involved in strategic decision making. Summary information on a periodic basis is adequate; there is usually no need for highly detailed or excessively accurate information. Strategic planning decisions are usually characterized by loosely structured information. The requirements for managerial control decisions fall in between those of operational control and strategic planning.

The characteristics of information described in this section are not mutually exclusive. For example, we can have historical information of a surprise nature that is loosely structured. Obviously, there are many ways to classify information, and this complicates the decision maker's problem in expressing what is desired as output from an information system. The most important thing for the user of information systems is to be aware of the intended use of information and the type of decision problem. Then the user should try to decide on the general characteristics of the information needed, using categories such as these as guidelines to develop more detailed information requirements. Consideration of characteristics similar to the ones described here should make it possible to avoid requesting grossly inappropriate information from an information system.

Table 2-2 Information Characteristics versus Decision Types

Characteristics	Decision type		
	Operational control	Managerial control	Strategic planning
Time frame	Historical	⟶	Predictive
Expectation	Anticipated	⟶	Surprise
Source	Largely internal	⟶	Largely external
Scope	Detailed	⟶	Summary
Frequency	Real time	⟶	Periodic
Organization	Highly structured	⟶	Loosely structured
Accuracy	Highly accurate	⟶	Not overly accurate

INDICATORS

An indicator is some summary statistic that is presented as information. The gross national product (GNP) is a single summary statistic used to indicate the general level of economic activity in a country. The cost-of-living indicator provides information about the rate of inflation and the decline in buying power of money. We use these summary statistics to reduce the amount of information presented and the amount of processing necessary to interpret it. Frequently we are confronted with a mass of data that contains very little potential information; an indicator summarizes and extracts the most pertinent information from such a mass of data.

Organizations and managers frequently develop indicators to measure their performance. An organization may use sales, net profit, earnings per share, or similar financial indicators for reports to stockholders. A credit analyst may use some of these statistics to decide whether or not to recommend a loan, and a manager may point out a favorable budget variance in talking with a superior. Frequently, information systems are designed to produce indicators for evaluation purposes. In designing these indicators, we need to consider carefully their credibility and bias. An example should help to illustrate some of the problems with indicators.

The national and local crime rates are often used as indicators of the moral fabric of society. The Uniform Crime Reports collected by the FBI are one source of data on the crime rate. Bidderman has written a scathing criticism of the crime rate as measured and reported in the 1960s (Bauer, 1967). The crime index at that time consisted of the crimes homicide, forcible rape, robbery, aggravated assault, burglary, larceny (theft greater than $50), and auto theft.

The first question one might ask is, What crimes are missing? The index presented above ignores crimes such as forgery, extortion, arson, and all white-collar crimes; also missing are narcotics and organized criminal activities. Given these omissions, how accurate is the crime index?

If a composite indicator is reported, are all crimes in this index equally serious? There are really two types of crimes represented above, those against property and those against persons. Yet in this simple index, with no weighting for seriousness, petty theft will be recorded on the same basis as homicide. (Recently the crime index has not been reported as a single summary statistic; it has been accompanied with statistics for each individual category.)

Over time, in what direction should the crime index above move? Undoubtedly it will increase. One trend in the world has been greater urbanization; as people crowd together and live in more densely populated areas, crime increases. Inflation also has a dramatic effect on the crime index—because of inflation, crimes classified as petty larceny will become grand larceny as the value of more items stolen exceeds $50. As citizens become more affluent, they buy more insurance and more crimes are reported to the police to collect insurance. Finally, as police forces improve, more crimes will be reported to and by the police. Thus, there will be many more reported crimes and a higher crime

RAILROAD APPLICATIONS

The Association of American Railroads is planning to expand a nationwide computer system that provides data on the location of over two million freight cars, trailers, and containers for some 27 railroads in North America. The Missouri Pacific Railroad is also expanding a computer-based car scheduling system; it will soon cover its entire 12,000 mile network.

The American Association of Railroads is using its system to send out car service directives advising railroads on how to move rolling stock from one region to another to respond to various shortages. Computer systems are paying off in the more efficient use of rolling stock and locomotives. Another benefit is less costly maintenance and better long range planning.

The trade group is studying whether new computer applications could be developed to eliminate waybill and other paper bottlenecks. These efforts are expected to become more important to rail operations, as the railroad industry is deregulated. The computer is the only way that the railroads will be able to analyze information and react to fare changes under deregulation.

The Santa Fe Railroad has a system that keeps track of every freight car and locomotive on the line. Every time a car enters a rail yard, a Santa Fe clerk enters an identification number into a central computer file. When a shipper requests a freight car, the system locates the nearest suitable one and sends dispatching instructions to the yard. A similar system, in use at the Southern Pacific Railroad resulted in a savings of $5 million per year.

The Missouri Pacific computerized its dispatching operation as well. Prior to the computer, a shipper had to call one of the companies 300 freight stations and wait while an agent searched for cars that might be available. The application that keeps track of rolling stock has resulted in a 10% average improvement in car utilization, savings which have exceeded the original expectation of an $8 million return from the $45 million system.

In 1978 the railroad began to schedule car movements along a 546 mile portion of the track, from Dallas to Memphis. If a freight car unexpectedly misses its train, the computer assigns it to the next one. Another 3,000 miles of track has been added to the computer system. Customers can also use the results of the computer system to help keep shipments on track; a computer at Ford Motor Company receives 50,000 reports a day on the location of its 31 railroad cars.

To speed up shipments railroads share information among themselves. The computers of the Missouri Pacific, Southern Pacific, Conrail and Burlington Northern often exchange information to obtain shipping data.

These applications are helping the railroads become far more efficient and compete with alternate modes of transportation. The investments are large, but the return on such operational systems can be extremely high.

Business Week, February 4, 1980.

index. even though the amount of actual crime may have increased less than the index. In the form above, the crime index is probably so biased that it is totally misleading.

Indicators are important; we cannot cope with the amount of raw data used to produce an indicator. However, we have to analyze statistics carefully to see what they actually indicate. A final problem with indicators occurs when they change from a measure to a motivator. Another example will help to illustrate this point.

A university administrator calculated the contribution of each department in a school. The total number of class hours taken by the students in the school was computed. This number divided into the total revenue of the school produced a dollar value for each student hour. The expenses for each department were then compared with the "revenue" it produced (the number of student-hours times the revenue dollars per student-hour plus any external funds raised by the department). The results were used in faculty salary, hiring, and promotion decisions. What would you predict the results would be from using this indicator?

Soon, the average class size began increasing rapidly, since the strategy of enlarging classes produced more income for a department. The indicator had become an incentive that motivated behavior. It began to drive the process it was designed to measure!

A manager who develops an indicator must consider its behavioral implications. Perhaps multiple indicators can be used to bracket the truth. If not, indicators may have to be eliminated; possibly, we should cast out all indicators every so often and invent new ones.

FORMAL THEORIES OF INFORMATION

So far, we have discussed broad, qualitative attributes of information and have appealed to intuition for their acceptance. Several formal theories of information also provide further insights into its nature.

Information is very precisely defined in the mathematical theory of communications (Davis, 1974). Information in communications is the average number of binary digits (a 0 or a 1) that must be transmitted to identify a given message from the set of all possible messages. This definition is used to develop and to identify messages. Binary coding is a convenient scheme, since most machines can produce signals based on one of two states.

To send one of four messages, we need two digits or bits:

Message	Bits
1 By land	00
2 By sea	01
3 By air	10
4 Not coming	11

If we code the messages according to the two bits in the right-hand column, and the decoder has the same table, we can transmit the messages very economically using fewer characters than the full messages contain.

MANAGEMENT PROBLEM 2-3

The sales manager of an apparel firm decided that he needed more information with which to evaluate sales representatives. The manager designed a new report to be completed by the sales force after making each call. Each sales representative was to indicate the number of lines shown and the name of the store.

This information was correlated with actual orders by the company's computer-based order entry and sales information system. The result was a report for the sales manager that showed the following information:

The number of stores on which the representative called
The number of lines shown
The number of lines sold to that store
The percentage of sales to calls
The ratio of lines sold to lines shown

The sales manager did not explain to the sales force the reason for the new information that was sent to them with their commission statements. However, it was rumored in the company that the method of compensation for the sales force was under study.

What do you think the results of this new information system were? Why? How do you think the sales force would interpret this information? What impact might it have on their behavior? Explain your reasoning.

Information content is defined by the formula

$$I = \log_2 n$$

where n is the number of possible messages and all messages are equally likely. In the example above, $I = \log_2 4$, or $I = 2$, since $2^2 = 4$.

Earlier, we said that information reduces uncertainty. If the codes are agreed on in advance, uncertainty is reduced to zero after the message is received. Partial information also reduces uncertainty. In the example above, receiving a right-most digit of 1 reduces our uncertainty by one-half. We know that the message is either 2 or 4, since each has a right-most digit of 1.

The use of information to reduce uncertainty can also provide a conceptual understanding of the value of information. Consider the example in Figure 2-3. We are planning to introduce a new product, and our prior belief is that the product has a 60 percent chance of success and a 40 percent chance of failure.

A market research firm offers to conduct a test to help us decide whether or not to offer the product. Unfortunately, the test is not 100 percent reliable, as shown in the figure. There is a possibility that the test will be wrong; for example, the upper right-hand box of Figure 2-3a says that there is a 20 percent chance that the test will indicate that the product will be a failure when it will actually be a success.

	Results B indicate product a success	Results B' indicate product a failure
A Product a success	P (B|A) = .8	P (B'|A) = .2
A' Product a failure	P (B|A') = .1	P (B'|A') = .9

(a)

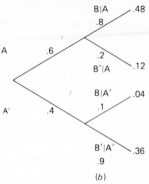

(b)

Figure 2-3 An example of information and uncertainty.

The information in Figure 2-3a is recast in the form of a decision tree in Figure 2-3b. The value of the test is in revising our prior probabilities, P(A) (successful product) and P(A') (unsuccessful product), on the basis of the test results. The marketing firm has provided us with the probability of the test results given the success of the product; for example, we know P(B'|A) is .2 as described above.

Our question now is this: What is the probability that the product will succeed, given that the test indicates success? Mathematically, Bayes' theorem helps us find the answer:

$$P(A|B) = \frac{P(A \wedge B)}{P(B)}$$

The conditional probability of A (the product is a success) given the test outcome B (the test says the product is a success) is equal to the probability of A and B together divided by the probability of B. In our numerical example,

$$P(A|B) = \frac{.48}{.04 + .48} = .92$$

The same calculation for the probability that the test indicates a failure and the product would fail is

$$p(A'|B') = \frac{p(A' \wedge B')}{p(B')} = \frac{.36}{.36 + .12} = .75$$

The market test, then, allows us to revise our prior probabilities. If the test predicts success for the product, our .6 probability of success would become .92. If the test predicts product failure, our .4 probability of failure would become .75. The value of the test can be calculated from these probabilities and compared with its cost. Clearly we would never rationally pay more for information than the value of the best decision we could make, given perfect information. Unfortunately, as a practical matter, it is very difficult to develop probabilities and costs for a conditional probability approach to ascertaining the value of information. However, this concept does provide a useful theoretical view of how information serves to reduce uncertainty.

KEY WORDS

Accuracy	Historical	Probability
Anticipated	Indicator	Problem finding
Bayesian analysis	Internal	Problem solving
Bias	Interpretive model	Real time
Binary	Intuitive model	Strategic planning
Choice	Logical flow model	Structured
Design	Managerial control	Summary
Detail	Mathematical model	Surprise
External	Operational control	Value of information
Frequency	Prediction	Verbal model

RECOMMENDED READINGS

Anthony, R.: *Planning and Control Systems: A Framework for Analysis,* Division of Research, Graduate School of Business Administration, Harvard University, Boston, 1965. (This short book explains Anthony's framework for decision making more fully and is well worth reading.)

Davis, G. B.: *Management Information Systems: Conceptual Foundations, Structure, and Development,* McGraw-Hill, New York, 1974. (See especially the first several chapters on the nature of information.)

Masterman, J.: *The Double-Cross System,* Avon, New York, 1972. (A most enjoyable book describing a system used by Allied intelligence, primarily the British, to feed false intelligence to the German high command during World War II. The book provides an excellent example of an analysis of a user's interpretational model and the development of information to suit that model.)

Pounds, W. F.: "The Process of Problem Finding," *The Industrial Management Review,* vol. 11, no. 1, 1969, pp. 1–20. (An insightful paper describing the nature of problem finding; the author gives several examples of different kinds of problems that managers in one company faced.)

Simon, H.: *The Shape of Automation for Men and Management,* Harper & Row, New York, 1965. (See especially the essay on the "New Science of Management Decision Making.")

DISCUSSION QUESTIONS

1 What alternative definitions for information can you propose?
2 What do you think selective perception is? How does it affect the design and use of information systems?
3 Why is information more than just data?

4 How would you measure cognitive style? How does this concept help in the interpretation of information and the design of information systems?

5 Can an organization bias the information it develops and uses?

6 How can different interpretations of information lead to conflict? How can this conflict be resolved?

7 Develop procedures for eliciting and defining information needs for a decision. How could you implement your plan? What are the problems?

8 How does the importance of a decision reflect itself in the users' interpretation of information?

9 Would you expect an analytical decision maker to be more favorably disposed toward computer-based reports than a heuristic one? Why or why not?

10 Pounds suggests that a problem exists when the decision maker's normative model of what should be conflicts with reality. How does this normative model relate to our information interpretation model? Are they completely independent?

11 Can the same information system be used by more than one decision maker?

12 How can we custom-tailor information systems to suit different decision makers at a reasonable cost?

13 Examine one particular indicator with which you are familiar for bias, reliability, etc. For example, how valid is a grade point average?

14 What other characteristics of information can you define beyond the ones listed in this chapter?

15 Are there information systems that deal with decisions or processes outside Anthony's categories for decisions? What types of systems are these?

16 What are the most frequent indicators for evaluating the performance of lower, middle, and top managers?

17 Is there any way to "beat" an indicator like a standardized aptitude test for college admissions? What kind of behavior does this indicator motivate?

18 Of what value are formal theories of information to a decision maker?

19 Why is there no formal theory of information systems?

20 In the example of Figure 2-3b, what is the probability that the product would succeed if the test indicates a failure? What is the probability that the product would fail given that the test predicts success?

Frameworks for Information Systems

CLASSIC VIEWS OF MANAGEMENT
    Different Approaches
MANAGERIAL ROLES
    The Research
    Interpersonal Roles
    Informational Roles
    Decisional Roles
    Managerial Activities
    Applicability of the Findings
FRAMEWORKS FOR INFORMATION SYSTEMS
    Anthony
    Simon
    Gorry–Scott Morton
✗ EXISTING INFORMATION SYSTEMS
    Churchill et al.
    Bay Area and Planning Studies
KEY WORDS
RECOMMENDED READINGS
DISCUSSION QUESTIONS

Frameworks for Information Systems

CHAPTER ISSUES

- What kind of information systems
  should be developed in the
  organization?
- What information should be
  provided by computer-based
  systems?

A "framework" is a conceptual model that helps us understand and communicate about information systems. The framework developed in this chapter will facilitate future discussions about different types of decisions, their information requirements, and different kinds of computer-based information systems.

We review the nature of managerial activities in the first part of the chapter. Many computer-based systems purport to be "management information systems," and an understanding of managerial activities aids in the analysis and design of such systems. Managers also allocate resources to information systems activities, so it is essential to understand the different roles of management within an organization.

CLASSIC VIEWS OF MANAGEMENT

One early view of management was set forth in the 1900s by Fayol, who suggested five basic managerial functions:

Planning $POCCC$
Organizing
Commanding
Coordinating
Controlling (Mintzberg, 1973)

Gulick coined an acronym in the 1930s that is even sometimes used today for describing management, "POSDCORB":

P   stands for *planning,* which is the development of an outline of what has to be done and the method to accomplish this goal;

O   is for *organizing,* which is setting up the formal structure of authority in an organization;

S   is for the *staffing* function, which refers to all matters dealing with the selection and recruitment of personnel;

D   stands for *directing,* which refers to making and carrying out decisions;

CO   is for *coordinating,* which is interrelating various components of work to see that they are accomplished;

R   means *reporting,* the activity of keeping supervisors and subordinates informed about one's activities;

B   is for *budgeting,* which encompasses financial planning, accounting, and control tasks of management.

Unfortunately, this early normative view of management is not very helpful, since the activities it describes are vague. This scheme presents the objective of managerial work; it does not characterize the work itself or how to accomplish the objectives (Mintzberg, 1973).

Different Approaches

Another attempt to describe managerial work has been called "the great man school" by Mintzberg. The great man school is typified by stories of successful managers found in popular journals and newspapers. These stories contain much detail, but there is little we can generalize from each case study. Also a number of books concentrate on an individual and his or her personality; however, they tell us that that person in a certain situation had a series of impressive accomplishments. Once again, it is very difficult to generalize from these stories.

On a more scientific basis, economists and management scientists have tried to describe how managers should act. These researchers unfortunately have to assume that managers are rational and profit-maximizing and that they should make certain mathematically specified choices. Decision theorists offer an approach to decision making based on the identification of probability utility functions and the use of Bayesian statistical procedures to recommend optimal decisions. These approaches are not really descriptive; instead they suggest how the rational manager should act given a certain decision problem. We have seen that human beings are very complex and that the simple assumptions of many of these models are inadequate. These scientific authors feel that managers should act in the way they specify, but their writings do not help us understand how managers actually do act.

① INTERPERSONAL
② INFORMATIONAL
③ DECISION.

MANAGERIAL ROLES

The Research

Mintzberg (1973) reviewed the small amount of literature available about managerial work and presented his own observational study of the activities of five top managers. Mintzberg spent a week recording the activities of each manager in detailed categories. This work identified 10 roles played by managers and divided them into three basic categories. A role is a position occupied by a manager; it can be identified by a set of activities. For example, a television actor may portray a detective in one show and a Western cowboy in another. The actor's activities and style along with the dress and set inform the audience which role is being played.

Roles are defined by grouping activities together and assigning descriptive labels. The most support for these roles comes from Mintzberg's own study, and therefore our discussion may be biased toward top managers since they were the subjects involved in the research. However, Mintzberg feels that the results are applicable to all managers and that only the proportion of the time spent in the different roles varies between a supervisor and a president. Additional studies are cited to support the author's observations.

① FIGUREHEAD ③ LIAISON POINT.
Interpersonal Roles ② LEADER.

There are three interpersonal roles characterized by their involvement with people both inside and outside an organization. The first is a figurehead role where the manager performs social or symbolic duties such as visiting a sick employee or working on a charity drive. A second interpersonal role is as leader: the manager must motivate workers and see that the organization is staffed and the work force well trained. The last interpersonal role finds a manager as a liaison: the manager makes contacts both inside and outside the organization to exchange information, problems, and ideas.

① MONITOR
Informational Roles ② DISSEMINATING DATA.

Managers have two informational roles that are clearly important in considering information systems. The manager in the first informational role acts as a monitor, observing and processing different types of information. Most of the information is current and has been developed from the organization and/or its surrounding environment. The manager is a nerve center for organizational information.

The next information-handling role finds the manager disseminating data. Information is transmitted to relevant colleagues, such as subordinates, superiors, and individuals outside the organization. Finally, a manager plays a minor role as spokesperson: the manager makes comments directed to individuals outside the organization to explain company policies and actions.

Decisional Roles

① ENTREPRENEUR.   ③ RESOURCE ALLOCATOR
② DISTURBANCE HANDLER. ④ NEGOTIATOR.

The manager's set of four decisional roles also has important bearing on information systems. First, the manager functions as an entrepreneur, searching for and initiating improvement projects to bring about positive changes in the organization. The manager is also a disturbance handler, taking action when the organization faces some unanticipated consequences. The resource allocation role involves decisions on the allocation of resources in the manager's area of responsibility. The final decisional role for the manager is as negotiator, trying to adjudicate disputes in the organization.

Managerial Activities

It is interesting to see how managers spend their time in the various activities constituting the roles described above. First, the manager's work consists primarily of verbal and written contacts. Many activities are fragmented, and frequent interruptions are the rule. The manager's work frequently seems never to be completed because of an awareness that something overlooked could improve the situation. Thus, the manager appears to be much like the student preparing for an examination: the student is never confident that an additional hour of study would be wasted because that hour could uncover the answer to a key question on a test. Since the work is never done, managers seem to work at a vigorous pace.

There are five main tools used by managers in their work, including the mail, telephone, scheduled meetings, unscheduled meetings, and observational tours. The managers observed appeared to favor verbal media; they spent much time in contact with people. Scheduled meetings consumed the greatest percentage of managerial time, and external contacts one-third to one-half of the time spent on interpersonal activities.

A recent study by the author examined the most important decisions faced by a sample of top managers, mostly at the chairperson or president level. The sample, however, was biased in favor of small businessmen and entrepreneurs. The results, though, seem logical when applied to other organizations. The problems could be grouped into four categories: marketing and regulation, organizational structure, personnel, and finance.

An example of a problem in the marketing category was the need to expand the market or the changing requirements of a government agency. The data involved in this problem were indicators that trouble existed, such as flat revenue growth or a poor profit and loss statement. In another instance, a government regulation was violated, which resulted in product seizures.

An organizational structure problem was the choice of a low-growth subsidiary for divestiture, a choice made through accounting reports of sales. A severe conflict of interest for a senior manager was an example of a personnel problem. The information that alerted the top manager of the firm of this problem came from outside vendors. A typical financial problem was the need to raise new capital; information from market forecasts, potential customers, the sales force, research and development, and company directors was significant in this decision.

Applicability of the Findings

How applicable are these findings, which are based primarily on the activities of top managers? Even though little data exist, the results seem intuitively appealing. Until further studies appear, this research offers the best evidence from which to describe the roles of managers in an organization.

Is it possible to generalize the results above to supervisors and clerical workers in the organization? First, some of the results were found to hold in a review of studies conducted before those by Mintzberg. Second, it does appear that various roles are descriptive of activities of individuals at different levels of management. We might, however, find that activities differ in importance between, say, a supervisor and the president of the company. The figurehead role is played far more often by the president than by the supervisor.

One might also expect the situations surrounding different roles to differ. The president of the company acting as a figurehead may talk to comparable leaders in the government or in other organizations. A first-line supervisor, on the other hand, may be a figurehead for a company baseball team or may preside over a retirement dinner for a subordinate in the department. One would also expect the tools used by management to differ among levels of managers. A supervisor spends more time on observational tours and less time answering mail than the president of the company.

FRAMEWORKS FOR INFORMATION SYSTEMS

Now that we have completed a review of managerial roles and examined information and decision making in the last chapter, we can construct a framework for viewing information systems. A framework, as we have seen, is a conceptual model for organizing thought and discussion about information systems.

We have stated that there is no one theory of information systems. However, a user or designer of a system needs some conceptual model of an information system. Unfortunately, there is no one clearly accepted framework for information systems. Because of the ill-structured nature of the field and its interdisciplinary origins, we can at best expect to develop an intuitive or a verbal model of information systems. We present several different approaches to frameworks, and adopt one for purposes of communicating in this text. It is not essential that everyone adopt the framework we use here. However, it is important for each individual dealing with information systems to have some conceptual model behind the decisions pertaining to these systems.

Anthony

Our first framework was actually presented in Chapter 2 when we discussed different types of information used for various kinds of decisions. These categories of decision types suggested by Anthony can be considered one framework for information systems. To review, Anthony proposed three types of decisions:

  1 Strategic planning is the process of deciding on organizational objectives and the means for achieving them; the planner focuses on the relationship between the environment and the organization.
  2 Managerial control decisions involve a manager ensuring that resources are used efficiently and effectively to achieve the objectives stated during strategic planning. Managerial control decisions are often subjective in their interpretation of information; interpersonal interaction is important in these decisions.
  3 Operational control decisions involve ensuring that specific tasks are completed efficiently and effectively.

AN INTERNATIONAL BANKING SYSTEM

SWIFT stands for the Society for Worldwide Interbank Financial Technology Communications. SWIFT provides users with a communication service for interbanking messages which, in the past, were sent by mail or cable. The prime objective of the system is to facilitate the automation of foreign banking departments.

The SWIFT Network covers most of Western Europe and North America. It is a two-center Financial Transaction Control System with the banks connected through terminals to concentrators in each country. Messages are temporarily stored at switching centers, and users are able to input transactions, whether the receiving terminal is available or not. Each of the operating centers has a fully duplicated computer configuration; the existence of two centers provides back-up at the center level as well.

The system offers two levels of priority, normal and urgent. Expected delivery times are within ten minutes and one minute, depending on the level of service. Access to the system is controlled for security reasons. All messages input to the system are numbered sequentially and the system checks for continuity to be sure that no messages are lost.

This system has helped to create standards among banks exchanging information at the international level. The system started with some fifteen countries. Two additional countries have joined and interest has been expressed in many other countries as well. It seems likely that this system will soon operate worldwide as originally envisioned. This kind of instant communications is only possible through the use of a computer system.

Education and Large Information Systems, A. Buckingham (ed.), North-Holland Publishing Company, 1977.

In Chapter 2, we stressed that different types of decisions require different types of information; for example, strategic planning decisions require infrequently updated, predictive, aggregated data from external sources. The reader should review the discussion on pages 27 through 29, and especially Table 2-2. The major contribution of Anthony is this distinction among types of decisions and their information requirements.

Simon

Earlier we discussed the decision-making stages proposed by Simon, including Intelligence, Design, and Choice. Anthony is concerned with the purpose of decision-making activities and Simon is concerned with methods and techniques of problem solving (Simon, 1965). In addition to the stages described above, Simon proposes that there are two types of decisions: programmed and nonprogrammed. Programmed decisions are routine and repetitive; some specified procedure may be applied to reach a decision each time the situation arises. Programmed decisions require little time spent in the Design stage.

On the other hand, decisions that are nonprogrammed are novel and unstructured. For these decisions, much time has to be spent in Design. There is no one solution to these nonprogrammed decisions, since the problem has probably not appeared before. Clearly, few decisions are at one polar extreme or the other. Just as with Anthony's decision types, decisions are expected to fall someplace along a continuum between programmed and nonprogrammed.

Different types of decision-making technology are suitable for attacking each type of problem. Programmed decisions have traditionally been made through habit, by clerical procedures, or with other accepted tools. More modern techniques for solving programmed decisions involve operations research, mathematical analysis, modeling, and simulation.

Nonprogrammed decisions tend to be solved through judgment, intuition, and rules of thumb. Modern approaches to nonprogrammed decisions include special data analysis programs on computers, training for decision makers in heuristic techniques, and heuristic computer programs, Over time we expect to see new technology providing more programming to nonprogrammed decisions; that is, decisions will tend to move toward the more programmed pole of the continuum.

Gorry–Scott Morton

Gorry and Scott Morton (1971) have synthesized the work of Anthony and Simon to develop a very appealing framework for information systems. The results of their efforts are shown in Table 3-1. This matrix classifies Anthony's decision types from operational control to strategic planning on a structured to unstructured scale (Gorry and Scott Morton feel that "structured" and "unstructured" are better terms than "programmed" and "nonprogrammed").

The three decision phases of Intelligence, Design, and Choice are structured for a fully structured decision. An unstructured problem means that all three phases are unstructured, and any decision between is semistructured. As

Table 3-1   The Gorry and Scott Morton Framework

Classification	Operational control	Management control	Strategic planning
Structured	Order processing Accounts payable	Budgets Personnel reports	Warehouse location Transportation mode mix
Semistructured	Inventory control Production planning	Analysis of variance	Introduction of new product
Unstructured	Cash management	Management of personnel	Planning for R&D

in Simon's framework, the line between structured and unstructured decisions shifts over time as new decision techniques are developed and applied to unstructured problems.

From Table 3-1 it appears that most existing information systems have attacked problems in the structured, operational control cell. These problems are similar in many organizations and are among the most easily understood. It is easier to mechanize these decisions and to predict and achieve cost savings than it is for less structured decisions or for strategic planning decisions. Since operational systems are important to the daily functioning of the firm, they are high-priority applications.

Many individuals in the information systems field believe that decisions with the greatest payoff for the organization are unstructured in nature. The development of systems for unstructured problems is a major challenge and is

---

MANAGEMENT PROBLEM 3-1

David Masters, vice president of finance for the Major Metals Company, is responsible for overall inventory levels in the firm. Major Metals is an integrated mining and metals-producing company with locations throughout the United States. The firm has several computer centers, all reporting to Masters at corporate headquarters in Chicago.

One of the major inventories in the company consists of spare parts for mining and metal-production operations. At one of the divisions, this inventory has a value of over $30 million and consists of around 60,000 items. Analysts at the computer center serving this division are developing a new inventory control system to replace the existing one. A number of new features are being added to this more advanced computer application, including an operations research model for determining reorder points and quantities.

Masters feels that the design of such a system should be under the control of the local design staff who know conditions best. However, he is disturbed about a report he received from the present system, which he does not find useful. Masters fears that this report will be continued in the new system.

Every month, Masters receives an inventory status report showing the quantity of each item in inventory, its usage during the month, the receipt of new merchandise, and the value of the item. Since there are 60,000 items in inventory, this report is voluminous.

Why do you suppose the analysts ever sent this report to the vice president? How does the material discussed in this chapter apply to the distribution of the inventory status report? What should Masters do?

MANAGEMENT PROBLEM 3-2

The recently hired director of information systems for a major manufacturing firm was contemplating his new position. After surveying existing applications in the firm, he found that most computer systems were mundane and primarily processed transactions. Users were happy with the service received from the information services department but had low expectations about the potential of computers.

The new director wanted to continue existing good service levels but also thought that computers could do a lot more for the firm. The director had the support of top management, but because of little user understanding of the potential for new systems, he knew that any innovative ideas would have to be his own.

How should the director proceed to bring more benefits from computer-based systems to the firm? How will the frameworks described in this chapter help him in this task? What problems do you expect the director will encounter?

---

undoubtedly more risky than the development of comparable systems for structured problems. The goals and design techniques for unstructured decisions differ from those for structured ones. In the structured case, the goal of an information system is usually to improve the processing of information. In an unstructured situation, the goal of the information system is more likely to be one of improving the organization and presentation of information inputs to the decision maker.

Using the Gorry–Scott Morton framework, we can obtain a better feeling for the nature of a management information system. Such an information system should support management decision making, not just routine processing. For our purposes, we shall restrict the term "management information system" (MIS) to systems that support managerial and strategic planning decisions. Because of its descriptive power and intuitive appeal, we adopt the Gorry–Scott Morton framework as our conceptual model for information systems in the rest of the text.

EXISTING INFORMATION SYSTEMS

From the Gorry–Scott Morton framework, we predict that most information systems fall into the structured operational control class. For the systems in this cell, the user is usually a clerk or production worker; few management information systems are represented here. We expect that most computer-based information systems are rather mundane in nature and have a relatively small impact on decision makers at the managerial level. Two of the three studies described below are somewhat dated, but the accumulated evidence tends to confirm these predictions.

Churchill et al.

A study performed by Churchill et al. involved interviews with users, managers, and computer department management in a number of companies. Based on the interviews, the researchers concluded that the present information systems literature presents a far more advanced picture than that which actually exists (Churchill et al., 1969).

Computers, as we predicted, have achieved much in clerical operations, but they have been used less frequently in other areas. The researchers noted a trend for the delegation of more decisions to computers. There was little or no impact from computers on higher levels of management in this study. Companies did appear to be moving toward more management-oriented systems. The new systems being planned in the companies were wider in scope than existing systems, and these new applications integrated more departments and crossed more functional boundaries.

Bay Area and Planning Studies

In a study by Lucas (1974a), seven San Francisco Bay area manufacturing firms provided data on their information systems. The study included 20 systems from a variety of applications selected with the consultation of the manager of the information services department. These applications were restricted to major systems involving multiple programs, several integrated processing stages, and reports with wide distribution in the firm. The systems required substantial time and cost to develop and served a large number of users.

About 75 percent of the reports dealt with transactions processing, systems that primarily automate clerical processing activities much the way assembly lines automated manufacturing. Thus, we should add another cell to the Gorry–Scott Morton framework, one of structured transactions-processing systems where almost no decision making is involved.

The Bay Area study is relatively old; there has been much progress in the development of information systems since that time. The next chapter and the short descriptions of applications throughout the text are intended to illustrate some of the diverse ways computer-based systems have served users, management, and the organization.

Although there are many more applications now than when the Bay Area study was conducted, we would expect to find much the same distribution of reports and systems. Most firms first develop transactions processing systems before moving to more sophisticated systems that report information useful for higher levels of management. These transactions systems are the most easily understood and have the greatest potential for demonstrable cost savings.

A more recent study of planning models also tends to confirm the emphasis on transactions and operational processing systems (Lucas 1976a). The research project examined the implementation of computer-based models in a sample of companies. This type of planning model is discussed further in Chapter 8, but essentially the planner uses the computer language to construct a representation of the firm. The resulting model is run on a computer to predict the outcome of various decision alternatives. Such a system has the potential to support strategic planning in the firm, but only 4 of 18 companies used the models for this purpose. The other 14 firms used their models to take immediate action on problems, generally at the operational control level.

HOSPITAL INFORMATION SYSTEMS

It has been estimated that ordering, inventory and supply functions consume 40% of a hospital's operating budget. Hospitals have done almost everything possible to hold down labor costs; in order to stay within government guidelines the materials handling function is now being examined.

Capitalizing on this need American Hospital Supply Corporation, the largest company in the hospital supply business with some $2 billion in sales, is assisting hospitals in better managing their materials.

American Hospital Supply is the only company currently offering automated order entry and inventory control systems to hospitals. It costs about $1,400 a month for most of the company's customers and the firm has signed up 3,000 of the 7,000 hospitals in the country.

These hospitals use computer terminals to communicate directly on-line with American's central computer in Illinois. Incoming orders are immediately routed by the computer to the company's regional distribution center located nearest the customer. There are some 90 of these regional centers around the United States. Within minutes of typing the purchase order on its terminal the hospital receives back a printed confirmation from the firm giving the price of the items and their delivery date. American claims that the system cuts the cost of a typical purchase by 20%. Hospitals can also save money by reducing inventories since American says that it ships 95% of all orders on the same day they are received.

The hospital is encouraged to combine the order entry system with an inventory control system to track incoming supplies, disbursements and stock levels and compare projected inventory with actual supplies on hand.

In addition to providing a service that generates revenue in its own right, hospitals are more likely to purchase supplies from American if they are using part of its systems. The average hospital order on the American system is for 5.8 items while the industry average is only 1.7 items per order. American supplies some 133,000 different items to hospitals.

Business Week, September 8, 1980.

The planning system described above is representative of a type of system that cuts across the Gorry–Scott Morton framework: a decision support system. Although there are several definitions of these systems, they generally are characterized by their focus on a single or limited group of decisions. Rather than encompassing the logic of an entire application such as order entry or inventory control, the system attempts to aid the human decision maker. Often these decision support systems are on-line and include complex operations research models. A decision support system can be used in any of the cells of the Gorry–Scott Morton framework and represents a type of system that is independent of decision level. (But one would be surprised to find a decision support system in a transactions-processing application since transactions-oriented systems feature almost no decision making.)

In summary, the picture that emerges is one of systems that have had fairly limited impact on managers, as predicted by the framework in this chapter. Most systems have focused on structured, operational control decisions and transactions processing. It is very difficult to serve the needs of managers given the variety of managerial activities described earlier in the chapter and the problems inherent in developing information systems.

We shall see in later chapters, however, that some organizations have developed extremely creative and useful applications. To succeed in these endeavors, one must understand the systems analysis and design process and be able to manage information processing activities in the organization.

KEY WORDS

Decision	Liaison	Programmed
Disseminator	Managerial control	Resource allocator
Disturbance handler	Management information	Spokesperson
Entrepreneur	systems	Semistructured
Exception reports	Monitor	Strategic planning
Figurehead role	Negotiator	Structured
Informational roles	Nonprogrammed	Transactions processing
Interpersonal roles	Operational control	Unstructured
Leader	POSDCORB	

RECOMMENDED READINGS

Anthony, R.: *Planning and Control Systems: A Framework for Analysis,* Division of Research, Graduate School of Business Administration, Harvard University, Boston, 1965. (A complete and readable exposition of Anthony's framework for decision making; it is highly recommended.)

Churchill, N. C., J. H. Kempster, and M. Uretsky: *Computer Based Information Systems for Management: A Survey,* National Association of Accountants, New York, 1969. (This early study of the impact of computers on organizations presents interesting findings that differ from popular literature. Though it is somewhat dated, it is good background reading.)

Gorry, G. A., and M. S. Scott Morton: "A Framework for Management Information Systems," *Sloan Management Review,* vol. 13, no. 1, 1971, pp. 55–70. (Consult this reference for more details on the framework adopted in this chapter.)

Lucas, H. C., Jr., K. W. Clowes, R. B. Kaplan: "Framework for Information Systems," *INFOR,* vol. 12, no. 3, October 1974b, pp. 245–260. (A review comparing and contrasting a number of frameworks for information systems. Each of the frameworks is evaluated, and the authors recommend the Gorry–Scott Morton framework.)

Mintzberg, H.: *The Nature of Managerial Work,* Harper & Row, New York, 1973. (Mintzberg's book is recommended reading for any student of information systems. The details of the study referenced in this chapter are presented along with the findings of other studies.)

Simon, H.: *The Shape of Automation for Men and Management,* Harper & Row, New York, 1965. (Essays by Simon describing some of his ideas on problem solving.)

DISCUSSION QUESTIONS

1 Why have so many transactions-processing computer systems been developed?
2 Keep a diary categorizing your daily activies according to the classifications used by Mintzberg. How do your activities compare with those of the managers in his study?

3 How could Mintzberg's technique of structured observation be used in designing an information system?

4 Describe the purposes of a framework. What kinds of problems are encountered when individuals with different backgrounds try to communicate without some common conceptual model?

5 Why is the line between structured and unstructured decisions shifting more toward structured? Are unstructured decisions being eliminated, or will we continue to be faced with this type of decision problem?

6 How would you define and recognize the characteristics of a management information system?

7 Sketch a framework for information systems of your own. How does it compare with the ones discussed in the chapter?

8 Several authors have suggested functional frameworks for information systems, for example, information systems to serve logistics, finance, and marketing functions. What are the advantages and disadvantages of this approach to frameworks?

9 What are the problems in developing an information system to support unstructured decision making?

10 What are the characteristics of an information system to support strategic planning activities in an organization?

11 What aspects of management are like a science? What aspects of management defy a scientific approach?

12 Compare and contrast an information system for processing orders with one for planning a corporate acquisition. On what technological characteristics would you expect these systems to differ? What types of information and to whom should the information be provided by each of these systems?

13 What type of technology would you expect to see used for operational control, managerial control, and strategic planning systems? For example, where would an on-line system be used versus a batch system?

14 What role can information serve for a decision maker acting as a disturbance handler? What role can information serve for a decision maker acting in the information, interpersonal, and decisional roles?

15 Can an information system be of any assistance to a manager acting as a negotiator?

16 What is wrong with the classic views of management activities?

17 What problems are created by providing the wrong type of information for a particular decision setting? What do the Simon, Anthony, and Gorry–Scott Morton frameworks suggest is likely to happen?

18 What level of management would you expect to be associated with different decision types; for example, who makes the preponderance of planning decisions in an organization?

19 Think of an example of a structured versus an unstructured decision problem and compare the two on the information differences presented by Anthony.

20 What top management functions and activities can be supported by a computer-based information system?

TYPES OF SYSTEMS
APPLICATIONS
    The Manager
    The Morning
    Lunch
    Afternoon
IN CONCLUSION
KEY WORDS
RECOMMENDED READINGS
DISCUSSION QUESTIONS

Chapter 4

An Overview of Computer-Based Information Systems

CHAPTER ISSUES

- Where can computer-based information systems be applied?
- What are some of the design features to be included in computer-based systems?

In this chapter, we discuss the general structure of information systems and look at examples of different kinds of systems. Our purpose is to gain an appreciation for the many different applications employing computer-based information systems.

TYPES OF SYSTEMS

Figure 4-1 is a simple illustration of the basic components of a computer-based information system. A system processes input that is provided by a user, for example, is a list of hours worked by employees. The input is first edited for errors and corrected, if necessary, through manual intervention. An entry that

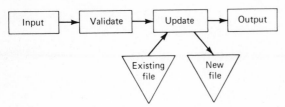

Figure 4-1   Components of a computer-based information system.

indicates someone worked 120 hours in a week is probably incorrect and should be questioned. The input becomes immediate output (a check) or is used to modify the files (pay records) of the system. Input can also be used to request the retrieval of information stored in the system, such as the names of all employees who worked overtime last week.

Files containing data are a major component of the information system. The files correspond to the information kept in folders, file cabinets, or notebooks in a manual information system. Information may be retrieved from a file or the file contents may be altered by modifying, adding, or deleting data in the file. We are also interested in some type of output from a system that may be a short response to an inquiry request for information from a file or the result of elaborate computations. Output is produced in many different formats and modes of presentation such as a printed report, a display on a televisionlike screen, or a verbal response.

It is helpful to distinguish among the types of information systems according to the technology employed. In a simple batch system, all input is processed at one point in time to produce the desired output. The input data are collected and used to update the files periodically, for example, daily, weekly, or monthly. The data are frequently out of date in this type of system, but batch processing is very economical. A payroll system is an example of an application that is usually operated in batch mode.

A simple inquiry system features on-line retrieval of information from files that are updated in batch mode. A system for production control might be updated overnight and have its files available for inquiry using a terminal during the day.

An inquiry and post system is similar to a simple inquiry system in processing retrieval requests for information. However, it also accepts and edits input on-line for later updating in batch mode. This input is saved on a file and is used to update the system later. The production control system above could be operated in this manner to accept input from factor-floor data terminals during the day. Then in the evening, when the computer schedule is less heavy, the files could be updated in a batch processing run.

An inquiry and on-line updating system actually makes modifications to files as the information is entered from terminals. These systems require more complicated technology and are exemplified by on-line reservations systems.

A command and control system or real-time system is one in which information has to be fed back instantaneously to control an operation. For example, sensors on a missile feed information to a computer that must process the data in time to provide guidance control for the missile.

Table 4-1 summarizes the types of systems and their characteristics, and provides an example of a typical application employing each type of technology.

APPLICATIONS

In the rest of this chapter, we present a survey of various computer-based information systems to illustrate the diversity of situations in which these systems have been used. Our vehicle for presentation will be to follow a hypothetical manager through a day's activities. We shall discuss the information systems encountered and briefly describe their characteristics. These information systems do not necessarily exist in exactly the form described here. However, all the applications areas suggested have been supported by computer-based information systems similar to the ones encountered below.

The Manager

Our hypothetical manager is Martha Johnson, the executive vice president of Diversified Products, Inc. Diversified is a medium-sized conglomerate whose major operation is the production of automobile parts for new car and replacement markets. Several smaller subsidiaries manufacture parts for other consumer durable products.

Martha has an M.B.A. from a leading business school and has been working for Diversified for about five years. She began as controller, having majored in accounting and finance. Martha was recently promoted to executive vice president, a position with major operating and financial responsibilities.

Table 4-1 Characteristics and Applications of Various Technologies

Type of system	Characteristics	Example
Simple batch system	Updating at one point in time	Payroll
Simple inquiry	Update in batch, retrieve on-line	Inventory status
Inquiry and post	Update in batch, retrieve on-line, enter and edit data on-line	Production control with factory-floor input
Fully on-line	All input, output, and updating done on-line through terminals	Reservations system
Command and control	Fully on-line and instantaneous feedback to control some process	Missile launching and guidance

The Morning

We join Martha on her way to work in the morning. She lives in a townhouse near a rail line serving the central city where Diversified's headquarters and main production facilities are located. This morning she listens to a weather forecast and decides to drive to the railroad station because showers are predicted.

A Weather System   Behind the forecast is a huge system of reporting stations and computer equipment: data from all over the world are collected and processed to study and predict the weather. Some of the largest computational programs for modern computers were developed for the task of weather forecasting. However, the general public rarely glimpses the people or machines monitoring the weather and generating these forecasts.

A Police System   While driving to the station, Martha encounters the well-known phenomenon of a radar speed trap, though fortunately she is heading in the opposite direction! She notices that immediately after stopping the offending motorist, the police officer does not leave the patrol car, but instead speaks on the car radio. Had she been able to overhear the conversation, Martha would have heard the officer checking with the dispatcher to get information about the automobile to be cited. What kind of data would the officer receive and how?

At the heart of this police information system is a computer-based file containing information on wants and warrants, and these data can be retrieved from the file on-line for an inquiring officer. The police officer in the field radios the command center and requests information on a given license number. At the center an operator, using a terminal connected to an on-line system, enters the

---

MANAGEMENT PROBLEM 4-1

The chief executive of a small firm specializing in the acquisition of cable TV companies feels that the major reason for the firm's success is its ability to perform an economic evaluation of a proposed acquisition in two or three days. Larger competitors, because of standards and bureaucratic procedures, are not able to move as rapidly.

However, there are several problems with the analysis conducted by the small firm. Because of the computational complexity of different financing arrangements and depreciation schemes, very few possibilities are computed. The controller of the firm uses a pocket calculator for the computations; there is not sufficient time for a complete analysis of the myriad possibilities available.

The chief executive thought that a computer might be able to help, but he does not know how to proceed. He fears that a computer might make procedures too rigid or that a system might be too expensive.

From what you know of the different kinds of computer systems available, what kind of computer processing, if any, would you recommend to the chief executive and why?

---

license number. The computer is programmed to search for any information on the file about a car with that license plate or the person to whom it is registered.

Typical questions would be, "Are there any outstanding tickets or warrants for the car or driver? Is the automobile stolen?" Information is retrieved and radioed back to the police officer. If the driver is wanted, the officer takes special precautions or calls for assistance in approaching the automobile. Such information has greatly increased the safety of the police officer.

However, as with any benefit, there are costs connected with such a system. Police systems have raised issues of invasion of privacy over the records of data maintained on them. These systems also can result in abuses to citizens if not updated properly. For example, in one city, stolen cars were later recovered, but the computer system was not updated. Several rightful owners of the returned automobiles were arrested later because the information system was not kept up to date!

A Sales Application   After arriving at work, Martha receives a summary management report on sales in Diversified's major division. Diversified employs about 150 sales representatives nationwide. Twenty-five of these representatives call on Detroit manufacturers to sell new car parts while the others concentrate on sales of auto replacement parts through chain stores and other retail outlets.

The company has developed a fairly elaborate batch sales information system as an outgrowth of its order entry computer system. Sales force members complete orders and send them to the data processing center where they are transcribed into a machine-readable medium. The orders are summarized by type and product and printed by due date for production control scheduling purposes. The orders are also analyzed to extract sales information; past sales history is kept on a computer file. Each sales representative receives a monthly report showing his or her accounts and 12 months of historical sales data. The reports also contain this-year-to-date and last-year-to-date figures on sales by unit and dollar volume.

There is a goal or quota for each sales representative that is also shown on the report. This system has eliminated much of the sales representatives' bookkeeping and allowed them to concentrate on sales. The sales information system also produces a summary report by territory and by product for management. A batch retrieval program allows managers to select different types of information based on their needs. Martha Johnson, for example, likes to receive a report of sales by product and sales by product within each geographical region. She uses this information to obtain a feeling for how different product groups are doing and to compare sales with inventories in different parts of the country.

The Production System   A 10 A.M. meeting is scheduled to discuss a request for a new production control system. Most of the operations of Diversified are classified as job shop as opposed to assembly-line production. There is a series of manufacturing operations on each product, and a number of different machines can be used for these operations; there is no one sequence of steps. Scheduling job shops is difficult because of the combinatorial number of paths through the shop for a given product.

Early in the days of computer use, Diversified developed a time-sharing simulation model to help in the scheduling process. A production control scheduler inputs the jobs to be completed to a terminal connected to a commercial firm selling time-sharing services. A model developed by a consulting firm simulates the flow of orders through the shop and prints the best schedule. The simulation program has a table showing all machinery requirements for different orders. Various scheduling rules are tried and the best scheduling rule in terms of time and cost is selected.

The purpose of the 10 A.M. meeting is to discuss a proposal for installing factory-floor data collection terminals to record the status of production. Several managers in the company have questioned the advisability and need for such data and the meeting continues until lunchtime.

Lunch

Computer-Aided Design   Martha lunches with the head of engineering for Diversified; they discuss a recent demonstration at a customer's location. The customer, one of the major automobile manufacturers, showed them its engineering research center. The manager of engineering was fascinated by the customer's computer-aided design system. Automobile designers sit in front of cathode-ray tube (CRT) terminals, which resemble a television set, and work interactively with the computer to design new products. An engineer uses a light pen to indicate changes on the screen and the computer system makes the changes on-line instantaneously. Several complete cars had been designed in this manner. However, the manufacturer admitted that the on-line computer system and programs to control the graphics displays (for example, line drawings of automobiles and their components) were very complex and costly. Martha and the engineering manager agree that such a tool is currently beyond economic feasibility for Diversified.

Two Customer-Oriented Systems   After lunch, Martha has a few minutes to conduct two items of personal business. First, she wishes to see if a check has been credited to her bank account. She stops at a branch of the bank and keys in her account number on a standard Touch-Tone phone. She receives a response giving the balance of her checking account: "four two oh one dollars and seven five cents."

This bank system is basically a batch on-line inquiry application. The telephone is a very inexpensive terminal; computer output is produced by an audio-response unit. Numbers are prerecorded on this device and the computer program accepts the account number, locates the balance on file, and gives instructions to the audio response unit on what numbers to "play" for output.

Back at the office, Martha decides to try another letter to *Modern Living* magazine (earlier she had resolved to cancel her subscription). First, her subscription was not renewed as requested. Then two copies of the magazine started arriving each month. Several letters also came demanding payment even after Martha sent a copy of her cancelled check. This time Martha is writing to the publisher in hopes of obtaining satisfaction.

At the magazine, chaos had prevailed since a consultant had designed and programmed a new subscription system. For some reason, unknown to the magazine staff, the new system did not work. The computer cancelled subscriptions after the magazine sent two copies each month. Customers cancelled other subscriptions because no copies were being received. Circulation dropped and the magazine had to resort to costly overprinting to be sure enough copies were available. Because of the decline in circulation, advertising revenue also decreased. Finally, after hiring some staff members with computer experience and turning to another consultant for help, the situation is improving. However, *Modern Living* was very close to bankruptcy at one point in time because the subscription system failed so badly.

Afternoon

Marketing Research   After lunch, Martha attends a meeting with the marketing department. This department is looking at marketing models to see how they could be used to assist the company. The department requested more funds in its budget to hire an operations research staff member and for time-sharing services. Several models were available to help in advertising decisions; there were also models to suggest strategies for new product selection and introduction. In addition to the models already available, a number of statistical techniques to answer different marketing questions could be applied to sales data that were collected already by the sales information system.

The marketing department also wants funds to use an existing information storage and retrieval system. Several vendors offer very large data bases of information useful for such research. For example, the Lockheed Dialog system contains some 40 million citations in a data base of 50 billion characters that can be accessed by customers for a fee. The user of these services dials a computer in California and employs a simple language to submit retrieval requests. A computer program searches for abstracts fitting the key words entered by the user. Abstracts can be printed at the computer center and mailed to the requester if a large number of citations are found.

Planning Systems   Later in the afternoon, Martha receives the output from the latest run of Diversified's planning model. Using a specially developed language for planning, a staff member constructed a model of the firm. Simple equations are used to express basic relationships among demand, production, sales, and inventory. The staff develops various scenarios and compares the output to predict the results of different courses of action.

Economic data obtained from a firm selling time-series data on the economy supplements the planning model. The vendor of economic data has a large computer model of the economy, constructed with sophisticated regression techniques. Information developed from this model is made available to customers; Diversified uses these data to provide information on general economic conditions for its own model.

Martha is particularly interested in a cash flow forecast for the next four or five years for a new subsidiary under consideration for acquisition. On the next run, she asks the analyst to show what would happen to cash flow projections if the new subsidiary is acquired this year and an existing, unprofitable subsidiary is sold in three years.

Airplane Reservations   Before leaving work Martha calls an airline to make a reservation for a trip the following week. The passenger agent who answers the phone converses with an on-line reservation system through an alphanumeric CRT terminal (unlike the graphics terminal for automated design, this TV-like terminal prints only letters and numbers). The agent obtains information on what flights are available from the computer system; a computer program checks the file of flights and times and displays them on the agent's screen.

Martha requests a round-trip flight. The agent enters the request; the computer system checks a file for the flight requested and indicates that space is available. The agent enters Martha's name and the computer program places it on a file. Later, plans can be changed easily. Martha's record can be consulted by the agent when she appears for her ticket and proceeds to the gate to board the plane.

A Supermarket System   On the way home, Martha stops at a supermarket that is experimenting with a new, automated check-out system. The system appears fast to Martha, but she wonders if it is economical. Each grocery item is coded with something called the Universal Product Code, and this code can be read by an optical scanner in the counter when the item and code are passed over the scanner. Price information is retrieved by a computer program that also maintains a running total of the groceries purchased by the customer. The clerk no longer has to operate a cash register. By knowing every item sold, the store can keep track of inventory and place appropriate reorders. However, these point-of-sale systems have aroused the fear of many consumer groups opposed to the lack of price information marked on grocery items, even though the price is marked on the shelf.

IN CONCLUSION

In this brief sketch, we observed a number of different information systems. These systems employ different types of computer technology and support different kinds of decisions (see Table 4-2). There are problems with some of the systems, and others appear to work well. In later chapters, we shall explain some

Table 4-2 Summary of Systems

System	Decision type	Technology
Weather	Operational	Batch, on-line
Police want/warrant	Operational	On-line
Sales, order entry	Transactional, operational, management	Batch
Production control	Operational	On-line (time-sharing)
Automobile design	Operational	On-line
Account inquiry	Transactional	On-line inquiry
Subscription	Transaction	Batch
Marketing models	Managerial and strategic	Time-sharing
Planning model	Strategic	Time-sharing
Reservations system	Transactional, operational	On-line
Supermarket system	Transactional, operational	On-line

of these problems and try to suggest how to make successful decisions about computer systems.

We should emphasize that the scenario described in this chapter is hypothetical; however, applications such as these do exist. It should be obvious that computer-based information systems have been applied to many diverse situations. Although we always are constrained by cost and technology, to a great extent we are limited only by our imagination, creativity, and ability to deal successfully with the changes created by computer-based information systems.

KEY WORDS

Alphanumeric	Graphics	On-line
Audio response	Edit	Output
Batch	Inquire and post	Posting
Command and control	Inquiry	Simulation
CRT	Models	Update
Files		

RECOMMENDED READINGS

Alter, S.: *Decision Support Systems: Current Practice and Continuing Challenges,* Addison Wesley, Reading, Mass., 1980. (This book presents a number of studies of systems primarily designed to support decisions.)

IBM Systems Journal, vol. 12, no. 2, 1973. (An issue that focuses on financial models using computer systems.)

IBM Systems Journal, vol. 14, no. 1, 1975. (Both supermarket and retail-store automatic check-out systems are described.)

Montgomery, D., and G. Urban: "Marketing Decisions Systems: An Emerging View," *Journal of Marketing Research,* vol. 7, May 1970, pp. 226–234. (A conceptual overview of the characteristics of a marketing decision system.)

Weiss, E. (ed.): *Computer Usage Applications,* McGraw-Hill, New York, 1970. (This book discusses a number of computer-based applications in various areas of a firm.)

DISCUSSION QUESTIONS

1   What are the advantages and disadvantages of batch computer systems?
2   Do you expect input editing to be easier for a batch or for an on-line system?
3   Why do you suppose inquiry and post systems were developed instead of fully on-line applications?
4   What are the advantages and disadvantages of fully on-line computer systems?
5   How do backup requirements differ between batch and on-line systems?
6   What applications, if any, exist for command and control systems in business?
7   How does time sharing differ in its use from both batch and on-line systems?
8   What are the drawbacks to mathematical models applied to management problems?
9   What are the problems with simulation as a tool in business analysis?
10 Why do so many batch computer systems exist?
11 What factors inhibit the development of on-line systems? (Hint: Think of the major components of such systems.)
12 What are the social issues involved in having massive files of personal data available on-line?
13 Computer-aided instruction has been suggested as one way to improve education. What do you think its limitations are?
14 Why are so many time-sharing applications developed in user departments rather than under the control of an internal information systems department?
15 One critic has suggested that management information can never be automated. What is your reaction to this statement?
16 Examine a computer application with which you are familiar. Describe its purpose, input, output, processing, and files.
17 Inventory control is one of the most popular computer applications. Why? What has its impact been on the economy?
18 An entire industry exists for selling information. Make a survey of some of the data for sale and classify it by functional area, for example. marketing, finance, economics.
19 Why is it useful to have interaction capabilities when working with a computer-based model?
20 What factors from a user's standpoint are different in the design of a batch versus an on-line system?
21 What are the major advantages and disadvantages of inquiry and post systems?

Part Two

Organizational Issues

In this part we review what is known about the impact of computer systems on the organization. Our emphasis is on the design of systems that have a positive impact on the organization and its members. The analysis is aided by two models: the first explains the development of power by different departments in an organization, and the second focuses specifically on information systems in the context of the organization.

The impact of computers on the organization is of key concern to management. Chapter 5 provides the preparation necessary to discuss the implementation of systems, in the section of the text on systems analysis and design.

Top management has a key role to play in the management of information processing activities in the organization. In this part we also discuss information systems policy; what are the key areas for the involvement of top management? What policy should top management establish for the information systems effort in the organization? A successful information services function begins with strong and effective leadership at the top levels of the organization.

IMPACT ON THE ORGANIZATION
    Early Predictions
    Distribution of Power
IMPACT ON INDIVIDUALS
    Early Predictions
    A Conflict Model
INFORMATION SYSTEMS IN THE CONTEXT OF THE
ORGANIZATION
    A Descriptive Model
    Implications for Systems Design
    Implications for Operations
IN CONCLUSION
KEY WORDS
RECOMMENDED READINGS
DISCUSSION QUESTIONS

Chapter 5

The Impact of Information Systems on the Organization

CHAPTER ISSUES

- How should the organization prepare for the impact of computers?
- How should the organization approach the design and operation of information systems?

Many times information systems have failed because the reactions of users were ignored or because designers did not consider the impact of the system on the organization. A technically elegant system is successful only if it is used. Most early studies of the impact of computers were completed after the systems had been installed; these studies were broad in nature and in general were not oriented toward the design of better information systems.

More recent research has led to the development of a model of information systems, in the context of the organization, that describes how information systems impact and interact with organizations. From this model it should be possible to predict the impact of systems in advance and plan for a successful interface with the organization. This topic is of vital concern to the user of information systems; anyone requesting a system is interested in its successful development. As we shall see, organizational factors are as important (or more so) than technological considerations in the design and operation of computer-based information systems.

IMPACT ON THE ORGANIZATION

Early Predictions

Leavitt and Whisler (1958) presented one of the best-known sets of predictions for the impact of computers on organizations. These authors suggested that firms would recentralize as a result of new computer technology; the availability of more information than previously possible would allow management to centralize. The trend until the development of computer systems had been toward decentralization because centralized management could not cope with the amount of information and the number of decisions required in a large organization. Computers offer the power to make centralized management possible so the organization can be tightly controlled by a group of top managers.

Little evidence supports this early prediction (Lucas, 1975). In a few cases, researchers have found examples of recentralization after computer systems were installed; however, there is no overall trend evident. Occasionally a system has replaced a level of management, for example, a military command and control system. Unfortunately, there have been too few studies, and research in this area is hard to conduct because so many variables besides computer systems affect the structure of an organization.

Another problem in validating predictions of computer impact occurs in defining variables such as centralization and decentralization. Moreover, early predictions assumed that decentralization is negatively motivated. However, there may be other reasons to decentralize—for example, to train managers or to provide more autonomy for supervisors.

There is no real reason why computer systems lead naturally to centralization. We can consider centralization and decentralization as variables in the systems design process. Certainly, centralization is not something that should be measured after a system has been implemented. Management should specify the goals of the organization and the degree of centralization desired. Given the sophisticated communications capabilities of on-line computer systems and large data-base systems, we can design a computer system that provides information for decision making at any level or geographical location in an organization.

Distribution of Power

As mentioned earlier, some of the first studies of the impact of the computer on organizations are not helpful because they have not really provided a basis for designing successful systems. The real problem with the impact of information systems on organizations is concerned with a subject not covered in past studies: information systems affect the distribution of power in the organization. "Power" is the potential to influence others to act according to our wishes. Different departments in organizations have different levels of power, and a theory proposed by Hickson et al. (1971) offers some insight into these power relationships. These authors suggest a model with four major conditions, described below, that produce a department having a high level of power. As we shall see, the information services department meets all these conditions for high power, and by its activities, this department alters the distribution of power in an organization.

One hypothesized determinant of power is the extent to which the department copes with uncertainty for other departments. Uncertainty is defined as the lack of information about future events that make their outcomes less predictable. An information services department copes with a great deal of uncertainty for user departments. When a new system is designed, the user often yields control over an operation to the information services department.

For example, consider the department that used to prepare budget statements manually but that has just implemented a computer system to process budgets. Before the computer system, when a group of clerks and analysts prepared the budget, the manager of the department had complete control. If the department was behind schedule, the manager could arrange overtime or employ temporary help to see that the job was completed. A solution to most problems was within the manager's own department. Now, with the computer system, the manager has added uncertainties about whether the information services department will finish processing on time and with acceptable accuracy. The development of this computer system has created uncertainty for the manager where none existed before. Interestingly enough, only the information services department can cope with this new uncertainty.

Information systems are designed to provide information for decision making and so the information services department is in the business of supplying information. We have defined information as some tangible or intangible entity that reduces uncertainty. Thus, the information services department supplies a product that reduces uncertainty by its very nature. Furthermore, in the operation of systems, there are many uncertainties, such as whether a job will be completed on time and whether the output will be satisfactory. This uncertainty also is controlled by the information services department.

A second hypothesized determinant of high power is whether or not a department can be replaced easily. These are a few alternatives to a mature information services department. Dissatisfied company management could hire an entirely new computer staff, but this would create chaos during the transition period. One can also turn to a service bureau for processing, but it would be difficult and expensive to convert all present applications. Another alternative to the information services department is a facilities management arrangement in which a consultant contracts to run an information services department.

However, most facilities management contractors hire a proportion of the people currently working in the information services department. A facilities management agreement also meets resistance from management, which is often uneasy about having another organization responsible for the processing of vital information. Thus, for a mature information services department, there are not many possible substitutes.

A third proposed determinant of high power for a department is the number of links between other departments and the department in question. The greater the number of links to a department, the greater its power. Clearly, here is another situation where the information services department has the potential for becoming quite powerful. The information services department may accept input from a wide variety of departments in the organization and provide them all with some type of service. The importance of each link also must be considered in assessing departmental power. If a link were separated, how long would it take for the organization to stop? The building and grounds department has a large number of links to each department. However, the lack of janitorial services would be only an inconvenience; in most organizations the final output would not be affected drastically.

For the information services department, the number of links and the importance of output depend on the type of applications developed. Transactional and operational control systems are usually associated with greater power, since these systems have an immediate impact on workloads in the company. Most organizations, for example, are heavily dependent on on-line transactions processing systems.

The degree of interdependence between the department of interest and all other departments in the organization is a final condition for power. The greater the dependence of department A on department B, the greater is department B's power. The information services department tends to exhibit reciprocal interdependence with user departments. That is, the information services department and user departments are mutually dependent on each other to process work, and unfortunately, this type of mutual dependence is the most demanding. An information services department depends on users during systems design to supply information and to provide an understanding of what is needed. On the other hand, the user is dependent on the information services department for the technical aspects of design and for seeing that a system is implemented. During operations, the user must supply input and help maintain the data base. The user in turn is dependent on the information services department to provide processing services.

The information services department has a potentially high score on all the conditions for power discussed above, particularly on coping with uncertainty. Limited evidence suggests that coping with uncertainty is the most important condition for high power (Hennings et al., 1974). As an information services department develops systems for different departments, it becomes more powerful in the organization. However, this trend is often not realized because no one stops to look at the department as a whole and consider the total of all applications. When there are significant power shifts in an organization, users can become resentful of dependence on the information services department, possibly without knowing the real reasons for dissatisfaction. As a result, users may stop working with systems or not seek added computer help when it could be of great assistance. Discomfort over changes in power relations has also been known to lead to personal conflict.

IMPACT ON INDIVIDUALS

Early Predictions

Many early studies of the impact of computer systems were concerned with user reactions. Some of these studies dealt with the psychological reaction of workers, and others concentrated on overall changes in levels of employment. Although isolated changes in employment have occurred, it is difficult to find an overall trend. It is safe to say that the impact of computers on unemployment levels has been no greater than that of any other technological change. The lack of an adverse impact is particularly significant in view of the short period of time that has elapsed since computers were introduced and the rapid development of computer systems.

Early writers were also interested in the impact of computer systems on jobs and job content. Turner (1980) presents an extensive review of the literature on the impact of computers on jobs and job content. He concludes from these studies that computer-based systems tend to make clerical jobs more demanding through increased workload and pace of work. Clerical jobs associated with

---

MANAGEMENT PROBLEM 5-1

A major United States bank was dependent on its computer systems for processing many different kinds of financial transactions. For several months, the information services department warned that it needed additional computer capacity but was out of physical space.

Bank management was relatively unconcerned; they were spending enough on computers at present. The decision to expand and obtain a new computer was deferred several times.

One day. the bank's computers were unable to process all the transactions. The bank lost track of its deposits and failed to clear its accounts with other banks on time. Such an incident cost the bank a large amount of money in fines and in lost interest on funds.

Bank management became very aware of the computer problem because of this malfunction and the attendant crisis. Now how do you think computers are viewed in the bank? What types of computer systems do you think result in the most power for the information services department? How can managers cope with the problems of power transfers in the organization because of computer systems?

computers tend to become more anxiety provoking as a result of greater strain and tension. Computers are also associated with job formalization at the clerical level since they generate more rules and procedures to follow. However, it does appear that computer use is associated with greater productivity as measured by output per worker. These studies do suffer from certain research problems and they are relatively few in number.

Turner's own study of clerical employees in banking found that high productivity, mental strain symptoms, and job dissatisfaction were associated with the use of computers. Stress on the job appeared to be the primary mechanism by which the use of computer systems affected clerical workers. In this study, systems with more structured processing were both more productive and more stressful than interactive systems.

Turner suggests creating jobs with more decision latitude and more opportunities for problem solving to mitigate the negative aspects of systems. This study and review of prior research are thought provoking. Although the results are still preliminary, management needs to consider carefully the impact of computer systems on users.

Other writers have speculated on the changes computers might bring to management. They have suggested that computers would assume more of top management's innovative activities and lead to a managerial elite. Computers would tend to accentuate differences among different levels of management (Leavitt and Whisler, 1958). Middle managers were expected to suffer the most from computer systems, and it was predicted that there would be fewer middle managers. Individuals holding middle management positions would need fewer skills and hence would receive lower pay. These workers would have less status in the organization and lower mobility. Early predictions also suggested that many nonmanagement employees would be replaced. For those remaining, jobs would become more boring, and the worker would have less self-control.

While only a few similar studies have been undertaken recently, they have all failed to confirm the predictions. First, it is hard to define middle management. Even still, the drastic changes forecasted do not appear to have occurred. Clerical personnel seem to have been replaced occasionally by a computer system, but the effect is not necessarily widespread. Often more work is done by the same number of workers than would have been possible before a computer system.

Although the research results are not extensive, it will become evident as we discuss systems analysis and design later in the text that computer systems do have the potential to affect individuals and their jobs. The design techniques to be suggested will help reduce the negative impact of the changes created through the implementation of computer-based systems.

A Conflict Model

A major impact of computers on an individual occurs when conflict arises between users and the information services department. Conflict can be caused by a number of conditions, one of which is the fact that power is transferred from users to an information services department. If a system does not fit users' needs or is not installed on schedule, there may also be conflict. Conflict is likely to result if the system is not operated according to specifications.

In addition to the problems listed above, there are a number of conditions that have the potential to create conflict in an organization (Walton and Dutton, 1969). We do not expect the relationships between each information services department and other departments to fulfill all conflict conditions, but the potential is there for such problems to arise.

Our first condition is mutual dependence, which increases the potential for conflict because the failure to perform by one party causes serious difficulties for the other. Dependence develops between an information services department and user departments as described earlier for the power model, so there is a high potential for conflict.

Task differences also create conflict. Computer work is highly specialized, and there are many differences between the tasks of a programmer and the average user. Uncertainty has also been known to lead to frustration and conflict, and we have seen that a large amount of uncertainty surrounds computer work. Conflict can also be fostered by ambiguities: In computer activities, who is responsible for a problem? Has the operations staff made an error or is the system badly designed? There is also the possibility that the error is the responsibility of the user.

Occasionally, when people depend on common resources, conflict arises. Computers may be seen as taking limited funds from a fixed budget in user departments, or several departments may compete for limited computer resources. Job dissatisfaction is another condition that leads to conflict. Users of the information services department may be unhappy in their job or jealous of other workers in the organization. Computer jobs have been known to pay more highly than other positions, and if a user feels service is bad, the fact that the computer staff is more highly paid may be resented. Computer staff members often keep rather strange hours, and a user seeing a programmer arrive at 2 P.M. may not realize that the programmer worked all night.

Communications obstacles have become a major problem between the computer staff and users. The computer field has developed its own jargon, and many computer professionals do not realize they are using strange and unfamiliar terminology. The user may feel that the information services department staff members are trying to demonstrate superior knowledge or avoid making an accurate explanation of a problem by using jargon. In certain situations an information services department staff member may also be confused by user jargon.

Performance rewards differ drastically among information services department staff members and users, and these differences have a potential for creating conflict. Reward structures are hard to assess, but a few companies appear to pay for harmonious relationships among users and the computer staff or for successfully designing and implementing systems. Personal characteristics and traits often differ among information systems staff members and users, which is

MANAGEMENT PROBLEM 5-2

A new payroll system is being implemented at the Old Shoe Company. While payroll is often considered to be a simple computer application, it often turns out to be very complex. At Old Shoe, the payroll system also collects data for the cost accounting system.

A single programmer-analyst has worked for several months to develop a new version of the system. The old version had to be replaced because Old Shoe had just acquired a new subsidiary. This new subsidiary increased the number of employees at the company beyond the number of digits in the employee identification number in the old system. Thus, there is intense time pressure to install the new system to run the total payroll for the company.

The head of the payroll section is very unhappy with the new system. She feels that the original system works well, despite examples that showed that it has errors in it.

The information services department is running a parallel test. That is, the old and new systems are being run simultaneously to check the results of one against the other. Of course, this type of test requires a lot of extra work. Duplicate input has to be prepared and the results of the two systems compared. Extensive overtime is required on the part of the payroll clerks.

The head of the payroll department refuses to accept the new system because the number of errors is "unreasonable." The programmer-analyst thinks that the payroll department head is unreasonable because the new system has actually shown some errors in the original one! He maintains that the few errors in the new system could easily be corrected after it is operational.

What type of information would you want to help you decide whether to install the new system? How would you resolve the dispute between the payroll department head and the programmer-analyst? What kind of problem is this?

---

also a condition leading to conflict. Technically, computer work can be very demanding and the staff member is usually highly committed to a career. Computer professionals may not empathize with and understand user problems, which often creates conflict.

Certainly not all the conditions described above exist in any one organization; however, the relationship between the computer staff and users has a potential for leading to disruptive conflict. As a result of this conflict, users may sabotage the information services department by withholding data or providing incorrect input. Because of the dependence of the information services department on users, it is easy for users to make the information services department appear in an unfavorable light.

On the other hand, the information services department can sabotage users through delays in processing or by withholding service. Controls can be relaxed, which will introduce more errors in the processing. In the case of heightened warfare, users may refuse to cooperate in the development of new systems, systems that could have a significant payoff for the organization. The computer

AIRLINE APPLICATIONS

Braniff International Airways is using computers for a variety of functions. The airline serves 79 airports including 57 in the U.S. The computer is helping to maintain complex fares which vary according to the class of trip, the length of stay, and how far in advance one makes a reservation. Braniff agents receive more than 2 million calls a month and the computer is helping them by displaying fares and special restrictions and advising travelers of all options. The computers can process over 200 messages a second.

The system has helped improve passenger service and agent productivity by automatically ticketing and by helping control passenger boarding operations. It takes less than ten seconds for the computer to print a ticket and a passenger itinerary.

Using the latest weather forecast, passenger load information from the reservations record, and anticipated cargo hauling, a computer program evaluates alternatives and produces a flight plan showing the best altitude and routing for each flight. The objective function of the system is to produce the lowest cost flight between the two airports. The computer advises the pilot of the altitudes to fly and the angle and rate of climb, and the rate of descent in order to optimize fuel use. When the flight is ready to depart, the flight plan produced by the computer calculates the aircraft weight and center of gravity to ensure the flight is within safety and balance limits.

Another application using the system is engine performance monitoring. Flight crews record in flight engine instrument readings and send them directly to the computer complex. Any deviation from a norm is a signal to an engineer to make the judgement as to whether the engine should be removed early for maintenance or other corrective action should be taken.

The Airline Industry has long had highly visible computer systems for reservations. These applications at Braniff also illustrate how the computer can be used for additional airline operations.

Computer World, November 19, 1979.

staff then tends to become discouraged, and the department experiences high turnover. New systems are not designed at all or are not well designed. As conditions worsen, we face a continuing spiral of poor performance and increasing levels of conflict.

INFORMATION SYSTEMS IN THE CONTEXT OF THE ORGANIZATION

Earlier we suggested that organizational factors are equally as important as technical details in the design and operation of computer-based information systems. The problem with the studies described above is their lack of emphasis on how we can develop successful systems. The power and conflict models discussed earlier in the chapter have helped to develop the model of computer-based information systems in the context of the organization presented below. The purpose of this model is to help understand the organizational impact of systems and to predict the results of implementing a system. The model, when validated, can help suggest ways to increase the probability of the successful design and operation of information systems.

A Descriptive Model

Figure 5-1 presents a descriptive model of information systems in the context of the organization. Boxes represent important components of information systems activities, and arrows between the boxes indicate predicted relationships.

The numbers on the arrows in the figure correspond to relationships stated formally as propositions in Table 5-1. While some of these relationships may appear to be self-evident, they are included to make the model complete. Experience has shown that it is important to subject even the most obvious relationship to scrutiny. Several times we have been confronted with counterintuitive results that required the revision of an "obvious" relationship.

The first part of the model deals with user attitudes and perceptions of information systems. Attitudes and perceptions are important in determining user reactions to systems and in influencing the use of the system. Attitudes have an action or behavioral component, especially when the attitude is related to something as specific as a particular computer system. If attitudes are highly negative, we expect little cooperation with a system, low levels of use, and in some instances, even sabotage of the system.

We expect that the systems design and operations policies of the information services department influence user attitudes and perceptions directly and indirectly. Direct influence comes from daily user contact with the department; if this contact is satisfactory, it should result in positive user attitudes. Indirect influence by the information services department on user attitudes comes primarily from the quality of service. Often contact between this department

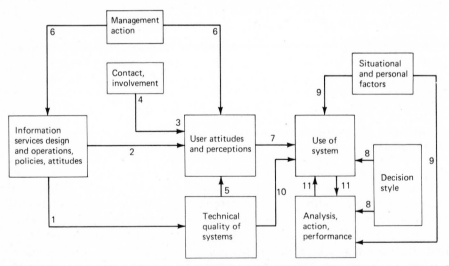

Figure 5-1 Information systems in the context of the organization. *(Adapted from Lucas, H. C., Jr.: Why Information Systems Fail, 1975, courtesy Columbia University Press.)*

Table 5-1   The Formal Propositions of the Model and Their Support

Proposition	Evidence
1 The systems design and operations policies of the information services department and the execution of these policies influence the technical quality of information systems	Some support
2 The systems design and operations policies of the information services department influence user attitudes and perception of information systems and the information services staff.	Reasonable support
3 User contact with information services staff members under adverse conditions leads to unfavorable user attitudes and perceptions of information systems and the information services staff.	Weak support
4 User involvement in the design and operation of information systems results in favorable user attitudes and perceptions of information systems and the information services staff.	Some support
5 Systems with higher technical quality result in more favorable user attitudes and perceptions of the information services staff.	Strong support
6 High levels of management support for and participation in information systems activities result in favorable information services staff attitudes toward their jobs and users, and favorable user attitudes and perceptions of information systems and the information services staff.	Reasonable support
7 Favorable user attitudes and perceptions of information systems and the information services staff lead to high levels of use of information systems.	Strong support
8 Individuals with differing decision styles have differing levels of use of information systems, perform different analyses of data, take different actions based on information, and have differing levels of performance.	Reasonable support
9 Different personal and situational factors lead to differing levels of use of an information system and different actions.	Reasonable support
10 High levels of system use result from a system with high technical quality.	Strong support
11 High levels of use of an information system make it more likely that a user will take action based on the information provided. Depending on the nature of the analysis, the problem, and the information, high levels of use may lead to high or low levels of performance or may be caused by low performance.	Some support

and users is initiated because of service problems. If systems are unreliable or if they are poorly designed and do not work properly, users will have contact with the information services department that is based in conflict, a condition leading to unfavorable attitudes.

User attitudes should also be influenced by management action and encouragement, for example, management support for the design of new systems and membership on steering committees. User attitudes and perceptions should also be influenced by contact and involvement in the design of systems.

Proposition 7 is based on the expectation that favorable user attitudes and perceptions lead to high levels of system use, especially if a system is of high technical quality. High technical quality should lead to more favorable attitudes and perceptions since a high-quality system is easier for a user to interact with and produces better output than a low-quality system.

The use of an information system is a very complex phenomenon. Different situational and personal factors should influence use; a supervisor with 20 years of experience operating a department one way would probably not use an inventory reorder report as extensively as one with six months on the job. Decision or cognitive style also can be expected to influence the use of the system. Quantitatively trained individuals may wish for different types of information than their counterparts who have a more intuitive decision style, as discussed earlier.

The relationship between the use of an information system and performance by the decision maker is very complex. High levels of performance depend on analyzing the output of an information system and taking action consistent with that output. On the other hand, low performance may stimulate the use of the system to determine the nature and cause of problems. It appears that different types of data are needed to support these different aspects of managerial decision making.

A manager is frequently concerned with problem-finding activities, that is, determining that a problem exists. Most computer-based information systems address this aspect of decision making through exception reports, comparisons of this year versus last year, or comparisons of budgeted with actual performance. Under these conditions, low performance would be associated with high levels of use of an information system as a decision maker tries to determine the reasons for poor performance.

After problem definition, the decision maker enters the problem-solving stage. We expect the use of problem-solving output from a system to be associated with high performance if the decision maker takes action consistent with the information. A problem-solving information system may provide such features as computational facilities and the simulation of different alternatives.

The results of six studies undertaken to test the model are summarized in Table 5-1, and in general, the model receives a high level of support from the data (Lucas, 1975). Several interesting findings from the analysis were not originally anticipated in the propositions.

First, multiple roles for information are provided for decision makers; the same information may have a different use for different individuals. A manager concerned about investment levels will respond differently to a report showing high levels of inventory than a warehouse manager concerned with service levels and stockouts. The same information, in fact, often plays different roles for the same individuals at different points in time. Historical data showing a trend toward decreasing sales may alert a decision maker to the existence of a

DECISION ANALYSIS AND SUPPORT

Decisions and Design, Inc. (DDI) of McLean, Va. is one of the few organizations that is dedicated solely to helping people make decisions. The firm encourages customers to come to its headquarters where they are isolated for two or three days during which they focus on a problem without interruption.

The process is supported by a computer system with a large number of terminals including color CRTs.; most programs are written in APL. The firm applies decision analysis to customer problems. The decision maker assigns a probability between 0 and 1 to represent his or her belief that an uncertain event will occur. Utility is a number between 0 and 1 that represents the degree of satisfaction an individual associates with a particular outcome of a decision.

The firm stresses methodology; it does not make decisions for clients. DDI helps define alternatives and structure possible outcomes. In one example, the firm worked with government strategists on where to locate the Sixth Fleet when it appeared that the evacuation of American personnel from a Middle Eastern country would be necessary. A business application examined whether a new plant facility should be built. The client obtained approval for the plant and then returned for help on the decision of where to locate the facility. A third conference was held to select the architect and engineers and a fourth to help design the plant. DDI has shown that computers can play a major role in supporting decisions.

Data Processor, September/October, 1980

---

problem. These same data may be used to develop a forecast to solve the problem of how much to produce for the next month.

Another finding is that we need more flexible information systems and the ability to custom-tailor output. Such flexibility can be provided through report-generator packages, different report formats, and the inquiry-answering capabilities of on-line systems. The technological capability to provide flexibility exists, but the user will have to provide guidance for the information services department to acquire and utilize the available technology.

Existing computer-based systems often provide too much data; users frequently have felt overloaded with information that could not possibly be analyzed. We need to concentrate on selecting the information necessary for decision making rather than on just providing more data. The user frequently is guilty of requesting large volumes of information just in case it is needed. Much information can be processed and saved for reference in archival form while only salient output is provided on a routine basis.

Implications for Systems Design

If we accept the model and results, what are some of the implications? From a systems design standpoint, the manager should consider the following action steps, which are intended to produce high levels of systems use and successful implementation.

1   Urge the formation of a steering committee of users and information services department staff members to determine priorities for the development of new applications.

2   Encourage training sessions for the information services department staff to help its members adopt a role as catalyst in the development process.

3   Insist that a user be placed in charge of the design team for a new system.

4   Provide sufficient resources so that the staff can spend time on systems design.

5   Work personally with a design team to show interest and commitment.

6   See that decisions and not just data flows are considered in systems design.

7   Ask probing questions to see if designers have considered the multiple roles of information for the organization and different decision makers.

8   Review all proposed output from a new system, be selective, and avoid information overload.

9   Examine the user interface with the system; see that users have experimented with the input and output and find it acceptable.

10   Plan for implementation for subordinates and colleagues, consider different personal and situational factors, and prepare for changes.

11   Ensure that adequate resources have been devoted to training and user documentation.

MANAGEMENT PROBLEM 5-3

A major bank has an information system designed to keep track of loan officer assignments to clients and calls made on clients. The system was intended for use by the commercial loan department.

The bank has a large number of loans, and one officer might have 50 or 60 clients. As a result, it is very difficult for officers to maintain their own records. The computer system is designed to solve this problem.

In theory, an officer simply fills out a form when establishing a relationship with a new client or after having visited an existing account. This form is used to update a computer file and a report is produced showing each officer's clients and the date of the most recent call on the client.

Unfortunately, the system has fallen into disuse. A number of clients are listed on the report but no longer do business with the bank. Some accounts are listed as belonging to retired or deceased loan officers!

An administrative assistant in the loan department sent corrections each month to the input/output control section of the information services department. For some unknown reason, only about half of these corrections were ever made, according to the next report. As a result, after several months of trying, the administrative assistant gave up and no longer submits input or corrections. However, the report continues to be produced on a regular basis, though it is never read by users.

Use the model of Figure 5-1 to analyze the situation described above. What are the key variables? What action is required to improve the situation?

Implications for Operations

After systems are designed, they have to be operated. What can a user of information systems do to improve the operation of existing systems?

1 Do not allow any new system to be developed until existing ones are operating satisfactorily.

2 Request the name of a single user representative in the information services department to handle all questions from you or your subordinates.

3 Urge the formation of a steering committee of users in the information services department staff to set priorities for the operation of information systems.

4 As a member of the steering committee, see that sufficient resources are set aside for making changes to existing systems and that a committee of users sets priorities on these modifications.

5 If an on-line system affects your activities, insist on adequate computer or manual backup in case of system failure.

6 Insist on a schedule of input and output for all batch computer system runs affecting you or your staff.

7 Conduct periodic surveys of your staff to solicit ideas for changes and to determine if service levels are satisfactory.

IN CONCLUSION

In this chapter, we reviewed the impact of information systems on the organization and individuals and presented a model of systems in the context of the organization. Managers and users of information systems have a crucial role to play in the design process. We shall explore this role further in Part Four when we discuss the implementation of systems in more detail.

KEY WORDS

Action	Decision style	Personal characteristics
Ambiguities	Design policies	and traits
Analysis	Job dissatisfaction	Power
Attitude	Management action	Situational and personal
Centralization	Mutual dependence	factors
Common resources	Operations policies	Task differences
Communications obstacles	Performance	Uncertainty
Decentralization	Performance rewards	Use

RECOMMENDED READINGS

Leavitt, H. J., and T. L. Whisler: "Management in the 1980's," *Harvard Business Review,* November–December, 1958, pp. 41–48. (A historic article presenting many of the early predictions of the impact of computers on the organization and individuals.)

Lucas, H. C., Jr.: *Why Information Systems Fail,* Columbia, New York, 1975. (This book presents in detail the model of information systems in the context of the organization discussed in this chapter and describes the research findings that test the propositions of the model.)

Mumford, E., and O. Banks: *The Computer and the Clerk,* Routledge, London, 1967. (A thorough study of the introduction of a computer system in several British banks.)

Walton, R. E., and J. M. Dutton: "The Management of Interdepartmental Conflict: A Model and Review," *Administrative Science Quarterly,* vol. 14, no. 1, March 1969, pp. 73–84. (This article contains, in much greater detail, the model of conflict discussed earlier in the chapter.)

Whisler, T. L.: *Information Technology and Organizational Change,* Wadsworth, Belmont, Calif., 1973. (Whisler's readable monograph discusses many of the early studies of the impact of information systems on the organization, and it is well worth reading.)

DISCUSSION QUESTIONS

1 Are the information services department staff members highly specialized? What other functional areas in the organization are highly specialized?

2 The information services department is often considered to provide a support function; can a support department really be powerful? Are there different kinds of power in the organization?

3 What kinds of management problems result from interdepartmental conflict?

4 Are there any organizations that are completely dependent on computers for their operations?

5 What kinds of employees are most likely to be replaced by a computer system? How does your answer depend on the type of computer system and the decision levels affected?

6 How would you measure the extent of unemployment created by the implementation of computer systems? What factors tend to mitigate the problem of increased unemployment if it actually occurs?

7 What signs might indicate the presence of conflict between two departments? How could this conflict be reduced?

8 Are computer systems creating more centralization in organizations? How do you define centralization? Why should computer systems have any impact at all on the degree of centralization?

9 How would you recognize a successful computer installation? What signs would you expect to find?

10 How can communications obstacles between users and the information services department be reduced?

11 How should users be involved in the allocation of scarce computer resources?

12 Two methods of charging for computer services, full charge-out to users and overhead charging, have been suggested. What are the advantages and disadvantages of each method?

13 Consider a typical manufacturing organization and describe the mutual dependence that exists among departments.

14 Why should users be involved in the design of systems? How much influence should they have?

15 What will happen to information systems if users have negative attitudes?

16 How are attitudes formed? How can they be changed?

17 What does the model of information systems in the context of organizations discussed in this chapter, suggest will be the result of an unresponsive information services department? What will happen if management fails to support computer-related activities?

18 How much does a manager have to understand about computer systems? What are the most important management decisions to be made about computer-based information systems?

19 What tools does the manager have available to influence computer activities in the organization?

20 As a user, where do you think the information services department should report? Should it be responsible to accounting?

21 Why do so many users turn to outside computer services, for example, to acquire time sharing or special packages?

22 Early forecasts suggested that middle managers would be reduced in number and stature as a result of the computer systems. Has this prediction been fulfilled? Why or why not?

23 Do computer systems have an impact beyond the organization, for example, on stockholders or customers? What kinds of impact and what problems are created for these groups?

BACKGROUND
    Symptoms
    The Impact of Computing
INFORMATION PROCESSING TECHNOLOGY AND
CORPORATE STRATEGY
    Capitalizing on Information Technology
MANAGING INFORMATION PROCESSING
    A Corporate Plan
    Organization Structure
    New Applications
    Operations
    Equipment/Staff Needs
    Charging
    Control
MANAGEMENT COMMITTEES
SUMMARY
KEY WORDS
RECOMMENDED READINGS
DISCUSSION QUESTIONS

Chapter 6

Top Management and Information Systems[1]

CHAPTER ISSUES

- How does information processing technology relate to corporate strategy?
- What are key management decisions about information systems?
- How much should the organization invest in information processing services?

Managers often experience difficulty taking advantage of information processing technology when formulating corporate strategy. Many top managers also seem unable to cope with the problems of controlling information processing activities in their organizations.

The president of a medium-sized manufacturing company remarked, "I receive about the same information today as was provided thirty years ago

[1]This chapter is based on the paper "A Top Management Policy for Information Systems" by Lucas and Turner, 1981.

before our computers. Only now I spend millions to get it." The chairperson of a three-billion-dollar conglomerate has commented repeatedly, "I get nothing from our computers."

This chapter (1) suggests an approach to incorporating information processing technology in the strategy formulation process and (2) presents a framework for top management to direct the information processing resource so that they may achieve strategic objectives.

BACKGROUND

Symptoms

Following are some common problems related to information processing:

- Managers and other users are uncomfortable with the method by which new applications are chosen.
- There appear to be no priorities for selecting new computer applications.
- One or more new computer applications is experiencing significant cost/schedule overruns.
- There are many complaints about the quality of information processing service.
- Requests for computer staff and equipment are escalating.
- The firm's information systems are not congruent with the firm's goals.
- Top management feels that information processing is not under its control.

If an organization has a number of these symptoms, it may be depriving itself of the opportunity to gain a major competitive advantage through the creative use of information technology. From the service sector to manufacturing, information processing technology can play a major role in managing the firm.

The Impact of Computing

When applying technology to a business problem, for instance, the introduction of a new manufacturing process, executives are usually concerned with the first-order effects of the technology; that is, they want to reduce manufacturing unit costs, improve product quality, etc. The impact of computing technology is different from the impact of many other types of technology in that the secondary effects of computing are often more important than their primary impact. As an example, consider a transactions processing system that is designed to automate the accounts receivable function. The primary objective of such a system might be to reduce errors in posting receivables and to maintain correct account balances. The secondary effect of this system in combination with a payments system is that the firm now knows its exact cash position at the end of each day. By reducing uncertainty in the firm's cash position, the treasurer may have a significant new source of funds for short-term investment.

Accurate cost data have permitted some firms to price products differentially in different parts of the country. In these cases the cost data collected for accounting purposes had a secondary effect on merchandising strategy. In addition the firm has the ability to reflect costs more accurately in setting prices, which should lead to higher revenue.

The firm should carefully manage and control information processing technology, because of its primary impact and because of its potential secondary effects.

INFORMATION PROCESSING TECHNOLOGY AND CORPORATE STRATEGY

A key task of top management is formulating corporate strategy. What does the corporation do well? Can it continue this activity at a high level of performance? What opportunities for new directions are available? What are competitors doing? A firm can continue its present course, maintaining momentum where it is doing well. Alternatively, the corporation can change its strategy dramatically by making a decision among competing alternatives for new ventures.

As an example, a single-product single-market firm might try to diversify to reduce cyclical fluctuations in product demand and to reduce the impact of a major change in consumer buying patterns. A large energy company has decided to enter the market for information processing equipment by purchasing a number of high-technology firms and integrating them into a new subsidiary. This new business is expected to grow and to help the energy producer cope with the uncertainties in its primary petroleum market.

There are three levels of integration of information processing technology with corporate strategy as shown in Table 6-1. At the lowest level of integration, we find independent information systems that help the firm implement strategy by creating greater operational efficiencies. These systems are not directly linked to the strategy formulation process or integrated with a strategic plan. The need

Table 6-1

Level of integration with strategy formulation	Primary objective	Secondary effect
Independent	Operational efficiency	Managerial information
Policy support	Aid repetitive decision making	Better understanding of problem dynamics
Fully integrated	Open new products, markets, directions	Change the decision-making process, alternatives considered, and evaluation criteria

for such a system is usually perceived by an operational unit, and its primary objective is to improve efficiency. Most existing information systems fall into the independent category: they process routine transactions, produce output that goes to customers, provide exception reporting, etc.

The second level of integration is characterized by policy support systems designed to aid the strategic planning process. In this case the system helps in formulating the plan but is not a part of it. That is, the system is not part of an end product or service produced by the firm. A good example of one of these policy support systems is in Chapter 18, which describes a planning application. The data needed for forecasting for a large conglomerate are contained in a common data base accessible through the computer. A set of analytic tools in the system includes a bank of models with a large mathematical programming routine that helps select a course of action to maximize corporate performance over a multiyear planning horizon. In addition econometric and risk analysis models are available.

The majority of firms do not appear to have reached the third and most important level of integration between information processing and corporate strategy. At this level the technology itself becomes a part of the strategy; it expands the range of strategic alternatives considered by the firm. At this third level, technology bears an integral relation to a company's strategic thinking by helping to define the range of possibilities. At the same time, it provides a good portion of the means by which the strategy, once chosen, is to be implemented. Several examples may help to illustrate this level of integration between technology and strategy.

A university professor of economics developed and marketed a model of the national economy through a new firm. Although such models were theoretically possible before the advent of electronic computers, computational requirements made them infeasible to solve. The development of information technology made it possible to create the kind of model that forms the nucleus of the firm's business. Furthermore, the company offers a variety of services in which the customer accesses its computer, services made possible only because of the options provided by information processing technology.

A major brokerage firm has set a goal of becoming one of the leading financial institutions in the U.S. This firm is offering a service in which a customer's cash in a brokerage account is automatically invested in the brokerage firm's liquid assets fund when the cash is not invested in securities. Thus as positions are liquidated or dividends paid, the cash immediately begins earning the highest interest available to the customer. The firm has expanded its market share and increased revenues to the extent that new business offsets the interest the brokerage firm loses from no longer being able to invest customer's idle cash for its own benefit.

On a smaller scale, information processing technology made it possible for a new market research firm to offer a service that could not be obtained from its competitors (*Business Week,* May 5, 1980). The company developed a strategy that is intertwined with information technology. The firm has purchased grocery store point-of-sale scanning equipment and given it free to 15 supermarkets in two towns selected on the basis of their demographic makeup. There are 2000 households in each of the two test markets using the scanning equipment; their purchases are recorded on the firm's computer in Chicago. Since each product is marked by the universal product code, researchers can pinpoint a family's purchases by price, brand, and size and then correlate the purchase information with any promotions such as coupons, free samples, price adjustments, advertising, and store displays.

This technology means that the company can conduct careful, scientific tests of marketing strategies to determine what is the most effective approach for its customers. For example, through cooperation with a cable TV network, the firm can target different TV spots to selected households and analyze the resulting purchases. The imaginative use of the technology has allowed the firm to gain a competitive lead over much larger, better established market research firms.

These examples illustrate how the integration of information processing technology with strategy formulation expanded the opportunities for each firm. The technology allowed the first firm to create an econometric model and then to use time-sharing services to market its product directly to the customer. Technology created the opportunity for a new form of business and expanded revenues. In the brokerage firm, the technology made it possible to offer a new service that probably expanded the market share of the firm and increased the size of its liquid assets fund. Technology helped the market research firm gain a competitive edge and set a new standard for service in the industry.

Capitalizing on Information Technology

How does the firm take advantage of information technology and achieve the highest level integration of technology and strategy? There are two steps to be followed by top management:

    1 Look for ways to incorporate technology in a product or service. Does information processing provide an opportunity for a new approach to business? Does the technology make it possible to differentiate a product and services from the competition? Technology can help open new markets or increase existing market share.

    2 To integrate technology with planning, the firm needs information about likely future technological developments. To conduct a technology assessment, the organization must invest resources in research and development. A small group of corporate researchers can collect information from a number of sources to estimate technological trends. The firm can invest selectively in university programs to keep up a research and can sponsor or subscribe to studies conducted by consulting firms.

One of the greatest impediments to using information technology for strategic purposes has been an inability on the part of top management to

OPTICAL SCANNING FOR MARKET RESEARCH

Early experiments with supermarket scanners for checkout have encouraged market researchers by their potential for collecting large amounts of data on purchases. However, supermarkets have been very slow to install laser scanning systems which identify purchases by optically reading Universal Product Codes printed on each grocery item. Market research firms, because of the relatively small number of scanner installations, still rely on relatively simple techniques such as asking shoppers to maintain diaries of their purchases.

A Chicago firm, Information Resources, Inc., purchased scanning equipment and provided it free to 15 supermarkets in two carefully selected towns, Marion, Indiana and Pittsfield, Massachusetts. These two cities have demographic makeups which makes them ideal as test markets. The company has enlisted 2,000 households in each of the two test markets. The householders have identification cards which are presented at the grocery store when they make a purchase. The card alerts the point of sale terminal to send an item by item list of the customer's purchases to the Information Resources computer in Chicago.

From the Universal Product Code, researchers at the company can determine purchases exactly according to price, brand and size. These data are related to any promotional experiments under way. As a result, Information Resources can monitor the grocery purchases of a representative sample of 4,000 households. The firm can determine how these consumers react to marketing strategies like television commercials, newspaper ads, displays in the store, coupons and free samples.

Through a cooperating cable television system, stations selectively broadcast commercials to target families on a house by house basis. The Chicago market research firm can experiment with different television commercials on selected households and compare the buying reactions in the store.

In one example, Information Resources attempted to determine the cost effectiveness of giving away a product sample. It divided household panelists into four groups of a 1,000 each and provided various combinations of samples and advertising. Sales doubled in all of the groups receiving samples during the period, but the group exposed to advertising was more loyal to the brand in subsequent weeks.

This innovative application demonstrates how computers can be used to offer a unique service and to collect data for market research.

Business Week, May 5, 1980.

manage the information systems function successfully. If executives do not believe that they can control information processing services, they probably will be unwilling to rely on this technology to accomplish strategic goals.

MANAGING INFORMATION PROCESSING

This section discusses the key variables and concerns for top management in managing information processing activities in the organization. Figure 6-1 presents a framework for viewing management decision areas involved in information processing; positive management action is needed in all areas illustrated in the figure. Without such action decisions will occur by default;

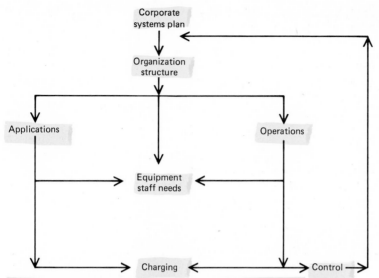

Figure 6-1 A framework for managing information processing.

management can and should control information processing. Table 6-2 summarizes the actions for management in each of the areas discussed below. Where possible, we offer recommendations for management policy. When the recommendations depend on circumstances unique to the firm, Table 6-2 lists some of the factors that should be taken into account in developing a policy.

A Corporate Plan

A plan for information processing should be coordinated with corporate strategy. The plan will serve as a road map to show the direction of the systems effort. It also furnishes the basis for later evaluation of the performance of the information processing function.

Many organizations agree that a plan is needed but do not develop one. A frequent reason is that the 3-to-5-year information-systems planning horizon is not compatible with the planning horizon of the organization. In other instances, the corporation does not have a plan at all. It is both possible and highly desirable to develop an information processing plan even without a formal corporate plan. The technology is too pervasive and important for planning to occur by default or solely through decisions made by personnel in the information services department.

A typical plan describes the breakdown in activities and resources required for the development of new applications and the operation of existing systems. A key task for the organization is to identify areas for new applications of technology. What are the applications areas with the highest return? What applications will most further the strategic goals of the corporation? What new opportunities does the technology provide?

Table 6-2 Summary of Issues and Recommendations

A corporate plan

See that a 3-to-5-year MIS plan is developed

Participate in the planning process

Issues	Recommendations
Mechanism	Operational plan of 1 year
	Longer-term plan of 3 to 5 years
	Technology assessment
	Link to organization plan
	Separate information systems planning officer
Involvement	User and management input
Contents and format	Applications needs
	Operations needs
	Implications for staff and equipment
Priorities	Steering committees to choose applications
Reporting	Annual report of information services department tied to plan

Organization structure

Evaluate various patterns for providing computing to choose the most effective alternative

Develop a policy that balances coordination costs and local autonomy

Issues	Alternatives
Type	Centralized distributed, decentralized for operations and analysis/design
Evaluation	Criteria: service levels, cost responsiveness, flexibility, history of organization
Control	Balance local autonomy with corporate needs

New applications

Convene a committee of users and managers to be affected by the system to choose an alternative for design

Be sure that a realistic number of alternatives are considered, including the status quo or the no-new-systems alternative

Issues	Recommendations
Generate new ideas	Also from plan, procedures for submission of requests, new applications
Selection	Use of committees; use formal approaches for selection
Development	Extensive user input, management involvement setting goals, reviewing system
Tools	Acquisition and use of tools-structured approaches

Table 6-2 (Continued)

Operations

Establish criteria for measuring the performance and service levels of computer operations

Measure and evaluate the operations function regularly

Issues	Recommendations
Measurement	Develop user-oriented measures
Evaluation	Administer regular evaluations including a variety of measures
Control	Are there adequate controls?

Equipment/staff needs

Review equipment recommendations

Authorize adequate staffing levels; systems design is labor intensive!

Issues	Recommendations
Evaluation and choice criteria	Develop evaluation methodology
Compatibility among vendors	Establish vendor compatibility policy
Technological assessment	Consider changes in technology in decisions
Staff increases	Examine alternatives such as adding to the staff, contract services, packaged programs, more user programming

Charging

Determine the objectives of a charging policy

Design and implement the policy

Issues	Alternatives
To charge	Yes-or-no advantage and disadvantages
Charging mechanism	Full or partial charge-out; accounting techniques

Control

Evaluate the contribution of information systems to corporate goals and strategy

Evaluate information services performance with respect to the plan

Take the needed corrective action to achieve the plan, e.g., add resources, modify schedules, etc.

Issues	Recommendations
Overall evaluation	Compare results to plan
Frequent feedback	Monitor progress on systems development projects, conduct user surveys as discussed under "Operations"

MANAGEMENT PROBLEM 6-1

The president of Ready-to-Wear, a medium-sized clothing manufacturer, was upset with information processing in his firm. "We have a system that was designed in 1939 and run on tabulating equipment. For its day, this was a good system. Now, we are spending over $500,000 a year on a computer, and I receive exactly the same information as the 1939 system. Only now it costs more and there are more errors and complaints."

The president has tried a succession of consultants to advise him, and there has been a new manager of the information services department about every six months. Interviews with users show them to be upset by computer processing and unwilling even to suggest new applications. The controller would like to eliminate the entire computer area and turn to an outside service bureau. In fact, this course was attempted several years ago.

The president is willing to give the computer one last chance. He has retained you to help him develop a set of systems that will meet the basic needs of the firm for order entry, accounting, production control, work-in-process inventory, finished-goods inventory, and raw materials and purchasing. What is your plan for helping the firm?

Table 6-3 contains a possible table of contents for an information systems plan. The plan first begins with an executive summary containing the key points in the plan. The document should have a section on the goals of information processing in the organization, both general and specific. One general goal might be to provide unique customer services, and a specific goal could be to complete a major on-line system during the year.

Any plan is based on certain assumptions about the business. Will the firm continue to pursue its current business strategy? Are major new lines of business contemplated? Is the organization divesting itself of certain components? It is mandatory for this plan to be linked to the organization's strategic plan.

Sometimes it is helpful to provide a short scenario of the information processing environment that will result from the execution of the plan. For example, the plan might describe an environment of distributed processing with extensive local computer power tied in a large network to central machines.

Table 6-3   Contents of an Information Systems Plan

Executive summary
Goals
Assumptions
Scenario—information processing environment
Applications areas
  status, cost, time, schedule
Operations
Maintenance and enhancements
Organizational structure—pattern of computing
Impact of plan on the organization—financial impact
Implementation—risks, obstacles

A critical element of the plan is the new applications areas being planned. Some systems will be in the process of development, and they should be identified along with a report of their status. For major new applications areas, there should be a breakdown of costs and schedules. For an insurance firm a major applications area might be the development of systems to report losses for customers being insured against factory accidents. Such an application area might have several potential systems developed for it.

The plan should outline and set priorities for applications areas; for example, marketing promotions, production control, etc. Once the priorities for applications development are identified, during the development of the applications, specific alternatives should be chosen for implementation, as we shall discuss later.

To set priorities, a corporate steering committee containing high-level representation of concerned managers should be convened. This committee can make the tradeoffs among functional areas. A committee ensures that the decision on priorities is a management decision, rather than a choice left to the information services staff.

The operation of existing systems must continue; the plan should identify the existing systems and the costs of maintaining them. Estimates are that a minimum of 50 percent of the total development budget in most organizations goes to maintenance and enhancement of existing applications.

The plan should also describe the existing and any new organizational structure for computing. Where will computers be located and how are they to be managed? Where does one find systems-analysis resources?

Management is also interested in the impact of a plan on the organization, particularly its financial impact. Finally, the plan should identify implementation risks and obstacles. For many ambitious plans, the availability of adequate

---

COMPUTERS ON THE RANCH

Until 1900, every summer cowboys from Gonzales, Texas herded cattle on the Chisholm Trail on the way to markets in Abilene and Wichita. The Harrell family are modern cattlemen who use different tools. The Harrells have switched record keeping chores from cowboys to computer systems, at a cost of some $30,000 a year.

The Harrells project the cost of their finished cattle and profitably trade futures contracts by plotting feedlot expenses and the herds' weight gain characteristics on the computer. It is anticipated that when the system is completed, the computer will supply 60 pieces of data on every animal on the ranch, including its father, its weight at weaning and its pasture of birth.

Because of these extensive records, the ranchers know which cows give birth to calves regularly, and have abundant milk. Those which do are retained or sold for breeding, and those who do not are turned into hamburger. While the Harrell operation is modern in many respects, and the computer only plays a small part in the business, it provides the owners with a competitive edge.

The Wall Street Journal, September 1, 1978.

numbers of computer staff professionals may be the key obstacle to implementation.

The information services department should also be encouraged to develop an annual report that discusses progress made during the year. The report should be tied to the goals in that year's plans, and it becomes an input for the preparation of the next plan.

Organization Structure

Existing information technology offers considerable flexibility in developing patterns for the structure of the information services function. The firm must identify possible processing patterns, evaluate them, and choose an alternative for implementation. Processing alternatives can be divided into three broad groups that represent points on a continuum. At one extreme is completely centralized processing; all systems analysis and design is performed by a central group and all equipment is operated centrally.

At the other extreme is complete decentralization; all equipment is resident at local sites, and these sites have their own staff for analysis and design work. Distributed processing occurs when local sites are tied together in some type of communications network.

Table 6-4 presents some of the evaluation criteria that can be used to select a particular structure for processing. These criteria, such as levels of service, system responsiveness, and reliability, are oriented toward the interests of the user. In general there is no rule as to what kinds of systems are most responsive or provide the highest level of service. Preliminary research indicates that local processing seems to be associated with more favorable user perceptions of service levels and greater responsiveness. The availability of a network of computers or of several computers at a central site provides high reliability. The least potential reliability is associated with a single system having no backup. Costs must be computed for every alternative; the cost of a particular pattern of

Table 6-4   Organizational Structure for Processing

Patterns

	Hardware	Systems development
Centralized	X	
Distributed		
Decentralized		X

Example: multidivision firm with a central computer group and analysts employed by the divisions

Evaluation Criteria
Level of service
Responsiveness
Reliability
Cost
Management task

processing depends on the configuration, the location of data, etc. The task of managing either a centralized or decentralized configuration is complex and will depend on the existing information processing organization.

The challenge of a centralized system is to make it responsive; that of decentralized and distributed systems is to make them coordinated. Management must trade off the benefits perceived by users in having and controlling their own computer equipment against the need for overall coordination in the organization. Allowing a proliferation of small computers can lead to high costs if the organization decides to connect diverse equipment through a network. Also, the firm must ask if there are opportunities to develop common systems that can be used in multiple locations to prevent the duplication of development efforts.

New Applications

Rarely today are totally infeasible applications suggested by users. Instead, some type of system can be undertaken to improve information processing that will be feasible. The question is what is both feasible and desirable? A corporate steering committee should have chosen applications areas as a part of developing a plan for information processing. Now, the task is to choose what type of system, if any, will be developed. Management must consider the existing portfolio of applications and provide guidance on the amount of investment possible and the balance of the portfolio. For example, the firm will want to have some low-risk projects under way to offset projects with a high risk of failure.

In Chapter 12 we advocate a procedure in which the information services department and users form a committee to select alternatives for new applications. Many firms have tried such selection committees and eventually disbanded them claiming that they do not work. A committee given both a proper role and information can succeed in this task. The committees that have failed are ones that were treated as rubber stamps for decisions already made elsewhere in the firm: the committee should make real decisions.

First, the committee should agree with the information services department on the number of alternatives to be considered for each system. Examples of alternatives for a single application are the use of an applications package, an on-line system, a batch system, or maintaining the status quo (Lucas and Moore, 1976). The selection committee and the information services department then agree on a series of criteria to be used to evaluate each of these alternatives. A scoring and weighting procedure is applied to help make the final selection.

Management must also see that a new application is implemented successfully after an alternative has been selected. It can take one to three years to develop a major new application, and we expect to use the new system for five to seven years. Thus a system may be around for the next decade, and the chances for making significant changes in it for the next five years are small.

Systems analysis and design is an area that requires a great deal of management attention. Managers must demonstrate that they are behind the development of a new system and see that there is adequate user input in the design process. Frequent group review meetings are important during the design process. Top management must participate in these meetings and make clear that it supports the changes that are likely to come from the system. Later in the text we discuss system analysis and design in more detail along with how the organization can implement systems so they are successful.

Operations

The major concerns in the operation of existing systems are credibility and service levels. It is very difficult to gain enthusiasm or cooperation in the development of new systems if existing service levels are unsatisfactory. Management must be sure the information services department is providing effective service as perceived by its customers. Often the measures used to evaluate service are created and evaluated in the information services department itself; they tend to have little meaning for users. However, management sees a report that describes the percentage of output reports processed on time, the availability of the computer, etc., and assumes that adequate measurement is taking place.

Table 6-5 lists some critical management concerns in the operation of existing information systems. Efficiency considerations include the utilization of equipment, the quality of scheduling, and smoothness of operations. As hardware becomes less expensive, having a machine that is fully utilized is less important than having adequate capacity for processing. A key task of operating management in the computer area is to schedule jobs on the computer so that all processing is done satisfactorily.

Efficiency is important, but most managers and users are more interested in effectiveness. One approach to measuring effectiveness is to conduct a user evaluation and survey at a detailed level. For example, one can ask about specific systems and reports. Measures of system "uptime" for an on-line system are also one good indicator of effectiveness. Adherence to schedules is important; so is the error experience of users. There will always be errors, but is their number reasonable and are there edit and error checks that catch errors?

Table 6-5   Operations

Efficiency
Utilization of equipment
Scheduling
Smooth operations
Effectiveness
User evaluation and survey
Uptime
Meeting schedules
Error experience
Control
Exposure analysis
Backup

The firm can conduct user surveys of service levels to supplement measures of on-time performance or computer uptime supplied by the computer operations group. These surveys can be treated statistically to extract key factors (combinations of items on the survey) that serve as a measure of performance. Over time the survey is repeated, the factors computed, and the progress of the operations function evaluated. Such a technique provides a measurement and an evaluation that include criteria important to users as well as indicators from the operations group.

As we shall discuss further in Chapter 19, management is responsible for control in the organization. Computer systems process vital transactions, and many applications are concerned with control. Thus, the computer area is one of extremely high exposure for most organizations. Management must assure itself that adequate controls exist within systems and that computers are applied effectively to the control of the organization. One major component of control is adequate backup. To determine the level of control, management can conduct an audit, a topic we shall discuss in Chapter 19.

Equipment/Staff Needs

The requirements to operate existing systems and the resources to develop new applications determine staff and equipment needs. One of the by-products of the planning process is the identification of needed resources; requirements are compared with available resources to determine what incremental equipment and staff are necessary. Top management must make the decision of what action

---

MANAGEMENT PROBLEM 6-2

AgChem is a major chemicals firm. Their chairman is the one quoted in this chapter as saying "I get nothing from our computers." The vice president of finance has the responsibility for information processing activities in the firm. He has just succeeded in making the department a division, the highest-level organizational entity in the firm. In addition, a new manager of the division has been recruited to try to "turn the computer area around."

The new manager and the vice president of finance are trying to develop a strategy for the turnaround beginning at the top and working through the various levels of the organization.

The vice president is very capable but has had no formal experience with computers. He knows, however, that there are many problems. Users constantly complain about information services. The new director of information processing has conferred with his staff. He feels that some of the criticism is justified but that a lot of the users and top management just do not realize the extent to which they and the entire firm are dependent on the computer.

The vice president and the new manager of information services would like some help in trying to improve the situation at AgChem. Can you suggest ways they might go about creating both better service and a better image for information processing?

---

to take when there is a discrepancy between the resources needed to accomplish the plan and the resources available.

There are a large number of options for equipment, and management must help develop criteria for comparing alternatives. One important issue today is the extent to which compatibility among different vendors is stressed. If many incompatible systems are acquired, the organization will not be able to take advantage of common software.

For the staff, the obvious way to expand resources is to hire more individuals. However, there is a limit to the number of people that can be absorbed productively into the organization. Another alternative is to use more packaged programs to improve staff productivity. Outside contractors can be employed to develop systems or supply staff members.

All trends in the future point to the conclusion that hardware costs will continue to decline and that there will be an insufficient number of computer professionals to develop systems. These observations suggest that the organization will have to give more responsibility to users for systems. The firm should acquire higher-higher level languages such as report generators and encourage users to retrieve their own data and design reports. Invest in a data-base management system and in a query language to extend the computer to the end user. The organization can prepare to use the technology better by making it widely available and easily understood. We shall discuss the acquisition of services and hardware in further detail in Chapter 11.

Charging

Two basic types of cost are associated with computer activities: development and operations. Development costs are incurred during the design of a new system. They can be estimated in advance, but our history has not been one of conspicuous success in staying within the estimated cost. Investment cost can be highly variable, especially if a project is not completed on time.

The major costs of systems development are personnel expenses. For most systems, the cost of computer time for testing and debugging is small compared with the labor cost. The systems analyst has to estimate both the number of days and the average costs necessary for computer department employees to design the system. Management may also want to allocate the salary expenses of users to the project when they are heavily involved in systems design activities.

In contrast to development costs, operations costs are usually more predictable, at least by the time program testing has begun. These costs include charges for computer time, supplies, and labor. Sometimes all the various components of computer cost are combined into one hourly charge keyed to computer resource utilization; for example, X dollars per CPU minute, Y dollars per 1000 lines printed, etc. Other charging algorithms are based on the units of work processed by the department, such as the number of checks processed, bills printed, etc.

There are two polar approaches to accounting for computer expenses: overhead charge-out and full charge-out to users. Table 6-6 describes the advantages of each approach (Dearden and Nolan, 1973).

Table 6-6   Comparison of Charging Mechanism for Overhead versus Charge-Out

Overhead advantages

Cheaper accounting
Responsibility for control remains with computer department
Makes all computer costs visible
Computer expenses reviewed by top management
Creates stability for computer department

Charge-out advantages

Users have to allocate resources to computer services and consider tradeoffs for other uses of funds
Shows how computer department is interacting with user departments
Provides data for comparison of external services with internal computer services
Provides information on relative costs of applications
User does not see computer as a free good

In one approach all expenses for computers are treated as company overhead. Accounting is cheaper and it is not necessary to keep track of many individual charges or go to the expense of developing and executing a charge-out procedure. Some advocates of this approach argue that it leaves ꓳecision making in the computer department where technical competence exists to make decisions. Because of the large expenditure charged against overhead for computer expenses, it is possible that top management will review computer expenses more under this charging system. Overhead charging does create stability for the computer department since it can count on the same processing load. For example, under a full charge-out scheme if user departments change their processing activities, there can be wide fluctuations in the computer department budget.

In a full charge-out scheme all computer expenses are charged to users. Users have to make resource allocation decisions; this approach leads to the complete decentralization of computer decisions. By examining the accounting system and comparing charges, management can see where the computer department is providing the most service and has developed the most applications. The charges make it possible to compare an internal department with an outside computer service organization, which is always an alternative to internal processing. Charging also provides data on the relative cost of each application. Since the computer is not a free good, users may exercise more restraint in requesting systems.

A partial charge-out approach offers a flexible alternative to full overhead or full charge-out accounting. The exact nature of the partial charge-out scheme depends on the individual organization. One approach that has been used is to charge users for operations since the amount involved is more certain. New applications are treated as a research and development effort and are charged to overhead. This partial charge-out approach recognizes that a new computer application is a capital investment, just as is adding a new piece of machinery.

An approach to selecting a charging mechanism based primarily on user and organizational considerations has been suggested by Dearden and Nolan (1973). If the user population is not too knowledgeable about computer systems, the opportunity for applications in the organization, and the cost and limitations of systems, then overhead accounting is favored. On the other hand, if users have widely diverse needs and are sophisticated and knowledgeable about computers, then full charge-out schemes are more appropriate.

We recommend a partial charge-out approach. For new systems development, at least a portion of the cost should be charged to overhead. Depending on organizational practices, management may insist on some matching investment funds from the user department or division. However, the user should not have to bear the full cost, especially given the uncertainty in cost and payoff in developing a new computer application.

For operations, develop a charge-out for users. It may be desirable to set up some type of flexible rate to help in allocating resources; for example, charge less for jobs that can be run on the third shift and charge more for daytime use of the computer. The cost allocation method should assure users of roughly the same charges for the same job; otherwise it is very difficult for them to budget.

Control

Management control is concerned with the broad question of whether information technology is making a contribution to corporate strategy. From our earlier discussions, this contribution could be in the form of independent systems, policy support systems for planning, or through a close linkage between technology and strategy formulation. One reason top management may feel uneasy about information processing is its realization that often managers are not controlling the technology. One way to gain control over information processing is to participate in the decisions mentioned above and to be knowledgeable about information processing activities in the organization.

On an operational level, one control mechanism is to compare actual results with the information processing plan. On a more frequent basis, user reactions to service levels can be measured and reported and progress on individual systems development projects monitored. Management should establish performance criteria and the information services department should report on them.

One major management problem is what action to take when it appears that some part or all the information processing function is out of control. A common solution, though not necessarily the best, is to replace the manager of the information services department. Instead of that reflex response, top management should take a careful look at how it is contributing to controlling information processing. The framework in Figure 6-1 is one starting point for such an examination. Has management helped develop a plan for information processing? Does management get involved in the selection of applications and the determination of priorities? Do top managers set the objectives for new systems and participate in their design?

In some instances changes in personnel may be appropriate when the operation is out of control. However, in others the best action may be to provide additional resources. Possibly processing schedules are not being met because of a lack of manpower or computer power. The design of new systems is a research and development activity with high uncertainty. If a high-risk complex system causes delays and yet appears well managed, the appropriate action may be to add resources or extend the schedule.

In summary, the first step in exerting control is knowing what to measure. The second step is conducting the evaluation. The third step is determining what action is most likely to improve the situation if part of the operation is out of control.

MANAGEMENT COMMITTEES

Because of the size of the investment involved and the importance of key systems to the organization, many firms are establishing committees to help manage information processing activities. A committee can bring to bear many different points of view on a problem, and it ensures widespread representation of functional areas and management levels in key decisions.

One large multinational firm has organized a series of committees to deal with planning for information systems and the review of proposals for new systems. An office of the president and of the chairperson are at the head of this firm. Each major line of business in this multinational is organized into a company with its own president and staff. There are also corporate vice presidents for various functional areas, such as a vice president of finance. Service units such as research and development and information processing are corporate divisions reporting to appropriate corporate vice presidents.

This firm has recently established a corporate level steering committee for information processing. Its objective is to review plans and determine the appropriate size of the firm's investment in information processing. The corporate committee reviews division plans, organizes and approves education about systems, and seeks areas for the development of common systems serving two or more suborganizations, such as two different companies with common information processing requirements. The purpose of a common system is to avoid the cost of developing a tailored application at each site.

Each division also has a local steering committee that is charged with the responsibility of developing and approving long-range plans for information processing in that suborganization. The local committee also reviews and approves short-term plans and the annual budget for information processing activities in the division. This committee serves to review proposals for new systems and to assign priorities to them. Finally, the local committee reviews and approves staffing requirements for information services.

The corporate and division committees could be supplemented by a separate committee to examine alternatives for a given application during the feasibility study for a new system. We shall discuss such a committee later in the section of the text on systems analysis and design. Another type of committee will also be recommended; a team composed of users, managers, and the information services department staff that works on the actual design of a computer-based system.

For the multinational firm discussed above, the corporate level and division level steering committees deal with policy. In a smaller firm, only a corporate level committee might be appropriate. However, the organization should develop a mechanism that involves users and the systems staff to (1) set policy and review plans, (2) select alternatives for a given application, and (3) participate in the actual design of a system.

SUMMARY

This chapter has presented a framework for examining the relationship between information processing and corporate strategy. The approach identifies three levels of the relationship between information technology and strategy formulation.

Most organizations appear to be at the first or second levels. At the first level, systems that are independent of the firm's strategy help achieve some stated objective through greater efficiency or better management. Second-level policy support systems contribute to the planning process directly. At the third level, information technology is merged with strategy formulation; technology serves to expand the range and number of strategic opportunities considered by the firm. In addition to the strategy formulation role for information processing, the technology also helps to implement the adopted strategy.

The second part of the chapter presented a framework for top management use in managing information processing activities in the organization. If information technology is to make a contribution to strategy formulation and to the operation of the firm, management must become more adept at coping with information processing activities. The framework for management stresses the importance of the planning process, the development of organizational structures for processing, the identification and development of new applications, the operation of existing systems, the identification of equipment and staff needs, and charging for services and monitoring information processing in general. The purpose of the framework is to assist top management in determining the key issues for concern in managing the information processing resource.

By including considerations of information technology in the development of corporate strategy and by effectively managing information processing activities in the organization, this technology will make its maximum contribution to the organization. Managers will no longer have to ask, "What am I getting from information technology?" Instead they will be able to point out the nature and extent of the contribution technology makes to the organization.

KEY WORDS

Acquisition
Alternative
Application
Charge-out
Control
Criteria

Equipment
Overhead
Operations
Plan
Processing pattern

Strategic
Structure
Tactical
Technology
Technology assessment

RECOMMENDED READINGS

Business Week, "Market Research by Scanner," May 5, 1980, pp. 113.

Deardon, J., and R. Nolan: "How to Control the Computer Resource, *Harvard Business Review,* November–December 1973, pp. 68–75. (A good paper on charging for service.)

Kantrow, A.: "The Strategy-Technology Connection," *Harvard Business Review,* July–August 1980, pp. 6–21. (A good paper on technology and strategy in general.)

Lucas, H. C., Jr.: *Why Information Systems Fail,* New York, Columbia University Press, 1975.

Lucas, H. C., Jr., and J. Moore: "A Multiple-Criterion Scoring Approach to Information Project Selection," *INFOR,* February 1976, pp. 1–12. (A procedure for a more rational selection of alternatives for a computer application.)

Nolan, R. L.: "Managing the Computer Resource: A Stage Hypothesis," *Communications of the ACM,* July 1973, pp. 399–440. (A famous and controversial paper describing the growth pattern of information services departments over time.)

DISCUSSION QUESTIONS

1 Locate an article in the popular business press about the strategy of a corporation. Describe the interrelationship between technology and the strategy of the firm. Compare two firms and note the differences.

2 Why did most firms first develop systems to improve operational efficiency?

3 Should a manager actually use a decision support system, or should there be a technical staff member to isolate the manager from the system?

4 What is the advantage of full charge-out for information processing costs?

5 How can users evaluate the level of service quality from an information services department?

6 One bank information services department developed 69 quality indicators for information processing. Do you think this was a good idea? What do you predict was the reaction of users?

7 What structural patterns of the organization would influence the structure of information processing?

8 Why do you think preliminary evidence indicates that users are more satisfied when the computer is located at their site?

9 Examine the trend toward distributed processing according to the conflict model in the previous chapter.

10 How does strategic planning differ between a firm that offers services and one that manufactures a product? Is there a difference in the impact of technology on strategy in the two types of firms?

11 How would management go about assessing the probable information processing technology available over the next five years?

12 What criteria are the most important for an organization in choosing among competing alternatives for a particular computer application?

13 Why should the decision on what applications to undertake not be left to the manager of the information services department?

14 What do you think the role of top management should be in the design of a specific information system?

15 Is it likely that the president of a firm who feels that he or she receives nothing from computers knows the contribution of computers to the organization?

16 It has been said that problems with information processing start at the top of the organization. What does this mean? Do you agree or disagree? Why?

17 Why do priorities have to be set on new computer applications?

18 Why do you think managers seem to know more about other functional areas than information processing?

19 What options are open to the organization if equipment and staff needs exceed available resources?

20 What actions can management take if information processing activities seem to be out of control? What different actions are suitable when the problem is in operations rather than systems analysis and design?

21 What is the role of external expertise in the development of a strategy for information systems?

22 Why have information services departments historically been reluctant to develop plans?

Part Three

Computer Technology

This section of the text contains the most technical material we shall discuss. Users and managers are often involved in important decisions about computer technology, as shown in the accompanying table. To make these decisions intelligently, the decision maker must understand some of the technical issues involved. As we discussed in the last chapter, a basic knowledge of technology is necessary to manage information processing activities effectively.

In Chapter 7 we discuss the fundamentals of computer hardware. Users and managers are often involved in the selection of the appropriate technology for a computer application. Should the system operate in batch mode or on-line? Should data be collected on-line but be processed in batch? For this application, what are the advantages and disadvantages of each alternative?

The user may be involved in the selection of the entire computer system; possibilities here range from a small minicomputer to a large, general-purpose computer system. It is also very likely that the user will have some say in the acquisition of specific devices, such as terminals for an on-line application. Finally, management must decide what pattern of processing is best for the organization. Where will computers be located, what will be their configuration, how will they communicate? What applications will each computer execute?

Management Decisions on Technology

Chapter	Decision area	Examples of alternatives
7 Hardware	Selection of technology Equipment selection for an entire system Selection of specific devices	Batch or on-line system General-purpose or minicomputer Terminals
8 Software	Choice of languages Acquisition of packages	Planning language Statistical analysis package Accounts receivable package
9 Files	Capabilities of application Response time of application Selection of data-base management system	Direct-access or sequential file organization On-line or batch processing Various data-management packages available
10 Future Trends	Planning	Strategic choices, new products, Services
11 Sources of services	Hardware Software	Service bureau, internal facility Consultant, internal staff, packages

There are also many important decisions concerning computer software, a topic discussed in Chapter 8. Should the organization purchase a proprietary, nonstandard language for some special application such as developing a planning model of the firm? Users and managers frequently must decide whether to recommend the acquisition of a software package and must work with the information services department to evaluate the package.

Computer files are the basic building block of a computer-based information system. Different types of file structures are necessary to support the requirements of different applications. The user who works on the design of a system must be conversant with the different options available with direct-access and sequential files. Decisions about response time also have implications for file design; if an application is to operate on-line, then direct-access files are required. Many organizations are investigating the development of a comprehensive data base for a number of important reasons. Very complex software packages known as data-base management systems are available and managers must decide whether to acquire a package and, if so, which one. Computer files are discussed in Chapter 9.

Future trends are important because they allow the manager to plan now for what will be happening. Hardware changes occur rapidly, and advances in software come at a slower pace. Managers need to be aware of how changes in the technology affect their range of strategic alternatives for managing the firm and offering products and services. By preparing now for the future, the organization will be in a position to profit from technological advances.

A manager is always concerned with the various sources available for products and services. In the computer field, there are options on suppliers for both hardware and software; we discuss some of the possibilities and their advantages and disadvantages in Chapter 11. Hardware capacity is available from service bureaus or through the development of an internal computer facility. Software is often available in the form of packages or it can be developed by an internal staff; staff members' efforts can also be supplemented through outside contractors and consultants.

The purpose of the material in this section is not to educate computer experts. Rather our objective is for the reader to gain enough understanding of computer hardware and software to make intelligent decisions about them. It is far more important to understand the concepts in this section than the specific details.

THE BASIC MODEL
COMPUTER GENERATIONS
PRIMARY MEMORY
    The Arithmetic Basis of Computers
    Memory Organization
    Memory Technology
X THE CENTRAL PROCESSING UNIT
    Components of the CPU
    Operation of the CPU
    Address Modification
    An Instruction Set
X MICROPROGRAMMING
    Background
    A Solution
    Applications of Microprogramming
DATA CHANNELS
X SPECIAL FEATURES
SECONDARY STORAGE
    Motivation
    Devices
I/O DEVICES
    Input
    Output
    Terminals
TYPES OF COMPUTERS
X ON-LINE SYSTEMS
    Motivation
    Hardware Requirements
    Telecommunications
X PATTERNS OF PROCESSING
    Patterns
    Computer Networks
    Evaluating Alternatives
SUMMARY
KEY WORDS
RECOMMENDED READINGS
DISCUSSION QUESTIONS

Chapter 7

Fundamentals of Computer Equipment

CHAPTER ISSUES

- What is the best technology for the organization?
- How does the organization select from the various options for computer equipment?
- What is an appropriate pattern of processing for the organization?

Why should users of information systems and managers in general be interested in computer equipment? In addition to making the important decisions described in the introduction to this section of the book, users and managers have to communicate with computer experts who are familiar with computer equipment. A knowledge of the concepts and vocabulary of computer hardware greatly facilitates this communication.

In this chapter we try to stress concepts independent of any particular computer equipment; our approach is a historical one tracing the development of computers through various "generations." In some places, however, it is

109

necessary to examine details as well as concepts. For example, it would be possible to describe primary memory as electronic devices capable of representing two states, a 0 or a 1. However, magnetic core storage has played a significant role in the development of computer systems, and "core" is a common term in every computer expert's vocabulary. For these reasons both core memory and the more modern semiconductor memory are discussed in some detail. However, sections containing more detailed information have been marked with an asterisk and can be omitted by readers interested primarily in an overview.

People invented computers and their associated equipment, and one of the most difficult aspects of computers is a consequence of this human involvement. Of the engineering and design decisions made during computer development, many often appear arbitrary. Computer science is thus unlike a field such as mathematics, in which theorems are developed and proved rigorously. The reasons for a certain design feature may not be obvious, even to a computer expert. Designers make decisions by balancing performance, estimates of how the computer will be used, and costs. Because of the arbitrary nature of design decisions, we shall try to discuss general concepts that underlie the operation of most computer systems, although specific machines differ from any general discussion.

The equipment we discuss in this chapter is often referred to as computer hardware—the parts of the computer that can be touched physically. The next chapter is about computer software, the instructions in the form of programs that command the hardware to perform tasks. Physically, programs are entered in the computer by punched cards, paper tape, a typewriter, or some similar device. However, once inside the computer, a program cannot be seen; it is represented electronically in computer memory.

THE BASIC MODEL

One view of an electronic computer system includes the four basic components shown in Figure 7-1. The central processing unit (CPU) is the heart of the computer; it contains all the logic that directs the operation of the machine. The CPU executes instructions such as add, subtract, etc.

Data to be processed by the CPU and instructions composing the programs are stored in primary memory. The CPU accesses this memory directly to retrieve and store instructions or data.

Secondary storage is cheaper than primary memory and usually has a much larger storage capacity. Examples of secondary storage devices include magnetic tape and magnetic disk. The contents of secondary storage cannot be accessed directly by the computer; instead, a data channel controls interchanges between the central processing unit and secondary storage.

Input/output (I/O) devices enable us to communicate with the computer. These devices include terminals, card readers and punches, and printers.

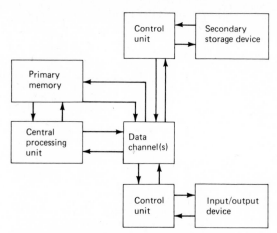

Figure 7-1   A basic computer system model.

Usually, a data channel also handles communications between I/O devices and the central processing unit. Control units are required to interface the data channel with each physically different secondary storage and I/O device. For example, the mechanical and electrical operations of a tape drive are different from those of a card reader. The controller helps the devices to present a more uniform appearance to the data channel.

COMPUTER GENERATIONS

Computer professionals frequently speak of different computer generations, each generation generally corresponding to the introduction of new computers with radically different hardware technologies from their predecessors. Changes in generations also have been accompanied by dramatic changes in performance. Each new generation has provided greatly increased computing speeds and more storage at lower cost than the equipment of the prior generation. (See Table 7-1.) Computer generations also can be characterized by changes in software, and in Chapter 8 we shall complete Table 7-1 by adding the software characteristics of each generation.

The first computer generation is characterized by vacuum-tube components and rotating memory on one of the most popular models, the IBM 560. (Note that IBM is used as an example in the text because its machines are the most familiar to computer professionals and users.) Second-generation computers use transistorized components for the central processing unit and magnetic cores for memory. Data channels appeared in this generation along with special features to improve central processing unit speeds. Computers were first used for commercial on-line systems involving communications and for time-sharing systems where users are presented with interactive computational capability through a terminal.

Table 7-1 Hardware Generations

Generation	Model	Monthly rental	Hardware characteristics	Organization	Cycle time microseconds (1)	Storage access (2)
First (1950s)	IBM 650	$3200†	Vacuum tubes, Memory = 3000 bits (600 digits), 1–4 K‡ of drum memory	5 bits/digit, 10 digits/ word	100	1 word (10 digits)
Second (1961)	IBM 1410	$4000	Transistorized CPU, data channel, memory = 10 K words	6 bits/digit, 1 digit/word	4.5	1 word (1 digit)
Third (1965)	IBM 360/40	$5300	Monolithic circuits, more CPU features, communications emphasis, memory = 65 K bytes	4 bits/digit, 2 digits/byte, 4 bytes/word	2.5	2 bytes (4 digits)
Third-and-a-half (1971)	IBM 370/135	$6400	Semiconductor primary memory, virtual memory, communications emphasis, memory = 98 K bytes	4 bits/digit, 2 digits/byte, 4 bytes/word	0.77	2 bytes (4 digits)
Fourth 1979	IBM 4331	$1900	Uses 64 K bit chip, 0.5 million bytes main memory, large disk storage	4 bits/digit, 2 digits/byte, 4 bytes/word	0.90	4 bytes (8 digits)

Table 7-1 (Continued)

Generation	Access time per digit (1) ÷ (2) microseconds (3)	Binary add time, microseconds (4)	Binary add size (5)	Add time per 2 digits (4) ÷ (5) microseconds (6)	2-digit adds per hour [1 ÷ (6)] (3600) millions (7)	Rental hour (monthly rental ÷ 176 hours) (8)	Cost per million 2-digit adds (8) ÷ (7) (9)*
First (1950s)	10	700	1 word (10 digits)	70	51.4	$18.18	35.00¢
Second (1961)	4.5	88	10 words (10 digits)	8.8	409	$22.73	5.56¢
Third (1965)	0.63	12	4 bytes (8 digits)	1.5	2400	$30.11	1.25¢
Third-and-a-half (1971)	0.19	4.2	4 bytes (8 digits)	0.53	6792	$36.36	0.54¢
Fourth 1979	0.11	3.4	4 bytes (8 digits)	0.43	8372	$10.80	0.13¢

*These figures are for comparison among machines; because of the limited configurations, the absolute costs are not meaningful.
†Costs are for rental of CPU and main memory; no peripherals are included. No adjustment has been made for inflation.
‡K = 1024

The third generation of computer hardware is characterized by more miniaturization and monolithic circuits (many electronic components on a chip) for central processing units. More CPU features to improve performance were added during this generation as well. Third-generation machines made it easier to develop on-line applications requiring telecommunication capabilities.

Third-generation computers evolved into the third-and-one-half generation through the use of semiconductor technology for main memory in some machines. A concept developed from time sharing called "virtual memory" has also been implemented through special hardware facilities (see the section on virtual memory in the next chapter.)

The fourth generation of computers is characterized by very large, fast semiconductor memories, small size, and lower power requirements. Fourth-generation machines are designed to ease the development of on-line applications and facilitate the use of large data bases.

PRIMARY MEMORY

Although the central processing unit controls the computer, we need to discuss primary memory before the CPU to demonstrate how data and instructions are stored in the computer. In the next section we shall see how the CPU processes the stored program and data to produce results.

The Arithmetic Basis of Computers

A computer can perform computations through an electronic counterpart to the arithmetic operations we perform on a routine basis. However, computer systems at their most fundamental level use a different number base than the common base 10 with which we are familiar.

The number 46 in base 10 can be represented as $4 \times 10 + 6 \times 1$. Furthermore, 10 is equal to 10^1 and 1 is equal to 10^0 (anything raised to the 0 power is 1 by definition). In our system of arithmetic, the position of a digit represents the power to which the base is raised before multiplication by the digit. For the number 46 above, 6 is in the "0 position," and 4 is in the 1 position. We can represent 46 then as $6 \times 10^0 + 4 \times 10^1$. This same procedure could be continued for more digits. For example, the number 346 can be represented as $6 \times 10^0 + 4 \times 10^1 + 3 \times 10^2$; now there is a 3 in the 10^2 position that adds 3×10^2, or 300, to the number.

There is no reason why we must use the base 10 for arithmetic; it is convenient for human beings, but not for computers. A computer can be designed most easily to base 2, or the binary system. The two digits of the binary system (0 and 1) can be represented as "on-off," for example, through the presence or absence of an electrical signal.

A binary number is represented in the same positional notation as a base 10 number. The number 1 0 1 1 1 0 in binary, starting with the right-most digit and working left, would be converted to base 10 as:

$$0 \times 2^0 = 0 \times 1 \ = \ 0$$
$$1 \times 2^1 = 1 \times 2 \ = \ 2$$
$$1 \times 2^2 = 1 \times 4 \ = \ 4$$
$$1 \times 2^3 = 1 \times 8 \ = \ 8$$
$$0 \times 2^4 = 0 \times 16 = \ 0$$
$$\underline{1 \times 2^5 = 1 \times 32 = 32}$$
$$46$$

which adds to 46 in base 10.

At the most basic level, computers store and process data in binary form; however, this is not an easy system for humans to use. Therefore, the binary digits in computer memory are grouped together to form other number bases for performing operations. For one series of machines, three binary digits are combined to produce an octal, or base-8, computer. Another popular line of computers groups four digits and is therefore a hexadecimal, or base-16, machine. Fortunately, even programmers rarely work at the binary level. For many applications, software or the design of the hardware makes the machine look as if it performs base-10 arithmetic from a programming standpoint.

All types of symbols can be coded and represented as binary numbers. For example, we could develop the following table to encode four alphabetic letters using two binary digits:

A = 00
B = 01
C = 10
D = 11

Thus, a series of binary digits can be coded to represent characters with which we are more familiar.

Memory Organization

Now that we have a convenient way to represent numbers and symbols, we need a way to store them in memory. Different computer designers have adopted different schemes for memory organization. Generally, all computers combine groups of bits (binary digits) to form characters, sometimes called bytes. The number of bits determines the size of the character set. From the example above, it should be evident that we can code 2^n distinct characters with a binary number of n digits. For example, if there are 4 bits, then there can be 2^4, or 16, symbols for alphanumeric data. Alphanumeric data are used for input and output display. Usually a different format for numbers is used for computation purposes. (See the section on arithmetic operations.) Many modern computers use an 8-bit character, or byte, giving a character set of 2^8, or 256, symbols.

After a character size and a set of symbols have been developed, the next design issue is to decide how to organize the memory of the machine. The basic use of memory is to store and fetch data, therefore we need some way to reference storage. An everyday example will help to clarify the problem. Suppose that we are expecting an important piece of mail. The mail delivery will be made to the mailbox at our street address; we know that by looking in the mailbox at our address we shall find the mail if it is there.

Now consider computer memory to be a group of mailboxes. We need an address to define each piece of data stored in memory so that it may be placed in a particular location (mailbox) and retrieved from that location. It is possible to have an address for each character in memory, or sometimes groups of characters are combined to form words and the words are given an address. In the IBM 360 and 370 series, four 8-bit bytes are combined to form a word, though each byte also has an address. A word structure is convenient because many numbers will fit within a single word as do many types of instructions.

Instructions, as well as data, must be stored in memory, and deciding on the instruction format is another design problem. At a minimum, the instruction must contain an operation code that specifies what operation is to be performed, for example, add or subtract. The operation code is combined with one or more addresses. For example, a single-address machine is designed with instructions that have one operation code and one address. For most instructions the single address specifies the memory location for one piece of data to be operated on by the instruction. In the case of an add, the address specifies the memory location whose content is to be added to some data already contained in the central processing unit. A machine with a two-address instruction format can have an add instruction that refers to both addresses in memory of the addends.

Memory Technology

From the standpoint of the programmer and the user, the technology used for primary memory is not important. However, a general understanding of memory technology helps in appreciating the characteristics of secondary storage and file structures, and these are topics of vital importance to users.

Core Storage   The earliest memory technology of interest to us is magnetic core storage. Most current computers do not use core storage for primary memory. However, this medium is used for large memories that can be attached to computers. Most computer professionals continue to refer to primary memory as "core storage" regardless of whether core technology is used or not!

Figure 7-2 is a diagram of a simple core memory. Remember that we are interested in representing 0 or 1 in memory. For core memory, these two states are determined by the direction of magnetization of the core. Each core in Figure 7-2 can be uniquely located by the two lines running through it. Each of these lines has one-half of the current necessary to reverse the direction of magnetization. When current is passed through a vertical line and a horizontal line, only the core at the intersection receives the full current necessary to reverse its direction of magnetization. Other cores—not at the intersection but on one of the two lines—receive one-half the current necessary to change their

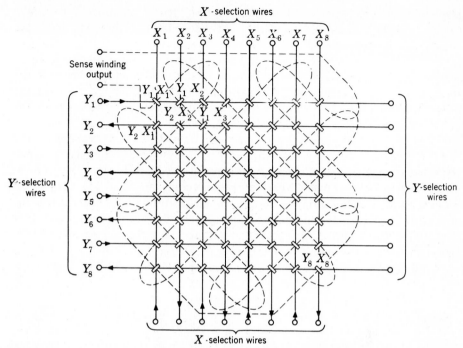

Figure 7-2 Core memory plane. *(From Bartee, T. C.: Digital Computer Fundamentals, 4th ed., McGraw-Hill, 1977.)*

state, so they are not affected. Core memories contain two additional lines—one to sense the direction of magnetization and one to aid in writing.

To read information from memory, current is passed through the two appropriate grid wires. If the core already is magnetized in the same direction as the current, nothing happens. Otherwise, the core changes its direction of magnetization. The change induces a current in a sense wire, and this current is interpreted to determine the original state of the core. The presence or absence of current in the wire can be interpreted as a 0 or 1. For cores in which the direction of magnetization was changed, the data have been "reversed." For the cores that were read, data have to be rewritten. An inhibit wire (omitted from Figure 7-2) blocks the rewrite current from the cores that did not change state during the read operation.

In summary, to read, we write into storage, sense any changes, and rewrite into storage to regenerate the original core state. Because of the need to rewrite data just read, core storage readout is referred to as "destructive" readout.

Semiconductor Memory Most modern computers have main memories of semiconductor devices. Semiconductor memories offer significant increases in speed over other memory technologies, are smaller, and are compatible with normal circuitry of the central processing unit. The major disadvantages of semiconductor memory are its volatility and high power dissipation. Semiconductor memories must be constantly powered and lose their contents (are volatile) if the power fails.

Figure 7-3*a* shows schematically how a typical semiconductor memory works. The memory is organized in an array of rows and columns; the cell at the intersection of each column and row stores one bit so that the diagram in Figure 7-3*a* contains 64 bits. Three binary digits specify the row (1 to 8) and three the column (1 to 8).

Figure 7-3*b* shows one cell storing a single bit in detail. A zero charge on the capacitor might represent a binary 0 and a very small charge a binary 1. When the selection line or row of the array is activated (row 4 in Figure 7-3*a*), it turns on all the transistor switches in each of the cells connected to it. The transistor is an on-off switch connecting the storage capacitor to its data line, which is the column of the array. When both the row and column lines are activated, they determine the cell selected for reading or writing (cell 4, 5 in Figure 7-3*a*.) Every few milliseconds the capacitor must have its charge regenerated because the charge is lost by being read and through leakage (Hodges, 1977).

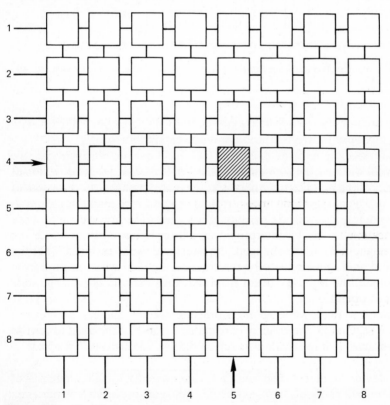

Figure 7-3a Semiconductor memory.

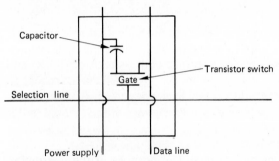

Figure 7-3b   Detail of cell. *(Adapted from "Microelectronic Memories," by O. Hodges,* Scientific American, *September 1977.)*

To produce integrated circuits containing many semiconductors special equipment is utilized to develop first a picture of an electronic circuit on a drafting board or computer terminal screen. A reduced image of the circuit is made into something called a mask, which is like a photographic negative. When light rays are projected through such a mask onto thin films of a liquid plastic, exposed areas harden. Unexposed plastic is washed away leaving a microscopic structure corresponding to the original drawing of the circuit. Acids are then used to cut away the surface of areas that were not covered by the plastic, producing an engraving of the original circuit. Chips are actually sandwiches of many of these layers.

To produce an integrated circuit a slice of semiconducting silicon is used as a base on which the circuit is engraved and built up with subsequent applications of the process described above. Parts of the semiconductor base must be turned into transistors. Foreign atoms (dopants) lodged in microscopic regions of a silicon crystal make the crystal either extra rich or extra poor in electrons. When such regions are placed together in a sandwich, they become transistors that act as on-off switches. The transistors allow current to flow when an external electrical field is applied but block current flow when the external field is removed. Other transistors are turned into capacitors for memory.

Most modern computers use semiconductors for main memory because the cost of fabricating these devices has dropped dramatically. For a class of computers called "microprocessors" the entire computer can be constructed on a single chip smaller than the end of a paper clip.

THE CENTRAL PROCESSING UNIT

As stated earlier, the CPU controls the operation of the computer; it contains most of the logic circuitry for the machine. Program instructions are stored in memory along with data. In a basic computer system the instructions are stored sequentially beginning at some location in memory. The CPU by convention always fetches the next instruction in sequence and executes it unless the program instructs it to do otherwise.

Components of the CPU

Figure 7-4 shows the CPU and primary memory in more detail than Figure 7-1. A discussion of CPU operations helps in understanding programming languages in the next chapter. Note the presence of a storage address register (SAR) and storage buffer register (SBR) in primary memory. The SAR is connected to memory in such a way that when an address is placed in it and a read command is given, the contents of the memory at that address appear in the storage buffer register. Similarly, when a write command is issued, the contents of the SBR are written into memory at the address location contained in the SAR.

The CPU contains a number of registers. The purpose of the instruction register is to hold instructions that are decoded and executed by the circuits of the CPU. The location counter keeps track of the address from which the next instructions should be fetched.

The arithmetic unit contains registers that hold data during the execution of arithmetic operations by CPU circuits. Several types of numbers can be processed by computers. A fixed-point number is an integer; the decimal point is fixed and is assumed to be to the right of the right-most digit. Examples of fixed-point numbers are 2, 512, and 671. A floating point number corresponds to scientific exponential notation; the position of the decimal point is indicated by digits associated with the number. For example, we might have a floating point format of .1632E03 meaning that the number 0.1632 is to be multiplied by 10^3. The number in conventional form, then, is 163.2. The number 16.32 would be presented by .1632E02. The exponent allows the decimal point to "float." It is also possible to have registers that perform decimal arithmetic.

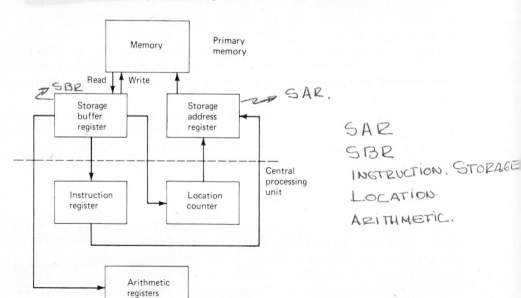

Figure 7-4 Central processing unit and memory.

Are arithmetic registers really necessary? One early computer had no registers; mathematical operations were performed by looking up information in tables in memory! The presence of arithmetic registers, however, speeds computations; if registers are not used, a program requiring memory and execution time must be written to stimulate desired arithmetic operations. However, several popular second-generation business-oriented computers had only fixed-point addition and subtraction capabilities. Multiplication was accomplished by successive additions, and division, by successive subtractions. In a similar manner, programs simulate floating-point operations on these computers. Most modern general-purpose computers feature fixed- and floating-point registers for addition, subtraction, multiplication, and division.

Operation of the CPU

Referring to Figure 7-4, we describe the fetch and execution phases of the instruction cycle of the CPU for a single-address computer (Hellerman, 1967).

The objective of the fetch cycle is to obtain an instruction from memory in preparation for executing the instruction. The steps are:

1 The address of the location counter is moved to the SAR, initiating a read-from-memory subcycle. At the completion of the read subcycle, the contents of the memory address in the SAR appear in the SBR.

2 The contents of the SBR are moved to the instruction register for interpretation by the logic circuits of the CPU.

3 The location counter is increased by 1 to point to the next instruction to be fetched.

4 The instruction is decoded to yield an effective address (see the discussion on address modification below).

During the execution cycle, the instruction is interpreted and the operation it signifies is performed:

1 The effective address of the data on which the operation is to take place is sent to the SAR. A read-access subcycle is started to fetch the datum that then appears in the SBR.

2 The datum is routed to a machine register.

3 The operation—for example, a subtract—is performed on the datum.

Address Modification*

In the section above, we mentioned the computation of an effective address. To provide added flexibility and power, many computers make it possible to modify an address contained in the instruction register before its execution. The first and most common modification is the use of an index register. The contents of this

---

*Sections marked with an asterisk contain detailed discussions and can be omitted on first reading or when the reader is interested only in an overview.

register are subtracted (or added, depending on the computer) to the data address in the instruction.

How is this capability used? Assume there are some data located in memory as shown in Table 7-2a. We could write a program (in a hypothetical language) that clears an arithmetic register and then adds the data from each location in memory. For example, in Table 7-2b the first add takes the contents of memory address 1024, the data 200, and adds it to the CPU add register. In this example, we have to use as many adds as there are numbers, say 25. This procedure produces a lengthy and inflexible program. What would happen if we wanted to add 40 numbers for the next computation?

In Table 7-2c, we write a program that uses an index register. The first instruction in our hypothetical program loads the index register with the number 24. The second instruction clears the arithmetic register in the CPU and the third begins a loop. This third instruction, an add, references the base location of 1024 where our data begin. The 1 in the add instruction refers to register 1. In this computer, assume the contents of the index register are subtracted from the address of the instruction; therefore, the add will fetch data from location 1024 minus 24, or 1000, where we said the data begin. The datum at location 1000 will be added to the arithmetic register in the CPU.

Table 7-2   An Example of Index Register Modification

Memory Location	Contents
a Data in memory	
1024	200
1023	150
1022	600
1021	432
1020	100
1019	700

Instruction	Address
b Program with no register	
CLEAR	
ADD	1024
ADD	1023
ADD	1022
ADD	1021
ADD	1020
ADD	1019
Etc.	

	c Program using index register 1	
	LOAD	1, 24
	CLEAR	
STEP1	ADD	1024, 1
	DEC	1, 1
	BRLZ	STEP1

The next instruction decreases the contents of the index register by 1, leaving 23 as its contents. The last instruction says go to the instruction labeled STEP1 if the contents of index register are not less than 0. Since the register contains the number 23, the program will branch back to STEP1 (a branch occurs by putting the address of the instruction at STEP1 into the location counter that results in the CPU taking that as the next instruction). On the last time through the loop, register 1 will contain 0. The last datum at location 1024 will be added to the sum accumulated so far. Then the register will be decremented by one making it less than 0 and the program will take the next instruction after the branch (not shown in Table 7-2c).

Another form of address modification is also useful for certain I/O operations and other functions. In indirect addressing, shown in Figure 7-4, the contents of a location are interpreted not as data, but as another address. In Figure 7-5, the instruction references address 412 indirectly. The CPU fetches the subtract instruction, decodes the address, and fetches the data at location 412. Because this is an indirect address, the CPU undertakes another fetch cycle to obtain the contents of location 637, the indirect address stored as data in location 412. Finally, the CPU uses the data at location 637, the number 10625, for the subtraction.

Some machines allow several levels of indirect addressing; for these computers, the data at location 637 could be another indirect address. In this manner, various pointers through memory to different locations can be established. This facility can be used for linking programs and data, for example, to connect a main program and its parts.

An Instruction Set

What operations can be performed by a typical computer? Table 7-3 contains the instruction set for an IBM 1130, a small third-generation scientific and engineering computer (Bell and Newell, 1971). Note the different classes of instructions in the table including data movement, arithmetic, logical comparison, and

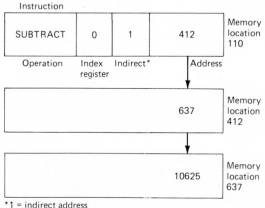

*1 = indirect address
 0 = no indirect address

Figure 7-5 Indirect addressing.

Table 7-3 Instruction Set for IBM 1130

Class	Instruction	Indirect addressing	Mnemonic symbol
Load and store	Load accumulator	Yes	LD
	Double load	Yes	LDD
	Store accumulator	Yes	STO
	Double store	Yes	STD
	Load index		LDX
	Store index	Yes	STX
	Load status	No	LDS
	Store status	Yes	STS
Arithmetic	Add	Yes	A
	Double add	Yes	AD
	Subtract	Yes	S
	Double subtract	Yes	SD
	Multiply	Yes	M
	Divide	Yes	D
	And	Yes	AND
	Or	Yes	OR
	Exclusive Or	Yes	EOR
Shift	Shift-left Instructions:		
	Shift left logical (A*)	No	SLA
	Shift left logical (AQ†)	No	SLT
	Shift left and count (AQ)	No	SLC
	Shift left and count (A)	No	SLCA
	Shift-right instructions:		
	Shift right logical (A)	No	SRA
	Shift right arithmetically (AQ)	No	SRT
	Rotate right (AQ)	No	RTE
Branch	Branch and store I‡	Yes	BSI
	Branch or skip on condition	Yes	BSC(BOSC)
	Modify index and skip		MDX
	Wait	No	WAIT
I/O	Execute I/O	Yes	XIO

*A = A 16-bit accumulator register which contains the results of any arithmetic operation
†Q = A 16-bit low-order expansion of the accumulator for multiplication, division, etc.
‡I = Instruction address register
Source: Adapted from G. Bell and A. Newell, *Computer Structures: Readings and Examples,* McGraw-Hill, New York, 1971.

branching. There are only 31 instructions, yet the machine is capable of performing a large number of tasks and supports the FORTRAN language discussed in the next chapter. Other large computers have repertoires of well over 100 instructions along with 10 or more registers capable of performing arithmetic operations or serving as index registers. These machines contain more operations and support several data formats. Because it is a simpler machine, the 1130 instruction set is easier to understand than more modern computers, and the example provides a good indication of the type of instructions found in a computer.

MICROPROGRAMMING

Background

When computer manufacturers planned third-generation computers, they faced a number of serious marketing problems. Unlike the transition to second generation from first, organizations had more substantial investments in programs for second-generation computers. These programs were frequently written in assembly language, a language that is generally unique for a given machine. That is, an assembly-language program cannot be executed on just any computer; it exhibits low compatibility among computers. How could a new machine be sold if it obsoleted a customer's program library so that all programs had to be replaced? How could customers convert? Would they have to keep a second-generation computer and a third-generation machine together while they translated their programs?

Second-generation computers were also characterized by several groups or families; for example, one dichotomy exists between business and scientific computers. Second-generation business machines featured limited arithmetic capabilities but excellent data editing and input/output features. A number of these machines had variable word lengths and were character-oriented. Scientific machines, on the other hand, had poor input/output features and fixed word lengths with many parallel operations. Scientific computers also featured high-speed arithmetic registers and floating-point hardware.

When a customer wanted to move up to a more powerful second-generation computer, it might have been necessary to switch to a new series of machines, requiring conversion. Computer manufacturers wanted to avoid major conversion problems in developing the third generation and also wanted to provide upward and downward compatibility. That is, there would be a family of machines, each capable of executing programs written for any "lower" member of that family. Of course, compatibility would only be possible within limits of memory and peripheral equipment.

To develop comparibility among computers in a family requires similar instruction sets. However, usually more powerful computers at the top of a product line have more extensive and capable repertoires of instructions than smaller members of the line. Thus, another major problem for computer manufacturers was how to develop identical instruction sets for small and large machines at a reasonable cost.

Several solutions can be suggested for the problem of conversion. For example, we could write a program to translate existing programs in second-generation assembly language to a third-generation higher-level language. Theoretically, this approach is easy. However, it becomes difficult in practice, and it was several years after the introduction of third-generation equipment before such a program was developed for one of the major manufacturers. (Even then, a customer and not a computer vendor wrote the program!)

Another possibility is a simulation program. Such a program would make third-generation computers look like second-generation machines; the new computer would execute second-generation programs. The only drawback here is speed; it takes several simulated instructions to execute each second-generation program instruction. The manufacturer could be in the position of trying to sell a new third-generation computer that took longer to execute programs than the second-generation computer being replaced! Moreover, neither of these solutions solves the instruction set compatibility problem.

A Solution

Certain operations in the CPU of Figure 7-3 are required by almost all instructions, for example, adding 1 to the contents of the location counter. The process of executing an instruction is made up of two types of activities: register-to-register transfers and control commands such as for clearing a register or initiating a memory read (the reader should review the discussion on page 121 about the basic instruction fetch and execution cycles of the CPU). Each instruction in machine language can be thought of as a series of more primitive or fundamental instructions such as:

> Move the contents of the arithmetic register to the SBR.
> Move the contents of the SBR to the arithmetic register.
> Add 1 to the location counter.
> Read from main storage.
> Write to main storage.
> Clear the arithmetic registers.

As an example of how an instruction is formed, suppose we wanted to store the results of an arithmetic operation back in main memory. The instruction in machine language would be something like STO 250; that is, store the contents of an arithmetic register at location 250. A microprogram for a hypothetical computer to accomplish this might appear something like:

> Move the contents of the arithmetic register to the SBR.
> Move the address portion of the instruction (250) to the SAR.
> Write into main memory.
> Add 1 to the location counter.

Following this approach, we have broken a machine-language instruction into a series of more fundamental instructions, or microinstructions. These more primitive instructions are combined into a "program" to produce a machine-language instruction like STO. The technique described above is called "microprogramming," and it represents a major advance in the design of computer hardware.

Applications of Microprogramming

How does microprogramming solve our marketing problems in selling third-generation computers? First, by combining different microinstructions, we can create a large variety of microprogrammed instructions at a reasonable cost. Microprogramming is cheaper than actually wiring the computer (called "hard-wiring") to perform, say, the STO instruction using circuits directly. In a microprogrammed family of computers, small, less capable models use micro-programming extensively, and larger models are hardwired. The hardware costs more for a hardwired machine, but a wired instruction executes faster than several microprogrammed steps. Microprogramming thus solves the problem of creating compatible instruction sets at a reasonable cost for a family of computers.

How does microprogramming help in conversion? A microprogramming feature can be used to simulate, with both hardware and software, one computer's instruction set on another computer—a process known as emulation. Microprogramming features are used to make a third-generation machine look like its second-generation counterpart. Under emulation, second-generation computer instructions are executed on a third-generation computer, by both software and microprogrammed steps. Emulation is considerably faster than simulation with a software program alone because the microprogrammed steps in the hardware execute faster than software instructions.

In addition to these original factors motivating the development of micro-programming, many other uses have developed for it. Manufacturers now use microprogramming to provide very complex instructions or to tailor a piece of equipment for a specific job. The extensive use of microprogramming for such special purposes has produced microprograms called "firmware." If some process has little chance of being changed, microprogramming offers greater speed than writing a software program. However, the cost is flexibility, since a software program is much easier to modify than a microprogram.

DATA CHANNELS

During the development of second-generation computers, it was recognized that the CPU spent much of its time interacting with input/output devices such as card readers and printers. The fact that these operations really do not require the full power of the central processing unit stimulated the development of the data channel. A data channel is a device that contains hardware logic capabilities like, but less complex than, those of the CPU.

The data channel accepts commands from the CPU and executes a channel program that controls input/output operations. The CPU is then free to operate in parallel with the data channel; both computations and I/O operations occur simultaneously, thereby improving the throughput (amount of work processed) of the computer.

In some second-generation computers, the central processing unit has an instruction to check if a channel is busy. Computations might stop to wait for a channel to finish supervising the printing of a line before the next line is printed. The CPU under these conditions waits until the channel is free. Most third-generation general-purpose computers have an interrupt structure. The CPU has special registers that save the status of the tasks on which it is working. By saving its place, the CPU can respond to an interrupt while maintaining the integrity of the currently executing program. Following interrupt processing, the CPU restores the interrupted program and then continues from where it stopped. An illustration that uses data channels will help to explain this very important capability.

Assume that a program on which the CPU is working needs to print a line on the printer. The CPU initiates the print operation through a command to the data channel. The data channel takes over to interpret the print instruction and give commands to the controller for the printer. The CPU continues with the program, performing a series of computations. When the data channel has finished printing, it interrupts the central processing unit. The CPU stores the status of what it is doing and answers the interrupt, for example, by noting that the print operation is now complete (which means that the next print operation can be undertaken). The the CPU resumes the task it was executing when the interrupt came from the data channel.

This capability may not seem like a major advance, given the ability of a second-generation computer to test for busy channels. However, in the next chapter, when we discuss operating systems and multiprogramming, the importance of interrupts should become more evident.

SPECIAL FEATURES

In the second- and third-generation computers, several special features were added to the central processing unit in some machines to improve speed. An example of such a feature is instruction look-ahead. The idea is to have the CPU accomplish several tasks in parallel; the look-ahead unit decodes program instructions in advance of their execution. While one part of the CPU is executing an instruction, another part of the CPU fetches instructions that follow the one being executed and decodes them. This concurrency of instruction fetch, decoding, and execution produces added speed.

Another feature that speeds processing is memory interleaving. Memory in this scheme is split into several modules, for example, four modules for four-way interleaving. Consecutive addresses are located in different modules so that four locations in sequence can be fetched at once. Interleaving can also be combined with look-ahead.

In multiprocessing, more than one central processing unit is present. Operations occur in parallel, similar to the parallel operations we discussed with the use of data channels.

Another innovation is the use of high-speed buffer memory to speed processing. A fast central processing unit is connected to a high-speed semiconductor memory with a cycle time of, say, 60 nanoseconds. This memory may be smaller than regular storage (tens of thousands of characters versus hundreds of thousands or millions of characters of main memory). Main memory is slower than the buffer; it might consist of main storage with a 1-microsecond cycle time. All computations are carried in buffer memory; the hardware automatically moves programs and data from main memory to the buffer cache memory when needed. Primary memory is assigned to a certain sector of cache memory. When a program or data are needed for main memory, hardware logic checks to see if they are in its buffer segment. If they are, computation proceeds; if not, the present contents of the buffer are written back to main memory (if the data in the sector have changed since it was loaded). The part of main memory required is now copied into the buffer sector. If there are few access references to main memory, execution will proceed at a speed near the cycle time of the high-speed buffer memory.

We shall postpone the discussion of another innovation, virtual memory, until the next chapter, since it involves software. All the features described here are invisible to a programmer; they are accomplished by hardware without explicit instructions from a program.

These approaches to hardware architecture have been designed to improve operations, that is, to gain speed at a reasonable cost. Many different approaches to the design of computers have been implemented, and the concepts discussed in this chapter should provide a good background for understanding specific design decisions.

SECONDARY STORAGE

Motivation

Secondary storage generally refers to storage devices that have to be accessed through a data channel; the CPU cannot fetch data or instructions directly from them. There are several reasons for the use of secondary storage devices. First, primary memory is very expensive; we often cannot afford to have sufficient primary memory to process large amounts of data. Some applications have files containing billions of characters of data, exceeding the capacity of the primary memory of any computer available today.

Even if we could afford enough primary memory and could physically attach it to our computer, we really would not want to fill it with data! Many programs use primary memory, each processing its own data. If we left all the data for one application in memory all the time, we would have to dedicate the entire computer or a significant part of it to just that application. Therefore, we do not want to store data in primary memory when they are not needed. Secondary storage devices provide a flexible storage capability for data and programs.

Devices

Table 7-4 contains a list of some of the important secondary storage devices arranged by average access time (how long, on the average, it takes to retrieve data from the device). In general, the cost per character of storage drops with access time; that is, faster devices—as we might expect—cost more. Note that, while the CPU and memory might operate at speeds of less than 100 nanoseconds (100×10^{-9} second), most secondary storage devices have access times in the millisecond (10^{-3} second) range, or nearly 10,000 times slower than primary

Table 7-4 Secondary Storage Devices

Device	Monthly rental	Average access time	Transfer rate bytes/sec	Capacity million bytes*†	Monthly rental/ million bytes	Type
Fixed-head disk	$ 5495 3245 $ 8740	2.5 milliseconds	3000 K‡	5.4	$1619.00	Direct
Semiconductor (16K chip) system including control unit (volatile storage, information lost when power off)	$ 4305**	0.4 millisecond	1750 K	12	$ 359.00	Direct
Movable-head disk and controller	$ 1450 2685 $ 4135	38.4 milliseconds (30.0 seek time, 8.4 rotational delay	806 K	200	$ 21.00	Direct
Movable and fixed-head disk and controller	$ 1915 2045 $ 3960	8.3 millisecond average rotational delay for 2.28 million characters, 25 millisecond seek, and 8.3 millisecond rotational delay for rest	1198 K	634	$ 6.25	Direct
Mass storage and controller	$12,937 3965 $16,902	15.5 seconds (5.5 to fetch cartridge; 10.0 to load, read to a disk, and unload)	874 K	35,300	$ .48	Direct
Magnetic tape and controller	$ 608 1101 $ 1709	Contingent on record size and density	470 K	180 (6250 bpi at 2400 feet)	Not applicable	Sequential

*Byte = 1 character or 2 digits.
†Ignoring interrecord gaps.
‡K = 1024.
**Based on 2-year lease contract.

MANAGEMENT PROBLEM 7-1

John Trout has just assumed a position as vice president for administration at Technical R&D, a diversified research and consulting firm. John's previous experience was in accounting and finance. At Technical, all information systems activities now report to him. Because of his lack of familiarity with computers, John has been reading widely in the field to prepare for his new assignment.

Mary Jackson is the director of information systems for Technical and reports to John. She has been supplying him with information about the use of computers at Technical and about computers in general. Technical employs computers for its own internal administrative work; in addition, large computers are used for scientific computations by the professional staff.

Mary explained the history of computers at Technical. In the second generation, Technical maintained complete separation between administrative and scientific processing. A separate, character-oriented business computer was used for all administrative work and a large, fixed-word-length scientific computer was utilized by the professional staff. Even though third-generation computers eliminated much of the distinction between business and scientific processing, Mary felt there were good management reasons for maintaining this separation at Technical R&D. Now, even with the latest equipment, Technical still has a separate computer for administrative processing and a larger machine in the same family for use by the professional staff.

John wondered what the "management considerations" were that convinced Mary two computers were necessary. What would the advantages be of using a single, large computer for all kinds of Technical's processing?

---

memory. Below, we briefly mention different secondary storage devices; we shall discuss these devices in greater detail in Chapter 9 on files.

Direct-access storage refers to the device's capability to locate information stored anyplace on it in roughly the same length of time. Direct-access storage contrasts with sequential storage, in which all the data are arranged in order and the device must be scanned in that order to find specific information. The fastest secondary storage device is constructed of semiconductors and has no moving parts. Rotating memories are slower and less reliable, because of their mechanical components.

The most popular mass-storage devices use magnetic tape strips arranged in cartridges that are retrieved, read, and transferred to a disk storage device. A mass-storage device might replace an entire magnetic tape library. Mass-storage devices are slow in placing the data on the disk, but once there, the data can be processed at disk speeds.

Magnetic tape is one of the oldest storage media. Data are stored in sequence on a tape; to retrieve the information we have to search one-half the tape, on the average. Magnetic tape is cheap and provides convenient off-line storage and backup.

All these devices share two common characteristics. We have to access them through the data channel at speeds considerably slower than we can access primary memory. Second, all use a magnetic medium of some type to store data.

Recently a new type of storage device has been employed for certain applications. One manufacturer offers a terminal with "bubble memory" that can record data in the field and then transmit it to a computer over a phone line. The telephone company is also using bubble memory to record certain routine messages that are played over the phone network such as, "This number has been disconnected."

A bubble memory consists of a thin film of magnetic material that is deposited (grown) on a nonmagnetic base material or substrate. A magnetic bubble is a cylindrical magnetic domain with poles the opposite direction of the magnetic material in which it is imbedded. The bubbles are uniformly spaced in the memory device so that the presence of a bubble signifies a "one" and its absence means a "zero."

A bubble memory can be thought of as a random access memory, but it also has some serial access features. Bubbles are located at a grid point but are configured in loops. (See Figure 7-6.) A bubble may or may not exist at each grid point as described above. As shown by the dotted lines in the figure, the grid is turned into a loop of bubbles by rotation of the bubbles within the loop. Each loop has a "window." To read or write, the entire loop is rotated until the bit of interest is in the window, the one position where the bubble can be sensed or altered. A bubble memory will have many loops of bubbles. Each loop can be accessed randomly, but within each loop an individual bit must be accessed serially (Osborne, 1980).

Although not in wide use yet, bubble memories are expected to have many applications for secondary storage, particularly where relatively fast access is needed for large amounts of data. Right now bubble memories are rather slow compared to disks, but they are becoming increasingly less expensive and therefore more competitive with other forms of secondary storage. Likely

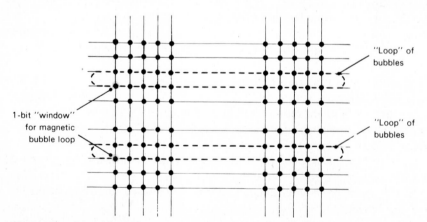

Figure 7-6 Magnetic bubble memory. *(From Osborne, A.:* Introduction to Microcomputers, *2d ed., vol. 1, Osborne/McGraw-Hill, 1980.)*

COMPUTER-AIDED DESIGN

When General Motors made the decision the Fall of 1974 to re-size its automobiles by 1977, the firm was already nine months late for such a major shift in the production schedule. General Motors used computer-aided design of manufacturing to develop the specifications for developing the resized cars. The 1977 versions of full-sized cars were 700 pounds lighter than their predecessors.

Some 15 years of effort have gone into the General Motors design console system. The system uses computers and CRT displays to perform design engineering and manufacturing functions. The system is so sophisticated that measurements taken from clay models can be used to produce dies to stamp out the actual sheet metal for the finished vehicle.

The system is used to evaluate the structural characteristics of designs. An engineer working with the system can assemble mathematical models of the components of a car and road test the car on a simulated drive route. The system makes it possible to alter the design with minimal risk, since the alterations are tested by the computer system. A lot of the trial and error process of design has been removed.

Another area with great potential for improving productivity is in the production process itself. In the past few years, General Motors has invested a large sum in basic machines to carry out traditional tasks of turning, boring, drilling or grinding metal parts. However, the design for these machines has not changed in many years, and productivity in relation to cost has actually declined.

To improve the productivity of these machines, GM is turning to computer controls. The President of General Motors has forecast that within 10 years computers will control about 90% of all new machines in manufacturing and assembly plants. The idea is not to replace workers, but supplement their skills.

Productivity is a national concern. The use of computers to aid product designers and to assist in the manufacturing process can contribute to increasing levels of productivity in the economy.

Datamation, May, 1978.

---

applications of bubble technology include use in special purpose terminals, such as word processing, banking, point of sale, etc. For minicomputers, bubble memory will probably be used as a disk replacement, and for mainframe computers, it will be applied as fast auxiliary memory.

I/O DEVICES

One of the largest bottlenecks in information systems is input/output. Devices to enter data generally have some mechanical component that requires human interaction. Consider a card reader capable of reading 80-column cards at a rate of 500 cards per minute. At this rate, $80 \times 500 \div 60$ or 667 characters per second are input to the computer. However, the computer may be capable of fetching over a million characters per second from primary memory. Output is also slow. Consider a standard 1000-line-per-minute printer. With 130 characters per line, the printer operates at $1000 \times 130 \div 60$ or 2167 characters per second. Below we discuss some of the common I/O devices in use today. (See Table 7-5.)

Table 7-5   Common Input/Output Devices

Input devices
  Paper tape
  Punched cards
  Key to tape
  Key to disk
  Magnetic-ink character recognition (MICR)
  Mark sense
  Optical character recognition (OCR)
  Terminals
  Voice
  Special devices (for example, analog to digital)

Output devices
  Paper tape
  Card punch
  Line printer
    Impact
    Nonimpact
  Computer output to microfilm (COM)
  Audio response
  Terminals
  Special devices (for example, digital to analog)

Terminals
  Remote job entry
  Interactive
  Hard copy
    Serial impact
    Nonimpact
  CRT (single or multiple color)
    Alphanumeric
    Graphics
      Dynamic
      Storage tube

Knowledge of this equipment is very important in making decisions on various alternatives in systems analysis and design.

Input

One of the earliest input media was punched paper tape, a narrow strip of tape punched with holes representing characters. A device reads the tape and transmits the characters to the computer. Paper tape is difficult to use and is not well suited to large volumes of input. Paper tape is essentially obsolete as an I/O medium for commercial computer applications.

The familiar punched card still is used extensively for input. An individual transcribes information to the cards using a keypunch. The information should be verified by another operator, who rekeys the original information and compares the holes in the cards and notes any discrepancies. An alternative is to have a computer punch cards, each containing information relevant to a particular user (for example, in a billing application). The card is sent to the customer, who returns it with payment. If the payment matches the amount billed, the card or "turnaround document" is entered directly into the computer.

To speed data transcription, key-to-tape and key-to-disk units have been developed. These devices may offer formatting aids beyond the card keypunch; they are also faster and quieter than the card-oriented keypunch. Several operators may use the same tape or disk, and the results may be aggregated and placed on a computer-compatible tape or disk for final input.

Magnetic-ink character recognition (MICR) has found its greatest acceptance in banking. All checks are coded with an account number and code identifying the bank. A human operator enters the amount on the check when it is processed, using a special coding device. The magnetic ink characters are read and the checks sorted by area and account number. However, a few applications beyond banking have been suggested for MICR.

Mark sensing can be used for input where there are a few alternatives that can be represented by simple choices. Mark sensing is a technique used to read answers in most standardized "machine-scored" tests. A question with four answers requires four columns on the answer sheet. The student darkens a choice for each question and a mark-sensing device reads the marks. Unfortunately, when there are many choices, mark sense forms become large because a space is required for each option. For example, consider the amount of space required to enter one's name on the test form compared with the space to answer questions.

Optical character recognition (OCR) is gaining increasing use as an input technique. OCR readers have a variety of capacities and costs and many employ laser technology to read data. The simplest OCR scanners are bar-code readers that optically scan information coded with bars such as those found on some credit cards. There are several OCR-type fonts that are easier for machines to read than standard printing such as the type in this book. These special OCR-type fonts can be read by equipment slightly more sophisticated than bar-code readers. A number of scanners can read documents typed using the OCR B-type element. More complex OCR devices also read hand-printed numbers and a few characters. The most advanced units read typed or hand-printed letters, although care must be taken preparing the data. With OCR, rejects may be high, but only rejected documents have to be keyed into the machine. Successfully read input reduces the transcription process and allows data to be captured closer to its source.

A variety of terminals is available for data input as well as output. The most general are described in the next section. There are also special input terminals that feature badge readers (to identify the individual entering data) and card readers for, say, a factory-floor production control application. Terminals make it possible to extend data collection to the original source of the data and reduce intermediate transcription.

Experiments are currently underway on voice-input devices. Voice input of numbers is being used in several instances where the individual providing information must have both hands free. However, there are many problems to overcome, and it remains to be seen how many applications there are for voice input. Finally, there are a number of special-purpose input devices. For example, for industrial process control, analog sensors (for continuous signals, as opposed to discrete or digital signals) may feed data to some device that converts them into digital signals for processing on a digital computer.

Output

A number of output devices are available. Equipment to punch cards or paper tape can be connected to many digital computers. Large general-purpose computers usually feature card equipment, and smaller special-purpose machines may have paper tape equipment.

The line printer is used heavily for output, especially in batch systems. An impact line printer has a print element that comes in physical contact with the paper; usually a type slug presses a ribbon against the paper when hit by a hammer device. Because of this physical impression, multiple copies can be created with carbon paper. Impact printers come in a variety of speeds, although the maximum currently available is in the neighborhood of 2000 lines per minute.

Nonimpact printers use other technologies to create an image. Some approaches are similar to commercial photocopying processes, and others employ charged particles of ink or print thermally. One printer uses special electrostatic paper and another uses a laser and a process similar to xerography to produce images. Nonimpact printers, with speeds in the range of 10,000 to 20,000 lines per minute, are considerably faster than impact printers. However, additional copies cannot be made with carbon paper; duplicate output must be printed or the original must be photocopied.

Computer output to microfilm (COM) offers one approach to reducing the bulk of the information printed by computers. Usually, the microfilm device is off-line; that is, it is not directly connected to the computer. The computer system produces an output magnetic tape at high speed. The tape is mounted on a computer output microfilm device, which produces the microfilm. Some devices require a separate step to develop the film, though at least one COM unit produces film directly from computer input. One limitation of microfilm is that a special viewing device is needed to read it; special equipment also is required to produce a paper copy.

Audio-response output units have been used for a number of applications in which there is a short inquiry and response—for example, in retrieving the balance in a bank account. Audio output devices record messages such as the phrase "your balance is" and a series of 10 digits. The program selects the appropriate digits and commands the device to play the entire message. New semiconductor devices that synthesize speech from its components are also available.

There are also a number of terminals that can be used for output, as described below. A myriad of special devices has been developed for output, especially for analog output for industrial process-control applications.

Terminals

Most terminals can be used for input or output. The remote job entry terminal (RJE) features a card reader and slow line printer as a minimum. This terminal device is connected by phone lines to a central computer, perhaps many miles away; more elaborate batch terminals feature card punches and tape drives. Often one of these terminals is a small computer that processes some local jobs; larger jobs are sent to the more powerful central machine. The major drawback of RJE is the lack of interaction with the computer.

Interactive terminals are designed for a single user who is communicating with a computer on-line (we shall discuss different on-line systems later in this chapter and in the next one). Some interactive terminals produce a hard copy, that is, a printed copy that can be removed from the terminal. However, cathode-ray tube (CRT) terminals and similar display devices produce output on a TV-like screen, and unless a special copying device is used, the next display will erase the current one.

Interactive hard-copy terminals usually have serial-print mechanisms. Such

---

MANAGEMENT PROBLEM 7-2

Mastercraft Tool Company manufactures a variety of manual and power tools for professional workers and home workshops. The tools are sold through specialty and hardware stores throughout the United States and abroad. For a number of years, the firm has been concerned over production-control problems.

Manufacturing a tool involves a sequence of steps requiring different machines; it is a classical "job shop" production situation. There are some 10 manufacturing departments at Mastercraft, much work in process, and large finished-goods inventories. The firm manufactures for inventory and fills orders from its stock of tools. There is limited back ordering for popular items.

The top management of Mastercraft has reviewed several proposals for computer-based processing to provide better production-control information. Because of the rather low skill level of some workers, management is concerned over the impact of a computer system on production employees.

At the present time, the nature of the system, either batch or on-line, is being considered. The president said, "I can see advantages and disadvantages to either possibility. Clearly we have to obtain input from workers or the system will fail. I just don't know how to evaluate the potential impact of batch forms versus a terminal for factory workers."

As a consultant to Mastercraft, can you help the president with his decision problem? What factors should he consider in evaluating different input and output alternatives? Which alternatives should he consider?

---

a terminal prints one character at a time, unlike a line printer, which produces an entire line of characters each time it prints. Hard-copy terminals are available in either impact or nonimpact form. Nonimpact devices may be thermal types in which a heated matrix of styli creates an impression on heat-sensitive paper. Other nonimpact terminals squirt an electronically controlled jet of ink at the paper to form characters. Nonimpact printers tend to be faster than impact terminals and are highly popular, since many interactive applications have no need for multiple copies.

Cathode-ray tube terminals are enjoying increasing popularity for input and output: they are quiet and very fast compared with printing terminals. Most CRTs feature one color, though multiple-color models are available. An alphanumeric CRT displays lines of characters and is a direct replacement for a printing terminal where no hard copy is required. Graphic CRTs make it possible to plot lines to form graphs or figures on the screen. A dynamic graphics CRT allows the program to change any part of the screen, erasing or adding information, without affecting the rest of the display. The computer scans a display list (a list of display commands) and refreshes the display many times each second. To change the display the program alters the display list. However, the constant refreshing of the screen demands attention from the CPU. As an alternative, local storage in the terminal itself may be used to refresh the screen and reduce the load on the central processing unit.

Storage-tube graphics units are cheaper than their dynamic graphics counterparts and are relatively easy to program. The screen is made of a special material so that the display remains visible for up to an hour without refreshing. Information can be added easily to the screen, but the entire screen must be erased to erase any part of the display. However, when operated at high speeds, redrawing a display of simple figures after an erasure is not too time consuming.

Many terminals have been developed with logic capabilities of their own. These terminals are referred to as "intelligent" because they can do more than respond to input from the user or output commands from the computer. Intelligent terminals may use their logic to perform editing functions before transmitting information to a main computer. Some terminals also have magnetic tape cassettes to record input off-line before sending it to a computer.

TYPES OF COMPUTERS

Our discussion so far about computers and how they work has been quite general. We have explored the characteristics of the various generations of computers primarily focusing on what are called "mainframe" computers. At first, these were the only machines available. However, during the third generation, advances in the fabrication of circuit components drastically reduced the cost of logic and memory. A fabrication process known as large-scale integration (LSI) has resulted in small circuit chips containing thousands of components. Very large-scale integration (VSLI) is expected to reduce that even further: millions of components are expected to be placed on wafers the size of postage stamps.

First, these small components were used to develop minicomputers, machines that typically had 16-bit word lengths and a simple, dedicated operating system, for example, for time sharing. At first, minicomputers were applied to a single task. Minicomputers have been used in process control applications and as the basis for intelligent terminals. One dynamic CRT graphics terminal is a TV set controlled by a minicomputer. Minicomputers have even been used on board yachts to compute variables during a race. Many businesses have purchased a minicomputer and used its time-sharing operating system to develop relatively inexpensive on-line processing systems.

Applications have expanded in two directions from the first minicomputers. The development of even less expensive fabrication techniques and logic has made it possible to expand the size and capabilities of the mini to create the "supermini." At the other extreme, is the development of computers on a chip. These small microcomputers have the promise for revolutionizing industry. A microcomputer usually has 8- or 16-bit words and is slower than a mini. However, a micro is frequently used in dedicated applications where extremely high speeds are not required. Micros have been employed in standard information processing tasks (for instance, as "personal computers") and in a variety of industrial products. For example, many automobiles use microprocessors to control fuel/air mixtures; the processors take into account parameters such as the load on the engine, pollution output of the car, temperature, etc. Microprocessors are appearing in more and more products because they offer sophisticated logic at low cost.

Table 7-6 describes the major characteristics that can be used to distinguish among types of computers from large mainframes to smaller micros.[1] Of course, the categories really represent points on a continuum; there is a great deal of overlap even within the line of a single manufacturer. Table 7-7 describes some examples of various minicomputers and their design features.

ON-LINE SYSTEMS

Motivation

During the second generation of computers, the need for a capability beyond batch data processing developed for two main reasons. First, there are a number of applications where individuals need access to a central data base from different geographical locations, in close to "real time." These individuals in different places need very recently updated information. The best example of this type of system is a reservations application; a passenger agent in Atlanta must be sure that a New York flight has a seat left before making a reservation.

[1] The author is indebted to Professor Norman White of New York University, who developed this classification.

Table 7-6 Types of Computer Systems

Type	Speed (mips*)	Cost (000)	Word size bits	Main memory K bytes	Secondary storage bytes	Software	Applications
Mainframes	0.5–10	300	32	500	5×10^8 to 10×10^9	Extensive operating systems, application packages	Batch, time sharing, on-line transactions processing simultaneously
Superminis	0.1–2	150–500	32	256+ Virtual	10^8 to 10^9	Time sharing Limited batch	Specialized, scientific, engineering, transactions processing
Minis	0.1–0.5	30–150	16–32	16–256	10^6 to 10^8	Time sharing	General-purpose time sharing, small commercial applications on-line
Micros	0.001–0.5	Under 30	4 8 16	8–128	5×10^6 to 1×10^7	Simple operating system	Dedicated applications, limited I/O; intelligent terminals, word processors, small business systems, personal computers

*MIPS = millions of instructions per second.

140

Table 7-7 Examples of Minicomputers

Model	Purchase price/ word size	Minimum main memory/ cycle time (microseconds)	Features
12 bit			
Digital Equipment PDP-8 (1965)	$18,000 12 bit	4 K words 1.5	Core memory; simple instruction set
16 bit			
Digital Equipment PDP-11/35 (1974)	$19,800 16+2 bit	8 K16 K words 1.07	Core memory; 8 registers, COBOL, FORTRAN, BASIC, and assembler
Hewlett-Packard HP-1000 M Series (1974)	$ 6950 16+1 bit	32 K bytes 0.65	MOS memory; FORTRAN, BASIC, and assembler
Honeywell Level 6 Model 33 (1976)	$ 7275 16+2 bit	16 K words 0.65	MOS memory; 1.9 microsecond add time, COBOL, FORTRAN, RPG, and assembler
Hewlett-Packard HP-3000 Series 30 (1979)	$28,525 16 bit	256 K bytes 0.86	MOS memory; COBOL, FORTRAN, BASIC, RPG, and assembler
Digital Equipment PDP-11/44 (1980)	$23,900 16+2 bit	256 K words 0.96	MOS memory with cache; 0.87 microsecond add time, COBOL, FORTRAN, BASIC, and assembler
32 bit			
Perkin-Elmer Model 8/32 (1975)	$51,900 32+2 bit	62 K words 0.3	Core memory; COBOL, FORTRAN IV, BASIC, RPG II, and assembler
Perkin-Elmer Model 3220 (1979)	$33,500 32+7 bit	131 K words 0.34	MOS memory; COBOL, FORTRAN IV, BASIC, RPG II, and assembler
Prime Computer 450 (1979)	$65,000 32 bit*	256 K bytes 0.75	MOS memory with bipolar cache; 1.1 microsecond add time; COBOL, FORTRAN, BASIC, RPG II, and assembler; virtual storage memory management
Digital Equipment VAX 11/780 (1979)	$10,500 32 bit	256 K bytes 0.29	MOS memory with 8 K-byte cache; COBOL, FORTRAN-IV-PLUS, BASIC-PLUS-2, RPG-II, and assembler; virtual storage memory management; real-time applications

*Also 16 bit

The Atlanta agent must be certain that some other agent in Los Angeles is not selling the same seat at the same time. By maintaining a continually updated central file of flights and reservations and providing on-line access through terminals, both the Atlanta and Los Angeles agents can check on up-to-the-second seat availability before making the reservation.

Time sharing can be considered a special case of on-line systems. Time sharing was motivated by the slow turnaround time (time from submitting a run until receipt of output) characteristic of early batch systems. Researchers at MIT recognized that there is a severe mismatch between human information process-ing and computer speeds. In early batch systems, a programmer might have only two or three runs a day at most because of the large number of people using the machine. The MIT Project MAC group developed a special on-line system that gave each user an individual computational ability through a terminal. It appeared to each user that the central computer was available solely to that individual, even though many users in actuality were sharing the CPU. The name "time sharing" reflects the sharing of a computer resource by multiple users.

Hardware Requirements

On-line systems were first created by adding special hardware to existing systems and by writing complex control programs, usually in assembly language. We shall explain more fully how these systems work in the next chapter, on software. In this section we discuss some of the hardware features, especially the communications necessary for on-line systems.

For the central computer, the major addition needed for on-line processing is a communications controller. An on-line system uses communications lines, such as those of the public phone system. Just as a printer or card reader needs a controller, so do communications lines.

The logic requirements for a transmission controller are very demanding. It must do the following:

1   Establish a circuit.
2   Recognize the line speed—for example, whether the speed is 30 or 120 characters per second.
3   Send a start-of-message signal.
4   Receive the message acknowledgement.
5   Translate from transmission code to computer code and vice versa.
6   Check for errors and for the completeness of the message.
7   Receive a retransmission if necessary.
8   Assemble the message.
9   Recognize the end of message.
10   Release the circuit.
11   Transmit the message to the CPU.

Many steps are necessary to perform these functions. Because of these require-ments, on-line systems frequently feature a communications "front end," a device with considerable logic capability that handles the communications functions to remove some of the load from the CPU.

Telecommunications   BAUD = 1 BIT/SECOND.

The communications network for an on-line system can be very complicated. Various classes of lines are used to send signals between a computer and remote devices (lines are also called circuits or channels). A simplex line can transmit data in only one direction. A half-duplex line can transmit data in two directions, but in only one direction at a time. A full-duplex line can transmit in both directions simultaneously; a full-duplex circuit might be two simplex lines, one in each direction.

We measure the speed of communications in bauds; a baud is generally 1 bit per second. A variety of communications lines is available from both the telephone company and private common carriers. A slow-speed line might have a capacity of 110 bauds, or about 10 characters per second, while high-speed channels can carry 50,000 characters per second. A normal voice-grade telephone line can transmit up to 2000 bauds (Watson, 1970). Public switched lines can be used for data transmission with the addition of special equipment described below. For higher speed and more error-free transmissions, leased lines are required.

If a remote terminal device is close to the computer, say within a mile, then a direct line can be used without too much signal attenuation. For greater distances, communications lines must be used to transmit the signal. Computers of the type described here are digital, which suggests that data communications should use digital signals. However, because most common carriers use analog transmission, digital communications for computers must be converted for transmission through a process known as modulation.

Analog transmission can be represented as a sine wave. A digital signal is modulated by a modem (modulator and demodulator) in some way so that a sine wave can be used to transmit the signal. At the receiving end, another modem converts the signals back into their original digital form. There are three approaches to encoding the digital signal: amplitude modulation, frequency modulation, and phase encoding. Amplitude modulation modifies the height of the wave, but this approach is subject to noise and distortion. Phase modulation involves sending two digital signals at different phases (Martin, 1969).

In frequency modulation, the modem at the sending end converts two direct current levels standing for a 1 and a 0 to two frequencies, which are then sent over analog circuits. At the receiving end, a modem converts the analog signal back to the direct current digital message (Watson, 1970). (See Figure 7-7.) A 1 might be represented by a frequency of 2000 cycles per second and a 0 by 1000 cycles per second, and transmission would be serial by bit. By using several frequency pairs, one line can be used to transmit several bits (forming a single character) in parallel.

Several common carriers now offer digital as opposed to analog transmission. Digital, or pulse-code, transmission makes it possible to send binary data

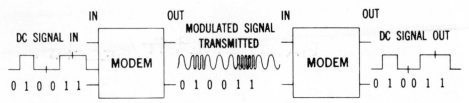

Figure 7-7 Use of frequency modulation for digital transmission. *(From Watson, R. W.:* Timesharing System Design Concepts, *McGraw-Hill, 1970.)*

without the use of a modem. If analog data, such as the human voice or music, are transmitted, the data must be converted to digital signals. In the future, increasing amounts of communications will be transmitted digitally.

Data transmission can be synchronous or asynchronous. For asynchronous transmission there are no timing requirements; the message is preceded by a start bit and ended with two stop bits, and the bits in between are the characters. Asynchronous transmission is used where a message is developed at random, for example, by a human operator who is sending data on a terminal. Asynchronous transmission is also used for low- or medium-speed devices where it is not worth the cost to synchronize.

For higher data-transfer rates and continuous transmission we usually find synchronous techniques. In synchronous transmission, sending and receiving units maintain exact synchronization by using timing generators. There is no need to send start and stop bits; however, the timing generators are usually synchronized by special timing codes that precede message transmission.

For a complex on-line system we must configure a communications network considering reliability and backup, speed, and cost. Tariffs for communications lines vary widely according to type of service, and there are a number of alternative common carriers for data. Some of these alternative services offer new communications technologies, for example, packet switching. A packet network charges for sending a chunk of data from one location to another independently of the distance traveled. The first of these networks was designed as an experiment to connect different types of computer systems, and now a commercial version is in operation using high-speed lines. In general network design is complicated; a number of communications specialists balance network performance against backup and cost.

Usually it is too costly to have one slow-speed circuit from each terminal to a computer. Instead we combine slow-speed circuits and send them on a single higher-speed line. A multiplexer combines several slow-speed lines through time-division or frequency-division multiplexing. Time-division multiplexing works by sampling separate incoming signals and combining them on a high-capacity output line. At the receiving end the signals are demultiplexed by reconstructing the sampled messages. Frequency-division multiplexing brings together different input lines and sends them over a higher-capacity line at different frequencies. The speed of the output line must equal the sum of the speeds of the input lines.

MANAGEMENT PROBLEM 7-3

A major bank, Eastern National, centralized all its information processing activities when third-generation computers were first installed. The prevailing argument in the industry at the time was that "economies of scale" justified centralization. Each larger member of a computer manufacturer's family provided more processing power per dollar. That is, moving from one machine to the next more powerful in the line might increase costs by 30 percent while processing power increased by 1 1/2 times. Thus, it made economic sense from the standpoint of hardware rentals to have a few large machines rather than many small machines located in different areas.

What do you think the disadvantages of centralization might be for Eastern National Bank? Are there other considerations beyond hardware cost that might enter into an analysis of centralization?

Currently, Eastern has reversed its trend toward centralization. A computer department spokesman said, "Now, with the availability of cheap minicomputers, the arguments for centralization are no longer valid. It is better to have each user develop applications for a dedicated minicomputer. Someday we will tie all the different minicomputers together. Right now, we can be more responsive to the user this way."

Are there management considerations that should be explored in Eastern's new approach, known in the industry as "distributed processing"? What technical problems might the proliferation of minicomputers in the bank create?

A concentrator is a small computer that collects messages from terminals and stores them if necessary. The concentrator sends the message over a higher-speed line to the computer. However, unlike the multiplexer, it can temporarily store data so the high-speed line does not have to equal the sum of the speeds of the slower lines. The computer transmits information using the reverse path; the computer sends device addresses so the message can be routed to the proper terminal.

In a multidrop configuration, several terminals are assigned to the same line. The message from the computer is preceded by a device address and completed with an end-of-message code. Messages are sent along the multidrop line, and all terminal devices decode the address. The device addressed connects itself to the line and accepts the message. To receive messages from the terminals the central computer polls them; the computer sends a message to each terminal in turn asking if it has something to transmit to the central computer. If the answer is "no," a message is sent to the next terminal; if the answer is "yes," the terminal transmits its message.

The central computer usually has a line buffer to convert serial bits into characters and to remove extraneous bits such as start and stop codes. The line buffer may also examine error-detection bits sent along with the incoming messages or add error correction bits to outbound messages. The line buffer sends connect and disconnect signals and often is responsible for synchronization; each line has a separate line buffer.

The communications controller discussed earlier can be attached to a channel. Sometimes the controller is a small computer that handles many of the communications tasks described above and removes some of the load from the CPU. Network design is very specialized; for further information see Martin (1969).

We should also comment that many organizations regard the transmission of digital data as one component of all communications. For example, a leased line might be used for voice communications during the day and data transmission at night. Communications in general is becoming a highly specialized area within organizations.

Patterns of Processing

The rapid advances in technology and the reduced cost of hardware discussed above have created a variety of possible patterns for computing. In the early days of information systems, batch computers were installed in various parts of the organization to handle processing, often to process transactions in the accounting area. During the second generation of systems that used transistorized circuits, the first-generation vacuum-tube machines were replaced, but the pattern of processing remained about the same.

Improvements in integrated circuits in the third generation of computers encouraged centralized computing sites. The increase in processing power exceeded the additional cost; that is, a large centralized computer operation exhibited significant economies of scale. During this time we saw the expansion of on-line systems to allow multiple access to a common data base; these systems usually operated from a single, centralized site.

Our ability to fabricate logic cheaply through Large Scale Integration (LSI) has dramatically reduced the cost of central processing units and memory, making it economical to install local or distributed intelligence. At first this trend toward distributed processing began by placing logic in terminals; one could edit some data locally and collect it in a buffer to be sent to the main computer, thus reducing the processing load on the central processor.

Patterns   Now a large number of alternatives are available for providing computer services. Table 7-8 presents a continuum of possibilities, though there are many variations on these alternatives.

In the totally centralized pattern, all processing is accomplished at a centralized site; there are no external input/output devices or terminals. This

Table 7-8   Patterns of Processing

Totally centralized
Batch centralized with remote input/output
Some local processing, batch centralized some on-line applications remote input/output
Sophisticated local processing, remote input/output, interactive capability
Totally decentralized

type of configuration represents one point on a continuum and is rare in a large organization. We might find this type of processing in a small company where there is only a single computer dedicated to a few applications.

From a totally centralized system, we move to remote input/output to a central site. The input/output is done through remote batch or on-line terminals. The next step toward more decentralized and distributed processing is to add a local processing capability but to maintain a centralized site running batch applications. There may also be a few on-line applications and remote terminals for on-line interaction. There are communications among local sites and the central site.

In a fully distributed system we expect to find extensive local processing, remote input/output, and an interactive capability. Retail point-of-sale systems are a good example of this type. Local store processors accept data from a centralized host computer, disconnect themselves, and function locally all day to register the purchase of merchandise and to control store inventory. Later the local computer is reconnected to the host to send summary data on the day's activity at the local store.

Finally one can have a totally decentralized system; all processing is local, and there is no data communications directly among systems. (Some individuals refer to this type as one type of distributed processing since there is no more central site; technically distributed processing describes a situation in which there are communications among several computer systems.) Total decentralization might be found in various subsidiaries of a large organization.

Computer Networks   Figure 7-8 shows patterns for interconnecting various processors. Just as one can develop a network for on-line processing, we can configure a system for distributed computers. In a hierarchical scheme, one computer controls a series of subordinate computers as in the earlier point-of-sale example. The star is similar, but here a single host or central computer can communicate with each remote processor. These local computers communicate with each other through the central system.

In a ring or loop all processors can communicate with their immediate neighbors. This pattern can be extended to allow communications from any processor to any other processor. One major problem in connecting computers is the fact that they must all be able to accept data transmitted from other computers and send data to them. In theory this problem is trivial, but in practice it can be difficult to achieve satisfactory connections.

The most important point from this discussion is that a variety of patterns for processing are available to the analyst. The problem is not one of too few choices, but rather one of too many alternatives to consider!

Evaluating Alternatives   One problem with this wide range of options is deciding on what pattern is best for a given situation. Table 7-9 suggests some design criteria for this decision. Is there a compelling reason for the data base for the application to reside in one location? If all data are generated in one location, then it may make some sense to locate the files and processing there.

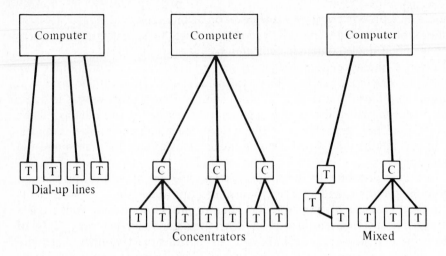

Examples of terminal connections

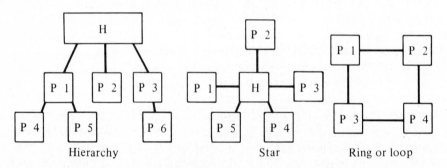

Examples of computer to computer connections.

H = host
P = processor

Figure 7-8 Network patterns.

Where is the data base to be updated? We may find that the transactions to update the files originate in a few, highly clustered locations. If others need limited access to these data, then consider distributing the data base and processing to each of these clusters.

One motivation for distributed processing is cost: large computers have overhead and are complex. Some experts argue that because of low-cost hardware, we can dedicate small, inexpensive computers to each application. However, if the distributed computers must communicate, there are communications costs to consider. Often these costs are less than the communications cost of a central on-line system since access to local data for a distributed system

Table 7-9   Criteria for Processing Alternatives

Physical location of data base
Location for updating and accessing the data base
Costs for equipment and communications
User reactions
Management considerations
  Control of applications
  Control of processing
  Communication
  Coordination

requires less data transmission. Also we must be sure that the computers are capable of exchanging data easily with each other.

Another major reason for distributed processing has been responsiveness to users. Many users feel that large, centralized systems are unresponsive to their needs, especially when located some distance away. Distributed computers mean that the user may have more control and influence over computer decisions. Distributed processing also is reliable and provides backup since multiple computers are available.

There are management considerations in making decisions to distribute or decentralize computing. If the applications/development effort is not coordinated, each location may develop new applications that are almost identical and incur high costs and duplication of effort. The same logic applies to control of

---

MANAGEMENT PROBLEM 7-4

Judy Sullivan was irate. Her bills from the information services department seemed to increase by 10 percent a month. Judy is the manager of accounting for Good Foods, a large chain of retail grocery stores. The firm operates a number of computer systems and many applications are in the accounting area. The company charges users for all computer applications based on standard rates set at the beginning of the year. The rates are estimated so that the computer center will be a zero cost center at the end of the year. Judy's increased bills, she was told, represented greater computer usage.

However, Judy was not mollified by the explanation. She said, "We have added one new computer after another. Everything I read says that computer power is getting cheaper. If this is true, why are my computer costs becoming more expensive all the time?"

The information services department indicated that there were offsetting trends that raised costs. "Of course," they said, "we justify new equipment on the grounds that it will save money. However, there is just more work and there are other costs besides equipment."

What are the costs of a computer operation? Why could Judy Sullivan's costs increase while the cost per computation for computers in general is dropping?

---

processing; there are strong arguments for some overall coordination of machine acquisition and operations policies.

In addition to considering machines, the computer department staff and users must also communicate. How do processing patterns affect human communications? How do they impact management control and coordination? Unfortunately, no one formula gives the best pattern of processing for an organization. There will probably be a mixture of different patterns for most large organizations, and each application will have to be evaluated to determine what type of processing is best.

SUMMARY

Electronic computers have evolved at a rapid rate. Today's desk-top computers have more power than first-generation computers that filled a room. The cost of computer hardware is continually being reduced as technological breakthroughs in the fabrication of components continue. Although fascinating in its own right, the technology becomes even more exciting when we apply it to problems in the organization. In the next chapter we discuss computer software followed by computer files. Then in Chapter 10 we return to examine trends in the technology and what they mean for management and the organization.

KEY WORDS

Analog	Direct access	Microprogram
Asynchronous	Execution cycle	Microsecond
Audio response	Fetch cycle	Minicomputer
Base	Firmware	Modem
Baud	Frequency modulation	Multiplexer
Binary	Full duplex	Multiprogramming
Bubble memory	Generations of computers	Nanosecond
Buffer	Graphics	Nonimpact
Cache	Half duplex	Nondestructive readout
Centralized processing	Hardware	OCR
CPU	Impact printer	Parallel
CRT	Index register	Primary memory
Capacitor	Indirect address	Register
Concentrator	Input/output	Secondary storage
Content addressable	Intelligence	Semiconductor memory
Core	Instruction set	Simplex
Controller	Large scale integration	Software
Cycle time	(LSI)	Storage-address register
Data channel	Location counter	Storage-buffer register
Data set	Look-ahead	Synchronous
Decentralized processing	MICR	Tape
Digital	Mark sense	Time-division multiplexing
Disk	Microfilm	Volatile storage
Distributed processing		

RECOMMENDED READINGS

Bartee, T. C.: *Digital Computer Fundamentals,* 4th ed., McGraw-Hill, New York, 1977. (Contains a great deal of information about computer hardware, especially input/output devices.)

Hellerman, H.: *Digital Computer Systems Principles,* McGraw-Hill, New York, 1967. (This book, while somewhat technical, contains an excellent description of computer processing.)

Martin, J.: *Telecommunications and the Computer,* Prentice-Hall, Englewood Cliffs, N.J., 1969. (A thorough explanation of the technology and problems of telecommunications.)

Osborne, A.: *An Introduction to Microcomputers,* 2d ed., vol. 1, Osborne/McGraw-Hill, New York, 1980. (A somewhat technical book on microcomputers and their programming.)

Rosin, R.: "Contemporary Concepts of Microprogramming and Emulation," *Computing Surveys,* vol. 1, no. 4, December 1969, pp. 197–212. (This somewhat difficult article describes microprogramming through the development of a hypothetical computer and instruction set. It is a very clear explanation of the concepts behind microprogramming and emulation.)

Watson, R. W.: *Timesharing System Design Concepts,* McGraw-Hill, New York, 1970. (About the development of a time-sharing system, with one particular computer as an illustrative example.)

Yourdon, E.: *Design of On-Line Computer Systems,* Prentice-Hall, Englewood Cliffs, N.J., 1972. (A complete description of the design considerations for on-line systems.)

DISCUSSION QUESTIONS

1 Why have electronic computers replaced electronic accounting machinery? What are the advantages of electronic computers?

2 Distinguish between computer hardware and software. With which is a manager most concerned?

3 What is the function of primary memory in the computer? How does it interact with the CPU?

4 Many data channels steal cycles from the central processing unit to access primary memory. For what purpose does the data channel access memory?

5 What is the purpose of a control unit? Could the same control unit control more than one type of device?

6 Why was conversion from first- to second-generation computers not much of a problem?

7 Why is it difficult to convert machine language for one computer to machine language for another?

8 What is the advantage of a data channel? How much logic must it contain?

9 Buffers are locations in memory reserved for storing data, for example, a group of data being entered from a card reader. How could multiple buffers be used to speed input/output operations?

10 What is the advantage of semiconductor over core memory? What are its disadvantages?

11 There are some very large storage devices using lasers to burn holes in a tape or disk,

the holes representing 0s or 1s. What are the disadvantages of such a device? For what applications is it best suited?

12   Why is the binary system suitable to computer operations?

13   Develop an addition table for binary arithmetic.

14   What are the differences between a character orientation and a word orientation for a computer? Which would you expect to be the faster? For which types of processing is each better suited?

15   Why did the distinction between business and scientific computers tend to disappear with third-generation machines?

16   Write a simple program in a hypothetical machine language to compute the average of 100 numbers. What is the advantage of an index register in this assignment?

17   What two major items are stored in main memory? How can we distinguish between them?

18   What is the advantage of having more than one address in an instruction?

19   Why is reading from core memory destructive? What are the problems in rewriting the data?

20   What are the functions of the sense and inhibit lines in core memory?

21   Take an instruction from the 1130 in Table 7-3 and explain how it is executed in detail by the CPU.

22   What is the advantage of having floating-point arithmetic registers? How do we provide the capability for floating-point arithmetic operations without hardware? What fundamental tradeoffs does this problem suggest?

23   What is the purpose of address modification?

24   Some computers have many register-to-register operations. What is the advantage of this capability?

25   For what are program loops used?

26   How do you suppose indirect addressing is used to link program modules together?

27   The presence of floating-point hardware increases the cost of the machine because of the additional circuitry and registers. What else has to be added?

28   How does multiprogramming help provide flexibility in the design of computer systems?

29   Why would we use microprogramming to make one computer look and act like another one?

30   Compare and contrast translators, simulators, and emulators as means for conversion from one type of machine to another.

31   Why is a computer manufacturer interested in compatibility within its own line of machines? Does a manufacturer want to be compatible with the computers of other manufacturers? What are the advantages and disadvantages of such a strategy?

32   What is a purpose of the location counter in the CPU? How do you suppose a branch instruction (GO TO) in the program is executed?

33   What is firmware? What are its advantages and disadvantages compared with software?

34   Why is an interrupt facility preferable to testing for a channel being busy?

35   What are the reasons for having secondary storage? Why not just add more primary memory?

36   How would the development of direct-access memory technology like core, but as inexpensive as tape, change information system processing?

37   What are the disadvantages of secondary storage?

38 Why is there such a mismatch between input/output and internal computer speeds? How can this mismatch be reduced? What I/O units are helping to solve this problem?

39 Why should we not necessarily be overjoyed with the development of ultra-high-speed printers?

40 What are the advantages and disadvantages of punched card input?

41 Why has paper tape been used as an input medium for minicomputers?

42 What is the advantage of OCR over mark sensing? What are its disadvantages?

43 What is the advantage of a nonimpact CRT terminal from a user's standpoint?

44 What factors underlie the trend toward on-line systems?

45 What would be the major use for voice input to computers if it were perfected?

46 What are the advantages and disadvantages of storage-tube terminals versus dynamic graphics terminals?

47 Why does high-speed data transmission require special "conditioned" lines?

48 What is the advantage of full-duplex transmission?

49 Several communications carriers offer digital transmission circuits. What are the advantages of these circuits?

50 Why have special design features been added to CPUs?

51 What is the advantage of a buffer cache memory? Under what conditions would its performance be best? Worst?

52 How are minicomputers extending computer power to small users? What problems do they create?

53 What are the advantages of connecting different computers to form a network? In what situations would this be most helpful?

54 What applications do you have for a personal computer?

PROGRAMMING LANGUAGES
    A Simple Computer
    Machine-Language Programming
    Assembly Language
    High-Level Languages
    Special-Purpose Languages
PACKAGE PROGRAMS
    Background
    Examples
OPERATING SYSTEMS
    Early Systems
    The Third Generation
    Evolutionary Advances
CONCLUSION
KEY WORDS
RECOMMENDED READINGS
DISCUSSION QUESTIONS

Chapter 8

Computer Software

CHAPTER ISSUES

- What computer languages are available and which one should be used for a particular application?
- What is the role of applications packages in the development of systems?

Why do managers or users need to know anything about computer programs and software? Because users help design systems, it is important for them to understand which programming tasks are easy and which are difficult. Should a packaged program be used for a particular application? There has been considerable difficulty in turning system specifications into working programs, and we have encountered serious problems in writing and managing program development. A basic understanding of software helps a user make intelligent management decisions about programming and project management. A manager may make decisions about programs, actually write simple programs, or supervise a subordinate developing a small decision-support system, as we discuss in Chapter 18.

In this chapter, we explore computer programs and languages along with different types of operating systems and packaged programs. Table 8-1 shows that the different hardware generations discussed in the last chapter can also be characterized by differences in computer software. (Remember we defined software as the instructions that tell a computer what actions to take.) In this chapter, we shall discuss these different types of software.

PROGRAMMING LANGUAGES

A Simple Computer

In the last chapter, we saw that binary representation is the fundamental language of computers; however, binary is difficult for people to use. Since the number base is not relevant to the concepts discussed below, we shall design a simple computer using base-10, or decimal, numbers.

In designing our computer, we must:

1   Select a character or word organization.
2   Define a character set.
3   Determine memory size.
4   Decide on the instruction set and data format.
5   Determine the type and number of arithmetic and other registers.
6   Define the instruction set.
7   Choose a machine base (we have already chosen decimal).

Table 8-1   Software Generations

Generation	Software
First	Machine language
	Assembly language
Second	Assembly language
	Higher-level languages
	Batch operating systems
	Dedicated on-line systems
	Experimental time sharing
Third	Preponderance of higher-level languages
	Expansion of packaged systems
	Operating system mandatory
	Mixed on-line and batch applications
	Virtual-memory time-sharing systems
Third-and-one-half	Expanded operating systems
	Virtual-memory batch systems
	Batch, on-line, and time sharing mixed
	Data-base and communication packages
Fourth	More applications programs
	Higher-higher level languages

We shall design a fixed-word-length computer with six digits per word to simplify some of our other tasks. Since we are developing a very simple machine, we use only decimal numbers for our character set: there will be no alphabetic characters. Furthermore, the computer will perform arithmetic on numbers in the same code as the input/output representation of these numbers.

Remember that memory contains both data and instructions so we must also define the format for each. The numbers in our computer will be signed integers with up to six digits, for example $+173426$ or -421376. Again because our computer is very simple, we shall limit the size of primary memory to 99 locations, numbered 1 through 99. (For a word size of six digits, normally the computer would have a much larger memory; to maintain simplicity our machine will be limited to 99 locations.)

An instruction consists of four digits; the first two are an operation code and the last two are the operand. The format is XXYY where XX is the two-digit instruction and YY the address of the operand. Since we are limiting the size of memory to 99 locations, we need only two decimal locations to address all memory. Note also that we have designed a single-address machine.

Since the machine is simple, we shall have only one register that can be accessed by a program. Of course, there is an instruction register, a location counter, and so forth, but these registers are a part of the CPU and do not concern a programmer. The accessible register is for arithmetic, and we shall call it the A register. The A register will be capable of addition, subtraction, multiplication, and division, making it a general-purpose arithmetic register.

Instructions that call for arithmetic operations such as add and subtract have one address for an operand in memory. The other number needed for the computation is assumed to be in the A register; that is, the A register is the implied address for these instructions. This assumption and method of performing computations are necessary since we are designing a single-address machine. We also have a condition indicator that can be tested by several instructions to make a decision about transferring to some other part of a program.

The instruction set for this simple computer is shown in Table 8-2. There are instructions to perform arithmetic and to test for various conditions and then transfer to another part of the program, as well as simple input/output instructions.

Machine-Language Programming

Table 8-3 contains a short program written for our simple computer in machine language. The program is designed to add a series of numbers and print their sum. The bottom half of Table 8-3 is a map of memory. Because our computer is so simple we have no provisions in the instruction set for writing a constant in the program. Every number has to be input to the program during execution. In location 99 we input and store the constant, which will be used as a counter to see how many numbers we have added.

Location 98 contains another input from the user—the number of items to be added. Location 97 is a counter; that is, the program will use this location to total the number of items added so far, such as a 2 for two numbers, a 3 for three

Table 8-2   Instruction Set for a Simple Computer

Operation code	Instruction
01	Subtract the contents of the memory location addressed from the contents of the A register.
02	Add the contents of the memory location addressed to the contents of the A register.
03	Multiply the contents of the A register by the contents of the memory location addressed. The product is in the A register.
04	Divide the contents of the A register by the contents of the memory location addressed. The quotient is in the A register.
05	Store the contents of the A register in the memory location addressed. (The contents of the memory location are replaced by the contents of the A register.)
06	Load the A register with the contents of the memory location addressed. (The contents of the A register are replaced by the contents of the memory location addressed.)
07	Print on the teletypewriter the contents of the memory location addressed.
08	Read a number entered from the teletypewriter and place it in the memory location addressed. (The user is prompted with the word "INPUT" before entering the data.)
09	The contents of the A register are compared with the contents of the memory location addressed, and a condition code indicator is set as follows:

Contents of A register	Contents of memory location	Condition code
>		+
=		0
<		−

10	Jump to the memory location addressed and execute that instruction next if the condition code is negative. If not, continue to execute the next instruction in sequence.
11	Jump to the memory location addressed and execute that instruction next if the condition code is zero. If not, continue to execute the next instruction in sequence.
12	Jump to the memory location addressed and execute that instruction next if the condition code is positive. If not, continue to execute the next instruction in sequence.
13	Jump to the memory location addressed and execute that instruction next unconditionally.
14	Stop executing the program.

Table 8-3   A Program to Add a Series of Numbers

Instruction address	Operation code	Memory location	Comment
1	08	99	Read a number (must be 1) into memory location 99
2	08	98	Read the number of items to be added into location 98
3	06	99	Load the A register with the 1 in location 99
4	01	99	Subtract the 1 from itself to get 0
5	05	97	Store the 0 in location 97 to be a counter
6	08	95	Read a number to be added into location 95
7	02	95	Add the new number to the A register
8	05	96	Store the sum in location 96
9	06	97	Load the counter into the A register
10	02	99	Add 1 to the counter
11	05	97	Store the incremented counter back in location 97
12	09	98	Compare the A register with location 98
13	06	96	Load the A register with the sum so far from location 96
14	10	06	Jump to location 06 if the A register is less than the number of items to be added
15	07	96	Write the sum from location 96
16	14	99	Halt

Memory map

Location	Contents
C 99	1
N 98	Number of items to be added
I 97	Counter of numbers added so far
S 96	Sum of numbers so far
A 95	The next number to be added

numbers, and so forth. In location 96 we keep the sum as it is accumulated. Finally, the next number to be added is stored in location 95.

The program begins in location 1 and requires 16 memory locations for all its instructions. The program first reads and stores the number 1. It then subtracts 1 from itself, giving zero, which is stored to initialize the counter. Next, the program reads the number of items to be added and stores it in location 98. The user of the program supplies this input.

Our strategy in the program is to add each number to the sum that has been accumulated so far, increase a counter by 1, and compare it with the number of items to be added. When the program has added this many numbers, it prints the results and stops. Until it has reached this total, the program loops back and picks up the next input item to be added. This loop is between the instructions stored at locations 6 and 14.

Each number to be added is read into location 95 and added to the A register. (The first time through, the A register is at zero because it has just been initialized. On subsequent passes through the program, the A register contains the total sum accumulated so far.) The counter is then incremented, stored, and compared with the number of items to be added from location 98. The comparison instruction is located at address 12, and this sets the condition code. Before testing the condition code, we use the instruction at location 13 to load the sum accumulated so far into the A register. The instruction in location 14 transfers control to the beginning of the loop, that is, the instruction located at location 6, if the counter does not equal the number of items to be added yet. If we loop back, the sum so far is ready in the A register for the next number. If we are done, the final sum is in the A register to be printed by the next-to-last instruction. Finally, the last instruction halts the program.

Table 8-4 shows the execution of this program and a map of computer memory and the A register before and after the execution of each instruction. Remember that each instruction is executed in sequence unless we explicitly tell

Table 8-4   Execution of the Program, that is, Table 8-3

Instruction		Computer memory before execution		Computer memory after execution	
0899 INPUT 1	READ A NUMBER 1 INTO LOCATION 99	99 98 97 A REGISTER		99 98 97 A REGISTER	<u>1</u>
0898 INPUT 2	READ NUMBER OF ADDENDS INTO LOCATION 98	99 98 97 A REGISTER	1	99 98 97 A REGISTER	1 <u>2</u>
0699	LOAD A REGISTER WITH 1 IN LOCATION 99	99 98 97 A REGISTER	1 2	99 98 97 A REGISTER	1 2 <u>1</u>
0199	SUBTRACT 1 FROM ITSELF TO GET 0	99 98 97 A REGISTER	1 2 1	99 98 97 A REGISTER	1 2 <u>0</u>
0597	STORE 0 IN LOCATION 97	99 98 97 A REGISTER	1 2 0	99 98 97 A REGISTER	1 2 <u>0</u> 0
0895 INPUT 250	READ ADDEND INTO LOCATION 95	99 98 97 96 95 A REGISTER	1 2 0 0	99 98 97 96 95 A REGISTER	1 2 0 <u>250</u> <u>0</u>

Table 8-4   (Continued)

	Instruction	Computer memory before execution		Computer memory after execution	
0295	ADD ADDEND TO A REGISTER	99 98 97 96 95 A REGISTER	1 2 0 250 0	99 98 97 96 95 A REGISTER	1 2 0 250 250
0596	STORE A REGISTER IN LOCATION 96	99 98 97 96 95 A REGISTER	1 2 0 250 250	99 98 97 96 95 A REGISTER	1 2 0 250 250 250
0697	LOAD COUNTER FROM LOCATION 97 INTO A REGISTER	99 98 97 96 95 A REGISTER	1 2 0 250 250 250	99 98 97 96 95 A REGISTER	1 2 0 250 250 0
0299	ADD 1 FROM LOCATION 99 TO COUNTER	99 98 97 96 95 A REGISTER	1 2 0 250 250 0	99 98 97 96 95 A REGISTER	1 2 0 250 250 1
0597	STORE COUNTER INTO LOCATION 97	99 98 97 96 95 A REGISTER	1 2 0 250 250 1	99 98 97 96 95 A REGISTER	1 2 1 250 250 1
0998 CONDITION CODE = −	COMPARE A REGISTER WITH LOCATION 98	99 98 97 96 95 A REGISTER	1 2 1 250 250 1	99 98 97 96 95 A REGISTER	1 2 1 250 250 1
0696	LOAD A REGISTER WITH SUM SO FAR FROM LOCATION 96	99 98 97 96 95 A REGISTER	1 2 1 250 250 1	99 98 97 96 95 A REGISTER	1 2 1 250 250 250
1006 CONDITION CODE = −	JUMP TO INSTRUCTION AT LOCATION 6 ON CONDITION CODE NEGATIVE	99 98 97 96 95 A REGISTER	1 2 1 250 250 250	99 98 97 96 95 A REGISTER	1 2 1 250 250 250
0895 INPUT 150	READ ADDEND INTO LOCATION 95	99 98 97 96 95 A REGISTER	1 2 1 250 250 250	99 98 97 96 95 A REGISTER	1 2 1 250 150 250
0295	ADD ADDEND TO A REGISTER	99 98 97 96 95 A REGISTER	1 2 1 250 150 250	99 98 97 96 95 A REGISTER	1 2 1 250 150 400

Table 8-4   (Continued)

	Instruction	Computer memory before execution		Computer memory after execution	
0596	STORE A REGISTER IN LOCATION 96	99 98 97 96 95 A REGISTER	1 2 1 250 150 400	99 98 97 96 95 A REGISTER	1 2 1 400 150 400
0697	LOAD COUNTER FROM LOCATION 97 INTO A REGISTER	99 98 97 96 95 A REGISTER	1 2 1 400 150 400	99 98 97 96 95 A REGISTER	1 2 1 400 150 1
0299	ADD 1 FROM LOCATION 99 TO COUNTER	99 98 97 96 95 A REGISTER	1 2 1 400 150 1	99 98 97 96 95 A REGISTER	1 2 1 400 150 2
0597	STORE COUNTER INTO LOCATION 97	99 98 97 96 95 A REGISTER	1 2 1 400 150 2	99 98 97 96 95 A REGISTER	1 2 2 400 150 2
0998 CONDITION CODE = 0	COMPARE A REGISTER WITH LOCATION 98	99 98 97 96 95 A REGISTER	1 2 2 400 150 2	99 98 97 96 95 A REGISTER	1 2 2 400 150 2
0696	LOAD A REGISTER WITH SUM SO FAR FROM LOCATION 96	99 98 97 96 95 A REGISTER	1 2 2 400 150 2	99 98 97 96 95 A REGISTER	1 2 2 400 150 400
1006 CONDITION CODE = 0	JUMP TO INSTRUCTION AT LOCATION 6 ON CONDITION CODE NEGATIVE	99 98 97 96 95 A REGISTER	1 2 2 400 150 400	99 98 97 96 95 A REGISTER	1 2 2 400 150 400
0796 OUTPUT 400	WRITE SUM FROM LOCATION 96	99 98 97 96 95 A REGISTER	1 2 2 400 150 400	99 98 97 96 95 A REGISTER	1 2 2 400 150 400
1499	HALT	99 98 97 96 95 A REGISTER	1 2 2 400 150 400	99 98 97 96 95 A REGISTER	1 2 2 400 150 400

*Changes underlined.

the computer to begin taking instructions from another location, as we do in the jump at location 14. Study the execution of this program carefully.

Assembly Language

One problem with machine language is remembering the operation codes and their numbers. For example, an add instruction is the number 2 and a subtract the number 1 in our simple computer. The first improvement to be made in this machine language is to substitute mnemonics for the operation codes. We would like to be able to write instructions of the form ADD, SUBTRACT, etc. Table 8-5 contains three-letter mnemonics for our simple decimal computer machine language.

The next aid in writing programs is to use symbols instead of address locations for data. In other words, we would like to introduce algebraic variables such as X, Y, and PAY. This enhancement involves more than just replacing a number with a group of alphabetic characters as we did with the operation code. We also want to give responsibility for memory management to the programming language. We would like to refer to a variable such as X without being concerned over where X is actually stored in memory. It is also desirable to have something called a statement label, a variable that labels the statement so that control can be transferred to the labeled instruction from some other place in a program.

The simple program of Table 8-3 is written in this new assembly language in Table 8-6. It is certainly much easier to write and understand the program in Table 8-6. What must be done to enable the computer to understand the assembly language? The computer is able to process machine language; it can execute the program of Table 8-3 directly. Unfortunately, the computer will not accept the program of Table 8-6.

The answer to our problem is to write a program in machine language, the

Table 8-5 Mnemonic Instructions for Simple Computer Example

Operation code	Mnemonic
01	SUB
02	ADD
03	MLT
04	DIV
05	STA
06	LDA
07	WRT
08	RDD
09	CMP
10	JLT
11	JEQ
12	JGT
13	JMP
14	HLT

Table 8-6 The Program of Table 8-3 in Simple Assembly Language

Label	Operation code	Operand	Comment
	RDD	C	Read a number (must be 1) as variable C
	RDD	N	Read the number of items to be added into variable N
	LDA	C	Load the A register with the 1 in variable C
	SUB	C	Subtract the 1 from itself to get 0
	STA	I	Store the 0 in I, a counter
B	RDD	A	Read a number to be added into A
	ADD	A	Add the new number to the A register
	STA	S	Store the sum in S
	LDA	I	Load the counter I into the A register
	ADD	C	Add 1 to the counter
	STA	I	Store the incremented counter back in I
	CMP	N	Compare the A register with the number of items to be added, N
	LDA	S	Load the A register with the sum so far, S
	JLT	B	Go to instruction labeled B if the A register contents are less than the number of items to be added
	WRT	S	Write the sum, S
	HLT	C	Halt

language of Table 8-2, to translate the assembly language in Table 8-6 into machine language. The language of Table 8-6 is called assembly language, and the program to translate it into machine language is called an "assembler." In general, an assembler produces one machine language instruction for each assembly language instruction in the program. Figure 8-1 illustrates the assembly process. The input to the translator is known as the "source language," and the output is the "object program."

We write the assembler in machine language. The plan is to scan the source program in assembly language twice from beginning to end; that is, we shall write a "two-pass" assembler. For example, the input might be on tape that is read once, rewound, and read again. On the first pass, the assembler constructs a symbol table in memory of the symbols used, for example, X and Y. The assembler also places the location of statement labels in this table. The assembler looks up in a table in memory similar to Table 8-5 the mnemonics for subtract, add, etc., and substitutes the decimal operation codes of 1, 2, etc.

Before the second pass through the input, the assembler processes the

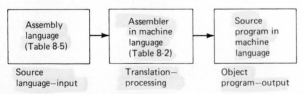

Figure 8-1 The assembly process.

symbol table and assigns memory locations to each symbol. It might place the symbols in order alphabetically or in the order encountered in the program, for example, C at location 99, N at location 98, etc. On the second pass through the input, the assembler substitutes the assigned locations for the symbols. It also places the address of the statement label wherever it encounters the label in the address field of the instruction.

The object program is complete at the end of the second pass of the assembler. During the assembly it is written on an output device, such as a tape. When ready to be run, the object program is loaded from the tape, and execution begins.

Unfortunately, we cannot actually write an assembler for our simple decimal computer because we have a limited character set: there are no alphabetic characters. However, we can add this capability with a slight redesign in the computer. (What changes would be needed?)

Assemblers have been developed with more features than the one in the example above. One of the most useful extensions is a macro capability, with which the programmer defines a series of steps called a "macro definition." For example, a program might define a macro to print a particular legend on a report. Every program wishing to use this macro issues a macro call. When the assembler encounters the macro call, it inserts the statements from the macro definition directly into the program. This feature makes it possible to avoid the manual repetition of duplicate sections of codes. An installation might write and make available a series of macros or provide macros written by the vendor for general use by all its programmers. Examples of these macros are routines for input and output or to compute dates.

A basic macro capability can be expanded to include parameters; that is, the program can pass variables to the macro through dummy arguments (the same principle behind the subroutine in a higher-level language). More extensive macro packages include the ability to nest macro calls, that is, to have a macro call within another macro call.

An assembler saves programming effort by assuming some of the more tedious programming tasks. The addition of macro capabilities greatly extends assembly language and further eases programming. However, with assembly language we are still very close to machine-language programming, and, with the exception of macros, it is still necessary to write one assembly language instruction for each machine-language instruction generated.

Higher-Level Languages

Higher-level languages make the computer easier to program and extend the use of computers to more individuals. The most significant of these languages appeared around 1957 and is called FORTRAN for FORmula TRANslation. This language is designed to facilitate the use of computers by scientists and engineers and is well suited to solving mathematically oriented problems on the computer. With FORTRAN we can write a complex formula in one statement, for example, $X = (A + B)*(C - D)/E$.

Table 8-7 An Assembly-Language Program for the FORTRAN Statement X = (A + B)*(C - D)/E

Program		Comment
LDA	A	Load A into A register
ADD	B	Add B to A register
STA	T	Store the sum in a temporary location
LDA	C	Load C into the A register
SUB	D	Subtract D from the A register
DIV	E	Divide the results by E
MLT	T	Multiply the results by T
STA	X	Store the final result in X

An assembly-language program to accomplish this computation is shown in Table 8-7. The assembly-language version requires eight instructions compared with a single line for the FORTRAN statement. For many problem solvers, particularly nonprofessional programmers, a higher-level language eases the conceptualization of program structure. A complete FORTRAN program is given in Table 8-8.

Table 8-8 A FORTRAN Program to Compute Rate of Return

```
C***********************************************************************
C* RATE OF RETURN PROGRAM                                            **
C* CALCULATES THE RATE OF RETURN WHEN INITIAL INVESTMENT AND CASH    **
C* FLOWS ARE KNOWN. ASSUMPTIONS ARE:                                 **
C* -THE ENTIRE INVESTMENT IS MADE AT ONE TIME AT BEGINNING           **
C* -CASH FLOW IS NET CASH SAVINGS FOR A PERIOD(DAY,WEEK,MONTH,OR YEAR)**
C* -CASH FLOW FOR EACH PERIOD IS INPUT WITH LIMIT OF 100 CASH FLOWS  **
C* -ERROR IF RATE OF RETURN NEGATIVE OR GREATER THAN 80 PERCENT      **
C* CARD INPUT-                                                       **
C* -FIRST CARD--PROBLEM NO IN COLS 1-10 RIGHT JUSTIFIED              **
C*              --NUMBER OF CASH FLOWS IN COLS 18-20 RIGHT JUSTIFIED  **
C*              --SUM INVESTED IN COLS 21-30 INPUT AS F10.2           **
C* -SUCEEDING CARDS--CASH FLOWS EIGHT PER CARD IN FIELDS OF F9.2      **
C* AUTHOR-ALISON DAVIS                                               **
C* DATE WRITTEN-2/17/76                                              **
C***********************************************************************
C
C
C***********************************************************************
C* DESCRIPTION OF VARIABLE NAMES                                     **
C* BRATE-LOWER VALUE IN TRIAL AND ERROR CALCULATIONS, INITIAL VALUE 0 **
C* CASH-CASH FLOWS AS AN ARRAY                                       **
C* NFLOWS-NUMBER OF PERIODS OF CASH FLOWS.                           **
C* NTRIAL NUMBER OF TRIALS BEFORE CLOSE-ENOUGH RESULT OBTAINED       **
C* NUMPRO-PROBLEM NUMBER                                             **
C* PVC-PRESENT VALUE OF CASH FLOWS USING TRIAL RATE                  **
C* RATE-RATE OF RETURN                                               **
C* URATE-UPPER RATE FOR TRIAL AND ERROR CALCULATIONS,INITIAL VALUE 80 **
C* VESTMT-INVESTMENT                                                 **
C* VSUM-CASH FLOW ACCUMULATOR FOR DATA VALIDATION                    **
C***********************************************************************
C
C
C***********************************************************************
C*DIMENSION-AND-INITIALIZE FOR INTIAL TRIAL                          **
C***********************************************************************
      DIMENSION CASH (100)
      URATE = .80
      BRATE = .0
      RATE = .40
```

Source: G. Davis, *Introduction to Computers*, 3d ed., McGraw-Hill, New York, 1977.

Table 8-8   (Continued)

```
C
C
C***********************************************************************
C* 100 INPUT AND INPUT VALIDATION. ERROR OUTPUT FOR NEGATIVE RETURN   **
C* OR RETURN GREATER THAN 80 PERCENT.                                 **
C***********************************************************************
  100 READ(1, 900) NUMPRO,NFLOWS,VESTMT
  900 FORMAT (2I10,F10.2)
      READ (1,910)(CASH(I),I=1,NFLOWS)
  910 FORMAT(8F9.2)
C                             *TEST FOR CASH FLOWS GR THAN INVESTMENT
      VSUM = 0
      DO 110 I=1,NFLOWS
         VSUM = VSUM + CASH(I)
  110 CONTINUE
      IF (VSUM .LE. VESTMT) WRITE (3,915) VSUM,VESTMT
  915 FORMAT (14H CASH FLOWS OF ,F10.2,18H AND INVESTMENT OF ,F10.2,
     -        21H MAKE NEGATIVE RETURN )
      IF (VSUM .LE. VESTMT) STOP
C                             *TEST FOR RETURN GREATER THAN 80 PERCENT
      PVC = 0
      DO 120 I=1,NFLOWS
         PVC = PVC + CASH(I)/(1.80**I)

  120 CONTINUE
      IF(PVC .GT. VESTMT) WRITE (3,920)
  920 FORMAT (39H RATE OF RETURN GREATER THAN 80 PERCENT)
      IF (PVC .GT. VESTMT) STOP
C                             *ELSE CONTINUE BECAUSE DATA IN VALID
C
C
C***********************************************************************
C* 200 PERFORM COMPUTATION TO OBTAIN RATE OF RETURN USING TRIAL RATE. **
C* RATE ADJUSTED AND COMPUTATION REPEATED UNTIL RATE CLOSE ENOUGH.    **
C* CLOSE ENOUGH IS ABSOLUTE DIFFERENCE BETWEEN INVESTMENT AND PRESENT **
C* VALUE OF CASH FLOWS NOT MORE THAN .001 AS FRACTION OF INVESTMENT.  **
C* IF CLOSE ENOUGH NOT OBTAINED BY 100 TRIALS, STOP PROCESSING AND    **
C* GIVE MESSAGE                                                       **
C***********************************************************************
  200 DO 220 ITRIAL=1,100
         NTRIAL = ITRIAL
         PVC = 0
         DO 210 I=1,NFLOWS
            PVC=PVC+CASH(I)/((1.0+RATE)**I)
  210    CONTINUE
         DIFFR = VESTMT - PVC
         IF((ABS(DIFFR/VESTMT).LE..001).OR.(DIFFR.EQ. 0)) GO TO 300
         IF (DIFFR.LT.0)BRATE = RATE
         IF (DIFFR.GT.0)URATE = RATE
         RATE = (URATE + BRATE)/ 2.0
  220 CONTINUE
C                             *NORMAL LOOP EXIT MEANS RATE NOT CLOSE
C                             *ENOUGH BY 100 TRIALS. WRITE MESSAGE
      WRITE (3,925) DIFFR
  925 FORMAT (41H TERMINATION AT 100 TRIALS. DIFFERENCE OF F10.3)
C
C
C***********************************************************************
C* 300 PRINT RESULTS AND STOP RUN                                     **
C***********************************************************************
  300 RATE = RATE * 100.0
      WRITE (3,930) NUMPRO,VESTMT,NFLOWS,NTRIAL,RATE
  930 FORMAT(15H PROBLEM NUMBER I16,/ 14H INVESTMENT OF F20.2,/
     -21H PERIODS OF CASH FLOW I10 / 14H NUMBER TRIALS I17 /
     -15H RATE OF RETURN F19.2, 8H PERCENT //)
      WRITE(3,935)(CASH(I),I=1,NFLOWS)
  935 FORMAT (11H CASH FLOWS  /, (6F10.2))
      STOP
      END
```

A number of other higher-level languages have been developed. Sammet describes about 120 of these basic languages, though only a few are in heavy use (Sammet, 1969). BASIC is a language very similar to FORTRAN except that it was designed for time sharing. APL is a very powerful time-sharing language that closely resembles mathematical notation; see Table 8-9 for an example of an APL program and its execution at a terminal.

COBOL (COmmon Business-Oriented Language) was developed to facilitate programming for business applications. An example of a COBOL program may be found in Table 8-10. Most commercial programs in the United States are written in COBOL, whereas most scientific computing employs FORTRAN.

Table 8-9   An APL Statistical Program

```
Beginning         ∇ STAT
       of   [1]    'ENTER DATA X'
   Program  [2]    X←,□
            [3]    N←ρX
            [4]    MIN←⌊/X
            [5]    MAX←⌈/X
            [6]    M←(+/X)÷N
            [7]    SD←((+/(X-M)*2)÷N)*0.5
            [8]    MED←0.5×+/(X[⍋X])[⌈(N+0,1)÷2]
            [9]    'NO. NUMBERS= ';N;' MIN= ';MIN;' MAX= ';MAX
            [10]   'MEAN= ';M;' STD.DEV.= ';SD;' COEF.OF VAR.= ';SD÷M
            [11]   'MEDIAN= ';MED
                 ∇

Beginning         STAT
       of   ENTER DATA X
  Execution □:
                  1
            NO. NUMBERS= 1 MIN= 1 MAX= 1
            MEAN= 1 STD.DEV.= 0 COEF.OF VAR.= 0
            MEDIAN= 1

                  STAT
            ENTER DATA X
            □:
                  1 2
            NO. NUMBERS= 2 MIN= 1 MAX= 2
            MEAN= 1.5 STD.DEV.= 0.5 COEF.OF VAR.= 0.3333333333
            MEDIAN= 1.5

                  STAT
            ENTER DATA X
            □:
                  3000 6000 5000 35000 8000 60000 7000
            NO. NUMBERS= 7 MIN= 3000 MAX= 60000
            MEAN= 17714.28571 STD.DEV.= 20040.77476 COEF.OF VAR.= 1.131334059
            MEDIAN= 7000
```

Source: H. Hellerman and I. Smith, *APL/360: Programming and Applications*, McGraw-Hill, New York, 1976.

Table 8-10   A Cobol Payroll Program and Sample Output

```
00001          IDENTIFICATION DIVISION.
00002          PROGRAM-ID. PAYROLL.
00003          AUTHOR. GORDON DAVIS.
00004          *SAMPLE SOLUTION TO PROBLEM 5 IN CHAPTER 19.
00005          *THIS PROGRAM READS HOURS-WORKED AND RATE-OF-PAY FOR EACH
00006          *EMPLOYEE AND COMPUTES GROSS-PAY.
00007          *
00008          *
00009          ENVIRONMENT DIVISION.
00010          CONFIGURATION SECTION.
00011          SOURCE-COMPUTER. CYBER-74.
00012          OBJECT-COMPUTER. CYBER-74.
00013          INPUT-OUTPUT SECTION.
00014          FILE-CONTROL.
00015              SELECT PAYROLL-FILE ASSIGN TO INPUT.
00016              SELECT PRINT-FILE ASSIGN TO OUTPUT.
00017          *
00018          *
00019          DATA DIVISION.
00020          FILE SECTION.
00021          FD  PAYROLL-FILE
00022              LABEL RECORD IS OMITTED.
00023              01  INPUT-RECORD           PICTURE X(80).
00024          *
00025          FD  PRINT-FILE
00026              LABEL RECORD OMITTED.
00027              01  PRINT-LINE             PICTURE X(132).
00028          *
00029          WORKING-STORAGE SECTION.
00030          77  OVERTIME-HOURS             PICTURE 99.
00031          77  REGULAR-HOURS              PICTURE 99.
00032          77  GROSS-PAY                  PICTURE 9999V99.
00033          77  REGULAR-PAY                PICTURE 9999V99.
00034          77  OVERTIME-PAY               PICTURE 9999V99.
00035          77  REGULAR-TOTAL              PICTURE 99999V99.
00036          77  OVERTIME-TOTAL             PICTURE 99999V99.
00037          77  GROSS-TOTAL                PICTURE 99999V99.
00038          77  MORE-CARDS                 PICTURE XXX.
00039          01  PAYROLL-DATA.
00040              05  NAME                   PICTURE X(30).
00041              05  RATE-OF-PAY            PICTURE 99V999.
00042              05  HOURS-WORKED           PICTURE 999.
00043              05  FILLER                 PICTURE X(42).
00044          01  DATE-RECORD.
00045              05  DATE-IN                PICTURE X(8).
00046              05  FILLER                 PICTURE X(72).
00047          01  COMPANY-HEADER.
00048              05  FILLER                 PICTURE X(58)   VALUE SPACES.
00049              05  FILLER                 PICTURE X(17)   VALUE
00050                               #THE SMALL COMPANY#.
00051              05  FILLER                 PICTURE X(57)   VALUE SPACES.
00052          01  WEEK-HEADER.
00053              05  FILLER                 PICTURE X(46)   VALUE SPACES.
00054              05  FILLER                 PICTURE X(31)   VALUE
00055                               #REPORT OF WAGES PAID WEEK OF #.
00056              05  DATE-OUT               PICTURE X(8).
00057              05  FILLER                 PICTURE X(47)   VALUE SPACES.
00058          01  DETAIL-HEADER-1.
00059              05  FILLER                 PICTURE X(56)   VALUE SPACES.
00060              05  FILLER                 PICTURE X(14)   VALUE
00061                               #HOURLY   HOURS#.
00062              05  FILLER                 PICTURE X(13)   VALUE SPACES.
00063              05  FILLER                 PICTURE X(27)   VALUE
00064                               #REGULAR  OVERTIME   TOTAL#.
00065              05  FILLER                 PICTURE X(22)   VALUE SPACES.
```

On the printer used, the card code for apostrophe (') printed as a not equal sign (=).

Table 8-10   (Continued)

```
00066              01  DETAIL-HEADER-2.
00067                  05  FILLER                  PICTURE X(20)   VALUE SPACES.
00068                  05  FILLER                  PICTURE X(13)   VALUE
00069                          *EMPLOYEE NAME*.
00070                  05  FILLER                  PICTURE X(24)   VALUE SPACES.
00071                  05  FILLER                  PICTURE X(14)   VALUE
00072                          *RATE     WORKED*.
00073                  05  FILLER                  PICTURE X(15)   VALUE SPACES.
00074                  05  FILLER                  PICTURE X(24)   VALUE
00075                          *PAY      PAY       PAY*.
00076                  05  FILLER                  PICTURE X(23)   VALUE SPACES.
00077              01  DETAIL-LINE.
00078                  05  FILLER                  PICTURE X(20)   VALUE SPACES.
00079                  05  NAME-PRINT              PICTURE X(30) .
00080                  05  FILLER                  PICTURE X(6)    VALUE SPACES.
00081                  05  RATE-PRINT              PICTURE Z9.999.
00082                  05  FILLER                  PICTURE X(5)    VALUE SPACES.
00083                  05  HOURS-PRINT             PICTURE ZZ9.
00084                  05  FILLER                  PICTURE X(13)   VALUE SPACES.
00085                  05  REGULAR-PAY-PRINT       PICTURE ZZZ9.99.
00086                  05  FILLER                  PICTURE X(3)    VALUE SPACES.
00087                  05  OVER-PAY-PRINT          PICTURE ZZZ9.99.
00088                  05  FILLER                  PICTURE X(3)    VALUE SPACES.
00089                  05  GROSS-PAY-PRINT         PICTURE ZZZ9.99.
00090                  05  FILLER                  PICTURE X(22)   VALUE SPACES.
00091              01  TOTAL-LINE.
00092                  05  FILLER                  PICTURE X(74)   VALUE SPACES.
00093                  05  FILLER                  PICTURE X(8)    VALUE *TOTALS *.
00094                  05  REGULAR-TOTAL-PRINT     PICTURE $ZZZ9.99.
00095                  05  FILLER                  PICTURE X(2)    VALUE SPACES.
00096                  05  OVER-TOTAL-PRINT        PICTURE $ZZZ9.99.
00097                  05  FILLER                  PICTURE X(2)    VALUE SPACES.
00098                  05  GROSS-TOTAL-PRINT       PICTURE $ZZZ9.99.
00099         *
00100         *
00101              PROCEDURE DIVISION.
00102              MAINLINE-CONTROL.
00103                  PERFORM INITIALIZATION.
00104                  PERFORM READ-AND-CHECK UNTIL MORE-CARDS = *NO*.
00105                  PERFORM CLOSING.
00106                  STOP RUN.
00107         *
00108              INITIALIZATION.
00109                  OPEN INPUT PAYROLL-FILE.
00110                  OPEN OUTPUT PRINT-FILE.
00111                  MOVE *YES* TO MORE-CARDS.
00112                  READ PAYROLL-FILE INTO DATE-RECORD AT END STOP RUN.
00113                  WRITE PRINT-LINE FROM COMPANY-HEADER AFTER ADVANCING
00114                      2 LINES.
00115                  MOVE DATE-IN TO DATE-OUT.
00116                  WRITE PRINT-LINE FROM WEEK-HEADER AFTER ADVANCING 2 LINES.
00117                  WRITE PRINT-LINE FROM DETAIL-HEADER-1 AFTER ADVANCING
00118                      2 LINES.
00119                  WRITE PRINT-LINE FROM DETAIL-HEADER-2 AFTER ADVANCING
00120                      1 LINES.
00121                  MOVE SPACES TO PRINT-LINE WRITE PRINT-LINE.
00122                  MOVE ZEROES TO REGULAR-TOTAL, OVERTIME-TOTAL, GROSS-TOTAL.
00123         *
00124              READ-AND-CHECK.
00125                  READ PAYROLL-FILE INTO PAYROLL-DATA AT END
00126                      MOVE *NO* TO MORE-CARDS.
00127                  IF MORE-CARDS = *YES* PERFORM PROCESS-AND-PRINT.
00128         *
```

Table 8-10   (Continued)

```
00129                    PROCESS-AND-PRINT.
00130                        IF HOURS-WORKED IS GREATER THAN 40
00131                            MOVE 40 TO REGULAR-HOURS
00132                            SUBTRACT 40 FROM HOURS-WORKED GIVING OVERTIME-HOURS
00133                            PERFORM OVERTIME-CALCULATION
00134                        ELSE
00135                            MOVE HOURS-WORKED TO REGULAR-HOURS
00136                            MOVE ZERO TO OVERTIME-PAY.
00137                        MULTIPLY RATE-OF-PAY BY REGULAR-HOURS GIVING REGULAR-PAY
00138                            ROUNDED.
00139                        ADD OVERTIME-PAY TO REGULAR-PAY GIVING GROSS-PAY.
00140                        ADD REGULAR-PAY TO REGULAR-TOTAL.
00141                        ADD OVERTIME-PAY TO OVERTIME-TOTAL.
00142                        ADD GROSS-PAY TO GROSS-TOTAL.
00143                        MOVE NAME TO NAME-PRINT.
00144                        MOVE RATE-OF-PAY TO RATE-PRINT.
00145                        MOVE HOURS-WORKED TO HOURS-PRINT.
00146                        MOVE REGULAR-PAY TO REGULAR-PAY-PRINT.
00147                        MOVE OVERTIME-PAY TO OVER-PAY-PRINT.
00148                        MOVE GROSS-PAY TO GROSS-PAY-PRINT.
00149                        WRITE PRINT-LINE FROM DETAIL-LINE.
00150                    *
00151                    OVERTIME-CALCULATION.
00152                        MULTIPLY RATE-OF-PAY BY OVERTIME-HOURS GIVING OVERTIME-PAY
00153                            ROUNDED.
00154                        MULTIPLY 1.5 BY OVERTIME-PAY ROUNDED.
00155                    *
00156                    CLOSING.
00157                        MOVE REGULAR-TOTAL TO REGULAR-TOTAL-PRINT.
00158                        MOVE OVERTIME-TOTAL TO OVER-TOTAL-PRINT.
00159                        MOVE GROSS-TOTAL TO GROSS-TOTAL-PRINT.
00160                        WRITE PRINT-LINE FROM TOTAL-LINE AFTER ADVANCING 2 LINES.
00161                        CLOSE PAYROLL-FILE, PRINT-FILE.
```

THE SMALL COMPANY

REPORT OF WAGES PAID   WEEK OF   75/07/25

EMPLOYEE NAME	HOURLY RATE	HOURS WORKED	REGULAR PAY	OVERTIME PAY	TOTAL PAY
RONALD JENKINS	9.750	25	243.75	0.00	243.75
BARBARA OLSON	3.500	42	140.00	10.50	150.50
MARGARET JOHNSON	2.500	58	100.00	67.50	167.50
NANCY BATES	8.025	35	280.88	0.00	280.88
JOHN WEBER	6.500	25	162.50	0.00	162.50
STEVE MILLER	10.000	30	300.00	0.00	300.00
			TOTALS $1227.13	$ 78.00	$1305.13

COBOL has been standardized to a greater extent than other languages, which gives the user the potential ability to transport COBOL programs from one system to another without a massive conversion effort. The language also features English-like sentences, easy program maintenance, and comprehensive data-editing capabilities.

Many organizations, particularly small ones, use a language called Report Program Generator, or RPG. This language is suitable for business applications. RPG provides fixed program logic automatically; programmers work from special RPG coding forms. The user defines the file, the output files, extra space for the compiler, input record formats, calculations, output, and any telecommunications interface. Because much of RPG is structured already, the programmer does not spend time with complex control logic. The language also makes it easy to update files, and many versions support direct access files with indices (see Chapter 9).

The programming language ALGOL (ALGOrithmic Language) is used frequently in Europe and has formed the basis for the design of one line of computers in the United States. PL/1 (Programming Language 1) is a language that combines the features of both COBOL and FORTAN. This language has very rich capabilities but is also quite complex: it is not a language for the novice programmer. An example of a PL/1 program is given in Table 8-11. The

Table 8-11   A PL/1 Sort Program

```
PROCEDURE OPTIONS(MAIN) ;

  /*              SORT A STRING ARRAY */
DECLARE (RECORD(0:1000), TEMP) CHARACTER(80) VARYING,
        BOOL BIT(1) INITIAL('1'B) ;
RECORD(0) = ' ';

DO I = 1 TO 1001 WHILE(RECORD(I−1) ¬ = 'END DATA');
    GET LIST(RECORD(I) ) ; END ;
N = I-2;

OUTER:   DO J = 1 TO N-1 WHILE(BOOL);
          BOOL = '0',
          INNER:  DO I = 1 TO N-J;
                  IF RECORD(I) > RECORD(I+1)  THEN DO;
                    TEMP = RECORD(I+1);
                    RECORD(I+1) = RECORD(I);
                    RECORD(I) = TEMP;
                    BOOL = '1';                END;
          END INNER;
END OUTER;

PUT DATA(J) PAGE;
PUT LIST((RECORD(I) DO I = 1 TO N)) SKIP(2);
END;

                              (INPUT DATA)
```

Source: W. Cole, Introduction to Computing, McGraw-Hill, New York, 1969.

Figure 8-2 The compilation process.

language PASCAL is becoming increasingly popular, especially on small computers. It features a simple yet powerful design and is oriented toward the preparation of clearly structured programs. Table 8-12 is an example of a PASCAL program.

How is a higher-level language translated into a machine language?* Just as we might expect, the early translators for higher-level languages—called compilers—first translated a source program into assembly language and then called on an existing assembler to produce machine language. Clearly this two-stage process is time consuming. One of the major contributions of computer science is the development of a mathematical theory of languages and a structured approach to writing compilers. See Figure 8-2 for a schematic of the compilation process.

The components of a modern compiler may be broken down into a series of modules or stages, although some of the stages interact with each other rather than follow each other in strict sequence.

The lexical analysis component of the compiler analyzes symbols in the source language statement and identifies them. For example, the FORTRAN statement $X = (A + B)*(C - D)/E$ contains three types of symbols. First, are the variables X, A, B, C, D, and E, and in some languages these variables could be composed of from 6 to 30 characters each. There are also operators, the $+$, $*$, $-$, and $/$. Finally, parentheses indicate the proper order of computations (some compilers classify parentheses with operators). Most languages have many other kinds of statements besides the computational one shown above, such as those for I/O, conditional tests (if a certain condition exists take the following action), looping, and others.

Usually lexical routines build tables and substitute codes for the symbols in the program. The mathematical field of automata theory provides an excellent basis for developing lexical analysis routines. Automata theory suggests an approach in which the analysis routine examines input, one symbol at a time, and advances to different states until a final accepting state is reached (Gries, 1971). At this stage, we know the input symbol is identified and is accepted or rejected as an error.

The next stage of the compiler is syntactic analysis, which examines the input program statements and tries to develop a syntactic representation of each statement (Cardenas et al., 1972). The set of rules specifying legal statements (symbol combinations) in a language is called the "syntax" of the language.

*This section can be omitted by the reader primarily interested in an overview of software.

Table 8-12 A PASCAL Program to Report Sales

```
00100      PROGRAM TAXCOM(INPUT,OUTPUT);
00200
00300      /* THIS PROGRAM READS A FILE OF LENGTH "N"
00400         CONTAINING SALES FIGURES.  BASED ON
00500         A CODE IT DETERMINES IF THE SALE WAS TAXABLE
00600         OR NOT. THE PROGRAM THEN CALCULATES
00700         THE TOTAL DOLLAR AMOUNT OF TAXABLE SALES,
00800         THE TOTAL DOLLAR AMOUNT OF NON-TAXABLE
00900         SALES AND THE APPROPRIATE TAX. */
01000
01100
01200      /* DECLARE VARIABLES AND CONSTANTS */
01300
01350      CONST TAXRATE =0.07;
01400      VAR I,N,CATEGORY: INTEGER;
01500          SALES1,SALES2,AMOUNT,TAX: REAL;
01600
01700    /* BEGIN PROCESSING */
01800
01900      BEGIN
02000
02100         SALES1 := 0.00;
02200         SALES2 := 0.00;
02300         AMOUNT := 0.00;
02400
02600        /* READ LENGTH OF FILE  */
02800         READLN(N);
02900
02902        /* ENTER LOOP */
03000         FOR I := 1 TO N DO
03100           BEGIN
03102
03104             /* READ FROM FILE TAX CATEGORY AND AMOUNT */
03200             READLN(CATEGORY,AMOUNT);
03201
03202             /* BASED ON CATEGORY CALCULATE */
03300               IF CATEGORY=1 THEN
03400                  SALES1 := SALES1+AMOUNT
03500               ELSE
03600                  SALES2 := SALES2+AMOUNT;
03700         END;
03750        /* END OF LOOP */
03775
03787     /* CALCULATE SALES TAX */
03800        TAX := SALES1 * TAXRATE;
03850
03875        /* PRINT RESULTS */
03900        WRITELN('TAXABLE SALES:  $', SALES1:5:2);
```

Table 8-12   (Continued)

```
04000          WRITELN('NON-TAXABLE SALES:   $', SALES2:5:2);
04100          WRITELN('TAX DUE ON SALES:   $', TAX:5:2);
04102
04104     /* END OF PROGRAM */
04200     END.
@
```

Data	Results
10	TAXABLE SALES: $ 129.90
1 12.45	NON-TAXABLE SALES: $ 84.15
1 30.00	TAX DUE ON SALES: $ 9.09
2 11.10	@
1 30.50	
1 09.95	
2 40.00	
2 23.05	
1 14.50	
1 32.50	
2 10.00	
@	

Here again computer science helped develop syntactic descriptions of programming languages to facilitate their analysis. These formalisms are called "metalanguages" because they are languages for describing computer languages.

A typical compiler in the syntactic analysis stage uses a formal representation of the language to screen input classified by lexical analysis routines. The input language is matched against permissible language structures, much as we might diagram an English sentence to see if it exhibits acceptable grammar. The matching process frequently involves the construction of a tree that classifies the various parts of the source statement according to their type. For example, in an English language statement such a tree would identify the verbs, prepositions, adjectives, and so on. Figure 8-2 is a possible parse tree for the FORTRAN expression discussed earlier. The syntactic analyzer routines call on the lexical analysis routine to classify each symbol (variable, operator, etc.) as the syntactic analyzer builds the tree. The entire process of lexical and syntactic analysis is referred to as "parsing" the input program.

Given a representation of the input in the form of a parse tree, the next step of the compiler is to interpret the parse tree. At this point we can produce a one-dimensional representation of the two-dimensional tree structure in machine language that the computer can execute directly. That is, the parse tree is used to generate a sequence of machine-language instructions: Figure 8-3 has to be converted into the machine language of Table 8-7. However, before machine-language instructions are generated, an intermediate linear language is produced called "pseudocode." Why bother with this step? Does it not just add time and complexity to compilation?

By accepting some inefficiency here we can produce a better program.

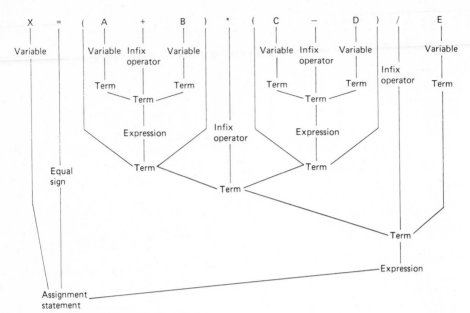

Figure 8-3 An example of a parse tree.

Frequently, in interpreting the parse tree, the compiler generates a number of redundant instructions. For example, the same value might be moved from a register to memory in one instruction and in the next instruction be loaded back into the same register. To avoid such unnecessary steps, the optimization phase examines the pseudocode and attempts to recognize and eliminate redundant operations, such as inefficiencies in register allocation, excessive use of temporary locations, and removal of invariant calculations in loops.

After optimization, the pseudocode is used to generate machine language, or object code. However, before the computer executes this code, one additional step is necessary. In many languages it is possible to employ subroutines. A subroutine is like a macro (they are called "closed macros") and is used to avoid repeating coding steps or to modularize a program. Subroutines may also be written by one programmer and saved in a library for use by others. Also, some languages are procedural; that is, a program consists of a series of modules called procedures. All these procedures and subroutines must be combined and the complete program loaded into memory for execution.

We would like to have flexibility in loading programs. As we shall see with different operating systems, a program may not be located in the same place in memory each time it is executed. Programs, therefore, are usually relocatable. A program called a "linking loader" links the various components of the program together and loads them into memory before execution.

There may be various types of compilers for the same language, each compiler with a different design objective. There is a tradeoff between the amount of time for compilation and the execution speed of the resulting output code. To produce fast-executing object code, we have to spend more time during compilation. For a job to be run many times we may compile the program once and save the object code. Here it makes sense to use an "optimizing compiler" that spends a great deal of time in the optimization phase.

For testing purposes, typically we compile a program many times and execute it for a short duration on limited test data. For this purpose we use an "in-core" compiler that translates the program and loads it into memory for execution during the translation process. Programs have to be a little smaller for this compiler because the compiler is in memory too. The output code is less efficient than for an optimizing compiler, but we do not plan to execute the program for a long period of time when we are just finding errors (debugging).

Special-Purpose Languages

Special-purpose languages are designed with the same philosophy as higher-level languages: to extend the capabilities of the computer to end users. Most frequently, special-purpose languages are translated into a higher-level language that is compiled to produce machine language.

An excellent example of a special-purpose language is the Statistical Package for the Social Sciences (SPSS) (Nie et al., 1975). This very complete statistical system is written in FORTRAN. It makes it possible to name variables for a particular study, save the variable names and data on a file, and create new

---

MANAGEMENT PROBLEM 8-1

The manager of production for Homeware, Inc., had just finished reading an article about how a time-sharing system was used by a manufacturing company to simulate different production schedules. The company in the article resembled Homeware; both firms operate more of a job shop than an assembly line.

The manager wondered if a similar system could not be developed for Homeware to solve some of its production problems. He approached the information services department with a proposal for a system. The response from the computer staff was fairly positive.

The manager worked with the computer staff to define the input language he would like to use and the logic of the simulation. The input language must be unique for each company, and the computer staff indicated that they would have to write an input parser especially for this application.

The manager did not really know what an input parser was, but it sounded rather formidable. The computer department also said they would have to hire a systems programmer (a programmer who specializes in software systems as opposed to applications programs) to write this routine. "It is a lot like writing part of a compiler," said the main representative from the computer staff. "We will have to use assembly language for a task like this," he added.

The manager really did not understand much of the conversation, but he was asked to authorize the new addition to the staff and to give his approval for developing the system. The investment for development would come from his budget. What should the manager do?

---

variables from logical relationships among existing variables. The package features extensive data-management facilities that are complemented by a number of statistical tests, including the preparation of frequency distributions, testing for differences among populations, calculating measures of association, performing analysis of variance, and performing a series of multivariate procedures such as regression analysis and factor analysis.

Table 8-13 contains an example of an SPSS program, and Table 8-14 presents the results of executing the program. The input program is for a multiple-regression run. The run name provides a title and the file name gives the data file a unique name. Data are envisioned as forming a matrix. The columns of the matrix represent variables such as GNP, and each row is one observation of the variables, for example, GNP for a given year. The variable list labels the different columns of data and the variable labels statement is

Table 8-13   SPSS Regression Run

```
1                      16
RUN NAME            MULTIPLE REGRESSION RUN USING CARD INPUT AND RAW DATA
FILE NAME           STOCKP    DATA FOR PREDICTION OF INVESTORS INDEX
VARIABLE LIST       INVINDEX,GNP,CORPPRCF,CORPDIV,YEAR
VAR LABELS          INVINDEX   INVESTORS INDEX 1949=0/
                    GNP        GROSS NATIONAL PRODUCT/
                    CORPPROF   CORPORATE PROFITS BEFORE TAXES/
                    CORPDIV    CORPORATE DIVIDENDS PAID
INPUT FORMAT        FIXED (F6.1,4F6.0)
PRINT FORMATS       INVINDEX(1) GNP TO CORPDIV(0)
N OF CASES          32
REGRESSION          VARIABLES =INVINDEX,GNP,CORPPROF,CORPDIV/
                    REGRESSION=INVINDEX WITH GNP TO CORPDIV(1)
READ INPUT DATA
    76.4   7678    269    216   1935
    99.5   8022    351    251   1936
   105.9   8820    403    250   1937
    86.7   8871    362    290   1938
    83.7   9536    541    304   1939
    70.7  10911    619    317   1940
    61.7  12486    801    273   1941
    58.7  14816    917    243   1942
    76.3  15357    882    233   1943
    76.6  15927    858    211   1944
    91.0  15552    852    195   1945
   105.8  15251    966    230   1946
    96.8  15446   1008    286   1947
   102.8  15735    908    240   1948
   100.0  16343    851    278   1949
   120.3  17471   1065    361   1950
   153.8  18547   1034    300   1951
   158.2  20027   1081    296   1952
   146.5  20794   1089    287   1953
   165.6  20186    953    282   1954
   212.7  21920   1206    321   1955
   245.9  23811   1313    340   1956
   236.0  24117   1202    364   1957
   218.8  24397   1242    371   1958
   242.6  25242   1378    388   1959
   256.9  15849   1295    397   1960
   326.1  25615   1314    436   1961
   314.4  28287   1422    470   1962
   336.0  29740   1525    511   1963
   394.0  31650   1718    583   1964
   433.1  33814   1836    629   1965
   408.5  35822   1762    655   1966
FINISH
```

Source: N. Nie et al., *Statistical Package for the Social Sciences*, 2d ed., McGraw-Hill, New York, 1975.

Table 8-14 Output from REGRESSION

```
MULTIPLE REGRESSION RUN USING CARD INPUT AND RAW DATA                              04/ 2/74     PAGE   2
FILE   STOCKP   (CREATION DATE = 04/12/74)   DATA FOR PREDICTION OF INVESTORS INDEX
* * * * * * * * * * * * * * * * * * * * * * *  M U L T I P L E   R E G R E S S I O N  * * * * * * * * * * * *  VARIABLE LIST  1
                                                                                                            REGRESSION LIST  1
DEPENDENT VARIABLE..    INVINDEX   INVESTORS INDEX 1949=0

VARIABLE(S) ENTERED ON STEP NUMBER  1..   CORPDIV    CORPORATE DIVIDENDS PAID

MULTIPLE R          0.93667                    ANALYSIS OF VARIANCE    DF     SUM OF SQUARES      MEAN SQUARE             F
R SQUARE           0.87735                    REGRESSION              1.      339486.57326      339486.57326        214.60000
ADJUSTED R SQUARE  0.87735                    RESIDUAL               30.       47458.51460        1581.95049
STANDARD ERROR    39.77374

----------------- VARIABLES IN THE EQUATION -----------------       ---------- VARIABLES NOT IN THE EQUATION ----------
VARIABLE        B          BETA      STD ERROR B      F         VARIABLE     BETA IN    PARTIAL    TOLERANCE       F
CORPDIV      0.87621     0.93667      0.05981      214.600      GNP          0.42296    0.63390     0.27549      19.481
(CONSTANT) -119.00286                                          CORPPROF      0.33527    0.54357     0.32240      12.162

* * * * * * * * * * * * * * * * * * * * * * * * * * * * * * * * * * * * * * * * * * * * * * * * * * * * * * *
VARIABLE(S) ENTERED ON STEP NUMBER  2..   GNP      GROSS NATIONAL PRODUCT

MULTIPLE R          0.96262                    ANALYSIS OF VARIANCE    DF     SUM OF SQUARES      MEAN SQUARE             F
R SQUARE           0.92664                    REGRESSION              2.      358556.98740      179278.49370        183.14280
ADJUSTED R SQUARE  0.92419                    RESIDUAL               29.       28388.10046         978.90002
STANDARD ERROR    31.28738

----------------- VARIABLES IN THE EQUATION -----------------       ---------- VARIABLES NOT IN THE EQUATION ----------
VARIABLE        B          BETA      STD ERROR B      F         VARIABLE     BETA IN    PARTIAL    TOLERANCE       F
CORPDIV      0.53943     0.57665      0.08964       36.211      CORPPROF    -0.00946   -0.01000     0.08193       0.003
GNP          0.00620     0.42296      0.00140       19.481
(CONSTANT) -123.06406

F-LEVEL OR TOLERANCE-LEVEL INSUFFICIENT FOR FURTHER COMPUTATION
```

```
MULTIPLE REGRESSION RUN USING CARD INPUT AND RAW DATA                              04/12/74     PAGE   3
FILE   STOCKP   (CREATION DATE = 04/12/74)   DATA FOR PREDICTION OF INVESTORS INDEX
* * * * * * * * * * * * * * * * * * * * * * *  M U L T I P L E   R E G R E S S I O N  * * * * * * * * * * * *  VARIABLE LIST  1
                                                                                                            REGRESSION LIST  1
DEPENDENT VARIABLE..    INVINDEX   INVESTORS INDEX 1949=0

                                              SUMMARY TABLE
VARIABLE                                 MULTIPLE R  R SQUARE  RSQ CHANGE  SIMPLE R        B           BETA
CORPDIV    CORPORATE DIVIDENDS PAID        0.93667    0.87735    0.87735    0.93667      0.53943      0.57665
GNP        GROSS NATIONAL PRODUCT          0.96262    0.92664    0.04928    0.91380      0.00620      0.42296
(CONSTANT)                                                                            -123.06406
```

Source: N. Nie et al., *Statistical Package for the Social Sciences*, 2d ed., McGraw-Hill, New York, 1975.

optional input that improves the readability of the output. The input format describes how the data are punched on cards, and the print format indicates the desired output.

There are 32 cases or observations. The regression statement invokes the procedure to compute a least squares equation using a stepwise algorithm. This very powerful language allows the user to perform complete statistical analyses using concise statements. Consider the number of program statements required in a language such as FORTRAN to accomplish what SPSS does with a dozen statements.

Our second example of a special-purpose language operates on-line and is designed to assist corporate planners (Boulden and Buffa, 1970). This particular language has four components: a planning system supervisory program, the model logic, a statistical series data file, and storage files.

The planning system supervisor is a program common to all users. It executes models written by the user and provides statistical routines, runs simulations, links data with the model, controls interaction between the model builder and user, and prepares all output reports. The supervisor can also access external files and data bases.

The supervisor controls input and output, a particularly necessary function if models are stored on files. It is helpful if users can build a series of command strings and save them to create an English-language-like input. A good supervisor provides the capability to create command files and name generalized commands. The planning system supervisor may also help the model builder link the planning model to other models such as a linear program. The user can specify variables and a range for parametic analysis; relative movements of input and output variables allow a sensitivity analysis. Some planning systems let a user designate an output value and search for the input value that results in this output.

The statistical series data files provide data on the economy as a whole, such as the gross national product, housing starts, and others. This file is available to all users.

The model builder provides two components, a company data file and the model logic. The company data file contains proprietary data on the company, such as production data, sales, and financial information. The corporate model logic is expressed in the statements of the planning language. This language is more closely related to planning activities than are general-purpose languages such as FORTRAN.

One planning language has parameters labeled P and data arrays labeled V. For example, PX might be the cost of product X and PY the cost of product Y. VX could represent the quantity of X needed each month and VY the quantity of Y required monthly. The model builder could define a new variable such as the total production, $EM = VX*PX$.

Variables such as the ones above are combined to form equations that constitute the planning model. The model, after validation, is used in a series of simulation runs to predict the impact of different plans.

Many organizations have found it useful to develop financial models of various aspects of their business. A proprietary language called EMPIRE developed by Applied Data Research helps the user to construct and execute such models. Table 8-15 is an example of an EMPIRE model of a movie theater. The first part of the table is the actual model execution; the second part is the listing of the model. Table 8-15 shows an execution of the model. First the user supplies data that are not contained in the model itself, and then the report is produced. One of the most powerful features of this system is the ability to make changes; for example, the user asks for a computation and printout of profits if ticket price is raised to $6 from the $5 in the first run. A language such as EMPIRE extends the power of the computer to the end user and does not require that a professional programmer be available to assist the model builder.

The advantages of special-purpose languages should be clear from these

Table 8-15   Example of an EMPIRE Model of a Movie Theater

```
empire

-----------
E M P I R E
 TRANSLATOR
   VER 2
-----------


ENTER COMMAND:    execute cinema

***TRANSLATING: CINEMA

    *MODEL *

***TRANSLATION COMPLETED***

FORTRAN: CINEMA
ADRSI
LINK:    Loading
[LNKXCT CINEMA execution]

-----------
E M P I R E
 EXECUTIVE
   VER 2
-----------


YES... verify
THE FOLLOWING ITEMS FLAGGED "INPUT" HAVE NO VALUE SET:
EXPSAL
LAB
TPRICE
TCOST
YES... data
->expsal(cin1)2000,2400
->lab(cin1)450,550
->tprice 5.00
->tcost 3.50
->end
YES... run
YES... print from incsmt
ADJUST PAPER, THEN ENTER A CARRIAGE RETURN TO PROCEED=>
```

Table 8-15 (Continued)

MODEL:CINEMA   DATE: 23-Apr-81   16:47   PAGE:1

CINEMA ONE AND TWO INC.
PROJECTED INCOME STATEMENT

	CINEMA ONE	CINEMA TWO	TOTAL BOTH CINEMAS
EXPECTED # TKTS SOLD	2,000	2,400	4,400
TICKET REVENUE	$ 10,000	$ 12,000	$ 22,000
FIXED COST OF SALES	$ 7,000	$ 8,400	$ 15,400
LABOR COSTS	$ 450	$ 550	$ 1,000
GROSS PROFIT	$ 2,550	$ 3,050	$ 5,600
INCOME TAX			$ 2,688
PROFITS AFTER TAX			$ 2,912

YES... what is profat if tprice=6.00

PROFAT   5200.000

YES... what is profat if tcost=3.75

PROFAT   2340.000

YES... what is profat if tprice=3.85

PROFAT   280.800

YES... what is prof if tcost=2.00

PROF   (CIN1)   5550.000
        (CIN2)   6650.000
        (TOTAL)   12200.000

YES... what is prof if tprice=5.5

PROF   (CIN1)   3550.000
        (CIN2)   4250.000
        (TOTAL)   7800.000

YES... exit

E M P I R E - END OF SESSION

Table 8-15 (Continued)

```
ty cinema.mod
00100    column section
00300    CIN1  "CINEMA/ONE"
00400    CIN2  "CINEMA/TWO"
00500    total "TOTAL BOTH/CINEMAS"
00600    row section
00700    expsal input "EXPECTED # TKTS SOLD"
00800    salr "TICKET REVENUE"
00900    csal "FIXED COST OF SALES"
00950    lab INPUT "LABOR COSTS"
01000    prof "GROSS PROFIT"
01100    scalar section
01200    tprice input "TICKET PRICE"
01300    tcost input "COST PER TKT"
01400    trate "INCOME TAX RATE" .48
01500    inctax "INCOME TAX"
01600    profat "PROFITS AFTER TAX"
01700    rules section
01800    for col=CIN1 to CIN2 do
01900    salr=expsal(col)*tprice
02000    csal=expsal(col)*tcost
02100    prof=salr-csal-lab(col)
02200    end
02300    total=CIN1+CIN2
02400    inctax=trate*prof(total)
02500    profat=prof(total)-inctax
@
```

```
ty incsmt.rep
00100    select CIN1:total
00200    columnwidth 15
00300    title 1 center "CINEMA ONE AND TWO INC."
00400    title 2 center "PROJECTED INCOME STATEMENT"//
00450    skip
00500    position 1
00600    print expsal
00700    skip
00800    prefix "$"
00900    print salr
01100    print csal
01150    print lab
01200    line
01300    print /,prof
01400    line
01500    print /,inctax@3,/ profat@3,/
@
```

examples. These languages are closer to the vocabulary of the user, making it more natural for a decision maker who is not a computer professional to interact with a computer. Special-purpose languages are extremely valuable to users of information systems because they provide the option of working directly with the computer without necessarily relying on a computer professional. We expect to see more of these languages as they are accepted and used increasingly in the future.

PACKAGE PROGRAMS

Background

A package program is a program written by a vendor for sale or lease. The software vendor tries to develop a computer application that can be used by a number of different organizations. Since it is not necessary for each organization to program its own system, costs can be reduced. This idea seems appealing; what are its advantages and disadvantages? We shall examine this question from the viewpoints of the vendor and the customer.

The vendor wants to produce a general package to increase market potential and reduce the need to modify the package. To accomplish this purpose, two strategies can be followed. A package can be produced that

---

GOURMET COMPUTERS

Computer systems are being adopted by fine food restaurants to help control costs. Typically these systems capture sales data at each cash register and convert the data into inventory, profitability, and productivity reports. The systems make it possible for management to keep track of the details that determine whether or not the establishment makes a profit. A computer can record each meal ordered and deduct the items consumed from inventory allowing management to determine whether all food has been accounted for properly.

In one system the computer compares the price of each dish with the cost of its ingredients to keep the menu prices at a group of restaurants up-to-date. The chain can react quickly and knows its costs; management feels it has already recovered the cost of the computer.

One Massachusetts restaurant with a $5 million annual gross put in a system for $60,000. The owners figure that the system has saved about $50,000 a year in food costs and has improved service. The server types orders into one of 16 terminals in the 500 seat dining room; drink orders print out at the bar and appetizers print at one unit in the kitchen while entrees appear on another. When the food is ready, a runner brings it to the server who now has more time to spend with the customer.

There are a number of packaged systems built around minicomputers and microcomputers as well as systems developed by individual restaurant owners. Some vendors claim that a restaurant with as little as $400,000 in gross sales can profit from a system.

Business Week, November 3, 1980.

---

features a number of input parameters or tables. The customer provides many of these parameters only once to initialize the package. Another approach is to develop a package with various modules; the client configures a package containing only the modules needed. Many times a vendor employs a combination of these two approaches.

From the customer's viewpoint, why use a package? First, the costs of developing information systems are steadily increasing. Designing and programming a computer-based information system is a labor-intensive task. Maintenance of existing systems requires 50 to 80 percent of programming time, leaving little for developing new applications. In addition 200 to 300 percent overruns on cost and time are not unusual in developing custom software in-house.

Packages offer one way to reduce costs and shorten development time. In addition, many small organizations do not wish to establish their own computer departments. With a package, the design and operation of computer systems can be left to an outside firm. One large beverage manufacturer buys 20 percent of its applications software externally, and other firms are following the same trend (*Business Week,* September 1, 1980).

The customer, however, often does not want a package as general as the vendor's product. The client wants the package to do a particular job. From a user's standpoint generality beyond what is needed is detrimental because it results in less efficient programs and more complex input and initialization efforts. We shall discuss package evaluation criteria in Chapter 10.

Examples

There are numerous examples of package programs. One vendor offers a batch data-management retrieval and report-generator package that has been highly successful. On the basis of input requests, the program reads data from several files and extracts the requested information by using logical combinations of variables specified by the user. It is possible to perform computations on the data and print totals and subtotals.

Output can be sorted and sequenced in a variety of ways. The package can also update the files (see Chapter 9), although many clients run the package after their own update program has executed.

The user employs structured forms to describe the information to be retrieved and the format of output reports. There is a heavy use of default options, that is, a standard value for an input. If the standard is acceptable, it is used by default and the parameter does not have to be entered. As an example, a package might automatically print the date and page number on the upper right-hand side of a report unless specifically requested otherwise. Default options reduce the input requirements for the average user.

The retrieval package above provides reporting flexibility, since each individual requesting a report can custom-tailor it to his or her needs. Some information services departments have succeeded in having user departments prepare input directly. A user rather than a computer professional is responsible for the use of the system in each department.

A similar package from Program Products called the Data Analyzer offers the user a great deal of power to create special-purpose programs. Users and managers often prepare simple programs to generate comprehensive reports after only a three-day class on how to use the language. See Table 8-16 for an example of a simple Data Analyzer run. Note the file definitions in the beginning of the table; the user has only to define the fields on the file of interest, ignoring all data fields that will not be used in preparing the report.

The Data Analyzer allows the user to match two files and extract data based on the value of variables in either file. A program can examine a record on a file being processed and decide whether or not to include that record in the report. Special computations can be performed during this extraction phase as well as during the report-writing phase of the program.

The extraction part of the Data Analyzer is a large program written mostly in assembly language. After the data are extracted and placed on a temporary file, they are sorted. Next, the user's report program is actually turned into a FORTRAN program that is compiled, loaded, and executed to produce the finished report. Computations can also be performed during the preparation of the report.

The Data Analyzer is a very powerful applications program. Simple run requests can be produced by users, and more complicated programs can be prepared by the expert. The program is used extensively in organizations by users and has also been employed to audit computer-based systems.

The SPSS package discussed earlier as an example of a special-purpose language can also be classified as a package. (The line between some very high level languages and package programs is indistinct.) Clearly, this type of

Table 8-16 A Data Analyzer Program

File definition

```
F INVENT  ISFB02552025525
D ITEM   00040005CA   04ITEM
D PACK   00170003CA   04PACK
D SLOT   01470005CA   04SLOT
D SIZE   00090008CA   04SIZE
D DESC   00200028CA   11DESCRIPTION
D VENDOR01610004CA   06VENDOR
D NETCST01650005CN2  08NET COST
D QUANT 00490005CN    13CASES ON HAND
D FAMILY01230002CA   06FAMILY
```

Program

```
TITLE,GROCERY    PHYSICAL INVENTORY – CURRENT PRICE 'FIFO' RUN D
SELECT,ITEM.LT.('27000').OR.ITEM.GT.('29999')
CALL,GETDATE
NEWFLD,EXT,FLO.2,'EXTENSION'
SORT,SLOT
COMP,DT,EXT–NETCST*QUANT
OPTION,STDSP–1
PRINT,ITEM,SLOT,PACK,SIZE,FAMILY,DESC,VENDOR,NETCST,QUANT(S),EXT(S)
END
```

MANAGEMENT PROBLEM 8-2

Martha Nixon recently received her M.B.A. and accepted a staff position with the planning department at H & M Foundries. H & M is a large, diversified metals concern that experiences much fluctuation in demand, depending on the economy. The planning department was formed last year as an attempt by management to consider the future in making current decisions.

Martha majored in finance in her M.B.A. program, and the idea of applying financial concepts to planning problems seemed very challenging. The head of the planning department has just asked Martha to take the responsibility for developing a model of the firm for simulating the impact of decisions.

Clearly, such a model will require computer processing and Martha wonders how to proceed. Should the planning department approach the information services department for help in developing a computer model? Is a computer expert needed to help program and implement the model? If so, should this individual come from the information services department, a consulting firm, or should the planning department hire its own computing staff?

Martha has also considered contacting several firms that offer proprietary computer languages designed expressly for planners. These vendors claim that even a planner who does not have computer experience can quickly learn to write models for a computer in these simple languages.

What factors should Martha consider in making this decision? Describe the ramifications of each alternative.

---

package extends the use of the computer to nonprofessional programmers. While every user must learn a small subset of the language for data definition and manipulation, only the actual statistical routines needed must be coded for any particular run. Thus, the user does not have to learn everything about the package; only features of immediate interest and relevance must be understood.

To illustrate the diversity of packages, out last example is a dedicated package, that is, a package to which an entire computer system is dedicated. One computer vendor developed a special operating system (we shall discuss operating systems in general in the next section) and series of applications programs for an airline passenger reservations system.

The development of such a system is a very complex undertaking; the vendor tries to reduce the costs and effort involved [the vendor expended an estimated 400 worker-years or more of effort in developing this package (Minini, 1969)]. However, the client airline still has to provide much data and will probably modify the package. It is necessary for the user to supply data that differ among airlines, such as routes and schedules.

The airline must also train agents and prepare for a massive implementation effort. Continued modification and maintenance are required after the installation of the system. To change and correct errors, the vendor continually updates the system, and these changes must be made in the user's version of the system.

These examples should illustrate the broad range of applications where packages have proved successful. Although these packages have many advantages and disadvantages, on balance we expect to see more use of packages in the future because of the high cost of developing special-purpose programs. We can afford to use computer hardware less efficiently as technology reduces the cost per computation, particularly as the cost of human resources increases.

OPERATING SYSTEMS

In the first generation of computers and for many second-generation installations, the operator of the computer system had a central role in controlling its use. The operator placed each new program in the card reader and loaded an assembler on tape. The assembler translated the object program and wrote it on tape, then a loading program loaded it and began execution. For production jobs to be run repeatedly, the object program would be saved on tape or on cards and loaded before execution; it would not be assembled each time it was used.

A good operator balanced jobs that needed many tape drives with jobs that needed few or no drives, so that the large tape job could be set up while the other job computed. In the case of a poor operator, the computer might be idle for a large part of the day while tapes were loaded and unloaded.

Programmers working on program development were given the entire computer for debugging, that is, for correcting the errors in their programs. The programmer operated the machine and when the program halted because of a bug, the programmer displayed memory locations on a computer-console typewriter. Because the program was written in assembly or machine language the programmer might "patch" (change) part of the object program in memory and run it again.

As the above scenario indicates, operations were very inefficient. It became clear that we could use the computer itself to help make operations proceed more smoothly. The first operating systems came into widespread use during the second generation of computers and most often customers, not computer vendors, wrote the first operating systems.

Early Systems

Batch Monitor   The earliest operating systems were simple batch monitors (monitor, executive program, and operating systems are synonymous for our purposes) that read special control cards. These cards might include a job card containing information about the programmer and the job, for example, run-time estimate, lines to be printed, and cards to be punched. Some systems also included information for accounting, such as an account or project number. Control cards were provided to tell the operator to set up tapes or to prepare any special paper required for the printer.

The next input card for the operating system might indicate what services the user desired, such as FORTRAN compile, load, and execution. The operating system examined this card and called the FORTRAN compiler to compile the program and put it on a secondary storage device. At the end of compilation the compiler returned control to the operating system. Next the loader was called to load the program and begin its execution. At the end of the program, control again was returned to the operating system, which read the next job and continued as above.

This monitor, though simple, sequenced jobs so that an entire stack or job stream of multiple jobs could be loaded at once. As disks became more common, compilers and work space were assigned to disks so the operator did not have to mount the compiler, loader, and program object tapes. Operating systems and disk storage have drastically improved the efficiency of computer operations.

Multiprocessing   During the second generation, at least one manufacturer offered a multiprocessing system, a computer system featuring more than one central processing unit. In reality, this system consisted of two complete computers; the smaller computer had an operating system and controlled both machines. The larger computer was a slave to the smaller machine. The small computer processed all input, and scheduled and printed all output using disks as a temporary storage area. An operating system in the large computer indicated to the control machine that it needed service—for example, when it needed a new program to process—and the control computer answered its request. This approach freed the more powerful slave computer from I/O and allowed it to concentrate on computations.

On-Line Systems   During the second generation of computers, the need for on-line computer access for applications such as inventory control and reservations became evident. The first on-line systems featured custom-designed operating system programs to control the computer resources. Applications programs in an on-line system express the logic of the application and are called by systems programs.

The supervisor in an on-line system establishes a series of queues and schedules service for them. First, an incoming message is assembled in a communications buffer; this message may have to be converted into a different code and moved to an input queue in memory by an applications program. The operating system notes the addition of this message to the messages-to-be-processed queue.

When the central processing unit is available, the supervisor assigns it to process a queue, say, the one with our input message. An applications program called by the operating system might verify the correctness of the message (correct format, etc.), after which the message is placed in a working queue.

The supervisor calls an applications program to parse and interpret the message, during which time the message may be moved along several different working queues. The supervisor calls different applications programs to process the message further and determine a response. Finally, an output message is assembled in another queue for transmission to the terminal. The supervisor schedules the CPU to send the output message.

The demands of such an on-line system are extensive. A great deal of bookkeeping is required to enforce and monitor queue disciplines. I/O operations also involve telecommunications activities. There must be adequate fallback and recovery facilities to prevent and handle system failures; for example, messages may be in process in one of a number of queues when the system fails. Recovery in these systems is complex, usually all input is logged on tape and periodically all data files are dumped to tape for backup.

A typical dedicated on-line system supervisor has the following responsibilities (Martin, 1967; Yourdon, 1972):

1   Scheduling all I/O operations, error checking and corrections, etc.
2   Assembling bits from communications lines into characters, and terminal control
3   Providing an edited, checked message to applications programs
4   Controlling displays and setting up output messages
5   Scheduling all message processing
6   Allocating machine resources
7   Building and processing queues, scheduling and queuing requests for service
8   Linking all programs and subroutines together and calling various

---

MANAGEMENT PROBLEM 8-3

Ted Armstrong is president of Advanced Airlines, a small regional carrier in the southwestern United States. Ted and several fellow pilots founded the airline in the early 1950s. Although operations were precarious at first, the firm is now in the position of making a small profit on its freight and passenger operations. In addition, the line has been slowly entering the charter market through contracts for private service with oil and utility companies.

Advanced Airlines has grown to the point where it now needs an automated reservation system for passengers and freight. Since the management of the firm generally consists of pilots with little exposure to computer systems, Ted has been exploring different possibilities himself.

Two options appear feasible. First, Advanced can obtain a packaged system from a major computer manufacturer. There would be substantial effort involved in initializing the package and installing it. Advanced would also have to lease or purchase its own computer. While the economics are in question, another regional airline has indicated an interest in joining Advanced so that the two lines would be able to share the cost of the system.

The alternative is to purchase reservations services from one of the large trunk carriers that operates its own extensive reservations system. Ted has discussed this possibility and at least two trunk carriers with excess computer capacity are interested.

Which option do you recommend?

---

applications programs for execution, loading, and relocating applications programs in memory

   9 Processing all interrupts

 10 Controlling the file system

 11 Initiating reliability and fault checks, running diagnostic programs,
possibly reconfiguring the system to isolate malfunctioning components

 12 Switching over to a backup computer when failure is diagnosed

 13 Recovering from errors that caused operations to cease

The Birth of Time Sharing As computer systems became more heavily
loaded during the first and second generation, the debugging of programs
became a frustrating and time-consuming process. A programmer might be
allowed only one test run a day or one run every several days. Programmers
found their schedules and lives controlled by machine availability.

A group of researchers in Project MAC at MIT began to work on a solution
of this problem, a solution that developed a new industry! There is a clear
mismatch between the speed with which humans think and mechanically enter
input or review output and the internal speeds of computers. Could we make
computer users feel that they have exclusive use of their own machine by rapidly
switching the computer from one user to another? One programmer's "think
time" would be used by the computer for serving other programmers. Each user
would share the time of the computer, especially the CPU and memory. This

---

A MANUFACTURING PACKAGE

*Gould, Inc., a diversified electronics firm, has installed a package program to control
production. The firm steadily reduced its inventory from 130 days supply to 89 days while
sales volume rose threefold. The applications package runs on-line and is accessed through
terminals. The system includes a bill of materials processor, inventory planning and
forecasting, inventory accounting, product costing, and shop order release.*

*The system is instrumental in materials requirements planning at any level of detail.
Before the system 25 percent of the dollar volume of inventory was distributed as
unplanned issues and the inventory shortage report was 20 pages long. The unfavorable
cost variance against standard in labor and materials was about 25 percent and profitability
one year declined for the first time.*

*Today the number of unplanned issues is small and the inventory shortage report is
less than 1 1/2 pages. Materials are at standard and labor and overhead variances reached a
favorable 50 percent necessitating a change in the standards. Pretax profits doubled in two
years. Improved inventory management held the unit cost of an item to the cost of 1 1/2
years earlier due to planned purchases from vendors in place of crisis buying.*

*The implementation of a major package like this requires a strong commitment from
management and cooperation throughout the company. The system is simple to use which
facilitates training. By using a package, the firm was able to implement a major application
in a relatively short period of time with impressive results.*

Data Processor, September/October, 1980.

---

special case of an on-line system provides the user with a computational capability and the ability to write and execute programs.

Early time-sharing systems required specially designed operating systems; Project MAC involved a few hardware modifications to a standard computer as well (primarily to add extra core memory).

The operation of early time-sharing systems is illustrated in Figure 8-4. In this representation only one program is executing at a time because there is only one central processing unit. A program executes for a short period of time until it is interrupted and "swapped" out of memory onto a secondary storage device (usually a drum).

Another user's program is swapped into primary memory and execution begins where it stopped when the program was previously swapped out of primary memory. In a simple round robin scheme, each user is given a maximum time slice in sequence. A program may be swapped out of primary memory even though it has used less than its time slice if it needs to send output or receive input, since these activities are handled by a data channel. The Project MAC computer could also run regular batch jobs simultaneously with time sharing; the CPU executed these tasks when not busy with time-sharing work (this is referred to as "background" processing).

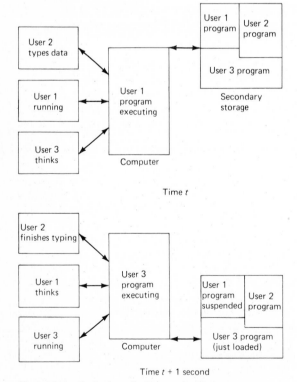

Figure 8-4   Early time-sharing processing.

The Third Generation

By the end of the second generation, most university and job-shop computer centers were using batch monitors, and the commercial time-sharing industry was becoming established. Many business users were also using operating systems for their second-generation equipment. When the third generation of computers was announced, manufacturers had clearly embraced the idea of an operating system. The IBM 360 line could not function without such a system; the operating system handles all input/output through interrupts. In fact, there are special instructions that can be performed by the computer only when it is in "supervisory state" under the control of the operating systems. These privileged instructions are unavailable to programmers, whose jobs run in the "problem state." The operating systems also require a certain amount of core for permanently resident routines. Other parts of the operating systems are stored on disk and brought into memory as needed.

Multisystems In our discussion of hardware we mentioned the development of data channels to take some of the I/O burden from the CPU. However, there was still an imbalance between CPU and I/O, even with channels. In most commercial systems with intensive input/output activities, we expect to find the central processing unit idle more than 50 percent of the time, primarily because it is waiting for input/output operations.

Third-generation batch operating systems introduced the concept of multiprogramming, a process very similar to the program-swapping techniques developed for time sharing. In multiprogramming, we have more than one program in a semiactive state in memory at one time; see Figure 8-5. Multiprogramming attempts to hide input/output latencies by switching the CPU to

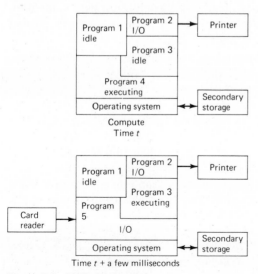

Figure 8-5 Multiprogramming.

another program when it can no longer process the one on which it is working because of an I/O request. In the top half of Figure 8-5 we see a multiprogramming scheme with four programs active. Just before time t, program 2 was executing; however it needed to print several lines on a report, and the CPU assigned this activity to a data channel.

The CPU then saved the status of program 2 and looked for another program on which to work. If many multiprogramming schemes, each program has a priority and in this instance the highest priority idle program would be executed. In Figure 8-5, assume that this is program 4.

The status of program 4 is restored from its last interruption and execution begins. When the data channel has completed the present operation for program 2, it interrupts the CPU, which stops program 4, saves its status, notes the completion of I/O for program 2, and checks to see what program to start next.

Assume program 2 has high priority, and the CPU therefore restores its status and executes it. Another interrupt occurs for output, and program 4 is resumed. Program 4 terminates and program 5 is loaded: execution begins but it is soon halted for input on a second data channel. The CPU now sees that it has only two candidates for work. Programs 2 and 5 are blocked; they are unready for execution because of I/O activities. The CPU has two programs ready, 1 and 3, and it chooses to execute program 3 according to preassigned priorities. The status of the system is shown now on the bottom half of Figure 8-5. Both data channels are active, one printing output for program 2 and the other reading input cards for program 5. In addition, program 3 is executing.

Multiprogramming has also provided spooling capabilities. Applications programs actually write their output to an output queue on a secondary storage device instead of directly to the printer. One system program schedules the printer and manages the output queue. Thus, a program is not held in memory because the printer is busy. Systems also spool input, for example, by putting cards in a disk input queue before beginning a job.

Multiprogramming has helped to increase throughput, the number of jobs processed per unit of time. However, it can take a single job longer to run under multiprogramming than under a unary processor (one job in the computer at a time) because of interruptions.

Multiprogramming should not be confused with multiprocessing. In a multiprogramming system, the central processing unit executes only one program at a time. Several programs are present in memory in a semiactive state; their execution has been suspended temporarily. Some third-generation systems also feature multiprocessing, the presence of more than one central processing unit. These processors are controlled by the operating system and, of course, are multiprogrammed since there is at least the potential for a program to be executing on each processor at the same time. In heavily compute-bound processing or for backup purposes, multiprocessor systems are often attractive. Several time-sharing systems, for example, employ multiprocessing.

MANAGEMENT PROBLEM 8-4

The president of Midwestern Bank is very concerned over the lack of progress on a new trust department computer system. This system is supposed to automate many of the clerical functions in the trust department. Instead of using a package, the bank decided to develop its own on-line system for use by clerks and trust officers.

However, the bank did acquire several packages to make the development of a custom-tailored on-line system easier. The bank has obtained a telecommunications control program, terminal input and output program, and data-base management program. However, it seems to require an inordinate amount of time to put all of the pieces together and construct the applications programs, as the computer staff calls them.

The president understands little about computer systems, but he does recognize that a tremendous investment has been made in the trust system. His computer staff complains that something known as the operating system is creating interface problems when attempts are made to install the packages. In addition, the applications programs do not work right, since the trust department keeps changing its specifications.

The president has asked you to help him understand what might be going wrong with the system. Are the excuses offered by the computer department reasonable? Is the trust department to blame for changing specifications? What action should the president take to put the project back on schedule?

On-Line Systems   During the third generation, operating systems came with more modules to facilitate the development of on-line systems, especially for supporting terminals and telecommunications processing. Systems were designed to support mixed batch processing and on-line inquiry. For example, a partition in a multiprogramming system could be devoted to an inquiry application while other partitions were devoted to batch processing. In this situation we assign the on-line partition a high priority since inquiries need to be answered quickly. Inquiries are also input/output intensive, which means they place a small burden on the CPU. Operating systems also facilitated the development of dedicated on-line systems during the third generation, for example, the airline on-line reservation package discussed earlier.

Time Sharing   During the third generation, Project MAC at MIT also developed a new time-sharing system called MULTICS. This system features an important innovation that influenced future computer systems. One goal of MULTICS was to provide the programmer with the appearance of a limitless memory, or a virtual memory several times larger than the actual memory. The Project MAC researchers also wanted to have pure procedures or reentrant programs. In such a program, several users execute the same program simultaneously. Each user does not need a separate copy of a reentrant compiler in memory, even though each is compiling separate programs.

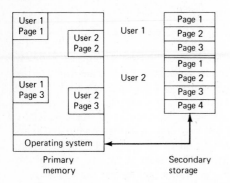

Figure 8-6   Paging.

Virtual memory can be produced by a combination of segmentation and paging, an approach that also facilitates the development of reentrant procedures. The idea behind this approach is shown in simplified form in Figure 8-6. Basically, a program and its data are broken into pages. Only the pages needed in primary memory at any one time are loaded; other pages are kept on secondary storage devices. In a demand paging scheme, a program executes in memory until it needs a page that is not in primary memory. A request for the page generates a page fault, and the supervisor locates and loads the needed page from secondary storage. In loading the page, the supervisor may replace an inactive page belonging to another program in primary memory. This entire process is transparent to the programmer, who sees a virtual memory as large as the total number of pages allowed, not the physical size of the computer's primary memory.

Paging also facilitates the sharing of programs. Figure 8-7 illustrates one possible scheme. Both users 1 and 2 are sharing the same program. A register loaded by the operating system points to the appropriate user data page (and a similar register points to the location of execution in the shared procedure). Data are accessed indirectly through this register. By switching user pointers in the register, user 1 can execute the same copy of the program; user 1 does not need a separate copy. Only the unique parts of user 1's and user 2's programs

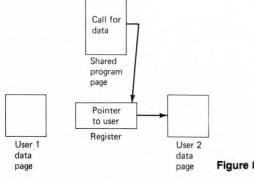

Figure 8-7   Sharing programs.

must be kept separate, for example, their data and place in executing the program. Shared code is also important in on-line applications and for the operating system itself. When multiple messages require the same applications program, only one copy needs to be in memory, thus precious primary memory space is saved.

Evolutionary Advances

The "third-and-a-half" generation of hardware brought improvements and modifications to operating systems. The major advance was to take virtual memory out of the exclusive domain of time sharing and include it in batch systems. To facilitate virtual memory schemes, one manufacturer added special hardware to help translate virtual addresses. Programs use addresses beyond the primary memory size of the computer in a virtual system, and it is necessary to map these addresses into physical memory space, as we saw in the discussion of time sharing. This mapping can be accomplished with software or hardware. (It should be noted that certain computer manufacturers offered this facility as early as the beginning of the 1960s. However, their machines were not widely used at the time.)

The mixing of systems continues with the third and fourth generations. Now we can have time-sharing, on-line, and batch applications all processing on the same computer system simultaneously. In addition, new packages are available to help reduce the problems of developing on-line systems. There are packages to handle inquiries and telecommunications tasks. These packages can be combined with data-base management systems, to be discussed in the next chapter, to facilitate the development of tailored on-line systems. Higher-higher level languages are also becoming available.

We have discussed the development of operating systems from a historical perspective. Where do we stand now? Madnick and Donovan (1974) present an insightful view of an operating system as a resource manager. The operating system consists of a series of managers, and each manager must accomplish the following: monitor resources; enforce policies on who, what, and how much of the resource is allocated; allocate the resource; and reclaim the resource. There are four major resource categories:

The *memory manager* keeps track of what parts of memory are in use and by whom, and what parts are free. In multiprogramming, this manager decides which process obtains what amount of memory at what point in time.

The *process manager* keeps track of the status of processes. It includes a job scheduler that chooses among jobs submitted and decides which one will be processed (it assigns resources like a CPU). The process manager must set up necessary hardware registers to allocate a CPU to a task and must reclaim the hardware at completion of the task.

The *device manager* monitors input/output resources, that is, anything connected to the computer through a data channel. It tries to schedule and allocate these resources efficiently.

The *information manager* controls the file system and its directories. Information must be protected, and this manager therefore sees that it is secure. The manager allocates and reclaims resources, for example, by opening and closing files.

Operating systems have become an integral part of computer systems and will continue to play a major role in the efficient utilization of computers. We are beginning to develop a better understanding of how operating systems should be designed, but there are many unresolved problems and operating systems are a topic of continuing research in computer science.

CONCLUSION

Software is the key to the expanded utilization of computers. As hardware becomes less expensive and more powerful, we shall continue to be constrained by the need to develop software programs for new computer applications. Programming can be a time-consuming and tedious task; however, in the space of two decades software has advanced and computer languages are becoming easier to use. There is still much to be done to remove the software bottleneck that exists in the computer field; but if users take advantage of some of the software tools that are available such as report generators, higher-higher level languages, and well-designed packages, they can accomplish a great deal.

KEY WORDS

Assembler	Macro	Queues
Assembly language	Mnemonic	Residency
Batch	Monitor	Shared code
COBOL	Multiprogramming	Source code
Compiler	Multiprocessing	Special-purpose language
FORTRAN	Object code	Spooling
Higher-higher level	Operating system	Subroutines
language	On-line system	Supervisor
Higher-level language	Packages	Translator
Interrupt	Paging	Variables
Instruction set	Partition	Virtual memory
Loader	Privileged instruction	
Machine language	PL/1	

RECOMMENDED READINGS

Boulden, J., and E. Buffa: "Corporate Models: On-line, Real Time Systems," *Harvard Business Review,* vol. 48, no. 4, July–August 1970, pp. 65–83. (A paper presenting several examples of how a higher-level planning language can be used to construct models for different organizations.)

Gries, D.: *Compiler Construction for Digital Computers,* Wiley, New York, 1971. (This advanced book gives a complete picture of modern compiler construction techniques.)

Madnick, S., and J. Donovan: *Operating Systems,* McGraw-Hill, New York, 1974. (A discussion of the features of modern operating systems containing many examples; the book is somewhat advanced.)

Nie, N., C. Hull, J. Jenkins, K. Steinbrunner, and D. H. Bent: *Statistical Package for the Social Sciences,* 2d ed., McGraw-Hill, New York, 1975. (This book describing the use of SPSS is one of the finest examples of system documentation extant.)

Sammet, J.: *Programming Languages: History and Fundamentals,* Prentice-Hall, Englewood Cliffs, N.J., 1969. (Catalogs and describes well over 100 higher-level languages.)

DISCUSSION QUESTIONS

1 What changes are needed in the simple computer designed in this chapter so that an assembler can be written for it?

2 What are the advantages of machine language and assembly language?

3 Why is programming such a time-consuming task?

4 Under what circumstances, if any, should managers ever write programs?

5 What are the advantages of standardized subsets of languages such as FORTRAN and COBOL, that is, a set of statements which is compatible across all compilers?

6 Develop a checklist of the factors to consider in evaluating a packaged program.

7 What is the major appeal of packaged programs for user departments? What is the major disadvantage of these packages for the information services department?

8 Computer science researchers have developed compiler compilers, that is, programs to help generate a compiler for a language defined by the user. What potential uses of such programs exist for information systems applications?

9 What are the advantages to using subroutines or other approaches to breaking up programs into small pieces?

10 How could knowledge of computer functions aid in developing a time-sharing application to support management decision making?

11 What was the motivation behind the development of operating systems?

12 How have time-sharing techniques influenced the development of operating systems?

13 What characteristics would be desirable in a text editor for an input program on a time-sharing system? How do needs differ for a novice user and an expert? How can these conflicting needs be resolved?

14 How does virtual memory contribute to the development of programs?

15 Where can problems occur with virtual memory? Under what conditions should we expect performance of a virtual memory system to be best? Worst?

16 What is the advantage of a simple programming language such as BASIC?

17 What factors influence the choice of a programming language for an application? Why should an organization have standards for languages?

18 Documentation (flowcharts, definitions of variables, etc.) describes a program. What is the benefit of documentation?

19 How should programs be tested? What types of data should be used and who should generate the data?

20 How has increased use of direct-access files enhanced the development of operating systems?

21 How has the widespread use of operating systems affected program testing?

22 How has time sharing aided program testing? To what extent can time sharing be used for testing programs? What limits its usefulness?

23 Remote batch processing systems often feature a text editor on-line (for example, a user can enter and edit a program from the terminal, submit the job for batch runs, and examine the printed output). What advantages does this provide for program development and testing? How does it compare with time sharing for this purpose?

24 What are the major advantages of special-purpose languages? How do they extend computer usage to more individuals?

25 Operating systems usually provide utility programs, such as file copy programs and sorting programs. Under what conditions should computer installations write their own sort programs instead of using one provided by a vendor?

26 What hardware and software characteristics are responsible for the overall performance of a computer system?

27 How can the quality of software be evaluated? What standards or measures can you suggest?

28 Various goals for programs have been found to influence programmer performance —goals such as minimum number of statements, minimal use of main memory, maximum output clarity, maximum program clarity, minimum number of runs to debug, and minimum execution time. Which of these goals are incompatible? Which ones should be emphasized by management?

29 Why is conversion from second- to third-generation computers so difficult? Why was emulation offered? What is the long-range solution to this type of conversion problem?

30 Does the extensive use of packages make it more or less difficult to change computer manufacturers? On what factors does the answer to this question depend?

31 It has been suggested that through microprogramming we can develop machines with a machine language of FORTRAN or some other higher-level language. What would be the advantages and disadvantages of such a computer?

32 By a combination of hardware and software it is possible to create virtual machines; that is, one computer operating system sets up separate computers for each user. Each user then chooses an operating system and proceeds to program applications on a virtual computer. What are the uses of such a system? What are the major problems?

33 What are the disadvantages of mixed processing in which batch, time-sharing, and on-line applications run simultaneously on the same computer system?

Computer Files, Data Structures, and Data Bases

FILE ELEMENTS
    Data
    Storage Devices
    Record Types
SEQUENTIAL FILES
    Storage Media
    Processing Sequential Files
DIRECT-ACCESS FILES
    Storage Media
    Processing Direct-Access Files
    More Complex Access
    Updating
ERROR CONTROL
DATA STRUCTURES
DATA-BASE MANAGEMENT SYSTEMS
    Complete Data-Base Systems
    An Example
FILE DESIGN CONSIDERATIONS
    Record Structure
    Response versus Cost
KEY WORDS
RECOMMENDED READINGS
DISCUSSION QUESTIONS
PROBLEMS

Chapter 9

Computer Files, Data Structures, and Data Bases

CHAPTER ISSUES

- What choices are available for computer files and data structures to support particular applications?
- Should the organization adopt a data base approach to design?

Files are the heart of a modern computer-based information system, and file design is the most technical topic we shall discuss in this text. Why should a manager care about files? First, in modifying an existing system, the structure of the files usually dictates the feasibility of a change. If we want added information on a report or a CRT screen, the cost of the change depends on whether the data we want are currently in a computer file or can be computed from data already in a file. If the data are not in a file and cannot easily be retrieved, the modifications will be more difficult and costly. To understand the requirements for a requested change, the user has to have knowledge of the file structure of the system.

In the next section, we discuss systems analysis and design and the crucial role users have to play in these activities. One of the main requirements for users to participate meaningfully in the design process is to have a basic understanding of computer files. Files are generally the first constraint we encounter in developing information systems. Sometimes the amount of data to be stored is too great for the capacity of the file storage devices to permit the desired response time. In other instances, complex information retrieval requirements for accessing the file make programs difficult to write or perhaps too large for the computer system.

From the standpoint of technology, files are the most important topic discussed in the text. If a manager understands input/output and files, there should be no mystery to computer-based information systems. A user with this knowledge should be able to make intelligent decisions about technical problems in the management of information systems.

FILE ELEMENTS

A file is a collection of data. A computer file is organized in some way; that is, there is some well-defined structure to the information in the file. A computer file consists of a collection of records, each of which is made up of fields. The various fields consist of groups of characters as described below.

Data

The smallest unit of storage of interest is the character, for example, the number 9 or the letter A. We generally do not work directly with characters, but rather with groups of characters that have some intrinsic meaning, for example, Smith or 599. These groupings of characters are called "fields" and we identify them with a name; for example, Smith is an employee's surname and 599 is Smith's department number.

Groups of fields are combined to form a logical record such as the one shown in Figure 9-1. This logical record contains all the data of interest about some entity; in this example it has all the data in the file about an individual employee.

A key to a record is some field of interest. In many files, we organize the file in order on a key. Last name is the primary key for a telephone book; that is, the telephone book is arranged in alphabetical order based on telephone subscribers' last names. We also can have secondary keys: in the case of the telephone book the secondary key is the first name or initial. The telephone book, then, is arranged in sequence on the primary key (last name) and within the primary key

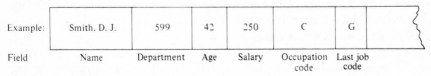

Figure 9-1   A logical record.

is arranged in order by the secondary key (first name). Fields designated as keys are also used as a basis for retrieving information from a file. For example, an inventory part number may be the key for retrieving information about the quantity of the part on hand from a computerized inventory file.

Storage Devices

Files of any size are usually stored on secondary storage devices. These devices are considerably cheaper than primary memory in the computer and have much greater capacity. We cannot expect to hold all the data in a file in primary memory. If we could hold these data in memory when the application is first installed, the amount of data processed for the application probably would expand over time beyond the capacity of primary memory. Therefore, most applications are designed so that any number of transactions can be processed and the files can expand in size.

Another reason for using secondary storage is that we probably do not want the data for an application to be available for computer access all the time. Secondary storage devices make it possible to store these data off-line at a reasonable cost. The off-line storage units can be mounted on a secondary storage device when we are ready to use them.

The mechanics of reading or writing data on secondary storage devices requires physical gaps between groups of characters. The number of characters actually transmitted between main computer memory and the file is called the physical record size. Between each physical record there is an interrecord gap, and we group logical records together to reduce the number of these interrecord gaps. For example, we might include 60 logical records in one physical record. This means that the blocking factor is 60; that is, there are 60 logical records blocked to form one physical record.

One reason for blocking records is to use space on the storage device more efficiently. Suppose the interrecord gap on a magnetic tape is 6/10 in. If we can record data at 1600 characters per inch, each gap could contain 960 characters if it did not have to be used as a gap. If a logical record were 500 characters long, grouping 60 together, we would have a physical record of

$$\frac{60 \text{ logical records} \times 500 \text{ characters/record}}{1600 \text{ characters/in.}}$$

$$+ \ 6/10 \text{ in. for a gap} = 19.35 \text{ in. of tape}$$

If the logical records were unblocked—that is, if the logical record were the same size as the physical record—we would have a physical record of

$$\left(\frac{500 \text{ characters}}{1600 \text{ characters/in.}} + 6/10 \text{ in. gap} \right) 60 \text{ records} = 54.75 \text{ in. of tape}$$

since there is one interrecord gap for each logical record. We would have used 35.4 in. more tape to store the 60 logical records by not blocking them.

More efficient utilization of space on the tape also means more efficient input and output operations. Since one physical record is transferred to main memory with each read (and the reverse on writing), blocking results in transfer of more information at one time and fewer read operations on the secondary storage device. The transfer rates of such devices are very fast, particularly when compared with the time required to being reading. Thus, reducing interrecord gaps by blocking increases both the utilization of the storage medium and the efficiency of input and output operations.

Record Types

Different applications require a variety of record types and file structures. One basic distinction is between fixed- and variable-length records. In a fixed-length record, we know the size of every field and the number of fields in the record in advance. We allow room for all the data that are of interest, as in the example in Figure 9-1. A new hire will not have a last job code and that field in Figure 9-1 would be blank. However, we do not expect many new hires compared with the total number of employees on the file, so that much wasted space is not a problem.

However, consider a system to keep track of patient visits to a medical clinic, type of test conducted, and results of the test. Assume that each test result can be described by 10 to 500 characters of data except for one test that requires 2000 characters of data. The patient also can have more than one test per visit. How could we possibly set up a fixed-length record for this system? Even if there were just one test per patient we could not afford to allow for 2000 characters of data in the record when only a few of the tests would ever need that much room.

The solution to this problem is a variable-length record; the number of fields and the length of a record do not have to be specified in advance. Of course, this adds to the complexity of our programs. Under a very general scheme for variable-length records, the program has to put a code in the record to identify what is there. In this example the record would have to specify what fields are present and the size of each field. We can carry either a single code at the beginning of a record or a code that indicates the contents of each field and its length before that field. In Figure 9-2 a code that precedes the record is shown. The first number in the code, 4, gives the length of the code in characters

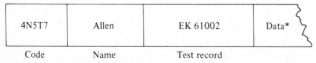

4N5T7	Allen	EK 61002	Data*
Code	Name	Test record	

Code length = 4
First name length = 5
Test name length = 7

*Another code could be used for the data on the test or there might be a standard format in the program for the data for each type of test.

Figure 9-2 A variable-length record code.

and the rest of the code tells what variables are present and how many characters were required to record each variable.

As an alternative, often we can specify several standard formats, each of a different length. That is, to avoid having to use codes, we may be able to establish three or four different formats of varying length, for example, 100 characters, 250 characters, and 2000 characters. Each of the formats for these records could be fixed in advance, but the combination of records for the file would be of varying length. There might be two records of 500 characters followed by one of 250 characters, etc.

We can see that this type of record structure adds complexity to file design and programming, but it does save file space. In some systems we lose space on the physical record in blocking variable-length records. There may be leftover space; for example, if the physical record is 1000 characters long and the sum of the variable-length records is 950 characters, it would be possible to waste 50 characters of space in the physical record. (Some systems will break a variable-length logical record into pieces to fill two physical blocks.)

Fortunately, another alternative to fixed- and variable-length records can be used if a problem is structured so there is a varying number of fixed-length records. As an example, consider a department store that wants to keep track of the departments where a salesperson has worked, the length of time on the job, department number, gross sales, and commissions while working in that department. In this example we have the same information for each department, but a clerk could work in several departments. One solution in designing a computer file for this information is to use header and trailer records (sometimes called master and detail records). We keep the benefits of fixed-length record processing by having header and trailer records of the same size, although it may be necessary to put the data for several departments in one trailer record. The header and trailer records are identified by a single code in Figure 9-3. There will be one header record for each employee along with a variable number of fixed-length trailer records.

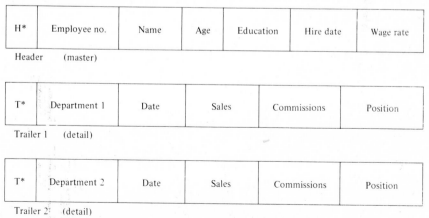

Header (master)

Trailer 1 (detail)

Trailer 2 (detail)

*Code identifying record type.

Figure 9-3 Header and trailer records of the same fixed length.

SEQUENTIAL FILES

The simplest kind of file is one in which all the records are in sequence according to some key, such as employee number, part number, etc. Many computer applications rely on sequential files, and although there is a trend to other types of files, sequential files will continue to be used heavily in the future.

Storage Media

Sequential files are most commonly associated with magnetic tape, but they can be supported on other file devices as well. In sequential files, the data are ordered on some key; for example, the telephone book is ordered on the last name, as we discussed earlier. It is also possible to have the file ordered on other keys, just as the telephone book uses a secondary key based on a subscriber's first name or initial.

A magnetic tape for computer storage is similar to the tape used on a home tape recorder. It has an underlying base that is covered with a magnetically sensitive coating. It is easiest to regard the tape as a matrix of bit positions, that is, nine rows or tracks of magnetic positions that can be either 1 or 0, stretching along the length of tape. Each character is represented by one column of bits: see Figure 9-4 (in this particular scheme eight bits are used to represent a character and one bit is used to check for errors).

The density of the tape is the number of characters that can be recorded in an inch, and is often referred to as bits per inch (which is really characters per inch). In the early days of computers, densities were quite low. In the late 1960s and early 1970s, 800 characters per inch was considered normal and 1600 characters per inch was classified as high density. Now tapes are available with a density of 6250 characters per inch.

Processing Sequential Files

Because sequential files are in a sequence (for example, numerical order) and must be kept in that sequence, much of sequential file processing involves

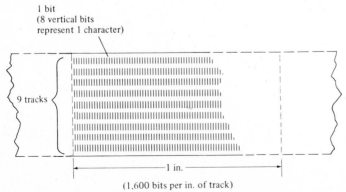

Figure 9-4 Schematic of a nine-channel tape showing capacity of 1600 bits per inch.

sorting data on some key. For example, all subscribers must be sorted on their last name and first name before a telephone book can be printed. There have been numerous books and articles written on various approaches to sorting (for example, Martin, 1971). Fortunately, most computer manufacturers supply sorting packages as a part of their operating systems. These packages are efficient and simple to use: all that is necessary is to indicate the fields, record sizes, and sort key, and to assign intermediate work areas for the sort to use.

Updating   A schematic for updating a sequential file is shown in Figure 9-5a. Since the master file is in order, input transactions must be sorted into the same order as the file before being processed. Note that a new file is created in the update process, since it is not good practice to try to read and write from the same tape file. (In fact, how could you possibly insert a new record and keep the tape in sequence?) The old file in the sequential update provides backup. If we keep the input transactions and the old file, any errors or the accidental destruction of the new tape can easily be remedied by running the update program again and updating the old file with the transactions.

On an update there are three possible actions. First, we can modify a record; that is, we can change some part of the record read from the old file and then put it on the new file. Second, we can add a record by placing it in proper sequence on the new file. Third, we can delete a record from the old file by simply not writing it on the new file.

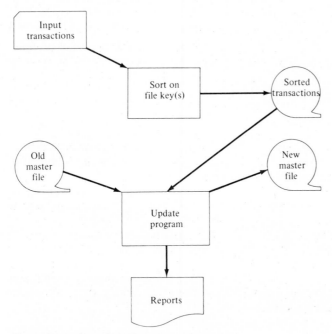

Figure 9-5a   Sequential file update schematic.

The logic of the sequential file update is complex because we should be able to add a record to the file, modify the new record by processing transactions against it, and delete the record, all on the same update run. (Consider someone who on the same day opens a bank account, writes several checks, and then closes the account.) This objective implies that transactions affecting a single record should be sequenced in the order of (1) add, (2) modify, and (3) delete. If there are nine types of transactions, transaction type 1 should be the creation of a new customer record, types 2 through 8 might be various other transactions that can occur, such as (in banking) deposits and withdrawals, and type 9 should be the delete. The transactions are processed in sequence by type number for each account.

The logic of a sequential file update is determined by the sequential nature of the file. The file must be maintained in sequence according to some key or keys. Incoming additions, modifications, and deletions must be in the same sequence as the file being updated. In the above banking example, the transaction file containing additions, modifications, and deletions to update the master file in the bank would be in exactly the same sequence by account number as the master file itself. Account number 10054 would appear on both files before account number 10056.

All transactions affecting the record for account number 10056 would be grouped together in the incoming group of transactions. The transactions affecting the record of account number 10056 should also be in order by transaction type. That is, the first transaction affecting 10056 would be an addition if this account number were being added to the file for the first time. Then all transactions of types 2 through 8 would appear, followed by transaction 9 if this record were to be deleted. Using this sequence for transactions, we cannot delete and add a record with the same key on the same run. For example, we are unable to close one account and assign that number to a new account on

---

MANAGEMENT PROBLEM 9-1

A small, special-interest magazine wishes to increase the number of issues published each year. Currently, the journal appears quarterly, but the editors desire to publish every other month. The magazine uses a computer system to print mailing labels and renewal notices. This old system is written in assembly language and allows only for the existing four issues a year. There seems to be no way to persuade the program to allow more frequent publication.

What do you think the original designer did in constructing the system to produce such inflexibility? How could the files have been designed originally to allow for more issues? Should the editors of the magazine try to modify the old system or develop a new one? What type of file design would you recommend if a new system is developed? How would the file design differ if the magazine decided to integrate the subscription system with an accounts receivable application?

---

the same run, since a delete has a higher transaction number than an addition and the transactions for each master file record are in ascending order by transaction number. Since the key is usually a field such as the account number or employee number, we would probably not want to reuse the deleted number immediately anyway.

An update program should be designed so that during the update, with proper authorization, it is possible to change any field in the record to correct errors. Of course, we cannot change the key field through a simple modification. Instead, if there is something wrong with a key, we delete the record with the wrong key and add a record with the correct key.

To place the transactions in the same order as the master file, we use a sort program as described at the beginning of this section. A utility sort program allows us to specify the keys and the order of the sort, either ascending or descending. Since we also want to have the transactions for each master file record in order by transaction number, we would specify a major and a minor (primary and secondary) sort key. For the above example, the major key would be account number and the minor key the transaction code. The sort program would produce as output a sorted transactions file with all transactions in the same order as the master file. Within the transactions affecting a single master file record, all transactions would be in order by transaction code.

An Example   The example in Figure 9-5b should help to clarify the logic of a sequential file update. The left column contains the record number of each record in the old master file. The center column contains the sorted record numbers of transactions: these transactions are sorted on record number as major sequence and transaction code as minor sequence. Finally, the right column shows the new master file.

To begin the update, the program reads an old master record, 110, and a transaction record, 115. By comparing these two numbers, the program knows that record 110 has no changes. (There is no transaction record less than 115 and since the file and transactions are in sequence, there is no transaction to modify

Old master file record number	Transaction			New master file
	Record	Code	Meaning	
110	115	1	Add	110
130	115	2	Modify	115*
150	130	2	Modify	130*
170	131	1	Add	150*
200	131	3	Modify	165
	131	9	Delete	170
	150	3	Modify	200
	165	1	Add	

*Refers to a modified record, that is, a record which has been updated by some transaction.

Figure 9-5b   Sequential file update example.

record 110.) Record 110 is written into the new master file and the program reads the old master record 130.

Because 130 is greater than the transaction record 115, the program knows that 115 must be the addition of a new record. (Any transaction with a key that does not match a key on the master file must be an addition or an error.) A check of the transaction code verifies that it is a new record, and the new record information is held in primary memory until there are no further transactions with the new record number 115. The next transaction is read and it does apply to the new record being constructed. The new record 115 is modified (indicated by an asterisk), and the next transaction is read.

This transaction is 130, so the program knows it can write the new record 115 into the new master file. Record 130 is already in memory and so transaction 130 is used to modify it. The next transaction is read, number 131. Because 131 is greater than 130, the program is done with record 130, and it can be written into the new master file. The old master file record 150 is read next. Record 131 is an addition to the file; the next transaction modifies this new record, and the last transaction affecting record 131 deletes it. A deletion is accomplished by simply not writing the deleted record into the new master file. The next transaction, this one affecting record 150, is read and used to modify record 150.

The program reads the next transaction, which affects record 165. Now record 150 can be written into the new master file and record 170 read. The transaction for record 165 adds it to the new master file and an end-of-file mark is encountered for the incoming transactions file. Therefore, the program only needs to copy old master file records into the new master file to complete the update.

Retrieval   Retrieval from a sequential file can be accomplished with a retrieval transaction request, and a retrieval report can be prepared during the update. If there is only one printer in the physical computer system, most operating systems allow multiple reports to be spooled for later printing, that is, to be placed on a secondary storage device and printed later. Even without this capability, one could put all the reports on a tape as the data are processed. If a report code is included on the tape, it can be sorted on the code and the different reports printed. Frequently, however, because we need complex retrieval logic that complicates the update program, or because we are using a file management package, we process retrievals in a separate run after updating the file.

One of the major disadvantages of sequential files on tape is the fact that we have to process the entire file to retrieve information. If only a few records are needed for retrieval, we still have to read the entire tape. Also, even if only a few records are changed during an update, it is necessary to update and rewrite the entire file.

DIRECT-ACCESS FILES

To overcome some of the problems above and to provide more rapid retrieval for on-line applications and more complex storage structures, direct-access files are used. These files allow more flexible file structures, but more work is required to use them.

Storage Media

The most common device for storing direct-access files is the magnetic disk (see Figure 9-6). One type of disk consists of a series of platters mounted on a spindle. The top and bottom of each platter (except for the very top and bottom ones) are coated with a magnetic material like that on a tape. Read and write heads are fitted between the platters. By moving the heads in and out we can access any track on the rotating disk. The maximum block size or physical record size for a disk file is limited by the physical capacity of each track. If the access arms do not move, each head reads or writes on the same track of each platter. Conceptually, these tracks form a cylinder, and, when using a disk file sequentially, we write on a given track of the first platter and then on the same track of the second platter and so on. This minimizes the access time since the heads do not have to move.

The total access time to read or write is made up of two components, seek time and rotational-delay time. Seek time is the time used in moving the read-write heads from one position to another. Rotational delay occurs because the data we want may not be directly under the read-write heads, even though they are located over the correct track. We have to wait for the disk to revolve to the beginning of the desired data.

A number of fixed-head disk drives often called head-per-track disks are also available. Since the largest component of average access time for a movable-head disk is seek time, fixed-head disks are considerably faster. For example, the average access time for one movable-head disk is 38 milliseconds, and, for the fixed-head counterpart, the average access time is 8 milliseconds. Recent trends in technology suggest that in the future we shall be moving more toward fixed secondary storage media and away from removable devices.

Each track on the disk has an address. Usually, manufacturer-supplied

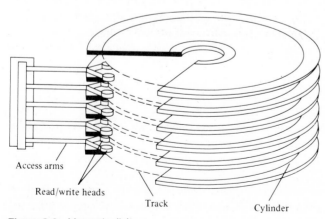

Access arms

Read/write heads

Track

Cylinder

Figure 9-6 Magnetic disk.

WEATHER MODELS

At Suitland, Maryland, forecasters use one of the largest computer centers in the United States to model and forecast the weather. The Center has three IBM Model 195 computers and some two dozen smaller systems for pre and post processing of weather data.

The simulation approach used for meterology divides the atmosphere into three dimensional units or rectangular blocks. These blocks cover the globe in two dimensions and extend vertically over 50,000 feet from sea level. Data describing the atmospheric conditions at the center of the block are derived from data for each of the block's corners. The two dimensional horizontal coordinates of the blocks form a grid which covers the area being examined by the researcher.

The third dimension of the imaginary block is the vertical level or layers into which the modelers divide the atmosphere. For example, a ten layer model would be one in which at any point there are ten imaginary blocks stacked on each other. Increasing the number of levels or decreasing the mesh size causes significant increase in the size and the power of the computer necessary to process the model.

Twice each day Worldwide Weather data is collected by airplane, ships, satellites and ground stations, and sent to Suitland. In addition to these data, the meterology service receives information from over 5,000 weather stations throughout the world four times per day. The Coast Guard sends ocean data; ocean buoys and over 2,500 ships provide data, and there are 1,200 observations from worldwide aircraft coming in about every six hours. Data are also received every two hours from polar orbiting synchronous satellites; two geostationary satellites provide data every half hour as well. Some 500 weather charts and 2,000 frames of digital facsimile are distributed to 52 regional forecast offices and 250 smaller service offices each weather forecasting cycle.

Meterorologists are convinced that if the resolution of current models could be doubled, there would be a dramatic improvement in the usefulness and accuracy of the resulting information. For this reason, large super computers are needed to solve weather models.

Datamation, May, 1978.

---

software lets us specify a file and record size and then retrieve a specific record. The records are numbered 1 through n, where n is the number of records in the file. Thus, we can treat a file as consisting of a group of separately numbered records without concern over the physical track address where the record is stored. The software associates the track address with a logical record and finds the desired record for us.

Processing Direct-Access Files

Basics There is no reason why the direct-access file cannot be processed sequentially in the same manner described in the last section for tape files. In fact, in many applications we update sequentially and retrieve records by direct access.

When processing the files directly, how do we locate the record wanted? If we request a record number, the file management software will supply it for us. However, we must associate the logical record number with the information desired. For example, in an inventory application, how do we know where information on inventory part number 1432 is located? What logical record contains data on part 1432? One solution is to begin at the first record on the file and read each record until we find part 1432, but this is simply scanning the file sequentially, which has no advantage over tape processing.

To relate a key of interest (part number 1432) to a logical record on the file, a directory is used. The directory is like a map that tells us where a particular address is located in a city. The problem of finding the location of a record for a particular key is called the key-to-address transformation problem. We have the value of a field, the key (part number 1432), and we want the record number (address) where the logical record with this key is located.

Direct   There are three basic methods or types of directories for transforming a key to an address. The first is called the direct method and is rarely applicable. Here we let the key be the address; for example, part number 10 is stored on record 10. It is not often that an application occurs where this approach is possible. Possibly in setting up an entirely new system we could assign a part number to the inventory and use the number as a record address.

Dictionaries   The second method for key-to-address transformation, called the dictionary approach, is probably the one used most often. A dictionary (a table in memory) relates keys to their location, for example:

Key	Dictionary entry	Record address
1432	1432-312	312
4293	4293-137	137

We search the dictionary in primary memory (which is several orders of magnitude faster than searching the disk itself) looking for the key. The dictionary entry tells at what record that key is located.

In the case of a very large file, the dictionary may become so big that it is stored on the disk file. Parts of the dictionary are brought into primary memory for searching. We usually try to keep dictionaries in order, so that it is not necessary to search them sequentially. A binary or some other rapid search is used to reduce search time.

In a binary search we divide the dictionary in half and compare the middle entry with the value of the key. If the key is in the bottom half of the table then we divide the bottom half in half. A comparison of this entry and the key indicates in what quarter of the dictionary the key is located. With each successive comparison, we reduce the number of possible dictionary entries in half. By the third comparison we look at one-eighth of the dictionary. When there are only a few entries left, it is possible to search sequentially. Remember that the key may not be in the dictionary because there is no record with this key in the file! (For example, information may be requested on a part number that is not stocked in inventory.)

When the dictionary is in order and we use a binary search, the need to store the dictionary on disk because it is so large is no problem. The various breakpoints—the value of the key in the dictionary at the ½, ¼, ⅛ positions, and so forth—are kept in primary memory. Then, the search key is compared with these numbers and the appropriate one-eighth, say, of the dictionary is brought into memory for searching. In this way, we have formed what can be considered a hierarchical directory. That is, a limited amount of information is maintained in primary memory as a directory to a more detailed directory on the disk.

Hashing   The final key-to-address transformation technique is randomizing or hash coding. Here we gain access speed at the expense of storage space. Randomizing refers to performing some calculation with the key and using the result of the calculation as an address. Clearly, there is no guarantee that the computation will not result in the same address for two different keys. Such an occurrence is called a "collision," and the keys with the same address are called "synonyms." In the case of collisions, we can recalculate the address or we can look for the next open record in the file and put the data there. For this approach to work we need a file with many open locations, or eventually processing will become sequential. Experience indicates that a file 50 percent larger than the total number of records is necessary for this approach to work.

Collisions or synonyms create a problem when hashed files are modified. Assume that we have a hashed file and are using the next sequential location that is available on the file for collisions. If two keys hashed to logical record 2365, and if record 2366 were empty, the second of the two incoming records would be placed at record 2366 on the file. Later, suppose that the first record, which was actually stored at file record 2365, is to be deleted. If we physically remove this record from the file, we shall "lose" the record at file location 2366!

This situation occurs because both records had the same address after hashing. The collision of keys forced us to put the second record in an adjoining location, 2366. When the second record is requested, it will still hash to 2365. When we examine location 2365 in the file, we find it empty and assume that the second record is not in the file. Thus, physically deleting the first record has destroyed the path to the second.

To solve this problem, we can simply use a delete indicator (a field we establish in each record) to signal whether a record is to be deleted. Periodically, the file is restructured physically, deleted records being dropped and all records being reassigned to new locations on the file. Now, when we try to retrieve the second record, we find the first record at location 2365 in the file. Since the key of this first record is not the one wanted, we look at the next sequential record at location 2366. Since its key matches the one for which we are looking, the desired record has been located. Later, when the file is restructured, the first record, with the delete indicator set, would be dropped and the second record would be stored at location 2365 in the new file.

One of the most frequent computations used in randomizing is to divide the key by the largest prime number smaller than the file size in records and use the

Table 9-1a File Example

Record no.	Part no.	Assembly	On hand	Vendor
1	4326	103	27	ACME
2	6742	607	51	JOHNSON
3	8137	12	100	DAWES
4	3218	103	13	FRAZIER
5	3762	607	43	ARMOR

remainder as the record address. The object of any transformation technique is to have a distribution of addresses that results in the minimum number of collisions. As an example, if a file had 1000 records the divisor would be 997. A key of 3722 would give a quotient of 3 with a remainder of 731, and 731 would become the record address for storage purposes.

More Complex Access

So far in the discussion of direct-access files, we have talked about how to locate a unique primary key such as an inventory part number. (This key is unique because there would be only one part with a given number.) More complex structures are also possible with direct-access files. For example, we can ask questions about how many parts are needed for a particular assembly and obtain a response. Clearly, all the same things could be accomplished with tape files and sorting, but the time and processing required would be inordinate.

Consider an inventory example in which it is desired to keep track of what parts belong in what assembly. This situation is depicted in Table 9-1a, and we wish to define a file structure to answer questions such as what parts in inventory are used to build assembly number 103. To find all parts used in assembly 103 it is possible to read each record and see if the assembly field is equal to 103. In Table 9-1a we read record 1, which is used in assembly 103. Then we read records 2 and 3 without finding assembly 103. We find it again at record 4, and so on. Clearly, this process is not very efficient; there could be a hundred records between each occurrence of assembly 103.

To avoid this reading time we use a pointer, which is a piece of data whose value points to another record; in this case it points to the next record where assembly 103 is found. The inclusion of pointers in the file is shown in Table 9-1b. The pointer in record 1 points to the next occurrence of assembly 103 in

Table 9-1b File Example

Record no.	Part no.	Assembly	On hand	Vendor	Pointer
1	4326	103	27	ACME	4
2	6742	607	51	JOHNSON	5
3	8137	12	100	DAWES	13
4	3218	103	13	FRAZIER	42
5	3762	607	43	ARMOR	106

record 4. Now, when looking for assembly 103, we retrieve record 1 and examine the pointer field; it tells us that the next occurrence of assembly 103 is at record 4. We follow the chain of pointers through the file to answer the retrieval question of what parts belong in assembly 103. This type of file structure is known as a "linked list" or a "chained file."

How do we find the record of the first part in assembly 103? We could read the file sequentially, but there might be 500 or 600 records before the first part in assembly 103 is located. This problem is easily solved using a directory like the one in Table 9-1c. This directory simply points to the first part contained in assembly 103: first we retrieve this record and then follow the chain of pointers in each record through the file.

It is also possible to remove the pointers from the file and put them all in the directory, which is then called an inverted directory, as shown in Table 9-1d. If there are multiple chains, questions can be answered, without accessing the file, just by processing the directory. Suppose that the file also has a directory for vendors, with the vendor ACME located in records 1, 16, and 42. By examining the directories for part and vendor, we see that Acme supplies two parts for assembly 103, since both ACME and assembly 103 can be found in records 1 and 42. All this processing can be done with the two directories without ever accessing the file! However, the price for this added flexibility is increased programming complexity and the need to create and maintain complex directories.

How are the directories and links built in the first place? One possibility is to use the program written to create the file originally. In creating the file, a program maintains a table in memory containing each part number. When the part number is encountered, the program places a pointer in the file to the last location in the file containing this part number and updates the pointer table. When the program is finished, the table becomes a directory and the pointers run backward through the file.

In the example of Table 9-1a the program keeps a list of inventory part numbers in primary memory. On encountering part number 103 in record 1, the program places a 0 in the pointer field of the record and a 1 in the record address portion of the directory. Processing is done the same way for records 2 and 3 (assemblies 607 and 12). When the program encounters assembly 103 at record

Table 9-1c Directory for Assemblies	
Assembly	Record
12	3
25	212
103	1
104	62
607	2

Table 9-1d Inverted Directory for Assemblies	
Assembly	Record
12	3, 13 . . .
25	212 . . .
103	1, 4, 42 . . .
104	62 . . .
607	2, 5, 106 . . .

MANAGEMENT PROBLEM 9-2

Scientific Laboratories, Inc., is interested in developing a new computer system to aid its researchers. Most of the members of the company are natural scientists engaged in basic research; these individuals place heavy demands on the library and support services. Currently the company uses a service bureau to develop and print a KWIC (Keyword in Context) index of articles.

This rather simple approach takes each major word in the title and alphabetizes articles on it. Thus, the same article may appear many times in the listing, once for each keyword that is major. As an example, consider a paper "The Use of PVC's and Diseases of the Lungs, Pancreas, and Liver." This article would appear five times in the KWIC index under PVC, Diseases, Lungs, Pancreas, and Liver.

The company would like to develop a more sophisticated retrieval system for the research staff. They would like to have a system that allows Boolean retrieval requests. For example, a researcher could ask for all papers that discuss PVC's and diseases of the lungs, pancreas, and liver. Such complex logic makes it possible to formulate a very specific retrieval request. The system should also be able to retrieve on journal and author's name. The library staff would provide keywords and abstracts of the papers that would be stored on-line. Copies of the articles would be available in filing cabinets in the library, and their location would be referenced by the abstract displayed on a CRT for the user.

You have been asked to sketch the basic file structures for such a system. What kind of files and keys would you choose? Show how retrieval requests would be processed.

4, it places the pointer from the directory (1) into the pointer field of record 4. Now, record 4 points back to record 1. Then the program updates the directory record address field to 4, and the directory points to record 4, which points to record 1. When finished, the record address field in the directory points to the most recent occurrence of assembly 103. That record points backward through succeeding records until the chain ends at record 1 with a pointer of 0. Another alternative to developing pointers in the file is to use a packaged software system. We shall discuss this topic later under data-base management systems.

Updating

Updating a direct-access file can be done randomly (direct) or sequentially. However, if we update on-line, then only the records that are actually changed need to be modified; it is not necessary to process the entire file. The disadvantage of this approach is that it is easy to lose an audit trail; records are changed and there is no backup copy as there is in the sequential update. To keep an old version of the file it is necessary to copy (dump) the file on some other storage medium, such as another disk file or tape.

What happens to pointers when records are added to, modified, and deleted from a direct-access file? Suppose part number 3218 in Table 9-1 is changed to assembly 607 from assembly 103. Can we just modify the assembly field in record 4? If it were not for the pointer chains running through the file, the answer to the question would be "yes." However, the modification would destroy the chain of pointers (see Figure 9-7). We could change the pointers, but in performing an update on record 4 we would have to know that the previous pointer was located at record 1.

Three choices are available. First, the program can look up assembly 103 and trace the chain of pointers through the file to find the one pointing to record 4. In this case, the program would change the pointer of record 1 from 4 to 42. Here we were lucky to find the record of interest on the first try; on the average, we would expect to follow a chain of pointers through half the file to locate the pointer immediately preceding the record to be changed.

A second alternative is to design the file with backward pointers for the assemblies; for example, a pointer from record 4 to record 1. Then, both sets of pointers have to be changed, but it is necessary only to access the three records that are involved for each change. This solves the problem of changing assembly 103. Here we save processing time at the cost of secondary storage and extra programming logic.

The third choice is to set a delete indicator and leave the record in the file just as we did with hash coding. In this case, we set a delete indicator at the old part number 3218 in record 4 and add a new record for part 3218 showing 607. Then we periodically restructure the file: the old file becomes input to the original file-creation program, which eliminates records with delete indicators and sets up new pointer chains and directories.

Any of these three choices solves the problem of modifying record 4 while

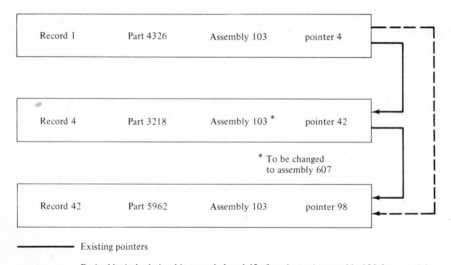

——————— Existing pointers

— — — — Desired logical relationship records 1 and 42 after change in assembly 103 for record 4

Figure 9-7 Changing chained files.

MANAGEMENT PROBLEM 9-3

Betty Martin, marketing manager for Interland Express Company, was amazed at the memorandum she had just received from the information services department. She had asked to have sales information for the company available for inquiry. In particular, she had wanted to know the performance for each sales representative and to retrieve information on sales by customer.

The information services department said that they had all these data, but they were not available on the right files. Betty did not understand exactly what this meant. The computer group went on to say that the data on sales were stored on a "sequential tape file"; her request would require the use of several sort programs and would produce two massive reports.

Betty knew that the company had just installed a new on-line retrieval system and asked why the data she wanted could not be made a part of that system. The information services department responded that this addition could be done but would require the design of new files and retrieval commands. The new files would be on disk and would require two directories, one on sales representatives and the other on customers.

Betty Martin was now completely perplexed. Could you explain to her the alternatives available to the computer staff in meeting her request? What are the pros and cons of each alternative? Which do you expect to be most expensive? Which is most responsive to Betty's needs?

---

maintaining the assembly 103 pointer chain. The last step is to modify record 4 and add assembly 607 to its chain. We can add assembly 607 to its chain simply by making the directory now point to it and letting its pointer field point to the old directory entry. That is, the directory record field for assembly 607 would now be 4 and the pointer in the new modified record 4 would be 2.

ERROR CONTROL

In any file operation, we should provide for some kind of backup. In a sequential or a batch system, backup is produced automatically. For an on-line system, we have to dump the files periodically if they are not updated sequentially.

Processing controls are also necessary to ensure the integrity of the file. An edit should be performed on each transaction to see if all numeric fields are filled with numeric data and to pinpoint transactions or data coding errors. It is also useful to include upper- or lower-bounds checks for reasonableness. Such a check specified by a user might be to determine if the number of items received is less than two times the number ordered. The program should keep processing but should issue notices that an error may have been made. Sometimes a record is flagged to ensure that a change is made on the next update.

For fields that are particularly crucial on the file, it may be desirable to verify all changes. For example, the program updating the file could carry a summary record at the end of the file with various totals on it. In the example used here, we could keep a total on the number of parts in inventory on a record at the end of the file. During file updating, the program would add all parts, keeping track of additions and usage. At the completion of the update, the summary record would be examined to determine if the old figure adjusted for additions and usage matches the new one.

DATA STRUCTURES

Data structures are the physical and logical relationships among records in computer files. A physical data structure is simply the way data are actually found on a storage device. In a sequential file all records are located in a linear sequence; they are usually related logically according to a sequence based on some key field. On a direct-access device, the physical data structure might include some directory records at the beginning of a physical location followed by portions of the record with data.

Of more interest to the analyst are logical data structures. We can develop many different logical structures to support different types of processing applications. In fact, we have seen several logical structures earlier in the chapter but have studied these primarily from the combined view of logical and physical structuring. For example, we indicated how we would include pointers and directories in a file. A completely logical view would simply have used arrows to show the connections among different fields. In designing physical data structures, we are concerned with how to represent best the desired logical structures on physical storage devices.

We have seen a list structure earlier in the chapter. We can redraw that structure as shown in Figure 9-8 to emphasize the logical relationship among records. The inverted list looks almost the same from logical considerations, but the actual implementation differs since the pointers are now in the directory rather than in the actual data records. A more complex structure with two lists is shown in Figure 9-9.

A list can easily be extended to become a ring as shown in Figure 9-10. In a ring the last record in a list points back to the first record of the ring, which contains a special symbol to show that it is first. One can follow the ring to find any record, for example, the preceding record, the next record, or the first record of the ring. One can also use a ring with connections in each direction (Dodd, 1969).

Three major types of data structures are generally defined in the literature today: hierarchical, plex or network structure, and a relational file.

A hierarchical file is a case of a tree structure as shown in Figure 9-11. The tree is composed of a hierarchy of nodes; the uppermost node is called the root. With the exception of this root, every node is related to a node at a higher level called its parent. No element can have more than one parent, though it can have more than one lower-level element called children. See Martin (1977).

A hierarchical file is one with a tree-structure relationship between the records, for example a master detail file with two record types. Such a

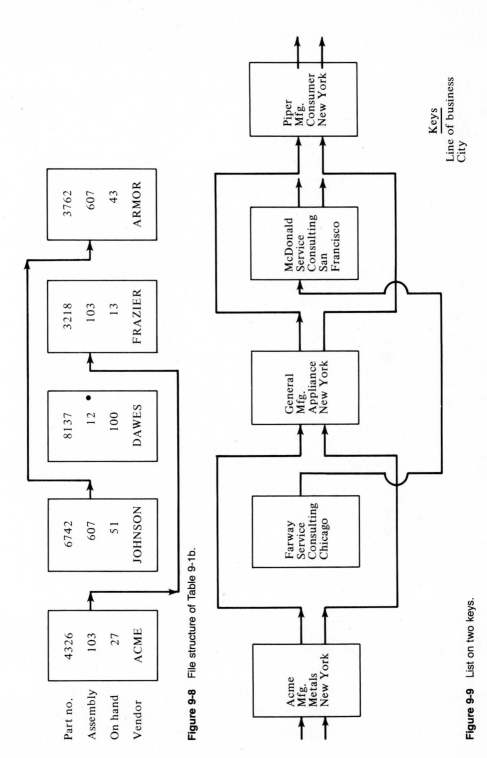

Figure 9-8 File structure of Table 9-1b.

Part no.	4326	6742	8137	3218	3762
Assembly	103	607	12	103	607
On hand	27	51	100	13	43
Vendor	ACME	JOHNSON	DAWES	FRAZIER	ARMOR

Acme Mfg. Metals New York	Farway Service Consulting Chicago	General Mfg. Appliance New York	McDonald Service Consulting San Francisco	Piper Mfg. Consumer New York

Keys
Line of business
City

Figure 9-9 List on two keys.

223

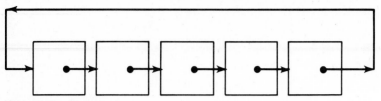

Figure 9-10   Ring structure.

representation is often very convenient because much data tend to be hierarchical in nature or can easily be cast into this structure.

A network or plex structure exists when a child in a data relationship has more than one parent. An item in such a structure can be linked to any other item; see Figure 9-12. Martin (1977) discusses simple plex structures in which the child-to-parent mapping is simple; that is, arrows do not go in both directions. The physical data structure to support complex plex structures are far more difficult to develop than for simple structures. An examination of Figure 9-12 should show the reasons for this difficulty.

There has been much research on yet a third type of data structure called "relational." The underlying concept of a relational file system is very simple; data are organized in two-dimensional tables such as the one in Figure 9-13. Such tables are easy for a user to develop and understand. One virtue of this

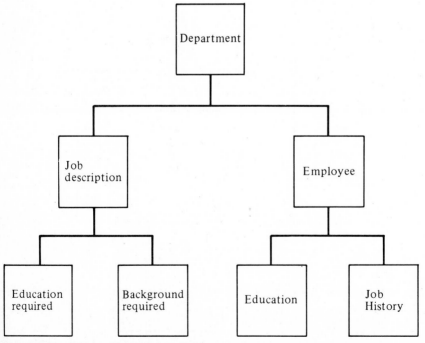

Figure 9-11   A tree or hierarchial structure.

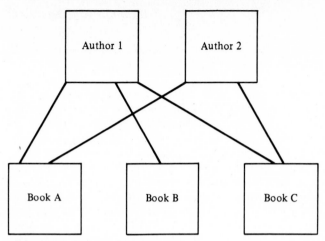

Figure 9-12 A plex structure.

Name	Address	Zip Code	City	Department no.
Smith	16 Main	92116	New York	302
Jones	37 Spencer	07901	Chicago	161
Morris	19 Old Way	83924	New York	302
Able	86 Fulton	10006	Denver	927
Charles	19 Hunter	11126	Chicago	161

Name	Profession	Income
Johnson	Bartender	15,000
Martin	Programmer	14,000
Jones	Systems Analyst	18,000
Carson	Manager	17,000
Smith	Systems Analyst	19,000

Join:
Name,	Address,	Zip Code,	Profession,	Income
Jones	37 Spencer,	07901,	Systems Analyst,	18,000

Project:
City,	Department
New York	302
Chicago	161
Denver	927

Figure 9-13 A relational data base.

SALES ALLOCATION

The Bell Telephone System which consists of 23 operating telephone companies has telecommunication service sales in an excess of $2 billion annually. A sales information and allocation system has been developed to help increase revenues from the sale of these services by identifying communications solutions to key business problems.

The data base for the system consists of business accounts and specific marketing information along with current communications billing data. The file system is structured so that location specific data can be linked together to form a corporate family, for each customer, that is, the relationship between corporate headquarters, subsidiaries and branches can be identified. These location specific data are merged with billing data from the operating phone company.

The combined file of data is then analyzed statistically. Profiles are built describing the characteristics of high potential businesses, and an analysis is performed to determine the sales potential of each business enterprise in the data base. Sales potential is defined as the difference between the expected revenue for a given service and the actual revenue being billed. Expected revenue is computed by estimating the revenues to be generated if the service is sold and multiplying this value by probability that a sale will be made. The system uses a number of statistical models, including nonlinear regression, for the purpose of estimating revenues.

The total file of some 5 million records is sorted first by sales region, then by potential within a given sales region. For each sales region, sales resources that are available are entered into the system. These sales resources are the number of field contacts and the direct telephone mail budget available in the region. The system allocates the highest potential sales to the highest cost sales action, for example, a direct field contact. Each lower potential sales lead is allocated to less expensive sales actions, direct telephone or mail contact. The philosophy behind the allocation is that the highest revenue potential businesses should receive the highest cost sales actions. The system actually prints field sales contact forms for each high potential direct contact lead. For other contacts, a direct telephone mail list is produced.

The system includes the capability to track performance. When the sales person completes a call, an evaluation of the type of sale and quantity of sale can be made. The sales person completes a customer tracking form to provide these data. Telephone interviews are also conducted later on a sample of customer classes to obtain their reactions to the sales contact. Billing data provides a final confirmation of whether or not a sale has been made.

In a pilot program, 71 out of 652 businesses contacted directly were sold communications products. For these 71 customers there was almost $1 1/2 million additional revenue generated or nearly $20,000 per sale. The actual average revenue per sale of businesses contacted during the same period was $8,300, so the model is directing sales efforts to accounts with the highest potential.

Interfaces, August, 1978.

type of structure is that it can be described mathematically, a most difficult task for other types of data structures. The name is derived from the fact that each table represents a relation.

Since different users see different sets of data and different relationships between them, it is necessary to extract subsets of the table columns for some users and to join tables together for others to form larger tables. The mathematics provides the basis for extracting some columns from the tables and for joining various columns. Martin (1977) argues that this capability to manipulate relations provides a flexibility not normally available in hierarchical or plex structures.

The subject of data structures is extremely complex and a number of good references are devoted entirely to this topic. The important thing for the analyst to realize is that there are many ways to represent different logical data structures. The flexibility and relatively low cost of direct-access storage make it possible to develop very complex logical data structures to support information systems. As we shall see in the next section, software exists to help implement many of these complex structures in a generalized manner.

DATA-BASE MANAGEMENT SYSTEMS

The objective of a data-base management system is to facilitate the creation of data structures and relieve the programmer of the problems of setting up complicated files. Data-base management systems have developed from a concept of the data base as something distinct from the programs accessing it. In addition to easing processing, this approach has tended to highlight the importance of data as a resource in the organization and as something that has to be carefully managed.

Most data-base management systems have grown from simple file-accessing aids and retrieval packages. The early file-management packages operated on sequential files. Users described the file records, and a retrieval language was used to express complex logical relationships among fields for retrieval. Many of these packages have been extended to include updating capabilities, thus eliminating the need to write a detailed program for retrieval and substituting a much higher-level, user-oriented language instead.

As direct-access files became more common, several vendors offered file-access packages for use in writing programs in computer languages such as COBOL. One of these accessing methods is known as the indexed sequential access method, or ISAM. This software package allows the COBOL programmer to develop a program to update and retrieve information from a direct-access file with a single access key without having to construct a directory or write search routines. The ISAM software maintains a directory (a dictionary in this case) for each record. The application program supplies a key, and the system retrieves the record. The current version of this package is called VSAM and it represents a major improvement in the system.

The software maintains overflow areas and pointers to keep the file in order sequentially. Thus, updating can be done sequentially, and retrieval can be accomplished on a direct-access basis. This type of file has been very popular because it is possible to update in batch but inquire on-line. As a file gets out of order and the overflow areas are filled, it is periodically necessary to restructure the file. Statistics are provided by the software as to when this updating is advisable. Simple access methods such as this and file-management packages have evolved into much more complex data-base management systems.

Complete Data-Base Systems

A data-base management system is a piece of software that allows an organization to develop data-base applications. The software automates many of the tasks of the programmer in setting up a data base and processing it.

A complete data-base management system separates the definition of data from the programs that access it. A new position is usually created in the organization that adopts data-base software, that of the data-base administrator. This individual is responsible for the definition and integrity of the data.

If a data-base system is to be used widely in an organization, it is mandatory that similar items be referred to by the same name. It would not be possible to call salary SALARY in one program and GROSS PAY in another, if both programs are referring to the same data on a file. For many organizations, the need to develop a common dictionary of data items is one of the largest costs in adopting data-base software. Various tools, such as data dictionaries, help in this process. In fact, some firms have acquired data-dictionary systems and begun work on them long before acquiring data-base management software.

The data-base administrator, or programmers, must use a special data-definition language with the data-base management system to describe the data and file structures to the system. Martin (1977) has described some of the characteristics a good data-definition language should have, which of course implies what characteristics a good data-base management system should include.

The language must identify various subdivisions of data, for example, items, segments, records, and files. There should be unique names for each data-item type, record type, file type, data base, etc. The language should specify how data items are grouped in aggregates, records, or other subdivisions and show repeating groups of items. The language must make it possible to designate data items as keys. It is also necessary to specify how various subdivision or record types are related to make different logical structures, and it should be possible to give names to relationships among data groupings. Martin also describes additional capabilities that the language may possess, including the specification of privacy locks to prevent unauthorized reading or modifications. He also argues that the language should be concerned only with logical data description, not specific addressing, indexing, or searching techniques or the placement of data on physical storage. These topics belong to the physical definition of the files, not the logical (Martin, 1977).

Given the data definition and the data base, the data-base management system constructs all pointers, linkages, and directories automatically. The applications program issues calls for the data it desires. The data-base management system examines the data request and determines where the records of interest are located; it returns the entire record or the field requested to the calling program. These systems also generally have a query language that facilitates data-base inquiry and report generation for data contained in the system.

With one of these systems, it is possible to design file structures much more easily and to set up a data base that can be used by a number of different applications programs. As a result the systems increase programmer productivity. These systems also try to avoid data redundancy; the same data are not maintained by a number of different systems, each having different files.

Data-base management systems can be very difficult to learn to use and install. As one can imagine, they are very complex programs and they tend to be inefficient in computer time and costly in storage. However, the importance of these costs is being reduced by the need for greater programming productivity. Machine costs are getting cheaper while human costs are getting higher.

Firms may also find it wasteful to have a significant proportion of their data on-line all the time. It really may not be desirable to integrate the data base, at least for some infrequently accessed data. However, new mass-storage devices are being developed and marketed that will reduce storage costs to the extent that we can afford to have huge amounts of data nearly on-line. For example, one of these devices uses disks as a staging area; some 472 billion characters of data can be stored with an average access time of around 10 to 20 seconds for the data to be transferred to a disk pack.

Many organizations have achieved impressive results using data-base management systems. However, it is necessary to study and evaluate the systems carefully. If you do not need the most complex system, do not acquire it. Clearly, the future trend is to use data-base management packages to save

---

MANAGEMENT PROBLEM 9-4

Marvin Thompson is president of Midwestern Bank and Trust. He has just returned from a bankers' convention at which the major topic was data-base systems. Midwestern has been studying the problem of central files for several years. The idea of a central file is to consolidate all the information about a customer of the bank. Currently, one system maintains data on loans to commercial customers, another one keeps track of demand deposits, a third keeps track of savings and certificates of deposit, and so forth.

The major advantage of central files is the better service they allow. The bank knows the total business picture of any given customer. However, as with any new system, there are disadvantages. Several representatives at the convention indicated that data-base management systems were not a panacea for computer problems. Because so much data were resident on expensive direct-access storage, costs were very high for central files.

Marvin wondered what major factors to consider in deciding whether or not Midwestern should move toward a central file system. If the file system is to be developed, should the bank program its own data-base routines or acquire a commercial data-base management package? What factors should it consider? Can you help Marvin structure the bank's decision problem?

---

programmer, analyst, and implementation time. Currently, there are few standards and there are wide differences among the packages. It is best to look at present and planned applications and then use references supplied by the package vendor to talk with other users. Try to determine the good and bad points of each package under consideration. For a discussion of various selection factors for data-base management systems, see Merten and Sibley (1973).

An Example

The different data-base management systems offer a variety of file structures, though the same file problem can usually be solved with the structure of each system. One data-base management system features two kinds of files, a master and a variable file. The master is accessed on some key and linked to the variable file. Within the variable file, associations among entries are linked by pointers.

Figure 9-14 shows examples of different logical file structures represented with this plex scheme. At the top of the figure we see a master file of inventory parts and their quantities in stock. This master file is linked to a variable file containing a history of usage of each part issued from the inventory.

A master file can have multiple variable files in this system. In the example of Figure 9-14, we can add another variable file to keep track of receipts of each part. It is also possible to have two master files accessing a single transaction file as shown in the bottom half of Figure 9-14. The parts and inventory master file is the same as the example in the top half of the figure. The second master file, a list of projects, is linked to all transactions that took place for a particular project. There would be two types of linkage in the variable file—one for transactions for the same part and the other for transactions for the same project. This same logical structure could be represented by data-base management systems using other forms such as a hierarchical tree structure.

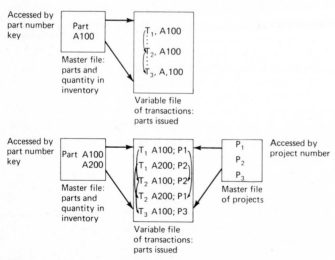

Figure 9-14 A network data-base example.

One major advantage is that data-base management systems set up all the directories and pointers automatically. The user specifies only the logical structure of the files; much of the complex programming for direct-access retrieval and updating is thus eliminated by the data-base management system.

FILE DESIGN CONSIDERATIONS

We have discussed a large amount of technical material in this chapter on file devices and logical file structures. However, we have not described how the systems designer should decide what kind of a file structure to use. Unfortunately, file design is more of an art at this time than a science. In this section, we attempt to provide some general guidelines for file design. However, much of the structure of the files for a computer system depends on the individual application, and the designer will have to make a number of decisions from the information developed during the systems analysis steps preceding file design.

Record Structure

The first file design decisions involve the data to be stored on the files. As the design for a new information system is developed, the requirements for information to be stored for subsequent retrieval will be specified. Related information is grouped into records, and several types of records may be in a single physical file. Record types must be defined, and so must the key fields for retrieval purposes.

Information in a file is typically updated in two ways. First, routine transactions occur that change fields in the file. For example, the receipt of a new shipment changes the balance due in an accounts-payable file and the quantity on hand in an inventory file. Other fields on the file are changed much less frequently—for example, vendors' addresses. The input for this type of change can be classified more realistically as file maintenance. In principle, it should be possible to change any field in the file with proper authorization, because errors can occur anywhere and provisions must be made to correct them. File maintenance input is usually processed by different users than in normal transaction processing, and the design of the input form and medium may differ for the two types of updates.

Having defined the basic information content of the files along with grouping of logical records, the designer approaches the problem of defining the record format. Fixed-length records are the easiest and simplest to use from a processing and programming standpoint. If there is a varying amount of fixed-length information, header and trailer records can be used. However, if the length of the record must vary, then variable-length records are necessary.

Response versus Cost

Having defined the contents and format of the file, the analyst next examines information on the nature, volume, frequency, and response-time requirements for retrievals and updates involving the file. We must balance response-time requirements against the costs of (1) creating the data base (including programming costs), (2) storing the data, (3) retrieving data, and (4) updating the data.

Some of the research on file design has resulted in the development of several models that aid the designer by forecasting the costs of alternative data-base configurations. Most of these models are in the research and development stage, but when they are refined, we hope that systems designers will be able to make routine use of them. In the future, the designer should be able to describe the physical file devices available, the structure of the data base and expected activities, and be able to work with a time-sharing computer system to compare different file design strategies. However, in the absence of these models or the time and resources to compute manually the tradeoffs between response and cost for different data-base configurations, what guidelines can be offered?

Batch Files   If there is no need for immediate inquiry or on-line updating, then batch sequential files are the cheapest to develop and maintain for most applications. In addition, these files offer good error-checking and backup features. However, even for a batch application, with seemingly no need for on-line access, direct-access files may be necessary because of processing requirements. For example, if a direct-access file structure were not used in the application of Table 9-1 to produce a bill of materials for each assembly, it would be necessary to sort the file many times and undertake very complicated processing, which might not be feasible.

Direct-Access Files   If processing or access response-time requirements justify the added cost, direct-access files can be selected by the designer. In the simplest case, only processing logic demands direct access, as in the example for the bill of materials processing above. For this application, it is not necessary to process retrieval requests on-line. The next level of design effort and complexity is represented by allowing on-line inquiry but updating the files in batch mode. This alternative is less costly and complex than on-line updating and offers better error control. If the only need for access is on a single key, then a simple package such as one of the available index sequential-access method (ISAM) programs is recommended.

If the information to be retrieved on-line must be up to date instantaneously —for example, in a reservations system or stolen-vehicle law-enforcement application—then on-line updating will be necessary. Of the three directory approaches discussed in this chapter, the easiest one to program is a dictionary with a linked or chained list of pointers through the file. If storage space is not a problem but speed is important, hash coding is the fastest key-to-address transformation technique. However, remember that a significant amount of extra file space must be available to realize this speed advantage. Inverted directories should be used only where there are complex retrieval requests or where presearch statistics are needed before the data file is actually accessed.

Data-Base Management Systems   The acquisition of a data-base management system may be warranted if systems currently being designed and ones planned for the future incorporate direct-access files for any of the purposes described above. As discussed earlier in this chapter, these systems offer a number of advantages. Although they may require a substantial investment in capital and labor, subsequent applications should be more easily designed and implemented. Clearly a growing trend in organizations is toward the adoption of data-base management systems to facilitate file and systems design for information systems.

KEY WORDS

Addition	Field	Plex
Average access time	File	Physical record
Backup	Fixed-length record	Pointer
Batch processing	Hash coding	Relational
Binary search	Header record	Retrieval
Blocking factor	Hierarchical	Ring
Chained file	Interrecord gap	Rotational-delay time
Character	Inverted directory	Secondary storage
Data-base management	Key	Seek time
system	Key-to-address	Sequential file
Deletion	transformation	Trailer record
Density	Linked lists	Transactions
Dictionary	Logical records	Tree
Direct access	Magnetic tape	Variable-length record
Directory	Modification	
Disk	Network	

RECOMMENDED READINGS

Davis, G. B.: *Computer Data Processing,* 2d ed., McGraw-Hill, New York, 1973. (See especially the chapter on computer files for a clear description of the data processing aspects of files.)

Dodd, G.: "Elements of Data Management Systems," *Computing Surveys,* vol. 1, no. 2, 1969, pp. 117–122. (An extremely well-written article describing possible file structures; read it several times to be sure you understand it.)

Martin, J.: *Computer Data Base Organization,* 2d ed., Prentice-Hall, Englewood Cliffs, N.J., 1977.

Merten, A. G., and E. H. Sibley: "Implementation of a Generalized Data Based Management System within an Organization," *Management Informatics,* vol. 2, no. 1, February 1973, pp. 21–31. (A good discussion on organizational philosophy. Some of the disadvantages of these systems are explained.)

DISCUSSION QUESTIONS

1 Why is a new file written during a batch update?
2 What are the advantages and disadvantages of batch updating?
3 What are the advantages and disadvantages of direct-access updating?

4   Where do users encounter computer files? Why is an understanding of their structure and operations important?

5   Compression techniques are often used to reduce file-storage requirements and input/output transfer times. Various schemes are used to compress information and eliminate redundant data. For example, we might remove blanks from a file of text and replace them with a special character and a number indicating the number of blanks that were removed. What are the advantages and disadvantages of compressing a file key along with the rest of the record for a direct-access file?

6   Is there any advantage to blocking records for direct-access retrieval?

7   What procedure do you recommend for providing file backup for an on-line system?

8   For a file of 1000-character records that contains 20,000 records would a dictionary or hash coding be fastest for retrieval on a single key? What are the advantages and disadvantages of each type of directory?

9   Why would programming for an inverted directory be more difficult than for a dictionary and a linked-list (chained) file?

10 What are the major capabilities a data-base management system should offer?

11 A relatively new mass-storage device was described in this chapter that is capable of holding hundreds of millions of characters. However, access to each record on a direct basis is relatively time consuming. In what types of applications do you think such a mass storage device might be used?

12 It has been suggested that the difficulty of updating is inversely related to the difficulty of retrieval. That is, a file structure that facilitates retrieval is likely to be very difficult to update. Do you agree with this observation? Why?

13 Why is it undesirable to have the same data stored on more than one file?

14 Data-base management systems stress independence between data and access programs. To what extent is this possible: that is, can a program ever be completely independent from the data it uses?

15 How does a data-base management system contribute to the flexibility of information systems?

16 For a mature computer installation with 50 or 100 different applications, what problems would you envision in the adoption of a data-base management system?

17 If a dictionary is so large that it cannot be stored in primary memory but must be placed on a disk, would you recommend that it be placed all at one location in a separate file or that the directory be interspersed with the actual data records? Why? If the directory were to be interspersed, what criteria would you use to determine where to place it relative to the data in the file? (Hint: consider the average access time for the disk, which consists of seek and rotational-delay times.)

18 Does the use of accessing techniques such as ISAM or complete data-base management packages mean that the analyst and programmer do not have to understand how files are structured or how the packages work? What problems can be created if the programmer and analyst are unaware of the physical and the logical structure of the data?

19 For the example in Figure 9-14, express the file structure as a hierarchical data base.

20 What are the major disadvantages of data-base management systems?

21 What difficulties would be created by having to add data to a file on tape, for example, to print a new piece of information on a report? What would the problem be if the information is to be retrieved on-line from a direct-access file? Would your answer differ if the added information is to be a retrieval key?

22 What are the basic differences between hierarchical and network data-base systems? Can you think of an application where one would be superior to the other?

23 Can a programmer really remain ignorant of the data-base management system when writing applications programs that use the system? Where might a programmer run into difficulties if he or she does not understand the retrieval logic of the data-base management system?

24 How is it possible for the logical view of data to differ from the physical storage layout of the data in a data-base system? (Hint: consider the discussion of direct-access files in this chapter and how those files are stored on different devices.)

25 The acquisition of a data-base management system is a major undertaking. It is unlikely that its first application can cost-justify the effort; instead the acquisition is amortized over a number of applications. How can the organization justify moving into a data-base system, given this problem?

26 Take a system that is relatively well known, like an airline reservations system. Make a list of the major transactions processed by such a system and then use it to sketch the data structures necessary to support the system.

27 Why is it such a problem for many organizations to adopt common identifiers for names that will become data in a data-base system? Why is it necessary to do so?

28 Data-base management systems usually provide for schema and subschema. The subschema is a different logical view of the data base than the schema and is often needed by different users. Can you think of an example where different users of the same data would tend to view it differently?

29 If massive amounts of computer storage become available at a low cost, will there still be the need to design secondary storage structures?

30 What problems do you think would be encountered in trying to convert from one data-base system to another?

PROBLEMS

1 Assume that you have been given the following information to be contained in a sequential tape file with fixed-length records:

Item	Size in characters
Social security number	9
Last name	15
Middle initial	4
First name	10
Address line 1	15
Address line 2	15
Address line 3	10
Zip code	5
Account number	7
Account balance	10

The file is used by a retail store for charge-account processing.

a On what key(s) would you organize this file if it is to be updated with purchases and payments?

b Given your file organization, how would you produce a report of customers by geographic area?

   c If you have a tape 2400 ft long and can record on it with a density of 1600 characters per inch, how many customers could you get on a reel, assuming a blocking factor of 1?

   d What would the answer be to *c* with a blocking factor of 10?

2 Given a sequential tape file, assume that it is desired to keep a record of each transaction during the year. Each customer may have 0 to an infinite number of these transactions.

   a What are two possible solutions for including these data?

   b What are the problems with each solution?

   c Which do you recommend?

3 A direct-access file on a disk has been proposed for a police on-line system to locate (1) stolen vehicles and (2) cars with outstanding tickets. Officers in the field will radio inquiries to a terminal operator. The officer can inquire about (1) license plate number, (2) auto make, (3) color, or (4) make and color together. It is estimated that the proportion of inquiries will be 70, 15, 10, and 5 percent, respectively.

   a Describe the organization of the file and the directory for your primary key.

   b For the other two access keys do you recommend a linked list or an inverted directory? Show how the file would appear under each alternative and explain the reasons behind your choice.

4 Consider the following job-matching system that is maintained on-line. A record consists of

   Social security number
   Employee's name
   Employee's address
   Salary requirements
   Skills code
   Area

The file is used for several purposes and it was decided to keep it on a disk in social security number order. You may assume that record addressing is relative to the beginning of the file and is independent of the physical track address.

   For one application, employer representatives call the employment office and a clerk enters their requests, which can be either by area, skills code, or some combination of the two.

   a How would you update this file (remember an update includes adding, deleting, and modifying records) if the skills code and area are referenced by a directory showing their initial file location and a linked list of pointers through the file? Describe how your update plan would affect subsequent inquiry file accessing.

   b What would your answer be to *a* if there were no points in the file and the area and skill codes were referenced through an inverted directory?

5 A request has just been made to include two additional fields in the file in problem 4. These fields would contain a code for the employee's last two jobs.

   a What problems would this change create both for files and programs?

   b Would the change be easier with an inverted directory or a linked-list file organization?

6 An analyst has just recommended that your company invest in the development of a financial data storage and retrieval system. The plan calls for using the system inside the company and for sales to other firms. The system will operate on-line.

   The major problem facing you is to evaluate the analyst's proposal for the file system. The use of a fully inverted directory and file—that is, inverted on every field—is recommended. The analyst feels that this file will enhance the marketability of the system, since it is difficult to anticipate all user requests.

Do you agree with the analyst? Why or why not?

The contents of the file are:

For each Fortune 500 company:
For each of the past 20 years:
Beginning stock price
Closing stock price
Average stock price
Dividends
Splits
Sales
Income
Profits
Number of shares outstanding

7 Anderson's is a chain of department stores in a large metropolitan area. There is one main department store downtown, and presently there are six suburban stores. Anderson's carries a full range of department store items from clothing to housewares to furniture. All merchandise is ordered centrally and distributed to stores from the central warehouse so that all stores carry approximately the same merchandise.

The company has a centralized computer located in their corporate offices near the main store. For customer billing and inventory, they are presently using a batch system and sequential files.

The inventory file contains fixed-length records in sequence by item number. Each record contains the following fields:

Field	Size in characters
Vendor number	10
Item number	10
Department	3
Quantity on hand	5
Quantity sold	5
Quantity on order	5
Wholesale price	7
Retail price	7

Anderson's keeps track only of total inventory; in other words, the "quantity on hand" field represents the total quantity of an item in all stores. Although they are considering ways to keep track of items by store, they presently do not have that capability.

The following three types of transactions may be included in an update run: (1) Orders of merchandise (remember that although some items will be reorders, many items will be new merchandise never before ordered), (2) receipt of merchandise (do not worry about distribution to stores—all orders are received at the central warehouse), (3) sale of merchandise (for each item sold, part of the price ticket is sent to the central warehouse to be keypunched and entered into the system).

a Describe and illustrate with a flowchart the process for updating the inventory file. Show how the contents of the file will be changed by each transaction type.

b The company presently has a separate system for keeping information about customer credit and making it available to each sales clerk. Next to each cash register is a small calculator-like terminal with a 10-key pad and a one-line screen for displaying a message to the sales clerk. The clerk enters the customer number from the charge plate and receives a message indicating how much above or below their credit limit the customer is or indicating that the customer cannot charge because the account is past due. The file for this system, which contains customer number, credit limit, amount due, and amount past due, is updated each night from the regular customer-billing file as part of the regular update run. What file organization would you suggest for this file with what key(s)? Justify your answer.

c Anderson does extensive mail advertising to its charge customers. Management wants a system developed that will select customers on certain criteria for selected mailings. For instance, they want to be able to select by geographical location, charge plan, age of customer, family versus single account, and credit limit. Using the customer master file (which contains all billing and address information for each charge customer) as a base, propose a file organization to accomplish this selection. Illustrate how your system works with a few records and one selection criterion.

8 General Products Corporation is a large company that produces, packages, and distributes a wide variety of grocery products nationwide. It has a customer base of about 3000 large grocery wholesalers and retail food chains. All ordering, shipping, and invoicing is coordinated through the central office. About 500 orders are received and processed per day.

The company presently uses a batch system to create customer invoices and to keep track of all payments to customer accounts. One daily processing run adds new invoices to a sequential file of outstanding invoices, and another program records all payments and removes paid invoices from the file.

a The invoice file includes, for each invoice, the following: invoice number, customer number (unique for each customer), date of order, date of invoice, total amount due, and date due. Invoice numbers are assigned in sequence as orders are processed. If the invoice file is to be stored sequentially on magnetic tape, what field or fields should be used as keys? Why? Given your choice of key, simply describe the update procedure and logic (1) to add new invoices to the file, (2) to remove paid invoices from the file.

b A separate sequential file contains detailed descriptive information about each customer, including address information, outstanding balance, outstanding overdue balance, credit limit, and other credit information. Each customer record is about 300 characters long. About 20 percent of the customers have special credit allowances for which additional information is needed, and management wants to add this information to the existing file. There are three categories of special customer credit allowances for which are needed 40, 60, and 10 additional characters, respectively. Suggest and explain a method for incorporating these data into the file.

c Because of the high volume of customer inquiries regarding their accounts and a need for better control of each account, the company wants to go to direct-access files for on-line retrieval and update of accounts receivable. Both the customer and invoice files will become direct-access files.

(1)For direct access to the invoice file, with invoice number as the key, what would be the most efficient direct-access method? Why?

(2)With direct access to invoice records, a customer may choose to pay on account by any of several methods: (a) by specific invoice number, (b) by oldest invoice first, (c) by most recent invoice first. Explain and illustrate with a few sample records how you would set up a linked list to process transaction types (b) and (c).

(3) Explain and show diagrammatically how the linked lists would be affected when a customer paid a specific invoice (not the oldest or the most recent).

HARDWARE
   Memory
   Summary
COMMUNICATIONS
INPUT-OUTPUT DEVICES
SOFTWARE
APPLICATIONS
   Office Automation
   Home Computer Use
SUMMARY
KEY WORDS
RECOMMENDED READINGS
DISCUSSION QUESTIONS

Chapter 10

Future Trends

CHAPTER ISSUES

- What should be done today to take advantage of tomorrow's technology?
- What can management do about the severe shortage of qualified computer analysts and programmers?

The manager and the user should prepare to take advantage of the opportunities provided by changes in information processing technology. It has been predicted that the information processing industry will soon reach $500 billion in yearly sales, making it one of the largest sectors of the economy. It is unlikely that any organization will remain untouched by this technology during the next decade. In this chapter we predict some of the trends in technology and their implications for managers and users.

HARDWARE

New computers will be smaller, faster, and have larger storage; their prices will continue to decrease.

In Chapter 7 we discussed some of the procedures for fabricating computer components. An engineer designs circuits using an interactive computer system. Photographic machines create reproductions of the circuit, and the displays are reduced in size until their individual components are in the micron range (one-thousandth of a millimeter). A photographic negative or mask is then made of the patterns. A machine projects ultraviolet light through the mask on a thin wafer of silicon that has been treated with a photo resist, a light-sensitive material. The photo resist is developed, and the patterns of the circuit emerge on the silicon surface. Dipping the wafer in acid eliminates the silicon where there was no photo resist. Metal is deposited for interconnections, and the process is repeated to add many layers to the wafer.

Very large scale integration (VLSI) will result in even more components per unit of area. One of the most promising techniques uses electron-beam lithography; electron beams expose the photo resist on a wafer. This process offers finer detail than the optical processes described earlier. As a result more complex circuits can be built far more cheaply and reliably. Currently more than 150,000 components can be fabricated and interconnected on a single chip of silicon no large than one-tenth the size of a postage stamp. The number of components per chip should grow dramatically for at least another decade.

VSLI offers a number of advantages. The first, of course, is extremely low cost electronics. A high-quality digital logic gate cost a few dollars 25 years ago, but today a high-quality gate costs only a few tenths of a cent, over a thousandfold reduction. VLSI produces circuits of high reliability; the mean time between failure for today's logic gate is a hundred thousand times greater than the gate of two decades ago, a trend that will continue. Very large scale integration also offers extremely small size, permitting space and energy savings. As more and more circuit elements can be packed onto a silicon chip, power requirements are lowered (*Computer World,* June 23, 1980).

Figure 10-1 shows the trends in processing speeds and a prediction for the future as a result of these improvements in technology. Figure 10-2 portrays the reductions in the average cost per calculation that have been achieved through improved technology.

Computers will employ different architectures to overcome physical limitations in their design. Research laboratories are working on new kinds of computers. An extremely fast computer is limited by the speed of light; electrical signals cannot travel faster than this constant. Therefore a computer with a cycle time of 1 nanosecond (10^{-9} second) would need about a billion chips all crammed within a box measuring just 3 inches square. The maximum distance between the two most distant chips would have to be inches, otherwise the signal between them would take too long to arrive since light travels only 6 inches in a nanosecond. With current technology the billion chips would consume 20,000 watts, and the moment the computer was switched on it would melt.

One experimental computer employs Josephson technology or super conductivity to achieve high speeds. Josephson technology relies on the fact that when certain materials are cooled to near absolute zero ($-269°C$), they exhibit almost no resistance to the flow of electrical current. These superconductors also

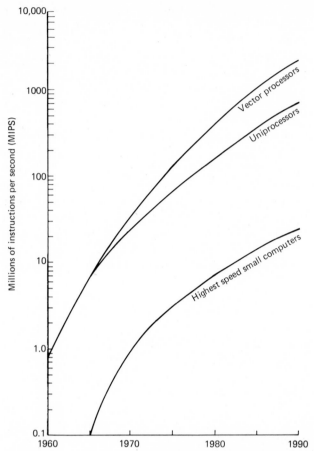

Figure 10-1 Trends in processing speed. *(Office of Technology Assessment, 1981.)*

require miniscule amounts of power because of the lack of resistance. Thus, Josephson junctions can be packed very tightly together. One computer manufacturer is developing this technology, and it represents one new method for increasing computer power (*The Economist*, December 8, 1979).

Memory

The exponential increase in the number of bits per memory chip and chip price reductions will continue.

Another use of large scale and very large scale integration is to develop memory devices. In addition to fabricating the logic of the central processing unit, VSLI offers very fast and large computer memories at reasonable cost. A single memory chip today contains the equivalent of entire computer memory of 15 years ago.

New technology will be applied to storage devices in general, reducing costs and increasing capabilities. Figure 10-3 is a cost projection for memory. In

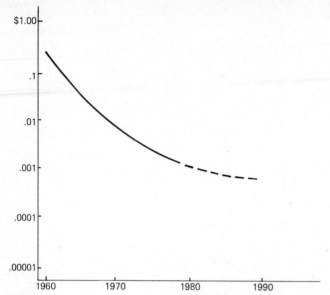

Figure 10-2 Drop in average cost per 100,000 calculations. *(Office of Technology Assessment, 1981.)*

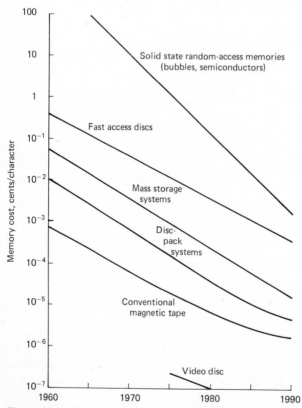

Figure 10-3 Cost projections for memory. *(Office of Technology Assessment, 1981.)*

addition to the use of transistors for primary memory, technology offers new advances in secondary storage devices. One group of researchers is working on a type of optical disk memory in which data can be erased and rewritten. Although optical memory systems exist today, they are limited because a laser is used to inscribe data permanently for storage. Since there are few applications (aside from large information storage and retrieval systems) where data do not have to be erased and updated, this kind of storage device has not seen widespread use. Optical disk technology is emerging, and it promises to increase the capacity of disks a hundredfold and reduce the costs of data storage.

In Chapter 7 we discussed bubble memories. The access to bubble memories is partially serial; stored bits circulate as if they were in a closed pipeline. In addition to bubbles, memories known as charge-coupled devices (CCD) have been developed. The area required for storage with CCD is somewhat smaller than it is for a semiconductor random-access memory. Also, the amount of address decoding required in a partially serial memory is less than it is for a random-access memory.

It is expected that memory in the future will be composed of a hierarchy of devices. Very large scale integration will continue the trend toward large primary memories consisting of semiconductor devices of extremely high speeds. For secondary storage there will be competition among charge-coupled devices, bubble memories, large core storage, and electromechanical devices like disks. The charge-coupled and magnetic bubble memories are filling an important price-performance gap between extremely fast semiconductor memory, and slower but less expensive drum, disk, and tape memories (see Figure 10-4). Fortunately, this storage hierarchy will be invisible to the user of the system. Instead, the user will see an extremely large data-base capability.

Summary

The implications of hardware technology for the central processing unit and memory are that computers will become faster, larger in storage capacity, and less expensive in the future. The reduction in cost will make it possible to use computer devices in a whole range of products and systems: computers will become even more pervasive in the future than they are now.

COMMUNICATIONS

Advances in communications depend on regulatory changes as well as technology.

Over the past decade the communications industry has undergone rapid change. In addition to trends toward deregulation and the entry of new carriers, entirely new types of services are now offered. For example, one company sells packet communications services; packets of data of a predefined size are sent anyplace in the United States at a flat rate per packet independent of distance.

New communications technologies aim at increasing the speed and reducing the costs of transmission.

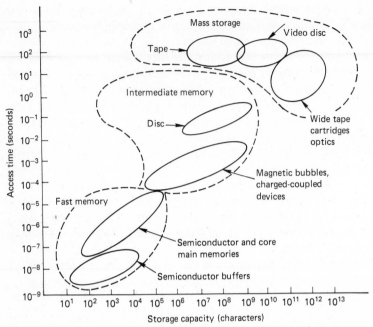

Figure 10-4 Capacity and access time of current memory technologies. *(Office of Technology Assessment, 1981.)*

In addition to influencing changes in communications industry regulations that allow more competition and new services, technology has made it possible to communicate in new and different ways. As an example Intelsat consists of a group of 95 nations that operate a network of satellites in orbit. The satellites furnish a combined capacity of over 40,000 circuits to six continents. Telephone, telegraph, and data transmissions account for 86 percent of the global satellite traffic, and television and special services make up the remainder. A total investment in excess of $650 million was required for the satellite system.

All Intelsat satellites operate in synchronous, equatorial orbits that make possible uninterrupted transmission and reception, with minimal tracking required by earth stations. The satellites receive signals transmitted from the ground, amplify, and retransmit them back to ground stations.

The first satellite had only 240 telephone circuits; the latest generation of satellites can carry 6000 simultaneous telephone circuits. Lifetime in orbit has advanced during the first decade, from 1.5 to 7 years. These improvements have resulted in the investment cost per circuit per year of $110 compared with an initial cost of $32,500 (Edelson, 1977). The space shuttle will provide new opportunities for the design of communications satellites. Shuttle-launched satellites can be much larger and heavier than current satellites. It will also be possible to erect large complex antenna arrays to allow the use of multiple frequencies and beams.

At present several companies are offering or plan to offer satellite services. Satellite Business Systems (a partnership of IBM, COMSAT, and Aetna Life and Casualty Co.) sells communication services on its own satellites. This service, designed for high-volume communications, offers speeds of up to three million bits per second. Another firm resells transmissions on satellite links rented from other carriers; now this firm is planning to purchase parts of an advanced satellite to expand its services. This competition means improved service and lower costs for the customer.

In addition to satellite new forms of communications are under development. One system carries voice data and video signals over underground optical cables connecting two telephone company switching offices. The underground cable consists of 24 optical fibers bound in two ribbons of 12 fibers each. The entire cable is only half an inch in diameter, yet the information capacity of each fiber is 44.7 million bits per second. (The laser light source for the fiber is turned on and off 44.7 million times per second.) A single fiber can carry 672 one-way voice signals, so that the entire cable can carry over 8000 two-way conversations. To match this capacity with copper wire would require a cable many times larger.

The hair-thin light guides are assembled into cables. They are coated for protection against humidity and abrasion and losses due to bending and then combined into flat, color-coded ribbons. Up to a dozen ribbons are closed in a cable that cushions and protects the individual fibers against damage. A technique has been developed to align all the fibers in the ends of the cable to an accuracy of 2 micrometers when it is necessary to splice the cables together.

FEEDING CATTLE

U.S. Department of Agriculture scientists have developed a computerized method of feeding cows faster and more economically with a new kind of feeding bowl. These engineers and scientists have invented a computerized feeding bowl to produce fast food stations for cows. A system currently installed with a single feeding stall now serves about 40 cows a day.

Researchers found that a cow spends less time eating if the bowl has a shape similar to a cow's lower jaw bone. This new bowl coupled with an electronic identification system appears to be working well. Each animal has a transponder attached to its collar so that when the cow sticks her head into the feeding bowl, the feeding unit is automatically activated to slowly dispense food. At the same time, the transponder's memory is charged. When the transponder's coded memory is fully charged, the dispenser stops. As time goes by, say twelve hours, the transponder's electronic charge dies off and the cow is able to eat again.

A minicomputer helps to determine exactly how much feed a given cow should receive. The system is designed to feed the cow in direct proportion to the amount of milk she produces. This system can be extended to perform other functions, for example, plans include implanting a small sensor under the cow's skin, which monitors the animal's temperature and indicates if it is ill.

Computers are being employed in a wide variety of unusual applications where the rapid processing of information and immediate feedback can improve efficiency or increase the level of quality of an operation.

Computer World, February 11, 1980.

Optical transmission offers a number of advantages over transmission by metallic conductors. The light is confined to the inner core of the fiber so that signals cannot leak between adjacent fibers and produce cross talk. The light guides are also not affected by electrical interference from other sources. Thus these cables offer distinct savings in materials compared with metallic cables of equivalent capacity.

This technology has a number of applications. Television signals can easily be carried over a single fiber, opening new possibilities for the entertainment industry. Buildings can be wired with almost invisible fibers for internal communications. The use of light fibers and lasers has also been suggested for communications among components in a computer system.

Both changes in the technology and in regulations should produce new opportunities for communications among machines and among individuals. However, because of continuing changes in industry regulations, cost reductions for communications are expected to be less dramatic than for computer technology.

INPUT-OUTPUT DEVICES

Input and output continue to be a major bottleneck in information processing, though new devices will improve the user interface with computers.

One type of technology involves touching terminals rather than keying data. Such a system was developed for a firm that wished to make it easier for users to work with the system. The computer displays a menu format on the screen of a CRT, and the user simply touches the answer desired on the screen. The system appears to work well for selecting choices from menus; however, it is awkward for entering data. It appears that the familiar keyboard is still best for data entry (*Datamation,* January 1977).

High-speed output devices are now available in the form of "intelligent printers." These devices are controlled by computers, which gives them considerable power. The printers rely on laser light beams to transform information in digital form into printed characters and graphics designs. Owing to their electronic method of printing (as opposed to mechanical), they can operate at speeds up to 40 times the speed of traditional impact, letter-quality printers. Some of the machines allow the user to transmit information to other locations; it is possible to change type styles easily and to have the devices print custom business forms along with the data (*Business Week,* December 15, 1980).

The use of computer graphics will increase.

Over the last several years interest in computer graphics has increased. Basic graphics applications feature simple pictures in black and white. Charts, graphs, maps, outlines, and business forms are examples of such displays that contain a great deal of information. More complex data often can only be communicated through the availability of multiple colors. Sometimes three-dimensional figures are required, or colored maps are produced.

Applications of this technology include a paper company that uses graphics to manage its forest inventory. Two sets of different forest maps generated by computers are displayed on top of each other so that management can see where and why disagreements occur.

In a marketing application an automobile manufacturer uses a graphics system to determine the best location for new dealers. All the automobiles of the manufacturer registered in a certain region and its dealers are represented by dots on a computer-drawn map. These data are combined with information on census tracts that satisfy criteria for dealer location based on variables such as traffic flow, population density, and land value to aid in making the decision on where new dealers should be located.

The automobile manufacturer uses graphics in a similar way to gauge the impact of competition on its business. Combining data on competitive registrations for cars in the same price class, the computer calculates the distribution of sales given the total expected sales of the make in a particular area. This information becomes an important part of an analysis of competition.

A food manufacturing company with 60 sales districts in the United States and multiple products found that computer graphics helped to manage the large amount of data generated by sales reports. These sales data on company brands are now presented graphically, and top managers quickly focus their attention on districts where sales seem to be lagging.

To develop a graphics system, a medium-sized computer and a graphic display device, usually a CRT with some kind of light pen, are generally employed. Often the CRT displays data in different colors. For systems featuring maps, two types of data bases are used. The first is cartographic or X-Y coordinate data base. This data base allows the shape of geographic zones to be defined in terms of states, standard metropolitan statistical areas, counties, census tracts, etc. A second type of data base is statistical and consists of commercial data from private companies such as A. C. Nielsen or Dun and Bradstreet. When these two data bases are combined, a great deal of information can be displayed for management.

In the future it is expected that reductions in the cost of display equipment will provide an impetus for more graphics output. The greatest contribution will be from CRT terminals that have built-in microprocessors. These terminals will be able to execute software and store some data locally at the user's site and then communicate with larger remote computers to access large data bases or to perform heavy computational processing (Takeuchi and Schmidt, 1980).

Systems will feature more graphics and nonkeyboard entry.

Several systems for computer-aided design use light pens or "joysticks" to control figures on the CRT. An individual can enter data using these devices without diverting attention from the display; the user is freed from the constraints of a keyboard. This same principle has been applied in at least one experimental system to aid the manager. The system can represent various papers and items on an executive's desk. An input device is used to signal the computer when a cursor (moving spot of light) is at a desired location, such as pointing to a function. Then, the computer executes the function. For example, a memorandum might be enlarged and read or filed in an electronic file. All this manipulation is accomplished with the input device rather than by striking keys on the terminal. Such systems should expand the appeal of computer use to many executives who are not comfortable with a keyboard.

Voice communication with computers will be applied in the development of information systems.

One of the most exciting areas for communicating with computers is by voice, both for input and output. Currently some systems are able to process limited speech input for a computer. For example, one chemical company uses voice input to sort 25,000 pieces of mail arriving each day. An operator wearing a microphone headset reads the initial of the recipient's first name and the first four letters of the surname. On a small CRT the employee's name and mail zone appear, and the operator places the package in the appropriate location for delivery. According to the chemical company the system has doubled the speed of mail processing. The operator could accomplish the same thing by keying in the characters, but both hands are occupied handling the mail because the mail is of nonstandard size and shape. The voice recognition system frees the operator's hands for the sorting job.

The system above is relatively simple: it is a discrete or isolated word recognition system. The speaker must pause briefly between words and the envelope of silence surrounding each word must be at least a tenth of a second. The user must train the system to recognize his or her speaking pattern and the words in the vocabulary.

Continuous speech recognition is a much more difficult task. Systems with limited context can make sense out of a 5- or 10-second-long utterance. Thus one can think of a system understanding a 10- or 12-digit number (*Datamation,* August 1976). Although there has been considerable commercial success with machines that recognize individual words spoken in isolation, it is still questionable as to whether we will ever achieve computer recognition of continuous speech for an unlimited vocabulary and grammar. Knowledge beyond the information contained in acoustic wave patterns making up words and sentences seems to be a necessary part of such a system. In the case of recognition of words spoken alone, the computer program is based on knowledge that the acoustic wave pattern corresponds to only a single word, and the machine decodes the word by a statistical pattern-matching technique.

For a computer to understand natural, continuous, fluid speech of humans, considerable knowledge about the structure of language and the context of the task must be programmed into the computer. The difficulty of devising strategies for providing this type of information has impeded the recognition of continuous speech.

The first operation in continuous speech recognition is to decompose the acoustic wave pattern into basic sounds called phonemes. Current speech recognition machines do this job with about 65 percent accuracy. The second operation is to arrange the phonemes into words and the words into sentences, taking into account the fact that a substantial number of phonemes may have been misidentified. The computer must have syntactic knowledge so that sentences are grammatically correct and semantic knowledge so that the sentences have a logical meaning. Thus, we are asking a computer program to have at least a rudimentary understanding of meaning, something that is not required in most other computer applications.

At least one computer manufacturer is currently working on a continuous speech recognition system and has reported some success with it. The computer manufacturer's first application is one of automatic dictation. Envision the manager being able to dictate a letter into a microphone and have the letter appear as rapidly as the words are spoken on a CRT screen. A system like this could be tolerant of some errors that could be fixed by the manager or by a secretary. The time-consuming, rather unpleasant chore of transcribing dictation copied manually or on some kind of recording device would be eliminated by such a system. Beyond the immediate application, a system like this would make it possible to consider the voice input of commands and questions into a computer system.

The generation of speech by computers is much further along than speech understanding. One commercially available product combines an optical character recognition device with a voice synthesizer to produce a reading machine for the blind. A book is placed flat over a glass plate, and the system converts the text into spoken words.

The difficulty in producing natural-sounding speech comes from many of the same problems that make continuous speech recognition difficult. We could store phonetic representations of all the words in the dictionary in the computer. When the machine needed to generate a sentence it could call up the pronunciation for each word and string the words together. However, the result would be a very jerky sentence with little modulation. Therefore, attempts are made to limit the complexity and the amount of knowledge the system must have to produce speech. Phrases may be recorded and recalled for playback, or other techniques can be used to make the speech sound more realistic (*Science*, February 1979, pp. 734–736).

SOFTWARE

Advances in software will be slower than those in hardware; software will continue to be a bottleneck.

The advances in hardware are innovative and exciting; advances in software are much more difficult to predict. The production of programs is a human intellectual task that so far has defied extensive automation. A report by the Office of Technology Assessment (1981) concluded, "The cost of information systems will be predominantly for the software, and the information industry will become increasingly labor-intensive."

Users will be forced to interact more closely with computers to satisfy their information processing needs.

MANAGEMENT PROBLEM 10-1

ECD is a manufacturer of electronic circuit components. The firm has plants in four locations in the United States and in five foreign countries. Currently all computing is centralized at one plant location in the northern U.S. The firm is wondering if they should consider decentralizing or distributing processing.

ECD has experienced rapid growth in sales volume and revenues. Compound growth has been in excess of 10 percent per year. The company is loosely structured, and the executives at remote locations have considerable discretion in making decisions.

The firm is concerned that it make plans that take advantage of trends in technology. They are particularly worried that they may introduce incompatibilities by wholesale distribution. ECD also is not sure of how to handle programming and systems development in a distributed environment.

How should ECD make its decision to go to distributed processing or remain with a centralized system? What changes in technology will have an impact on its decision for both the location of hardware and the development staff for new systems? Can you give the firm advice on how to proceed?

If software is becoming increasingly labor-intensive, we might ask who will write programs. A recent survey suggested that many organizations spend over 50 percent of their software development budgets on the maintenance of existing applications (Lientz et al., 1978). As more new applications enter the organization's portfolio, increasing efforts will be required for maintenance and enhancements. As a result the number of people available to develop new systems could actually decline if the technical staff is not increased.

Unfortunately there is a critical shortage of programmers and systems analysts, which is expected to continue over the next several decades. The question of who will write programs is a very important one. The computer revolution, to a large extent, is limited by the availability of professionals to work on software.

A study by Kendall (1977) suggests one possible approach to reducing the software bottleneck. Data were collected from a number of jobs at typical computer centers in industry. Although the sample of data is primarily from a few sites using the same brand of computer, the authors argue that the data are representative of many commercial installations in the country today.

The study found that half the programs observed·accounted for only 2 percent of the machine running time. On the other hand, 2 percent of the programs accounted for nearly half the running time of the machine. This 2 percent of the programs that take half the CPU time should be carefully written and tested. However, the large number of programs that demand little computer time do not have to be written by highly skilled computer professionals. Instead, users of systems can write these programs using very high level languages, report generators, and/or query languages as a part of a data-base management system.

Another study, this one of users, also suggests that the software gap is real and that less reliance will have to be placed on computer professionals for software. Users reported extensive backlogs in requests for new information systems. Even more discouraging was the finding that many latent applications existed that had not yet been suggested. Users were discouraged by the existing backlog and had not formally requested further applications, even though they would have liked to have them developed.

All these factors, the shortage of personnel, the real and hidden backlog of applications, the increasing costs of maintenance, and the large number of programs that do not consume computer resources, suggest that users will play a greater role in system development. We shall discuss the nature of this role and other alternatives to reduce the software gap below.

There will be an expansion in the use of applications packages and outside services.

The lack of computer professionals also suggests that more packaged applications will be used. Organizations will change their procedures, particularly small firms, to take advantage of existing program products. Companies will buy turnkey systems, systems that have been programmed for particular industries, and will adapt their procedures to them. Organizations that cannot change procedures or are unique may use packages but modify them heavily to try to save development time.

Organizations will move rapidly toward data-base environments.

The advantages of the data-base approach to information processing were discussed in Chapter 9. Firms often acquire a data-base management system for a single application and then use it for the development of many subsequent applications. Once the system has been installed and the staff understands how to use it, data-base management systems can dramatically reduce the length of time required to implement a new application. Special development tools for the programmer are also available with some of the systems. For example, one system aids the programmer in writing software. The programmer uses an interactive terminal to define the structure of an application, and the system generates code in COBOL.

Other such high-level application development systems have been announced with even more capabilities. The objective is to move to an environment in which one defines the data base, transactions, and their editing requirements and output while the system does the rest. Of course, it will always be necessary to specify some processing logic, but perhaps the specification will be at a high level instead of at the detailed level of conventional programming languages.

The query languages associated with data-base management systems are an important feature. Some of these languages are quite suitable for users in an organization. In order to access data for ad hoc inquiries, users will have to employ these languages and become familiar with the names of data in the data base.

Evidence also suggests that some of the functions of a data base management system will be taken over by hardware. The literature has presented examples of "data-base machines," computers dedicated to data processing that are used in conjunction with computers that run the applications programs.

There will be more extensive use of prototyping in systems development.

To assist users in visualizing a system, designers will make greater use of prototypes. That is, a simulated version of a system or a part of the system will be developed quickly and demonstrated to the user. Then the user can provide immediate feedback based on what he or she experiences. The prototype is done quickly and replaces a large, functional specification that is hard for the user to understand.

Some of the very high level languages, report generators, time-sharing systems, and development tools available now can be used to produce simple prototypes. Users and managers should request this approach whenever it seems feasible. Many functional areas will want to consider developing their own prototype systems rather than calling on a professional designer. For many applications, a simple prototype developed by the user may suffice for the final application after a few rounds of changes and modifications.

Users will write programs in very high level languages.

Ultra high level languages will be used more extensively in the future. One of these packages, offered by IBM, is a good example of this type of system. "Query by Example" can be learned relatively easily and requires little data processing background. All the data are visualized as existing in a series of two-dimensional tables, that is, a table consisting of columns and rows.

To perform an operation, the user fills in an example of the solution in a blank skeleton table that is associated with an actual table. The user can input examples of the data required or actual data values. A series of retrieval examples will demonstrate some of the power of this particular system. The first inquiry is for a list of the names and departments of all employees in a simple personnel data base (IBM 5796 − PKT).

EMP	NAME	SALARY	MGR	DEPT
	P.			P.

In a qualified retrieval, the user requests the name, salary, manager, and department of any employee who earns less than or equal to $16,000 and works for Morgan. The P symbol asks that the data be printed.

EMP	NAME	SALARY	MGR	DEPT
	P.	P. < = 16000	P. MORGAN	P.

A more complicated example allows one to link multiple tables together. In this example the D1 used in the department column is an example element. It establishes a link between two or more entries in the same row or two or more rows of different tables. The same example, D1, must be used in both tables to link the tables together. This query says print the names of the employees that work in a department, D1, such that department D1 sells perfume.

EMP	NAME	SALARY	MGR	DEPT
	P.			__D1

SALES	DEPARTMENT	ITEM
	__D1	PERFUME

One advantage of this type of system is that the information services department can react to user needs immediately, not in several months. Also those needs can be met without writing extensive programs. The Query by Example system has cut programming requests at one firm and maintenance requirements over 30 percent and has eliminated many hard copy reports (*Data Processor,* June/July 1980).

Using packages such as Query by Example, Mark IV, and the Data Analyzer, users will become more involved in the actual preparation of programs in the future. Many of these programs will be nonprocedural; that is, it will appear that the user is telling the computer more what he or she wants than how to do it. Underlying these request processors will be extensive software systems. The software systems will make relatively inefficient use of the computing hardware, but as we have seen, computing hardware is becoming much less costly and the real bottleneck in information systems is the availability of people to apply the technology.

More applications will display "Artificial Intelligence."

Artificial Intelligence (AI) refers to computer systems that exhibit some of the characteristics of human information processors. Early AI programs simulated human behavior, learned how to improve their ability to play games such as checkers, and helped diagnose medical problems.

Some of the systems attempt to store the knowledge of experts in a field and then apply it to solving a problem. Several medical diagnostic systems work in this fashion. The systems feature a knowledge base of facts and their interconnection and an inference procedure that draws implications or conclusions after processing input to the system.

Another area that employs AI techniques is *robotics.* Today intelligent machines are performing tasks sometimes beyond the capabilities of humans. One refined robot assembles a critical, fragile part on the electron beam of a CRT. Humans frequently break the part, but the robot does not.

AI techniques are also used extensively in the speech recognition and generation systems described above. AI is moving from the laboratory into practical and useful applications. The need for decision support and diagnostic systems to aid management offers exciting opportunities for the use of AI in information systems.

APPLICATIONS

The number and scope of computer applications will continue to increase dramatically.

It is difficult to predict what types of applications will be developed in the future since they are governed by the needs of individual organizations. The technology is making more and more applications cost effective that might not have been considered in the past. In particular, we expect to see increasing use of systems that require large amounts of data to be available on-line. Reduced storage costs, communications costs, and more easily developed on-line systems suggest this trend. Most processing in the future will move from batch to on-line. No longer does on-line processing have to be justified by the need for simultaneous access to data. Instead on-line processing can be justified on the basis of improved input and retrieval capabilities. Changes in hardware and software technology will contribute to the expansion of applications in general. The primary limit on applications will be our imagination and resources to implement new systems.

Office Automation

Computer systems will be applied to nontraditional situations such as office processing.

The stimulus for the application of computers to office procedures comes from the relatively low investment in capital for an office worker combined with the large percentage of the work force involved in information processing activities. It has been estimated that the average capital equipment investment for a U.S. factory worker is $25 to $50 thousand, and that the average investment for an office worker is about $2 to $3 thousand. A U.S. government study estimated that over half the work force actually processed information rather than provided a service or a product. To improve productivity in the economy, additional capital equipment will have to be provided for the office worker, much of which will be computer-based.

Generally an office automation system includes some type of electronic mail, text editing and word processing, a calendar and/or reminder system, and some type of electronic filing of messages.

Computer technology can be applied to human communications through "electronic mail." Each user of a system has a mailbox that consists of records of textual information stored in a computer file. When the user logs onto the computer he or she is notified that messages await (see Table 10-1). The user can read the subject matter of the messages and choose to read the entire message now or at a later time. The user is able to reply to messages in a similar fashion.

Table 10-1   An Example of Electronic Mail

```
 Msg 117 (705 chars) --      ---------
DATE: 25-Sep-80 20:37
FROM: B20.H-LUCAS
TO: B20.C-LARSON


Subject: Revised morning schedule


Thank you for the messages on the system-they were waiting when I
returned from my trip today.  I called Mr. Smith at home and it is
very important that I see him first thing.  This morning, then I
shall be with him at 269-2861.

I ran into Marsha Johnson in Philadelphia today and she asked if we
could send her a copy of the End User Survey. It is quite germane to
some work she is doing now, so could you please get it off airmail
special delivery to her in Los Angeles this morning?

Thank you very much.  I will be in around noon.

Hank
    ========
```

Electronic mail makes it possible for individuals to communicate over long distances asynchronously. Statistics indicate that a little less than a third of all telephone calls are actually completed the first time dialed. Electronic message systems make it possible to send information that is not critical, and the recipient can look at it when convenient. The systems offer advantages particularly to multinational firms that must contend with time zone differences.

Text editing and word processing facilities improve the speed and quality with which documents can be prepared. The document is entered into a computer system using special commands that later will direct a program to format the document and print it. Changes can be made to parts of a document without having to retype the entire piece. Word processing has been used extensively where multiple copies of the same document must be changed only slightly for each recipient, for example, a large mailing of letters to different individuals.

A calendar system helps individuals schedule appointments. A user can ask what is the first hour at which it is possible to have a meeting with a group of other individuals. As long as all participants make use of the electronic calendar, the system responds with free times for all to attend the meeting.

A reminder system operates in conjunction with an electronic mail system. The reminder system allows an individual to define a reminder (a message) to be sent at some time in the future. When the computer scans the reminder file and sees that the date has arrived, the message is dispatched to the recipient (see Table 10-2).

Table 10-2   A Reminder System

```
@remind

>>> REMINDER SYSTEM


>> Please type     A  for ADD        I  for INQUIRY
                   H  for HELP        Q  for QUIT
>>>  A

     Today is  14-Oct-80
>>> Please enter REMIND date as above      >>>    5-Jan-81

>>> REMIND  Recipients     >>>  b20.h-lucas

>>> COURTESY COPIES TO     >>>  b20.c-larson

>>> SUBJECT              >>>   Universal Products

>>> PROJECT             >>>    Plant construction bid

>>> MESSAGE (TERMINATE WITH A CARRIAGE RETURN, FOLLOWED BY A CTRL-Z.)
The bid for building a new plant for Universal must be in final
typing by today to meet the bid date.
^Z

>>> DO YOU WANT TO VERIFY YOUR REMINDER ?      >>>    n


>> YOU MAY CHANGE ANY ITEM OF THIS REMINDER

using   D  for DATE        R  for RECIPIENTS     C  for COURTESY COPIES
        S  for SUBJECT     P  for PROJECT        M  for MESSAGE
        [V  for VERIFY]
  -or-  N  for NO (further) CHANGE(s).
  >>>  CODE?  >>>  n

UPDATING...

>>> REMINDER PROCESSED.
```

One common feature of all these applications is that instead of processing data, the computer is working with text. Since the machine is not expected to understand the contents of the messages or the documents, a different type of processing and language is used for text editing and text processing than for numerical computation.

Office automation systems, while they can be used at a single site, offer the greatest versatility when they serve multiple geographic areas. Thus office automation, if it moves from an emerging to an established technology, will require extensive telecommunications facilities. Several U.S.-based companies with many different locations around the world have developed successful electronic mail systems.

Office automation is also sometimes defined to include teleconferencing or electronic meetings. In one system a group of individuals meets in a studio with communications equipment. The simplest machine is a type of "electronic blackboard" in which data written on a blackboard in one location appear on a television screen at a remote location. Such a system can be supplemented with video images through the use of closed circuit television. Generally it is recommended that the individuals involved in this kind of communications process meet beforehand. The greatest success has been reported where the people all know each other reasonably well before an electronic conference is undertaken.

The purpose of this application of technology is to reduce costs and to improve communications. Rising energy costs rapidly increase the expense of travel. If travel can be reduced or eliminated through electronic means, then large savings are possible.

However, the technology is so new that its impact on individuals and on the organization is not clear. Will video conferencing change the outcome of meetings because certain individuals will be more dominant through an electron-

---

MANAGEMENT PROBLEM 10-2

Nationwide Insurance, a large multiline firm, is investigating the possibility of starting a major office automation project. The firm recognizes that many of its activities revolve around information processing. While long a user of computers for basic policy processing and accounting, the firm has recently become aware of its extremely high volume of memoranda and messages transmitted primarily on paper and through the mail.

Nationwide has reviewed the literature on office automation and is trying to determine how best to apply various functions in these systems to its operations. The company operates in 25 countries around the world and in 40 of the 50 United States. The mail causes it considerable problems and phone calls are sometimes difficult because of different time zones. Although local managers have a fair degree of autonomy, a high volume of information still flows from the field to headquarters and vice versa.

Nationwide is also concerned about its escalating travel costs. They see advantages to electronic communications but wonder about the impact of the new technology on employees and the firm.

What features of office automation do you think would be the most suitable to Nationwide? What functions should they implement first? How would you advise the firm to approach the implementation problem for such a system? How does one evaluate the benefits and the costs? What would be required for office automation to help Nationwide?

---

ic medium than in person? Will office automation meet high resistance from managers or will they accept the use of computer terminal-like devices? Will jobs at the clerical level be more dehumanized because of the equipment introduced? The answers to these questions will come from further research and experience in the application of this new technology.

Home Computer Use

The use of inexpensive home computers connected to national networks will increase.

The development of microcomputers costing a few hundred dollars has created a vast new market for computers. These devices, which often use a television set as the display device, have been sold in large numbers to individual consumers. Extremely powerful software is available for these systems for a variety of applications ranging from the calculation of income taxes to plotting investment strategies.

There are several large, national computer networks to which home users can connect their computers over phone lines to access special programs and

---

TELECONFERENCING

The chairman of Atlantic Richfield Company (ARCO) complains that he has traveled 600 to 700 miles every day of his life for 35 years. As a result, ARCO has begun an ambitious two year project to build a $20 million telecommunication network. The basis of the network will be a two way video teleconferencing service that will eliminate the need for the chairman and other ARCO executives to make a trip for many of their face-to-face meetings. Up to six managers will be able to meet their counterparts in another city, on wide screen color television. A group of geologists in Anchorage could see as well as talk back and forth to a vice president of explorations in Los Angeles.

The company initially will link by satellite eight of its regional centers, in states like California, New York, Texas and Alaska, for video conferencing. The conference room will be equipped with two large screens, one to display participants and the other to show graphics, statistics and photographs. A manager in New York could simply walk down the hall to meet with a life size image of a colleague sitting in an identical room some 3,000 miles distant. Planners of the system are convinced that video conferencing will preserve the face-to-face communication that is essential in making important decisions.

One motivation for developing the system was spiraling travel costs. ARCO figures that it can cut travel costs by 20% with the new video teleconferencing service. The company has been spending up to $50 million on travel per annum.

The digital communications network will also offer electronic mail service, facsimile transmission of documents and computer-to-computer data transfers. The company plans to equip ten to fifteen of its oil and gas exploration teams with small field computers to tie into the large network. Seismic data, which are now recorded on magnetic tapes and flown to Dallas for analysis on a large computer, could then be sent over the network for instantaneous processing.

Business Week, July 7, 1980.

---

data. For example, the home user can dial locally into an Ohio service bureau via a communications network and obtain up-to-date stock market closing prices. The system also features electronic mailboxes for each user so that various home computers can communicate with each other. The Ohio firm offers programs that can be loaded into the user's machine and executed. The home computer can also be used like a terminal to access programs run on a mainframe computer.

Although many of these systems are sold and used for game playing, there are a large number of more serious applications. Microcomputers are also being adopted by small businesses as a sole processor and by larger companies to complement their computer services. Home computers add to the proliferation of computing devices in general and suggest that this technology will become ever more pervasive in the future.

SUMMARY

The implications of the trends that we foresee in technology and in applications are important for the user and manager. First, we expect there to be more computer power at a lower cost. This trend will result in a proliferation of opportunities to apply the technology to develop new systems. (We do not expect to see total computing costs decrease; rather more processing will be available per dollar spent.) There is a chance to alter and improve communications patterns dramatically within organizations through office automation systems. We can change the structure of the organization more easily now that new ways to communicate are becoming available.

To achieve these benefits and to develop more applications, users and managers will have to become more heavily involved in systems analysis and design; they will program simple retrievals and applications themselves. There simply are not enough computer professionals to provide the services desired. Thus, the user is going to have to take matters into his or her own hands to achieve the benefits of computer-based processing.

Users and managers who are prepared now will be able to take advantage of these trends in technology. They and their organizations will have a competitive edge over others who are not ready to exploit the new opportunities offered by information processing.

KEY WORDS

Bubble memory	Laser	Voice I/O
Calendar systems	Light guide	Very large scale
Charge-coupled device	Large scale integration	integration (VLSI)
(CCD)	Maintenance	Telecommunication
Earth station	Query by Example	Teleconferencing
Electronic mail	Retrieval languages	Text editing
Enhancements	Satellite	Word processing
Graphics	Superconductivity	

RECOMMENDED READINGS

Johnson, R., J. Valee, and K. Spangler: *Electronic Meetings, Technical Alternatives and Social Choices,* Addison-Wesley, Reading, Mass., 1979. (A book describing teleconferencing with a hypothetical example describing the pro's and con's of this approach.)

Scientific American, vol. 237, no. 3, September 1977. (A series of articles on microelectronics, the development of electronic circuits on chips, and their application.)

Uhling, R. P., D. J. Farber, and J. H. Bair: *The Office of the Future,* North Holland Publishing Co., Amsterdam, 1979. (A book that describes some of the capabilities and features of the office of the future.)

Zloof, M. N.: "Query by Example: A Data Base Language," *IBM Systems Journal,* vol. 16, no. 4, 1977, pp. 324–343. (An explanation of the capabilities and the development of the Query by Example system.)

DISCUSSION QUESTIONS

1   Why do scientists constantly try to reduce the size of computer components?
2   What uses can you envision for a home computer?
3   What are the advantages of charge-coupled devices and bubble memories? Where do they fit in the memory hierarchy?
4   Why would the development of an erasable optical memory be advantageous?
5   What can be done to alleviate the labor-intensive nature of programming?
6   What kind of tools does a user or manager need to develop systems?
7   How can the organization identify what applications requests are best handled by users themselves?
8   What are the disadvantages of systems like Query by Example?
9   What do you think the advantages of electronic mail are?
10   Can you think of problems with text editing and word processing applications? (Hint: consider the input process.)
11   Why might individuals resist the use of a calendar system?
12   What forms of resistance would you expect to see to office automation in general?
13   What are the major impediments to the recognition of continuous speech?
14   What kind of breakthroughs would speech recognition produce for information systems?
15   What are the major applications areas for computer graphics?
16   Why is input/output such a bottleneck in a computer system?
17   What are the implications of having greater computer power and lower costs?
18   Why is software apparently not subject to technological breakthroughs?
19   Do you have an suggestions as to what can be done to improve the productivity of programmers and systems analysts?
20   What do you think the disadvantages might be to teleconferencing?
21   Can you see any practical limits to the ability to communicate using satellites?
22   Why should it be necessary to invest in the maintenance of software; after all, programs do not wear out, or do they?
23   What kind of flexibility do on-line systems and the availability of computer networks provide for the organization in developing its information processing services?

System Alternatives and Acquisition

HARDWARE
    Service
    Remote Batch Processing
    Internal Systems
SOFTWARE
    Software Houses
    Packages
    Internal Staff
COMPARISON OF SOURCES
    Hardware
    Software
    The Decision
ACQUISITION STRATEGY
PERFORMANCE EVALUATION
    Early Approaches
    Contemporary Evaluation Techniques
    Recommendations
ACQUISITION OF A NEW COMPUTER SYSTEM
    Request for Proposal
    Performance
    Proposal Evaluation
SOFTWARE PACKAGES
    Criteria
    Decision
    Expanding Role
KEY WORDS
RECOMMENDED READINGS
DISCUSSION QUESTIONS

System Alternatives and Acquisition

CHAPTER ISSUES

- What are the sources for computer equipment and services?
- What processing alternatives are best for this organization?
- How should the organization select computers, software, and services?

Management is frequently involved in decisions on the acquisition of computer equipment and services, and these decisions have major implications for the organization. For some organizations, the decision to acquire computer capabilities will lead to the creation of an information services department requiring the investment of substantial resources. The firm adopting a package or turnkey system may change its procedures to adapt to the system. For an organization with a mature information services department, users frequently must choose between internal services and the special services offered by external vendors of computer time and/or software. In this chapter, we discuss some of the considerations in deciding between internal and external sources for hardware, systems, and software. We also explore major evaluation criteria for both hardware and software.

HARDWARE

There is a wide range of sources for computer power (see Table 11-1). We shall discuss the alternatives of a service bureau, remote processing, and an internal computer system for batch, on-line, or time-sharing services.

Service

Many organizations with no computer systems gain their first experience with information systems through service bureaus. Most service bureaus provide a range of services, from keypunching data through the processing and return of output. A number of service bureaus offer specialized packages, for example, payroll or accounts receivable. For batch work, the computer is located at the service bureau.

Table 11-1   Sources of Hardware and Software

Hardware alternatives			
	Service bureau	Remote	Internal
Batch	At service bureau	Batch terminal	General-purpose or minicomputer
On-line	Through large time-sharing network or local computer	Not applicable	Mixed or dedicated general-purpose, or dedicated minicomputer
Time sharing	Interactive terminals connected to central computer(s)	Not applicable	Mixed general-purpose, or dedicated minicomputer

Software alternatives			
	Software consultant/vendor	Applications package	Internal staff
Batch	Contract programming and design	Modifications by vendor or staff	Develop from beginning
On-line	Contract programming and design	Large system requires modification, small system may be operational without changes	Will use some packages, develop own applications program
Time sharing	Only for modifications	Use as is or modify	Modifications or write programs

For on-line systems using the external services alternative, a nationwide time-sharing network is often employed. The customer takes advantage of the vendor's existing operating systems and communications network; it is only necessary to write applications programs. One automobile manufacturer has adopted this approach for providing certain information to dealers so that a dedicated on-line system is not needed. If a dealer in one city decides to subscribe to the service now, long after the system was installed, the manufacturer only has to modify the basic tables in the system; there is no need to reconfigure the computer network, since the system uses an existing, national communications network.

Several service bureaus also rent or sell their customers a local computer to be installed at the customer's location. The local computer operates on-line and can be connected to the computers at the service bureau when a processing task requires a larger computer. Also, a large data base can be maintained by the service bureau computers and accessed through the local computer.

Many service bureaus provide time-sharing services; here the user has one or more interactive terminals that are usually connected by dial-up telephone lines to the computer. A service bureau owns and operates the computer. A user dials a connection phone call to establish a connection between the terminal and one of several service bureaus. There are a number of highly specialized service bureaus; for example, one offers services primarily to the financial community. This company has a number of proprietary data bases available and a special-purpose, high-level language to manipulate these data. Other bureaus offer general computational time-sharing services, though pure computing power is so inexpensive today that a vendor generally must offer special programs or data bases.

Remote Batch Processing

A remote system is similar to a service bureau in the sense that the central computer is not at the user's own location; instead a local terminal is used primarily for batch processing. The terminal features a card reader and line printer and often a card punch. Frequently a tape drive is at the batch terminal; the terminal may be a minicomputer or even a small general-purpose computer. With this processing alternative, an organization must have a computer department of some type, but it need not invest a large sum of money in a large general-purpose computer. Instead, this computer is at a service bureau and data are transmitted to and from it over telephone lines. Usually this alternative employs leased lines that offer higher speeds than voice-grade circuits. Remote batch work has somewhat the same characteristics as time sharing on a large computer. For example, one company that performs many engineering computations uses a remote batch system because it can buy only the computer services it needs. When the firm had its own computer system, it could not afford a computer with enough power to run large compute-bound engineering jobs efficiently. Now the firm pays for only the capacity it uses on a much larger general-purpose computer than it used previously.

A primary advantage of this approach to processing, then, is sharing. We still must have a computer department; in fact, all input/output preparation proceeds just as if the computer were on site. Instead of having a large general-purpose computer located within the organization, however, we have a terminal sending the same type of data to and receiving it from a central computer at a remote location. For backup purposes, several different vendors can be accessed from the same remote terminal.

Internal Systems

Our last alternative is an internal computer system; here, the organization owns, rents, or leases computer equipment. Large organizations typically have a mix of general-purpose computers and minicomputers for special jobs. A mature information services department usually undertakes a variety of activities from the operation and maintenance of existing systems to the design of new computer applications. The typical department includes an operations section with control clerks, data transcription personnel, computer operators, and possibly maintenance programmers. There is also a systems development group with analysts and programmers; some installations have systems programmers as well.

Small organizations in the last few years have acquired mini- and microcomputers at a rapid rate. These small, less expensive machines have expanded computer power to organizations that had no computer resources or could use only a service bureau. A minicomputer can be used for batch work of a general-purpose nature. On-line terminals connected directly to the computer

---

MANAGEMENT PROBLEM 11-1

Woolen Works, a small manufacturer of men's and boy's sweaters, has expanded steadily during the last decade. A rapid growth in sales strained existing information processing, especially for order entry. The president of the firm finally decided that some action was necessary and hired a consultant. The consultant recommended that the firm develop a computer-based order-entry system.

The president agreed that something was needed, but was unsure how to continue from the consultant's recommendation. Woolen could acquire its own computer and set up an information systems department. However, the president did not like the idea of becoming dependent on a few people to process information and did not feel he knew enough to manage a computer department.

A service bureau was also suggested. However, this meant that Woolen would be completely dependent on another organization. What if a service bureau could not meet the daily processing demanded by Woolen's order-entry system? A final alternative was to acquire a packaged system built around a dedicated minicomputer. One firm has been trying to interest him in such a system for several months. The drawback here is that Woolen would have to adapt to the system; the vendor will not change it to meet Woolen's unique requirements.

What other factors should the president of Woolen consider? Develop a scenario describing the development and operation of a system under each alternative.

---

are often used to key source data into the machine. When this mode of operation takes too much available computer time, devices that record data off-line are substituted, and the operation resembles the data preparation activities of a large computer department with general-purpose computers.

For on-line work, a large organization may have a dedicated on-line system or operate in mixed mode, with both on-line and batch work processed simultaneously on one computer. A small organization may use a dedicated minicomputer for on-line systems. A number of consultants and software vendors have developed packaged on-line systems on mini- and microcomputers. For example, one such system handles the routine information processing of a garment manufacturing firm, including order entry, accounts receivable, accounts payable, general ledger, production reports, sales analysis, and other processing.

Time sharing can be provided as one component of a general-purpose computer system or on a dedicated computer. Most time sharing on large general-purpose computers features remote batch processing as well as interactive time sharing. There are also a number of minicomputers whose manufacturers offer time-sharing operating systems, languages, and file packages.

SOFTWARE

In the early days of computers, manufacturers offered hardware and software together as a package or "bundle." Because of complaints from companies trying to develop and sell software and because of antitrust fears, major manufacturers have "unbundled" hardware and software. The customer usually acquires the computer hardware and operating system as one package since the hardware cannot really operate without this control program. However, compilers, special applications packages, and so on are purchased or rented separately. Unbundling has stimulated more software competition, which, of course, is good for the customer. However, it also has increased the range of software sources and the complexity of acquisition. Table 11-1 lists some of the software alternatives available. We shall discuss software vendors, applications packages, and the internal staff for developing batch, on-line, and time-sharing software.

Software Houses

Software consultants or vendors (software houses) offer programming and systems design services for both batch and on-line systems and some offer special packages as well. The software vendor may contract to manage an entire systems development effort or furnish programmers to perform work assigned by the client. The staff of the software house writes and tests batch and/or on-line programs. However, it is unusual for the average organization to have such a firm develop a time-sharing application; most organizations adopt an existing time-sharing package or users write their own programs.

A "turnkey system" is a variation on contract services made possible by the development of mini- and microcomputers. The turnkey vendor is a private contractor who provides the computer, in addition to programming, training, and installation support. The user contracts with the vendor for a complete system, and most frequently these systems involve a minicomputer. Some turnkey vendors have developed applications packages for a particular industry that suit many of the firms in that industry, such as the garment system example mentioned above. The customer owns the computer but does not have to manage a computer department or staff. Most systems are designed so that someone already employed by the customer can operate the system: computer professionals are not needed. Turnkey systems have proved very popular for small organizations that would like to take advantage of computer processing without establishing a computer department. Large organizations also use turnkey services to supplement the efforts of their own computer staff.

Packages

A contract software firm will analyze a proposed application and then bid for developing the needed software. Applications packages, such as those discussed in Chapter 8, represent another alternative to developing our own programs. A software house might sell and install its package; it also would make needed modifications to it as a part of a purchase or rental price or for an additional fee.

For an on-line package, such as the airline example in Chapter 8, the package vendor expects to make changes. The user may have to develop some of the applications programs to accompany the routines in the package. For a minicomputer-based on-line package, the system may be operational when acquired. A small organization might well choose to modify its procedures to use the package rather than incur the expense of modifying the computer programs.

Internal Staff

Many organizations have their own internal information services department staff writing programs and systems. These staff members may develop new applications from the beginning or use packages as building blocks, particularly for systems functions in an on-line application. In addition to developing new applications, the staff also fixes errors in existing applications and enhances these systems.

COMPARISON OF SOURCES

What are the advantages and disadvantages of different sources for hardware and software? We can look at the two extremes for discussion purposes: all activities are undertaken either internally or externally through an outside organization (see Table 11-2).

Hardware

With an internal computer department, an organization has to deal with the problem of managing the computer; overhead is introduced into the organization. For this price, management gains control over its own computer operations. Data remain exclusively within organizational confines and are accessible

Table 11-2 Comparison of Internal versus External Services

	Internal	External
Hardware		
Management	Must manage computer department	Contractual arrangement; no line management responsible except for data preparation
Control	Control potential high	Only through contract, influence, withholding payment
Security	Under own responsibility; data remains at internal location	Data in hands of external organization; other customers a threat
Priorities	Assigned by own employees	Determined by external management
Resources	Must accommodate peak loads; high fixed cost	Variable cost, pay only for what is used (beyond possible minimum charge)
Capacity	Limited to what is needed	Frequently more powerful equipment than could be justified by clients
Backup	Limited by internal resources	Usually available because of higher capacity
Software		
Management	Must manage program development	Contractual arrangements, specifications on cost, time, performance
Staff	May have to hire experts	Expect vendors to have expertise
Implementation	Probably easier in terms of user reaction to internal staff	May be more difficult for "outsiders"

only to employees. Processing priorities are established internally and no other organization can preempt time from an organization with its own system. Management must provide sufficient resources to accommodate peak loads, so there can be high fixed costs for computer equipment that may not be fully utilized under this alternative. Usually, extra capacity is not provided because of the cost. Backup may be limited by the resources management is able to provide.

Organizations choosing to rely on external services have a contractual agreement with the servicing firm. There are few management responsibilities of a supervisory nature because these tasks have been delegated to an outside company. Control may be less than under the internal alternative because litigation over contracts is costly and time consuming. Instead, the customer seeks to influence the service organization. Many firms worry about having sensitive data in the hands of another organization, particularly when other companies have access to the same computer resources. The priority for applications is also in the hand of the organization providing services; management influences, but does not control, processing priorities. With an outside organization, the customer incurs a variable cost and pays only for the resources consumed. Frequently, the client has access to more powerful equipment than would be installed internally, since it is being shared among a number of users. Availability is less of a problem because the service bureau has high capacity to serve all the customers.

Software

With internal software development, we must manage the development process. Internal program development often results in duplication; there may be a tendency to start from the beginning with each new system. Because there are "not-invented-here" complexes, packages are not adequately investigated. Implementation problems, however, should be minimized because internal employees deal directly with the users in the firm.

External software services are handled on a contractual basis. However, a customer may still need some individual who is familiar with computer technology to work with the contractor and monitor progress, although, for the most part, clients will rely on the vendor's expertise. Implementation can be difficult for "outsiders"; however, the client may be able to take advantage of an existing package or set of routines whose cost has been amortized over a large group of users.

The Decision

Unfortunately, it is not possible to determine how all these factors should be balanced; every organization must make its own decisions. One typical path is to begin with a service bureau to gain some familiarity with systems and technology. When a cost analysis indicates that an internal system is justified, the organization acquires equipment and hires a staff or acquires a turnkey system. Once the system is in operation, we may still use external services, for example, for time sharing or for special software tasks beyond the experience of the internal staff.

ACQUISITION STRATEGY

No matter what alternative is selected, the customer has to acquire computer equipment and/or services. How do we approach this problem? There are several considerations a potential customer should have in mind. First, check a vendor's financial condition; a number of small companies have gone bankrupt in the computer industry. Even major firms have sold or discontinued their computer manufacturing activities. How likely is a vendor to be around in the future to service the product and improve it?

What kind of documentation is available, particularly for software, since modifications may be necessary? Documentation describes how the system works and how it can be used, and without it, a customer has very little information on the product purchased. What kind of vendor support is available? Does the price include installation and training by the vendor?

An extremely important research activity for a customer is to contact present users of a product to determine their level of satisfaction. How well does the product or service meet vendor claims? What problems did users have? If possible, visit users without a vendor representative to ask these questions. If it is not possible to see a product demonstrated, do not buy it. Too often, announced products are delivered years late: insist on a demonstration and attempt to evaluate the performance of the product.

Before we discuss some of the factors to be considered in the acquisition of computer systems and software, we examine techniques for evaluating computer system performance. Performance evaluation is important for a number of reasons, and it should be a component of most acquisition decisions.

PERFORMANCE EVALUATION

One of the major activities in acquiring new equipment or software is the evaluation of product performance. There are many approaches to performance evaluation, and the following suggestions are taken from Lucas (1976b).

Early Approaches

Early approaches to hardware evaluation really did not consider software because, at that time, most programming was done in machine language, and software was not a major factor in performance. The first attempts to compare computers used central processing unit cycle time and add time as performance indicators. Unfortunately, these numbers ignore the organization of the machine and any special hardware or software features.

Instruction mixes extend cycle- and add-time comparisons. In a mix, the frequency of execution for typical instructions is used to compute a weighted average execution time, and this average is compared for several computers. For business computers, as an example, one might multiply a weighting factor by the manufacturer's specified time to execute additions, subtractions, data moves, and certain input/output operations. The weighted sources are added to give a total estimate of performance for a particular machine. Unfortunately, the mix technique omits any consideration of special hardware features and also totally ignores software.

A kernel is a program coded for the machine in question; however, it is not actually executed. The time required to execute the kernel program is developed from the manufacturers' specifications for the execution time of each instruction in the computer. The kernel, then, must be specified in assembly or machine language for timing purposes. Because a kernel uses the actual instructions of the computer, special features can be included. However, again, the technique does not include any consideration of software.

Contemporary Evaluation Techniques

The above approaches are used only to get a very rough indication of the performance differences among machines. For serious evaluation efforts, the methods presented below must be used instead.

Analytic Modeling   Analytic modeling is a performance evaluation technique focusing on mathematical analysis. It is best suited for design calculations —for example, for a queuing model of an on-line system. These models are extremely difficult to develop and validate; for the average information services department, consulting help is usually needed to develop such a model. Generally, these analytical approaches do not model software and therefore do not have wide applicability to the average computer installation.

Simulation   Simulation has been used extensively to evaluate the performance of computer systems. Simulation is not suitable for the selection of a specific piece of software such as an applications program, but it can include software considerations in evaluating the performance of a complete computer system. Various types of simulators are available, or users can write their own, using special-purpose simulation languages. However, writing a simulation is a

---

MANAGEMENT PROBLEM 11-2

Marilyn Davidson is manager of new business development for the First National Bank. Her job, a new one in the bank, is to perform analysis and undertake special projects for major bank clients. As a result, she and her staff are frequently called upon to perform massive computational chores. After much manual and clerical processing, the frustrations, errors, and delays caused by this method of information processing became intolerable to both the bank and its customers.

Marilyn has begun to investigate actively some type of computer processing. The bank has an extensive array of computers, but discussions with the information services department were not encouraging. The manager of the computer staff explained that Marilyn would be making requests at odd times for unusual runs that might never be repeated. His large batch computers were better suited to printing large volumes of repetitive information.

Marilyn was discouraged until she talked with a friend in another department in the bank. Her colleague said, "Oh, the internal computer department always responds that way—their conception of a computer is quite old-fashioned. We have turned to time-sharing for our needs since the computer staff is so unresponsive."

Marilyn wonders about time sharing and whether it would be a good choice for the analyses in her department. If she acquired time-sharing services, would she need a computer programmer or could she use packages? If new programs are needed, should she have her own staff learn how to program the computer or rely on outside contractors? Should she hire professional programmers to work for her department instead?

---

research project and the average user is not encouraged to undertake such an effort.

Benchmark   A benchmark is a sample of an existing workload and it does include software considerations. Any aspect of a system can be evaluated using benchmarks, from an entire computer to a file-management package. A benchmark is an existing job (or combination of jobs) that has been recoded if necessary so it can be executed on the system being evaluated. The benchmark job is executed on the new equipment. The use of a benchmark is based on the assumption that the existing job mix or one particular application is representative of how the product under evaluation will be used. For a thorough evaluation using benchmarks, many different benchmarks may have to be developed and executed. This technique offers a high degree of flexibility because the evaluation effort can be tailored to the importance of the decision. For a major acquisition, a large number of benchmarks can be used; for a less important alternative, only a few are selected.

Synthetic Modules   The synthetic job is a mix between a kernal program and a benchmark. Like a kernal program, it is coded to represent a typical function and is not restricted to being an existing application. Like a benchmark, a synthetic program is actually executed on the equipment under evaluation. Synthetic modules offer a great deal of flexibility because it is possible to include estimates of how the job load will change in the future when the modules are constructed. For example, certain activities such as file processing can be more highly weighted in an evaluation if a new data-base application is planned.

It is possible to use a small group of synthetic modules to model a much larger workload by combining and weighting these different components. As with benchmarks, the evaluator can perform a number of experiments consistent with the importance of the decision. An extensive group of synthetic modules can be developed and scientific experiments planned for evaluation. As an alternate approach, a few modules and a small number of runs may be employed to obtain a rough estimate of performance.

Monitoring   Monitoring falls into a different category of performance evaluation than the approaches described above. Monitoring is primarily oriented toward evaluating existing hardware and software. The techniques above are most useful in deciding whether to acquire something new, and monitors are usually used to tune or improve the performance of an existing computer system. Although there are two types of monitors currently available, the distinction between them is blurring because they have been combined to produce hybrid or integrated monitors.

A hardware monitor contains a set of probes that are attached at critical points to the computer component being monitored. The monitoring device collects data on elapsed time or the count of some value such as the number of disk-file accesses. The data recorded by the monitors are input to a separate batch program that reduces and analyzes them. The major disadvantage of the hardware monitor is limitations on what can be measured and the fact that it is often difficult to relate the data collected to software performance.

A software monitor is a program embedded within an operating system. The operating system calls it as a high-priority task every so often to collect statistics on the status of the machine. The data gathered by the software monitor are also generally analyzed after the end of the monitoring period. Since this monitor has access to all operating system tables and data, it can keep track of more items than a hardware monitor. Unfortunately, because this measurement tool is a program, it interacts with what is being measured; that is, a software monitor's execution affects the system it is measuring.

Integrated or hybrid monitors use software and hardware to collect data. The hardware monitor may be a minicomputer operating under program control. These monitors will undoubtedly become more common in the future because of their flexibility and measurement capabilities.

Monitoring can be very useful, and many installations have experienced impressive savings by tuning their computer systems. However, there are some drawbacks to monitoring. It is necessary to sample the system for a short period of time, which may be unrepresentative. Far too much activity occurs in a short period of time when machines operate in the 50-nanosecond (10^{-9} second) range. Even with a small sampling period, large amounts of data will have to be analyzed. A user must study the data and determine in what way to modify the system to improve performance. The monitor shows the existence of a bottleneck, but it does not indicate whether performance will improve by a small amount or by a major increment if the bottleneck is removed. If the system is tuned for one particular workload or some portion of it, can we say that this job is representative of the entire processing load on the system? What will happen if other jobs are added or the workload changes?

Recommendations

A number of performance evaluation techniques have been discussed above, and, certainly, there are drawbacks with each one. How should a typical user proceed in evaluating performance? For acquiring a new product, the best alternative is probably to use benchmarks if the future job load can be predicted reasonably well from existing applications. Synthetic jobs can be used as an alternative if the job mix is expected to change in the future. The user can construct a series of experiments to evaluate the product under consideration.

When a computer system is operating, it is probably a good idea to use a hardware or software monitor periodically—every 6 months or year—for tuning purposes. Tuning may indicate the need for a new device or make it possible to postpone the acquisition of a larger system by making minor improvements in existing hardware or software.

Software monitors can also be used to tune programs that are under development. These monitors provide frequency counts for different program

---

MANGEMENT PROBLEM 11-3

David Klein is a senior consultant for Computer Associates Limited. He has hung up the phone from a conversation with a potential client, a major manufacturer of consumer durables. The firm's technical computer staff wanted to evaluate the computer vendor's newest operating system, which provides a virtual memory facility. The manufacturing company wishes to determine if the new operating system would improve throughput. The technical staff, according to the caller, had begun to write a simulation of their computer for the purpose of performing the analysis. However, the staff had quickly become mired in details and was looking for help. David made an appointment to see them the next week.

David had been active in computer performance evaluation for a number of years. However, this was the first time anyone had suggested employing simulation for this type of problem. At least, he had never heard of a user of computer systems writing such a simulation. He knew of computer vendors who had used simulation to help develop operating systems, but the manufacturing firm's approach was new to him.

Why was David surprised by the phone call? Why does he think simulation is probably not the best alternative for the manufacturing company? How do you think the computer vendor used simulation in the design of an operating system? What performance evaluation technique would you recommend to the manufacturing company?

---

instructions, so the programmer can optimize the parts of the program that are executed most frequently. However, in today's environment we are usually more interested in stressing prompt completion and clarity of coding rather than extremely efficient program execution.

ACQUISITION OF A NEW COMPUTER SYSTEM

Periodically, it may be necessary to upgrade a computer system or to acquire an entirely new computer system. The acquisition of a system is a complicated decision and usually involves a number of people in the organization, including both users and members of the information services department.

Request for Proposal

After the need for a new system has been identified, the potential buyer usually prepares a carefully written request for bids or proposals (RFP). This request is sent to various vendors, who in turn propose equipment. The buyer often attempts to have a manufacturer do most of this work. Table 11-3 shows some of the factors that should be included in the request for a proposal.

All present applications should be described in detail in the proposal. The vendors will consider these and recommend the equipment from their product lines that they think is best for the workload. Plans for a new application should also be included; the vendor should be asked to specify and support reliability data for the equipment. Are there redundant components in the system to

Table 11-3 Items Included in Request for Proposal

1 Present applications
File characteristics
Input/output
Volume
Frequency
Batch or on-line
2 Same as **1** for proposed systems
3 Vendor service
4 Reliability data
5 Backup
6 Demonstration
7 Evaluation arrangements
8 Conversion and transition
9 Descriptive material (hardware and software)
10 Price

provide backup? Can a faulty component be isolated while the system continues to run in a possibly degraded model? The customer would also like to have information about similar installations in the area that could be used in an emergency.

The vendor should provide arrangements for demonstration and describe how the customer can access the proposed configuration to evaluate its performance. The installation of a new computer or the transition to a new system is a major undertaking and the vendor should present a transition plan. Table 11-4 contains some of the descriptive material that might be requested from the vendor to obtain an idea of the type of equipment being proposed. Certainly the price for the recommended system should be provided in detail both for software and hardware components.

Performance

The customer should prepare to test the proposed equipment while the vendor develops a proposal. A typical customer will use benchmarks or possibly synthetic modules to model the existing and proposed plan workload. Benchmarks also are an excellent technique for indicating difficulties that can be expected during the transition from an existing computer system to a new system. The customer attempts to execute several existing jobs without changes to see how easy it is to run them on the new system.

A large number of benchmarks or synthetic jobs (often more than 20 or 30 are needed) should be run in several experiments on the proposed equipment. If an entirely new computer system is being acquired and performance is an important criterion, compilers as well as operating systems should be examined. For the turnkey vendor or for packages, the user can visit a firm that uses the system with the same volume of transactions and observe performance. This way the potential customer is able to see exactly what is to be acquired.

Table 11-4   Example of Descriptive Proposal Material

Hardware	Speed
CPU cycle time	Transfer rate
Memory cycle time and hierarchy	Tracks
Data path	Disks
Registers	Seek time
Type	Rotational-delay time
Number	Average access time
Microprogramming features	Capacity
Instruction set	Removable or fixed
Fixed point	Bulk storage
Floating point	Access time
Decimal	Size
Precision	Data path
Interrupt structure	I/O peripherals
Number	Input/output speed
Type	Reject rate (e.g., OCR scanners)
Priority	Software support
Memory size (each hierarchical element)	Software
Memory organization	Operating system
Data	Job and task management
Instructions	Multiprogramming
Special features	Partitions
Parallel operations	Size
Instruction look-ahead	Priority
Multiple processors	Overhead (time and space)
Data channels	Control language
Number	Documentation
Type	Utilities
Transfer rate	Special features
Control units	Compilers
Device assignment	Subset or superset of language supported
Effect on CPU	Extensions to language
Storage devices	File-accessing capabilities
Tapes	Storage requirements
Density	Applications programs

Proposal Evaluation

Currently, many organizations employ extremely subjective methods to evaluate proposals. Meaningful criteria should be established for evaluating each proposal from the different vendors. Examples of these criteria include performance, presence of certain software, ease of conversion, the availability of special applications packages, and the response of other users having the equipment. The evaluation team should assign a weight to each criterion. It may be possible to eliminate certain vendors because of one dominant failing, for example, the lack of a key applications package that is critical for the customer. If it is not possible to eliminate vendors one by one, then a formal evaluation procedure is necessary.

A RETAIL SYSTEM

Hudsons headquartered in Detroit has seventeen stores in three states and annual sales of over $600,000,000. Hudsons has a new computer-based system to help solve the continuing problem of controlling the flow of merchandise. This flow begins with the order of a product from a supplier and ends when the product is delivered to the sales floor.

The merchandise processing system includes a company-wide communications network and a central data base that tracks merchandise from the buy order until it is placed in the destination store's stock. Orders are entered on-line when the buyer issues a purchase order. All subsequent receiving movement and transactions are keyed into the system on-line. On-line access to the system is available at buyer warehouse and store and management levels.

The system services all the stores in Michigan, Indiana, and Ohio. Company officials feel they could not have handled the much larger volume of purchased goods that move through their warehouses to stores during the past year without the system. The heavier work load was handled easily while operating costs dropped by $4,000,000.

Approximately 350 buyers and assistant buyers for 380 departments of Hudsons placed an average of 300 orders a day via the system. Terminals in the buying department are used to enter the purchase order data including vendor name, items and quantities, and prices and store department destinations. The initial transaction sets up the data base record that will follow the ordered merchandise to the selling floor. The system automatically generates a detailed fully extended purchase order which is ready for mailing to the vendor.

One of the major savings is not only time but also the number of documents generated. A preliminary study showed that before the on-line system, the typical purchase order ultimately multiplied itself into 107 paper copies. If a change was made, an additional 115 pieces of paper were generated. Now virtually all of this paper is eliminated. Buyers have more time for a closer evaluation of their open to buy positions and for more effective buying. The clerical staff assigned to each buyer has been sharply reduced.

Receiving is also handled on-line in the warehouse. By entering the purchase order number of the incoming shipment, a detailed receiving document can be printed. The actual item quantity delivered when entered creates merchandise tickets with all of the information required from the current purchase order.

Merchandise that arrives on hangers, apparel in cartons, case goods, furniture and appliances are quantity checked, unit by unit. Any discrepancies between the delivered quantity and the amount ordered are noted on the receiving document which becomes input to accounts payable processing. Merchandise is magnetically ticketed on-line at the warehouse for immediate sales floor use on arrival at a destination store, completing the cycle from purchase order generation to becoming available for sale.

Data Processor, June/July 1980.

One approach is to assign the interval scores to each vendor on each criterion and multiply this score by the weights of the criteria. These weighted scores are added to produce a final weighted total. However, the results are often quite close, and the evaluation team may not have much confidence in minor numerical differences among the vendors. Another alternative is to prepare a brief scenario of how the computer department and the company would function with each alternative system. What transitional activities would have to take place? Then the decision-making body rank-orders the scenarios and chooses the most desirable one. Because there are usually few alternatives, three to six at the most, it is far easier to rank scenarios than to make a decision based on small differences in numerical scores.

SOFTWARE PACKAGES

Some of the benefits and problems of software packages were discussed earlier in Chapter 8. In this section we consider some criteria for evaluating different packages.

Criteria

It was recommended earlier that the information services department and steering committee agree on screening criteria for packages. Many times packages will be considered as an alternative to developing a system in-house. Table 11-5 lists some of the possible evaluation criteria for decisions on applications packages. The major reason for acquiring a package is that it performs a desired function. The customer wants to know how many desired functions are included and what effort would be required to modify the package.

It is also important to consider the user interface; that is, how difficult is it to use the package? How much information does the user have to supply? Is it simple to prepare and understand the input? Is the package flexible? Can it be used if any requirements change somewhat?

The evaluation is concerned with how long the package takes to run and how it might impact current computer operations. Execution time considerations are not too important for a simple application that is run infrequently, but execution time can be very important for a major, dedicated system. The user will also want to know how much present procedures will have to change for the new package.

Table 11-5   Considerations in Evaluating Software Packages

Functions included
Modifications required to package
Installation effort
User interface
Flexibility
Execution time
Changes required in existing system to use package
Vendor support
Updating of package
Documentation
Cost and terms

Just as with hardware, it is necessary to evaluate the software vendor's support and the likelihood that a vendor will remain in business. It does not require much in the way of resources to program and sell software packages. Updates and improvements to the package should be forthcoming, and we are dependent on the vendor's remaining in business.

With software packages, documentation is extremely important; the information services department staff may have to modify the package and will undoubtedly have to correct errors that occur. Users are extremely interested in documentation as well, since documentation—combined with whatever training the vendor provides—must be sufficient to allow users to interact with the package. The final consideration is cost, although we should remember that we usually underestimate the cost of developing a comparable system ourselves and overestimate the cost of modifying a package!

Many of the criteria in Table 11-5 require the analysis of package documentation by a systems analysis and programming staff. We should also contact present users to answer questions about vendor claims and support. Almost all the recommended criteria are subjective, and therefore several individuals should rank the package on each criteria, for example, on a 1-to-7 scale. The responses can then be averaged for each criterion and a score developed for the package.

Decision

It is probably best to have a two-stage decision for applications packages. That is, we divide the criteria for package selection into essential and nonessential groups. We can insist that a package obtain a passing score established in advance on each essential criterion to be considered for acquisition. This procedure protects the information services department, which often has legitimate reasons for opposing a package. For example, reasons such as poor documentation or inability to understand and modify the code because of its lack of clarity are sufficient to warrant the rejection of a package.

If a package is acceptable and is the only alternative under consideration, we should probably acquire it. However, if several packages are available, then the ones that pass the screening test can be compared by ratings or scenarios as described in the last section. If the package under consideration is an alternative to the development of an in-house system, the criteria established before the acquisition effort by the steering committee should be used to evaluate this package in comparison with other processing alternatives.

Expanding Role

Given the high cost of developing new applications, packaged programs are becoming increasingly important in the entire decision process for obtaining computer services. For some organizations, the presence of an adequate software package is even more important than the computer on which it runs. For example, when a firm acquires a turnkey system, it will be more interested in how the package fits its needs than with the specific aspects of the computer that executes the package.

Even for large organizations that do a substantial amount of custom programming with an internal staff, the availability of a package can make the difference in deciding what computer system to acquire. Over the past two decades, the emphasis on evaluation has shifted from the capabilities of the hardware to the ease of use and power of software. It is expected that this trend will continue and that more of the evaluation effort in the future will be devoted to comparing the functions of software and its ease of use with the requirements of the organization.

KEY WORDS

Analytic models	Hybrid monitor	Scenarios
Backup	Independent manufacturer	Service bureau
Benchmarks	Instruction mixes	Simulation
Capacity	Internal services	Software monitor
Contractual relationships	Kernal programs	Software vendor
Cycle and add times	Packages	Synthetic programs
External services	Performance evaluation	Unbundling
Hardware monitor	Remote processing	

RECOMMENDED READINGS

Davis, G. B.: *Computer Data Processing,* 2d ed., McGraw-Hill, New York, 1973. (See especially the section on performance evaluation.)

Nie, N., C. Hull, J. Jenkins, K. Steinbrenner, and D. H. Bent: *Statistical Package for the Social Sciences,* 2d ed., McGraw-Hill, New York, 1975. (An example of excellent user documentation for a software package; it is a standard by which other documentation can be judged.)

Timmreck, E. M.: "Computer Selection Methodology," *Computing Surveys,* vol. 5, no. 4, December 1973, pp. 199–222. (A good survey of approaches to the computer selection decision.)

Walton, R. E., and J. N. Dutton: "The Management of Interdepartmental Conflict: A Model and Review," *Administrative Science Quarterly,* vol. 14, no. 1, March 1969, pp. 73–84. (How do the conditions of the conflict model apply to the relationship between the customer and computer product and service vendors?)

DISCUSSION QUESTIONS

1 What are the tradeoffs in acquiring hardware from various alternatives such as a service bureau?

2 What are the advantages and disadvantages of using contract programming services versus an internal staff? How would you expect documentation to differ between these two alternatives?

3   Developing a nationwide on-line system by using a commercial time-sharing system can save development time and effort. What is the cost of this approach versus the cost of a dedicated on-line system, developed and operated internally?

4   What do you think the most important factors are in influencing management on the decision whether to use external or develop internal computer services?

5   What are the problems of managing an information services department? Why do managers resist the development of an internal department?

6   Does entering a relationship with a service bureau solve the management problems of computer-based information systems? What areas of difficulty still remain?

7   What is wrong with the use of cycle and add times or instruction mixes for performance evaluation?

8   What is the major difference between monitoring and other types of performance evaluation?

9   What are the problems involved in using a monitor to tune a system?

10 What are the drawbacks of analytic models and simulation models for the average computer installation?

11 Why should a computer installation consider the use of application packages; what are the advantages and disadvantages?

12 In what situation would you expect applications packages to be most satisfactory?

13 What would your reaction be to the development of a set of industrywide synthetic modules to be used in performance evaluation?

14 How would you characterize an existing computer workload for performance evaluation purposes?

15 What performance evaluation technique would you use, and why, if the workload is expected to change drastically in the next 5 years?

16 To what extent should vendors other than the one currently supplying a computer be included in bidding for a new system?

17 What are the advantages and disadvantages of mixed-vendor installations—for example, when the computer and main memory are from one company and the peripherals are from another?

18 What factors inhibit the conversion to a different vendor's computer? Has the development of higher-level languages affected this type of conversion? Will the use of more applications packages impact the conversion to a different computer vendor?

19 What types of questions and information would you desire from a survey of other users of computer equipment under consideration for acquisition?

20 How can regular levels of service be maintained during the conversion to new computer equipment? What are the dangers of acquiring new equipment?

21 What are the disadvantages of using a weighted score for ranking competing proposals for computer equipment? What advantages are presented by scenarios to describe how an information services department and organization would function under each alternative for a new computer system?

22 Is it a good idea to be a pioneer with the new equipment or software? Should an installation wait before acquiring a newly developed computer system component?

23 How can an information services department avoid having to make frequent requests for additional computer capacity? As the manager, what is your response to this

strategy? Does the development of a plan for information systems activities affect this problem?

24 Computer systems can be purchased, rented, or leased from a third party. What are the advantages and disadvantages of each alternative?

25 Why should applications packages be seriously considered as an alternative to programming and implementing a system with an internal computer staff? What are the most significant difficulties with these packages? How can the ease of modifying a package be determined before its acquisition?

Part Four

Systems Analysis and Design

One of the most exciting activities in the information systems field is the design of a new computer-based system. In this part of the book we follow the life cycle of a system from its inception through final installation. From the considerations discussed in Part Two, on organizational issues, we recommend an approach to systems analysis and design in which users have control over the design process; the chapters in this part of the text stress the role of the manager and user in each stage of systems analysis and design. The systems analyst aids the user in making crucial decisions and performs the technical tasks necessary to develop the system. We complete this part with a short discussion of project management, since so many information systems have failed to achieve time and budget targets, especially during the programming stage.

WHAT IS A SYSTEM?

THE SYSTEMS LIFE CYCLE

RESPONSIBILITIES DURING THE LIFE CYCLE

RESOURCES FOR NEW SYSTEMS
    Demands and Resources
    A Resource Allocation Problem

PROBLEMS IN THE LIFE CYCLE

USER-ORIENTED DESIGN
    Problems with the Conventional View
    Predicted Results
    Required Knowledge
    Design Team

DATA COLLECTION
    Observation
    Interviews
    Questionnaires
    Comparison

DESIGN TOOLS
    Flowcharts
    Decision Tables
    Other Techniques

SUMMARY

KEY WORDS

RECOMMENDED READINGS

DISCUSSION QUESTIONS

Chapter 12

Introduction and Overview

- How does one develop a computer-based information system?
- What tools and techniques can be used in systems analysis and design?
- What resources should management make available for systems analysis and design?

The design of a new computer-based information system is an exciting and demanding undertaking. First, someone calls attention to a problem with existing information processing procedures. A design team assesses the benefits of using a computer to improve these procedures. Then an abstract model of present processing procedures is developed and designers create a new information processing system. The new procedures are converted into systems specifi-

cations and finally into computer programs. During the final stages of development, the system is tested and converted and becomes operational.

The design of an information system is a creative and labor-intensive task. It
is creative because we are building a new set of information processing
procedures just as an architect designs a new building. Systems analysis and
design is a human, intellectual task. There are some portions of design that can
be automated, but most of the creative aspects require human thought.

What are the roles of the user and manager in systems analysis and design?
In this chapter we introduce the systems life cycle and discuss the resources
available for developing new systems. We shall see that users and managers have
crucial roles in all aspects of systems analysis and design.

WHAT IS A SYSTEM?

In Chapter 4 we saw a number of examples of information systems, and in each
chapter we have presented one or two applications briefs describing how a
computer has been applied to an information processing problem. A system is
made up of a number of interrelated components only some of which are easily
seen. For example, it is difficult to characterize the actions of individuals who are
involved in making decisions as a part of an information system. The flow of
information and the processing of data by computer programs and/or individuals
can also be obscure.

One of the major tasks in systems analysis and design is to describe systems,
both existing systems and proposed new systems. Later in this chapter we shall
discuss some of the tools available for preparing descriptions of systems, but for
now we present an overview of a system.

Information systems can be described by four of their key components:

1 Decisions
2 Transactions and processing
3 Information and its flow
4 Individuals or functions involved

It is difficult to observe the decision process, though we can see and review the
results of a decision. Transactions are usually more visible, though many current
systems use computer programs, which are not easy to understand, to process
transactions. In principle an observer can see information and its flows.
Individuals can be observed too, but it is not always easy to figure out the
information processing functions they perform.

Much of systems analysis and design, as we mentioned above, consists
of developing a sufficient understanding of a system to document it. Consider
the following example of a simple inventory system; we can describe it as
follows:

Decisions

1 What to reorder
2 When to reorder it
3 How much to reorder

Transactions

1 Place an order
2 Receive merchandise
3 Withdraw goods from inventory

Information

1 Quantity on hand for each item
2 Historical usage for each item
3 Cost of the item
4 Holding costs
5 Reorder costs
6 Interest cost (to finance inventory)

Individuals/functions

1 Warehouse supervisors
2 Stock clerk
3 Receiving clerks
4 Purchasing agents

Several other systems are also related to this one, including purchasing and accounts payable. The information above serves only to describe the simple inventory system. We could further document this system by going into more details, especially concerning the flow of information. We could prepare flowcharts, which we discuss at the end of this chapter to help visualize how the system works. Also we can document the various decisions in narrative form to provide a better understanding of the inventory system.

This example illustrates the difficulty of describing and defining a system. Unfortunately there is no one standard for what constitutes a system or how to document it. A number of different approaches are used, and individuals have to develop descriptive techniques that help them conceptualize a system. Most people find it easiest to start at a very high level and then work toward filling in the details. In our example above, we described the system first as being concerned with inventory. To anyone with experience in working with inventories, this description should stimulate thoughts of how inventory systems operate in general. By listing decisions, transactions, information flows, and functions, we add details to the inventory system. Further details can be added in a top-down fashion as our knowledge increases about this particular system. In the end, everyone involved in trying to learn about this system should share a common concept of the system and an understanding of the documents describing it.

THE SYSTEMS LIFE CYCLE

A computer-based information system has a life cycle, just like a living organism or a new product. The various stages in the life cycle of a system are shown in Table 12-1. The idea for a new information system is stimulated by a need to improve information processing procedures. This need leads to the preliminary survey to determine if a system can be developed to solve these processing problems. If the results of the survey are positive, it is refined to produce a more detailed feasibility study. From the outcome of the feasibility study, a decision is made whether to proceed with the design of a system. One of the alternatives sketched in the feasibility study is chosen for development if a positive decision is made.

Table 12-1   The Systems Life Cycle

Inception
   Preliminary survey
Feasibility study
   Existing procedures
   Alternative systems
   Cost estimates
Systems analysis
   Details of present procedures
   Collection of data on volumes, input/output, files
Design
   Ideal system unconstrained
   Revisions to make ideal acceptable
Specifications
   Processing logic
   File design
   Input/output
   Programming requirements
   Manual procedures
Programming
Testing
   Unit tests
   Combined module tests
   Acceptance tests
Training
Conversion and installation
Operations
   Maintenance
   Enhancements

In systems analysis, the existing information processing procedures are documented in detail. One major task during this phase is to define the boundaries of the system. Does the problem just concern inventory control, or should any new system also consider the problems in purchasing when inventory has to be replenished? Data are also collected during analysis on the volume of transactions, decision points, and existing files.

The most challenging and creative part of the life cycle is the design of a new system. One approach to this task is to develop an ideal system relatively unconstrained by cost or technology; this ideal system is then refined until it becomes feasible. Detailed specifications must be prepared for the system just designed. The exact logic to be followed in processing and the contents and structure of the files must be specified. Input and output devices are selected, and the formats for I/O are developed. These requirements for processing, files, and I/O activities lead to the specification of programming requirements; these requirements can be turned over to a programming staff for coding.

In the programming stage, the actual computer programs necessary to perform the logical operations of processing are written. In some organizations this task is done by a separate group of programmers; other organizations use analyst-programmers. The same individuals who perform the systems analysis and design also code the resulting programs. Programs have to be tested carefully, first as units and then in combined modules. Usually a programming task is broken down into a series of smaller subtasks or modules; all the individual modules must operate together if the system is to work properly. During the final stages of testing, there will be some type of acceptance test in which users verify that the system works satisfactorily.

Since one purpose of the new information processing system is to change existing procedures, training is crucial. All individuals have to understand what is required by the new system. When training has been completed, it is possible to undertake conversion; it may be necessary to write special programs to convert existing files into new ones or to create files from manual records. Finally, after all these stages, the system is installed.

After the problems of installation have been resolved and the organization has adjusted to the changes created by the new system, the operational stage is begun; that is, the system now operates on a routine basis. However, this does not mean that it remains unchanged: there is a constant need for maintenance and enhancements. Maintenance is required because programs inevitably have errors that must be corrected when they appear. Because of the creative nature of design, users and the computer staff may not have communicated accurately, so that certain aspects of the system must be modified as operational experience is gained with it. As users work with the system, they will learn more about it and will develop ideas for change and enhancements. It is unreasonable to consider a computer-based information system finished; the system continues to evolve throughout its life cycle if, in fact, it is successful.

Figure 12-1 shows the resources required during each stage of the life cycle

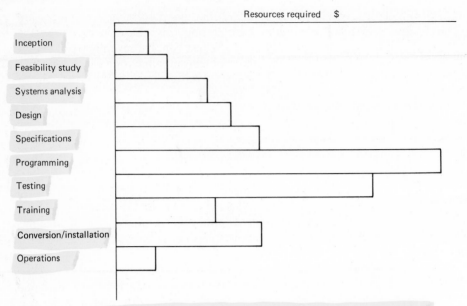

Figure 12-1 Resources required during each stage of the life cycle for a typical system.

for a typical system. (The pattern of time required would be much the same.) Few resources are usually required during the inception and feasibility study. Once systems analysis is begun, more expenses will be incurred as analysts and users work on the system and its design. These stages culminate in the preparation of specifications from which programming can begin. The programming stage is intensive and requires the most resources. For a large project, the entire process of design can last two years or more, of which over a year may be required to write programs and test them. Training will occur in parallel with the later stages of programming, and finally the system will be converted and installed. After this time, the system reverts to operational status and is run on a routine basis. The resources required at this stage are steady with some increases as the system becomes older and more changes are requested.

One noticeable trend in the industry is to move more of the design process forward, that is, to spend more time in analysis and design. If a system is well specified, there are fewer changes during programming. These later changes often require major redesign of programs and files, a very costly process. The entire systems life cycle can be compared to constructing a building. Changes are relatively inexpensive in the early conceptual stages. They become a little more expensive at the blueprint stage and exorbitant when the walls are erected. For systems, changes are much the same; in the conceptual stages of analysis and design they are reasonable. However, when programs are being written and some are complete, major design changes have the potential to create huge time and cost overruns.

RESPONSIBILITIES DURING THE LIFE CYCLE

Users, management, and the information services department staff interact in a number of ways during the analysis, design, and operation of information systems. In this part of the text on systems analysis and design, we shall often refer to the responsibilities of each of these groups in the development of successful systems. Because this task is so complex and demanding, it is essential that all three groups cooperate during the analysis and design process. Table 12-2 restates the stages in the systems life cycle and suggests the appropriate roles for users, management, and the information services department.

The user initiates the preliminary survey by suggesting a potential application. The information services department responds with a rough estimate of its desirability and with several alternative systems, for example, improvements to present information processing activities, a batch system, a package, or even an on-line system, each meeting some percentage of user needs. Management must approve of the basic suggestion and the idea of a new computer application in this area of the firm. Management should also participate in setting the objectives for any new system. A preliminary survey evaluates each alternative on criteria developed by a selection committee. The selection committee, with management participation, authorizes a feasibility study, possibly eliminating some alternatives suggested in the preliminary survey.

The information services department staff conducts the feasibility study with help and advice from users. Users conduct an analysis of the existing system and help the information services department evaluate various alternatives on criteria specified by the selection committee. Management reviews the feasibility of the proposed alternatives and develops an understanding of what the system will accomplish. The selection committee selects the alternative for implementation with participation and review by management. Possibly the committee chooses the alternative of no new system, in which case the application may be held in abeyance until changing conditions make it feasible.

If the decision is to proceed with the development of a new system, users and the information services department staff collaborate to analyze the existing system. Users aid by explaining existing processing procedures and providing data. The computer staff uses this information to document the existing system and help establish the boundaries of a new system. Management has a key role to play in this stage: it must provide adequate resources both for the information services department and for users. It may be necessary to hire additional staff so that users can participate or additional analysts to work on the project.

Next the design of a new system begins; we advocate that users design their own output and input and basic processing logic. The information services department acts as a catalyst, presenting alternatives for users to consider. Management encourages user design through its own attendance at review meetings. Management may provide special rewards, prizes, or other incentives to help encourage user participation in design. Management also must plan for

Table 12-2 Responsibilities during the System Life Cycle

Stages	Users	Responsibilities of	
		Management	Information services staff
Inception	Initiate study, suggest application, sketch information needs, describe existing processing procedures	Approve area for application, set objectives	Listen to requirements, respond to questions, devise alternatives, assess using rough estimates, prepare preliminary survey
Feasibility study	Help evaluate existing system and proposed alternatives, select alternative for design	Review feasibility, understand proposal, choose alternative	Evaluate alternatives using agreed-upon criteria
Systems analysis	Help describe existing system, collect and analyze data	Provide resources, attend reviews	Conduct analysis, collect data, and document findings
Design	Design output, input, processing logic; plan for conversion and forecast impact on users; design manual procedures; remain aware of file structures and design	Encourage user design, provide rewards, attend reviews, plan impact	Present alternatives and tradeoffs to users for their decisions
Specifications	Review specifications, help develop specifications for manual procedures	Understand high-level logic, key features	Combine user needs with technical requirements to develop specifications, develop technical conversion plan
Programming	Monitor progress	Monitor, provide buffer, extra resources	Organize programming, design modules, code programs, report progress
Testing	Generate test data and evaluate results	Review	Test program modules individually and in entire system
Training	Develop materials, conduct training sessions	Review	Aid in preparation of materials and train operations staff
Conversion and installation	Phase conversion, provide resources, conduct postimplementation audit	Attend user sessions, demonstrate management commitment	Coordinate conversion, perform conversion processing tasks, help in postimplementation audit
Operations	Provide data and utilize output, monitor system use and quality suggest modifications and enhancements	Monitor	Process data to produce output reliably, respond to enhancement requests, suggest improvements, monitor service

the impact of the system on the organization at this point. Will the structure of the organization be changed? How will work groups be affected? What will specific individuals do as a result of the system? A plan for conversion, including a forecast of the impact of the system on all potential users, should be developed. A conversion plan can be started at this point and users can work on the design of any manual procedures associated with the new system.

The information services staff develops detailed specifications based on the logic and requirements specified by users; the staff also prepares a technical conversion plan. The users on the design team review the technical plans and also work on the development of specifications for manual procedures. It is vitally important at this stage for both users and managers to understand the system. Users must be familiar with the output, input, and processing logic. Management must understand the overall flow of the system and be aware of key decisions. For example, management should be aware if inventory items are to be grouped into classes and different reordering rules applied to each class. Management should help set the classification and reorder rules and understand how the logic is to work.

The user and management role during programming is one of monitoring progress. Are modern techniques being used to manage programming? Is a project schedule maintained and are resources reallocated as necessary to achieve installation on schedule? The bulk of the responsibility during this design stage rests with the information services department. The staff has to design program modules, code them, and test them both alone and in combination. Management should realize that they need to help when problems arise. The development of a computer-based system is similar to a research and development project; it is very difficult to anticipate every contingency. There will be project slippages, budget overruns, and other problems. The role of management is to provide a buffer for the project and furnish additional resources where they will help.

During testing, users should define data for test programs and an attempt should be made to generate data with errors to be sure the system will catch them. Users should carefully examine test results and evaluate the adequacy of processing. Management should also participate in the reviews of data processed by the system. Some kind of acceptance test should also be conducted by the information services department and the results evaluated by users. A parallel test of old and new procedures or pilot studies may be used for this purpose.

Training is essential for smooth conversion and installation. Users develop materials and actually conduct the training sessions. Management remains aware of the training program, attends occasional sessions to communicate support for the system, and checks that its knowledge of the system is accurate. Training can often be combined with testing; the preparation of test data serves to help train users. The information services staff aids in the preparation of materials and has the responsibility of training the operations staff.

Conversion is a crucial part of the systems life cycle and should be done in phases if possible. For example, can one department or geographic area be converted first? The information services department coordinates conversion and performs conversion procedures such as creating initial files for the new system. Users and the information services department should jointly conduct a postimplementation audit and report the results to management. How well does the system meet specifications? How good were the specifications; that is, how do users react to the system now? How do the original estimates compare with what was achieved? These data can be helpful in making estimates for future projects.

Finally, during operations, users furnish data for input and work with the output. Users and management will probably suggest enhancements and modifications to the system over time. The information services department should also look for improvements itself and respond to modifications suggested by users.

RESOURCES FOR NEW SYSTEMS

Originally, in many organizations, the information services department had to search for new computer applications. Now, for most mature computer installations, there is more demand for services than resources available to satisfy the demand. Typically, the budget for developing new computer-based systems is only one part of the total budget for the information services department.

Demands and Resources

What are the demands on the information services department? There are a number of responsibilities for the typical information services department:

MANAGEMENT PROBLEM 12-1

The president of Farway Manufacturing Company was pondering the firm's recent disastrous attempt to develop a computer-based system for factory-floor data collection. The company wished to improve scheduling and control over work-in-process inventories. A consultant was hired who recommended the development of a computer-based production control system.

The recommendations of the consultant were accepted and he was hired to design the system. It turned out that the consultant had designed a similar system for another manufacturing company and proposed to transfer it to Farway. This seemed like a very economical approach, so the president quickly agreed.

The consultant set about his task with zeal; within six months the necessary programming changes had been made and the system was ready to begin operation. Over one weekend, terminals were installed in all departments and on Monday morning, workers were supposed to begin using the new system to report production. The workers are paid on piece rate and are unionized.

For reasons not completely understood by the president, the system failed completely. No one provided input and the little data collected were all erroneous. What happened? Why did the systems development effort fail so miserably?

---

1 One of the first concerns is operating existing systems; that is, the information systems developed in the past must be executed on a routine basis.

2 Maintenance also requires resources. Where many existing systems are in operation, it is necessary to make repairs and to maintain computer programs.

3 Enhancements to existing systems are frequently requested by users; if a system is used, individuals will make suggestions for improvements. These modifications entail programming changes and sometimes even require new computer equipment.

4 The development of a new information system requires a major commitment of resources.

Many individuals outside the information services department see only the operation of existing systems and the development of new ones. However, maintenance and enhancements require over 50 percent of the programming effort in many firms.

What are the resources available to the information services department? There are two major categories of information services resources: people and machines. Machine capabilities are necessary to develop and operate computer-based information systems. Different types of information systems require different equipment, for example, an on-line system necessitates equipment for communications and terminals. A large data-base application makes demands for data storage devices.

On the human side, many of the resources of the information services department are not interchangeable among jobs. We can identify a number of positions in this department:

1 Operators are trained to operate the computer and its peripheral equipment.

2 Clerical personnel manually process input and output; they may separate copies of reports and prepare output for distribution, and may also check input and output for accuracy.

3 Input specialists transcribe data to machine-readable form by, for example, keypunching cards or keying information onto a magnetic tape or disk.

4 Maintenance programmers repair errors in the programs that direct the computer (see Chapter 8). These individuals may also be responsible for enhancements to existing systems.

5 Systems analysts work with users to define specifications for a new system.

6 Applications programmers convert system specifications into the computer programs necessary to process data and produce the desired output.

7 Systems programmers are found in large installations; they work with the control software of the computer (see Chapter 8).

8 Managers of various functions such as operations and systems design are also employed by an information services department, if it is large enough.

A Resource Allocation Problem

The basic allocation problem is to match demands for services against resources (see Table 12-3). How much discretion do we have in this process? Unless some

Table 12-3   Demands and Resources of the Information Services Department

Demands	Resources
Operating existing information systems	Equipment
Maintenance	Human
Enhancements	Operators
Development of new information systems	Clerical personnel
	Input specialists
	Maintenance programmers
	Systems analysts
	Applications programmers
	Systems programmers
	Managers

applications are to be eliminated, the information services department has to maintain equipment and needs operators, clerical personnel, control, and maintenance programmers to operate existing systems. (Some installations also need a systems programmer for this purpose.) Discretionary resources can be used for enhancements and the development of new information systems. Systems analysts, applications programmers, and necessary managers, plus machine capacity, constitute the discretionary resources available to the department.

How easily can these resources be increased? Machine capacity can be enlarged, although usually it takes many months to obtain and install new computer equipment. New personnel can, of course, be added; however, there is a limit to how rapidly new employees can be integrated into the organization and become productive. Thus, in the short run, there is probably little that can be done to increase the resources devoted to the development of new systems within an organization. However, added resources can be used to purchase applications packages and/or consulting services from outside the organization. In the long run, if users are dissatisfied with the amount of resources devoted to the development of new systems, they will have to undertake efforts to increase the discretionary portion of the information services department budget.

PROBLEMS IN THE LIFE CYCLE

It is widely recommended that the stages in the systems life cycle described in Table 12-1 be followed. However, when we have seen them followed as rigorously as a checklist, usually the result has been systems that fail. What is wrong with the life cycle? Is the concept invalid? There are two major difficulties with following these stages rigidly in the development of a system. First, the stages tend to focus attention on a particular type of application, and second, they mislead analysts as to their role in the systems design process.

The first problem of the checklist is its orientation toward transactions systems and paperwork automation. Notice a complete lack of mention in the checklist of designing systems to support decision making. This approach is oriented toward tabulating operations that use punched cards, and the list was probably developed before the advent of modern electronic computers. The old card systems were directed toward transactions processing, and the systems design stages reflect this bias. Certainly there are good reasons to develop transactions-processing information systems. However, if we have faith in the potential of information systems to improve managerial decision making, then we should focus on decisions as well as document flows in systems design.

A second problem of the checklist is even more serious. The stages suggest that a systems analyst must be in charge of the systems analysis and design activity: the analyst alone has the tools and techniques for designing the system. Any mention of users is conspicuously absent in these design steps. In Chapter 5 we discussed some of the organizational problems of systems, the fact that systems can affect power relationships and create conflict in an organization. We need to develop an entirely different role for the analyst and user to overcome these problems.

USER-ORIENTED DESIGN

Problems with the Conventional View

In the conventional approach to systems analysis and design described above, the analyst is a skilled leader. The analyst interviews users, collects data, and returns to the information services department to create a new system. In recognition of the fact that this approach usually does not work in systems analysis and design, numerous periodicals suggest that user participation is necessary to ensure successful systems. The writers in these journals suggest that the analyst spend more time with users, show them report formats, and so forth. However, in their viewpoint, the analyst is still clearly in charge. We label this as "pseudoparticipation"; we are consulted, but few changes are made in the system on the basis of the users' suggestions. The analyst and the information services department are still very much in charge of the project.

Instead of viewing the analyst as the designer of the system, we recommend strongly that users should design their own systems. Does this mean that we actually undertake some of the tasks normally carried out by the analyst? The answer is definitely "yes." Our recommended approach raises two questions: first, why should users assume this role, second, how can users do so? Our experience indicates that users are capable of responding to this approach and that successful results can be achieved (Lucas, 1974c).

There are a number of good reasons for participation and user design of systems. User involvement should not be criticized, only the way in which involvement has been attempted in the past. Real involvement requires time; users must understand the system and their recommendations have to prevail.

A more user-oriented approach to design may require deviations from the standard life cycle. Although the conceptual steps represented in the cycle may be followed, innovations will be included. For example, design is often facilitated by prototyping. A prototype is a smaller scale version of a planned feature for

MANAGEMENT PROBLEM 12-2

As a new attempt at designing a planning system is about to begin, Robert Johnson is contemplating a previous disaster. Johnson is the director of planning for Petrochem, a diversified manufacturer of petrochemicals. The company has an ambitious acquisition program and frequently enters joint ventures with other firms.

Planning includes detailed computations of various possible outcomes from entering these ventures. The return to the company and forecasted cash flow are of particular importance to the firm. Johnson and his staff currently use calculators to make projections, and each suggested project requires a monumental clerical effort to evaluate.

Several years ago, Johnson approached the firm's information services department to ask for help. His project was rejected a number of times in favor of what he considers mundane, low-return projects, for example, putting the company telephone directory on the computer.

Finally, two years later, the information services department sent an analyst to study his problems. The analyst spent about one week in the planning department and then designed a simple batch system to automate some of the calculations. On attempting to use the system, the planning staff found that it would not perform any of the calculations needed. The staff also could not understand how to complete the input forms for the system.

After a great deal of work, Johnson persuaded the president of the company to intercede. Now, the information services department is back to try again. However, Johnson wonders how to avoid the same outcome that the last attempt produced.

What should Johnson do? Who is responsible for the problems at Petrochem? Is it Johnson, the information services department, the president, or all three?

---

a new system. A good example is sales forecasting: we can code the new forecasting routine on a time-sharing system and analyze past data for a limited number of products. Users will be intimately involved in this test so that they can provide feedback on the prototype and evaluate its output. When they are satisfied, the prototype can be programmed in final form with more error routines, data manipulation features, etc, that were excluded to keep the prototype simple.

Predicted Results

User participation eliminates potential difficulties of an organizational nature in systems design; it particularly helps to reduce problems created by power transfers and conflict. Users, by taking charge of the systems design activity, retain control over their information processing activities. All these factors combine to reduce the amount of power transferred from users to the information services department and the potential for conflict. Because of participation, we are not so dependent on the information services department. Knowledge gained through participating in and influencing the new system means the information services department copes with less uncertainty for users, reducing

A SYSTEM FOR HUMAN BLOOD MANAGEMENT

In the United States human blood has a legal life time of 21 days from collection. During this time it can be used for transfusion to a patient of the same blood type. However, at the end of the time it must be discarded. The blood is collected from donations at regional sites and after a series of tests it is shipped to blood banks at hospitals in the region. Blood is issued from this blood bank during its legal life time. Because some issued blood is not used it can be returned and reissued.

It is difficult to evaluate the performance of a regional blood system. The most common measures used are the percentage of days when extra deliveries have to be made to satisfy a hospital's demand and the outdate rate, the percentage of a hospital's supply that becomes outdated for each hospital in the region. A system has been designed to arrive at decision support mechanisms for regional blood centers. This system addresses the following inventory management questions:

1. What is the minimal achievable outdate and shortage target which can be set for a region?

2. What type of distribution policy is necessary to achieve these targets?

3. What should the level of regional supply of blood be in order to achieve different targets?

This decision support system is based on a mathematical programming model. The primary objective of the model is to optimize the allocation of the regional blood resources and at the same time to observe policy constraints. The model features centralized management of blood rather than management by individual hospitals, prescheduled deliveries and a distribution system through which blood may be rotated among hospitals.

This decision support system was implemented in the 38 hospital region of Long Island, New York, and has been operational there for some three years. The system has been established as routine and has drastically reduced the outdating and shortage incidents in the region. Plans are being made to introduce the system in other regions in the U.S. and abroad.

G. P. Prastacos and E. Brodheim, *Management Science,* vol. 26. no. 5, May 1980.

the amount of power the users surrender in developing a system. Mutual dependence is actually changed to cooperation in an effort to accomplish the common goal of developing and implementing a successful system. The user understands the system better by being in charge of it, and therefore, the amount of uncertainty associated with the project is reduced.

By performing some of the information services department tasks, user departments reduce task differences between them and the information services department and thus reduce the potential for conflict. By working together, the information services department and users develop more understanding of each other's problems, and thus help to reduce ambiguities. Heavy user participation also leads to more understanding of the jobs of information services department staff members, and vice versa, reducing job differences. Users also become more familiar with computer jargon, so that communication obstacles are reduced between the information services department and users.

Heavy user participation is not always necessary or advisable. Certainly some systems have been successfully designed with limited or no user involvement. For systems in the transactions processing and operational control category it is possible to design a system with less user input because the application is so highly structured. However, user involvement can still help in creating acceptance of the changes produced by the new computer system.

As information systems design moves toward managerial and strategic planning applications and less structured systems in general, as discussed in Chapter 2, we predict that user participation will become more important. Less structured applications need more input and enthusiasm to succeed, since the use of many of these systems is voluntary. A certain amount of user participation in the design of any system is important. However, the nature of the application influences the extent to which users need to be involved.

How can we participate where conditions are not favorable, for example, in a single application to be used by many different individuals? Imagine a grocery store planning to install point-of-sales terminals for check-out operations. If a chain has several hundred or thousand checkers, all of them cannot participate in the design of the system. However, in this situation representatives of the checkers could participate in the design. These representatives can meet with their coworkers at each store as the system is implemented; any questions or problems during the design process can be explored with the checkers using these representatives as liaison agents.

There can, of course, be problems with user participation to the extent advocated here. An individual whose ideas are rejected by the group may become alienated. It may not be possible to satisfy expectations raised about future participation in, for example, operation of the system. Certainly,

---

MANAGEMENT PROBLEM 12-3

The information services department at Madison Drugs is trying to stimulate heavy user participation in the design of information systems. A new system for financial management is in the planning stages, but problems with users seem to occupy most of the planning sessions in the department.

One of the key figures in the new system is a user named Keith Ryan. Keith has been at Madison for 20 years and is responsible for all financial transactions. The information services department chose him as the most obvious user to head the design effort. Keith is in sympathy with this selection, but says, "I don't have time to spend designing a system: I work 60 hours a week now."

The information services department recognizes the extent of Keith's efforts and devotion to the company. However, they ask why cannot additional staff be hired to remove some of the load from Keith? Keith says that he has tried to break in new people, but the demands of the job are too rigorous and they all leave.

The president of Madison wants to know why the design of this new system is taking so long. What should the manager of the information services department do? What can he suggest to the president?

---

participation is time consuming and costly; added time for participation means that systems will cost more to develop. We are usually under pressure when we request a system; now it is necessary for users to take time to design a system when they are already under time pressures. Finally, there are the dangers of pseudoparticipation. Where users do not have a real say, but only go through the motions of participation, their frustration will increase. On balance, it seems fair to say that there is too little participation at present. Whether we agree on the extent of user design or not, most organizations should be striving for more user input in the design process.

Does a user have enough knowledge and training to participate in the design of a system? In the next section we discuss the user requirements of this philosophy of systems design. They are not too severe, since the user is specifying parts of the system that are familiar; the user is certainly not programming a system.

A more serious problem with this approach is the attitude of the analyst: the ideas above may seem quite radical. Management will have to adopt the approach suggested here and influence the information services department to implement these user-design procedures. Although the analyst may perceive a diminished role at first, the more successful systems and better relationships with the users that should result from the approach will help to assuage the analyst's misgivings.

The proposed extensive involvement and influence of users is time consuming and costly. Systems undoubtedly take longer to develop in this manner and cost more. However, we must examine the incremental costs and time of this approach and compare them with those for the conventional method of systems design. If user-controlled design results in successful systems, then a fairly small increment in cost and time should be worthwhile in view of the problems of many information systems developed under conventional procedures.

Required Knowledge

What does the user have to know to be able to design a system? There are four components of design for which users should have elementary knowledge and extensive control:

1 Output
2 Input
3 File contents
4 Processing logic

First, users should consider the different aspects of information and decision making discussed in Chapters 2, 3, and 5. What output from a new information processing system do we desire? Working with an analyst who explains different alternatives, users develop drafts of the output, for example, a printed report or display for a CRT. Review the various hardware alternatives in Chapter 7 to see the range of possibilities.

All information and output must come either directly from an input, from a file, or from computations based on input and file data. With the output defined, the contents of files and inputs can be determined. Users then design actual input forms; see Chapter 7 for a discussion of various alternatives for input.

Analysts may define the files by working with users. However, with no more background than Chapter 9, users should be able to make a major contribution to the definition of file contents and structure. Certainly users are in the best position to indicate the size of data items and to specify updating needs.

The response time, the degree to which data must be up to date, and the volumes of input/output activities help determine the type of system needed, for example, batch, inquiry, or on-line updating. If data do need to be up to the minute, or various geographical locations must be coordinated as in a reservations application, an on-line updating system is necessary. If a user must be able to obtain immediate response, then at least on-line input/output for inquiry purposes must be provided. We have also found that many organizations are moving toward on-line systems to reduce the heavy volume of input/output processing. Input can be captured on-line and posted to files later, and the files can be made available for inquiry without on-line updating. See the discussion of systems alternatives on pages 53 to 55.

Our final task is to specify basic processing logic. What computations does the user require to produce the desired output? How can output fields be derived? What file data are updated on a regular basis? What editing and line checks should be performed on the input?

A user who has understood and mastered the material in the text so far is in an excellent position to design input, output, processing logic, and file contents for a computer-based information system, with guidance from a computer professional.

Design Team

To coordinate users and the information services department staff, we recommend the formation of a design team with a user as head of the team. Having a user in charge makes the user role apparent, ensures that time will be available from other users, and demonstrates a strong commitment to users on the part of the information services department. Normal job activities should be reduced for the user placed in charge of the design team.

In cases where there are too many individuals for all of them to be involved, liaison representatives are suggested. These people interview other users and brief them on the system as it is developed. They are responsible for soliciting participation in phases where it is meaningful.

The information services department systems designer guides the design team, teaching the tools and techniques necessary to complete the design and providing required technical advice and support, for example, by developing detailed file structures after users complete the logical file design. Systems designers monitor the project, describe the different stages, and help to schedule them. However, the actual analysis and design work is done by the users with the assistance of the analyst, rather than vice versa as in conventional systems design.

DATA COLLECTION

What techniques are available to the design team for collecting data? As discussed earlier, the objective is to develop an understanding of key decisions and how they are supported with information. The team needs to examine decisions, the flow of information in the organization, and the types of processing undertaken.

Observation

One technique for collecting data on a process is to observe that process. Frequently in systems analysis and design we will "walk through" a system observing crucial information flows and decision points. Then we may use one of the graphical techniques described later in this chapter to prepare documentation of our understanding of how the system functions.

Observations can also be quite structured; we may develop a rating form of some type to collect data on the frequency of inquiries, say, in a credit office. The analyst prepares a form showing the possible inquiries and then during a sample of different days and hours codes the actual inquiries.

Interviews

The systems analyst spends a great deal of time interacting with others, particularly in interview settings. Interviews have varying degrees of structure; for a first meeting there may be no structure at all. The analyst may be getting acquainted with the user and gaining a broad understanding of the problem area.

Often, as the project progresses, more structured interviews are conducted. The analyst may wish to prepare in advance an interview schedule containing the questions to be asked and the points to be covered. The main thing is to be prepared.

One of the most common problems in interviewing is probing for the answer. The interviewer, perhaps unconsciously, encourages the interviewee to give a desired response. Often people being interviewed follow these cues and try to help the interviewer. It is very important from the standpoint of systems design to be sure that the data collected are as accurate as possible.

Questionnaires

A questionnaire allows us to obtain data from a relatively large number of people at a reasonable cost. A questionnaire can be thought of as a structured interview form with questions designed so they can be answered without a face-to-face encounter. The design of a good questionnaire is a difficult task. Although the idea is an extension of a structured interview form, the questionnaire is, in principle, capable of being completed by the respondent alone without an interviewer being present.

Table 12-4 presents some examples of questionnaire and/or structured interview questions. (A questionnaire can also be completed in an interview setting.) The example illustrates several different types of questions. The questions with a 1-through-7 number scale assess subjective perceptions and attitudes; no real unit such as dollars, degrees, etc., measures these variables.

Another type of question is open-ended. Here we simply ask the respondent to write a short paragraph to answer our inquiry. Such a question might be, "Please indicate the four most important pieces of information that you use in your work."

Fixed alternative questions are difficult to construct because we must be sure to bracket the range of alternatives. For example, we might ask, "What is the average value of an invoice in your department?" and provide four choices:

1 Under $2000
2 $2000 to $5000
3 $5000 to $10,000
4 Over $10,000

This question looks all right; however, there may be a problem if the average value of invoices for the firm is $25,000. The answer would be 4 for virtually all respondents and we would get very little information. Most of the time in systems analysis and design, we are interested in more exact figures, so we would actually collect a sample of invoices and compute the average and variance, or we would ask a question and leave a blank so that users could provide their own estimate.

As a part of our effort to determine attitudes during the design process, we may also use questionnaires and interviews. Knowing attitudes helps us prepare for how different users will respond to a new system. In fact, we could use these attitudinal ratings to include some of the least receptive people who are important potential users on a design team.

Comparison

Both questionnaires and interviews are important for the analyst, though interviewing will probably be used more. The advantage of the interview is that a new tangent can be followed. The respondent is not constrained by the limitations of the questions but can expand in other directions. If the question is ambiguous, the interviewer can explain what is desired. Interviews are the best technique in an unstructured setting and when it is necessary to probe issues in depth.

Questionnaires offer the advantage of being relatively inexpensive to administer to a large group of respondents. They are well suited to expanding data collection beyond the interview. For example, assume that a system is being developed that will be used by a number of sales representatives nationwide. If the firm has 500 sales representatives, it is impossible to include all of them on a design team; instead we would use representatives chosen to be typical of the

Table 12-4 Sample Interview and Questionnaire Items

Attitude Questions

Directions: Circle the number which best represents your opinion.

For example: The temperature inside today is:

Too cold _____ Too hot

1 2 3 4 5 (6) 7

The answer indicates that the temperature is hot.

1 My general impression of the data processing staff is that they

are uninterested in the user	_____	are interested in the user
	1 2 3 4 5 6 7	
are not too competent technically	_____	are highly competent technically
	1 2 3 4 5 6 7	
are not too good in dealing with people	_____	are good in dealing with people
	1 2 3 4 5 6 7	
do low-quality work	_____	do high-quality work
	1 2 3 4 5 6 7	

2 How do you think a computer might benefit you? (You may answer more than one.)

1 Reduce the time I spend processing papers
2 Reduce errors
3 Make my job more interesting
4 Make it easier to find information
5 Make it easier to use information
6 I don't know specifically how, but feel it would help
Comments _____

3 What do you think the major problems with a computer would be? (You may answer more than one.)

1 It would make things more complicated
2 It would make more mistakes
3 It would be harder to use
4 It would take more of my time
5 It would lose information
6 It would make our jobs boring
7 I don't know specifically what, but feel there would be problems
Comments _____

4 If we use a computer here, the company will not need me anymore.

1 Strongly agree 2 Agree 3 Neutral 4 Disagree 5 Strongly disagree

Design Information

Please rate the following reports on the indicated characteristics

Inventory Status Report

1	Highly accurate	_____	Highly inaccurate
		1 2 3 4 5 6 7	
2	Out of date	_____	Timely
		1 2 3 4 5 6 7	
3	Useful	_____	Useless
		1 2 3 4 5 6 7	

Sales Analysis Report

4	Highly accurate	_____	Highly inaccurate
		1 2 3 4 5 6 7	
5	Out of date	_____	Timely
		1 2 3 4 5 6 7	
6	Useful	_____	Useless
		1 2 3 4 5 6 7	

types of salespersons on the force. This group might assist in developing a questionnaire for the rest of the sales force that has, until now, been uninvolved in the design. The questionnaire could explain some of the chosen tradeoffs and characteristics of the system to all potential users to obtain their input and feedback. Valuable attitudinal data could also be collected at the same time. Questionnaires are also a good way to obtain feedback in a postimplementation audit.

DESIGN TOOLS

In the remainder of this chapter we present an overview of some of the tools that have been developed to assist the designer.

Flowcharts

Probably the oldest graphic design aid is the flowchart. Each organization may have its own standards for flowcharting; in addition, the American National Standards Institute (ANSI) has published a standard for flowcharts.

A flowchart consists of a series of symbols and connections among them. A chart can depict a number of information processing activities ranging from a computer configuration through the detailed steps of a program. (However, flowcharting of programs at a detailed level has been declining in popularity because of the effort involved and because of failure to update flowcharts when programs change.)

Figure 12-2 contains the basic symbols in the ANSI standard. Input and output activities irrespective of media or format are represented by a parallelogram. However, specialized symbols may be used instead for punched cards or a terminal. The process outline is a rectangle and is used for any kind of data processing; it is the symbol to use when no other special one is available. This symbol can stand for data transformation, movement, or logic operations.

The flowlines show the sequence among steps and the transmission of information among operations. An arrow is used to specify direction when it is not implicit in the diagram. ANSI specifies that arrows are not necessary when the flow is from top to bottom and from left to right.

An open rectangle with a dotted line connecting it to the flowchart is used to annotate the flowchart. Because charts rarely fit on a single sheet, different pieces are cross-referenced. Out-connectors are used to indicate that the flow is to be continued on another page, and an in-connector shows that another page contains the preceding processing.

An interrupt symbol shows a beginning, an end, or a break in the usual line of flow. Communications links indicate the transmission of data from one location to another.

The next set of symbols in Figure 12-2 is specialized and augments the standard processing symbols. One of the most important of these is the diamond, which represents a decision point. Multiple paths representing possible outcomes of the decision exit from this symbol.

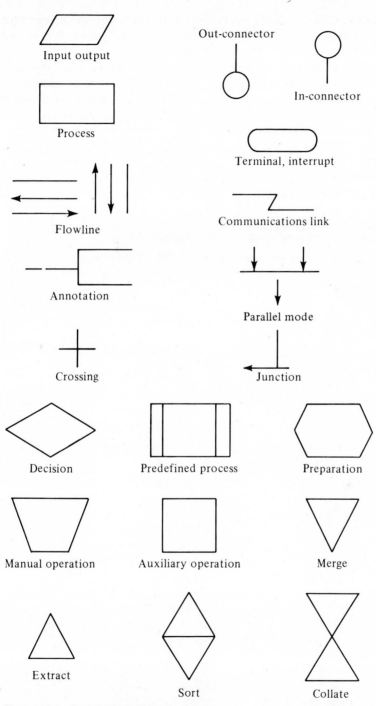

Figure 12-2 Basic and specialized symbols.

Figure 12-3 shows some of the input/output special symbols that represent various types of media. This figure also contains additional symbols that can be used to represent specific computer equipment such as a disk or drum.

Given these symbols we can represent a wide variety of processes graphically. For the analyst, flowcharts of the existing system can be of great assistance in visualizing how it operates. We shall see many flowcharts of manual procedures in subsequent chapters. These charts can be used to communicate with users as well as within a design team; they also are valuable for training purposes.

Unfortunately, the many ways to combine these symbols into flowcharts can make it difficult to read and share charts among different individuals. We can offer some guidelines to facilitate the construction and the later readability of the charts (Chapin, 1976):

Use simple symbols where possible; avoid overly elaborate charts.
Try to maintain the same level of detail on the charts.
Consider using hierarchies of charts; one chart is at a high level and succeeding levels of detail are shown in charts that expand the symbols in the higher-level chart.

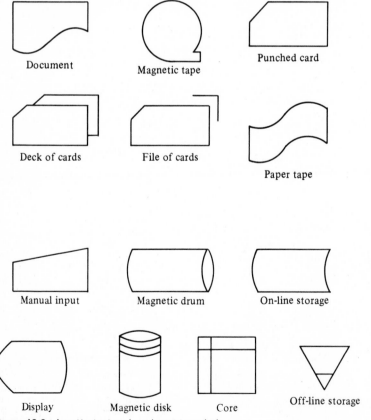

Figure 12-3   Input/output and equipment symbols.

Develop the chart to suit the reader; if the chart is for communications with users, it should be annotated and clear.

Try to develop a standard or use the existing standard in the organization so that the charts can be more easily read by others.

Although the use of flowcharting is not being recommended today for programs, flowcharts are very important in systems analysis and design. Charts show the structure of a system, the flow of information, and decision logic. Flowcharts also help communications between designers and users.

Figure 12-4 is an example of a very high level flowchart of the information flows in a hypothetical manufacturing company. The chart depicts the arrival of orders at the firm; these data are combined with sales forecasts and economic data to arrive at a production plan. Information on various inventories is also vital to the production planning process. Orders are filled resulting in shipments that decrease finished goods inventory. At the same time, manufacturing operations replenish finished goods inventory and cause a corresponding decrease in work-in-process stocks. Shipments generate invoices that create a receivable on the accounts-receivable files. Manufacturing requires the purchase of raw materials, which means that the manufacturing company must enter a transaction on its accounts-payable files.

Each of the subsystems in the flowchart in Figure 12-4 can be broken down into more detail, for example, the flowchart of accounts receivable. However, the high-level diagram illustrates the key parts of a flowchart. It shows the flow of information and key processing/decision points. The chart also shows major files of data that are created and manipulated in processing information. To have a narrative description of the flowchart also helps facilitate understanding.

The process of creating a flowchart is really a part of systems analysis and design. In the next chapters we shall discuss information flows and processing; a flowchart as well as the other techniques described in this chapter is one way to document the analyst's and the users' understanding of an information processing system.

Decision Tables

A decision table is another graphical technique to facilitate communications between users and analysts. As a side benefit automatic decision table translators or manual algorithms exist so that a program can easily be generated from a decision table. The decision table expresses a series of conditions; when the conditions are fulfilled, then a rule associated with the condition is executed.

Figure 12-5 shows the basic decision table format. A header is used to identify the table and condition stubs describe the various conditions. A rule is a procedure for checking the different conditions, and the action statement tells what action to take when a rule is true. The table is read until the conditions for a rule are met and the action described is taken. Then the next scan of the table begins.

The decision tables in Figures 12-6 and 12-7 represent the logic for a credit card purchase authorization. In this example, a purchase under $50 is approved

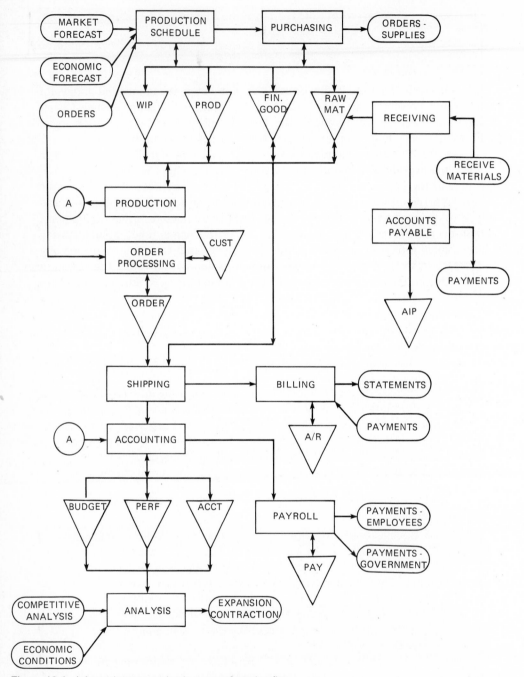

Figure 12-4 Information processing in a manufacturing firm.

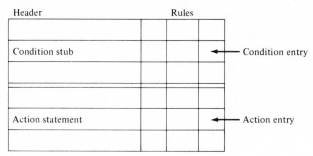

Figure 12-5 Decision table format.

automatically. Purchases between $50 and $10() are given an authorization number. Finally, for purchases over $100 we give an authorization number and place a "hold" on the customer's account for the amount of the purchase.

Figures 12-6 and 12-7 illustrate two different forms of decision tables. The first figure is a limited-entry table that allows only a "yes" or a "no" entry for the rules. In this type of a table, each possible condition has to be expressed in a statement. The extended-entry form in Figure 12-7 allows us to use logical conditions as entries and save space. Readers should assure themselves that these tables adequately describe the logic for the credit card example and that the two tables are equivalent.

Decision tables have a number of advantages. First they can facilitate communications between analysts and users. In fact, users can often learn rather easily to describe the logic of their decisions using decision tables. Decision tables are compact and express far more logic in a small location than a comparable flowchart. They are a good form of documentation that can be updated easily (Murdick and Ross, 1975). Computer programs are available that translate decision tables into COBOL and FORTRAN programs automatically.

	Rules			
Credit card authorization	1	2	3	4
Is purchase less than $50	Y	N	N	N
Is purchase between $50 and $100		Y	N	N
Is purchase over $100			Y	N
Approve with no action	X			
Give authorization no.		X	X	
Place hold on account			X	
Error				X

Figure 12-6 Limited-entry example.

Rules

Credit card authorization	1	2	3
Is purchase p	$p > \$100$	$\$50 \leqslant p \geqslant \$100$	$0 < p < \$50$
Approve with no action			X
Give authorization	X	X	
Place hold on account	X		

Figure 12-7   Extended-entry example.

Some guidelines have been offered for table construction. First, avoid making tables too large; often several small tables are better than one. (A rule in one table can be to execute another table.) All possible rules must be presented and every rule must have an action associated with that rule. The action is to be taken if the set of conditions hold. (Tables can be action tables that consist of a single rule.)

Decision tables should be analyzed to be certain that they are complete and to avoid excessive rules, contradictions, and possible redundancies. See Fergus in Couger (1979). A table is complete if it accounts for the correct number of independent rules to cover all combinations of possible conditions. The number of rules to be accounted for is equal to the number of unique condition combinations possible. This number of possible conditions is the product of the values each condition might assume.

In the example in Figure 12-7 are three conditions, each of which could be answered with two values "yes" or "no." To be complete, the table should then have $2 \times 2 \times 2$ or 8 rules. However, note that the possibilities of having two "yes" answers for a rule would be contradictory; a purchase could not be less than $50 and greater than $100 at the same time. Therefore, there is no need for rules that would have all three "yes" values.

If all the conditions in a table have the same number of values, the number or rules needed to satisfy all combinations is the number of values raised to the power of the number of conditions. Figure 12-7 has three conditions, each of which has two possible values, yielding 2^3 or 8 possible rules. However, as mentioned above, not all possible rules will make sense, and editing is necessary.

The rules themselves must be unique and independent; they cannot contradict one another, and only one rule can apply in a given situation. It does not matter in what sequence rules are presented since only one set of conditions can be satisfied at a time.

The rules consist of relationships among the various conditions. That is, if there are three conditions in a rule—A, B, and C—then A and B and C must be true for the rule to be satisfied. Finally, if the rule is satisfied, then the logic of the table dictates that the action is to be executed (Murdick and Ross, 1975).

Other Techniques

Several other techniques for systems analysis and design have been developed. Canning (1979) has reviewed two of these approaches, Information Analysis and Structured Analysis and Design Technique (SADT). There are reports that both of these approaches have been used successfully in systems design; the approaches have been credited with reducing costs and development time and improving the quality of the final system.

Information Analysis Information Analysis involves the use of a simple, large form. A square on the form represents the bounds of what is being included in the system. The analyst constructs small boxes outside the square to represent documents or materials flowing into and out of the system. The analyst identifies three to six activities that constitute a function. The analyst describes the inputs and outputs and represents the actual activities by dots in the square.

The purpose of the dots is to force the analyst to refrain from thinking about the details of the activity at this point; he or she notes only that the activity exists. Such a technique forces one to use a level-of-abstraction approach where each step in design proceeds to a more detailed level of analysis.

Next the analyst connects input boxes to one or more of the activity dots. The analyst looks then at each activity dot in the square to determine what major types of information and output are produced by that activity. Information and/or materials flowing outside the function require lines drawn to boxes at the bottom of the square representing the output of the whole system.

A high-level diagram might have five or six information and material input boxes at the top of the square and five or six output boxes at the bottom with several activity dots. There are two types of diagrams: activity graphs and information analysis graphs.

Figure 12-8 is an example of how we might construct an activity graph for a simple inventory control system for a wholesale supplier. The wholesaler orders merchandise from manufacturers and stores it in a warehouse. The customer of the wholesaler orders merchandise, which is shipped to the customer from the warehouse.

The inventory control department receives shipments from suppliers and is responsible for seeing that enough merchandise is available for filling orders. Incoming orders from customers enter the warehouse's order processing operation and a shipping order is written for their inventory control department. The inventory control department uses an inventory status report from the computer department to send reorder notices to the purchasing department. This department in turn generates purchase orders, which go to suppliers, an action that generates shipments from suppliers, which are placed in inventory.

As we might expect, the next step is to examine much of the activities in the high-level diagram and draw subsidiary diagrams. Through this process the system is decomposed into lower levels of detail. The entire process is known as activity analysis.

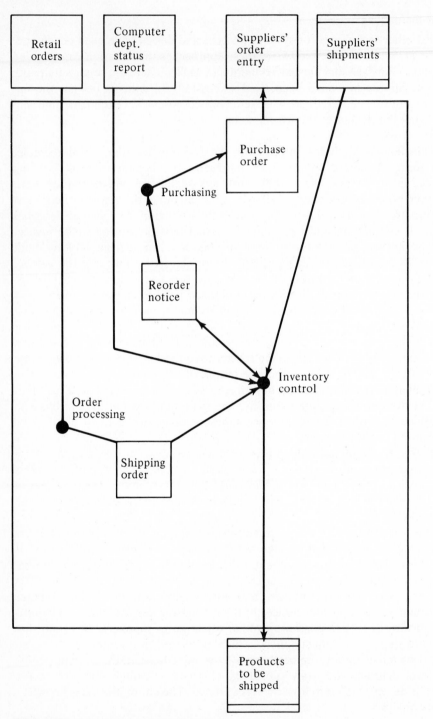

Figure 12-8 An example of an activity graph.

Following activity analysis is information analysis: each information-handling activity from the activity diagram is analyzed on a separate information flow diagram. The inputs are identified on the top of a square by boxes and the output similarly at the bottom as before. Now the analyst identifies the information processes needed to transform inputs into outputs; he or she also must specify the sequence required for processing.

Information analysis shows what information must be available at each processing step and what information is produced as output. Again, the information processes from a diagram are decomposed and shown on separate forms. At the lowest level of decomposition, the information is displayed with a listing of data types that make it up. Finally the data are broken down into fields and records.

Now the analyst is ready to develop a process table showing what inputs are needed, what calculations must be performed, and what outputs are produced. Detailed procedures have thus been postponed until this stage, which is consistent with the principle of top-down in design.

SADT   Structured Analysis and Design Technique was developed by a private firm. This proprietary system consists of a graphical language for building models, a method for developing models, and management practices for controlling the development of the models. The SADT package is similar in concept to others that are offered; the objective is to force structure on the unstructured systems analysis and design task.

SADT seeks a top-down decomposition of a problem, using a graphical modeling language. The development of a typical system will involve a number of different models, such as functional models that define what the system should do, implementation models to tell how the system is to accomplish its tasks, conversion models, and so on. Both activities and data are modeled top-down using a graphical language. The technique is designed for large projects requiring 4 to 6 analysts and from 6 to 9 months.

Activity diagrams and data diagrams are used. The former use boxes to represent activities and lines connect the boxes to show data interfaces. The rule is to keep the number of boxes between three and six on any diagram.

The approach emphasizes the concept of bounded context; each box and all its arrows must completely describe its activity and nothing outside that activity. Arrows on the left of an activity box represent data inputs, and arrows from the right side are outputs. Control arrows enter the top of the box and mechanisms exit from the bottom. Control arrows indicate the conditions under which an activity is to be performed. Mechanism arrows show resources used to perform activities such as an individual or a computer.

An output from one box can be a control or input to other boxes on the diagram. The top-level activity diagram represents the complete system being investigated; the boundaries of these diagrams are retained throughout the design process. The diagrams force the analyst to think carefully about the contents of the function boxes and how they are to be decomposed. The graphical technique helps guide the analyst in decomposing the system into lower levels of abstraction.

The boxes contain short statements about the activity. As with other techniques, higher-level boxes are decomposed at each step. The diagrams are a part of developing the specification; they are not necessarily intended to be used after the design is complete as documentation.

After the activity model is completed, the analyst undertakes a top-down decomposition of the data by drawing levels of a data model. The boxes in this diagram represent data classes at the current level of decomposition. This process frequently results in changes being made to the activity model.

The approach also involves individuals who read the various diagrams and comment on them. Design is not done in isolation; there is review and feedback. However, the role of users in this design process is not clear. For more details on information analysis and SADT see Canning (1979).

SUMMARY

Systems analysis and design is an activity that requires teamwork among managers, the systems staff, and users. It is a creative and exciting process that can bring about substantial change in the organization. This chapter has described the life cycle of a system, the responsibilities of various parties in developing a system, and the process of analysis and design. We have also presented some tools to assist in this process. Because a system may have a design time of 2 or 3 years and a useful life of 5 to 7 years, the decisions that are made today will influence information processing for up to a decade. The manager and user must be involved in these decisions and see that the systems that are designed are beneficial to them and to the organization.

KEY WORDS

Analysis	Estimates	Programmer
Analyst	Feasibility study	Programming
Budgets	Flowcharts	SADT
Conversion	Information analysis	Structured analysis
Data collection	Installation	Systems life cycle
Decision tables	Maintenance	Testing
Design	Operations	Training
Enhancements	Preliminary survey	User-controlled design

RECOMMENDED READINGS

Canning, R.: "The Analysis of User Needs," *EDP Analyzer,* vol. 17, no. 1, January 1979. (A good discussion of methods for defining the requirements for a new system.)
Chapin, N.: "Flowcharting with the ANSI Standard: A Tutorial," *Computing Surveys,* vol. 2, no. 2, June 1970, pp. 89–110. (A thorough discussion of flowcharting.)

Lucas, H. C., Jr.: *Toward Creative Systems Design,* Columbia, New York, 1974. (A short monograph containing many more details on user-controlled system analysis and design.)

Mintzberg, H.: *The Nature of Managerial Work,* Harper & Row, New York, 1973. (This book describes managerial activities and is helpful in the design of systems for managerial decision making.)

Murdick, R. G., and J. E. Ross: *Information Systems for Modern Management,* 2d ed., Prentice-Hall, Englewood Cliffs, N.J., 1975. (A book with many details about systems analysis and design.)

Yourdon, E.: *Design of On-Line Computer Systems,* Prentice-Hall, Englewood Cliffs, N.J., 1972. (A thorough discussion of the design of on-line systems.)

DISCUSSION QUESTIONS

1 What are the advantages of user-controlled design?
2 What are the disadvantages for the systems design staff and users of user-controlled design?
3 Would you expect user-controlled design to be more or less costly than conventional approaches?
4 What is the role of top management in managing the information services department?
5 What type of planning should be undertaken by the information services department?
6 Does a long-range information services department plan make any sense when technology is rapidly changing?
7 How should new systems development projects be charged in the organization? Should overhead, the information services department, or user department budgets absorb the cost?
8 Why have so many existing systems concentrated on information flows and transactions processing?
9 What are the problems of putting a user in charge of a design team for a new system for the information services department?
10 What are the implications of user-controlled design for the information services department? What view will have to be adopted by this department to make the recommended approach to systems design work?
11 Develop a questionnaire for obtaining data from potential users of a system on their attitudes, expectations, and thoughts for the goals of a new system.
12 The design of information systems is one of the few activities in most organizations best accomplished by a team. What possible conflicts might this create for other employees? How should the team structure be presented to reduce these problems?
13 If users design systems, will changes still be necessary after conversion when the system is in operation? Should as many changes be needed as under conventional design? Why or why not?
14 How can users be heavily involved in systems analysis and design in a large organization when there are many potential users who should be included?
15 Can top managers also participate in systems analysis and design if they will be users? Is this activity important enough for their participation?

16 How can management help a user to participate in the design of systems? What are the major factors inhibiting full participation?

17 How should the information services department budget be developed for new applications and enhancements?

18 Are there decisions in the operation of existing systems that should be influenced by users?

19 How does scarce machine capacity influence decisions on new applications?

20 To what extent can personnel resources be reallocated within the information services department to provide more flexibility in meeting demands for service?

21 Programs are available that will translate a decision table into a COBOL program that contains the logic expressed in the decision table. How would the use of such a program increase programmer productivity?

22 What are the disadvantages of flowcharts and decision tables?

23 Why do many members of the computer profession resist making changes requested in operational systems?

24 When on a cost-cutting drive, management will sometimes dictate an across-the-board budget reduction of some number, say 10 percent. Does this approach make sense for the information services department? What alternatives are available?

25 What is the most likely reason that a proposed system will be infeasible?

26 How do changes in technology, especially advances in hardware, affect the feasibility of new computer applications?

27 Where are the largest bottlenecks in the systems life cycle; that is, where are the most problems and delays probably encountered in developing a system?

28 Explain the term "bounded context"; why is it important in systems analysis and design?

29 How should one choose among the different design tools and techniques discussed in this chapter?

30 Is there one design approach that is best in all situations?

31 What design approach would you choose for a system to process incoming orders for a manufacturing firm?

32 What design approach would you recommend for an interactive decision support system to be used by the treasurer of the firm to manage cash deposits?

Inception through Specifications

ANALYSIS OF THE EXISTING SYSTEM
SURVEY AND FEASIBILITY STUDY CONTENTS
    New Systems
    System Alternatives
    Organizational Impact
DETERMINING FEASIBILITY AND CHOOSING AN
ALTERNATIVE
    Selection Committee
    Problems with Committees
    Committee Responsibilities
THE SELECTION PROCESS
    Decision Information
    The Decision
SYSTEMS ANALYSIS
SYSTEMS DESIGN
    Results
    Work Responsibilities
    Tradeoffs
GENERAL DESIGN CONSIDERATIONS
    Output
    Input
    Manual Procedures
    Errors
    Backup
    Security and Fraud
SYSTEM SPECIFICATIONS
KEY WORDS
RECOMMENDED READINGS
DISCUSSION QUESTIONS
SYSTEM DESIGN PROBLEMS

Inception through Specifications

CHAPTER ISSUES

- How should the organization select alternatives for a given computer application?
- What alternatives are available for the detailed design of a system?
- How does the user trade off various design alternatives for a new system?

In this chapter we examine the first stages of the systems life cycle. We begin with the preliminary survey and the feasibility study. The output from these two studies is used to determine whether to proceed with the design of a computer-based information system and to select one processing alternative if the system is approved. If a system is feasible, the analysis and design stages are undertaken, and the design team prepares detailed specifications.

ANALYSIS OF THE EXISTING SYSTEM

Analysis is the study of a problem, generally done before undertaking some action to solve the problem (DeMarco, 1979). In the case of systems analysis, the first task is understand and describe existing information processing procedures in the area where a new system has been proposed. Many of the techniques recommended in the last chapter can be used to document our understanding of the present processing system, for example, flowcharts, decision tables, and some of the structured diagrams of information processing. In many instances it will be hard to identify any organized set of procedures that represent the existing information processing system. We need to enumerate problems and determine what motivated the suggestion that a computer system might help in processing information. Whether there is a well-defined system or not, we should develop the specific information listed in Table 13-1. First, we should identify decisions that have to be made and the decision maker who is to be responsible. What are the inputs and outputs, what is the frequency of the decision, and what are the levels of cost involved?

Next, we should identify crucial information flows including the source, frequency, and volume of information. Information can be characterized according to the decision-making framework of Chapter 3. For example, we can look at the form in which data are gathered and processed, either written or verbal. If documents are involved, how many are there and what is their information content? What types of decisions are supported?

We also need to identify what processing is done to information as it flows through a system; by whom is the information processed, and what are the peak

**Table 13-1   Analyzing
the Existing System**

Decisions
   Decision maker
   Input
   Output
   Frequency of decision
   Level of costs
Information
   Flow
   Characteristics
   Form
   Source
   Retention
Transactions and processing
   Operations
   By whom performed
   Peak load
   Average load
Individuals/functions

and average loads? Finally, we should estimate the current cost of information processing.

For the preliminary survey we develop very rough estimates and collect samples of documents. We may interview only a few people and use approximations. After a list of objectives for the system is developed, we use the data gathered to make a rough sketch of several alternative new systems.

The feasibility study goes into much more detail and instead of approximations, we actually sample the documents and develop more refined estimates. In the feasibility study we trace the flow of information through the system and spend time with the various individuals who originate and process the data. Thus, the same framework used in the preliminary survey can be used for the feasibility study though our analysis will be much more detailed for the feasibility study.

SURVEY AND FEASIBILITY STUDY CONTENTS

In this section we present recommendations for the contents of the preliminary survey and feasibility study. Basically, each of these documents consists of two parts: the present system and an alternative. The alternatives section actually presents several potential alternatives and evaluates them on technical, economic, and operational criteria. We must estimate technical and operational feasibility and compare costs with benefits.

New Systems

From a technical standpoint, what is the state of the art? This analysis is related to the discussion of risk, since very few organizations should be pioneers in the development of all their new systems. Some pioneering may be desirable, but an attempt should be made to estimate exactly what is involved. Will existing technology as experienced by members of this organization be adequate for the application under consideration?

Operational feasibility addresses the question of whether or not we can run the system. Are schedules for processing realistic? Can input data actually be collected, errors corrected, and the system run on schedule? In one example an inventory system was planned in which files would be updated every 3 days. There were so many errors in the input that could not be corrected in time that the system had to move to a weekly updating schedule, reducing some of the benefits.

In examining costs versus benefits, there are a large number of factors to consider. System costs include

Development
  Computer time
  Systems analyst time
  Programmer time
  User time

Operations
    Computer costs
    Communications costs
    Operating staff costs
    Incremental user costs
    Maintenance costs

Development costs refer to the actual cost of analysis, design, and installation for the system. These costs are highly sensitive to the amount of time that must be spent to develop the system and are directly proportional to the number of analysts, programmers, and user staff involved and the length of their involvement. Computer time for testing tends to be far less expensive than the cost of staff time. Historically, the profession has done a very poor job of estimating the time required to design and install a system.

We should not forget the cost of operating a new system when assessing total costs. A new system will require the use of part of the time available on an existing computer or may necessitate an upgrade on the present system or even a new computer(s). Many modern systems involve telecommunications, which can be very costly. Incremental staff in the computer center and for users may be required to operate the system. Finally, there are the costs of routine maintenance and enhancements. No system is ever finished; "bugs" will need repairs, and users will request periodic enhancements as they work with a system.

Traditionally, benefits have been analyzed from the point of view of tangible cost savings from a computer system. Often these savings have been measured by the reduction of employees currently employed or by an estimate of the number of future employees who would have been hired without the system. (Many times savings projected in personnel have proved illusory.) Tangible savings also come from more efficient processing. For example, an inventory control system may reduce inventory balances while maintaining service levels. The firm saves the interest charges on the money previously required to finance the level of inventory needed before the computer system.

Tangible cost savings can be difficult to estimate in some cases. Emery (1974) has suggested looking at the value of perfect information as providing an upper bound on possible benefits. For example, in a forecasting application, what is the maximum benefit from having a perfect forecast of sales, that is, knowing exactly what sales will be in advance? If the cost of developing the system exceeds the maximum benefit under perfect information, then the application will undoubtedly be rejected immediately. If, however, the benefits look higher than costs, then we can make various assumptions about the impact of forecasts from the proposed system that are less than perfect.

To refine the benefits estimates a prototype of the forecasting system could be applied using a calculator or simple computerized version of the forecast. Historical data are processed by the model to provide an estimate of the improvements the model would produce over the existing forecasting procedures.

We should not only look at tangible cost savings, but we must also consider intangibles and unquantifiable savings. This is particularly true as we move from transactions processing systems toward operational and managerial control systems where intangible benefits are more important.

The following list of benefits may prove helpful in this analysis (Kanter, 1972).

1   The ability to obtain information previously unavailable
2   The receipt of information on a more timely basis
3   Improvements in operations
4   The ability to perform calculations not possible before (for example, the simulation of production schedules)
5   Reduction in clerical activity
6   Maintenance of a competitive position
7   Improvements in decision making
8   Improvements in image, customer service, etc.

Emery also discusses some of the problems of quantifying the benefits from intangible savings. For example, suppose an automobile manufacturer can increase from 90 to 95 percent the probability that a dealer will have parts in stock. How can the manufacturer quantify (in dollars) the increased customer satisfaction and goodwill that results from getting his or her car repaired without having to wait for a part? Of course, where a system can be justified on the grounds of tangible savings alone, the quantification of intangible savings will not be necessary.

Although intangible savings data may not be concrete, they can be evaluated. The automobile company could survey a sample of its dealers to determine their estimates of the monetary value of reduced stockouts. Although crude, the estimate is far better than making no attempt to include this factor in the analysis of the new system. As Emery points out, if we develop only systems that show tangible savings, we may ignore many of the benefits of computer-based information systems. It is very difficult to justify a planning system or decision support aid on the basis of tangible cost savings.

In this section we have discussed categories of costs and benefits for information systems. Senn (1978) lists a number of techniques that can be used to compare the costs and the benefits to determine whether or not a system should be developed. Using the net present value concept, future savings are rolled back to their present discounted value and compared with the discounted value of the investment and operating costs for the system. If the discounted benefits exceed the costs, then the system is attractive from a cost-benefit standpoint.

A similar computation can be used to determine the internal rate of return of a project. Here, the analyst attempts to determine the interest rate at which discounted benefits equal discounted costs. The payback period is a simpler approach since it ignores interest rates. It is simply the length of time before the benefits exceed the costs; that is, how long will it be before the benefits of the system pay back the cost of developing it?

Some organizations also use subjective techniques to determine whether or not a project is desirable from a cost-benefit standpoint. They argue that with intangible benefits uncertain, one still has to decide whether or not a system appears justified. These decision makers use their subjective feelings for what a reasonable cost is for the benefits provided by the system.

Regardless of the sophistication of the cost-benefit analysis, we need to develop a list of costs and benefits as a part of a feasibility study. Then agreement should be reached by all involved that the system is worth developing before proceeding.

Systems Alternatives

General   One of the major activities during the survey or feasibility study will be to sketch possible alternatives for a new information processing system. Each of these alternatives has to be evaluated on standard criteria selected in advance. The reports should show manual procedures, input and output, files, and processing schedules to characterize each alternative.

It also will be necessary to estimate development time and effort. Unfortunately, making these time and effort estimates is a very difficult task. At least one author provides guidelines on programmer productivity to help in making estimates (Kelly, 1970). However, there is a wide variance in programmer and systems designer performance among organizations and individuals. In a later chapter we shall discuss project management and suggest some new approaches to programming. Since these approaches are not in widespread use yet, we do not have historical data on which to base estimates. Our approach will be to record development data as projects are implemented so that each organization can make estimates based on its own past experience.

Finally, for evaluating the alternatives, the survey and feasibility studies should include estimates of the costs and effort involved in operating each alternative if implemented. Since we have far more experience and better data on operations than on systems design, this presents less of a problem than the estimates discussed above.

Packages   For many proposed systems, an applications package offers one alternative. Frequently, large amounts of money and time can be saved through the use of one of these packages, though there can be a number of drawbacks to packages. An applications package is a program or system of programs written by someone for sale. The package vendor tries to make the product very general; users supply the data parameters that apply to their situation and the package does the processing.

The major issue with the use of packages is the tradeoff between efficiency and generality. The vendor wants to make the package as general as possible so that a larger number of potential customers can use the package. However, the more general the package is, the less efficient is its processing and the more complex is the input required. The user, of course, wants the simplest input and the most efficient processing.

Generally, we overestimate the effort needed to install a package and underestimate the effort required to program the same system ourselves. In fact, most programmers prefer to design a new system than to install a package. The former activity is far more creative and challenging than working with someone else's program.

Since computer power is becoming cheaper per computation, it makes sense in many instances to acquire a package that uses computer hardware inefficiently to have an application functioning earlier. However, there can be legitimate reasons not to use packages. A set of criteria should be developed for the technical requirements a package has to meet to qualify for consideration. As a partial list of requirements consider the following:

1 Quality and reliability. A survey of existing users should be undertaken to determine how the package has actually performed.

2 Documentation. Can the computer department fully understand the system and is it capable of making the necessary modifications based on the documentation provided?

3 Vendor stability and support. Will the vendor stay in business and is the vendor committed to improving the package and issuing subsequent versions of it?

4 Compatibility with current equipment and applications. If it is necessary to spend 50 percent of the package price to modify the package, it is probably not worth it.

In summary, packages are a viable alternative, and they should be evaluated where they exist. After passing the screening requirements, packages should be considered in the same way as any other alternative and included in the survey and feasibility studies. It is still necessary to study the existing system and make estimates of technical, economic, and operational factors when an applications package is one alternative.

Organization Impact

An attempt also should be made to estimate the impact of each alternative system on the organization. What departments and individuals will be affected by the system and what jobs will be changed? Will any existing work groups be reassigned and what will happen to any employees who are replaced by a system?

Contents

The contents of one possible format for a survey or feasibility study are outlined in Table 13-2. The summary presents a brief overview of the reasons for the study and ranks each processing alternative (including the present system) on the criteria established by the steering committee. This summary is the primary input for decision making. Existing systems should be described according to the

Table 13-2 Outline of Preliminary Survey and Feasibility Study Contents

---

I Summary
    A Goals
    B For each alternative evaluation on standard criteria
II The existing system
    A Problems
    B Goals of new system
    C Decision considerations
    D Information flow
    E Processing
III For each alternative proposed
    A Overview—percentage of goals achieved, benefits
    B Decisions
    C Information flows
    D Technical (files, I/O, processing)
    E Development effort, schedule, and cost
    F Operational aspects
    G Impact on the organization
    H Total costs and benefits

---

analysis above. Finally, each alternative is presented in detail. Here it is helpful to include a scenario; that is, a short story on how the system would actually be used including management, user, and computer department activities under each alternative.

DETERMINING FEASIBILITY AND CHOOSING AN ALTERNATIVE

In the early days of computer systems, the information services department usually decided what applications to undertake. As demands for services increased, problems began to develop because some user requests had to be denied. As more systems of importance to the organization developed, many information services departments felt they were placed in a difficult position if forced to choose among competing applications. The information services department is not in a position to decide whether a system is feasible or which processing alternative should be chosen if the system is to be developed.

Selection Committee

One answer to the information systems selection problem is to convene a selection committee of users and other managers and information services department personnel. When representatives of various functional areas are included, each department is able to see why certain decisions are made. Selection of applications alternatives seems less arbitrary under these conditions. With management guidance, the committee can select applications and

MANAGEMENT PROBLEM 13-1

The order processing department manager at Leisure Clothing has a serious problem. She cannot understand why the information services department is so unresponsive to her requests. The firm has an elaborate on-line order-entry system that serves the entire United States. For the past 6 months, the order processing manager has logged the requests she has made for changes to the system. The total number of requests now stands at 15 and only three of the changes have been implemented!

When the manager of the order-entry system from the information services department stopped to see her, she indicated displeasure over the lack of progress and suggested two new modifications.

The weary systems manager asked, "Do these new changes have priority over the five you suggested last week, or should we try to do those first?"

The conversation grew more heated until finally both parties were shouting at each other. What do you suppose is responsible for this conflict? What steps can each individual take to resolve the conflict? What does the department manager need to appreciate? What action should the information services department take?

---

processing alternatives that it feels are consistent with functions currently emphasized in the organization.

Problems with Committees

If the ideas expressed above are good, why have a number of organizations become dissatisfied with selection committees? First. the goals of the committees are often not clear, resulting in little direction or continuity during meetings. Frequently the committees appear to be ratifying decisions already made by the information services department. No alternatives for a given application are suggested. Instead, the information services department presents the option of developing a complete, elaborate system or doing nothing. Almost no systems are rejected at the feasibility stage.

When decisions are made, there seems to be a failure to apply consistent decision criteria. Finally, in making any decision where costs and benefits are difficult to estimate, it is important to include subjective considerations. Members of committees have reported the lack of a mechanism for successfully including subjective factors in the decision process.

Committee Responsibilities

In Chapter 6 we discussed the applications selection process and recommended that a corporate steering committee review plans for systems and set priorities for different applications areas. An applications selection committee will generally consist of lower levels of management combined with users and members of the information services staff.

Few applications are really infeasible, though certain alternatives may be infeasible or undesirable. The role of the selection committee is to choose an alternative for a given system, though that alternative may be the status quo, that is, doing nothing. This role for the committee means that there will probably be several different selection committees, each dealing with systems for different functional areas. There might also be a committee with a variety of users on it to make decisions about small projects that do not involve a major commitment of funds.

THE SELECTION PROCESS

It is desirable to have all new systems suggested and investigated at one point in time so that all possibilities can be considered and some subset selected for implementation. Unfortunately, ideas for systems arise almost at random; some

---

GROCERY CHECKOUT

All 88 outlets of Ralph's, a leading southern California grocery chain, use computer-based laser scanning at the checkout stand. The operation utilizes point of sales terminals that include a laser scanner, a scale and a keyboard. Some 92% of the shelf items now carry the universal produce code, a series of parallel bars which the scanner can recognize as the grocery item is passed across a window in the checkout counter. Meat and other items are hand keyed and produce items are calculated using the scale and a keyed number. As each transaction occurs, it is flashed on an electronic panel visible to customers. At the end of the checkout process, the terminal prints a receipt including a specific description of each item as well as its price.

Ralph's produces a series of management reports that analyze everything from dollar volume per check stand to bottle returns. The company has found that the scanning device produces improved service and shorter lines at the checkout counters. By examining the statistics on the reports, management can see the cost of an average item and know what is selling well in a particular neighborhood. Ralph's feels that it can service its customers better when it knows their buying habits and preferences.

With scanners the company has been able to cut down from twelve checkout stands to nine while still getting customers through the stores 20% faster than before. Chain store executives believe customers view the length of the line as second only to price when they decide where to shop. Not only the customers but the checkout clerks are enthusiastic about the scanning devices.

If the store's controller quits operating, an identical unit at another Ralph's can pick up the slack within 15 seconds, though the scanning process is a bit slower. In the 15 months that the system has been operating at a Pasadena store, the unit has yet to fail. Each installation's scanners and controllers cost between $175,000 and $200,000. The company, however, feels it's getting a two year payback at most stores due to increased productivity and reduced inventory loss. Even more remarkable, there have been significant sales gains in stores which the company felt had already achieved their maximum volume.

Data Processor, June/July 1980.

---

length of time is required to study the suggestions before a decision is made on whether to undertake a suggested application. The decision process recommended below, therefore, concentrates on the selection of an alternative for a single proposed application. It does not attempt to evaluate an entire portfolio of projects because we are rarely in a position to compare the entire set of proposed projects at one point in time. The commitment of resources to past projects and the characteristics of systems currently under development can be reflected in the weights assigned to the criteria described below.

Decision Information

The approach suggested here can be used for decisions at either the preliminary survey or the feasibility study stage. The major difference between the two studies is that the feasibility study contains more data than the preliminary survey and presents more refined cost estimates.

The first task of the selection committee is to agree with the information services department on the number of alternatives for a single project and how the alternatives should be developed. As an example, suppose that one user department has proposed an inventory control system. The alternatives might include (1) doing nothing, (2) setting up a very basic batch system, (3) purchasing a packaged program from a computer services vendor, and (4) establishing an on-line system. Each of these alternatives for an inventory control system meets some percentage of user needs at different costs. Probably three to five alternatives for each proposed application are sufficient; however, there should always be more than one alternative for a new system. The selection of the first alternative, doing nothing, is equivalent to a decision that a new system is infeasible.

The next step is for the committee to agree on a set of criteria to be used by the information services department in evaluating each alternative. Table 13-3 contains examples of possible criteria, although criteria will probably be unique for each organization. The set of criteria should be as complete as possible so that no important evaluation factors are overlooked. However, the selection committee should avoid enumerating too many criteria or the data collection and processing requirements for evaluation become a burden. The inclusion of relatively minor criteria similarly should be avoided.

There is no one correct number of criteria to use, but experience indicates that five to ten should be adequate. Criteria can be voted upon by the committee and rank-ordered for selection, or a group consensus on important criteria may be possible without the voting. It is also desirable to avoid as much overlap in the criteria as possible to avoid overweighting one factor.

Each criterion should be measurable on a natural or artificial scale. It is necessary to assign a value to each criterion, such as a dollar amount or a number from a questionnaire scale. Criterion measurement is a difficult and time-consuming process; much effort is required to develop scales and assign scores during evaluation.

Once the criteria have been determined, it is necessary to develop weights

Table 13-3 Some Potential Criteria for Evaluating Alternatives in Project Selection

Tangible and intangible benefits
  User satisfaction
  Percentage of needs met
  Maximum potential of application
  Costs of development
  Costs of operations
Timing of costs
Timing of benefits
Impact on existing operations
Development time
Time to implement
Manpower required
  Analyst
  Programmer
  User
Probability of success
Probability of meeting estimates
New equipment required
Priority of function

Source: H. C. Lucas, Jr., and J. R. Moore, Jr.: "A Multiple-Criterion Scoring Approach to Information System Project Selection," *Infor,* vol. 14, no. 1, February 1976.

that indicate the relative importance of each criterion in arriving at the application selection decision. It is unlikely that each criterion will be regarded as equally important by all committee members, and some method will have to be used to weight the criteria for different individuals. Approaches to this process range from simple rank-ordering schemes to partial and paired comparison. The weights are of paramount importance to project selection because they reflect the priorities of the selection committee. The committee, of course, cannot expect conditions to remain constant; shifts in management policies and user needs necessitate revisions to weights over time.

The Decision

If the recommendations above are followed, the steering committee should be in a position to review a series of alternatives for each application proposed for implementation. Each alternative should have been evaluated on the criteria established by the committee. Consider the example in Table 13-4. In this hypothetical decision problem, the steering committee is considering three alternatives: a batch inventory-control system, an applications package, and an on-line inventory system.

The first column in the table lists the criteria agreed on by the committee and the information services department, and the second column contains the weights assigned to each criterion by the committee. The remainder of the table contains the scores for each alternative as evaluated by the information services department.

There are several ways to arrive at a decision, given this information. One

Table 13-4 Applications Selection Example

Criterion	Weight	Batch system	Package	On-line system
Percent of user needs met	0.35	60%	75%	90%
Cost of development	0.20	$25,000	$12,000	$30,000
Cost of operations	0.10	$ 3,000	$10,000	$ 7,000
Workers to develop	0.15	3	1	3
Probability of success	0.20	.85	.95	.75

approach is to work toward a consensus among committee members. In this example, the applications package would probably emerge as the preferred choice because of its high rating on the important criteria of percent of user needs met, low development cost, and high probability of success. As an alternative to this qualitative approach to selecting an alternative, more formal methods are available in which historical and survey data are used to develop a single numeric score for each alternative (Lucas and Moore, 1976c).

As conditions change, the committee can modify the weights to reflect new priorities. Also criteria can be dropped and/or added to reflect new circumstances. The major advantage of the recommended approach is the fact that it forces an objective evaluation of several alternatives for each proposed application, while providing a consistent but flexible framework for making decisions on applications.

SYSTEMS ANALYSIS

If a system is feasible and one alternative is chosen for development, detailed systems analysis is the next stage. There are few guidelines on the depth of analysis required when the design team examines present information processing procedures. All aspects of the present processing method must be understood and documented, and the analysis should seek to identify key decisions as well as flows of data.

It is important to sample existing documents and files of data. The design team should count all types of documents and classify the information contained on them; what are both the peak and the average flows of information? What time pressure is on managers who must make key decisions in the system? Some of these questions were asked in collecting data for the survey and feasibility studies; however, now the task is to obtain all relevant details.

The design team must also decide where to place the boundary on its studies; it is too easy to expand a simple processing problem into a huge system. What initially looks like an order-entry process turns into an accounts-receivable system and a production-control system because eager designers expand the boundaries of the problem into other areas. In some instances, an expansive boundary may be appropriate, but a design team is well advised to take steps slowly in order to outline a manageable task.

The designers should document their understanding of present procedures with information memoranda and reports. Flowcharts and decision tables should

MANAGEMENT PROBLEM 13-2

The top management of Eastern Bank and Trust practices group decision making. The highest four officers, including the chairman of the board, the president, and two executive vice presidents, meet together to make all major decisions. This committee approves the budget for the information services department and also decides on new applications.

Because of pressing business, information-systems-related decisions often are postponed from one meeting until the next. The budget director for the information services department indicated that he waited in the reception area for four meetings before his budget presentation was reached on the agenda.

The budget director's major objective is to have the information services department budget approved with as few questions as possible. The budget includes the funding for major systems development projects in the bank for the coming year. Therefore, approving the budget also involves selecting the major new applications for the coming year.

The members of the management committee are very dissatisfied with the current approach to information systems project selection decisions. They admit that no project has ever reached the feasibility study stage and been rejected. The managers indicate that they are not really making decisions, they are just ratifying the proposals of the information services department.

How can the bank solve this problem and develop a more effective project selection procedure? Why is this management committee not working well for information-systems-related decisions?

---

be constructed and reviewed with users who are not on the design team. When satisfied with its understanding of the present processing procedures, in effect, the design team should hold a "walk-through" with all users involved as a final check on the analysis.

SYSTEMS DESIGN

The most creative part of the systems life cycle is the design of new alternatives for processing. Although these ideas were sketched in the preliminary survey or feasibility study, they have to be developed in far more detail now. For example, in the last section we chose a packaged program for inventory control; (see Table 13-4). Suppose instead that the on-line system had been selected for development. The information in the feasibility study is general: the details of that system must be designed before programming can begin. What equipment is required? What are the I/O formats and file structures?

Results

The results of this study should be complete specifications for the new system as shown in Table 13-5. Usually, we begin by specifying the desired output; that is,

Table 13-5   Detailed Systems Design Specifications

Output	Errors
Destination and use	Design decisions
Medium	Modules
Reports (samples)	Processing
Frequency	Conversion programs
Input	Input
Source	Output
Medium	Errors
Document (sample)	Design decisions
Fields	Modules
Estimated volume	Processing
Files	Manual procedures
Medium	Error control
Contents	Input error conditions
Record format, field names	Processing errors
File structure (linkages, directories)	File integrity
Estimated file size	Output errors
Estimated activity	Backup
Updating frequency	Security
Processing	Work plan
System flow	Program schedule, milestones
Program specifications	Time estimates
Input	Personnel required, assignments
Output	

what does the user want from the system? Then it is necessary to determine what input is required to produce this desired output. A comparison of input and output identifies the data that must be maintained on files.

Next, we consider processing; that is, how are the input data transformed and used to modify the files? How often does a file have to be updated? How are the input and the contents of files processed to produce the desired output? Also, at this point the design team should specify manual procedures for other activities associated with the system.

For input and output files and processing, it is necessary to determine what kinds of errors are likely to occur and design procedures to locate or prevent errors. The final output of the specifications for the system should be a work plan and schedule for implementation.

Work Responsibilities

At various times during the development of detailed specifications we will need to develop more data; there is no such thing as "a completed design." By this time, the design team should have developed many contacts with the rest of the organization, so returning to users for additional information should be easy.

During this stage users on the design team still have major tasks to perform and computer department representatives continue to guide design activities. For example, user team members should develop the report contents with actual users of the report. The computer department staff can then design a format for the report and draw up pro forma examples. Alternatively, users can actually draw examples of the reports they would like. Pro forma examples are reviewed thoroughly by users before programming.

Given a brief tutorial it should also be possible for users to design the input for the system and specify most of the file contents. The computer department staff certainly has to specify the details of processing and file structures, but users can supply the overall logic. Users also specify manual procedures that accompany the system. Both users and the information services department staff should think independently of possible errors and the necessary audit trails for the system. (An audit trail is a logical path by which a transaction can be traced through the computer system.)

Tradeoffs

All during the design process, the analyst and user are making tradeoffs among the various alternatives as we have discussed in the previous chapter. With user-centered design as advocated here, the analyst does not make all decisions unilaterally. The analyst can and should narrow the choices to a reasonable number, but the user and the analyst should jointly make final selection of design alternatives.

In one of the examples described later an incident occurs that illustrates this approach. In the design of a system to process accounts receivable on a minicomputer, a question arose as to how one could maintain an alphabetical sequence for a customer listing. Because the minicomputer had limited input/output capabilities and was slow in sorting. the analyst suggested that a numbering scheme be used to create the desired sequence.

By leaving a large number of digits between successive customers, the user could create a pseudoalphabetic listing. For example, if customer Adams were assigned number 1000, the next customer, Adamson, would be given 1010. If a new customer named Adamsen were to be added to the file, the number 1005 would be given. Over time, exact alphabetic order would not be maintained, but the results would be quite close. Certainly this process would be easier for the programmer and more efficient for computer.

The user was presented with the tradeoffs in nontechnical terms. The analyst explained the reasons for the programming choice, and the user was asked to think about how work could be done with the numbering scheme as opposed to the alternative of sorting the customer file alphabetically. The user indicated that a large number of new customers were added to the accounts receivable system each selling season. In addition, a large amount of work was involved in locating customers quickly on a printed report instead of one of the CRT terminals.

In this case since alphabetic sorts are the most time consuming, the tradeoffs were between machine time and efficiency and programming ease versus user convenience. It was clear, when the analyst examined the cogent reasons of the user and empathized with her, that the tradeoffs should be decided in favor of sorting the customers alphabetically as the user requested.

Although this detail is small, it could be an important one for the acceptance of the system. In the conventional approach, the analyst or programmer might have made the opposite decision unilaterally, and the results could have been disastrous. A large number of users would be inconvenienced; for them, the use of the system might constitute 40 to 60 percent of their daily activities. The out-of-sequence customer list would affect them every day in their jobs and would become a major irritant.

This one decision at a fairly late stage in the design process illustrates the kind of tradeoffs that must be made continually during design. Our philosophy of user-centered design means that the analyst eliminates grossly inappropriate alternatives and presents the user with feasible choices to consider. Together the user and the analyst determine what the important evaluation criteria are. In our example, criteria were user convenience versus machine time and programming ease. The user makes the final choice given the pros and cons of the decision alternatives. It is important to emphasize that this tradeoff activity is the essence of systems analysis and design; hundreds and even thousands of such tradeoffs will be made during each design project.

GENERAL DESIGN CONSIDERATIONS

One approach to the design task is to develop an ideal system unconstrained by cost or technology. Then this system is refined through successive iterations until it is realistic. It is in this creative process of design that a team of designers is most important; one individual cannot hope to originate all the features of a system. It is through the synergy of the group that a new system is created.

Below we discuss guidelines for batch or on-line systems. When we discussed patterns of processing in Chapter 7, we saw that many combinations of equipment and response are possible, from centralized through distributed to decentralized systems in some combination of batch or on-line processing. These alternatives will impart the options available to the analyst. However, the discussion below can be easily applied to designs for these various patterns of processing.

Output

The output of the computer system is the primary contact between the system and most users. The quality of this output and its usefulness determine whether the system will be used, so it is essential to have the best possible output. Through much of our research on the use of information systems, we have found that users have different requirements. Some users want exception reports; they wish to be notified only if sales fall, say, 5 percent from last year's level. Other users may want summary information, while still others prefer complete details. To determine the different types of output desired, the design team can employ user surveys or have user members of the design team observe how other users work with information. Users should be provided with samples of reports for several weeks so they can think about their contents and format.

How can designers provide output flexibility? Clearly, data have to be maintained at the lowest level of detail required for reporting purposes. There is no reason, however, why everyone must receive the same output. Summaries can be developed from detailed data for those who desire it. Designers should consider keeping a file of user preferences regarding report formats if there are substantial differences in requests for output. A report can then be produced according to the preferred format of each user.

Another possibility to enhance output flexibility is to employ file management packages or to develop a retrieval program that makes it easy to custom-tailor reports. The use of such packages also makes it much easier to change reports as experience with the system grows.

The design team should stress clarity in format and headings for output. One of the most frequent complaints we hear is that users cannot understand reports; it is essential to use clear, descriptive titles for different fields on a report and to avoid the use of obscure or little-known codes. If the data on a report are not obvious, a footnote should be added, explaining how the numbers were derived or referring to the appropriate documentation for an explanation. Perhaps the first page of the report should include a short description of how the computations were performed.

When it is necessary to print exception or error messages, the system should provide as polite a response as possible. Here again, it is not desirable to use code numbers, such as "Error 13B." Instead, the error message should explain what is wrong and provide feedback so one can learn from mistakes.

Another chronic complaint is that the computer systems produce too much data. Information can be made available and printed only when needed. Will an exception report do? Are data needed only infrequently? Can they be saved on a tape and printed only if necessary? If we must maintain large amounts of

---

WAREHOUSE CONTROL

A computer that is used as a part of the point of sales scanning at Ralphs Grocery Stores also provides around the clock on-line control of four of the company's seven Los Angeles area warehouses. As soon as merchandise is received on the warehouse dock, it is entered into an on-line inventory management system via a display terminal. The system immediately assigns each pallet to a specific warehouse slot. Simultaneously a printer produces an adhesive location label giving a description of the product, number of cases, the purchase order number and where the pallet is to be stored in the warehouse. The printer also produces a summary label listing all activities relating to each purchase order including the warehouse location of each pallet received. The summary label provides both an audit trail and a document that can be forwarded to accounts payable to reconcile billing problems.

After each billing, the system determines which pallets need to be moved from a secondary or reserve location to a primary or picking location. Labels are printed again to direct the forklift operators. By using this method, warehouse scratches (items shown in inventory but not shipped because they cannot be located) have diminished from 14,000 to less than a 1,000 a week.

Data Processor, June/July 1980.

MANAGEMENT PROBLEM 13-3

Susan Friedman, the director of sales for the Trumbull department-store chain, is concerned over the complaints she has been receiving from store managers about the company's sales information system. The system has been highly successful until now; it provides information for store managers that most competitors do not have.

However, a recent survey sent to each department store in the chain indicated significant differences in how the information on the report is used. Susan has been meeting with the computer staff to review the comments from users. It seems that there are two choices: either managers can be trained to use the existing batch report produced by the system, or a more responsive output can be designed.

Susan does not like the idea of forcing the managers to use the system in a predetermined manner. She says, "The real beauty of this system is that it contains enough data to make all of the different store managers happy. They all have different ways of managing and I don't think we would be successful enforcing uniformity."

The computer staff has indicated that there are a number of possibilities for changing the output from the system, but has asked for help from Susan and the managers to determine what changes are desired.

What different output alternatives might be examined? How should they be investigated? What are the implications of each alternative for the present system, particularly for the current system, which has a sequential file structure?

---

archival data for historical or legal purposes, it may be possible to use microfilm. The design team should also consider whether the addition of an on-line inquiry facility would eliminate the need for many printed reports.

The discussion above has referred primarily to batch processing output, and there are a few additional considerations that should be included in the design of on-line output. First, there should be a key on the terminal the user can depress to obtain help. The "help" function provides an on-line set of instructions to show how to obtain information. In addition to a "help" key, there may be several levels of prompting in the system. For example, a more detailed mode of comments can be used for the novice and a terser mode for the frequent, experienced user.

Another important feature of an on-line system is adequate response time. Users who become dependent upon on-line processing are very sensitive to degraded response times; backup should therefore be provided. Users have been known to become enraged when a crucial on-line system is not functioning. It is also helpful to use pleasing terminals; can a CRT be used if hard copy is not needed? Perhaps silent printers can be used where a permanent record is necessary.

Input

In the past few years, the trend in information systems has been toward collecting data as close to its source as possible. The objective of this philosophy is to eliminate data transcription wherever possible, for purposes of avoiding errors and reducing the time required to enter the data into the computer. The ultimate in automatic data collection, of course, is sensors attached to the input of a real-time system, such as a computer monitoring a patient in a hospital. In most commercial computer systems, a popular source-data collection technique is to use an on-line terminal.

However, there are alternatives to on-line input that are usually less costly. It may be possible to use a turnaround document in dealing with customers. For example, a bill is punched on a card and sent to a customer who returns the card with payment. If the customer pays the amount due, the return card can be processed directly. If the customer does not pay the full amount, then some kind of a keying operation is necessary to record the amount actually paid.

Another method to avoid data transcription—one that is gaining rapidly in popularity—is the use of optical character recognition (OCR) equipment. For a large sales force, it would be too expensive to have computer terminals for each salesperson. Communications and equipment costs would be too high, and it is not clear that it would even be desirable for sales personnel to use a typewriter terminal to record sales. Instead, if numbers are printed carefully, the actual order form prepared by each person can be used as an input to the computer system through a scanner. In fact, the use of the scanner might actually be faster than an on-line terminal, since undoubtedly the sales personnel would have to write orders before they could key them into a terminal. By taking a few more minutes to write clearly, the order form itself is entered directly into the computer system.

It is also possible to use mark sensing for input where the user darkens a box or circle corresponding to the user's choice for input. However, optical character recognition is easier for the user to understand than mark sensing and generally is preferred except where input data are very simple. Unless there are just a few alternatives, the mark sense forms become clumsy, since a separate box or circle must be provided for each possible answer.

Batch input, unfortunately, suffers from rigidity. Since most batch input requires information in a strict format, there is also a lack of immediate feedback on errors with batch processing. However, batch input is very economical and these systems have several advantages, including backup and processing error control. Whenever possible, the design team should consider the use of existing documents for input, since these will minimize problems in understanding new and possibly more complicated forms. It is important to be sure that data to be entered can be provided legibly on the form. If a document has to be transcribed by a keying operation, it is helpful to use boxes for each character. If this is not possible, a separate well-delimited space should be provided for each character since this helps the keying operator justify the input.

For input forms intended for optical character recognition or mark sensing, it is best to work with manufacturers' representatives to determine the demands for their particular machinery. OCR has very exacting requirements for the location of information and the quality of printing on forms.

On-line interaction should be clear and polite; one should try to avoid a cumbersome input command structure and emphasize natural response. For on-line data entry, the system should provide courteous error messages and the opportunity to rekey data that are in error; messages should be polite and explain the error. It might be advisable to give no explanation unless the user types a question mark or presses some other key after receiving an error message. That way those familiar with the system can avoid tedious error messages really designed for someone with less experience.

Manual Procedures

The systems design is not complete until we specify the manual processing procedures surrounding the computer system. What volume of activity will there be? How much time is required to perform these manual tasks? We should specify what processing the user has to perform and indicate the flow of information and the time required to complete processing. Manual input procedures are an often-overlooked part of systems design, yet poorly planned manual procedures have caused many otherwise well-designed systems to fail.

Errors

A well-designed system handles errors; that is, it corrects them or notifies someone of the errors and continues producing valid output. It is not unusual to find more than half the instructions in a program devoted to error detection and handling, especially in an on-line system. Detection of errors in processing is the responsibility of the information services department and these problems are usually technological in nature. However, the user design team should be aware of input error possibilities and design procedures to minimize the likelihood of their occurrence and any adverse impact on the organization. One of the advantages of batch input is the error control it allows, since the data are all entered together in batches.

Whenever data are transcribed by some keying operation, they are usually key-verified to check for reporting errors. The first operator keys the data and a separate individual verifies them, using a machine that compares the keying of the original operator with the keystrokes of the verification operator. The verification process shows discrepancies that are then corrected by the operator. We assume that the data are recorded accurately on the document being keyed; however, there is nothing that guarantees accuracy.

It is not always necessary or desirable to key-verify all input fields. The use of a check digit, described below, lets the computer catch transcription errors. Some input fields such as names or descriptive information are not crucial for every application. When batch totals are used, the designer must decide whether or not it is necessary to key-verify the amount field since the computer checks it when totaling the batches on input.

We also may include a set of checks after transcription to see that data were correctly entered into the computer. For crucial fields, such as those dealing with monetary amounts, we usually employ a batch control total. A batch total is computed by keeping track of the dollar amount of a field in one batch of around

50 input documents. The batch total is entered in a batch control record that follows the documents in a batch. The computer program reading the input adds the data fields and compares them with the batch total. If the fields do not match, the program indicates an error. Batch totals provide assurances that the data, as prepared, are entered into the computer and furnish another check on the keying operation.

After checking data transformations and making sure that the data are entered, a program should perform logical checks on the source of the information. Did the originator provide correct data? For numbers that are used as keys, such as an identification number, we can use a check digit. Assume that the identification number for a part in inventory is four digits long, for example, part number 4326. During processing, we add a fifth digit to the number to serve as a check. We might compute the check digit by dividing the identification number by 11 and using the remainder as the check digit. The remainder when 4326 is divided by 11 is 2, so the number should appear in a parts catalog, in all input documents and on file as 43262. The computer programs that process the identification part number perform the same calculation; that is, a program divides 4326 by 11 and takes the remainder, checking to see that it is the same as the digit 2 in the units position.

A variety of other verification schemes also employ check digits, such as weighting each digit by a certain number. These calculations all have the same objective: to detect transposition and entry errors. Check digits are especially crucial when optical character recognition or mark sensing is used because of the possibility that the machine might make reading errors.

During the editing stage, we examine individual fields to be sure that no alphabetic characters have been placed in positions that should be all numeric. For example, if all inventory part numbers begin with the letter A or M or R, we should check to see that the first input character is one of these characters. If it is possible, we place boundaries on the input data to recognize invalid data; for example, we may be able to say that no transaction should be less than 50 cents or over $1,000,000. In a sequential update, it is likely that for many error checks we shall have to wait until the file is actually updated. The data at the edit processing stage are likely to be unsorted, and the data affecting a single master file record will not be all together.

In later stages, when sorted input is being processed, we can check the number of transactions affecting a single record to see if the amount of activity is reasonable. If there are too many transactions, there may be a problem that should be checked. For example, if usage of a part exceeds 200 percent of the prior month's usage, human intervention may be necessary to determine the reason for such abnormally high usage.

On-Line Systems   One of the major efforts in the design of on-line input is error detection; it is difficult to catch errors such as the transposition or transcription mistakes we discussed under batch processing. With on-line processing, transactions are frequently not entered together in a group, so batch

MANAGEMENT PROBLEM 13-4

John Washington is the manager of sales for Farway Manufacturing Company, a firm specializing in the manufacture of yard and garden supplies. The firm's products are sold in hardware stores and nurseries throughout the world by a large force of field sales representatives.

Currently, Farway is involved in the design of a new order-entry and sales-information system, and John is the user in charge of the project. The design team is in the process of choosing a method for data input and is divided over which of two alternatives would be most desirable.

One group in the firm favors optical character recognition for order entry; the sales force would be trained to print carefully when preparing order forms. The forms would be input directly to an OCR scanner connected to the firm's computer system, eliminating the need for any data transcription. Adherents of this approach point to the savings inherent in not having to transcribe order information into machine-readable form. Those opposing this alternative worry that the sales force will be uncooperative because of the changes required and the added time to print orders very carefully.

A second group that is uneasy about OCR has proposed continuing with the same, familiar order form; all changes would take place at the factory and would not be noticed by the sales force. When the orders arrive at the factory, they would be grouped into batches of 50 and entered by operators using a CRT on-line to the computer. This alternative features the advantage of batch error control combined with immediate feedback as the data are entered.

John Washington is trying to determine what criteria to use in deciding between these two alternatives for input. Which alternative sounds best to you? How should John resolve this deadlock on the design team?

---

totals are not possible. These applications will probably make use of check digits and will also require logical checks on input. Frequently, with on-line transactions, we have access to files, therefore more complete checks can be performed on the data as they are entered. On-line input has the major advantage of providing immediate feedback on errors, however.

It is certainly possible to perform the same type of field checking as in batch processing, that is, checking the upper and lower bounds on the values of input numbers. Input fields can also be scanned to be sure that numeric fields do not contain alphabetic data. On-line processing generally includes inconsistency checks; if a room clerk books two hotel reservations, then the clerk should also enter the names of two guests. In the case of extremely critical data that cannot be verified, the system should echo them back to the user and ask for confirmation.

Some systems collect data on-line, post them to a transaction file, and update the master file later in batch mode. As long as the data on the files do not have to be up to the minute, this processing strategy presents an alternative to a fully on-line updating system. It is also customary to record all input transactions on magnetic tape in an on-line system to produce an input audit trail and for backup.

The first on-line applications were developed to give individuals at different locations access to a centralized data base, generally for rather simple transactions such as making a reservation. Today, many organizations are applying on-line technology to what, in the past, would have been batch input. For example, consider an order-entry application in which the sales force sends a completed order form to the factory. In the factory, a day's receipts of orders could be placed in a batch and the number of pieces ordered added to provide a batch total.

Then an operator working on-line at a CRT enters the information from each order. First, the operator types in the customer number, and the computer retrieves and displays the customer name and address; the operator checks the computer-retrieved data against the order. If there is an error, the operator corrects the account number and continues. Each item on the order is keyed in, and the computer checks to see if the item numbers are legitimate. For example, do we make style 3245 in color 37 (blue)? Various totals are computed on the order as a further check: for example, all the items entered from the CRT can be added and the total compared with that manually computed on the order. A listing of the day's orders with a batch total should correspond to the manual batch total computed for the orders before they are entered into the system.

This type of on-line input combines the advantages of batch control checking with on-line interaction. The interface with the operator entering information is much more pleasant than a keypunch device and very little special training is needed for most applications. We expect to see a continuation of the trend toward more on-line data entry for this type of operation.

Output Errors   If input is correct, and processing up to the output stage has been carefully checked, we expect correct output to result. However, it may still be necessary to take certain precautions. It is likely that a report program will read data from the output of some other programs. We may want to have control totals on the different amount fields if report contents are written into an intermediate file. The report-writing program computes the same totals and checks them against the intermediate file. When the reports are actually printed, the report-printing program checks different calculations, for example, by "crossfooting" various output totals (that is, computing the same total more than one way—perhaps horizontally and vertically on a statement). We should also be alert to rounding problems, although most computer languages for information systems now feature decimal arithmetic capabilities. Some older machines that had only binary arithmetic created errors when financial statements were off by several pennies because of poor rounding procedures in programs. In one company, the inaccuracies were not appreciated by the accounting department, which lost all faith in computer processing because of this easily corrected error.

Error Action   Many of the input and processing checks described above are designed to ensure file integrity, that is, to avoid the introduction of erroneous data or the destruction of portions of a file. This goal must be balanced against having a system that is overcontrolled, that is, a system with so many error checks that it is never able to run to completion.

For gross processing errors, such as an incorrect file, it is necessary to avoid processing until the problem can be corrected. If a series of transactions appears to be incorrect when a file is updated, the particular record in error can be skipped and an error notification issued. Alternatively, that record can be updated, but a field on the record should be used to indicate that some type of authorization for the change must be received on the next updating cycle. If control totals do not match at the end of a run, then appropriate notices have to be issued and the operations staff has to decide whether a rerun is necessary.

Backup

In addition to error controls during processing, we must consider the availability of backup. An audit trail is necessary; that is, there must be some way to trace transactions through a system from input to output. In an on-line system, one reason for keeping a tape of transactions is to make sure there is an audit trail. Special audit transactions may be created as a legitimate type of input for use by auditors in checking the system.

Batch updating provides automatic backup and security in the form of the old master file plus a record of transactions; we can recreate the new master file easily if anything happens to it. Usually two versions of the master file are kept, giving rise to what is called "the grandfather-son backup strategy." For on-line systems, the contents of the file are dumped to tape, possibly several times a day. If a catastrophic failure occurs, the operator reloads the dumped files and uses the transaction-log tape to restore file changes.

Because batch computer systems also occasionally fail for hardware and software reasons, batch file updates may make use of checkpoint procedures so that a complete rerun is not necessary if an error is encountered. Some computer languages feature automatic checkpoint facilities; during a sequential update, for example, a request for a checkpoint causes the recording of all data areas and the program status on a file. In addition, information on the records that are finished processing is recorded. If the system fails for some reason, the operator can restart the program at the last checkpoint without returning to the beginning of processing.

The major problem with restarting on-line systems is that we do not know how many transactions were in process at the time of failure. Because of the time involved, we may not want to reload the dump tape, but would like to recover from a minor failure as quickly as possible. It may be feasible to ask terminal users to verify their last transactions after we update the file. Alternatively, the time of update may be a field on the file and the recovery program could identify suspected transactions which were entered, but not completely processed, at the time of the failure. On-line error control is a very specialized topic; for further discussions see Yourdon (1972).

Security and Fraud   There has been a great deal of publicity about the problems of fraud and security with computer systems. In designing a system, we have to take reasonable precautions to avoid the possibility of fraud. Independent programmers should be used for critical parts of the system, and multiple users should be involved. Procedurally, we should avoid giving authorization for sensitive changes to only one person. One of the easiest ways to develop reasonable precautions is to include an internal auditor on the design team. Security is enhanced not only by having backup files, but by storing them in separate physical locations.

SYSTEM SPECIFICATIONS

The final design must be converted into system specifications, a task best undertaken by the staff of the information services department. The specifications must reflect the processing logic of the new system and describe the format, contents, and structure of each file in the system. Input and output must be specified in detail including the form, medium, format, and examples. The designers should explain programming requirements, and both users and the computer staff can work on the documentation of manual procedures. An example of system specifications is presented in Chapter 17, and Table 13-5 contains a list of the items that should be included in this report.

KEY WORDS

Analyst	Documentation	Resource allocation
Alternatives	Error control	Resources
Backup	Exception reporting	Response time
Batch controls	Feasibility study	Risk
Check digit	Flexibility	Source data collection
Control totals	Input specifications	Steering committee
Conversion program	Manual procedures	Verification
Criterion	Priorities	Weight
Data transcription	Processing alternatives	
Demands	Reasonableness checks	

RECOMMENDED READINGS

Ackoff, R. L.: "Management Misinformation Systems," *Management Science,* vol. 14, no. 4, December 1967, pp. B140–B156. (This classic article describes a number of myths about information systems design.)

Lucas, H. C., Jr., and J. R. Moore, Jr.: "A Multiple Criterion Scoring Approach to Information System Project Selection," *Infor,* vol. 14, no. 2, February 1976, pp. 1–12. (This paper describes in detail the scoring model referred to in this chapter.)

Martin, J.: *The Design of Real-Time Systems*, Prentice-Hall, Englewood Cliffs, N.J., 1967. (In this and several other books referenced in the bibliography, Martin describes many of the considerations in the development of on-line systems.)

Moore, J. R., Jr., and N. R. Baker: "Computational Analysis of Scoring Models for R&D Project Selection," *Management Science,* vol. 16, no. 4, December 1969, pp. B212–B232. (This paper presents the results of a simulation of some of the properties of scoring models; it is technical, but provides good background on this type of model compared with others.)

Yourdon, E.: *Design of On-Line Computer Systems,* Prentice-Hall, Englewood Cliffs, N.J., 1972. (This book contains a great deal of detail on the design of on-line systems.)

DISCUSSION QUESTIONS

1 Why is the selection of an information systems project so important to an organization?

2 What are the major sources of frustrations in selecting computer applications?

3 How does the conflict model of earlier chapters apply to selection of information systems projects if the information services department is in charge of this process and makes unilateral decisions?

4 What is source data collection? What are its advantages?

5 How would you expect an information services department to react to the idea of evaluating several different alternatives for a single system?

6 What kind of output equipment has the most pleasing user interface, in your opinion? What is the cost of more desirable equipment compared with that of a less pleasant interface?

7 Can systems design be described as a science? What is scientific about it? What characteristics make it appear to be an art?

8 What type of computer system—for example, batch or on-line—is most flexible in meeting user needs when in operation? What type is most flexible when changes are made after implementation?

9 What is the drawback for users in serving on a selection committee and/or design teams?

10 What other approaches to selection of information systems projects can you suggest?

11 Who should be on a selection committee for project selection decisions?

12 Suggest a mechanism for deciding which enhancements to existing systems should be undertaken. How does this problem differ from selecting new applications? How are the two decisions similar?

13 Why present multiple alternatives in preliminary surveys and feasibility studies?

14 How do projects already under way influence decisions on undertaking a proposed application?

15 How can one find out what applications packages might be available as a possible source of processing in a proposed system?

16 How should risk be considered in evaluating proposed applications? What are the risks in systems analysis and design? Should an organization have a portfolio of projects balanced on risk?

17 What is an audit trail in an information system? Why is such a trail of transactions necessary?

18   What are the reasons for using on-line technology if there is no need for decentralized coordination of users who access a common data base?

19   Are there manual procedures with an on-line system? If so, what type? How important are they?

20   Why are some managers unsatisfied with exception reports? How can their fears be eased?

21   Are error checks more demanding for a batch system or for a system that operates on-line? What types of error checks differ for the two systems?

22   What contribution can the user make to a preliminary survey and feasibility study? How can the use of this information lead to biased recommendations?

23   How can the amount of computer output be reduced while still meeting user needs?

24   What other creative tasks are there in the organization in addition to the design of new information systems? How do they differ from this activity?

25   What are the prospects for automating systems design tasks? Where could automation be fruitfully applied in the systems life cycle?

26   Design a procedure for developing criteria and assigning them for project selection.

27   Does a system have to use the most modern technology to be successful? Why or why not? Are there disadvantages to utilizing the most up-to-date technology?

SYSTEMS DESIGN PROBLEMS

1   One of the most common computer applications is payroll. Many organizations have custom-designed payroll systems, and a large number of service bureaus offer packages to compute an organization's payroll. The logic of the payroll process is fairly simple and is common across many organizations.

Usually a payroll master file contains data about each individual who is on the payroll. Examples of the data to be included in setting up this file for employees would be:

NAME
NUMBER OF DEPENDENTS
MARITAL STATUS
DEDUCTIONS
UNION DUES
HOSPITAL PLAN
MEDICAL PLAN
PENSION
EMPLOYEE NUMBER
WAGE RATE
SOCIAL SECURITY NUMBER

On a periodic basis, such as weekly or monthly, input must originate to trigger the computation of the payroll and the production of a check for each employee. This weekly input would have to include at a minimum:

Employee number
Regular hours worked
Overtime hours worked
Sick leave
Special deductions

Once the system is run on a periodic basis, checks should be produced along with various accumulations for different year-to-date categories. The computer program would subtract all deductions and withhold funds for tax purposes. Also included in the output would normally be a payroll register. On an annual basis, the computer system would produce W2 forms, which are summaries of earnings and taxes withheld from wages, for the IRS.

a Design the input forms to be used to place a new employee on the payroll file, and the forms to be completed weekly for each employee to be paid.

b List the file contents and approximate field sizes for the payroll master file. Do not forget to include year-to-date totals.

c Draw a system flowchart for this payroll application.

d Describe the modifications necessary for the system to mail automatically a check to the bank, if the employee so elects, and to include a notice to the employee.

e Design the file maintenance and change cards necessary to alter information about employees.

2 Most organizations have some kind of accounts receivable, whether they are in manufacturing or a service company. Accounts receivable was one of the first applications undertaken by many firms when computer systems were acquired. Service bureaus also offer accounts-receivable packages for sale or rent. In the early days of computers, most accounts-receivable packages were typically batch applications; today, however, there is growing interest in on-line input and payment processing.

Consider an on-line accounts-receivable system. An accounts-receivable transaction is generated by a shipment of a product to a customer. An operator at a terminal enters the following information:

Order number
Shipment number
For each shipment:
Product code
Quantity
Date
Shipping costs
Special shipping mode
Special discounts
Comments

The program accepting this input responds with the customer name and address once the order number is entered: it also prints the product descriptions, the price extension, and the total invoice cost.

The customer receives the statement and sends in payment for one or more invoices. The next task is for an operator to enter the payments and to match them against invoices. The operator enters the invoice number, the total payment, and exceptions to indicate partial payments for items on an invoice that are not paid.

In addition to the printed invoices, invoice register, and monthly statements, the system would provide an accounts-receivable listing, a daily cash balance, and exception reports for invoices that were partially paid or have not been paid at all. There would also be a function to allow on-line inquiry concerning payment history.

Of course, as with any system, it is necessary to establish a new customer. The new customer information would have to include:

The account number
Name and address

Credit
Payment terms
Normal shipping mode
a   Design the customer master file, the shipment and invoice files, and show any directories necessary to access these files.
b   Describe the overall logic of file access.
c   Design the screens for data input and inquiry using a CRT.
d   List the edits and controls that would be necessary on this system.

3   Accounts Payable

Accounts payable has also traditionally been a batch processing application; however, on-line input improves the editing and the user interface with this system. To add a new vendor with whom a firm does business, it is necessary to assign a vendor number and include a name, address, and list any terms and discount that apply.

The first activity that generates an accounts payable is the issuance of a purchase order. The purchase order must contain:

Vendor number
For each item:
Item number
Item description
Quantity
Cost
Cost for the whole order, shipping costs, and special discounts

For on-line accounts payable, the system would respond with the vendor, name, and address as soon as the vendor number was entered, and would perform all the extensions of price times quantity. The output from this part of the system would be a printed purchase order. It would be also desirable to allow the purchasing department to make inquiries on a purchase order number.

The purchase order would be used as a document for receiving. The receiving department enters a purchase order number when merchandise arrives and notes any exceptions on the items, such as a particular item that was not received, or a quantity that is not what was indicated on the purchase order.

Next, the organization receives a bill from the vendor. This bill should contain the company's purchase order number and the amount owed. An individual in the accounts-payable section accesses a terminal, enters the purchase order number, and compares the bill with the original purchase order and the quantities received. On authorization for payment, the system prints a check ready for mailing to the vendor and a check register.

a   Design the system flow for this system.
b   Design the vendor and the open purchase order files.
c   Design the input edits and controls for the system and the displays for a CRT screen.

4   Sales reporting can be a very important computer application. Often, data for sales reports come directly from shipping and/or invoicing systems in the organization. At a minimum, this application requires a customer file including a customer number, geographic code, shipment date, order number, item number, quantity shipped, and price.

From these data, it is possible to generate an output sales report. This report might be summarized by product, product type, region, or salesperson.

    a Would you recommend that this system operate in batch or on-line mode?

    b Design an inquiry system that would answer questions interactively concerning customers or products. Would these answers be computed on-line or would a summary file be developed?

    c Assume that historical data are available on sales for the last 10 years. What kind of forecasting system would you design for this organization? What would be your considerations in choosing a forecasting system?

5 The manufacturing or production function in an organization includes many activities, such as materials acquisition, production scheduling and control, work-in-process inventory control, and finished goods inventory control.

    One way to start the manufacturing process is with the preparation of a bill of materials. A bill of materials lists all the components necessary to manufacture a product. Usually the input that is provided is the number of new products identified by product number and quantity. The output from this system is a list of subassemblies and the quantity required; that list contains all the parts needed to manufacture the particular product.

    a Design the file structures for a bill-of-materials processor.

    b Describe the logic of the explosion program.

    c Assume the input to the bill-of-materials processor contains the product and the date it is to be shipped to the customer. Design a system to produce a report on products that must be manufactured by a given due date.

6 A budget is a fundamental managerial control tool in an organization. In setting up budgets, minimal input includes an account number, the type of account, a description, and where a control break is to be taken to add up the totals for a subaccount. Then for each budget cycle, input is provided on the account number, the budgeted amount of money, and the actual money spent.

    The output from such a system is the budget report. It shows the account, the description, the budgeted amount, the actual amount, variance amounts, and usually percentage totals as well.

    Design a master file for a budget application and describe the format of a budget report.

7 One unusual application was suggested for a retail grocery chain. This particular organization computes what is called a markup and markdown plan each week. The markup is the general gross profit the store wishes to obtain on groceries; this markup might be 20 percent. The markdown is the amount of margin acceptable when the regular and special discount items are sold; so, for example, if a special is to be held on frozen peas, the sale on frozen peas might be 10 percent off, which is estimated to reduce the total gross profit to a level of 18 percent, which is the markdown.

    In this grocery chain, pricing specialists make estimates of the sales of discount special items and the sales of all items sold at regular price. The markup goal is then compared with the estimates for the actual markup to determine if the markdown resulting from sales plan specials is acceptable.

    A consultant has recommended this activity as a possible computer application. What kind of computer application does this suggest? What would be the interface between the pricing specialist and the computer? What mode of operation do you recommend?

    a Design the files for this system.

    b Describe the interaction between the system and the pricing specialist.

    c Design an output report that shows the prices to be charged for items on special.

8 General ledger is an accounting application to produce a final consolidation of all financial transactions in a company. A file must be created showing the chart of accounts for the firm. Many subsystems automatically produce entries for the general ledger, and other input comes from journal entries. Examples of input from different subsystems include payroll, vendor invoices, accounts payable, cash receipts, check writing, work in process, fixed assets, and shipments.

General ledger programs traditionally include a trial balance that is run before the final general ledger for the month. The output of the system is a detailed general ledger showing transactions against individual accounts and a consolidated ledger at the account level.

a Design the files necessary to produce a consolidated and a detailed general ledger.

b Draw a flowchart of the general ledger system showing the inputs from other systems.

c Design the logic for the production of financial statements (an income statement and balance sheet) from the general ledger. What alterations have to be made in the file design in **a** above to produce the financial reports?

9 Computer technology is being applied to the retail industry, particularly to supermarket check-out operations. In these systems, some type of optical character recognition scanner reads the universal product code on items sold in the store. A minicomputer in the store contains a file with the universal produce code numbers and the current price. As the items are scanned, their price is read from the file and the entire cost of the grocery order is computed.

All during the day the computer in the store maintains a record of items sold. In the evening, the data can be transferred to a central host computer to update master records, which represent sales and, more important, inventory balances. These inventory data can then be used to restock the supermarket, so that it is not necessary for store personnel to place formal orders with the warehouse.

Such systems were designed to speed the check-out process and to ensure more rapid response for the resupply of grocery products.

a Design the files for the local grocery store and the files for the central host computer.

b Develop a backup plan that will become operative if the minicomputer in the supermarket fails.

c What reports could be generated from the system for the use of store management?

Programming through Installation

PROGRAMMING
    Programming Goals
    Egoless Programming
    Programmer Teams
    Modularization
    Stepwise Refinement and Structured Programming
    Top-Down Programming
    Reviews
TESTING
    Unit Testing
    Combined Module Testing
    Testing Manual Procedures
    Acceptance Tests
TRAINING
CONVERSION AND INSTALLATION
DOCUMENTATION
    Design Documentation
    Training Documentation
    Operations Documentation
    User Reference Documentation
POSTCONVERSION ACTIVITIES
KEY WORDS
RECOMMENDED READINGS
DISCUSSION QUESTIONS

Programming through Installation

PROGRAMMING
TESTING
TRAINNING
CONVERSION
INSTALLATION.

CHAPTER ISSUES

- How can management monitor and aid the development of systems?
- What management actions are needed to ensure adequate training and smooth conversion to a new system?

The next stages in the development of a new information system are programming, testing, training, conversion, and installation. Programming is a highly technical and time-consuming task, and in this chapter we suggest some modern approaches to programming to improve productivity. Careful testing and planning for installation are essential; many systems have failed because attention was not paid to these activities. What roles do the user and manager have in testing and planning for training, conversion, and installation? In this chapter we explore activities during these stages.

PROGRAMMING

The most technical parts of computer project management and the greatest amount of uncertainty are associated with the task of writing and testing programs. In the past, we have not been able to estimate completion times effectively or to coordinate people working on different parts of a program. In this section we present some new ideas and approaches to these tasks that should help to improve programming productivity.

Programming Goals

In many development projects, management does not realize that there are different objectives in writing programs and does not inform programmers what they should adopt as a design goal. In an experiment, Weinberg (1972b) found that by giving a group of programmers explicit objectives, each group ranked first on the achievement of its objective. The objectives in this experiment were minimum core usage, output clarity, program clarity, minimum number of statements, or minimum hours of development time. The study also showed that some of the goals were incompatible, for example, the goal of output clarity and the use of minimum number of statements.

The implications of this experiment for management are quite significant: managers should make programming goals clear and explicit. Lacking goals, the programming staff may make different assumptions; one programmer may stress minimum completion time while another tries for the minimum number of statements in the program. For most organizations developing information systems, the overriding goal probably will be clarity of program coding and output. In developing information systems we usually do not want elegant and sophisticated programs. Clarity of output is important to the users, and clarity of coding is important to programming management so that program changes can be made easily.

Egoless Programming

For the most part we have always thought of programming as an individual task. Programmers are often detached from their coworkers, but are highly attached to the programs they write. Errors in programs are taken personally and programmers tend to be highly defensive about their programs. Weinberg (1972a) has suggested a new approach to programming (he calls it "egoless programming") that treats programming as a group activity rather than as an individual effort. Management must create an environment in which the programmer expects errors in the code and recognizes that help is needed to find them. Programmers in a group trade programs and look at each other's codes. Many examples are cited by Weinberg that show the advantages aside from easier debugging and faster completion time. First, each programmer becomes better aware of the entire system and develops an understanding of how different modules fit together because of this involvement in the construction of other parts of the system. Also, more backup is provided, since several people are familiar with each module.

Programmer Teams

A structure that incorporates egoless programming teams and has the potential for greatly improving project management has been suggested by Baker (1972). The chief programmer team consists of a senior chief programmer, one or more backup programmers, one to five junior programmers, and a programming secretary (Mills, 1971). The chief programmer directs the activities of the group, holding a position similar to that of a senior engineer. Programming is often viewed as a profession leading to a system analyst or management position, but one of the advantages of the team concept is that a highly paid chief programmer position can be viewed as a senior staff position in an organization. This approach presents a better career path for programmers and recognizes that skilled programming is a worthy profession in itself.

All other programmers report to the chief programmer, whose job is to design and code programs, and who will program the most critical segments of the system. This person also works with other programmers to define modules for them. The chief programmer is responsible for the management of the team as a whole, and has the opportunity to be a high-level creative programmer and, at the same time, a professional manager.

A backup programmer who is equivalent in talent with the chief programmer becomes totally familiar with the activities of the chief programmer and provides backup. As long as the chief programmer is able to continue to manage the project, the backup programmer serves as a research associate to help develop new ideas and program test data.

A programming secretary maintains records of the project, including a complete file or library of programs, flowcharts, and program specifications. An index or directory to each part of the library is also maintained. The librarian is responsible for keeping a list of all the data elements so that all data are called by the same identifier in each program. Old versions of programs are maintained in the archives so that useful information is not thrown out. For the same reason, copies of test data and test runs are filed in an archive; this practice maintains the status of the programs and the project to facilitate programmers' work. Therefore a complete and accurate directory or index to the items in the file is required.

The entire programming team functions as a group. Various programmers follow the guidance of the chief programmer; they work on different modules and read each other's programs. Heavy use is made of the library to build, store, and retrieve information for the team. For large projects it may be necessary to have several levels of teams, with the highest level reporting to the project manager. To implement this approach management must make an extensive effort to provide an environment for and to encourage group-related activities.

Modularization

In the early days of programming, the practice was to write a single large program to accomplish a major task, for example, the entire update of a major file. Large individual programs have proved very hard to write because of their complexity, and extremely difficult to debug and modify. Modern programming techniques call for dividing programs into modules that are reasonably small. Each module accomplishes one processing function. The modules should be written so that they are easy to understand and so that control enters at the beginning of the module and exists at the end without intervening transfers. The task of partitioning a system into modules is very difficult and not well understood today.

It is helpful to make a list of design decisions and to construct program modules around these decisions to hide them from other design decisions. (A program will usually consist of several modules.) Consider the following example, which is for the design of input for an application.

The decision on the format for card input should be hidden from other parts of the system by having one module of the input program read the data from the card. This module should pass the fields of data independently of the format or their layout on the card to the other parts of the input program for further processing. Later, if it is decided to use a different card layout or input device, it would be necessary to change only the module that reads the card, not the entire input program.

This breakdown of programs into smaller modules makes it easier to debug the system and modify it. Of course, program specifications must be developed for each module. We should list all the data entering from another module, the

---

MANAGEMENT PROBLEM 14-1

David Schwartz is controller of Play Toys, a manufacturer of high-quality children's toys. He has recently served as the user in charge of the development of a new integrated accounting system for the company. The specifications are complete, and the system is now being programmed by the information services department at Play Toys. David, although not managing the programming, has tried to stay in touch with progress.

He is very concerned about the problems the computer staff apparently is having with the project. There are four programmers assigned to write different portions of the system. As the computer staff manager explained it to David, there has been a great deal of frustration when the components written by each of the four programmers do not fit together. As David understands it, the programs fail to "cooperate" in the way they should.

David now has the feeling that the manager of programming for the new accounting system really is no longer in control of the project. This manager is just responding to problems and pressures. When David asks to see a schedule or tries to obtain a status report, the manager of programming is evasive and does not appear to know the answer. David feels the company needs the system very badly. If the company misses the conversion date, it may be necessary to wait an entire year because they are planning to install the new system at the beginning of the fiscal year.

What can David Schwartz as a user do to rescue the accounting project?

number of characters and format of any source documents to be read, and, finally, any data to be read from a file. Output for reports or output that is to be passed to another module should also be specified.

Finally, we must specify any processing to be done by the module. How are the inputs and information derived from files processed? What should the program accomplish? The processing should be described in the form of an algorithm, that is, an effective procedure for accomplishing the goals of the module. The algorithm can be expressed in English, in symbols, or in some combination of the two.

In addition to specifying the programs that will constitute the system when it is in operation, we must also define any conversion programs needed to create files or manipulate data before the installation of the system. Since these programs will be run only once for the most part, efficiency is not as important as clarity and the speed of program development.

Stepwise Refinement and Structured Programming

In addition to modularization, we also suggest the use of structured programming (Baker, 1972; Mills, 1971). Structured programming is a methodical approach to developing programs. The term "stepwise refinement" is usually associated with structured programming. In fact, we have borrowed this terminology in our discussions of the task of systems analysis and design.

The idea behind stepwise refinement is that we move to successively lower levels of detail. At the highest level, the plans for a program are abstract and global. In successive stages, we break the program down into more detail; the last of these successive refinements is the coded program. Just as with systems analysis and design, stepwise refinement lets us cope better with the complexity of the programming task. The highest level of abstraction gives us an overview; then we can concentrate on details of what are usually smaller pieces at lower levels of abstraction. By recording the intermediate steps, we document mental processes and design decisions. Many days later when questions arise, there are no unrecorded insights to recall to understand part of a system. Stepwise refinement aids in making logical design decisions and in reviewing them at a later date.

Structured programming follows from stepwise refinement. It is based on the fact that any program can be constructed using the following statement types:

Sequential operations (including procedures calls)
IF THEN ELSE
DO WHILE

The most conspicuously absent type of statement is the GO TO; by eliminating GO TO statements a much more readable program results. It is not possible to find a transfer of control within a program segment. In a well-structured program there is only one entry point and one exit per module. Therefore, a programmer can read a program segment from top to bottom without worrying about intervening jumps. This technique makes it much easier to modify existing programs.

Clearly, it takes more skill and planning to write such a code, but it is much easier to understand and change. This approach to structured programming should be combined with modularization, the use of program comments that describe what each segment of code is meant to accomplish, and code indentation to make the structure of the program clear. For example, statements in the range of DO loop are indented, and different conditions in an IF THEN ELSE grouping are indented. This practice also enhances the readibility of code by grouping related portions of logic together. The programmer should also attempt to have one comment for each related block of code or at least one comment every four or five statements.

Top-Down Programming

Most systems are designed from the top level down; that is, a general plan is developed and refined to greater levels of detail. But systems tend to be implemented from the bottom up; that is, basic modules are written first and then integrated into subsystems.

Some evidence suggests that it may be better to reverse the implementation process (Baker, 1972; Mills, 1971). Under this top-down approach, we write the highest-level programs and test them while the next lowest level is being written. Dummy subroutine and procedure calls are used for lower-level modules that have not been written yet. Top-down programming makes the status of work clear and shows the functions that must be performed by lower-level routines. The interface between modules can be defined before the functions are actually coded. We can avoid the redesign of lower-level modules that would have been required because of some oversight discovered when lower-level modules were combined for use by a higher-level routine.

Reviews

Design reviews in which processing is described in detail should be scheduled for different parts of the system. For example, the logic of an input error check could be presented by the programmer in charge of the module to an audience of other programming team members and perhaps a user representative from the design team. The audience notes errors and inconsistencies and makes suggestions for improvements in the module. Someone in the meeting records these comments for the person making the presentation. The purpose of these reviews is constructive; we are trying to find what has been omitted or what errors in logic are included in the design. The review is not held for employee evaluation; the goal is to improve the product, not to criticize the speaker. Clearly, this approach requires an open and nondefensive attitude that is consistent with the environment required for "egoless" programming.

TESTING

Users have an important role to play in testing. While programmers design a certain amount of test data, users should help develop test data for system verification. Users should not provide only average transactions, but should also generate test data with errors and data that encompass as many different conditions as possible. For example, one should try to violate rules for input by putting wrong characters in columns, such as alphabetic data where numeric data belong. These test practices ensure that programs have adequate error checking and editing features.

Next, the user should try to make illegal changes in files, for example, by updating an invalid field and using incorrect transaction codes. These errors will occur in actual operations of the system, and we should be sure that the system has been programmed to detect them so they will not damage files and lead to incorrect output.

Testing also includes checking the basic logic of each program and verifying that the entire system works properly. We cannot be exhaustive in program testing because there is an overwhelming number of paths in a program. Testing individual programs involves an attempt to be sure that the most likely paths work properly. Programmers facilitate testing by coding as clearly as possible; however, we should remember the saying that no program is fully debugged. Systems should be planned so that errors are easy to find and correct. As users, we must expect to encounter occasional errors, even after installation of the system; the purpose of testing is to reduce their frequency and severity.

Unit Testing

After the systems design, programmers write and test basic program modules. At this stage programmers usually construct their own test data or use a program that generates these data. One problem is common to all testing: if programmers make up their own test data, only the conditions thought of in advance by the programmer will be tested. Unit testing with programmer data is necessary, of course, but it is not sufficient. Although it is important to know if the logic included in the program works properly, we are also concerned about conditions that the programmer did not include in the program. Egoless programming and team approaches help here, as they provide for input from other programmers who might think of missing logic. Structured review sessions also point out omissions. However, it is still best to have an independent source of test data for users to augment each programmer's tests, and one activity for the backup programmer is to generate data for testing individual programs.

Combined Module Testing

Modules are combined for testing after they pass individual unit tests. Top-down programming helps here, since errors frequently occur in calling sequences. Programming lower-level modules first creates major changes when we program higher-level routines and recognize an omission in a lower-level module. By carefully specifying the interface for high-level modules, programming them first, and by keeping a systems library up to date, many interface problems are avoided.

At this point in combined module testing, we also stress independent test data generation. It is important for users to be included in developing test data because the data will be less contrived and more realistic. In one instance, management offered a prize to the user who designed the best error-detection scheme and the best processing module for the user's department's processing. The idea was to create input data that would cause another department's processing logic to fail (Lucas 1974c). This "game" resulted in the development of realistic test data to run against the program logic developed in each user area.

Testing Manual Procedures

The testing described above is concerned with programs. Another major activity occurring simultaneously with the development of programs is the design and testing of manual procedures. Manual procedures are sometimes overlooked, but they can determine the success of a system.

In one case, an airline developed an automatic seat-assignment option as part of its on-line computer reservations system. This on-line CRT-based system replaced the old approach of using cardboard cutouts of the seats torn from an outline of the plane's body. The new system was implemented at a peak holiday travel season. At one San Francisco gate, a spotlight was directed on the CRT screen at the check-in counter—a lighting effect that made it difficult to read the CRT. In addition, the device was positioned so that the agent operating the console could not stand straight; he had to bend over slightly. Long lines formed while a nontypist agent tried to assign seats and enter passenger names on the terminal. The old way of tearing off the seat stub from the cutout and handing it to the passenger was several times faster.

What happened in this example? The airline spent millions of dollars on a computer system and obviously spent no time on testing manual procedures. The design team could have employed a very simple queuing model, or even written a small simulation to test manual operations. In fact, the airline might even have programmed a simple version of the system on a time-sharing computer and actually had airline employees or real passengers simulate the boarding process.

Where there are major changes in existing manual procedures, pilot testing is essential, especially with a terminal with a system that interfaces directly with customers. It is relatively easy to simulate parts of a system by developing a few input forms and having users work with these forms. However, it is important to design pilot tests so they are real experiments. One company conducted a pilot test, but had the entire computer department present in the small user department to answer questions and help with the test. Because of the attention and extra help, the experiment succeeded; it could not really have failed.

COMPUTERS AND HEALTH CARE

Health care institutions have long used computers for standard business functions, such as billing and accounting. Computers can also make a direct contribution to patient care by improving the efficiency of clinical facilities and relieving the physician of certain routine, data processing tasks. A system at the Regenstrief Institute for Health Care and the Indiana University Department of Medicine helps reduce physician errors by providing summaries of patient medical records. The system also suggests appropriate action based on that information.

The system contains treatment and diagnosis data from hospital stays, medicine and clinic encounters, and any visits to the emergency room. Currently there are about 32,000 outpatient medical records in the system from three clinics in the health center which experience some 40,000 patient visits per year. The system processes the information in the data base according to rules specified by a physician. For example, a physician can ask the machine to verify that a child's immunizations are up-to-date, or to remind the doctor when they are not. The physician asks the computer to perform many of his or her simple information processing tasks.

This particular system does not require a physician to use terminals. The doctors interact with the computer through three paper reports which are produced for each patient at each visit. A patient summary report contains all numerical test results as well as a coded output of narrative diagnostic reports. A patient encounter form serves as a primary record for each patient's visit. It contains the patient's current problem list, observations and tests suggested by rules entered by the physician. The physicians write on this form and one copy of it is entered into the computer system to update medical records.

A surveillance report produces messages generated by the rules physicians define. Such messages call attention to clinical conditions that might require further treatment or investigation. The messages also provide information from recent medical publications, and some cases even suggest very simple diagnoses.

An administrative part of the system processes demographic, administrative and appointment data for the patients whose records are in the system. The computers contain a file of 7,000 active appointments for the 150 physicians who use the clinic. Appointments are entered into the computer from terminals in a reception area.

Another application on the system processes 80% of the clinical laboratory workload. This application accepts laboratory requests and provides working documents for laboratory production; it helps generate lab reports for physicians and offers administrative research and billing information. A similar application helps support operation in the pharmacy.

Systems such as these have the potential for drastically improving the quality of health care while at the same time reducing costs.

Mini-micro Systems, October 1979.

However, when the system was introduced in the whole manufacturing plant, it was a total disaster. The experiment was not a fair test because it was not representative of what would happen during actual operations.

Users are an essential component of manual procedures testing since they are the individuals who will execute these manual procedures. Can we simulate the procedures to be sure they work properly? The process of testing procedures results in users who are well trained before conversion, since they will try the procedures before they actually have to be used.

Acceptance Tests

Some formal procedure is generally employed to certify that a system is ready for installation; users must view the test results and "accept" the system. When feasible, a parallel test may be conducted in which the new system is run along with the old. The results of the two systems are compared to assess the validity of the new system. Parallel testing requires much extra work for users, since two systems are operated simultaneously. In the case of some systems—for example, those that are on-line—parallel operations may not be possible logically. Other approaches to acceptance testing include the development of special data by users who then validate the output of the system; such test data must be carefully developed and as comprehensive as possible. Regardless of the approach used, some type of acceptance test is necessary before the conversion and installation of a new system.

TRAINING

Heavy user participation in design pays dividends during training. All individuals who will be affected by a new system should receive some training. The design team develops training materials such as sample forms to be completed by users or samples of screens that will appear on a CRT. For terminal-based systems, users should have the opportunity to operate a special training version or simulated version of the new system in order to gain familiarity with it.

Several on-line systems, including the one discussed in Chapter 17, have successfully employed computer-aided instruction (CAI) to train terminal operators. CAI is a programmed learning approach in which the computer is a tutor that drills the student while recording student progress. For large systems with many operators distributed widely from a geographic standpoint, CAI may be the only economical way to provide training. The CAI programs maintain a record of progress and can be designed to let operators exercise only those functions for which they have received training.

In planning for training, all people potentially affected by the system should be considered. One approach is to predict the reaction of each individual, for example, in the form of a balance sheet (Mumford and Ward, 1968). What are the costs and benefits of the change for each affected individual? A change plan can then be customized to each individual; in some instances the design team may change the system to minimize the costs to certain users.

CONVERSION AND INSTALLATION

Conversion is the process of preparing for the first live operation of the new system; what activities are required for the system to begin running? Usually

MANAGEMENT PROBLEM 14-2

The new manager of information services for a major West Coast bank is trying to improve relations with users. The bank has a history of conflict between the computer department and user departments. One approach the manager has adopted is to increase user participation in systems design. However, his own observations have confirmed those of the computer staff: users are woefully ignorant of computer systems. Furthermore, they really do not want to learn about them because of the stormy computer history of the bank.

The president of the bank has given her commitment to the project and has offered whatever resources are needed. The manager of the information services department is trying to solve the following problems:

1 How does he gain the support of department heads to encourage users to participate in training and systems design?

2 What are the most essential topics for user training?

3 What kind of courses should be offered? Who should teach them and when?

4 Who should attend the training sessions—should only those users who will be working on a system next be invited, or should there be general invitations?

5 Is similiar training needed for the information services department staff?

6 How can he evaluate the results of the training program?

Can you help answer these questions and design an action plan for the manager?

---

new files are created from either manual or existing machine-readable records. Existing procedures have to be terminated and the new ones phased into operation. The conversion date is a target that should be well publicized in order to encourage readiness.

The major consideration in planning for conversion and installation is to proceed gradually; never convert and install a system at the peak season for the organization. It may be possible to phase in a system by department, geographic region, or on some other basis. A great deal is learned from the first unit implemented, which can be used to prepare for the next portion of the cutover. Full-scale cutover of an entire system at one point in time runs a high risk of disaster. If the system has to be installed at once because of some special requirements, then extra effort should be taken in training and users should have a chance to work on a simulated version of the system.

DOCUMENTATION

Documentation is a term used to describe all the instructions programs, and narratives, that is, almost anything written about the information system. Documentation serves a number of purposes. First, during systems design, it is the evolving product developed by the design team. After implementation, it is the basis for making changes to the system. The quality of documentation determines in part how much flexibility the information services department has in responding to user requests. Good documentation serves to reduce conflict between users and the information services department, since a well-documented system is easier for users to understand. Good documentation means that an adequate reference is available when problems arise, and this helps us learn how to solve problems with the system.

If a user is in charge of the design team, it is that user's responsibility to see that good documentation is developed as part of the design effort. Unfortunately, the information services department staff generally does not like to document systems; this activity is viewed as a tedious job and something that does not contribute to progress on the system. Like programming management, documentation is an activity to which time must be devoted if the system is to succeed. It is interesting to note that the new technology for programming management discussed earlier in the chapter requires far more documentation than older, more haphazard approaches. The user leader of the design team must be aware of the types of documentation needed and work to influence the information services department to prepare it. Users on the design team can help by preparing the training and user-reference documentation for a system.

Design Documentation

During design, the purpose of documentation is to aid in control by providing a record of what has been developed and of what has been changed. It is important to be sure that all parts of a system are considered and that those responsible for the components affected by the change are notified. What program modules and what programmers are involved if a file format or the contents of a file are altered?

Control is also the ability to retrieve past test runs and old versions of programs or files. Design documentation builds an excellent data base for making future estimates of how long it will take to develop similar systems. The systems librarian should maintain a copy of all runs and progress reports so that a complete description of project activities can be found easily.

Training Documentation

Training documentation prepares us for conversion, installation, and the eventual use of the system. Most of the information needed for training can be developed from the systems documentation discussed above. User-training documentation is used to bridge the gap between old existing procedures and those required for the new system. This documentation should be developed by user members of the design team in conjunction with other users in the organization.

We have found it best to begin training by looking at the output of a system. Output documentation should focus on key decisions and reports. Having discussed output, we can cover the input and files necessary to produce the desired output. Finally, the computer processing logic and other procedures involved are discussed. It is important to include error conditions and the remedial actions taken in training documentation.

User training should also include considerations of transitional effects, especially testing and conversion. These problems can be presented to the user group for help in developing a solution. In fact, it is best at first not to have a completely detailed plan formulated. After plans have been jointly developed for these stages, they can be documented as conversion procedures.

Operations Documentation

The operations section of the information services department has to operate a system after it has been converted. The operations group needs information on normal operating procedures and how to respond to errors. This information is best prepared by the systems analysts and programmers, and much of it can be derived from design documentation.

User Reference Documentation

The last type of documentation that should be developed is for user reference after the system has become operational. This information should be referred to first when we have a question or a problem. If this documentation is of sufficient quality, users can answer their own questions without having to contact the information services department, and thus the potential for conflict is reduced. There is a tremendous amount of frustration when something goes wrong with an information system and we do not understand why, or know how to fix it.

Fortunately, most of this material can be taken directly from other documentation, for example, the procedures parts of the training documents. This documentation should be assembled into a reference manual such as a loose-leaf binder that can be updated easily as the system evolves over time. A detailed table of contents is necessary to make this documentation easy to use as a reference. We should make available a complete discussion of the input, output, and processing logic. One of the most important components in this documentation is a list of error conditions and "fixes" (how to correct the error). It is helpful to include the names of the most knowledgeable user and the maintenance programmer who is now in charge of the system.

POSTCONVERSION ACTIVITIES

At some point near the cutover, it is necessary to "freeze" a system temporarily as far as changes are concerned. During this critical period, all resources have to be devoted to conversion. However, the freeze in changes should be considered clearly temporary in nature; we hold changes that are suggested in abeyance until conversion is completed.

If systems are to serve us, we shall make continuing requests for changes. In fact, a responsive information services department looks for changes and suggests them to users. The fact that users are heavily involved with the design should reduce the number of modifications necessary. However, we shall make important requests for alterations as we gain experience with the system. Another reason for structured programming and good documentation is to facilitate these changes. A system is literally never finished, but as it matures changes should become less frequent.

After the system appears to be working smoothly, it is time to examine what was accomplished and the resources required in a postimplementation audit. Now is the time for the design team to assess reactions to the system. What could be done better next time? Were the tangible savings that were forecast achieved? How do we evaluate the intangible benefits?

We should also look at the original estimates and determine if they were achieved. The accuracy of forecasts and the experience with this system provide the data from which to make estimates in the future. These data reflect what can be done by this design team in this organization. Past experience is the best source of information available for estimating the requirements for the next system for this team and organization.

KEY WORDS

Backup programmer	Impact of system	Review session
Changes	Independent test data	Structured programming
Chief programmer team	Modularization	System library
Combined module testing	Operations documentation	Top-down programming
Conversion and	Parallel testing	Training documentation
installation	Participation	Unit testing
Documentation	Postimplementation audit	User-reference
Egoless programming	Programming goals	documentation

RECOMMENDED READINGS

Baker, F. T.: "Chief Programmer Team Management of Production Programming," *IBM Systems Journal,* vol. 11, no. 1, 1972, pp. 66–73. (An article describing the uses of a chief programmer team and many of the techniques discussed in this chapter to develop a retrieval system for the *New York Times.*)

Mumford, E., and T. Ward: *Computers, Planning for People,* B. T. Batsford, London, 1968. (This excellent book presents suggestions for planning for the impact of a system on individuals.)

Nie, N., C. Hull, J. Jenkins, K. Steinbrenner, and D. H. Bent: *Statistical Package for the Social Sciences,* 2d ed., McGraw-Hill, New York, 1975. (This package program for statistical analysis is one of the best-documented systems in existence. It is a standard by which other documentation can be judged.)

Weinberg, G. M.: *The Psychology of Computer Programming,* Van Nostrand, New York, 1972. (A revolutionary book suggesting the concept of egoless programming.)

————: "The Psychology of Improved Programmer Performance," *Datamation,* vol. 18, no. 11, November 1972, pp. 82–85. (An experiment is described in which different programming teams are given different goals in writing a program.)

DISCUSSION QUESTIONS

1   What are the reasons for user participation in testing a system and planning conversion and installation?
2   What issues should be examined in a postimplementation audit?
3   Who should conduct the postimplementation audit and what should be done with the results?

4 Who should accept a system; that is, who is responsible for indicating that a system is working properly and can be considered fully converted?

5 Describe different approaches to the gradual implementation of:
  a A batch computer system
  b An on-line system

6 What are the problems and disadvantages of parallel testing?

7 After conversion, are the responsibilities of the design team ended? If not, what other tasks should the team attempt to accomplish?

8 Why is it unwise for programmers to design all their own test data?

9 Do conversion programs need to be documented carefully? Why or why not?

10 What action should a design team take if it expects sabotage or user resistance for some aspects of a new system? Of what is such resistance a sign?

11 Why is it unwise to make a major change in the organization (such as departmental restructuring) concomitantly with the conversion of a new information system?

12 How does good documentation serve to reduce user conflict with the information services department and staff?

13 Why is documentation generally the weakest part of a system's design?

14 How does the presence of a systems librarian aid documentation?

15 What can be done to facilitate and encourage documentation besides employing a systems librarian? Are there any mechanical tools that will encourage documentation?

16 What is the role of documentation after a system has been converted successfully?

17 What role does documentation play in subsequent changes to a program or system?

18 How should program changes be controlled? Is it necessary to have more than one person agree on the change? Why or why not?

19 Why should test results be kept as part of the documentation of an information system?

20 Why do users need to have documentation on the data files in the system?

21 How can the computer operator use documentation to determine if an error has occurred because of a programming problem, a data problem, or a malfunction of the computer itself?

22 How can the design team leader influence documentation standards of the information services department? Why should agreement on documentation formats and contents be reached?

23 Why should users design the training program? How can users on the design team gather data on potential change resisters and evaluate different personal and situational factors that are likely to affect implementation?

24 How does the development of the chief programmer position change the career path for computer professionals? What benefits does this have for users?

25 Is programming such a craftlike trade that it defies management?

MANAGEMENT TASKS
    Uncertainties
    User Responsibilities
PROJECT SCHEDULING
    Estimates
AUTOMATED DESIGN APPROACHES
KEY WORDS
RECOMMENDED READINGS
DISCUSSION QUESTIONS

Chapter 15

Project Management

CHAPTER ISSUES

- What is the role of general management and users in managing information systems development projects?
- What techniques are available to aid in project management?

We have already seen that a computer project should be managed jointly by users, managers, and the information services department during its early stages. The information services department directs the preliminary survey and feasibility study. Analysts guide users, who control most of the design activities. The final schedule is agreed on jointly; the exact amount of time required depends on the nature of the system and the availability of analysts and user representatives on the design team. What tasks are required for managing the project? What are the roles of the user and manager in these tasks? In this chapter we explore the answers to these questions.

MANAGEMENT TASKS

Unfortunately, there has been a notable lack of success in managing systems design projects. A number of problems have been reported: schedules are not met on time, systems do not meet original specifications, and there are often high cost overruns. Programming was regarded at first as a craftlike trade that did not need managing; today, the need to manage the entire development process of a system is recognized.

Uncertainties

One of the major problems in systems analysis and design is the high level of uncertainty associated with these activities. Users are often unaware of the problems creating the need for an information system, yet they must work with the design team to develop the data for designing the system. The activities of the design team also create uncertainty for users who are asked to describe their information needs. Can users adequately explain their decision and information processing requirements?

Lack of certainty is also reflected in the development of the system itself. Is the model developed by the design team close to reality; that is, do the specifications adequately represent the needed information processing procedures? Once given the system design, programmers have to interpret the specifications and write programs. It is difficult to forecast what is involved in writing, testing, and debugging a program. There is usually uncertainty about the time required, whether or not the program will work, and whether or not it will meet specifications.

If the program and system meet specifications, then user acceptance tests are undertaken to see if the design, as represented by systems specifications, fits user needs. The task of project management is to attempt to reduce all these uncertainties, coordinate the activities of the diverse parties working on the project, and ensure that the project is completed within time and cost estimates.

User Responsibilities

As mentioned above, users in the systems design staff can to some extent control progress through the development of specifications. Under the approach of user-controlled design, who should manage the remaining tasks? Can the user be expected to manage technical activities such as programming? Clearly the answer to this question is "no." We do not expect or advocate that users be placed in this role.

Although users do not necessarily have detailed technical knowledge, they can still monitor a project with assistance from technical staff members from the information services department. First, users can ensure that modern tools and techniques are being used by the programming staff by influencing management in the organization and the information services department. They should see that project control techniques are used and should be kept advised of critical milestones and progress. When it is clear that there are problems in maintaining the schedule, the manager should work with information services department management to see that resources are reallocated and/or new resources are added.

In the rest of this chapter, we discuss a scheduling technique for project management. Users do not have to be expert in these areas, but they should be aware that technical and management aids exist and should urge the information services department staff to employ them. Because programming is the area where most difficulties have been encountered, the suggested scheduling techniques will be applied to this stage in the life cycle. Of course, any project management technique for scheduling and monitoring progress can be applied at other stages in development as well.

PROJECT SCHEDULING

To establish control over a project, it is necessary to have a schedule, milestones, data on progress, and some structure for analysis purposes. Consider the programming stage as an example; a schedule should first be estimated during the feasibility study. As systems design progresses, the schedule becomes more

---

MANAGEMENT PROBLEM 15-1

Jane Braun works for the information services department at National Insurance Company. This large insurance firm specializes in life and casualty insurance and has been very successful since its founding in the early 1900s. The company has a number of modern computers, although most existing applications deal with transactions processing as opposed to decision-making applications.

Jane is excited about the new system she has helped to design for National. The application is for the investment department and appears to have a significant potential for supporting some of the important decisions made by this group. Having worked on the design, Jane was chosen to manage the programming phases of the project.

Five programmers are working on the new system, four of whom seem to cooperate very well. The fifth programmer, Stan Elton, has been with National for 10 years and is considered to be an experienced programmer. Stan's past work has generally been on systems where he was the sole programmer or where he worked with one junior partner. This is his first real assignment with a larger group of programmers, and it is the first time he has not been left on his own devices for managing his own programming efforts. Computer management at National, realizing the importance of the new system, did not want to have problems with it. Therefore, they asked Jane to manage the programming part of the project.

Jane was having a great deal of trouble communicating with Stan. For every suggestion she made, Stan responded with some reason why it was not possible. Stan also refused to give estimates for when his programs would be complete. The other programmers indicated that it was difficult to coordinate with him since he preferred to work alone. What should Jane do to solve this problem with Stan?

---

concrete as the magnitude of each task becomes clearer. During the feasibility study, the developers do not know how many programs are needed or how complex they are. However, by the time program specifications are completed, these requirements will be known with greater certainty.

The selection of milestones for managing programming and testing has been a difficult process. Some possibilities are:

Program modules defined
Program module flowcharted
Program module coded
Program module compiled
Testing with programmer data
Tests with independently generated data
Tests with other modules
Tests with "live" data

One guideline is to define tasks that are estimated to take 20 to 50 hours to complete. A shorter task makes the number of tasks too large, and longer ones do not provide sufficient warning that a project is behind schedule.

We have not had great success in estimating completion times for the steps above nor in achieving them. Studies of programmer performance have shown high variances among individuals, which complicates forecasting. It is hoped that

---

A COMPUTER-BASED MARKET

Some 24,000 cotton producers in Texas and Oklahoma meet electronically to transact cotton sales at the best competitive price. The system they are using is called Telecot and was developed by the Plains Cotton Cooperative Association. It is viewed as a model by the U.S. Department of Agriculture and is being studied for applicability in other markets, such as feeder cattle, cows, eggs and hogs. The system links 160 cotton gins through the computer and another 50 are in touch with the center via telephones. About 45 buyers' offices are also connected to the central system through CRTs.

Telecot helps to improve the interaction between cotton producers by putting them directly in touch with the marketing system for Southwest cotton. The network includes all major handlers of Southwestern cotton, as well as a percentage of the smaller firms in central and remote markets.

A video display unit and printer are located in each buyer's office. The buyer can display all data on all lots offered for sale as well as results of trades. The buyer uses the terminal to enter bids and the printer produces a hard copy of any data desired. The computer awards the cotton to the highest bidder at the end of a 15 minute period, providing that the best bid exceeds the minimum price acceptable to the seller. In one of its early years Telecot handled a million bales of cotton and processed more than 500,000 inquiries. Computers offer the power to establish such market systems and to make information available where it is needed for decision making.

Data Processor, June/July 1979.

programmer teams will help to reduce some of the individual variances and make estimates more accurate.

Having defined milestones, we are faced with the problem of knowing that a milestone has been achieved; the 90-percent complete program that remains that way for a year is legend! The milestones suggested above are designed to be concrete. Also, the milestones do not reflect quality; it may be easy to write a poor program module on schedule. It is important to be sure that the milestone can be observed and evaluated. For example, a program module is defined as complete when it has passed a quality test established independently of the programmer writing the module. The manager of the project must be able to verify independently of the person reporting that the milestone has actually been achieved.

In the final analysis, we are dependent on the technical staff's cooperation in managing programming. If accurate reporting is rewarded rather than punished, then programmers should cooperate. The first step is to include programmers in management and let them see the need to keep track of a project. When milestones are not met, additional resources should be furnished in the form of assistance, a shift in workload, more teams, and so forth. In this fashion, honest reporting will be encouraged. Finally, we need a formal mechanism for analyzing the data of progress and determining where there is slack available, that is, where added resources can be obtained and where resources are in critically short supply. One useful project management technique is the "critical path" method.

The critical path method, or CPM, was developed from a military system called PERT, for Project Evaluation and Review Technique. PERT uses probability distributions to compute the most likely completion time for the major events in a project. CPM is conceptually simpler than PERT and is better suited to the development of computer systems. The critical path method breaks a project down into a series of subtasks and arranges the activities according to precedence relationships. We indicate that one task must precede another task, as a survey precedes a feasibility study. The length of time required for each task is estimated, and the various tasks are arranged in a network reflecting precedence relationships. The critical path, that is, the path through the network requiring the greatest amount of time, is identified. As tasks are completed and estimates for completion times for remaining tasks are changed, the critical path also changes. Project management can add extra resources to critical activities on the path.

The major reason CPM has not been widely used in managing programming projects is that it requires time to measure and report on progress. The approach to obtaining progress reports described above should help ameliorate some of the data collection problems. Users who are familiar with management can appreciate the need to devote resources to the management of the programming task itself. Users may have to see that time is taken to obtain estimates and update the CPM chart. Fortunately, a number of time-sharing programs are available that perform all the calculations and print the charts so that mechanical

MANAGEMENT PROBLEM 15-2

The president of American Moving and Storage has just dismissed the company's manager of information systems. The president commented, "I have finally had enough with these computer types. We have spent millions of dollars on the design of new systems, and we never seem to implement one. The trucking system was the final straw. It is over a year late and has cost us 50 percent more than the original estimates."

The president turned to his administrative vice president and said, "It's your responsibility now. From this point on, the computer department reports to you. I want things straightened out; you have 3 months."

The vice president of administrative services has no computer experience. He has been a user of some of the systems developed by the computer department and shares the president's concern over their lack of success in meeting deadlines and budgets. However, the vice president wondered what to do now. Should he try to run the department himself or hire a new manager for it?

If he takes responsibility, will the lack of any computer background hinder his ability to understand the problems of the department? What actually is responsible for all of the computer difficulties at American? If he hires a new manager for the computer department, what characteristics and skills should this new employee possess?

---

computations for CPM are automatic. In fact at least one CPM-based system exists specifically for computer applications project control. The system is based on the idea that tasks are assigned to individuals who must report on progress. Original estimates are updated periodically by the programming staff and the system generates a number of useful reports for the project manager. Such tools and the information they provide are extremely important in project management.

Estimates

For all stages of project management, we need estimates of the time required for various tasks. Historically, these estimates have been difficult to develop and have been inaccurate because of the uncertainty involved. For example, because of the way in which programming has been viewed, the time required for a program to be written is highly dependent on the talent of a single programmer. There are various rules of thumb for estimating analyst and programmer time, such as the number of lines of debugged code expected per programmer per month. However, these old ideas are not too helpful if we plan to follow the new approaches suggested in the last chapter. In fact, it is not clear that such generalizations across all organizations and projects will always be possible.

Instead of these rules, we need to develop data within each organization. The systems librarian already maintains some of the data needed to develop estimates and should also keep track of original estimates and the actual results. These results are used not to embarrass programmers but to adjust future estimates to make them more accurate. Gradually, we can build a set of data to determine if estimates are unique to the staff, the design team, the project, or the organization. We do not have enough information at the present time to develop valid guidelines for the number of lines of debugged code per programmer or to know if such guidelines will ever be meaningful.

AUTOMATED DESIGN APPROACHES

Many of the technical activities we have described in systems design are highly repetitive among systems—for example, the conversion of specifications into programs. The most creative part of the systems design task is the definition of requirements and specifications. This is, at present, a highly unstructured and unprogrammed task. However, a number of researchers have tried to develop tools to assist in the technical part of systems development.

We have discussed some simple techniques, such as the use of flowcharts and decision tables. However, many single-purpose design aids also assist in program development, such as test data generators and programs to convert shorthand notation to COBOL programs. Project management should evaluate these tools carefully to be sure they contribute to improved productivity and do not make the systems development effort dependent on some unique or nonstandard approach. Some of these products have the potential to improve the technical aspects of systems design, and they should be used where they make a positive contribution.

In addition to the products described above, there have been several efforts to automate a large portion of the technical part of systems development (Couger, 1973). Approaches to automation of the systems design project differ widely. One commercially available product requires the systems analyst to complete structured forms containing system specifications, including a definition of file records and data elements. These specifications are input to a proprietary program that produces as output a COBOL program to do the processing described in the input specifications. Another automation approach is based on a special high-level design language used by the systems analyst. A translator accepts this language as input and produces computer programs for the problem described by the input. This very high level language allows the analyst to concentrate on information processing problems rather than on specifications for a computer system. (See also the discussion of software trends in Chapter 10.)

These automated techniques offer exciting possibilities for systems design, particularly since we are currently limited by the availability of personnel in developing systems. Systems design is a labor-intensive task, and these approaches, far from replacing the computer professional, allow more time for the development of information systems of high quality. Any resources freed from technical tasks can be applied to creating new systems and improving the productivity of those who work on information systems design projects.

KEY WORDS

Automated design	Librarian	Subtasks
Completion time	Milestones	Tasks
CPM	Network	Uncertainty
Design aids	Precedence relation	Variance
Documentation	Productivity	
Estimates	Schedule	

RECOMMENDED READINGS

Improved Technology for Application Development: Management Overview, IBM Corp., 1973. (A summary of various techniques for improving productivity in the development of applications.)

Lucas, H. C., Jr.: *The Design, Analysis, and Implementation of Information Systems,* 2d ed., McGraw-Hill, New York, 1981. (See especially the chapter on project management.)

Olsen, R. A.: *Manufacturing Management: A Quantitative Approach,* International Textbook, Scranton, Pa., 1968. (See the chapter on project management and CPM techniques.)

DISCUSSION QUESTIONS

1 What motivated the development of network project management techniques such as CPM?

2 Why should users review schedules during project execution?

3 Why do we suggest that most organizations are interested in the program goals of prompt completion and clear and readable code?

4 What is the precedence relationship among the major tasks in systems analysis and design?

5 Compare and contrast information systems development projects with a project to design a new airplane.

6 In the systems life cycle, what are the points where the most serious delays are likely to occur? How do these points relate to uncertainty?

7 Where are the major risks in the development of a manual information system? How can these risks be reduced?

8 From a management standpoint, what are the disadvantages of using assembly language for information system projects?

9 What advantages are there to using package programs from the standpoint of project management? What are their major disadvantages?

10 Why do programmers resist making changes in a working program after an information system has been installed? How do the techniques suggested in this chapter affect this resistance?

11 What reporting from a programming team is necessary for project management? How can this output be obtained without disrupting progress on the programs?

12 Why do so many information services departments avoid formal project-scheduling techniques?

13 Does user management have to understand programming to be able to monitor the programming part of a project? What knowledge is required?

14 What impact will automated design techniques have on users and on the information services department?

15 Are there any types of systems for which the user should not have any role during programming? What types? What are some of the management problems expected for these systems?

16 Occasionally, organizations have used managers with nontechnical backgrounds as chief executives for the information services department. What problems does such an executive encounter? Compare these problems with those of a user who is in control of a systems design project.

17 The previous chapter discusses the design team and special management tools. How does this special task force and project organization contrast with normal managerial activities? What problems are created for the user managing such a project?

18 How does the design team facilitate making future estimates of completion times for programming projects?

PROBLEM AREAS
IMPLEMENTATION
    Definition
    Success or Failure
RESEARCH ON IMPLEMENTATION
AN IMPLEMENTATION STRATEGY
CREATIVE SYSTEMS DESIGN
    A New Design Method
    Advantages
    Disadvantages
    Some Experiences
IN CONCLUSION
KEY WORDS
RECOMMENDED READINGS
DISCUSSION QUESTIONS

Chapter 16

Successful Implementation

CHAPTER ISSUES

- How does the organization plan systems implementation?
- How should an organization approach the relationship between the designer and user of a system?
- What is the proper manager/user role in systems analysis and design?

Managers frequently complain about the low return they receive on their organization's large investment in computer-based information systems. Many of these systems are not used to their potential or are not used at all.

• In one manufacturing company, the manager of the information services department had not distributed computer output reports for two months because he was not completely satisfied with them. Interviews with users indicated that the reports had not really been missed!

- A mining company spent several years designing a complex inventory system at its largest division. The system was finally installed and showed definite cost savings. Several years later, some managers in the company were still successfully resisting the installation of the new system in their divisions.
- A major university developed a sophisticated on-line computer system to automate a number of administrative functions. On a survey, most users expressed the desire to return to a manual system or the old batch-computer reports, because of problems with the newer system.
- Two computer systems at a major bank were supposed to calculate the internal transfer price for borrowing and lending among branches. Each system produced a different number on its reports. Bank managers tended to doubt both figures and were afraid to rely on any of the data in the two reports because of this inconsistency.

Managers and other users of systems want to be certain that the systems work when installed. In this chapter, we explore some of the problems associated with implementation, which is basically a behavioral process. Our goal is to develop an implementation strategy that minimizes the problems of developing and operating successful information systems.

PROBLEM AREAS

The problems described above have several sources:

1 The original design of the system
2 The interface of a system with the user
3 The process of design and implementation
4 The operation of systems

The original design of the system may have been faulty; for example, some systems do not provide the information needed by the decision maker. As we have seen, different information is required for different tasks. Other systems do not work technically; for example, there may be so many errors that no one trusts the output from the system.

The interface of the system with the user refers to the way in which we come in contact with the system, for example, through printed input forms, terminals and their associated input language, or batch reports. In one system, terminal input was so complicated that no one submitted data and the system had to be discontinued.

Implementation refers to the entire change effort associated with a new system. We design a system to improve information processing, and improvement implies that we must change existing information processing procedures. The operation of a system involves longer-term issues after a system has been designed and installed. If the operations section of the information services department does not provide good service (for example, meeting schedules for batch systems and having on-line systems available as needed), systems will not achieve their potential.

IMPLEMENTATION

Definition

What is implementation? In the discussion above, we stated that implementation is part of the process of designing a system and that it is also a component of organizational change. We develop a new information system to change existing information processing procedures. Implementation as we use the term should not be confused with a step in systems design. This definition, frequently used by computer professionals, is too narrow. Their definition generally refers to the last steps of systems design, which we shall refer to as conversion and installation of a new system.

Our definition stresses the long-term nature of implementation; it is a part of a process that begins with the very first idea for a system and the changes it will bring. Implementation terminates when the system has been successfully integrated with the operations of the organization. We expect most of implementation to be concerned with behavioral phenomena, since people are expected to change their information processing activities.

Success or Failure

How do we know that we have successfully implemented a system? Researchers have not really agreed on an indicator for successful implementation. One appealing approach is a cost-benefit study. In this evaluation, one totals the costs of developing a system and compares them with the dollar benefits resulting from the system.

In theory, this sounds like a good indicator of success, but in practice it is difficult to provide meaningful estimates. Obtaining the cost side of the ratio is not too much of a problem if adequate records are kept during the development stages of the system. However, an evaluation of the benefits of a computer-based information system has eluded most analysts. How do we value the benefits of improved information processing? With transactions processing and some operational control systems, we can usually show tangible savings. For example, many transactions systems have resulted in increased productivity in processing paperwork without a proportional increase in cost. Operational control systems, such as those used to control inventories, may reduce inventory balances, saving storage and investment costs while maintaining existing service levels. For systems that aid a decision maker or provide customer service, it is much more difficult to estimate the benefits and there are few examples of any such attempts.

In lieu of the more preferable cost-benefit analysis, we can adopt one of two indicators of successful implementation, depending on the type of system involved. For many information systems, use of the system is voluntary. A manager or other user receives a report but does not have to use the information on it or even read the report. Examples of such reports are summary data on sales for sales management, and a forecast for the marketing manager. Systems that provide on-line retrieval of information from a data bank can also often be classified as voluntary; the use of such a system is frequently at the discretion of the user. For this type of system where use is voluntary, we shall adopt high levels of use as a sign of successful implementation. We can measure use by interviews with users, through questionnaires, or in some instances by building a monitor into the system to actual use.

For systems whose use is mandatory, such as an on-line production control system, we shall employ the user's evaluation of the system as a measure of success. For example, one can examine user satisfaction, although it will probably be necessary to measure several facets of satisfaction such as the quality of service, the timeliness and accuracy of information, and the quality of the schedule for operations. An evaluation might also include a panel of information processing experts to review the design and operation of the system. We should also note that managers might well consider a system to be successful if it accomplishes its objectives. However, to accomplish its objectives, a system must be used. We would also hope that one objective of a system would be extensive use and a high degree of user satisfaction with the system.

RESEARCH ON IMPLEMENTATION

In recent years, the amount of research on implementation has increased dramatically. Since the implementation of computer-based information systems is similar to the implementation of operations research or management science models, we can also learn from studies of model implementation. For summaries of some of this research, see Lucas (1976a, 1981) and Schultz and Slevin (1975).

Most research on implementation has been an attempt to discover factors associated with success; that is, what independent variables are related to successful implementation as defined by the researchers? If there is any basis for believing a causal connection exists between independent and dependent variables, we can then develop an implementation strategy around the independent variables. For example, suppose we found in several studies using different research methodologies that top management's requesting a new system and following through with participation in its design is associated with successful implementation. If there were sufficient evidence to support this finding, we might develop an implementation strategy that emphasized top-management action.

While individual studies of implementation have addressed a number of independent variables, there is no real consensus in the field on an explanation of successful implementation or on a single implementation strategy. Table 16-1 contains a list of some of the variables in past implementation studies. The

Table 16-1   Variables Associated with Implementation Studies

Independent variables

Information services department
  Policies
  System design practices
  Operations policies

Involvement
  User origination of systems
  Involvement and influence
  Appreciation

Situational and personal factors
  Personality type
  Business history
  Social history
  Structural factors
  Past experience

User attitudes
  Expectations
  Interpersonal relations

Technical quality of systems
  Quality
  Model characteristics

Decision style
  Cognitive style

Management
  Actions
  Consultant/client relations
  Support
  Location of researcher
  Managerial style

User performance

Dependent variables

Implementation
  Frequency of inquiries
  Reported use
  Monitored frequency of use
  User satisfaction

dependent variables used to measure implementation success generally can be classified as measures of usage, intended use, and/or satisfaction with a system. The independent variables fall into several classes, as shown in the table. Although researchers have different methods of applying the variables in each study to operations, the variables can be placed into classes similar to ones contained in the descriptive model of information systems in the last chapter.

One of the central variables in our model is the use of the system. We are concerned with factors leading to high levels of use, which we have also adopted as a measure of successful implementation. Thus, we can use the model we have already developed to help us understand the implementation process.

Favorable attitudes on the part of users should be extremely important in implementation; attitudes have an action component, and favorable attitudes are consistent with high levels of use and satisfaction with a system. The technical quality of systems is important; it directly affects our attitudes as users and also makes it easier to use the system physically. For example, a system with difficult input requirements or a difficult language for user input will be used less than one with a good technical design.

As we have seen in our discussion of information, personal and situational factors make a difference in an individual's approach to an information system. We can predict that the new manager will be more interested in an acquisition planning model than the 20-year veteran. Decision style is also important in determining system use; does an analytic decision maker use the same information as a heuristic one? The future use of an information system is also

---

AGRICULTURAL INFORMATION

Faculty members at the University of Nebraska have designed a computer network for direct use by farmers and ranchers along with agricultural specialists. There are now over a thousand users of the AGNET system. The system delivers information to clients located in 30 states and Canada.

There are two broad classes of system users: agricultural specialists who advise others and individuals, business and agencies making direct use of system services. Many users access the system rarely, once or twice a month or even seasonally. There are over 200 management and information programs in the library. The system is customized with respect to data for participating states. Thus, a user in Montana deals with data that are applicable to that state.

Examples of some of the programs include FEEDMIX which helps calculate the best ration for feed using locally available foodstuffs. PUMP is used in the classroom to teach engineering students how irrigation costs are affected by changes in application rates, altitude or water depth. A rancher might use BEEFGROWER to estimate when a particular lot of cattle will be ready for sale and what the cost of weight gain will be. The cost of production for various crops can be calculated using CROPBUDGET and the economic value of land estimated with BUYLAND. The system also provides news items and a message service.

During the eruptions of Mount St. Helens, the system was used as a local communications link for the Washington State University Cooperative Extension Service. The system transmitted information to county extension agents. The Secretary of Agriculture in Washington, DC and departmental personnel used information from the areas to coordinate disaster relief programs.

Perspectives, October 1980.

---

influenced by past experience in analyzing the information and in taking action. Successful use of information will make it more likely that a decision maker will use the system when faced with a similar problem in the future.

AN IMPLEMENTATION STRATEGY

The research and model described in Chapter 5 suggests an implementation strategy based on our view of information systems design as a planned change in activity in the organization. We stated earlier that the reason for developing a new computer-based information system is to create change. Dissatisfaction with present processing procedures stimulates the development of a new information system. However, change can create almost insurmountable problems in the development of a system if only technical factors are considered by system designers.

What do we predict will happen as a result of the major changes undertaken during the development of a new information system? The model in Figure 5-1 helps in forecasting the results. Suppose that change is treated by a rational engineering approach. People are expected to cooperate with the design of a system because it is in their best interest to do so; we make no special efforts to ease the change process.

First, we predict that forcing change on a potential user of a system will create unfavorable attitudes; change is always difficult and threatening. If users develop negative attitudes and are afraid to cooperate with the systems design staff, the technical quality of the system will suffer because the input of users is needed to design a good system from a technical standpoint. Poor attitudes and low technical quality are likely to lead to little use of the system—a state we defined as implementation failure.

How do we avoid this type of outcome? The first step in the prevention of information system failure is to adopt an implementation strategy that recognizes systems design as a planned change activity and stresses that successful implementation requires behavioral changes on the part of users.

Psychologists have suggested that a change approach based on user participation is most likely to be successful. A number of experiments and field studies have supported the importance of participation in making changes. Some of the reasons for the participation strategy are:

1 Participation is ego-enhancing and builds self-esteem, which result in more favorable attitudes.

2 Participation can be challenging and intrinsically satisfying, leading to positive attitudes.

3 Participation usually results in more commitment to change; commitment in this case means that a system will be used more.

4 Participating users become more knowledgeable about the change. Therefore users get to control more of the technical qualities of the system and become better trained to use it.

5 Technical quality will be better because participants know more about the old system than the information services department staff.
6 Users retain much of the control over their activities and should therefore have more favorable attitudes.

How should users participate in the design of a system? Participation requires the efforts of both the information services department staff and the users. The information services department staff has to encourage participation, while users have to be willing to participate and devote considerable efforts to design work. In the past, although most information services departments have attempted to involve users, the effort frequently produced what would have to be classified as "pseudoinvolvement." To bring about the necessary involvement, a suggestion has been made that users should actually design their own systems. We shall explore this idea further in the next section.

CREATIVE SYSTEMS DESIGN

The suggestion of having users actually design systems is aimed at solving the critical organizational behavior problems in the development and operation of computer-based information systems. This approach is based on the argument that systems design is a planned change activity in the organization. Technology is important in the development of computer-based systems, but user reactions determine the success of a system. We design systems to change and improve

---

MANAGEMENT PROBLEM 16-1

A major stock brokerage firm developed a sophisticated operations-research model to help customers decide what stocks to buy and when to enter and leave the market. The model is "solved" each week by a large computer system; reports are distributed regularly to brokers across the country.

In a study, each broker was found to have a slightly different way of using the recommendations. Some of the brokers call their clients who are interested in the model to give them the results. Other brokers assimilate the results and then call clients with recommendations based on the reports but do not reveal the source of their recommendations.

Some brokers do not use the system at all while other brokers use it primarily as a sales tool. That is, they show a brochure on the model to prospective customers to demonstrate the advantage of opening an account with their firm. One type of broker becomes an expert in the use of the model. However, instead of working with customers, this broker spends too much time studying the model.

From the discussion in this chapter and the model of information systems, in the context of the organization, presented in an earlier chapter, how do you explain the different reactions of brokers to this model? As a manager in the brokerage firm, what steps would you undertake to obtain the best results from the modeling effort?

A FIRE RESEARCH SYSTEM

The Los Angeles Fire Prevention Bureau uses a minicomputer to log data collected from tests. These data are to be used to establish a nationwide standard for residential fire-protection sprinkler systems. Tests are conducted in a two story house that was condemned by the city to extend the Los Angeles airport.

The rooms are set up with furniture and various monitoring probes to collect temperature, air velocity, smoke density, oxygen levels and carbon monoxide at various levels in the room. Then sprinkler design alternatives are tested such as the head spacings, water pressure and volume by setting various types of fires in the rooms.

The programs on the minicomputer convert the data into graphs displayed on a CRT. The system makes it possible to monitor the tests on-line and then to analyze the data in greater depth at a later time. Previous tests were recorded on conventional devices and it took almost a year to analyze the data. With the computer system the entire testing process proceeds much more quickly.

Mini-Micro Systems, September 1980.

---

existing processing procedures, and this requires modifications of human behavior (Lucas, 1974c).

A New Design Method

The new philosophy of creative systems design has three major components:

1 User-controlled systems design
2 A definition of system quality according to user criteria
3 Special attention to the design of the interface between user and the system

The most important and radical component of the design method is user control of systems design. Why do we make this suggestion? Creative systems design places the responsibility for the design of a system with the user. The computer professional acts as a catalyst to help the user construct the system and translate it into technical specifications for computer processing. Creative design places the user in control of the design of the system.

The analyst helps direct the efforts of the user and indicates what tasks must be accomplished. For example, the first task delineated by the analyst might be the specification of output. The user is asked to think about the information it would be desirable to receive and to draw up a rough report. The analyst suggests that the user keep the report for several weeks while thinking about how it could be used. Should the information be available in inquiry form on-line? Does the information have to be updated on-line? The analyst, from knowledge of the capabilities of computer systems, presents alternatives for the user to consider.

The user might be asked to develop a method for obtaining input for the new system. The user determines the contents of forms for input after the analyst discusses alternatives such as a terminal, an optical character recognition system, or a batch-input form.

The user is then shown how the computer files are developed and the logic of computer processing. Working with the analyst, the user defines processing logic and the file structures for the system. In a similar manner, with guidance from the analyst, the user prepares plans for conversion and implementation.

The second component of creative design relates to system quality. We should evaluate the quality of information systems according to user criteria and not the criteria of the information services department and staff. In one instance, the computer department developed a new on-line system featuring the latest in communications and data-base management techniques. However, users were irritated because the command language was hard to use and because the system had a number of errors in it. In addition, users no longer had their old familiar reports, yet the new system was available to retrieve information for only four hours during the day! Computer professionals rated this system highly because of its technical elegance. Unfortunately, the enthusiasm of the computer staff was not shared widely by users. Instead, users were highly dissatisfied because the technology, more than the needs of the user, had intrigued the designers.

The interface between the user and the system is extremely important and attention to the interface is a third and final creative design component. A great deal of effort should be expended to ensure that a high-quality interface is developed. Care should be taken in determining the input and output with which the user has contact. Experimentation here is strongly recommended; users should have the opportunity to work with the new input and output forms and devices before they are made part of the system. Users should design the input or output form and choose the appropriate technology (for example, optical character recognition or on-line terminals).

Advantages

What are the benefits of this design approach? User participation in and control over the design process has a number of payoffs for the organization. The new system is more likely to be utilized because the user, instead of the information department services staff, has psychological ownership of it. The user has invested time and ideas in the system. Because of exposure to the system during design, users will understand the system and become trained in how to use it for the conversion and installation phase.

Because of their influence, users will surrender less power and less control over their activities to the information services department. Systems should have higher quality because the user is in charge. The user knows what is needed for the application, and, since the user is in control, quality will be defined according to user criteria. The user interface with the system will be appropriate because the user will have designed it.

MANAGEMENT PROBLEM 16-2

The Major Mining Company hired a consulting firm to design a new computer system for inventory control. The consultant was supposed to coordinate his efforts with the company's computer centers located in two parts of the United States.. The consultant was retained because the existing workload at the company centers prevented them from developing the system and because the consulting firm had extensive technical expertise.

The computer center designated to work most closely with the consultant was extremely hostile. The standard reaction of the personnel in the center to the consultant was, "It's your system, you design it." The consultant had a rather low opinion of the staff in the computer center but knew that the staff would have to program any system designed. Therefore, the consultant tried to obtain systems analysis and programming personnel from the center. Much time was spent on this rather unproductive activity and progress on the new system was very slow.

The consultant described these problems to the vice president who had retained the firm. Although the vice president could order the computer center staff to cooperate, he knew that it was impossible to force cooperation. What can the vice president do to solve this problem? Is the problem solely at the computer center? What can the consultant do?

Disadvantages

The method for systems design suggested above will not be easy to implement. Resistance can be expected from information services department staff members who will probably perceive a diminished role in systems design. Experience, however, should show that systems design jobs become more satisfying under this new approach because the designers' efforts will be successful. It is far more exciting to be a catalyst in the development of a successful system than to be in charge of the development of a system that fails. In addition, the technical challenge of systems design has not been removed from the duties of the information services department staff.

Resistance to these new suggestions can be expected from users too. Users may fear computer technology and question their own ability to take charge of or contribute to a systems design effort. Management support and encouragement will be necessary to help users overcome their initial fears. Once into the design process, these doubts should quickly disappear as users are caught up in the challenge and excitement of designing their own systems.

A final problem in adopting the participatory systems design method is cost, both in time and money. Extensive participation requires time, usually from employees who are already overcommitted, and added resources will be needed to free these users to work on a system. As a result, the design of each system will take longer and cost more than under more traditional approaches. However, we feel that the results in terms of successful systems will be worth the effort.

Some Experiences

Can the user design information systems? The procedures for systems design recommended above have been used for the development of several information systems. In one instance, a feasibility study and systems design were carried out for a grass-roots labor organization. The design team consisted of union members and faculty and students from a university. The union members in general had a low level of formal education, and the design team was concerned over the impact of computer technology on the union and on its individual members. Because of hectic union organizing activities, the union staff could not devote the amount of time needed to the development of a system, although eventually several full-time union staff members began to work on the project.

To begin the analysis, the university design team interviewed members of the union staff and gathered data on existing procedures and requirements. After jointly determining that a system was feasible, the design team developed a rough design. To turn the ownership of the system over to the union, and to be sure that they were in control of the system, a day-long review meeting was held to present the draft of the system. At this meeting, the union president explained that there were many tasks to be done and that no one would be replaced by a computer. He stated that, instead, workers probably would have more interesting jobs, and he asked members to think about how the system could help the union.

The design team began its part of the meeting by stressing that the session would be successful only if at least half of the system presented was changed: the team was offering ideas and not a finished product. Elaborate flowcharts and visual aids were not used. Instead, a very simple tutorial on computer systems began the presentation. The designers spoke from rough notes and listed report contents, files, and inputs on a blackboard. The highly motivated union staff quickly grasped the relationship among reports, files, and input documents. Substantial changes to the rough system were made in front of the audience during the meeting.

Several weeks later, a follow-up meeting was held with union leaders who suggested management-oriented reports. The design team helped the union develop specifications for bids and worked on a consulting basis with the union staff that finally developed a system. The designers intentionally reduced their role as the union became more capable in the computer area. The system was successfully implemented; the level of use was high and users from the union president to clerical personnel appeared pleased with the system.

In another situation, a system was developed to support the decisions of a group of three managers (see Scott Morton, 1971). These managers had responsibility for setting production schedules in the commercial laundry products division of a major manufacturing company. The production manager wanted to minimize setups and have long product runs. The marketing manager wanted to have wide product availability at warehouses throughout the country to provide high levels of customer service. The market planning manager had to resolve differences in objectives so the three managers could develop a feasible production plan. Because future production depended on the decision for the next month, a 12-month planning horizon was used.

In the original manual system, the managers generated possible solutions that were analyzed by clerical personnel who performed a large number of manual calculations. Upon evaluation, it was usually found that a solution had to be modified because some part of it was infeasible. More meetings and more clerical computations were required. Sometimes, almost the entire month elapsed before the next month's schedule was ready.

The research group trying to improve this decision process observed the managers at work for some 6 months. After 3 months, a rough system featuring an interactive graphics display terminal was developed. The first prototype system was shown to the market planning manager, who learned how to operate it. This manager made many suggestions for changes, which the designers incorporated into the system. Then, the market planning manager trained the production and marketing managers in the use of the system. They, too, had numerous suggestions for modifications that were incorporated into the system. Over time, the researchers modified the system for the managers in this

---

MANAGEMENT PROBLEM 16-3

The Airflow Manufacturing Company has retained a consultant to help design an order-entry and accounts-receivable computer system. Airflow manufactures precision parts for the aerospace and automotive industries.

The consultant believes in the creative design techniques discussed in this chapter. As a result, she stresses the importance of extensive user involvement in the design of the system. The president of the company agrees intellectually with the consultant's advice, but recognizes there could be problems in trying to obtain the needed cooperation.

The most serious bottleneck appears to be one key employee in the office. Most of the work on processing orders and receivables is under the supervision of this one individual. There is no real second in command, even though the president tried unsuccessfully for a number of years to have an assistant trained. Several had been hired, but left during the training period because of unknown problems.

Because of the lack of an assistant and the increased information processing load created by a good business year, the president knows that obtaining help from this key supervisor will be difficult. However, the consultant, after a few days working in the firm, indicates that this individual is probably the most logical person to place in charge of the design effort.

What can the president do? Can he afford to have this key supervisor in charge of the system? If there is no alternative, what steps can the president take to be sure that the system is designed well and that normal information processing tasks are completed?

---

particular decision situation. The managers were very satisfied with the system and resisted attempts by the computer department to discontinue it after the research project was officially completed.

These efforts so far have been with small groups of users who have not had complete control over design, but the techniques are promising and should be applicable to other settings. Certainly more time is required on the part of the user to participate so fully in systems design. However, the time is well spent, since a significant component of a user's activities is likely to be affected by a new computer-based information system. Given the failure of so many information systems, users must spend time on the design of systems and encourage the adoption of more participatory design techniques.

IN CONCLUSION

One of the problems of the design approach presented here is user knowledge. In the examples presented, users with little background quickly developed the needed skills to control the design of systems. Parts Three and Four of this text presented the basic material necessary for the user of an information system to understand enough about computer technology and systems design to partici-pate successfully in the development of a system.

KEY WORDS

Attitudes	Independent variable	Pseudoparticipation
Change	Operations research model	Quality of systems
Dependent variable	Participation	Satisfaction
Failure of systems	Planned change	Successful implementation
Implementation	Process of design	User interface

RECOMMENDED READINGS

Lucas, H. C., Jr.: *Implementation: The Key to Successful Information Systems,* Colum-bia, New York, 1981. (Presents a review of implementation literature and a new framework for approaching implementation.)
————: *The Implementation of Computer-Based Models.* National Association of Ac-countants, New York, 1976. (Presents the results of a study of the implementation of planning models written in a higher-level computer language.)
————: *Toward Creative Systems Design,* Columbia, New York, 1974. (This short monograph describes in more detail the philosophy of systems design introduced in this chapter.)
Mumford, E., and T. B. Ward: *Computers: Planning for People,* Batsford, London, 1968. (An excellent discussion of the factors that should be considered in designing information systems so that they will be used.)
Schultz, R., and D. Slevin: *Implementing Operations Research/Management Science,* American Elsevier, New York, 1975. (Contains the results of a conference on the implementation of OR models; many interesting studies provide insights on the implementation process.)

DISCUSSION QUESTIONS

1 Why are favorable attitudes important for successful implementation?
2 What other definitions and measures of successful implementation can you suggest besides the ones in this chapter?
3 What are the responsibilities of users in the systems design process?
4 How do the responsibilities of managers and, say, the clerical staff differ during systems design?
5 What are the crucial differences between an operations research model and computer-based information systems from the standpoint of implementation? What are the key similarities?
6 What is the role of a consultant in helping design information systems? How does this role change under the creative systems design policies suggested in this chapter?
7 What approaches are there to evaluating the benefits of information systems?
8 How would you measure the impact of an information system on decision making?
9 How do you suppose cognitive style affects implementation? Can cognitive style act as a constraint on successful implementation?
10 How could you take cognitive style into account in designing a system?
11 What problems does user-controlled design create for users, their management, and the information services department?
12 Can user-controlled design work for a system encompassing large numbers of people, for example, a reservation system involving hundreds or thousands of agents? What strategy could be adopted in this situation?
13 How would you study the implementation process? How could such a study be used to improve implementation?
14 Why do so many information services departments resort to pseudoparticipation?
15 What are the origins of the rational engineering approach to change? Contrast this approach with more participatory techniques.
16 What are the dangers of participation? (Hint: think about raised expectations.)
17 What is the role of the information services department analyst in the design techniques discussed in this chapter?
18 As a potential or present user of information systems, how do you respond to the idea of being in charge of the design of such a system?
19 What is the key distinction between planned change and change in general?
20 Are the techniques suggested here applicable in other contexts? What situations can you suggest in which user control might be more successful than control by a group of technological experts?
21 How does the technique of creative design affect the conditions of the conflict model discussed earlier?
22 How do the change techniques suggested here relate to the power model presented earlier?
23 When does planning for successful implementation begin in designing an information system?
24 Who should suggest the development of a new information system—users or the information services department? Why?
25 Who should suggest modifications and improvement to existing systems—users or the information services department? Why?

Part Five

Examples of
Information Systems

This part of the test attempts to integrate the material in the previous chapters through a series of examples. The first chapter in the section presents two different information systems, one a simple batch application and the other a nationwide, on-line system of great complexity. Chapter 18 describes three decision support systems that illustrate the use of computers to aid more sophisticated and less structured decision problems than the applications in Chapter 17. These two chapters and their examples illustrate how decision requirements, information needs, users, organizational considerations, technology and the process of systems analysis and design combine to make computer-based information systems.

HARDSERVE
    Background
    Preliminary Survey
SPECIFICATIONS
HARDSERVE ON-LINE
    Order Entry
    Receipt of Merchandise
    Ordering for Inventory
    Inquiries
    Picking Slips
    Reconcilement
    Extensions
    File Structures
    Errors and Modifications
    Summary
AN ON-LINE ADMINISTRATIVE SYSTEM
    Background
    Objective
    Special Features
    The System
SUMMARY
KEY WORDS
RECOMMENDED READINGS
DISCUSSION QUESTIONS

Chapter 17

General Information Systems

- What systems alternatives are
  available for an organization?
- What kind of technology should
  be employed by the organization?

In this chapter we discuss two different information systems to support transactions processing and operational control decisions. Our purpose is to integrate material covered so far on computer technology and systems design. The first example presents specifications for a hypothetical system, and because the system was designed for illustrative purposes, it is simple enough to be presented in some detail. The second system is a large, on-line administrative application featuring many terminals, large files, and multiple computers for processing and is one of the most advanced systems currently in operation.

HARDSERVE

Background
Hardserve is a company that specializes in the wholesale distribution of merchandise to retail hardware stores.[1] Hardserve buys goods from manufactur-

---

[1]Hardserve is a subsidiary of a diversified holding company named Manhold.

ers and stocks them in a warehouse; retail hardware stores order merchandise from Hardserve, which then ships it from inventory. If Hardserve does not have the goods requested by the retail store, the store will go elsewhere. Hardserve has usually been the first choice for retail stores trying to find an item. Because of its efficient operations, it has been able to keep prices slightly lower than competitors. Naturally, the demand for goods fluctuates drastically by season. For example, tree stands are a big item just before Christmas but there is very little demand for them in July. By the same token, lawn mowers move very rapidly during the spring but only a few western stores need them in stock all year long.

The company recently developed an inventory-control system. This system provides better service for customers and assists in reordering and controlling inventory balances.

Preliminary Survey

A design team was formed of users and of information services department personnel, and a steering committee judged the recommendations of a preliminary survey and feasibility study. Below we present the results of the preliminary survey.

Hardserve Preliminary Survey

EXECUTIVE SUMMARY

For several weeks we have been conducting a preliminary survey on the advisability of developing a computerized inventory-control system. This document presents our findings for consideration by the steering committee.

Goals

We have identified the following goals for an inventory system:

1 Reduce inventory levels while maintaining a desired level of customer service
2 Improve reorder policies
3 Improve inventory management for seasonal and slow-moving items
4 Capture sales data so purchasing can analyze trends and stock the proper merchandise

Alternatives

We identified one package program and developed two alternatives for new systems for consideration by the steering committee. The results of our analysis are summarized below.

1 Minor improvements in the present system
   a Percentage of goals met—5 percent
   b Tangible savings—$5000 per year
   c Intangible benefits*—10 percent

    d Time to implement—3 months
    e Total cost—$10,000
2 A batch computer system with a simple economic order-quantity model
    a Percentage of goals met—75 percent
    b Tangible savings—$20,000 per year
    c Intangible benefits*—30 percent
    d Time to implement—18 months
    e Total cost—$50,000
3 Computech inventory-control package
    a Percentage of goals met—60 percent
    b Tangible savings—$15,000 per year
    c Intangible benefits*—25 percent
    d Time to implement—6 months
    e Total cost—$55,000 ($40,000 for package, $15,000 to install and modify)
4 An on-line inventory system
    a Percentage of goals met—95 percent
    b Tangible savings—$15,000 per year
    c Intangible benefits*—50 percent
    d Time to implement—24+ months
    e Total cost—$80,000

*Intangible benefits were rated on a scale of 0 to 100 percent and include consideration of such things as the user interface with the system, ease of use, improved decision making, and so forth.

THE EXISTING SYSTEM

Problems

The existing system is illustrated in the flowchart of Exhibit 1. At the present time we have manual processing of papers and no real inventory control. For some items we tend to overstock out of fear of running out, and for others we miss a reorder point and incur a stockout. Purchasing hears from the warehouse when a particular item has reached a reorder point marked on the bin. This reorder point is set by the warehouse manager and is based on experience. We also have no real sales forecasting because we don't know what items are moving. Accounting analyzes the physical inventory and at the end of the year purchasing looks at what items have sold. However, it's too late to do any good by that time.

Goals

The goals for improvement in the system are stated in the Executive Summary.

Decision Considerations

We have identified the following crucial decisions in processing inventory:

    1 What should be ordered for each new season?
    2 What should be reordered during the season and when?
    3 How much should be reordered each time?
    4 What items should be dropped from inventory?

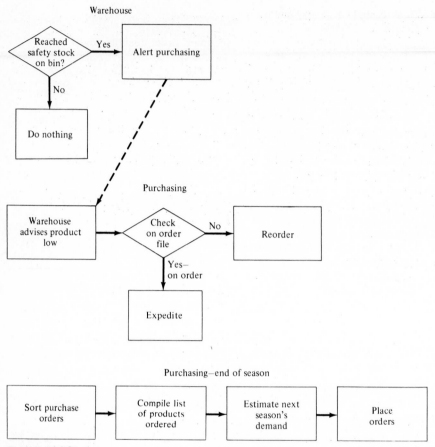

Exhibit 1 of Survey

Information Flows

Information processing at Hardserve is shown in Exhibit 1. The warehouse supervisor notices when the physical stock has dropped below the reorder point and prepares a report that is sent to purchasing at the end of the day. The purchasing agent either reorders the item, if it is not on order, or expedites it if an order has already been placed. At the end of the season, the purchasing department analyzes purchase orders and estimates what quantities will be needed for the next season. Decisions on the reorder amount are based on the purchasing agent's negotiations with the supplier. Approximate volumes of orders and other related data are given in Exhibit 2.

ANALYSIS OF EACH ALTERNATIVE

Improvements to the Present System

Overview   With minimal impact and cost we can make some improvements to the present system. For example, we can set up tables for economic order-quantity amounts and put better reorder points on the bins.

Exhibit 2   Approximate Monthly Values

	Average number of orders
January	4,100
February	6,700
March	7,800
April	8,400
May	5,400
June	4,600
July	5,000
August	5,100
September	6,200
October	9,500
November	10,100
December	8,200
	81,100

Average orders per month   6758
Maximum orders in a day   500
Average orders per day   311
Average number of items per order   5.1

Decisions and Information Flows   These improvements would help us reorder a more economic quantity of goods each time, and we would do so at a better reorder point. However, these improvements would do little for other decisions or information processing.

Technical   There will be no computer processing involved in this alternative.

Development Schedule   A very few months would be required to implement these changes. We might use a computer program to set the economic order quantities and lot sizes, but this could be done very inexpensively on a time-shared system.

Impact on the Organization   There should be minimal changes and a very small impact on organizations or on jobs. The purchasing agent would have to consult a table, which would make decisions on economic order quantities more routine. However, this lets the purchasing agent shop for a better deal, for example, by looking for a better discount or lower price. Warehouse managers should be happy to have a better system of reorder points, since the current haphazard way of establishing them is of concern to the manager.

Operational Aspects   The only change this system needs is for purchasing to use a series of tables on the proper economic order quantities. Instead of the warehouse supervisor deciding on the reorder point, a more scientific calculation could be used.

Costs and Benefits   The costs in the Summary were estimated to include computer programs and printing the tables for the economic order quantity. We can use the computer for this task. The benefits from this system are estimates of savings through economic ordering and reductions in the number of stockouts.

A Batch System

Overview   This system would be updated once or twice a week with inputs from order processing providing data on usage. Information from the warehouse would show arrivals of merchandise. When a reorder point is nearing, the computer would notify the purchasing agent, who would place the order and notify the computer that goods were on order. Whenever desired, we could produce a usage report.

Decisions_and Information Flows   This system would provide data for all decisions discussed in the Goals section. Information flows would be altered; the computer department would receive information from the warehouse on order processing and would send information to purchasing.

Technical   We would use punched card input and reports would be printed for purchasing. We would send copies of the inventory report to accounting as well. We would probably have one file on tape with all the data on inventory.

Development Schedule   Development should take about 12 months, but we have allowed 18 to be safe. The system would be run on our holding company's computer and we would have a remote batch terminal here for input and output. It should be easy to manage two or three updates a week, and we could vary the number of updates depending on the season.

Impact on Organization   It would be necessary for us to add a data preparation and control department at Hardserve, and we would want to have a liaison here to interact with the central computer facility. We would remove the reorder notice burden from the warehouse supervisor. In interviews, the supervisors indicated that this would be a welcome change. It is a tedious and error-prone job now, and they would rather spend time supervising their employees. The purchasing agents, too, indicated that the idea of better planning and sales data would be very appealing. They now are confronted with too many emergency orders and the necessity to expedite orders all too frequently.

Operational Aspects   The major changes in operations have been described. Almost all departments are affected, although the changes are relatively minor. There will be a number of reports produced, and certain existing documents will have to be sent to keypunching for input into the computer system. However, there is very little additional work created for any individuals as far as manual processing is concerned.

Costs and Benefits   Benefit estimates were based on savings on inventory balance and a reduction in the number of stockouts. We did not really include a better service level for customers, although we think that this will be provided. Cost estimates are based upon a comparable system developed by our holding company's computer staff.

A Package Program

Overview   We also looked at several package programs and selected the best one for consideration by the steering committee. This package does much the same thing as our batch system, but has some functions we don't need and lacks certain features we would like to have.

Decisions and Information Flows Basically, a package program would cover the same decisions as the batch system discussed above. In fact, all the items discussed above are similar for the package except for the development schedule, costs, and benefits.

Development Effort The development effort includes installing and modifying the program to produce the types of reports we would like to have. We estimate this will require less time than developing a system from scratch.

Costs and Benefits The benefits of the new system would be much the same as the batch system described above. A large portion of the cost is the purchase price for the package. We would also have a small operating cost from subscribing to changes and improvements that are made in the package over time.

An On-line System

Overview This alternative is the most sophisticated one presented for consideration. It offers the advantage of not having to transcribe any data by keypunching. Instead, there would be terminals in the warehouse, receiving department, and purchasing department. Data would all be entered by the user.

Decisions and Information Flows We will again cover the same decisions and have basically identical information flows except that now we would not use existing documents. Instead, information would be keyed into the system by various users.

Technical The input and output are clearly different for this system. We would have to use direct-access files. Output would be selective, although we would probably still want to print some batch reports for a historical record.

Development Effort This system will take more effort to develop, even though our holding company has several on-line systems running now. Moving to on-line processing requires a more sophisticated technology, and this is reflected in the development effort.

Operational Aspects Operationally, the system will be easier to use and there will be far fewer documents. However, we are somewhat concerned about whether people will be able to use the terminals in the various locations. In some respects, paper processing may almost be easier since it is already familiar.

Impact on the Organization This system would have the greatest impact on the organization because purchasing agents, warehouse personnel, and others would use terminals directly. There is also the possibility of problems with backup and computer downtime.

Costs and Benefits Benefits are the highest here because data are captured at the source and are up to date when on-line. We would expect to have the same tangible savings as with the batch systems, but operating costs are somewhat higher, reducing total benefits.

SPECIFICATIONS

After the design team completed the Hardserve preliminary survey, they submitted it to the steering committee. Members of the steering committee read the report and discussed it at length. They decided that a new system would make a positive contribution to the company, and that it should be implemented. The steering committee rejected the package system for a number of reasons[2] and asked the design team to compare two alternatives in the feasibility study: the batch and the on-line systems. The design team spent two weeks refining the estimates in the preliminary survey. Further study convinced them that the cost and the time estimates had been too conservative. The estimates for the batch system were revised to 12 months and $80,000, while the new estimates for the on-line system were 18 months of development time and a cost of $110,000.

The steering committee examined the feasibility study and focused primarily on the percentage of the original goals met and the impact of the system on the organization. They felt that, given Hardserve's limited experience, the best approach would be to develop a batch system and implement it successfully before moving on to a more sophisticated system. However, the committee did ask the design team to develop a system that could be converted easily to on-line inquiry in the future. Below we present the specifications developed by the design team.

In the specifications that follow, the reader should note that all parts in inventory are currently identified with a seven-digit number. The first two digits of the number are the class code for the type of item (such as lawn care) and the remaining five digits are the item number within the class. For the purposes of the computer system, a check digit will be added to this number.

Output The major reports from the system are shown in Table 17-1. (Normally samples of report formats would be developed by the users on the design team for inclusion in the specifications.) Users agreed that they needed an inventory balance report to check inquiries and for historical records. However, several users confirmed that this report would be referred to infrequently. The systems design team suggested the use of microfilm with one reader each in order processing, accounting, warehousing, and purchasing.

One of the major goals of the system was to speed reorder information to purchasing on a regular basis, and the reorder report will be prepared each updating cycle to accomplish this. The recommended order quantities and the reorder point are computed in a program by a simple formula (see Buffa, 1961):

$$Q = \sqrt{\frac{2RS}{Ci}}$$

---

[2]In a real situation, the committee would have seriously considered the option of the package, as it is a good way to quickly implement a system and gain experience. However, for the purposes of the example, we shall eliminate the package so we can illustrate the design of a system in detail.

MANAGEMENT PROBLEM 17-1

Howard Atkins just became chief executive officer of Dorman's Dairies. Dorman's began as a small local dairy in the Midwest and gradually expanded to include several cities. Atkins came to Dorman's when it was acquired by a major conglomerate in the food industry.

Dorman's is fairly conservative and has no computer processing. All production, inventory, and order information is processed manually. Atkins, on the other hand, had extensive experience as a user of information systems at the parent company and felt that Dorman's profit margins could be improved substantially if the costs of information processing could be reduced. Fortunately Atkins is on good terms with the computer department at the corporate headquarters of the conglomerate so that obtaining computer time and service should be easy. In addition, Dorman can use the parent's computers until it becomes necessary to acquire its own.

Atkins is faced with two major problems. First, the employees of the dairy are not used to thinking in terms of systems. He recognizes that there will be significant problems in obtaining enthusiasm and cooperation in designing systems. The other problem is the selection of applications. What areas are most crucial? Where is the greatest potential for savings? What types of information systems should be developed? Atkins is searching for some mechanism to solve these two problems. What do you recommend?

---

where Q = order quantity
     R = requirement or usage rate
     S = ordering cost
     i = the carrying cost as a percentage of inventory
     C = cost of an item

All these data needed to compute Q are readily available from purchasing records.

The economic order quantity is first computed when a new item is added to the inventory, or when costs change. When the balance on hand reaches the reorder point, a reorder notice is included on the order report for the item. The reorder point computation is based on the estimated usage during the lead time. To compute this point the usage for the last month is divided by the number of days in the month. This figure is multiplied by the lead time in days to obtain the expected usage during the lead time as the reorder point. A percentage is included in the calculation to let us increase the safety stock if we experience too many stockouts. There are more sophisticated approaches to setting a reorder point and safety stock; however, this rule of thumb should be adequate for Hardserve.

The order analysis report was developed by the purchasing agents to assist in planning. The agents hope it will allow them to see trends and decide what to order during each season. Purchasing agents will override the reorder report on

Table 17-1   Output Reports

1 Inventory balance report
   Distribution: Order processing
                  Warehouse
                  Purchasing
                  Accounting
   Form: Microfilm
   Sequence: (1) Inventory class (first two digits of item number)
                  (2) Item number (next five digits of item number)
   Frequency: Each update
   Contents: Item number
                  Description
                  Units
                  Previous month's balance
                  Current month's balance
                  Current month's usage
                  Current month's receipts
                  12 months' usage
                  Reorder quantity
                  Reorder point
                  Cost
                  Physical location in warehouse
                  On-order quantity
                  Average balance
                  Leadtime

2 Reorder report
   Distribution: Purchasing
   Form: Printed
   Sequence: (1) Inventory class
                  (2) Item number
   Frequency: Each update
   Contents: Item number
                  Description
                  Units
                  Previous month's balance
                  Current month's balance
                  Current month's usage
                  12 months' usage
                  Reorder quantity
                  Reorder point
                  Cost
                  On-order quantity
                  Number of stockouts
                  Average balance
                  Expedite (if already on order)
                  Leadtime

3 Order analysis report
   Distribution: Purchasing
   Form: Printed
   Sequence: (1) Inventory class
                  (2) Item number
                    or

Table 17-1   (Continued)

	(1) By number of units ordered	
	or	
	(1) By number of units ordered by class	
Frequency:	As requested	
Contents:	Item number	
	Description	
	Units	
	Yearly orders	
	Reorder quantity	
	Reorder point	
	Number of stockouts	

4 Inventory turnover report

Distribution:	Purchasing	
	Accounting	
Form:	Printed (summary or detailed)	
Frequency:	As requested	
Sequence:	(1) Class	
	(2) Item number	
Contents:	Item number	(or class)
	Description	Description
	Units	—
	Balance	Balance
	12 months' usage	12 months' usage
	Reorder quantity	—
	Reorder point	—
	Cost	Cost
	Average balance	Average balance
	Total usage	Total usage
	Average usage	Average usage
	Turnover	Turnover

5 Physical inventory adjustment report

Distribution:	Accounting
Form:	Printed
Sequence:	(1) Inventory class
	(2) Item number
Contents:	Item number
	Description
	Units
	Previous 12 months' balance
	Current balance (book)
	Previous 12 months' usage
	Current month (usage)
	Date of physical inventory
	Adjustment quantity

Note: For size and type of fields, see file specifications.

seasonal items; for example, they do not need to stock many lawn-care items during November. When it wants, the purchasing department can request the order-analysis report, and it will be prepared as a part of the update. The report will be produced by item number in detail or will be sorted and presented by decreasing usage. The purpose of this inventory review report is to allow analysis of items that are selling well. The report can be obtained by inventory class summarized for all the items in the class, or by individual item.

The inventory adjustment report was requested by accounting. Periodically, accounting takes physical inventory and adjusts the book inventory to reflect quantities actually in storage. (Discrepancies come from loss, damage, etc.) Not shown in Table 17-1 is a generalized retrieval report for management. In observing management, the design team found requests for inventory information were erratic. It would be very difficult to satisfy management with a formal, prescribed report. Instead, managers wanted an inquiry capability to support their decision making. At first the information services department staff members would formulate inquiries for the program; later, perhaps, managers will learn to prepare the input themselves.

Input   Four types of inputs in the system are shown in Table 17-2. First, customer orders come into order processing; these orders represent the demand for goods. Receipts for merchandise reflect items that have been ordered by purchasing to replenish inventory; these items arrive at the warehouse, are uncrated, and put on shelves. On-order data come from purchasing so that the reorder program will know whether something has actually been placed on order. Error corrections come from a number of places; these corrections include file maintenance for correcting errors and for physical inventory adjustment.

Files   Table 17-3 lists the three major files in the system. First, a file is created from editing the input transactions (file a in Figure 17-1). This file is the input to a sort routine that places transactions on input file b in Figure 17-1 in the same order as the master file for updating purposes. Finally, there is the master file itself (file c in Figure 17-1).

The master file for this application is placed on disk for two reasons. First, there is a plan to move to on-line inquiry in the future. Second, the president makes unusual requests for information on fairly short notice. He spends much of his time meeting with customers and vendors. With vendors, the president tries to obtain the best price possible, and in times of short supply tries to get what Hardserve has ordered. It helps him to see what types of items are purchased from a particular vendor before meeting with that vendor. The president is curious to find out both the amount and dollar volume of business that is done with the vendor firm so that he can negotiate better service. To answer his inquiries on short notice, the designers included a directory and a linked list of pointers on vendor number for up to three vendors per item. A

Table 17-2   Inputs

1 Orders
   Source: Current purchase order
   Medium: Card (one card per item ordered)
   Fields:

	Columns	Type
Customer number	1–8	Numeric
Item number	9–17	Numeric
Quantity	18–23	Numeric
Vendor number	24–29	Numeric
Price	30–37	Numeric (two decimal positions)

   Estimated card volume:
      Average 1600 per day
      Maximum 2500 per day

2 Receipt of merchandise
   Source: Warehouse copy of Hardserve purchase order
   Medium: Card (one card per item received)
   Fields:

	Columns	Type
Item number	1–8	Numeric
Quantity	9–15	Numeric
Vendor number	16–21	Numeric
Purchase order date	22–27	Numeric

   Estimated card volume
      Average 800 per day
      Peak 1500 per day

3 On order
   Source: Purchasing department
   Medium: Card (one card per item ordered)
   Fields:

	Columns	Type
Item number	1–8	Numeric
Quantity	9–15	Numeric

4 Error correction
   Source: All users
   Medium: Card
   Fields: To be designed by update programmer

Note: The programmer should number transaction type and assign the numbers to columns, for example, 79–80.

study showed that, in general, no more than two vendors were ever used for a single product.[3]

Processing   Figure 17-1 presents the overall system flowchart. All input enters the editing program and is edited at one time. Then the input transactions are sorted to update the file. During the file update, various reports are spooled to an intermediate file and error notices are printed. The report print program uses the report file to output each report, and a special retrieval program uses the master file to produce custom-tailored output reports.

[3]This is a fairly unusual request and is included to illustrate use of directories and a linked-list file organization.

Table 17-3 Files

1 Master file
   Medium: disk

Fields:	Size	Type
Item number (key)	8	Numeric
Description	50	Alphanumeric
Units	5	Alphanumeric
Previous month's balance	8	Numeric
Current month's balance	8	Numeric
Past 12 months' balance	8@ = 96	Numeric
Current month's usage	6	Numeric
Past 12 months' usage	6@ = 72	Numeric
Reorder quantity	8	Numeric
Usage during leadtime	6	Numeric
Most recent cost	9	Numeric (two decimal places)
On-order quantity	8	Numeric
On-order date	6	Numeric
Number of stockouts	3	Numeric
Three most recent vendors	6@ = 18	Numeric
Number of orders this year	3@ = 9	Numeric
Dollar value of orders this year	7@ = 21	Numeric
Vendor address pointers*	6@ = 18	Numeric
Leadtime (days)	3	Numeric
Delete indicator	1	Numeric
Expansion space	20	Numeric

2 Transaction file
   Medium: Tape
   Fields: Card image input—see forms
3 Directories (item number and vendor number)
   Medium: Disk
   Fields: To be designed by programmer

*For linked-list direct-access file.

Manual Processing Basic manual processing operations are shown in Figure 17-2. Order entry in Figure 17-2a begins with the receipt of a customer order and the production of copies. The order is divided into warehouse locations where the different items can be found. That is, orders are divided into the regions of the warehouse where the merchandise is shelved to make picking easier. Four copies of the order are filed for the day on which they are to be filled (picked) in the warehouse.

Before that date the orders are removed from the file and sent to the warehouse. As the order is filled, the picker marks whether the full order requested is shipped or not and turns in the form with the shipment. One copy of this form now goes to the information services department, and this is the only change in procedures for order processing.

The activities in placing an order are shown in Figure 17-2b. The purchasing agent makes out an order, but now works from a computer report instead of a notice from the warehouse. Four copies of the purchase order go to the

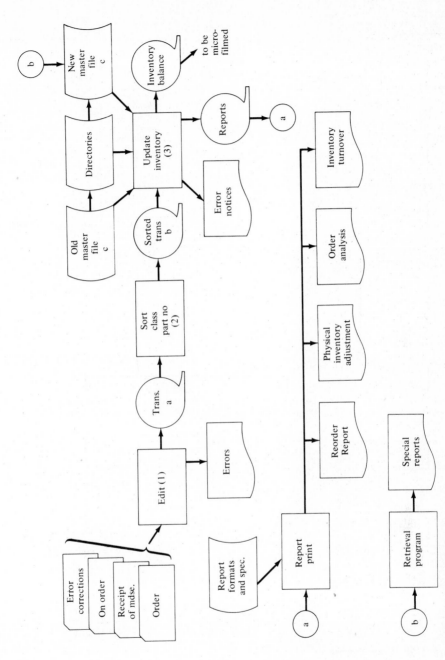

Figure 17-1 System flowchart.

417

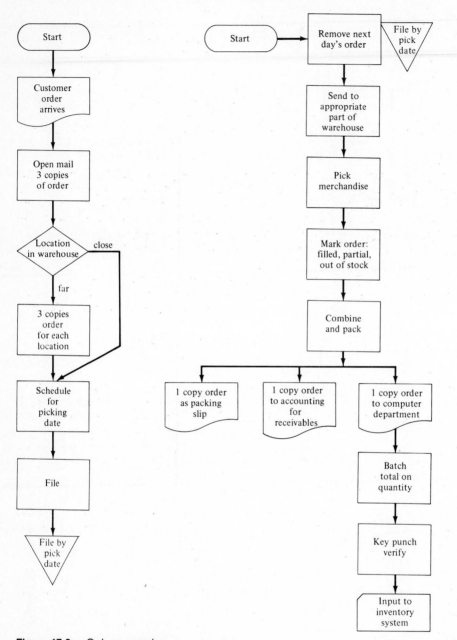

Figure 17-2a Order processing.

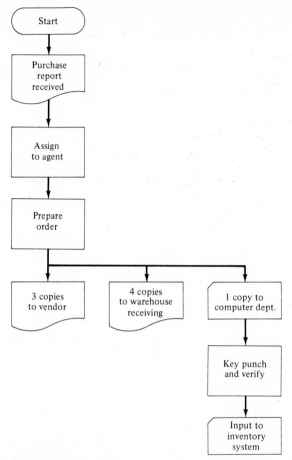

Figure 17-2b On order.

warehouse to be filed under purchase order number for receipt of the item. One copy goes to the information services department, and this is the only other change in purchasing procedures.

Receipt of the merchandise in the warehouse is shown in Figure 17-2c. When the item is ordered, four copies of the purchase order are placed on file in the warehouse by purchase order number. When a shipment arrives, purchase orders are pulled to check whether it is a complete or partial shipment. If it is a partial shipment, two copies are filed to be used when the back order arrives. The extra copy of the marked purchase order indicating arrival is sent to the information services department to indicate receipt, and this is the only change in receiving procedures.

Error correction procedures are shown in Figure 17-2d. The supervisor in each user area must authorize the change in the file by signing a form. An

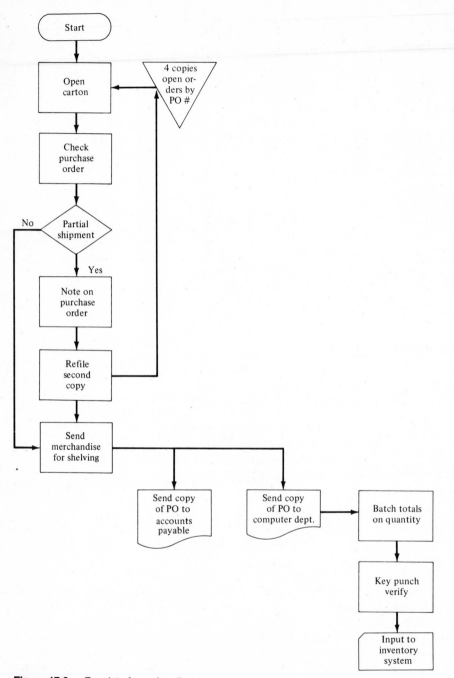

Figure 17-2c   Receipt of merchandise.

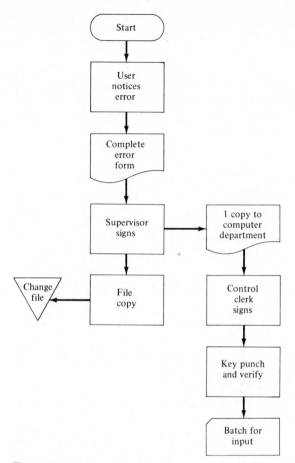

Figure 17-2d Error corrections.

individual in the data control section of the information services department also examines and authorizes each change.

HARDSERVE ON-LINE

In this section we present a revised version of the system at Hardserve, one that operates on-line. By studying this new version, one should be able to obtain a good idea of the differences between on-line and batch processing from both a design and user standpoint. We think the conclusion perhaps will be that the on-line version offers a substantially more pleasant user interface and processing environment at a cost of increased complexity.

The specifications that follow are preliminary; the on-line system will be changed as it is refined and users begin to contribute more to its design. However, the specifications presented here show how an on-line system might appear and illustrate how radically it differs from the original batch processing version.

Table 17-4 is a sample of the type of input menu selected by users for communicating with the system. Table 17-5 presents the major types of transactions that will be processed by the system and provides an overview of its capabilities. In the batch system, we spoke of output, input, files, and processing. In the on-line example, it is clearer to present a discussion based on major transactions that are processed by the system. Figure 17-3 shows the overall structure of the system.

Order Entry

A major activity in the new system is order entry. To provide the input for processing and inventory control, we include an on-line order-entry capability. Table 17-6 contains the expanded data that must be keyed at the CRT as an order is being entered. To begin operations, the order-entry clerk would log on to the terminal. After entering his or her identification and password, the display shown in Table 17-4 would appear, asking for a selection of function from the menu. The clerk enters a 1, producing the screen shown in Figure 17-4. Table 17-6 shows the data that have to be entered, while Figure 17-4 is one possible screen layout for the CRT. Note that the system responds with the capital letters in the figure, and the operator fills in the blanks that are shown in italics.

The order-entry program leads the operator through each order. For

Table 17-4 Sample Menu Selection

Hardserve On-Line System

DO YOU WISH TO:
  1 ENTER ORDERS FROM CUSTOMERS
  2 ENTER MERCHANDISE RECEIPTS
  3 INDICATE AN ORDER HAS BEEN PLACED
  4 INQUIRE
  5 PRODUCE PICKING SLIPS
  6 RECONCILE INVENTORY
  7 CORRECT ERRORS, MODIFICATIONS
ENTER NUMBER OF FUNCTION DESIRED _4_

(a)

INQUIRY
  1 INVENTORY ITEM
  2 CUSTOMER ORDER (BY ORDER NUMBER, SHIP DATE DESIRED, CUSTOMER NUMBER, SEARCH-BY-DATE ORDER)
  3 CUSTOMER
  4 PURCHASE ORDER NUMBER
  5 SHIPMENTS DUE IN
  6 CUSTOMER NAME/NUMBER
  7 VENDOR NAME/NUMBER
ENTER NUMBER __

(b)

Table 17-5 Processing Logic for Major Transactions

1 Order entry from customer
 a Key in customer number, and ship date using fill-in-blanks on formatted screen. System responds with name, address
 b For each item ordered, enter item number, vendor desired, price, and quantity. System responds with item description. See sample screen format

2 Receipt of merchandise
 a Display purchase order
 b Enter quantity received if different from purchase order in additional column next to ordered quantities

3 Order placed
 a Enter purchase order number and vendor number using fill-in-blanks on formatted screen. System responds with vendor name and address
 b Enter date due, route code, carrier, terms
 c For each item ordered, enter item number, quantity, description, price. System responds with item description
 d Key in total price of purchase order for check against system computed total

4 Inquiry: retrieve requested data from appropriate file
 a Inventory item: display inventory record
 b Customer order: display customer order status including customer's name, address from customer file. Option to retrieve by order number, ship date (all orders), customer number following order date
 c Customer: Display customer file record
 d Purchase order number: Display purchase order including vendor name, address from vendor file
 e Shipments due in: for date entered, display one screen at a time the purchase orders to be received on that date
 f Customer name: use first six consonants to retrieve Hardserve customer number
 g Vendor name: use first six consonants of vendor name to search directory for vendor name and display name, address, and Hardserve vendor number

5 Produce picking slips
 a Enter date due or customer order number for slips
 b Compare order to inventory, update inventory, modify order to show actual amount shipped

6 Reconcile inventory
 a Display requested customer orders
 b Enter deviations in shipping
 c Adjust inventory file, order file

example, the operator enters only the customer number. The system retrieves the data on the name and address of the customer from the customer file and displays it. At this point, the operator should check that the address on the screen corresponds to the name and address on the order. If not, some type of escape facility would permit hitting a special key to renew the screen or backspacing over the customer number to erase it and retype the correct number. (The specific form of error recovery depends on the computer system

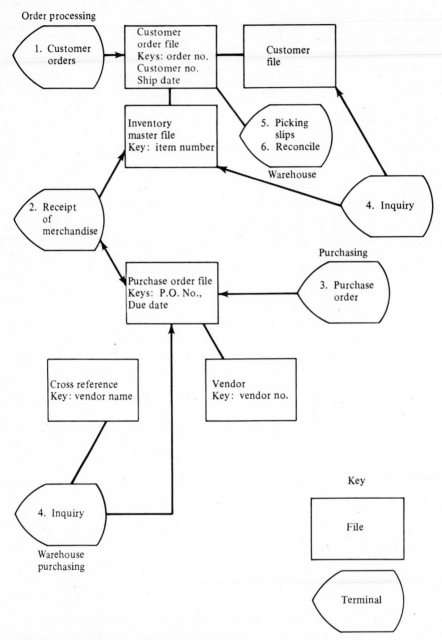

Figure 17-3 Hardserve on-line system overview.

and terminals being used. For all subsequent discussions, assume that it is possible to make these typing corrections when they are noticed by the operator.)

The operator continues to enter the items indicated. The computer program

Table 17-6   On-Order Input

Expanded On-Order Input	Characters	Type
Purchase order number	10	Alphanumeric
Vendor number	6	Numeric
For each item ordered		
Item number	8	Numeric
Quantity	7	Numeric
Description	40	Alphabetic
Price	8	Numeric
Date ordered	6	Numeric
Date due in	6	Numeric
Route code	8	Alphanumeric
Carrier for delivery	15	Alphanumeric
Terms	10	Alphanumeric

automatically performs the extensions and adds the total for the purchase order. The operator enters the total amount of the order, and the computer checks this total against its own total. If there is a discrepancy, the operator is asked to correct the order. If the order is acceptable, the operator so indicates, and a new screen is started for the next order. Another key is depressed to stop order entry.

Depending on the type of application, it might be desirable to compute a running total of all the orders entered and compare them with the total on a batch of orders obtained from an adding machine. In a very high volume operation, such an additional check might be in order to be certain that all orders are entered each day.

HARDSERVE ORDER ENTRY 4/15/81

CUSTOMER NUMBER *12345*   JONES HARDWARE
                                       75 MAIN STREET
                                       BOSTON, MASS. 02139

ORDER NUMBER 89654321   SHIP DATE 5/12/81 ACTUAL

ITEM	DESCRIPTION	VENDOR	QUANTITY	PRICE	EXTENSION
7777777	SHOVEL	*672931*	*12*	12.00	144.00
8888888	HAMMER	*473612*	*24*	5.00	120.00
					264.00

(Computer generated messages in capital letters, User entry in italics.)

Figure 17-4   Draft customer order entry screen.

Receipt of Merchandise

The warehouse uses the system to check in merchandise that has been ordered. The Hardserve purchase order number should be included on the packing slip with the merchandise. From this number, the warehouse staff displays the purchase order. A clerk enters any discrepancies between what was ordered and what was received. These data update the inventory files at the same time that they update the file of purchase orders.[4]

If the purchase order number is missing, the clerk can enter the due date and browse through the file until the right purchase order is located. It might be necessary to enter several due dates because the shipment might not be exactly on schedule. Before the system is programmed, the systems staff should ask the warehouse to research the number of shipments that do not contain a purchase order number. If there are too many, it may be necessary to establish an inquiry based on vendor or some other piece of data included on the packing slip or bill of lading that accompanies a shipment.

Ordering for Inventory

A major addition to the new on-line system will be the installation of terminals in the purchasing department. This department will now have the responsibility for entering the data on purchase orders as they are prepared for vendors. The operators should key the data using a CRT; the data can be used to produce a printed copy for mailing to the vendor. This screen follows the same general pattern as the order-entry example; it will be a fill-in-the-blanks format, and the program will lead the clerk through each of the pieces of data to be entered.

Inquiries

One of the major advantages of an on-line system is the powerful inquiry facility it can provide. For Hardserve there will be a number of inquiries for different groups in the firm.

1   The warehouse and order-entry and purchasing functions will be interested in inventory balances; they need to be able to inquire on inventory-item number and obtain display of the pertinent data about the item.

2   The system will be able to display a customer order; retrieval will be possible by order number, customer name with a link to each successive date (in case the customer phones and does not know the order number), and by ship date (primarily for the warehouse).

3   The contents of the customer file record can be displayed.

4   By entering the purchase order number, an operator obtains a display of the order.

5   By entering a date, warehouse personnel can display (one at a time) the purchase orders with merchandise due on that certain date.

---

[4]The possibility of including a back-order capability is being evaluated. The design team is collecting data to determine how many back orders occur when Hardserve is out of stock, and whether goods would be received in sufficient time to fill the back order.

6 By entering the customer's name, the system will retrieve customeı names and numbers that match, based on the first six consonants of the name. The purpose of this facility is to locate a customer's number given only the customer's name.

7 Vendor name: using the same approach as (6) above, an operator can obtain a vendor's number.

Picking Slips

The warehouse can now call for picking slips as they are needed. The operator enters a due date or specific customer order numbers to obtain the picking slips. The system checks available inventory, produces the slip, decreases the quantity in inventory, and sorts and prints the list.

Reconcilement

After the order has been picked, it is necessary to reconcile the picking slip with the order. Frequently, there is a discrepancy between physical inventory and book inventory. The system may suggest that something can be picked when, in fact, the item is out of stock. While filling the order, the picker crosses out the quantity ordered and writes in the quantity actually selected if there is a difference. These differences must be input to the system to maintain an accurate record of what has been shipped to the customer. At the same time, depending on company policy and control questions, the book inventory may be adjusted to reflect the stockout.

Extensions

As with the batch example, we have tried to keep the on-line system relatively simple. A number of possible extensions would be fairly easy to implement; for example, we could provide for backordering when an item is out of stock. It would also be very easy to produce statements for customers based on the order file. However, the system sketched here provides a good basis for an on-line system for Hardserve.

File Structures

Tables 17-7 and 17-8 contain the new and revised files for the on-line system. The first major addition is a customer order file that is also one of the most complex. There are trailer records for the actual items ordered since there will be a different number for each order. Trailers may be created through the provision of extra records between orders with a chain to an overflow area or through a separate file of trailers that are chained to the order record and chained to each other.

This file has a directory on the Hardserve order number and another one on customer number. Since there may be several orders for the same customer, a date chain of pointers in the file connects each order for a given customer to the next most recent order. The directory to the customer points to the most

Table 17-7 Hardserve Customer Order File

Customer order file (medium: disk)

Fields	Size	Type
Order number	8	Numeric
Customer number	8	Numeric
Order date	6	Numeric
Order date pointer	6	Numeric
Ship date desired	6	Numeric
Ship date pointer	6	Numeric
Ship date actual	6	Numeric

For each item ordered

Item number	8	Numeric
Vendor desired	6	Numeric
Quantity	7	Numeric
Price	8	Numeric (2 decimal)

Directory: Order number
          Customer number (note order date pointers within customer number)
          Ship date

recently placed order. There is also a directory and pointers on ship date for the warehouse. Figure 17-5 shows the file.

Another new file contains data on the customer. Since each order for a customer refers to the same basic information, it would be wasteful of input time and file space to key name, address, credit, terms, etc., for each order. Therefore we create one file, keyed on customer number, to contain all the constant information about the customer.

The next major file is the one containing purchase orders prepared by Hardserve. Like the order file, it uses trailer records to contain the data on each item included on the purchase order. The key for the file is purchase order number; also a directory and a linked list on the date the shipment is due serves to help the warehouse receiving area.

A vendor file—similar to the customer file—is needed to contain fixed information about the vendor. Because there is a frequent need to locate a vendor's number assigned by Hardserve (the vendor is unlikely to keep track of a number assigned to it by each of its customers), the system has a cross-reference file. Each time a vendor is added, this file is recreated by sorting the vendor name and number into alphabetical order, based on the name. A simple directory is constructed, based on the first six consonants of the vendor name to support inquiries to determine vendor number given the name.

Errors and Modifications

We have not talked about errors or modifications yet. From the discussion on the files, it should be clear that there will be a need to make changes as customer

Table 17-8 Other New and Modified Files

Customer file (medium: disk)

Fields	Size	Type
Customer number	6	Numeric
Customer name	30	Alphabetic
Customer address—line 1	25	Alphabetic
Customer address—line 2	25	Alphabetic
Customer address—line 3	25	Alphanumeric
Customer address—line 4	25	Alphanumeric
Credit rating	4	Alphabetic
Volume year-to-date	6	Numeric

Directories: Customer number
First six consonants of customer name

Purchase order file (medium: disk)

Fields	Size	Type
Purchase order number (key)	10	Alphanumeric
Vendor number	6	Numeric
Date due in	6	Numeric
Due date pointer	6	Numeric
Date ordered	6	Numeric
Route code	8	Alphanumeric
Carrier for delivery	15	Alphanumeric
Terms	10	Alphanumeric

For each item ordered (trailer records)

Item number	8	Numeric
Quantity	7	Numeric
Price	8	Numeric (2 decimal places)
Description	40	Alphabetic

Directories: Purchase order number
Due date

Vendor file (medium: disk)

Fields	Size	Type
Vendor number	6	Numeric
Vendor name	30	Alphabetic
Vendor address line 1	25	Alphabetic
Vendor address line 2	25	Alphabetic
Vendor address line 3	25	Alphanumeric
Vendor address line 4	25	Alphanumeric

Directory: Index sequential on vendor number

Cross-reference file (created by sort of vendor file when new vendors added). (medium: disk)

Fields	Size	Type
Vendor name	30	Alphabetic
Vendor number	6	Numeric

Directory: First six consonants of vendor name

Order no.	Customer no.	Order date	Ship date	Actual	Item Trailer Section
12345678	8765432	04 22 81	05 13 81		
12345679	8888888	04 24 81	05 15 81		b
12345680	8765432	04 25 81	05 15 81		
12345681	9999999	04 25 81	05 13 81		

Notes: Directory points to Customer number, then customer orders are linked by order
        date for customer (a link) above, ship date directory points to beginning of
        chain for each ship date (b links above)

Figure 17-5 Customer order file linkages (examples).

orders change, delivery dates are altered on merchandise due in, and for a number of other reasons. These changes must be defined along with the impact on each file. A major effort will have to be devoted to this exercise because the system must be able to alter data that will change during the course of business.

Summary

In this section we have presented a sketch of a possible on-line system for Hardserve. Comparing this system with the batch system should demonstrate the more pleasant user interface and higher levels of responsiveness of the on-line system. Now, users have instantaneous response to inquiries; much paperwork is eliminated. Errors in data entry are corrected as they are made, for the most part. The warehouse problem with merchandise due in from customers should be alleviated, and the work of the purchasing department should be simplified.

AN ON-LINE ADMINISTRATIVE SYSTEM

International Business Machines Corporation (IBM) operates our next example of an information system. This on-line system performs many of the administrative functions of branch and regional offices and features CRT terminals. Because of the immense size and complexity of this system we cannot present it in the same detail as the Hardserve example; however, in the remainder of this chapter we shall try to describe the system's functions and enough of its underlying technology to provide a notion of its capabilities. Much of the discussion comes from Wimbrow (1971), although this source has been updated through demonstrations and company material on the system.

Background

IBM is a large manufacturer of business and computer equipment. Branch offices sell computer equipment, software, and education and maintain contact with customers. Before the development of the Advanced Administrative

MANAGEMENT PROBLEM 17-2

Hardserve is developing a batch processing system for inventory control. Management has a number of good reasons for this decision, especially the desire to begin working with computers in a modest way. However, management feels that, at some point in the future, the on-line system described in this chapter will probably be justified but is unsure at what point on-line response becomes desirable.

They have asked for assistance in outlining the criteria that should be used to decide when to operate on-line. Management knows that a commitment to on-line processing will be costly and wants to be certain that there is an adequate return. Some of the important criteria in the decision to adopt on-line processing, they feel, are the volume of input and output and the need for instantaneous updating. However, management thinks there must be other factors to consider. They have asked your help to outline a decision framework for when to replace the new batch system with an on-line version.

System (AAS), IBM's order-entry system[5] was being strained by increasing sales volume and the increasing complexity of computer equipment that could be ordered by a customer.

For these reasons, AAS was initially developed to perform order entry and some 450 other logical transactions interactively. The order-entry process consists of the following steps:

1 The order is entered.
2 Validity checking takes place during entry.
3 The system assigns a delivery schedule.
4 Confirmation notices are sent to the branch office and to the customer.
5 Commission activity is generated.
6 Orders are forwarded to manufacturing.
7 Customer inventory records are created at the time of installation.
8 Billing activity is generated.

There are many opportunities for delay in this process. In the original system, before AAS, acknowledgments and delivery dates were transmitted through the mail. The validity check for an order was time consuming when performed manually. A validity check is necessary because of the complexity of computer systems; each system usually involves a number of systems components that are interdependent. For example, certain peripherals and controllers can be used only on certain central processing units. A validity check is performed to ensure that all prerequisite devices are present on the original

---

[5]The reader should not be confused because the company in this example is a manufacturer of computer equipment. The system under discussion is an application of computers within the company.

order and to be certain that all configurations ordered can be manufactured and operated. In the original manual system, errors in orders resulted in a cyclical revision that delayed order processing further. These revisions also created inventory control and management difficulties in reconciling on-order backlogs and order totals at manufacturing plants.

Management and inventory control in the original system consisted of three files: (1) open orders, (2) installed inventory, and (3) uninstalled inventory (manufactured but not yet installed). The installed inventory file is the source of rental invoices sent to customers. The original system had difficulty coping with geographic mismatches between payment receiving centers and customer paying centers, which complicated the billing process.

All these problems were compounded in the mid-1960s when IBM planned the introduction of the 360 computer system, which dramatically increased the number of possible configurations for systems. Projections indicated that the complexity of the order-entry process and a growing volume of orders would seriously overload existing information processing procedures for order entry.

Objective

By 1965, a study group recommended a new order system that would (1) operate interactively, that is, on-line; (2) connect branch offices, regional offices, plants and headquarters, some 320 geographical locations requiring about 1500 terminals; and (3) operate in a conversational mode.

One important feature of the new system would be conversational, on-line interaction. A user provides one item of information at one point in time and in several minutes enters more data. The underlying computer system associates the information with each operator without exclusively dedicating itself to any one terminal. The approach is the same we observed with time-sharing and on-line systems in general. The on-line computer appears to the user as if it is maintaining a continuous and exclusive conversation with that user, although actually several hundred users are having "exclusive" conversations at the same time.

The system was originally designed to handle order-entry processing, inventory control, and accounts receivable. However, the design expanded to 16 application areas with 980 transactions, including order entry, delivery scheduling, territory assignment, payroll, commissions, publications, validation of computer group configurations, accounts receivable, customer master record, inventory of installed machines, billing, customer-student enrollment in IBM courses, and user training through computer-aided instruction (CAI).

The system has dramatically reduced the prior 2 to 4 week order-confirmation cycle. Four years after installation, IBM was processing 30 percent more transactions with 18 percent fewer people, a productivity gain of greater than 12 percent a year! The flexibility of the system is illustrated by the ability of the company to reorganize completely the assignment of clients to branch offices over a weekend.

Special Features

One problem with a large-scale system is ensuring that only those with authorization are permitted to use it. Managers are authorized to have access, but they usually delegate this authority to operators. The manager registers employees who then receive security codes generated by the system. The manager and operator must be recognized by the system, and neither can perform functions for which they are not authorized.

The system gives the operator two attempts to enter a security code. An attempt to execute transactions for which the operator is not authorized or for which the operator is untrained brings a reminder on the first attempt from the system. If the operator makes a second attempt to enter an unauthorized transaction, or to log on with an error, or makes any other security error, the system locks the terminal. The terminal remains locked until an authorized security individual unlocks it.

The initial need to train over 5000 operators in branches throughout the country led to the inclusion of computer-aided instruction in the system. Classroom training would have been too expensive and time consuming. Training courses are designed in a modular fashion for the overall system and for each different application. The system keeps track of operator progress and training, and an operator is not allowed to execute transactions for which he or she has not completed the appropriate CAI course.

The System

The closest analogy to the type of system envisioned by the designers was SABRE, the first on-line airline reservation system. This second generation system was developed on a dedicated computer using a specially coded supervisor in assembly language. Because of the progress between the second and third generations of computers in the development of operating systems, IBM utilized a more general-purpose operating system for the on-line AAS system. The AAS system was first developed under an operating system developed for real-time operations for NASA. When the version of a standard IBM operating system (OS/MVS) became available, the designers converted AAS to it.

Input/output devices for the system include more than 8000 terminals and low-speed printers in approximately 1300 branch office, plant, and headquarters locations. There are some 25,000 users of the system. Data are sent over medium-speed lines and concentrated by five distributed computers for transmission over high-speed lines to two central computer sites. Original system design parameters included a 5-second response to 95 percent of the input. Designers had estimated that it would be necessary to process 1.5 million inputs per 12-hour day, or an average of 50 inputs per second. By late 1980, the system was processing 1.3 million inputs per day with an average response time of 5 seconds.

The basic programming structure of this system is illustrated in Figure 17-6. There is an expanding number of applications, each having a group of transac-

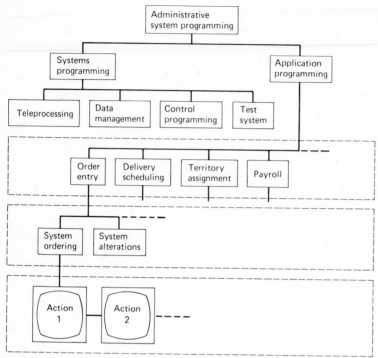

Figure 17-6 Organization of administrative system programming. *(From Wimbrow, J. H.: "A Large-Scale Interactive Administration System," 1971, courtesy* IBM Systems Journal.)

tions. For example, order entry consists of a number of transactions, such as locating a customer record and entering a new equipment order. The lowest level consists of action programs that interact with the operator at the terminal. An example of an action program is one that lists available colors for a computer system. By 1977 there were about 10,000 applications programs in total.

The system stores action programs on secondary storage. The more heavily used programs are prefetched into main storage and remain there. Others are fetched as needed. Action programs are the applications programs; they provide all logical operations necessary to service the user at the terminal. Each message processor has a series of entry blocks that are used for entering messages from terminals, processing information, and transmitting responses back to terminals. There are fewer message and data blocks than terminals, so the system must process messages rapidly enough to prevent delays. The system assigns messages awaiting service to a queue in the teleprocessing monitor. (If the input queue becomes full, the teleprocessing monitor stops polling terminals, so the system runs out of time, but not space.) Enough capacity is provided for most actions to be processed in 5 seconds.

The data base is structured hierarchically; an individual file will contain individual records and may also contain strings of records and groups of strings. A record is a series of logically related fields (see Table 17-9). One record, for

Table 17-9   Installed Machine File

Record key (serial number)	String key (system number)	Group key (customer number)	Description	Date of manufacture	Color
1234	A9421	27123.00	2401 tape unit	xx/xx/xx	Blue
2345	A9421	27123.00	CPU card reader		
3456	A9421	27123.00			
0112	B0942	27123.00			
0479	B0942	27123.00			
4823	B0942	27123.00			
7894	B0942	27123.00			
3168	A9111	87941.00			
.	.	.			
.	.	.			
.	.	.			

Source: *IBM Systems Journal.*

example, is for a 2401 tape unit installed at a particular customer location. This record contains complete information about the unit, including description, manufacturing date, system number, serial number, color, and so forth. All fields in the record are stored contiguously in the data base.

All records related to installed machines are stored in the same file, and the records in Table 17-9 constitute the installed machine file. The format and the length of the records vary widely by individual file. However, all records in a given file adhere to the same format and length. Each record has a unique key such as the serial number in Table 17-9.

Logically associated records in a file are called strings. The tape unit in Table 17-9 is associated with its control unit CPU, and so forth, to make up a configured computer system. This system is identified by the system number (the string key in the table).

We also have associations among strings called groups. A group could be used to relate all systems (string keys) belonging to a specific customer (group key). In Table 17-9, a customer with group number 27123.00 has more than one system, each of which in turn consists of several machines. The file logic is illustrated in Figure 17-7.

Collections of identical types of records, which can possibly contain strings and groups, form files. The complete data base has about 512 such files. A file may have up to three primary keys (record, string, and group) and seven secondary keys although it does not have to; for example, only two levels of association are found in the accounts-receivable file. Naturally directories connect keys to logical records in the file. Each key field has its own directory or index file. For record keys there must be one entry in a directory for each record. String keys, however, take advantage of physical contiguity in the file, and pointers in the directory reference only the first record in a string. The system retrieves subsequent records in the string by reading sequentially.

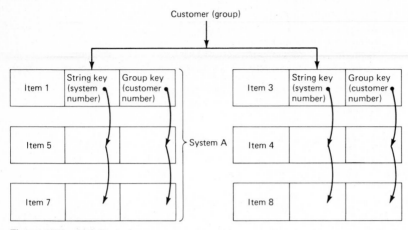

Figure 17-7 AAS file logic.

The system places new data records in an overflow area allocated when the file is loaded, and modifies or creates directory records to reflect the addition. Periodically files are reorganized as retrieval time degrades because of the necessity to refer to overflow areas in the directory files. As discussed in Chapter 9, reorganization consists of reading the old file, writing data in proper sequence in another location, and eliminating the original file. The system recreates directories to point to the new locations. The size of the data base in late 1980 was more than 61 million data records and about 59 million directory records; there are approximately 12.2 billion characters of data in the system and over 1 billion characters of directories.

It is also necessary to provide for reconstructing the data base in an on-line system in case of failure. The designers of the AAS system chose to minimize day-to-day backup costs and incur higher emergency reconstruction costs. The system also includes a trail to allow determination of what data were changed, by whom, and when. All changes to the data base are journalized in the data file journal and appropriate cross-references are noted. Changes include additions, modifications, and deletions of records. The system creates journal records and logs them on to tape. This record consists of the new version of the record after a change, and the signature of the "requester" (application program name and user terminal location code).

Each record of the data base has a control field to record a folio number for the last update. When a record is created, modified, or deleted, the system posts the number of the data-file journal tape currently being used by the system to the folio field in the record (each journal tape is sequentially numbered from the time the system became operational). The previous contents of the folio field associated with the record are also recorded on the journal to show where the previous journal entry for this record is located.

The journal fields forming the audit trails can also be used to recreate the files, although, because of the volume of activity, it would be impractical to

MANAGEMENT PROBLEM 17-3

Astro Electronics is a major producer and retailer of electronic equipment, specializing in audio and television products. The firm sells to department and hi-fi stores throughout the United States. Regional offices and warehouses are in almost all major U.S. cities. Business has been expanding rapidly because of the increased level of affluence in general and the increasing consumption of audio and TV equipment by young adults.

The firm is designing a new sales information system to keep track of sales to retailers and to maintain information on the status of inventories. Because of the large amount of input and output and the need for recently updated information, the company decided to develop an on-line system.

Currently, Astro is organized on a regional basis for sales. However, management thinks that, at some time in the future, it may be necessary to organize both by region and by product line. For example, TV equipment might be handled separately from audio products.

Top management of Astro wants the design team for the new system to be sure that they do not constrain the firm's prerogatives by creating an inflexible system. The computer department thinks the most likely problem area will be in the file structures of the new system. How can they design the files so that the company can easily reorganize its sales activities?

---

begin from where the system first started. Therefore, periodically the system copies the data files to tape. Whenever a file is reorganized, the system creates an image tape containing an exact copy of the new file. The time of reorganization and the first folio number reflecting the reorganization are recorded. If files are damaged, the system processes journal tapes since the last reorganization to remove and compact records affected by the damaged file (compaction is used to eliminate duplicate updates, since only the most recent version of the record is needed). The system reloads the latest image tape and uses the transactions affecting the file to update it.

SUMMARY

In this chapter we have reviewed in some detail systems for transactions processing and operational-control decision making. The AAS system is also used for managerial control purposes. Each of these systems has inputs, files, processing, and output. The hypothetical Hardserve example is very simple and was presented in detail in both a batch and an on-line version. The AAS system is extremely complex and demonstrates some of the advantages of on-line interaction in a high-volume transactional system: there was a need to coordinate geographically decentralized activities on-line. Another major advantage of this on-line system is its ability to collect data at its source and to make immediate corrections interactively. In the next chapter we turn to more decision-oriented information systems to illustrate further different types of applications.

KEY WORDS

Action program	Entry blocks	Preliminary survey
Audit trail	Economic order quantity	Records
Computer-aided	Feasibility study	Steering committees
instruction (CAI)	Groups	Strings
Concentrator	Manual procedures	Telecommunications
Criteria	Message processing	monitor
Directories	Packages	

RECOMMENDED READINGS

IBM Systems Journal, vol. 12, no. 2, 1973. (This issue is devoted to various financial models.)

IBM Systems Journal, vol. 14, no. 1, 1975. (An issue containing an interesting series of articles on an operational-control, transactions-processing system for grocery and retail store point-of-sale data collection systems.)

Lucas, H. C., Jr.: *The Analysis, Design, and Implementation of Information Systems,* 2d ed., McGraw-Hill, New York, 1981. (See Chapter 15 of this reference for complete details on the Hardserve system.)

Wimbrow, J. H.: "A Large Scale Interactive Administrative System," *IBM Systems Journal,* vol. 10, no. 4, 1971, pp. 260–282. (An article containing details and a description of the IBM AAS system).

Yourdon, E.: *Design of On-Line Computer Systems,* Prentice-Hall, Englewood Cliffs, N.J., 1972. (This text presents detailed considerations in the design of an on-line system.)

DISCUSSION QUESTIONS

1 How would you classify the Hardserve system? What decisions are supported in each department?

2 Where should the greatest savings come from using the new system at Hardserve?

3 Develop a procedure for taking physical inventory at Hardserve. How do you enter physical inventory information into the system accurately, given the lead time between counting the items in the bin and updating the computer system?

4 How would you identify each of the different input cards and number the transactions for Hardserve?

5 How can a request for information on how much business has been done with each vendor be satisfied without using a chained direct-access file in the Hardserve example?

6 Why are so many existing forms continued in the new Hardserve system?

7 What extensions of the Hardserve system do you recommend for accounting, warehousing, and purchasing areas?

8 Is there any way to eliminate manual files of purchase orders in the warehouse and receiving station at Hardserve?

9 If the Hardserve system is placed on-line at some time, what kind of inquiries would you expect from each department? Design the files and directories to answer these questions.

10 Besides the files and directories, what other major changes will be needed to develop an on-line version of the Hardserve system?

11 Where do you anticipate the greatest behavioral problems in implementing a new system at Hardserve?

12 What conversion steps will be necessary before the new Hardserve system can begin operating?

13 Design a training program for the users of the Hardserve system.

14 What role should the members of the Hardserve steering committee play during the implementation?

15 Does it make sense for Hardserve to begin planning other applications now? Why or why not?

16 How does extensive user involvement in design prepare Hardserve for the implementation and operation of a system?

17 Why are such stringent authorization procedures necessary in a system like AAS?

18 Is a backup processor often required in on-line systems?

19 What is the purpose of a concentrator in the AAS system?

20 Why is a printer also used at branch offices in the AAS system along with CRTs?

21 Would transferring accounts among branch offices be difficult or easy in the AAS system? How would such a change be accomplished?

22 Compare and contrast AAS with an on-line airline reservation system.

23 Could a system like AAS be developed using packaged programs, for example, for telecommunications and data-base management? If so, why were such packages not used?

24 Why is CAI successful in training people for the use of AAS? How does this training differ, say, from training students in high school or college?

25 How can a company like Hardserve afford on-line systems? What advances in technology make this option a possibility for small firms?

26 What kinds of inquiries do you think customers would make of AAS? Are the record keys and directories sufficient to answer these requests?

27 Are there manual procedures in the AAS system? What controls do you recommend over orders and order-entry processing?

28 How could AAS backup procedures be modified to reduce the cost of recovering from damaged files? What added costs would your solution incur?

29 Why is an audit trail needed in an on-line system? What is its equivalent in a batch system, specifically in the Hardserve example?

30 How is the Hardserve system backed up in case of failure?

31 How would you estimate requirements for on-line systems equipment? What data would you collect?

32 How is conversion to an on-line system different than that for a batch system?

33 What is the purpose of the preliminary survey and feasibility studies?

34 What are the advantages from the user's standpoint of on-line systems for data entry and retrieval; what are the drawbacks?

35 Would you predict that the two systems described in this chapter would upgrade or downgrade the skills required of clerical users?

36 What management information could be developed from each of the systems discussed in this chapter?

CONNOISSEUR FOODS
    Aggregate Market Response Models
    Data Retrieval
    Use of the System
A PORTFOLIO SYSTEM
    Background
    A New System
    Results
A STRATEGIC PLANNING SYSTEM
    Background
    An Example
    The System: An Overview
    Subsystems
    Summary
IMPLICATIONS
KEY WORDS
RECOMMENDED READINGS
DISCUSSION QUESTIONS

Chapter 18

Decision Support Systems

- Can this organization develop
  and does it have a use for
  decision support systems?
- What is the proper level of
  sophistication and information
  processing for this organization?

In this chapter we discuss three systems that are markedly different from the two in the last chapter. The first "system" is really a collection of evolving tools to support marketing decisions. The second system was developed as a research project but was soon converted into a proprietary product for commercial purposes. Various banks in the United States are currently installing revised versions of this system. The third system was recently developed to assist strategic planning in a large company. All these systems exhibit the strong user-orientation required of a decision support system, and the use of these systems is clearly discretionary on the part of the decision maker.

CONNOISSEUR FOODS

Connoisseur Foods is a large, multidivisional food company whose management decided in 1969 to encourage the development of computer models and systems (Alter, 1980). As business grew, Connoisseur Foods split into separate divisions for beverages and farm products (canned goods). Later a division for frozen foods was created, and more recently, the firm has diversified into the toiletries market; they have also acquired a number of subsidiaries. Approximately three to ten major brands are in each division along with a number of minor brands and products in the prototype stage. A brand manager is generally in charge of one or two major brands or a number of minor brands. There is a marketing, production, and distribution department in each division cutting across the brand-manager structure.

The divisions enjoy different histories and personnel with different management styles. The Farm Products Division is considered to be "old line" with managers who have worked their way up through the company ranks. These managers tend to rely on their lengthy experience in the market when making major decisions. In this division, brand managers have the responsibility for many aspects of brand administration, but their superiors generally make strategic decisions and advertising allocations. The Frozen Foods Division is a study in contrasts; it has younger personnel and tends to be somewhat more aggressive and more quantitatively oriented. The division has more clearly defined lines of responsibility, and its brand managers have a greater range of decision-making responsibility.

In 1969 Connoisseur Foods and a consulting company, Business Software Corporation (BSC), began to work together. The effort began with a series of seminars at Connoisseur Foods to prepare management for some of the opportunities available from computer-based systems. During a 5-year period, slow progress was made. During this period certain support tools have played an important role in some decision making, a role that is expected to expand in the future.

Aggregate Market Response Models

Connoisseur Foods applies aggregate market response models to products where there is a reasonable data base reflecting sales experience. These models are used to aid decisions about advertising, pricing, promotion, etc., and then to help monitor those decisions.

To develop a model, the decision maker has to establish reference conditions. Definitions usually come from sales and marketing activities during the recent past. One purpose of future sales and marketing decisions is to create some change in market conditions relative to the reference period. The impact of marketing decisions can be expressed by response functions.

A response multiplier curve such as the one shown in Figure 18-1 indicates that an advertising level at point a will produce sales equal to .7 times the sales in the reference period. Frequently these response curves are "s-shaped" with both

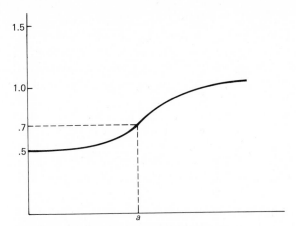

Figure 18-1 Response multiplier curve.

upper and lower limits. A curve of this shape expresses a belief that, past a certain point, additional expenditures for advertising will have no further short run impact on sales.

A model builder develops a response multiplier curve for each controllable variable so that each decision variable is a basis for estimating the impact of any given marketing plan. If a marketing plan for a product includes advertising, promotion, and price that have multipliers from their three response curves of 1.1, .95, and 1.15, the estimated sales of the product would be 1.1 × .95 × 1.15 of the sales during the reference period.

The model building team also is likely to develop curves that reflect seasonality and sales trends. Sometimes the response curves for competitive products are incorporated into the analysis to determine their impact on the sales of Connoisseur Foods. In developing the curves, hard data on historical sales are combined with intuition and judgment.

As described above, the market response model for a product can be used to estimate the effect of various mixes of promotional activity. Such an explicit mathematical model forces the user to segment the problems into a number of smaller, more manageable parts. One's best judgment can be brought to bear without worrying at first about the interaction of the parts. Instead of relying on only one or two key variables, the decision maker can consider more effects and their interactions.

At Connoisseur Foods the models are executed interactively through a computer terminal. The analyst enters a marketing plan and the computer program prints a forecast of the results. The analyst can then evaluate variations on the plan until a satisfactory one is complete. The models are generally developed by a team, and they can be time consuming and stressful to create. Generally one starts with a few main factors such as seasonality, sales trends, advertising, and promotions. The model can be made more sophisticated later.

Data Retrieval

At Connoisseur Foods the original seminars conducted by the consultant showed that the computer-based marketing support was rather poor. Clerks performed hours of hand calculations and retabulations to modify and recast the basic sales reports printed monthly. Special requests for reports on the computer involved delays of almost a month.

To improve this situation the consulting firm, BSC, developed a data retrieval system to allow the generation of desired reports from a large sales data base on a routine and on an ad hoc basis. The consultant followed an evolutionary approach; an experimental system was installed for the Farm Products Division with a plan for later expansion. At the most disaggregated level, the information in the data base consists of sales in dollars and number of units for 13 periods per year for all item codes at each of the sales branches of the firm. The data retrieval system will produce certain standard reports periodically and it will support the ad hoc generation of other reports and data retrieval in general. The system has three levels of user interaction: the Programmer, Expert, and User. The Programmer mode features technical features of the computer that are invisible to simpler levels. Expert mode is for the manager or analyst who wants more flexibility than the User mode; these individuals must be willing to spend more time and effort learning how to specify desired reports.

The simplest level is the User mode. Here the user initiates a report specification simply by naming the type of report needed. The system prompts with a series of questions that leads the user through the logical specification of the report. In this mode, the user only needs to know the type of report desired and the data to be included. The system assumes the responsibility for ensuring the logical completeness of the specification and for finding the data and producing the report.

The following reports can be requested in User mode:

1 **Display** Sales of a product or product class in a given branch or region during a given period

2 **Compare** Compare data such as the sales for a period versus sales during the same period last year; compare sales for one region versus sales for other regions

3 **Variance reports** Forecasted versus actual sales by forecasting units

4 **Sorted listings** Products listed in order of percentage gains or losses compared to last year

5 **Exception listing** All products more than 15 percent below last year's sales

6 **Area test** Evaluation of the impact of a promotional activity

Because of the size of the data base for the Farm Products Division, dollar and unit sales for 400 items across 300 sales branches for 13 periods, the data base will be maintained permanently on a tape. The most recent data of this 20 to 40 million number data base will.be on disk. A user will specify the data desired and if it is available on-line, the report will be produced immediately. If the data are on tape, the system will store the request, which will be processed by a data extraction program run during the night. The next day the data will be available to the user on a disk.

Use of the System

The aggregate response models have been used primarily for planning and tracking; they generate estimates of sales and profits for different promotional plans for a brand. The models are also used to monitor and evaluate brand performance and the effectiveness of a marketing strategy. One of the reasons for the eventual acceptance of several brand models was their high accuracy, within 3 percent of actual sales. The level of use of a model is highly dependent on the brand manager and how much he or she likes to work with models.

One manager thought that the main impact of modeling efforts in the Farm Products Division was to help learn more about the business. The firm now understands more about how their most important product works in the marketplace. There were some disagreements about whether the models have had an important impact on decisions to date. There seems to be good support from top management for modeling, but less at the middle management level. For expanded use of the models by brand managers, management probably would have to give more support.

The data retrieval system, after about a year of use, requires the assistance of technical intermediaries. A brand manager decides that a report is needed and discusses it with the representative in the information services department. The firm wants to eliminate the intermediary and move to a mode of operation where the manager will type a request at a terminal to find out if the data are available on the disk. Assistance will be needed only for exceptional conditions rather than constantly, as it is now. It is hoped that within one year four or five brand managers will use the system regularly without needing help from the computer staff.

There have been a number of implementation problems with the various tools. Some brand managers reason intuitively and do not like quantitative models. Top management thinks that the analytic techniques are new and that it will take time for the staff to become comfortable with them. Some of the brand managers have embraced the models, and the models are having a definite impact on the way they think about their markets. The managers report a more explicit understanding of the market process. For more details of the Connoisseur Foods decision support system, see Alter (1980).

A PORTFOLIO SYSTEM

Background

The system described in this section was developed as a research project and is documented in a paper by Gerrity (1971). The system has been expanded and converted into a commercial product, and more recent information for our

MANAGEMENT PROBLEM 18-1

Sheila Renati joined Kaufman Brothers, an investment banking firm, after obtaining an M.B.A. from a leading business school. Sheila majored in finance and minored in information systems. At Kaufman she has enjoyed working on a number of different projects. Her most recent challenge is the design of a small decision support system for a group of managers working on client mergers and acquisitions.

This system works on a time-sharing computer and provides many different analyses for the managers involved. It is particularly useful in making the projections necessary to analyze a merger between two large firms. The managers remarked that the computer had allowed them to save significant amounts of time and explore many different possibilities for mergers and acquisitions. As a result, they were serving clients better and had more time to handle additional business.

Sheila worked very closely with the three key managers in the department and the system reflected their approach to decisions. Fortunately, much of the programming needed for the computer system was not original. The time-sharing company offers a number of interactive packages and Sheila was able to interface these packages to satisfy the needs of the managers.

A recent reorganization has resulted in one of the three key managers moving to another department; a new member of the firm has taken his place. The new merger and acquisition team is worried because its newest member has many ideas for changing the computer system. They are surprised, however, when Sheila states that she expects to make changes and that the modifications will not be too costly. What makes it possible for Sheila to respond in this manner?

---

description was developed from a study of the system. The prototype version of this portfolio management system was developed for a pension-fund management section of a major bank. The trust officer manages assets for a trust, buying and selling securities to maximize the objectives of the trust, such as growth in capital and maximum return. The bank receives a management fee for its efforts.

Under the conditions existing before the system was developed, managers of the portfolio had three main sources of information: (1) portfolio-related information showing the holding structure of each portfolio, (2) security-related information of historical and predictive variables for alternative investments, and (3) security prices.

The accounting group provided the portfolio information, and security data came from investment research groups. Newspapers furnished security prices. Managers received only fully priced portfolio status reports monthly from the accounting group.

The available information was fragmented and focused on individual security holdings rather than total portfolio status. Management tended to define problems in terms of single security holdings, although from a normative view, overall portfolio structure is what determines performance.

The manager's activities were carefully analyzed through observation and the administration of psychological tests. A number of problems with the current system were discovered in addition to those above.

1 The prices on status reports were often out of date and had to be updated manually.

2 Data were fragmented into two files, one on portfolio holdings and the other on stock history and performance data. The managers needed to see the research information juxtaposed with the account information.

3 There was a lack of an aggregate measure of portfolio status and structure that would enable a manager to look at the distribution of the portfolio on a single dimension or to compare two variables.

4 There was a lack of formal mechanism to compare portfolio status with goals.

5 There were rigid report formats; for example, the holdings were listed only by industry groups. It was not possible to obtain a listing of portfolio contents, say, in order by earnings per share.

6 Managers tended to search locally for stock buy and sell candidates. They rarely considered the entire list of 350 approved stocks for investment because of the effort involved in searching the list for stocks with certain criteria, for example, a price/earnings ratio less than 20.

7 There was no method to consider alternatives, that is, to develop and monitor a hypothetical portfolio.

8 In general, information sources exhibited a slow response.

A New System

The designers tried to solve some of the problems above by providing an interactive decision system with a graphics CRT. The original system operated on an existing time-sharing computer, although present versions run as a part of a standard operating system capable of supporting mixed batch and on-line systems. Most potential users can operate this system on their own internal computer.

One version of the system currently in use has the following functions:

1 **Directory** This function provides a tabular overview of all accounts under the manager's jurisdiction. The table generated can be sorted on a number of fields, such as account identifier, market value, or fixed income performance. The manager can compare whole portfolios in a number of different ways in addition to simply listing the ones under the manager's jurisdiction.

2 **Scan** This operator allows the user to view the holdings of a particular security across a group of accounts. The manager selects the security, a sort key, and other information; a report is produced that includes the units of the security held for each account and certain data on that security, such as the percentage of the account devoted to the security.

3 **Groups** This operator produces a picture of the distribution of the holdings of an account by broad industry groups, such as consumer, petrochemical, and so forth. The display is a graphic histogram.

4   Table   This function provides a way for the managers to design their own reports for reviewing the holdings of an account. The user types the account name and a list of the data items desired for each holding, and a report containing this information appears on the screen.

5   Histogram   The histogram operator allows the manager to view the distribution of any available data item for all the holdings of an account; for example, the user might want a histogram of the total market value of accounts.

6   Scatter   The scatter operator provides the manager with the capability of viewing the relationship between two data items associated with the securities in an account. An example of such a plot is the relationship of current price/earnings ratio against 10-year average price/earnings ratios for the holdings in the account.

7   Summary   The summary function displays various account summary data such as holdings, type of account, and account description.

8   Issue   The issue operator displays all the information pertaining to a specified issue on the list of issues approved by the bank for investment. Examples of such information include price/earnings ratio, historical price/ earnings ratios, and dividends.

It is interesting to note that the designers did not take a fully normative approach. The theories of normative portfolio construction and the "efficient market hypothesis" are not included in the system. Instead, a true decision support system was developed so that the managers could use information in a manner consistent with their own decision styles.

Results

A monitor in the experimental version of the system showed that managers made heavy use of the graphics commands and switched back and forth among portfolios. Sessions tended to be lengthy and to generate a number of reports. Almost all the functions were used; there was no concentration on one function, for example, obtaining the status of the portfolio. Later studies of the system in full-scale operation found that the number of sessions dropped, as did the number of reports produced per session.[1] There tended to be much more of a focus on a single function by each user.

The designers of the original system felt it would provide the tools necessary for managers to change their approach to decision making. They could now focus on a single portfolio; they were not forced to look only at a single stock. The follow-up research indicated that this type of change did not occur. However, from our discussion of change and model of information systems in the organization, these results are not too surprising. The system could be used to support existing security-by-security approaches to decision making. There is no reason why a normative portfolio-centered approach should necessarily be adopted unless the individual decision maker feels that it is best. Did the managers all desire to adopt a more portfolio-centered view, or were they basically content with their current decision process?

---

[1]Charles Stabell, discussion at MIT Conference on Implementation, April 1975.

We have said that organizational change should not be implemented through information systems. Organizational and behavioral changes should be made and then a system to support the new style can be developed. It appears in this case that the new system could be used to improve existing decision approaches or to change one's approach to decision making. Apparently there was no pressing need felt by the decision makers to change their approach, so they used the system to support existing patterns of decision making.

A STRATEGIC PLANNING SYSTEM

Few examples of computer-based information systems support decision making at the strategic level; the system described in this section is a notable exception. This planning system features a number of advanced operations research techniques integrated through a user-oriented interactive computer system. We hope to illustrate some of the exciting possibilities of how information systems can be used to support management decision making with this example.

Background

Strategic financial planning is an important activity for an organization, especially large multidivisional firms. The decision maker is confronted with many competing alternatives for investment and numerous sources of funds. Government regulations and other conditions place restrictions on these decision

---

MANAGEMENT PROBLEM 18-2

Jim Gilmore is executive vice president of Precious Metals, a firm that buys and processes rare metals such as gold and silver. Recent price fluctuations on the world market have created many problems for Precious Metals and Jim has tried to find some way to predict price changes.

He knew that some firms had been successful building computer models of various economic markets. With this in mind, he hired Management Models, a consulting firm, to investigate the possibility of building models for each of the commodities purchased by Precious Metals. The company and industry have very good data on historical prices and other economic indicators.

The modeling effort proceeded very smoothly. The resulting model produced valid results when confronted with the rapid price fluctuations of recent years. Management Models indicated that short-range forecasts should be very good, but the model should not be trusted for extrapolations past one year.

Jim Gilmore now wondered how to integrate the model into purchasing decisions. For a long time, the brokers at Precious Metals had based their decisions on intuition and experience with the market in making purchases. The new model was available on a time-sharing computer system and Gilmore wanted the brokers to use it. However, he felt sure that none of them would take advantage of it if just told that it existed. Jim wondered how to obtain acceptance of this new tool.

makers (Moses, 1975). One of the most important goals of a system for planning is to increase the effective use of executive time by:

1 Focusing attention on key variables
2 Providing rapid feedback
3 Evaluating alternative allocations of resources
4 Providing computer capacity to analyze a large number of alternatives

For planning purposes, alternatives can be classified into the following categories (Hamilton and Moses, 1974):

1 Momentum strategies representing continuation of the present lines of business
2 Development strategies representing incremental effects of proposed changes in momentum
3 Financing strategies including alternatives on how to fund existing and proposed activities for the corporation and divisions
4 Divestment strategies including the sale of a unit in an effort to discontinue a policy
5 Acquisition strategies for different ways to enter a new activity or expand.

An Example

Before discussing the structure of the planning system, we shall present a scenario to demonstrate how the system can be used. Assume that a user has created the necessary data bases and wishes to run an operations research optimization model contained in the system.

First, the user logs on to the system; the system responds with guided instruction after the user types the key words "OPT. PHASE" to select the part of the system to be used. The instructions ask the user to specify the different files for this run of the model (to provide flexibility, designers separated models from data so that the models can be used on many sets of data contained in different files). File specifications are required for a permanent file and a temporary file and to guide preparation of the output reports.

Next the user has the option to print or modify the data base. In this case the user does not wish to make changes; however, if changes were desired, an edit program would be called automatically.

The system asks for specifications of different data and options; for example, what predefined strategies are to be included? Is group-level financing to be in the form of a long-term debt or common or preferred stock? The user proceeds interactively by answering questions. If the answer is long-term debt, the user responds to questions about the year of debt issue, interest, principal, compensating balances, and so forth. When all parameters have been specified, the system saves the data as an input file for an optimization run.

The user types the key word "OPT. PHASE" and the system requests file names and performance options. The user again is given the opportunity to change input parameters. The system asks the user to choose between two objective functions, maximizing either earnings per share or return on equity. After answering several more questions, the system begins its optimization calculations. The user can wait for the results or come back later to display the output. The user can run several analyses changing parameters to reflect different strategies.

When finished with the runs, the user can undertake postoptimality analysis. This analysis might include changing the "right-hand side" constraints of a model by providing a range of parameters to test. The system responds with results for each parameterization step. In the reporting stage, the user can graph various results using bars, lines, or special characters. The user can also generate standard or custom-tailored printed reports to display results. Finally, at the completion of the run, the user logs off.

The System: An Overview

One of the major advances represented by this system is its large number of integrated components. It is not just a single model, but instead the planning system represents a collection of models coordinated by a computer system. The corporate level focus, financial orientation, and long-range planning horizon clearly make this a model to support strategic planning. (See Figure 18-2.) The central analytical component is a large mixed integer mathematical programming model that maximizes corporate performance over a multiperiod planning horizon. The model selects appropriate operations, acquisitions, and financing strategies. A corporate simulation model computes the detailed implications of alternatives and projected financial statements for each set of inputs. A third econometric model supplies external data and projections for the national economy, specific industries, or subsidiaries. The user can employ risk-analysis models to evaluate the business mix and the implications of various strategic alternatives.

To use the model, corporate management communicates its assumptions on planning to the group management and subsidiary management that control strategic planning units. This communication process ensures uniform global assumptions. The strategic planning units submit as a minimum (a) a profit-and-loss statement, balance sheet, and sources and applications of funds for the case where all proposed marketing, development, acquisition, and financing strategies were accepted; (2) an abbreviated profit-and-loss statement showing the source and application of funds for each development and acquisition strategy; (3) financial data for each existing or proposed financial investment showing principal amount, payment schedule, compensating balance, category type, and restrictions on funds.

These data are assembled at corporate headquarters and used as input to economic models that generate alternative data bases. The risk-analysis system prepares other data bases to determine confidence levels for the performance of selected strategic planning units. Information from these activities is transferred to the optimization subsystem to formulate a goal constraint plan for each

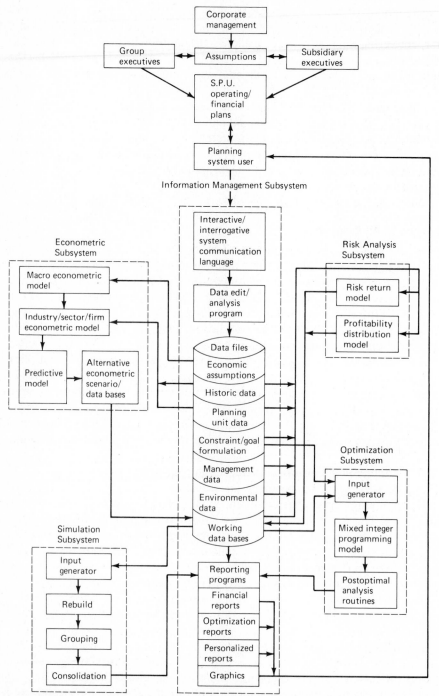

Figure 18-2 The strategic planning system. *(From Hamilton, W. F., and M. A. Moses: "A Computer-Based Corporate Planning System," 1974, courtesy The Institute of Management Sciences.)*

alternative data base. The simulation subsystem determines the financial impact of the plans in the form of profit-and-loss statements and various other financial output. Nonfeasible alternatives will arise, and an iterative process is required to develop a plan acceptable to management.

Subsystems

There are several discrete subsystems in Figure 18-2. The information subsystem controls all information flows in the planning system. It contains an executive program, input editors, output generator, data-editing routines, and the system data base. The executive program organizes the flow of information and controls the conversational time-sharing mode of operation. The input editors organize raw inputs in card-image form on strategic planning units and place them in the data base. These data are edited for reasonableness and compared with historical data and economic projections. The input editor organizes data in the strategic planning unit files, strategic files, and financial files. (There are also files for historical data at the corporate level and for strategic planning unit management and environmental data such as tax rates, prime interest rates, and so forth.) The output generator is responsible for all output report preparation and includes a graphics option for producing graphs and charts.

The consolidated simulation subsystem conducts deterministic, as opposed to stochastic, financial simulations for predetermined sets of strategies. This model is based largely on accepted financial accounting variables and relationships. A rebuilding facility allows the consolidation and definition of new strategic planning units. These units can be configured into a group, and then the model is used to generate group financial projections. A consolidation model is used to eliminate interest flows, to finance deficits from a corporate pool, and to produce annual consolidated statements of corporate financial conditions.

The corporate optimization subsystem maximizes corporate performance over the multiperiod planning horizon. It selects an optimal set of strategic funds sources while considering a complex set of financial, legal, and operational limitations at the corporate and strategic planning unit levels. A mixed integer mathematical programming model is the most important component of this subsystem; several performance measures may be maximized by the model. Planning variables include all available momentum, development, acquisition, divestment, and financing strategies. Restrictions on the pattern of growth in earnings per share, return on assets and equity, corporate cash flow, and various ratios consistent with management desires are considered by the model. The data necessary for the model are drawn from the data base and placed in a matrix for analysis. The data in the matrix are frequently a function of basic input parameters, so there is a matrix modification module to perform computations and create new variables.

The economic subsystem provides projections for the economy and industry where the company is planning to operate or is currently operating. This subsystem contains national- and industry-level models. The economic models were not built especially for the planning model but are among many commercially available economic forecasting models. Another part of the model uses computerized financial information available from proprietary sources to generate financial-planning data for companies being considered for acquisition.

The risk-analysis subsystem generates alternative data bases to show the effect of the variability present in the point estimates provided by planners. For example, one model in conjunction with forecasting models determines the probability distribution of performance for strategic planning units based on historical data and subjective input from management. These data are used to generate confidence intervals for different levels of profits.

New profit estimates are used by the simulation subsystem to create the required financial data. A worst-case minimum profit is derived for every strategy and becomes a constraint in the optimization analysis. All strategies selected during the optimization phase must exceed this minimum level by an amount specified by management. A separate model computes the proportion of corporate assets in businesses of different characteristics. A business-mix evaluation uses portfolio-type analysis to recommend the allocation of corporate assets to different lines of business to maximize expected return on equity for different variances. The optimization subsystem is used again to search for an optimal solution within the bounds of the new allocation of assets.

MANAGEMENT PROBLEM 18-3

Nancy Swanson is vice president of planning for Beauty Aid, a major manufacturer of cosmetics. The top management at Beauty Aid recently heard a presentation on planning and felt that the firm should be looking into this area. Beauty Aid has grown rapidly through its own efforts and by acquiring several smaller companies. Because of its highly profitable business and good cash position, it has been able to make acquisitions easily.

However, top management realizes that business is becoming more complicated and that the next round of acquisitions will involve far larger companies than in the past. Therefore, the computational burdens of evaluating potential acquisitions and projecting conditions after the acquisition would become even more severe.

Nancy is investigating the use of computer models to help in the planning process. After conducting research on the possibilities, she has narrowed her consideration to the following alternatives:

    1 Hire a group of consultants to build a model of the firm.

    2 Develop the internal staff in the planning department to construct a model using a general-purpose computer language.

    3 Design a model with the present planning staff using a higher-level planning language.

What are the advantages and disadvantages of each alternative? What course of action do you recommend to Beauty Aid?

Summary

The computer-based planning system described here is a sophisticated approach to top-management decision making. It can be used for periodic studies or as a part of the annual planning process. The system can also be used for special planning activities that arise on an ad hoc basis. The objective is to assist in developing strategies, and exact solutions with detailed accuracy are not as important as rank-order consistency. Although a system like this is expensive to develop—in the neighborhood of one-quarter to one million dollars—it can provide significant benefits to management.

IMPLICATIONS

The three systems described in this chapter differ considerably from the Hardserve and AAS systems discussed earlier. The differences are not really pronounced in terms of computer technology; rather the major contrast is the type of decision supported. The immediate requirements for information in systems such as AAS necessitate instantaneous updating. In the decision support systems, most of the updating does not have to be done in real time. In these systems, it is the decision maker's need for on-line interaction that necessitates an on-line system; instant conversational response means that the decision process does not have to be interrupted to wait for the computer.

The systems dealing with transactions processing and operational control decisions in Chapter 17 become a part of the control process in the organization. They tend to embody a few decisions that are actually programmed in the procedures of the system; a certain minimal level of use is mandatory, since the systems are installed. Certainly the systems are capable of providing management with information for making decisions, but this is not the major reason the systems were developed.

On the other hand, the systems in this chapter provide very little in the way of routine information processing: their use is almost exclusively voluntary. These three systems provide information to support decisions; they do not actually make the decisions. A number of decisions are programmed into the systems, but they are required to evaluate different alternatives and process information that is presented to and acted on by the decision maker. This type of system is risky to develop, potentially expensive, and almost impossible to justify on a cost-benefit basis. What is the value of better planning? How do we know the decision makers using these systems perform better than under previous manual systems?

Will decision support systems be limited to research projects or to organizations with large amounts of capital to invest? Ten years ago the answer to this question would probably have been "yes." However, recent advances in technology may make decision support systems easier to develop for one-shot or novel decisions. Now economical time-sharing systems are available based on minicomputers that can be acquired for internal use in the company. If more computer power is required, a number of external time-sharing service bureaus offer services, and the user pays only for what is consumed. Low-cost graphics terminals are also available to provide a variety of output alternatives.

More suitable hardware for developing decision support systems has also been accompanied by better software. Simple time-sharing languages are available so that even a novice can program a small decision support application. Many service bureaus have packaged programs that can be used alone or in combination (for example, by interfacing them through a file) to solve management decision problems. For some applications, special-purpose higher-level languages, such as the planning languages discussed in Chapter 8, can be utilized. These languages are designed for the nonprofessional programmer who wants to develop a system in a language more natural than most general-purpose computer languages. As the complexity of the application increases, more elaborate packages and more computer processing power are available. Also, many organizations now have implemented data-base management systems, so much of the internal data for use in management decision making already exists. Only the analysis routines and external data need to be added.

As more transactions systems are completed and we look to support decision making, the technology is present to facilitate the development of advanced applications. These systems, it is hoped, will become regarded as a standard tool for management in the coming years. The manager who is aware of the potential of such decision aids and knowledgeable about computers and information systems should be at a distinct advantage.

KEY WORDS

Alternatives	Hypothetical portfolio	Parameters
Bottlenecks	Integer programming	Portfolio
Conflict	Interactive response	Postoptimality analysis
Consolidation	Mathematical	Report generator
CRT	programming	Response functions
Decision support	Multiplier	Risk analysis
Editor	Normative models	Simulation
External data	On-line updating	Strategic planning
Graphics	Optimization	

RECOMMENDED READINGS

Alter, S.: *Decision Support Systems: Current Practice and Continuing Challenges,* Addison-Wesley, Reading, Mass., 1980. (A book with several good examples of decision support systems.)

Boulden, J., and E. Buffa: "Corporate Models: On-line Real Time Systems," *Harvard Business Review,* vol. 48, no. 4, July–August 1970, pp. 65–83. (This article describes a higher-level language for constructing planning models.)

Gerrity, T. P.: "Design of Man-Machine Decision Systems and Application to Portfolio Management, " *Sloan Management Review,* vol. 12, no. 2, winter 1971, pp. 59–75.

(An article describing the portfolio management system of this chapter in more detail.)

Hamilton, W. F., and M. A. Moses: "A Computer Based Corporate Planning System," *Management Science,* vol. 21, no. 2, October 1974, pp. 148–159. (An article presenting useful insights on the planning system discussed in this chapter.)

Keen, P. G., and M. S. Scott Morton: *Decision Support Systems: An Organizational Perspective,* Addison-Wesley, Reading, Mass., 1978. (This book presents a good overview of decision support systems and the problems of developing them.)

Moses, M. A.: "Implementation of Analytical Planning Systems," *Management Science,* vol. 21, no. 10, June 1975, pp. 1133–1143. (This paper describes some of the implementation efforts associated with the planning system in the last part of the chapter.)

DISCUSSION QUESTIONS

1 Why was graphics necessary in the OPM system?
2 Does the level of technology of this early decision support system matter?
3 How would the systems design approach differ for Connoisseur's system and a batch system such as Hardserve?
4 How would a new manager react to custom-tailored systems like the market response and planning decision support system? What problems does this suggest?
5 Suppose that the decision support system helped the manager to understand problems better and the system could then be discontinued. Would such a system be a success or a failure?
6 What types of decisions are supported by each of the systems in this chapter?
7 Describe the underlying technology, for example, batch and time sharing, for each of the systems in this and previous chapters. How does the technology compare with the types of decisions supported in the system?
8 What is the major difference between the Connoisseur system and previous manual systems? What are the advantages of the past systems from an implementation standpoint?
9 How could managers have been prepared to take a normative approach to portfolio selection before the introduction of the portfolio system described in this chapter?
10 All the interactive applications create problems for users when not working because of computer or systems problems. Why do users become so dependent on these systems? How does the batch system provide a buffer between the user on the one hand and the information services department and the computer on the other?
11 What decisions have you encountered where one of these systems would have been useful?
12 How does an information system serve to integrate the components of the planning system in this chapter?
13 Is an operations research model a form of an information system?
14 How can management justify the expense of a strategic planning model that costs over a quarter of a million dollars?
15 One author has claimed that strategic planning information can come from a company's transactions-oriented data base. Does the example of a planning system in this chapter agree with this observation? What else is needed?
16 How has technology changed the cost-benefit ratio for these decision support systems since the early ones were developed in the late 1960s?

17 How might decision or cognitive style affect a manager's reactions to graphic output?

18 Why have information services departments generally not developed decision support systems? Why do they seem to concern themselves more with transactions-processing applications?

19 Why is on-line updating not always a requirement with decision support systems, while, most of the time, interactive response is necessary?

20 What software advances are needed to facilitate the development of decision support systems?

21 How can we evaluate the effectiveness of the systems in this chapter after they are installed?

22 Make a list of the types of computer systems we have discussed, from transactions through strategic planning, and describe them in terms of the benefits you would expect from each. What does your list suggest about problems with feasibility studies?

23 Why does it make sense for most organizations to develop transactions-processing systems before strategic planning applications?

24 One author has suggested that management information can never be automated. After reading about the systems in this chapter, do you agree or disagree? Has information really been automated?

25 What would be the capabilities of a general-purpose decision support system that could be used across a number of applications by different decision makers? Do you think such a system could be developed and would be advisable? What might the implementation problems be?

26 What type of system is a recent management-school graduate likely to develop, a transactions-processing or decision support system? What skills are necessary for the development of each system?

27 How would you approach the development of a personalized decision support system for a superior?

Part Six

Special Management Concerns

We conclude the book with an examination of special management concerns about information systems. What are the special problems of managing the information services department? We examine some of the crucial considerations in a management audit of the information services department. Finally, the last chapter expands the boundaries of computer-based information systems beyond the organization to include society at large. What are the social implications that the manager should consider when making decisions about computer-based information systems?

The Information Services Department Manager
Managerial Influence
Responsibility of the Information Services Department
OPERATIONAL ISSUES
CONTROL
A MANAGEMENT AUDIT
Computer Center Procedures
Telecommunications
Processing
Input/Output Procedures
Documentation
Conclusion
KEY WORDS
RECOMMENDED READINGS
DISCUSSION QUESTIONS

Chapter 19

Information Systems Issues
for Management

CHAPTER ISSUES

- How does general management
  work with the manager of the
  information services department?
- How can management control
  information processing activities?

In the preceding chapters we discussed a number of organizational, technical, and systems analysis topics to prepare managers to make intelligent decisions about information systems. Having covered these background matters, we are now in a position to discuss some of the problems faced by a nontechnical manager to whom the information services department manager reports. We conclude the chapter with a discussion of auditing and computer-based information systems. Although many aspects of control should be established during systems analysis and design, controls over computer operations should also be insisted on by management.

The Information Services Department Manager

Many user and management problems with information services revolve around the manager of this department. Understanding this individual's position helps in developing a relationship between the information services department and users. In an insightful paper, Nolan (1973) has described the plight of managers of information services departments.

First, these managers have a wide variety of subordinates reporting to them, ranging from highly technical computer professionals to clerical personnel. Second, the department is responsible for a broad range of activities from creative systems design work to routine clerical chores. Third, the department impacts many, if not all, areas of the organization. The manager controls a large budget and is responsible for a major investment in equipment. As the department becomes larger and needs become less technical, the emphasis shifts more toward managerial problems. Unfortunately, we often find managers of information services departments with no management background because their experience is all on the technical side of computing.

Management of the organization has tended to treat the information services department manager as a scapegoat. More seriously, top level management often views the information services department manager only as a technical specialist; they assume that the manager has no desire or ability to progress further in the organization. Given this set of attitudes, the only option open to the information services department manager is to become the manager of a larger or better department in another organization.

How should the top management of the organization respond to the information services department manager? First, top management should see the manager of the information services department as change agent and give support to the manager's activities within the organization. Management must provide extra resources and encourage users to join design teams. Management should also consider the broad exposure that the information services department manager obtains to all other areas of the organization. Is this person not a good candidate for other managerial positions? Top management should not view the information services department manager as necessarily in a terminal position in the organization.

Managerial Influence

How does a manager who is not directly responsible for the information services department influence that department's activities? What can a user or manager do when faced with an unresponsive information services department?

The framework suggested in Chapter 6 is one place to begin. Management should be certain that a plan is developed for information processing that is related to the organization's plan. Attention should be paid to identifying areas where information systems should be developed and to giving priority to potential applications. An appropriate organizational structure for processing must be developed, for example, centralized or distributed processing.

Managers and users must select a particular alternative for a given application that is to be developed, such as an on-line system, a system based on a minicomputer, or an applications package. Operations of a computer facility also need to be carefully managed. The organization should measure service levels and establish performance criteria that are meaningful to users.

A manager responsible for information processing must also be sure that there is adequate staff and equipment. Charging for services is generally instituted to help allocate computer resources. Finally, manàgement must control information processing to see that performance is in line with plans.

The material summarized above and explored in detail in Chapter 6 requires cooperation from senior levels of management in the firm. How does a middle-level manager do when confronted with an unresponsive information services department? Several steps can be taken to influence this department:

1 Urge the formation of steering and selection committees.
2 Request user representatives.
3 Insist that existing information systems work properly.
4 Request a schedule for services.
5 Conduct a user survey to rank various information systems and use the results to work with the information services department on improvements.
6 Insist on the inclusion of users as a part of the design team.
7 Review new systems input and output specifications and plan for implementation.
8 See that the user department staff is adequately trained.

Unfortunately, in many organizations the information services department has become so totally unresponsive that even these steps are hard to achieve. We see users who are totally frustrated with the information services department and turn to external services, for example, a batch or time-sharing service bureau. Other managers acquire their own mini- and microcomputers to satisfy their needs.

Is there any other solution to the problems of an unresponsive information services department when they have reached this level of severity? The major difficulty in this situation is with top management; top management is either unaware of the situation or unable to act to correct it. One approach is to bring in an external consultant to provide some perspective on the information services department. However, there is no guarantee that the consultant will adopt a user-oriented set of criteria in evaluating the department.

A solution more under the control of the manager is to create an informal committee of managers within user departments. These managers should develop a program, including the steps recommended above. Then the committee should meet with the manager of the information services department to present ideas in a helpful manner. If the response is highly negative, the committee should meet with top management of the organization to discuss the problems and possible solutions.

This procedure serves two purposes. It brings problems to the attention of top management if they are unaware of the difficulties. Presenting a program for action also helps management formulate a solution. Top managers may know about the problem but be unsure of what steps to take. Now they have concrete proposals plus evidence of the information services department manager's attitudes toward users and their needs.

Responsibility for the Information Services Department

The discussion above refers primarily to managers who are in departments parallel to the information services department; they have no direct responsibility for the information services department. What about the problems of the nontechnical manager to whom an information services department reports? Some organizations have vice presidents of information systems or administration with computer backgrounds. However, in many organizations the information services department reports to a nontechnical manager.

The nontechnical manager is in an excellent position to implement the steps suggested above and in Chapter 6. For managerial decisions about information services department policy, the nontechnical manager needs no greater technical knowledge than that contained in this text. If management doubts the quality of the recommendations received from technical staff, then an objective opinion can be obtained from a consultant.

It is not appropriate for the high-level manager to deal with highly technical computer details. Rather, that manager's responsibility is to help set policy for the information services department and serve as a liaison with users and other managers. The recommendations we have made for management in the early part of this text—especially in Part Two—should be carefully considered by the top-level manager to whom the information services department reports. Also, the systems analysis and design approach recommended here can be strongly recommended to the information services department by top management.

MANAGEMENT PROBLEM 19-1

Roberta Hobart is president of Fashion News, a monthly magazine for the fashion industry and consumers. The company has a computer department that operates a number of systems in the areas of accounting, advertiser billing, and subscription processing. Recently, the manager of the computer department left to accept a position with another firm.

Two good candidates to become manager of the computer department are Bill McDonald and Lynn Phister. Bill is really not a computer professional. He began his career as an accountant but has been very involved in computer work. Roberta feels that he is probably quite knowledgeable except in the most technical computer areas. Lynn, on the other hand, is a true computer professional. His past jobs have included working for a computer manufacturer designing software and programming for several firms. At Fashion News, he has been manager of systems and programming. In this task, he has performed very competently, especially in solving technical problems.

Roberta feels that both men could do an adequate job. She is worried about Bill's lack of technical experience, but gives him high marks on management. The opposite evaluation applies to Lynn. He should be superb at solving technical problems, but Roberta is worried about his lack of experience as a manager, particularly in working with users.

What are the essential components of the job? Can you help Roberta make her decision? What additional information about each candidate would you like?

MANAGEMENT PROBLEM 19-2

Cookwell is a manufacturer of cooking utensils; its products are sold in department and specialty stores throughout the world. The company has a large information services department and many computer applications in accounting, production, and sales. Historically, there have been a number of problems with computers at Cookwell. There have been five data processing managers in the last 4 years!

Systems seem to be late or are never implemented at all. Users in all departments are highly dissatisfied with computer services. Reports are always late and there seem to be an inordinate number of errors. The computer staff generally blames users for all the problems. Typical comments are, "The users never get us the input on time. When it does arrive, the data are wrong and we have to correct them. Then users get mad because the output is late."

Users, on the other hand, say, "The computer staff is the most arrogant group of people in this company. Whenever we ask them to do something, there is always some excuse why it cannot be done. Every new suggestion is rejected; if an application looks good, they come back with such an unrealistic cost estimate that no one will pay for it. We would be better with no computer at all."

The president of the company has avoided computer problems as long as possible. However, things have become so serious that some action is required. Rather than fire the present manager of the department, who has been on the job only 4 months, the president has decided to try a new strategy. The president has hired a vice president for administration, and the computer department now reports to him. This man has no computer experience, but he is a competent general manager. What should he do to solve the computer problems?

OPERATIONAL ISSUES

Three areas of operational policy require management attention. The first is the development of a data retention policy. Although it may seem mundane, data retention is a major problem for many organizations; for example, insurance companies process thousands of pieces of paper, many with legal significance. Do they need to save the originals, copies, or even microfilm versions of these documents?

Computers generate large volumes of output in a short period of time; some of these records are vital, but which ones? The Internal Revenue Service may make certain demands on firms to supply records; generally a ruling can be obtained from the IRS as to what will be required. A more uncertain request comes from discovery procedures during litigation. What documents are available if a firm is sued? What documents are available to service a customer who needs a historical record? Legislation may also affect record retention; for example, equal opportunity laws require extensive personnel record keeping.

Many firms are using some form of microfilm to store critical data to reduce storage space requirements. Some companies have even developed computerized indices to their microfilm data base so that retrieval will be relatively fast, such as with bulky personnel records.

Second, management must also consider privacy, a topic of broad social concern as we shall see in the next chapter. Privacy issues include who shall have access to data, what data are actually stored, the appeal right of individuals about whom data are maintained, and the implications of potential legislative action on the firm's records. Organizations store vast amounts of data about their employees and their customers. Policy needs to be established in each of these areas to protect the firm, its employees, and its customers.

The third area of management concern is backup and security, a topic we have discussed elsewhere as well. Management must see that the essential operations of the firm can be processed; if a computer center is destroyed, could the firm remain in business? Are there adequate copies of data maintained off-site? Could the firm recover from a major catastrophe? A number of precautions should be taken in addition to the off-site storage of copies of critical records, programs, and documentation. For example, many organizations have arrangements with other firms to use their computers in the case of an emergency. Few firms try to execute their systems on the computers that are available for backup or know whether the firm with the backup machine has adequate capacity to process information for them.

CONTROL

- In 1979 air defense alarms signaled the launching of Soviet missiles aimed at the United States from both land bases and submarines. Officers in charge of the system suspected that something was wrong with the data, however. The missiles supposedly in flight had appeared on only one sensor and not on others. However, the defense command remained on alert status for more than 5 minutes and fighter planes were sent aloft while the data were checked.

The monitors were wrong; through a human error, a connection was made between an off-line computer running a simulation exercise of the firing of land and submarine-based missiles and the on-line computer monitoring air defense at the time. Because the test tape did not simulate data from all sensors, the officers in command were suspicious. What would have happened, however, if the simulation had been complete? (See the *New York Times*, December 16, 1979.)

- The computer operator in a medical institution forgot to remove the file protect ring on a tape that contained the only record of $500,000 in cash receipts. He accidentally mounted the tape on the wrong drive and it was erased; past due receivables could not be identified and pursued. About the time the reconstruction of the file was finally complete, the same accident occurred again.

- Programmers in a financial institution computed interest calculations on savings accounts as if there were 31 days in every month. In the 5 months it took to discover the error, over $100,000 in excess interest was paid.

- Programmers and analysts in a large mail-order house designed a "perfect" system; it would operate only if all errors were eliminated. After installation, auditors discovered that errors were occurring at the rate of almost

50 percent. The system collapsed and had to be abandoned after an investment of approximately a quarter of a million dollars. (For a discussion of these and other similar problems, see W. C. Mair et al., 1978.)

These examples all represent the failure of control in the organization. A control system compares actual performance with some desired state. A household thermostat is an elementary control device; when the temperature in the room falls below the desired setting, the thermostat turns on the furnace to raise the temperature to the desired level.

For a control system to work, then, the organization must have a model of its desired states. Often this model is in the form of routine procedures or generally accepted accounting practices. For problems like controlling a sales representative, standards are less clear, as is our ability to influence behavior.

All levels of control in the organization are the responsibility of management. The Foreign Corrupt Practices Act makes control a legal as well as a normal management task. This act requires that publicly held companies devise and maintain a system of internal accounting controls sufficient to provide reasonable assurances that:

1 Transactions are executed according to management authorization.

2 Transactions are recorded as necessary to permit the preparation of financial statements according to generally accepted accounting principles.

3 Records of assets are compared with existing assets at reasonable intervals and that action is taken when there are differences.

Computer-based information systems have given organizations the ability to process large numbers of transactions in an efficient manner. However, these same computer-based systems create significant control problems and challenges. With thousands of transactions being processed in a short period of time, an error can spread through an immense number of transactions in minutes. Control failures can become costly; firms have been forced out of business because of their inability to control information processing activities.

There are many opportunities for errors to occur in computer-based processing. Figure 19-1 is a diagram of the most difficult case: an on-line computer system with widespread access available from outside the organization. The figure highlights eight areas where the system is vulnerable.

1 The operating system is a piece of software that controls the operations of the computer and allocates computer resources. Operating systems can and have been penetrated; they also have errors in coding just as any other program. No one has devised a satisfactory way to check on the actions of the systems programming group that is responsible for the maintenance and any modification of the operating system.

2 Applications programs contain the logic of individual systems operated in the organization. These programs may have errors or may be incomplete in

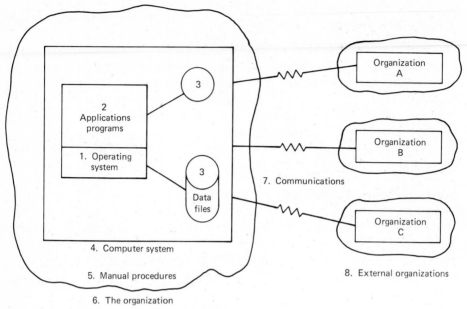

Figure 19-1 Components of an on-line system.

their editing and error checking for input and processing. For an on-line system, users also are executing these programs and may in some way misuse them or create errors the programs cannot handle.

3 Data exist on files in the computer center; these data are often proprietary or confidential within the organization. Are the data safe from accidents? Does the system allow a user or programmer to have unauthorized access to sensitive data?

4 The entire computer system must operate reliably if transactions are to be processed effectively. Is there adequate backup? Is the computer site physically vulnerable?

5 Most computer systems have a number of associated manual procedures for the submission of input and the processing of output after it has been produced by the system. These procedures must be developed with adequate controls to ensure the accuracy and integrity of processing.

6 At a higher level than the individual user, the organization itself must be structured with control in mind. Management must take its responsibilities seriously and emphasize control.

7 On-line systems feature communications among users and systems. Communications links are subject to failure, penetration, and sabotage.

8 Many systems are also available to external users from other organizations. These individuals may make mistakes or intentionally try to misuse a computer system. Controls must protect the system from these users and the users from themselves.

A DAIRY FARM SYSTEM

Managing a modern dairy farm is a complex task. The farmer must maintain records on breeding history, milk production, butterfat content, gestation and lactation cycles for each animal. Many dairy farms operate on a very small profit margin which means that these data must be accurately monitored and used in making decisions.

One West Virginia dairy farm uses a system sponsored by a local cooperative. A USDA official from Washington measures production one day each month for each cow; milk is sampled for analysis. The dairyman or a firm providing artificial insemination services supplies breeding information. The data are processed in Washington through a computer service firm in Utah. The user of the system receives four reports each month.

The individual cow record contains historical information on breeding and production. The report extrapolates the total 305 day lactation production quantity from current data. Another report groups animals into various categories such as "cows to breed," or "check for pregnancy." A third report helps the dairyman evaluate the success of the breeding program. A final report repeats some of the other information in a different format and provides other data like the average calving interval.

The system is used in a number of ways by the farmer. For example, the reports help in making the decision on which cows to sell because of production or breeding problems. Records of production make it possible to evaluate the breeding program. The approach has proven its value as most of the dairy farms in the U.S. employ some type of computer-based record system.

A MANAGEMENT AUDIT

Currently a great deal of effort is being devoted to developing adequate controls for organizations and their computer-based systems. The first step in this process is usually an audit of the organization's existing control system. In the remainder of this chapter we present guidelines for an audit of computer-related controls.

The audit is directed toward computer center procedures, processing controls, input/output procedures, and documentation. Note that for the prototype system described above, these procedures do not adequately address the control problems with the operating system and communications lines. These two technical areas are complex and adequate controls have not been reported in the audit and control literature. The audit procedures below do include consideration of the applications programs, data security and integrity, telecommunications, the entire computer system, manual procedures, and organizational controls in general.

Computer Center Procedures

Table 19-1 contains a list of points raised in an audit of computer center procedures. The auditor checks an organization chart showing staffing of the center, focusing on the separation of functions between operations and control.

Table 19-1   Computer Center Audit Guidelines

Organization chart of staff and center
Separation of functions between staff; operations versus control
Separation of functions between programming and operations
Maintenance of control logs for input and output
Presence of a schedule for regular jobs
Records of jobs run, beginning, ending, errors, restarts, and reruns
File backup procedures; second copies stored in separate locations
Program backup procedures; second copies (including documentation) stored in separate
    locations
Backup arrangement for processing with another organization, including actual attempts to
    make runs
Insurance for recreating bad files, programs, payment for alternative processing
Procedures to check changes to programs
Program library and verification, for example, number of cards in deck; also logs of program
    changes
Disk and tape library controls
External labeling of files
Control of blank forms like checks

The opportunity for fraud exists if one individual is responsible for all processing and control for a system; one classic control technique is separation of functions.

Control logs make it less likely that input or output will be lost, and logging applications in and out also makes it easier to answer questions about job status. Records of job runs and reruns are useful for making corrections and help ensure that a fraudulent run is not being disguised as an error.

Many organizations are lax in providing backup copies of crucial files and programs. It is quite possible for fire or other disasters to destroy a computer center. If backup copies of programs and files are not maintained in a safe location, usually off-site, the organization is quite vulnerable. Its entire inventory of information systems and records vital to the functioning of the organization could be irretrievably lost. The firm should check backup procedures to be run on other systems by executing programs periodically; this practice ensures that the backup system is compatible with the organization's computer.

Programming changes should be authorized and checked to ensure that changes do not create undesired consequences and to guard against fraud. The computer center probably has a disk pack and tape library. The computer center should control access to material in the library because the library contains vital records for the organization. Finally, the organization should control blank forms such as checks, for example, through control numbers on the checks that are recorded as the checks are used.

Telecommunications

Computer systems are making increasing use of communications, either for remote input and output or to connect multiple computers in a network. Because the communications networks are generally outside the direct control of the organization, data security and integrity are difficult to ensure. One technique that is used is the encryption of data. Here some type of key is used as a basis for coding data, such as following a standard algorithm. Basically a number of calculations are performed on the data to transform them to another encrypted stream of data. Without the key or the ability to execute the algorithm the data cannot be decoded. One such algorithm has been established as a national standard and is available from at least one computer manufacturer.

Aside from encryption, communications controls revolve around error detection and correction. Hardware devices must function properly and be able to detect errors. Sometimes the errors can be corrected; if not, the device requests retransmission of the data. In applications programs all data have to be submitted. In one organization, the firm searched for a week because of a processing error; it was finally determined that the transmission of data from a remote location had been terminated before all the data had been received.

Finally, the organization also has to be concerned about the reliability and backup for the network. With many on-line systems and networks of computers, the unavailability of alternative transmission paths can seriously disrupt the operations of the organization. See Table 19-2 for telecommunications audit guidelines.

Processing

Audit considerations in processing not only protect assets and liabilities, they also help ensure accurate processing for users. See Table 19-3. Clearly, the organization must protect files of data. For a sequential file, we check the sequence of the file during update and also confirm the sequence of incoming transactions. We check input during the update to see if transaction values are reasonable when compared with the existing contents of the file.

Table 19-2 Telecommunications Audit Guidelines

Telecommunications
Encryption
Need for encoding
Access to keys
Algorithm employed
Error detection
Error correction
Retransmission
Reliability of network
Backup for network
Applications programs
Error checking
Checks on completeness of data
Backup
Logging of messages

Table 19-3   Processing Audit Guidelines

Processing
Files
Sequence checks
Reasonableness checks on input fields
Reasonableness checks on updating
Record counts, hash totals to ensure integrity
Trailer records with totals
Error notices for unmatched transactions
Use of file labels and error checking on labels for all runs
Checks on sequence of program execution (interprocess communication)
Trial balances and output checks
Audit trail records, especially for on-line updating
Ability to trace all transactions through the system
Backup and restart capability for long runs
Complete record of file changes

Record counts ensure that records are not accidentally lost or destroyed. A hash total is a calculation on some field: for example, the value of each item in inventory is added and carried as a control total at the end of the file. The update program computes the old totals and a new one. The computed total is checked with the total on the old master file and a new total is written to the new master file if all figures agree.

Interim notices for transactions that do not match the file should be printed, because these transactions may represent an attempt to misuse the system. Most operating systems provide the capability to put machine-readable labels on a file; this information should contain as a minimum the name of the file and date created. The program should always check for the correct file to be sure that the operator has not made a mistake in mounting it.

Particularly in a batch system, a number of programs are executed in sequence. Each program should check—for example, through the use of a small communications file—that its predecessor has finished processing. Trial balances are used to develop adjustments for closing books. Output checks ensure that all output is printed and that various totals match. Audit trails make it possible to follow a flow of transactions through a system, and they are crucial to tracing an inquiry. Some long batch runs keep intermediate progress records so in case of failure they can be resorted at the intermediate step. Finally, all file changes should be recorded; see the discussion of the AAS system in Chapter 15 for an example of an audit trail for an on-line system.

Input/Output Procedures

Input/output involves many manual procedures, and often the lack of control inherent in these operations jeopardizes computer-based processing. These procedures apply to both individual programs and systems (see Table 19-4). We should use transaction counts, batch totals, control logs, and so forth to verify

Table 19-4   Input/Output Audit Guidelines

Input/output procedures

Manual processing
  Verification that all transactions have been received for processing (for example, by item counts)
  Incentives to provide data by source
  Review of proper authorization for file changes
  Data transmission checks
  Data conversion checks (for example, record counts, hash totals, control totals on card-to-tape run)
  Action taken if control totals do not match
  Proof and control function performed by other than machine operator
  Follow-up to see that all errors are corrected
  Schedule of outputs to go to users
  Checking of output reports

Machine processing
  Input control
    Batch control records, duplicate computations by computer
    Editing on fields (alpha or numeric)
    Check digits
    Missing data checks
    Prevention of duplicate processing of same input
  Output control
    Record counts on output reports
    Control totals

that all data are received for processing. The system should be designed so that there is as much positive incentive as possible to provide data. File changes should be authorized. When data are transmitted over a distance, the receiving end should check to be sure that all data are received correctly.

When data are converted, for example from paper to magnetic medium, some technique should be used to verify conversion. This verification may take the form of a key verifier, or in other instances we can use control totals or check digits.

What action should be taken when there are errors? For many applications we continue processing, dropping the transaction in error and issuing a notice that an error has occurred. When input/output is controlled properly, a separate section, either in the information services department or a user department, proofs input and output; computer operators should not be responsible for I/O control.

We should see that someone follows up errors and checks output as well as input. Entry to the computer system should also be examined. Batch control totals are used to see that all input is entered correctly. For example, in keypunching, a group of 50 documents is totaled on one field manually and a record is punched with this total. The computer input program adds the fields and compares its total to the final total; an error represents an error in keypunching or the omission of an input record. We should also edit input as processed; for example, an edit program may look for alphabetic characters in numerical fields. Check digits as described above are also useful as a check for missing data. Besides looking for missing or omitted data, we need to protect the system from processing the same input twice, which could happen if, for example, the operator loads input a second time accidentally. Output can also be checked with control totals and record counts to be sure all output is produced, especially reports placed on a temporary print file.

Documentation

We have discussed documentation during systems design. Its importance there was in training users and providing information on how to maintain and repair the system; documentation also provides backup (see Table 19-5). The information services department should have a list of all applications and their status (discontinued, active, under development). Systems design documentation serves as a reference or library during the development of the system, and after

Table 19-5   Documentation Audit Guidelines

Documentation	
List of applications	User documentation
Systems design and maintenance	Output—how to interpret
Table of contents	Input—how to complete and submit
Feasibility study	Files
Existing system	Processing procedures
Specifications for new system	Errors
Output	Transitional considerations
Input—examples of actual forms, codes	Testing
File layout and organization	Conversion
Program modules	Operator documentation
System flowchart	System flowchart
For each program	List of programs
Listing of each version	For each program:
Flowchart/decision tables	Input and format
Variable cross-reference list	Files
Module interface cross-reference	Processing narrative
Variables and identifiers (library)	Output produced
Tests	Error conditions and action
Design	Restart
Data	Distribution and processing (for example,
Results	decollating) of reports
Manual procedures	Programmer responsible for system
Flowcharts	User responsible for system
Narrative	Cutoff for submission on input
Error controls	Scheduled run time (batch) or availability
Work plans	(on-line)
Progress reports	Setup requirements
	List of machine components used

conversion, it is used for maintenance purposes. This library contains all information about the system, including the feasibility study and specifications of the new system. We should have examples of input/output forms, file layouts, flowcharts, and decision tables. Each program should be documented in detail, including an actual listing, a flowchart, a variable list, a module list, etc. Testing records are also needed as a reference when errors occur or enhancements are made. Finally, manual procedures should be documented.

User documentation is designed to help reduce questions and simplify the use of a system. It should contain easy-to-follow instructions and examples of output and input along with descriptions of file contents. What are the major processing steps? What kinds of errors occur and how are they corrected by users?

Finally, the installation needs operator documentation to run each application. This documentation includes a system flowchart, a list of programs and their requirements (input files output), and so forth. Error conditions and operator action should be noted. What should be done with output? It is also helpful to have the name of the programmer and user responsible for the system, along with a schedule for input cutoff and the run time for a batch system or the system availability schedule for an on-line application. Finally, the operator needs a list of the machine components used and any setup requirements for the components, for example, special forms.

Conclusion

Adequate control and security require attention to detail, which can be hard to enforce. Periodic reviews are necessary to be certain that the organization's investment in computer-based information systems and processing equipment is protected. One firm reportedly has a group of traveling internal auditors that enter a computer center and "pull the plug" on all machines to simulate a fire or disaster. Management of the division and the information services department must then demonstrate backup procedures. Creative techniques like this may be necessary to maintain the vigilance necessary for the adequate control and security of computer processing.

KEY WORDS

Applications programs
Audit trail
Auditor
Backup
Batch total
Check digit
Communications
Control logs
Documentation
Encryption

Errors
Fixed-based activities
Hash totals
Internal auditor
Labels (internal and external)
Operating system
Operator documentation
Postimplementation audit
Reasonableness checks

Record counts
Responsiveness
Schedules
Security
Sequence checks
Testing
Training
Transmission
User documentation
Verification

RECOMMENDED READINGS

Burch, J. G., and J. L. Sardinas, Jr.: *Computer Control and Audit Systems,* Wiley, New York, 1978. (A good text on the audit and control of computers.)

Caroll, J. M.: *Computer Security,* Security World, Los Angeles, 1977. (A good reference on developing greater security for computers and systems.)

Jancura, E.: *Audit and Control of Computer Systems,* Petrocelli/Charter, New York, 1974. (A comprehensive view of auditing for computer systems.)

McFarlan, F. W.: "Management Audit of the EDP Department," *Harvard Business Review,* vol. 51, no. 3, May–June 1973, pp. 131–142. (This article contains a number of ideas on the effective operation of computer departments.)

Mair, W. C., D. W. Wood, and K. W. Davis: *Computer Control & Audit,* Institute of Internal Auditors, Wellesley, Mass., 1978. (One of the most frequently cited references on audit and control for computer systems.)

Nolan, R. L.: "Plight of the EDP Manager," *Harvard Business Review,* vol. 51, no. 3, May–June 1973, pp. 143–152. (An excellent paper presenting the dilemma of the information services department manager.)

Wimbrow, J. H.: "A Large-Scale Interactive Administrative System," *IBM Systems Journal,* vol. 10, no. 4, 1973, pp. 260–280. (Examine this description of the advanced administrative system for the on-line logging and audit trails contained in the system.)

DISCUSSION QUESTIONS

1 What stages in the systems life cycle are most critical for users? For the information services department staff?
2 Why should users initiate a suggestion for an information system?
3 How can users monitor programming progress, since this is primarily a technical task and the responsibility of the information services department?
4 Describe the format and contents of good user documentation.
5 How could a system like AAS (in Chapter 15) be converted gradually?
6 Develop a conversion plan for the Hardserve example in Chapter 15.
7 How should users generate test data? What should the data include? Should users familiar with the system or those unexposed to it develop these data?
8 What is the purpose of the postimplementation audit? How should it be conducted, and what variables are important?
9 Why has the information services department manager been considered primarily a technician? What historical conditions account for this? Are there information services department managers who are in fact not suitable for their managerial posts? What should be done about this situation?
10 Steering committees are sometimes called integrating devices. What other integrators for user and information services departments can you suggest?
11 Why does the top-level manager (to whom the information services department reports) not need a detailed knowledge of technical factors?
12 Under what conditions is an audit for a computer center's efficiency a good idea?
13 Design an audit procedure for the effectiveness of computer operations.
14 How could audit requirements be taken into account during systems design?
15 What is the fundamental role of a C.P.A. in conducting an audit?
16 Can we expect to catch fraud with computer systems?

17 Have computer-based information systems made fraud easier? Do you think more or less can be embezzled from a computer system than from a manual system?

18 Is there any way to detect fraud if there is widespread collusion among information services department personnel and management?

19 Describe the reasons for the separation of functions among individuals processing information.

20 Of what use are control logs for input and output?

21 What kind of file backup procedures are needed in the average organization?

22 What good does a sequence check on a file do? Against what errors does it protect?

23 What is the purpose of an audit trail beyond control? How does it help users?

24 Why are manual procedures so critical to good control?

25 Can an information system be overcontrolled? What might happen under such conditions?

26 What input controls are available? Are most of these suited for both batch and on-line processing? What checks are possible with an on-line system?

27 What are the functions of different types of documentation? What problems are encountered if documentation is inadequate or nonexistent?

SOCIAL RESPONSIBILITIES
    Issues for Public Policy
    Alienation
    Some Suggested Solutions
THE FUTURE OF COMPUTER-BASED INFORMATION
SYSTEMS
    Technology
    Applications
KEY WORDS
RECOMMENDED READINGS
DISCUSSION QUESTIONS

Chapter 20

Societal Implications

CHAPTER ISSUES

- What are the significant societal problems created by computer-based information systems and do they apply to systems in this organization?
- What actions should management take to alleviate any potential systems problems at the societal level?

Computer-based information systems have an impact beyond any one organization. A user of systems may be affected by them directly as a member of an organization or indirectly as a citizen: computer-based systems can transcend the boundaries of an organization. In this chapter we discuss some of the implications of systems to become aware of the social responsibilities associated with information systems. At the end of the chapter we offer a forecast for information systems of the future.

SOCIAL RESPONSIBILITIES

Issues for Public Policy

A committee on computers and public policy of the Association for Computing Machinery (ACM) published a report defining a problem list of issues for computers and public policy. We highlight the various questions raised by this report (ACM, 1974) and update the report with points raised by a Congressional Office of Technology Assessment study (OTA, 1981).

Home Information Services   There are many opportunities for personal information processing services to be offered in the home, particularly through the use of two-way cable communications networks for television. One experimental system allows viewers to vote on a question through a two-way cable TV installation.

Other possibilities include the use of satellites to beam signals to a wide area of receivers. There are a number of current applications and experiments. One European service, which is being tested in the United States, makes a wide variety of information available on a television set equipped with a special decoding device. The viewer can access weather forecasts, plane, train, and bus schedules, up-to-the-minute news, etc.

The microprocessor has given birth to the personal computer; for a few hundred or thousand dollars, an individual can buy a small computer that has a surprisingly large set of features. National networks have been developed through which these personal computer users can access common programs and communicate with each other through electronic mail and bulletin boards. One firm has recently made the entire contents of a newspaper available to a computer user in the home or office; the paper can be displayed on the CRT at will.

Such capabilities raise a number of policy questions. Should an information utility offering this type of service be public, private, or private with some regulation? Are these uses of computers good from a broad public policy viewpoint? Is it possible that such systems would tend to create greater isolation among different groups in society? Another question concerns the basic economics of specific proposals. In addition to economics, we must consider the possibility that people are not really interested in many of the services that might be offered.

If such information and communicating capabilities are available, what will be their impact on mobility and personal habits? If these suggestions were ever implemented throughout the country, they might significantly reduce the number of occasions on which people leave their homes.

We have to be concerned about whether security and privacy can be provided effectively in such systems. Can the owner or operator of an information utility use the information for personal gain, such as conducting marketing research surveys?

Another policy question concerns a capability for a national referendum. Is it desirable to present issues in this manner and ask for public response? Will people become tired of this invasion of privacy and lose interest in the legislative process? It is also possible that such a service would be too expensive, thus disenfranchising certain groups who are unable to afford it. Such a proposal raises the specter of sabotage or of attempts to influence the outcome of elections illegally. How easy would it be to abuse the information available for the purposes of controlling the people?

Computers and Money   Electronic funds transfer systems have been studied extensively during the past decade and a number of systems have been proposed. To implement such a system, it would be necessary to rewrite many of the present laws concerning credit and money. However, we do not really know the present public attitude toward electronic funds transfer. Questions of privacy also are involved here; for example, information on checks could be potentially useful to different segments of society or such information could be used for surveillance purposes. The point-of-sale recorders in stores would make it possible to keep track of where a person is at the time of any transaction and thus keep a record of an individual's travels.

Computers and Elections   Computers have been used routinely to predict the outcome of elections and to tally votes. Some political candidates have used computers widely to custom-tailor campaigns to individual areas, ethnic groups, and even individuals. Are the sophisticated computer predictions actually discouraging people from voting since they "know the outcome" in advance?

Computers in Education   Computers and computer-aided instruction have not revolutionized education. Many of these systems have turned out to be more expensive than traditional methods and have had mixed results. Can these systems be used for something more than drill, and, if so, will they replace or supplement the teacher? Could the use of more computer-aided instruction decentralize the education process so the students can spend more time at home and less time in school?

Privacy   Certainly one of the most widely debated topics relating to society is the issue of an individual's right to privacy. Many bills and acts have been proposed to ensure the individual's privacy. At what point does the right to privacy come in conflict with other rights? Recent revelations about government agency data banks and misuse of information have also heightened concern over privacy. On the other hand, society certainly has the need and the right to have certain kinds of information that contributes to the general welfare. Demographic information and information on income levels are vitally important in establishing national policy. However, information on wages and financial condition is considered to be extremely sensitive by most individuals.

Certainly, current thinking is that individuals should have the right to ascertain whether information held about them is correct and to force the correction of errors. There is less agreement on the types of penalties that should be imposed for the misuse of private information maintained in some type of data bank. Other questions arise as to whether individuals should have the right to know who has requested information about them from a data bank. Some countries have become very concerned about this trend; for example, Sweden has enacted a comprehensive program to regulate the development of data banks.

A number of solutions have been proposed, and the federal government has passed legislation affecting only federal agencies. Suggestions have been made to extend the federal law to the private sector. As it stands now, the legislation requires a large amount of record keeping about the pattern of access to records that contain any personal information. There are fears that the proposals for the private sector may prove extremely costly for organizations. One important issue, then, is what should be the balance between the individual's rights and the burdens and costs of protection and record keeping?

Employment   Labor leaders have been extremely concerned about the possibility of wide-scale unemployment because of computers. The computer industry is now a very large component of the United States economy and it has created hundreds of thousands of jobs. Naturally, the implementation of some information systems has eliminated or modified jobs, although there are few statistics to indicate the overall impact on employment.

Clearly, there are implications from the implementation of information systems on the pace of technological change, job security, and the importance of retraining workers when jobs change. Has the opportunity to exercise individual initiative and has the interest of jobs been reduced by computers?

Productivity   On the positive side, computer-based systems can make a major contribution to productivity. If the estimates are correct that over half the U.S. working population is involved in activities dealing with information processing, then the computer will become the new productivity engine. The major form of capital investment for the office and knowledge worker is the computer. Estimates vary, but it is generally accepted that the average farm worker in the United States has about $70,000 of capital investment behind him or her. For the factory worker, the number is in the $25 to $30 thousand range; for the office worker it is more in the range of $2 to $3 thousand. Through a variety of information processing systems and office automation systems, computers can contribute to the productivity of a postindustrial, information-intensive economy.

Computers and Power   We have discussed the fact that computers can change power relationships within organizations; the same trend may occur in society as a whole. Is it possible that, through the acquisition of data stored in computer data banks, an organization such as a credit bureau might increase significantly the amount of power that it has over citizens? Is it true that a candidate for national office who cannot afford to use a computer may be at an insurmountable disadvantage? If there are gross inbalances in power, what can we do about it? How much responsibility does the producer of a tool have for its use?

The Technology Gap There is a serious question of whether or not computer and communications technology will accentuate the gulf that exists between the "haves" and the "have nots" both within society and among countries. Will those who are able to acquire computer systems or the knowledge of how to use them become the new elite? Will individuals who are not literate about computers find themselves confined to a second-class existence? It is unlikely that such extremes will evolve, but the likelihood is that significant segments of the population will become less able to deal with an economy that depends on computer-processed information.

Computer Knowledge There is a widespread lack of understanding in the world concerning the capabilities of computers. Some individuals believe that the computer can do almost anything. Once the author was asked if the only thing necessary to use a computer was simply to pick up a microphone and talk to the machine! Other individuals think the computer can be used only for performing simple, repetitive chores. What are the responsibilities of the society to help educate the population concerning the actual capabilities and use of computers?

Computers and Communications One major trend in computing is toward more telecommunications. For traditional information processing applications we see more on-line systems, distributed processing, and computer networks. The expansion of office automation will create a high demand for telecommunications facilities for sending messages, documents, and data over long distances. These trends raise major policy issues with respect to government regulation of the communications industry.

Early in the history of the computer and communications industries, the government posture was that computer firms could not offer common carrier services and that regulated common carriers could not offer data processing services. It now appears that regulated carriers may be able to offer computer services through separate, arms-length subsidiaries. The rationale behind this policy is that a monopoly carrier should not be able to use revenues from a regulated business to subsidize a nonregulated business. As more options have become available for communications, for example, the use of satellites instead of communications systems employing cables or microwave towers, the government has allowed a number of competitors to offer communications services in addition to the existing common carriers.

As a result of these developments the nature of the entire telecommunications industry is changing; more competitors and services are available. We expect these changes to continue and to create more issues for public policy.

A WELFARE SYSTEM

Many governmental welfare programs suffer delays in determining applicant eligibility for economic aid, and experience inconsistency in applying eligibility and benefit rules. A distributed computer system has been implemented in Wisconsin to help solve these problems and to save money for the state.

Local operators use on-line CRT terminals to enter applicant data; the system guides the terminal operator step-by-step through the data entry process. If the data passes the edit checks, and the host computer is currently available, a local computer transmits the application to the host. Should the host not be available, the local computer queues and stores the data that has passed the pre-edit test to be sent as soon as the host becomes available.

The host computer has many functions in the system. Applicant data from the local computer is posted to a daily activity base, which is used by the host to determine eligibility and benefits. The central computer has a case data base which stores updated records of 100,000 AFDC* medical assistance and food stamp cases. A case is a welfare unit which averages about three individuals per household.

The host computer first checks to determine whether the applicant is known to the system, and if he or she is currently receiving economic assistance. A complex formula is used by the system to determine aid benefits. However, this determination is completely objective. When the benefit determination is completed, the host transmits the findings back to the local computer where a sheet is printed for use by local administrators. In the evening the central computer goes off-line to process the day's activity data against the case data base to update these records.

In even the most populous counties a determination of eligibility is generally made the same day the application is entered. The system also assists local eligibility workers in conducting scheduled reviews of welfare cases.

*Aid for Dependent Children
Computer World, July 28, 1980.

Complexity and Integrity   Society in general is becoming more complex as are batch and on-line computer systems. What is the interaction between computers and complexity? Will computers create additional complexity or will they help us cope with the growing complexity inherent in a postindustrial, information-based economy? The answer to both questions is probably yes. We may be able to trade off some organizational and societal complexity for information systems, but these systems in turn are likely to be complex in their own right.

Consider the Connoisseur Foods system for supporting decisions in Chapter 18. Although a complex system technologically, it helped brand managers cope with the complexities of the marketplace. They seemed to understand the dynamics of the market better having used the powerful analytical tools provided by the decision support system. However, many of the managers still felt uncomfortable with the type of decision making represented by the computer system. Some of this unease was undoubtedly from a lack of understanding of the technology as a result of its complexity.

Reliability and Failure   In the last chapter we discussed some of the problems of control and system reliability. Computer-based systems are extremely complex. Although systems in the future are expected to feature more redundancy and lower failure rates, there will still be the possibility of a system failing. The results of such a systems failure range from inconvenience to catastrophe. There is a serious public concern in seeing that systems are designed and installed with adequate considerations of reliability and backup. For critical systems there should be backup capabilities. For example, critical on-board systems in airliners have long featured redundancy, that is, several separate and independent hydraulic systems. For the most part, the computer profession has not yet approached such levels of redundancy. Some systems have extensive hardware redundancy, but very few systems have been reported where the software is independently developed and executed on separate machines to provide reliability and backup. Obviously such an approach is costly, but for certain kinds of systems envisioned in the future, such as electronic funds transfer applications, it may become necessary.

More research is needed to conduct the kind of cost-benefit analysis needed to select the proper design for reliability. The computer profession in general does not have a well-developed procedure for the analysis of the risks of various types of system failures. Without this assessment capability, it is very difficult to determine what kind of steps need to be taken to achieve acceptable levels of reliability for any given system.

Security   Closely related to problems of privacy is the issue of system security. There are many possible threats to the security and integrity of a computer system, particularly on-line systems where there is widespread access by individuals outside the organization. Researchers in the field are working on methods of encrypting data so that they cannot be intercepted and decoded by an unfriendly user. Such concerns are very important given the existence of highly sensitive data in on-line data bases.

Liability   Computer systems are an important part of many business operations. A few companies have already gone into bankruptcy because of errors in processing, and others have turned profitable operations into losses. It is also possible, as one recent scandal has shown, to use a computer to help perpetrate widespread fraud.

There is no way to pinpoint responsibility when a computer system fails. We have stressed that systems design is a creative task; it is possible to have errors in logic and processing that are not caught until actual operations begin. Auditing firms are particularly concerned over the use of computers to process and maintain basic information on the operations of a firm. It is very difficult to audit computer-based systems and to be certain that controls are adequate.

Data Flows and Trade Barriers   In the last few years a number of important issues have arisen around the rapid growth of the information processing industry. A large, multinational firm might wish to install common systems in several subsidiaries located in different countries. At a minimum, the firm might want to have all its subsidiaries transmit data on a periodic basis to a central computer site for reporting purposes. A midwestern bank serves all its foreign subsidiaries through a data center located in Chicago; each day transactions are transmitted from Europe to Chicago for processing to generate reports that are transmitted back to the European offices.

For the multinational and for the bank above, laws in a number of companies are threatening this type of operation. Countries with the stated purpose of controlling and protecting the personal data of their citizens are passing laws to restrict the transmission of data across their borders. One country is already limiting the ability of a bank to transmit and process data outside the country. If each country passes different legislation, it will become almost impossible to transmit data freely.

Is privacy the only reason for these governmental concerns? Many computer professionals think that other motives may be more important. First, the United States exports a considerable volume of computers and information processing equipment; foreign regulations can act as nontariff trade barriers. Third-world countries see the regulations as a way to protect the development of infant industries and as a way to prevent the domination of their economies by multinationals. Some developing countries have instituted strict regulations virtually to the extent of prohibiting the importation of certain software products. These nations do not want to become dependent on the industrialized countries.

The United States must examine all the ramifications of proposed legislation and rules governing the use of information processing technology in foreign countries. The comparative advantage that this country enjoys in exporting technology and the fundamental ability of U.S. firms to use the technology to conduct their business are at stake. The problem affects all of us whether directly involved in the computer industry or not.

Computers and Underdeveloped Countries   Is it possible to use computers to help accelerate the development of preindustrialized countries? If so, how do we transfer the required technical expertise to these countries? It will be necessary to work with the leadership of such nations to develop priorities for applications and to train nationals to carry out the work.

Harassment   Too many times it appears we are being harassed by computers. Systems are designed to send automatically second, third, and even further overdue notices even when a customer has a legitimate complaint about a bill. Systems appear unresponsive to an individual's problems because of the need to process large volumes of information quickly. Some systems may be flexible, but require cumbersome manual procedures to update records and keep them accurate. If a clerk makes an error or omission, the computer will continue sending letters to the customer. In other situations, employees learn to rely on computer-based systems and do not provide customer service when a system is unavailable. One bank installed an on-line inquiry system for tellers cashing checks. The tellers were provided with the same hard-copy microfilm used before the on-line system for backup. However, when the new computer system was unavailable because of a malfunction, many tellers refused to cash checks and told customers to come back when the computer was working.

A Canadian survey found that 40 percent of the individuals returning questionnaires had at least one problem related to computer processing in the previous year (Stirling, 1979). Of those reporting errors, 81 percent were in billing and 8 percent in banking transactions. The largest number of errors were charges for nonexistent expenditures, inappropriate interest charges, and overcharges. Eight percent of the respondents who reported an error made no attempt to correct it, and 7 percent who tried to correct the error failed in their attempt. It took a reported average of 2.6 hours to correct an error, but 20 percent of the cases required 20 hours or more of effort to obtain satisfaction. These figures are probably good approximations for experiences in the U.S. as well; the picture they present is not one that inspires confidence in the way organizations respond to customer problems with computer-based systems.

Alienation

All these problems and frustrations create the most significant social issue: widespread alienation from information systems. If the population is alienated by stories of abuses and harassment, and if people deal with poorly designed systems, clumsy interfaces, and unresponsive information services departments, the future of computer-based information systems is dim. Alienation will undoubtedly result in a lack of cooperation with systems and the failure to develop new, potentially effective applications. How can we prevent widespread alienation?

Some Suggested Solutions

Education   Can we provide the general public with more education about computers and information systems? If individuals better understand computers and the problems with information systems, they are better able to cope with them. One reason for widespread participation in systems is to provide users with education and training about systems.

Education about computer-based information systems should be a part of every high-school curriculum, and certainly each college graduate should be exposed to computers. Continuing-education programs on computers should also be encouraged for citizens who want more general knowledge, as opposed to those who want to enter the computer profession. Companies can do their part by providing general education and training in the effective use of computer-based information systems.

Technical Safeguards   Some problems of the misuse of computer-based information systems are technical in nature. We should attempt to make systems as secure as possible to avoid penetration by the unscrupulous. Thorough testing is needed to prevent programs from accidentally disclosing sensitive data. There should be technical checks to procedures to prevent accidental entry by unauthorized individuals; for example, consider the AAS system in Chapter 17, which locks terminals if there are two attempts at unauthorized access.

A more difficult challenge is to design a system to be secure from skilled agents, or from individuals who commit fraud through the system. Protection here may take the form of monitoring to keep track of users (Hoffman, 1969), or special encoding algorithms, to maintain security. Unfortunately, there is almost always some weak point in system control; for example, one could bribe an employee of the computer center. For more details on technical safeguards, see Martin and Norman (1970).

Controls　Some of the controls discussed in the last chapter on auditing procedures can help to prevent certain social problems from occurring. Requiring several individuals to authorize changes in programming and files and checking input carefully help to prevent problems. Controls that require that all data be processed help to solve problems such as files not being updated to reflect payments. Controls are important to the extent that they ensure accurate processing and screen out requests where access is aimed at fraud and/or mischief.

Ombudsman　Because individuals often know so little about computer-based information systems, they are often baffled, frustrated, and alienated when confronted with computer-related problems. One device used in Europe since the eighteenth century is an independent ombudsman to whom citizens can turn for help. In the U.S. there are reporters for newspapers, radio, and television who check consumer complaints and play a role similar to that of the ombudsman.

The Association for Computing Machinery, a group of computer professionals, has an information ombudsman program for citizens. However, it is not clear that the average citizen knows of the association's existence or where to turn for help. The idea of an expert who can assist citizens with grievances about computer-based information systems is excellent, although in a society as large as that of the United States, it may not be feasible. One alternative approach would be for each organization using computer-based information systems to have its own ombudsman. In fact, two such individuals may be necessary; one for employees, similar to a user representative suggested earlier, and one for customers or the population at large.

Legislation　Another solution to some of the social issues, particularly privacy and abuse of power, is legislation. In 1973, Sweden enacted a law regulating personal data maintained about individuals. The act establishes a data inspection board that grants permission to keep a data bank of personal information. Sensitive data such as a criminal conviction can be maintained only by an agency charged by statute with keeping these records. Once permission is granted, the data inspection board issues regulations to prevent undue encroachment on privacy. Responsibility for maintaining the correct data lies with the organization maintaining the data bank, not the individual whose records are in the bank. Those organizations whose key records are in error must make corrections demanded by the individual. Damages are specified for violations of these regulations.

In 1974, a comprehensive Federal Privacy Act was passed requiring government agencies to keep elaborate records of the use of personal information. Records of inquiries by those whose records are kept must also be provided. To extend these requirements or a similar set to private-sector firms, some of the following are usually proposed in privacy legislation (Goldstein, 1975):

1   Notification of the subject about the existence of a record
2   Responding to inquiries on the contents of data and the use of records
3   Investigating complaints
4   Obtaining consent for each use of the data
5   Checking authorization for requests
6   Keeping a log of all accesses
7   Providing subject statements when disputed data are released
8   Sending corrections and/or subject statements to past recipients of information
9   Ensuring the accurate compilation of records
10   Providing additional data to give a fair picture
11   Providing a secure system

Although many of these requirements would prevent abuses of data, the regulations are potentially expensive to implement (Goldstein, 1975).

System Design   Although undoubtedly some of the above solutions will be implemented and will help solve some of the social problems with computer-based information systems, are they really sufficient? To a large extent, many social implications are determined in the process of designing a system. By asking the appropriate questions during the design process, we can assess some of the potential problems with the impact of the system on society. For example, we can ask the following about each application:

1   Is the application a potential threat to anyone's rights? What could go wrong? For example, do the files contain rumors, hearsay information, or unevaluated reports on individuals?
2   Is there a natural disincentive to use the system? For example, does it act to police workers who must contribute the data?
3   Is it difficult for someone to use the system? That is, could an individual fill out the forms, understand the input, enter data through a terminal, or do whatever is required?

4 How many ways could someone find to defraud the system?

5 If one wanted to misuse the data of the system, how could he or she evade the procedures that safeguard it? What could someone do to misuse the data?

6 Is the system sufficiently reliable?

The design team should encourage independent attempts to penetrate the system along the lines suggested above to verify the completeness and the viability of the design. A well-designed system is the best guarantee against harassment, abuse, privacy violations, and alienation.

THE FUTURE OF COMPUTER-BASED INFORMATION SYSTEMS

What are the likely future trends in information processing that will affect managers and users of systems?

Technology

As we discussed in Chapter 10, the cost of computing is decreasing at the same time that computer performance is increasing. Computers are becoming smaller and faster, and the amount of high-speed primary and secondary memory is increasing. We also expect to see greater communications within a given application and between computers. Further in the future voice input to systems should be widespread. Graphics output will expand, and there will be more use of nonkeyboard data entry for communicating with systems.

Unfortunately the advances in software are slower than in hardware. Software is labor-intensive, and increasing amounts of effort have to be devoted to the maintenance of existing systems rather than the development of new applications. The trend toward faster, cheaper computers means that we can afford to use hardware inefficiently to save human time and effort. As a result we expect to see more use of packages and turnkey systems; organizations will modify packages slightly or even change their own procedures to utilize software that is already available.

Very high level languages and applications generators will be used more when custom systems have to be developed. More firms will move to a data-base environment to increase the efficiency and reduce the time required to develop new systems. The use of a data-base system also facilitates changes to a system, reducing the impact of maintenance and enhancements on the programming staff.

At the same time, more responsibility for accessing data will be given to the user. Through high-level query languages and report generators, users will be expected to satisfy their own demands by retrieving data from the data base. Users will also have to spend more time evaluating packages and participating in the design of custom systems.

Applications

The changes in hardware and software technology have made it easier and more feasible to develop on-line systems with large data bases and this trend will continue. On-line access is justified today for ease of entry retrieval and the advantages of up-to-date information. With the availability of mini- and microcomputers with on-line capabilities and time-sharing operating systems to support on-line applications, even small organizations can enjoy the benefits of this mode of processing.

We expect to see continued emphasis on the automation of transactions-processing systems where savings can be demonstrated or where there will be better service. This automation will be particularly important in the service industry where added productivity is hard to achieve and salaries are a large component of costs: automated information processing is one way to improve productivity.

Computers are also expanding their role in the office. We expect this trend to continue, and it has significant implications for management. Many existing information processing systems do not affect managers directly; office automation will have a major impact on users if it succeeds. Now computers have the potential to alter dramatically the flow of communications in the organization; we hope they will assist the manager in carrying out his or her duties by facilitating the communications process.

Because of the expansion of office automation and telecommunications in general, we expect to see the convergence of computer-based processing, office support services, automated offices, and the communications function under one subunit of the organization. This administrative services function will take on increasing importance because information processing, communications, and control are vital to the success of any organization.

Considering the Gorry and Scott Morton framework in Chapter 3, we expect to see increasing emphasis on managerial control and strategic planning applications. Some of these systems will be quite similar to the decision support applications discussed in Chapter 18. Models and higher-level language combined with time sharing will help to make the development of these systems easier and less costly, though system benefits will be hard to evaluate quantitatively. These systems do provide information to support decision making.

We also expect more attempts to develop unstructured applications in general, though clearly this is a high-risk activity. Systems for unstructured problems will probably feature more man-machine interaction and will let computers and people perform the information processing activities to which they are each best suited.

In conclusion, the future of computing rests on the efforts of individuals. If the organization and its managers are able to manage information processing effectively, then it can make a major contribution to the organization and society. Users and managers must cooperate with the staff of the information services department to develop and operate systems. The greatest impediment to the further application of computers is not the technology; it is our ability to apply and manage the technology.

KEY WORDS

Alienation	Home services	Social impact
Control	Legislation	Structured
Decision support	Misuse of information	Transactions processing
Employment	Ombudsman	Unstructured
Fraud	Power	
Harassment	Privacy	

RECOMMENDED READINGS

ACM Committee on Computers and Public Policy: "A Problem List of Issues Concerning Computers and Public Policy," *Communications of the ACM,* vol. 17, no. 9, September 1974, pp. 494–503. (An article containing a detailed list of policy issues concerning the use of computers in society.)

Goldstein, R. G.: "The Costs of Privacy," *Datamation,* October 1975, pp. 65–69. (This article attempts to assess some of the possible costs of privacy legislation to organizations maintaining large data banks.)

Hoffman, L.: "Computers and Privacy: A Survey," *Computing Surveys,* vol. 1, no. 2, 1969, pp. 89–104. (An article discussing technological solutions to invasions of privacy and the misuse of computer systems.)

Martin, J., and R. Norman: *The Computerized Society,* Prentice-Hall, Englewood Cliffs, N.J., 1970. (This entire book is devoted to some of the problems and solutions to social issues with computers.)

Office of Technology Assessment, "The Impact of Emerging New Computer Technologies on Public Policy," 1981. (A comprehensive survey of information processing and the policy issues it raises.)

DISCUSSION QUESTIONS

1 Why is the use of a system the responsibility of the systems design team and the organization?
2 Is there any such thing as a right to privacy?
3 Does the presence of computer equipment make it easier to violate an individual's privacy?
4 Is fraud easier with a computer system than with its manual predecessor?
5 What would your response be to a proposal for a national data bank of information on citizens for purposes of social science research?
6 What kind of home computer applications would you envision that would use a television- or telephone-type terminal in private residences?
7 It has been suggested that an electronic funds transfer system could eliminate "float," that is, the use of money by a purchaser who has not yet been billed for goods or services. Would the elimination of float be desirable? How would an electronic funds transfer system affect the public?

8 In your opinion, would it be possible for a group to utilize computers to rig a nationwide election?

9 Why has computer-aided education been less successful than originally envisioned? What types of educational activities can best make use of this type of computer system? Where might computer-aided instruction be used in the design of information systems?

10 Do computers make it easier to violate an individual's right to privacy? What are the dangers of centralized government records on each citizen? What are the advantages?

11 Do employers have a responsibility to retrain workers who might be replaced by a computer system?

12 Why is the public so badly informed about the capabilities of computer systems? Do you feel most problems seen by the public are the responsibility of the computer, the manual procedures associated with the system, or the original systems design?

13 What can be done to reduce the possibility of a computer-based fraud that would cause the failure of a business?

14 How could computers and communications be used to solve some of the pressing problems of society, such as reducing the amount of energy consumed?

15 What priorities should be used by underdeveloped countries in trying to develop computer capabilities?

16 Is it possible that computer systems will become so pervasive that an elite of computer specialists will acquire dangerous amounts of power? What factors reduce the possibility of such a power shift?

17 What are the reasons for developing transaction-processing and operational-control information systems?

18 During what economic conditions would you expect the emphasis on transactions processing, as opposed to strategic planning systems, to be greatest?

19 Can strategic planning systems ever be shown to save money?

20 Why are unstructured systems risky? Under what conditions should they be developed?

21 How can an organization decide between centralized and distributed processing?

22 What management and control problems are created by distributed processing?

23 What advances in computer technology are needed to facilitate decision support systems and the development of unstructured applications?

24 Does the design of human-machine systems require a different approach than the design of transactions processing systems?

25 What is the role of the user in the development and operation of computer-based information systems?

Glossary

Access time   The time required to retrieve data from secondary storage and move it to primary memory.

Address   The location of a character or word in computer memory. Also the location of ,a track or record on a random-access device.

Address modification   The use of index registers or indirect addressing to change the address specified in an instruction.

Algorithm   An effective procedure for accomplishing some task. A set of repetitive steps that, when followed, terminates in a solution.

Application package   A program or series of programs intended for use by more than one group of users.

Application program   A set of instructions that embody the logic of an application. It should be distinguished from a supervisory program, which controls the operations of the computer.

Arithmetic/logic unit   The portion of the central processing unit that performs computations.

Arithmetic registers   CPU registers that actually perform arithmetic operations on data.

Assembler   A translator that accepts assembly language as input and produces machine language as output.

Assembly language   A language that closely resembles machine language, although mnemonics are substituted for numeric codes in instructions and addresses. Generally, one machine-language statement is produced for each assembly-language statement during the translation process.

Asynchronous operation   Any operation that occurs out of phase with other operations. For example, in certain CPU's an instruction look-ahead feature, which fetches instructions before they are needed, operates asynchronously with regular instruction processing.

Audio response   Vocal output produced by a special device that contains prerecorded syllables or synthesizes speech.

Audit trail   A means for tracing data on a source document to an output such as a report, or for tracing an output to its source.

Background program   In a multiprogramming environment, a program that can be executed whenever the computer is not executing a program having higher priority. Contrast with foreground program.

Backup   Alternative procedures available for temporary or emergency use in case of system failure.

Bandwidth   The range of frequencies for signaling; the difference between the highest and lowest frequencies available on a channel.

Batch computer system   A computer system characterized by indeterminant turnaround time for output. Data and programs are collected into groups, or batches, and processed sequentially.

Bench mark   An existing "typical" program that is executed on a machine to evaluate machine performance.

Bit   A binary digit, either zero or one; the smallest unit of information storage.

Blocking factor   The number of logical records per physical record on a storage device.

Bubble memory   Storage constructed of tiny cylinder-shaped magnetic domains in a thin, crystalline film.

Buffer   A storage area set aside, e.g., in primary memory for temporary storage of input or output data.

Byte   Generally, an eight-bit grouping that represents one character or two digits, and is operated on as a unit.

Cache   A small, high-speed computer memory.

Channel   A computer component with logic capabilities that transfers input and output from main memory to secondary memory or peripherals, and vice versa.

Check bit   A word or a fixed-length group of characters to detect errors.

Check digit   A number added to a key as a result of some calculation on the key. When data are entered, the computation is performed again and compared with the check digit to ensure correct entry.

Cognitive style   The orientation of an individual to approach decisions in a particular way, e.g., from an analytic or heuristic view.

Compatibility   The extent to which one can use programs, data, and/or devices of one computer system on another without modification.

Compiler   A translator for high-level languages. Generally, several machine-language statements are generated for each high-level language statement.

Computer-Aided Instruction (CAI)   The use of an interactive computer to provide or supplement instruction on some topic.

Concentrator   A device with some local storage that accepts data from several low-speed lines and transmits it over a single high-speed line to a computer installation.

Control of computer systems   Techniques to ensure the integrity and accuracy of computer processing.

Control unit   A device that serves as an interface between channel commands and secondary storage or peripheral devices.

Core storage   A medium of computer storage; for most second- and third-generation computers, the term is used synonymously with "primary memory."

CPU (central processing unit)   The part of the computer that controls the interpretation and execution of instructions, the arithmetic functions, and the I/O channels; the CPU contains a number of registers.

Critical path method (CPM)   A project scheduling and control technique focusing on the activities that contribute to the total elapsed time to completion of a project.

CRT (cathode-ray tube)   A terminal resembling an ordinary television set that can display a large number of characters rapidly; many also have graphics capabilities.

Cycle time   Either the time required to access information from primary storage and bring it to the CPU, or the time required to fetch, decode, and execute an instruction within the CPU itself.

Data base   A comprehensive, integrated collection of data organized to avoid duplication of data and permit easy retrieval of information.

Data-base management system   Software that organizes, catalogs, stores, retrieves, and maintains data in a data base.

Data structures   The relationship among different fields of data on secondary storage.

Debugging   The task of finding and correcting mistakes in a program.

Decision support system   A computer system that focuses on a specific decision area; usually it is interactive and its use is highly voluntary.

Demodulation   The process of decoding the information from a modulated carrier wave; the reverse of modulation.

Directory   A dictionary or an algorithm for obtaining the address of logical records on a storage device.

Disk   A random-access magnetic device used for secondary storage in computer systems.

Distributed processing   The dispersion and use of computers among geographically separated locations; the computers are connected by a communication network.

Documentation   Written descriptions about a system usually with instructions on how to operate the system.

EAM (electronic accounting machine) equipment   The first devices used to manipulate punched cards. These devices had wired logic plugboards but no stored programs.

Effective address   An address produced by indexing or indirect addressing; the address actually used to fetch the contents of the desired storage location.

Emulation   A technique that uses both hardware and software to execute programs written for one computer on another.

Encryption   The coding of a data stream to prevent unauthorized access to the data.

Enhancements   The process of making changes and improvements in operations programs.

Execute cycle   The CPU interprets an instruction and carries out the operation it signifies.

Executive program   The control program that schedules and manages the computer's resources.

Fetch cycle   Retrieving data or instructions from memory and moving them to the CPU.

Field   A group of bit positions within an instruction. A subdivision of a record, consisting of a group of characters.

Firmware   A combination of software and microprogrammed hardware used to control the operations of a particular computer.

Fixed-length record   A record in which the length and position of each field in the record is fixed for all processing.

Fixed point   The representation of numbers as integers with no digits to the right of the decimal point.

Floating point   The representation of a number as a quantity times a base raised to a power; for example, the number 472 as 4.72 times 10^2.

Foreground program   The highest priority program in a multiprogramming environment.

Graphics   A feature that permits the construction of lines and other geometric shapes on a CRT or plotting device.

Hardware   The physical components of the computer system.

Hash coding   The use of a mathematical calculation on a key to generate a storage address for a direct-access file.

Heuristic programs   Programs that are not guaranteed to arrive at an optimal or even acceptable solution; nonalgorithmic coding.

Higher-higher level languages   User-oriented languages that have single commands that would require many lines of code in a compiler level language.

High-level language   A language closer to English than assembler language that, when translated, produces many machine-language instructions for each input statement.

Identifiers   The mnemonic symbols assigned to variables in a program.

Index   Some type of table to relate keys to addresses on a direct-access file.

Index registers   Computer registers used to hold data for address modification, subroutine linkage, etc.

Indicator   A piece of data used as a summary statistic, e.g., the GNP as a measure of economic activity.

Indirect address   An address (formed by the contents of a particular storage location) that points to another storage location, which may contain either a direct address or another indirect address.

Information   The interpretation of data to provide meaning by an individual; tangible or intangible entity that reduces uncertainty about a state or event.

Inquiry-and-post system   A system in which inquiries are made, and data are entered and posted to a file for later updating.

Inquiry system   A computer system in which inquiries are processed, but updating is done in batch mode.

Intelligent devices   The addition of logic to a device or product, usually through the incorporation of a microcomputer. *

Interface   The boundary between two entities that interact.

Interpreter   A hardware or software program that examines an instruction and executes it.

Interrecord gap   The physical gap that separates records on a secondary storage device.

Interrupt   A signal that causes the current program in the CPU to terminate execution. Depending on the nature of the interrupt, a different program may be loaded and executed.

Instruction location counter   A register in the CPU that points to the next instruction to be fetched for execution.

Instruction register   A CPU register that holds the instruction, decodes it, and then executes it.

Instruction set   The repertoire of instructions available on a computer.

Iteration   A single cycle of a repetitively executed series of steps.

Kernel   A series of programmed instructions that are timed from published timings and used to evaluate the performance of a specific computer or system.

Key   The part of a record that is used for identification and reference; for example, an employee number.

Latency   The time required for a mechanical storage device to begin transmitting data after a request. For a movable-head disk drive, the seek time to position the read/write heads plus the rotational delay time.

List   A group of logically related items that are stored with pointers to the next item on the list. Also, a series of pointers running through a storage file.

Loader   A program that places a translated computer program in primary memory before its execution.

Logical record   A collection or an association of fields on the basis of their relationship to each other.

Machine language   The actual string of digits the computer hardware interprets and executes.

Magnetic core   A small piece of magnetic material that can be used to represent a zero and a one.

Magnetic tape unit   A sequential storage medium that operates like a home tape recorder.

Mainframe   A large general-purpose computer with high instruction-execution rates, extensive peripherals, and large primary and secondary storage.

Maintenance   The process of modifying operational programs to fix errors.

Managerial-control decisions   Decisions primarily concerned with personnel and financial control; concerned with ensuring that resources are applied to achieving the goals of the organization.

Megahertz   A measure of transmission frequencies; megacycle or millions of cycles per second.

MICR (magnetic-ink-character recognition)   The machine reading of characters printed in magnetic ink; primarily used in check processing.

Microcomputer   A very small computer with limited word size and processing speed but with extremely low cost; micros are used to provide logic to a number of devices such as "intelligent" terminals.

Microprogramming   The combining of series of elementary hardware functions (invisible to the programmer) to make a single instruction.

Minicomputer   A computer with smaller memory than a mainframe and fewer peripherals; often dedicated to a single application such as time sharing.

Mixes   The weighting of a representative series of instructions for the purpose of evaluating machine performance.

Mnemonics   The alphabetic symbols that are used in place of numeric codes to facilitate recognition and use of computer instructions.

Model   A tangible or intangible representation of some physical event, entity, or process.

MODEM (modulate and demodulate)   A device that converts digital computer signals into analog form and modulates them for transmission. Demodulation is the reverse process that occurs at the receiving point.

Modular programming   The subdivision of a system and programming requirements into small building blocks to reduce programming complexity and take advantage of common routines.

Modulation   The process of encoding digital information on an analog carrier wave.

Monitor   The control program that schedules and manages the computer's resources.

Multiplexor   A device that combines signals received from a series of low-speed lines and transmits them over a high-speed line. No storage is provided and signals must be demultiplexed on the receiving end.

Multiprocessing   A technique for executing two or more instruction sequences simultaneously in one computer system by the use of more than one processing unit.

Nonprogrammed decisions   Decisions that are unstructured and for which an algorithm for solution cannot be specified.

Multiprogramming   The presence of more than one semiactive program in primary memory at the same time; by switching from program to program, the computer appears to be executing all concurrently.

Object language   The output of a translator, usually machine language.

OCR (optical-character recognition)   The machine recognition of certain type styles and/or printed and handwritten characters.

Off-line   Any operation that is not directly controlled by the CPU.

On-line system   A system that has the capability to provide direct communication between the computer and remote terminals; files are updated immediately as data are entered.

On-line updating   Pertaining to a system in which the data entered are used to update the files immediately.

Operating system   A control program that schedules and manages the computer's resources.

Operational-control decisions   Day-to-day decisions concerned with the continuing operations of a company, such as inventory management.

Overlap   The ability of the CPU to continue processing while input/output operations are underway.

Package program   A program written for a user by multiple groups or organizations.

Packet switching   A message is broken into small units, or packets, for independent transmission over the different routes and then reassembled at its destination.

Paging   The segmentation of storage into small units that are moved automatically, by hardware or software, between primary and secondary storage to give the programmer a virtual memory that is larger than primary memory.

Parallel test   The test of a new system at the same time an existing system is in operation. The results from both systems are compared.

Parse   The separation of an input string of symbols into its basic components.

Peripherals   Input/output devices connected to a computer system.

Physical record   One or more logical records read into or written from main storage as a unit.

Pointer   Data that indicate the location of a variable or record of interest.

Power   The ability to influence behavior.

Primary memory   The memory in which programs and data are stored and from which they are generally executed; main storage.

Problem program   A user-written program that uses only nonprivileged instructions. It should be distinguished from a supervisory, or control, program, which may have privileged instructions.

Problem-oriented language   A language specifically designed for one particular type of problem, such as civil-engineering computations.

Procedural language   A language designed to facilitate the coding of algorithms to solve a problem, e.g., PL/1.

Program   A set of instructions that directs the computer to perform a specific series of operations.

Programmed decisions   Generally, decisions that can be made automatically by following certain rules and procedures.

Protection   The maintenance of the integrity of information in storage by preventing unauthorized changes.

Pure procedure   A program in which no part of the code modifies itself. Because a reentrant program is not modified during execution, it can be used by many users.

Random access   The ability to retrieve records without serially searching a file.

Reasonableness checks   General range checks on data to be sure that values are within reason.

Record, logical   A collection of related data items.

Record, physical   One or more logical records combined to increase input/output speeds and to reduce space required for storage.

Reentrant program   Synonymous with *pure procedure* (which see).

Refreshing   The regeneration of an image on a cathode-ray tube. Certain storage-tube devices eliminate the need for refreshing.

Registers   In general, storage locations capable of holding data. In particular, index registers that can be used to modify instruction addresses, or arithmetic registers that perform calculations.

Remote batch system   A type of computer system in which batch jobs are entered into the computer from a remote location, and the output returned to that location.

Report generator   A program that reads information concerning items to be retrieved from a file and their required output format, processes the file to retrieve the desired records, and produces a report according to the specified format.

Response time   The time from submission of a request until the computer responds.

Rotational delay   On rotating secondary memory devices, the time required for a particular record to arrive under the read/write head.

Satellite communications   The use of orbiting satellites to receive, amplify, and retransmit data to earth stations.

Scratch file   A file on which data are stored temporarily and which is not saved.

Secondary memory   Random-access devices such as disks and drums; programs are not executed from secondary memory devices but must be loaded into primary memory.

Seek time   For movable-arm disks, the time required for the reading mechanism to position itself over the track desired.

Semantics   The meaning of a programming language statement, or groups of statements.

Semiconductor   A small component having an electrical conductivity that lies between the high conductivity of metals and the low conductivity of insulators.

Semiconductor memory   Memory consisting of transistor devices; generally faster than core storage.

Serial access   A sequentially organized file from which information can be retrieved only by processing through the file in order.

Simulation   The modeling of some process that often involves the use of a computer program and probability distributions.

Simulator   A software program that is used to execute programs written for one machine on another.

Software   Instructions that control the physical hardware of the computer system.

Source language   The input language to a translation process.

Spooling   The simultaneous operation of peripherals using a disk to store output and/or input for multiple programs at the same time.

Storage address register   A register that holds the address of a memory location being referenced by the CPU or channel.

Storage buffer register   A register that holds data to be moved to or from main memory.

Strategic-planning decisions   Decisions of a long-term nature that deal with setting the strategy and objectives of the firm.

Structured programming   A modular approach to program development that emphasizes stepwise refinement, simple control structures, and short one-entry-point/one-exit-point modules.

Supervisor   The control program that schedules and manages the computer's resources.

Synchronous   Events that are coordinated and controlled.

Syntax   The physical structure of a programming language or statement.

Synthetic program   A specially constructed program (but one that is not used for production) that is used to measure and evaluate the performance of a computer system.

Systems programmer   A programmer who works on the software associated with an operating or supervisory system.

Telecommunications   The transmission of signals over a long distance, either through private or public carriers.

Terminals   A device used to communicate with a central computer from a remote location, usually featuring a typewriterlike keyboard.

Throughput   The amount of processing done by a system in a given unit of time.

Time sharing   An on-line system that provides computer services (including computational capacity) to a number of users at geographically dispersed terminals.

Top-down design   Planning a system by looking first at the major function, then at its subfunctions, and so on, until the scope and details of the system are fully understood.

Trade-off   The pros and cons of different alternatives; one often is forced to trade cost savings for performance.

Transaction   A basic communication with a computer system, e.g., the receipt of cash from a customer.

Transactions-processing systems   Basic systems that process routine transactions in an organization such as the entry of customer orders.

Translator   A program that accepts a source language and produces an output, or target, language that differs in some respects from the source language.

Turnaround document   A computer-prepared document, usually a punched card or printed report, that is sent to a customer. When returned to the sender, the document can frequently be reentered into the computer without modification.

Turnaround time   The length of time elapsing between the submission of input and the receipt of the output.

Turnkey system   A complete computer system with customer software installed for customer use.

Unbundling   The separation of prices for computer services and hardware.

Uncertainty   Lack of knowledge about a state or event.

Variable-length records   A record in which the number and/or length of fields may vary from other records accessed by the same program.

Virtual machine   The computer system as it appears to the user. The term was first used to refer to the extension of main memory to almost infinite capacity by the automatic use of secondary storage. The operating system moves portions of a program that are too large for primary memory to and from secondary memory automatically.

Virtual memory   Addressable space beyond physical memory that appears to the user as real; it is provided through a combination of hardware and software techniques.

Word   A combination of bits that form a logical storage grouping. A word may be further subdivided into bytes, which can be addressed by instructions.

Bibliography

Aaron, J. D.: "Information Systems in Perspective," *Computing Surveys,* Vol. 1, no. 4, December 1969, pp. 213–236.

ACM Committee on Computers and Public Policy: "A Problem List of Issues Concerning Computers and Public Policy," *Communications of the ACM,* vol. 17, no. 9, September 1974, pp. 495–503.

Ackoff, R. L.: "Management Misinformation Systems," *Management Science,* vol. 14, no. 4, December 1967, pp. B140–B156.

Alter, S.: *Decision Support Systems: Current Practice and Continuing Challenges,* Addison-Wesley, Reading, Mass., 1980.

Anthony, R.: *Planning and Control Systems: A Framework for Analysis,* Division of Research, Graduate School and Business Administration, Harvard University, Boston, 1965.

Baker, F. T.: "Chief Programmer Team Management of Production Programming," *IBM Systems Journal,* vol. 11, no. 1, 1972, pp. 63–73.

Bartee, T. C.: *Digital Computer Fundamentals,* 4th ed., McGraw-Hill, New York, 1977.

Bauer, R. (ed.): *Social Indicators,* MIT, Cambridge, Mass., 1967.

Bell, G., and A. Newell: *Computer Structures: Readings and Examples,* McGraw-Hill, New York, 1971.

Blumenthal, S.: *MIS—A Framework for Planning and Development,* Prentice-Hall, Englewood Cliffs, N.J., 1969.

Boulden, J., and E. Buffa: "Corporate Models: On-Line, Realtime Systems," *Harvard Business Review,* vol. 48, no. 4, July–August 1970, pp. 65–83.

Burch, J. G., and J. L. Sardinas, Jr.: *Computer Control and Audit Systems,* Wiley, New York, 1978.

Buffa, E. S.: *Modern Production Management,* Wiley, New York, 1961.

Canning, R.: "The Analysis of User Needs," *EDP Analyzer,* vol. 17, no. 1, January 1979.

Chapin, N.: "Flowcharting with the ANSI Standard: A Tutorial," *Computing Surveys,* vol. 2, no. 2, June 1970, pp. 89–110.

Cardenas, A., L. Presser, and M. Marin (eds.), *Computer Science,* Wiley-Interscience, New York, 1972.

Carroll, J. M.: *Computer Security,* Security World, Los Angeles, 1977.

Churchill, N. C., J. H. Kempster, and M. Uretsky: *Computer-Based Information Systems for Management: A Survey,* National Association of Accountants, New York, 1967.

Couger, J. D.: "Evaluation of Business Systems Analysis Techniques," *Computing Surveys,* vol. 6, no. 3, September 1973, pp. 167–198.

————, and R. W. Knapp: *Systems Analysis Techniques,* New York, Wiley, 1979.

Davis, G. B.: *Management Information Systems: Conceptual Foundations, Structure, and Development,* McGraw-Hill, New York, 1974.

Dearborn, O., and H. Simon: "Selective Perception: A Note on the Departmental Identification of Executives," *Sociometry,* vol. 21, 1958, pp. 140–144.

Dearden, S.: "MIS is a Mirage," *Harvard Business Review,* January–February 1972, pp. 90–99.

De Marco, T.: *Structured Analysis and System Specification,* Prentice-Hall, Englewood Cliffs, N.J., 1979.

Dodd, G.: "Elements of Data Management Systems," *Computing Surveys,* vol. 1, no. 7, June 1969, pp. 117–133.

Doktor, R., and W. Hamilton: "Cognitive Style and the Acceptance of Management Science Recommendations," *Management Science,* vol. 19, no. 8, April 1973, pp. 884–894.

Edelson, B. I.: "Global Satellite Communication," *Scientific American,* February 1977, vol. 22, no. 8, pp. 58–74.

Emery, J.: "Cost/Benefit Analysis of Information Systems," in J. D. Couger and R. W. Knapp (eds.), *Systems Analysis Techniques,* Wiley, New York, 1974.

Fitzgerald, J., and A. Fitzgerald: *Fundamentals of Systems Analysis,* Wiley, New York, 1973.

Gerrity, T. P.: "Design of Man-Machine Decision Systems: An Application to Portfolio Management," *Sloan Management Review,* vol. 12, no. 2, winter 1971, pp. 59–75.

Goldstein, R. G.: "The Costs of Privacy," *Datamation,* October 1975, pp. 65–69.

Gorry, G. A., and M. S. Scott Morton: "A Framework for Management Information Systems," *Sloan Management Review,* vol. 13, no. 1, 1971, pp. 55–70.

Gries, D.: *Compiler Construction for Digital Computers,* Wiley, New York, 1971.

Hamilton, W. F., and M. A. Moses: "A Computer-Based Corporate Planning System," *Management Science,* vol. 21, no. 2, October 1974, pp. 148–159.

Hellerman, H.: *Digital Computer System Principles,* McGraw-Hill, New York, 1967.

Hennings, C. R., D. J. Hickson, J. M. Pennings, and R. E. Schneck: "Structural Conditions of Intraorganizational Power," *Administrative Science Quarterly,* vol. 19, no. 1, March 1974, pp. 22–44.

Hickson, P. J., C. R. Hennings, C. A. Lee, R. R. Schneck, and J. M. Pennings: "Strategic Contingencies Theory of Interorganizational Power," *Administrative Science Quarterly,* vol. 16, no. 2, June 1971, pp. 216–219.

Hodges, D.: "Microelectronic Memories," *Scientific American,* vol. 237, no. 3, September, 1977, pp. 130–145.

Hoffman, L.: "Computers and Privacy: A Survey," *Computing Surveys,* vol. 1, no. 2, June 1969, pp. 85–104.

Husson, S.: *Microprogramming Principles and Practices,* Prentice-Hall, Englewood Cliffs, N.J., 1970.

IBM: *Improved Technology for Application Development—Management Overview,* IBM Corp., 1973.

IBM Systems Journal, vol. 4, nos. 2 and 3, 1965.

IBM Systems Journal, vol. 12, no. 2, 1973.

IBM Systems Journal, vol. 14, no. 1, 1975.

Jancura, E.: *Audit and Control of Computer Systems,* Petrocelli/Charter, New York, 1974.

Johnson, R., J. Vallee, and K. Spangler: *Electronic Meetings, Technological Alternatives and Social Choices,* Addison-Wesley, Reading, Mass., 1979.

Kanter, J.: *Management-Oriented Management Information Systems,* Prentice-Hall, Englewood Cliffs, N.J., 1972.

Keen, P. W., and M. S. Scott Morton: *Decision Support Systems: An Organizational Perspective,* Addison-Wesley, Reading, Mass., 1978.

Kelly, J. F.: *Computerized Management Information Systems,* Macmillan, New York, 1970.

Kendall, R. C.: "Management Perspectives on Programs, Programming and Productivity," Guide Meeting, 1977.

Leavitt, H. J., and T. L. Whisler: "Management in the 1980's," *Harvard Business Review,* November–December 1958, pp. 41–48.

Lientz, B. P., E. B. Swanson, and G. E. Tompkins: "Characteristics of Application Software Maintenance," *Communications of the ACM,* vol. 21, no. 6, June 19, 1978, pp. 466–471.

Lucas, H. C., Jr.: "An Empirical Study of a Framework for Information Systems," *Decision Sciences,* vol. 5, no. 1, January 1974*a,* pp. 102–113.

———, K. W. Clowes, and R. B. Kaplan: "Frameworks for Information Systems," *Infor,* vol. 12, no. 3, October 1974*b,* pp. 245–260.

———: *Toward Creative Systems Design,* Columbia, New York, 1974*c.*

———: *Why Information Systems Fail,* Columbia, New York, 1975.

———: *The Implementation of Computer-Based Models,* National Association of Accountants, New York, 1976*a.*

———: *The Analysis, Design, and Implementation of Information Systems,* McGraw-Hill, New York, 1976*b.*

———, and J. R. Moore, Jr.: "A Multiple-Criterion Scoring Approach to Information System Project Selection," *Infor,* vol. 14, no. 1, February 1976*c,* pp. 1–12.

———, and J. Turner: "A Top Management Policy for Information Systems," NYU Center for Research on Information Systems Working Paper," New York, 1981.

———: *Implementation: The Key to Successful Information Systems,* Columbia, New York, 1981.

McFarlan, F. W.: "Management Audit of the EDP Department," *Harvard Business Review,* vol. 51, no. 3, May–June, 1973, pp. 131–142.

Madnick, S., and J. Donovan: *Operating Systems,* McGraw-Hill, New York, 1974.

Mair, W. C., D. W. Wood, and K. W. Davis: *Computer Control & Audit,* Institute of Internal Auditors, Wellesley, Mass., 1978.

Martin, J.: *The Design of Real-Time Systems,* Prentice-Hall, Englewood Cliffs, N.J., 1967.

———: *Telecommunications and The Computer,* Prentice-Hall, Englewood Cliffs, N.J., 1969.

———, and P. Norman: *The Computerized Society,* Prentice-Hall, Englewood Cliffs, N.J., 1970.

Martin, W. A.: "Sorting," *Computing Surveys,* vol. 3, no. 4, December 1971, pp. 147–174.

Mason, R., and I. Mitroff: "A Program for Research in Management Information Systems," *Management Science,* vol. 19, no. 5, January 1973, pp. 475–487.

Masterman, J.: *The Double-Cross System,* Avon, New York, 1972.

Merten, A. G., and E. H. Sibley: "Implementation of a Generalized Data Base Management System Within an Organization," *Management Informatics,* vol. 2, no. 1, February 1973, pp. 21–31.

Mills, H. D.: "Chief Programmer Team's Principles and Procedures," IBM Federal System Division, Gaithersburg, Md., 1971.

Mintzberg, H.: *The Nature of Managerial Work,* Harper & Row, New York, 1973.

Montgomery, D., and G. Urban: *Management Science in Marketing,* Prentice-Hall, Englewood Cliffs, N.J., 1969.

———: "Marketing Decision Systems: An Emerging View," *Journal of Marketing Research,* vol. 7, May 1970, pp. 226–234.

Moore, J. R., Jr., and N. R. Baker: "Computational Analysis of Scoring Models for Rand D Project Selection," *Management Science,* vol. 16, no. 4, December 1969a, pp. B212–B232.

Moses, M.A., "Implementation of Analytical Planning Systems," *Management Science,* vol. 21, no. 10, June 1975, pp. 1133–1143.

Mumford, E., and O. Banks: *The Computer and The Clerk,* Routlege, London, 1967.

———, and T. B. Ward: *Computers: Planning for People,* B. T. Batsford, London, 1968.

Murdick, R. G., and J. E. Ross: *Information Systems for Modern Management,* 2d ed., Prentice-Hall, Englewood Cliffs, N.J., 1975.

Nie, N., C. Hull, J. Jenkins, K. Steinbrenner, and D. H. Bent: *Statistical Package for the Social Sciences,* 2d ed., McGraw-Hill, New York, 1975.

Nolan, R. L.: "Plight of the EDP Manager," *Harvard Business Review,* vol. 51, no. 3, May–June 1973, pp. 143–152.

Office of Technology Assessment, "The Impact of Emerging New Computer Technologies on Public Policy," 1981.

Olsen, R. A.: *Manufacturing Management: A Quantitative Approach,* International Textbook, Scranton, Pa., 1968.

Osborne, A.: *An Introduction to Microcomputers,* 2d ed., vol. 1, Osborne/McGraw-Hill, Berkeley, Calif., 1980.

Pounds, W. F.: "The Process of Problem Finding," *The Industrial Management Review,* vol. 11, no. 1, fall 1969, pp. 1–20.

Rosen, R.: "Contemporary Concepts of Microprogramming and Emulation," *Computing Surveys,* vol. 1, no. 4, December 1969, pp. 197–212.

Rothman, S., and C. Mosmann: *Computers and Society,* Science Research Associates, Chicago, 1972.

Sammet, J.: *Programming Languages: History and Fundamentals,* Prentice-Hall, Englewood Cliffs, N.J., 1969.

Senn, J.: *Information Systems in Management,* Wadsworth, Belmont, Calif., 1978.

Schultz, R., and D. Slevin: *Implementing Operations Research/Management Science,* American Elsevier, New York, 1975.

Scott Morton, M. S.: *Management Decision Systems,* Division of Research, Graduate School of Business Administration, Harvard University, 1971.

Simon, H.: *The Shape of Automation for Men and Management,* Harper & Row, New York, 1965.

Stirling, T. D.: "Consumer Difficulties with Computerized Transactions: An Empirical Investigation," *Communications of the ACM,* vol. 22, no. 5, May 1979, pp. 283–289.

Takeuchi, H., and A. H. Schmidt: "New Promise of Computer Graphics," *Harvard Business Review,* vol. 58, no. 1, January–February 1980, pp. 122–131.

Timmreck, E. M.: "Computer Selection Methodology," *Computing Surveys,* vol. 5, no. 4, December 1973, pp. 199–222.

Turn, R.: *Computers in the 1980s,* Columbia, New York, 1974.

Turner, J.: "Computers in Bank Clerical Functions: Implications for Productivity and the Quality of Working Life," unpublished doctoral dissertation, Columbia University, New York, 1980.

Walton, R. E., and J. M. Dutton: "The Management of Interdepartmental Conflict: A Model and Review," *Administrative Science Quarterly,* vol. 14, no. 1, March 1969, pp. 73–84.

Watson, R. W.: *Timesharing System Design Concepts,* McGraw-Hill, New York, 1970.

Weinberg, G. M.: *The Psychology of Computer Programming,* Van Nostrand, New York, 1972a.

Weinberg, G. M.: "The Psychology of Improved Programming Performance," *Datamation,* vol. 18, no. 11, November 1972b, pp. 82–85.

Weiss, E. (ed.): *Computer Usage Applications,* McGraw-Hill, New York, 1970.

Whisler, T. L.: *Information Technology and Organizational Change,* Wadsworth, Belmont, Calif., 1970.

Wimbrow, J. H.: "A Large-Scale Interactive Administrative System," *IBM Systems Journal,* vol. 10, no. 4, 1971, pp. 260–282.

Yourdon, E.: *Design of On-Line Computer Systems,* Prentice-Hall, Englewood Cliffs, N.J., 1972.

Index

Acceptance tests, 368
Access time, 129 – 131, 213 – 214
Acquisition of hardware, 272 – 281
Action programs in AAS, 434
Add time, 273
Address, 115 – 116
    indirect, 123
Address modification, 121 – 123
Aiken, Howard, 7
ALGOL, 173
Alienation of users, 487
Alphanumeric data, 115
Analytic models, 274
Anthony, Robert, 26 – 29
Anthony framework, 44 – 45
APL, 168
Applications briefs:
    agriculture information system, 390
    airline applications, 73
    blood management system, 303
    cattle feeding, 247
    computer-aided design, 133

Applications briefs (*Cont.*):
    cotton market, 378
    dairy farm system, 469
    department store system, 280
    DSS in a utility, 26
    fire research system, 393
    gourmet computers, 184
    grocery checkout system, 334
    health care application, 367
    hospital system, 49
    production control example, 191
    railroad applications, 31
    ranch systems, 93
    teleconferencing at ARCO, 260
    telephone sales system, 226
    warehouse control, 342
    weather models, 214
    welfare system, 484
Applications packages:
    criteria for selection of, 281 – 283
    general, 184 – 188
Applications programmers, 299

Applications selection, 95
Arithmetic/logic unit, 120 – 121
Arithmetic registers, 120 – 121
Artificial intelligence, 255 – 256
Assembler, 163 – 165
Assembly language, 163 – 165
Asynchronous data transmission, 144
Audio response, 136
Audit trail in AAS, 436 – 437
Auditing (*see* Information services
        department, audit of)

Backup, 349 – 350
    in file processing, 221 – 222
BASIC, 168
Batch computer system, 53 – 55
Batch monitor, 188 – 189
    functions of, 197 – 198
Bayesian information theory, 33 – 35
Benchmark programs, 275
Benefits of information systems,
        328 – 330
Binary number system, 114 – 115
Bits, 115 – 116
Blocking factor, 205 – 206
Bubble memory, 132 – 133
Buffer memory, 128 – 129
Byte, 115

Cache, 128 – 129
CAI (computer-aided instruction), 481
    in AAS, 432 – 433
Cathode-ray tube (*see* CRT)
CCD (charge-coupled devices), 245
Central processing unit (*see* CPU)
Centralization, 66
Channels, data, 110 – 111, 127 – 128
Character set, 115, 156 – 157
Charge-coupled devices (CCD), 245
Charging for services, 98 – 101
Check digits, 345 – 346
Chief programmer teams, 361
COBOL, 168 – 172
Cognitive style, 75 – 76, 389 – 391
Committees for information systems,
        101 – 102

Communications issues involving
        computers, 483
Communications subsystem, 143 – 146
Compatibility among computers,
        125 – 127
Compiler, 173 – 177
Computer-aided instruction (*see* CAI)
Computer output to microfilm, 136
Computer types, 138 – 140
Concentrator, 145
Conflict conditions, 70 – 73
Control of computer systems, 466 – 468
Control logs, 470
Control totals, 345 – 346
Control unit, 111
Controls to prevent computer errors,
        345 – 349
Conversion and installation of new
        systems, 368 – 369
Core memory, 116 – 117
Core storage, 116 – 117
Cost-benefit analysis, 327 – 330
CPU (central processing unit), 119 – 121
    cycles of, 121
Critical path method (CPM), 379 – 380
CRT (cathode-ray tube), 137 – 138
    graphics, 138
Cycle time, 273

Data analyzer, 186
Data-base management system,
        227 – 231, 253 – 254
    example, 230 – 231
Data channels, 110 – 111, 127 – 128
Data structures, 222 – 227
Debugging, 376
Decentralization, 66
Decision-making stages, 25 – 26
Decision style, 75 – 76, 389 – 391
Decision tables, 313 – 316
Decisions:
    on new applications, 334 – 337
    structured, 45
    unstructured, 45
Demodulation, 143
Design team, 306 – 307
Dictionaries, 215 – 216
Direct-access devices, 213 – 214

Direct-access files, 212–221
  chained, 217–219
  directories, 214–217
    dictionaries, 215–216
    hash coding, 216–217
    inverted, 218
    linked list, 217–219
    updating, 219–221
Directories (see Direct-access files,
  directories)
Disk devices, 213–214
Distributed processing, 146–147
Documentation of new systems,
  369–371
  design, 370
  operations, 371
  training, 370–371
  user, 371

EAM equipment, 7
Eckert, J. P., 7
Economic order quantity (EOQ),
  410–411
Effective address, 121–123
Egoless programming, 360
Elections, use of computers in, 481
Electronic funds transfer systems, 481
Electronic mail, 256–260
EMPIRE, 180–184
Employment, impact of computers on,
  482
Emulation, 127
Encryption, 470–471
Enhancements to existing systems, 299
ENIAC, 7
EOQ (economic order quantity),
  410–411
Error control, 345–349
Estimates for project scheduling,
  380–381
Execute cycle, 121
Executive program, 188–198

Feasibility study, 327–332
Fetch cycle, 121
Fields, 204–205
File design considerations, 231–233

Firmware, 127
Fixed-length record, 206
Flowcharting, 310–314
Foreign Corrupt Practices Act, 467
FORTRAN, 166–168
Frameworks for information systems:
  Anthony, 44–45
  Gorry-Scott Morton, 45–47
  Simon, 45
Future of computer-based systems,
  490–492

Generations of computers, 111–114
Gorry-Scott Morton framework, 45–47
Graphics, 248–250
  example, 447–449

Harassment from computer systems,
  486–487
Hardware, 105, 110
Hash coding, 216–217
Hash totals, 472
Hierarchical data structure, 222–224
Higher-level languages, 165–177
  (See also Special-purpose languages)
Hollerith, Herman, 7
Home information services, 260–261,
  480–481

Impact of information systems:
  on individuals, 69–73
  on organizations, 66–69
Implementation, 387–395
  research, 388–391
  strategy, 391–392
Inception of new system, 326–332
Index registers, 121–122
Indicators, 30–32
Indirect address, 123
Information:
  characteristics of, 27–30
  communications theory, 32–35
  definition of, 8, 19–20
  formal theories of, 32–35
  interpretation of, 20–24
  value of, 33–35

Information analysis, 317–319
Information services department:
  audit of, 469–475
    computer center procedures,
      469–470
    documentation, 474–475
    I/O procedures, 472–474
    processing, 471–472
    telecommunications, 470–471
  demands on, 298–299
  manager of, 461–462
  managerial influence on, 462–463
  plan, 89–94
  reporting relationship, 462
  resources of, 299
Information systems:
  basic functions, 8–10
  definition of, 8–9, 19–20
  types of, 54–55
    batch, 54
    command and control, 55
    inquiry and post, 54
    on-line updating, 54
    simple inquiry, 54
Instruction location counter, 120–121
Instruction look-ahead, 128
Instruction mixes, 273
Instruction register, 120–121
Instruction set, 123–124
Instructions, 123–124
Intelligent devices, 138
Interrecord gap, 205–206
Interrupt, 127–128, 183–184
Inverted directory, 218
I/O devices, 110–111, 133–138

Kernel program, 273
Key, 204–205
Key-to-address transformation, 214–215
Key-to-tape/disk, 135

Large-scale integration (LSI), 138
Legislation to relieve computer abuse,
  488–489
Liability for computer errors, 485
Life cycle (*see* Systems life cycle)
List, 222–223

Loader, 176–177
Logical record, 205
LSI (large-scale integration), 138

Machine language instructions, 123–124
  microprogram steps, 126
Magnetic core, 116–117
Magnetic-ink character recognition
  (MICR), 135
Magnetic tape, 131
Mainframe, 138–140
Maintenance programmers, 299
Managerial control decisions, 27
Manual procedures, 345
Mark sensing, 135
Mass storage devices, 131
Mauchly, John, 7
Memory:
  core, 116–117
  semiconductor, 117–119
Memory interleaving, 128
MICR (magnetic-ink character
  recognition), 135
Microcomputers, 139
Microprogramming, 125–127
Milestones, 378–379
Minicomputers, 138–141
Mintzberg, H., 41–43
Mixes, instruction, 273
Mnemonics, 163
Models, 22–24
Modem, 143–144
Modular programming, 361–363
Modularization, 361–363
Modulation, 143–144
Monitoring, 275–276
Multiplexing, 144
Multiprocessing, 189, 193–194
Multiprogramming, 193–194

Network data structure, 224
Networks, 147
Nonprogrammed decisions, 45

Object language, 176
OCR (optical character recognition), 135

Office automation, 256 – 260
Ombudsman for computer problems, 488
On-line systems, 54 – 55, 139, 142,
    189 – 191
  errors in, 346 – 349
On-line updating, 54 – 55
Operating systems, 188 – 198
Operations, 96 – 97
Optical cables, 247 – 248
Optical character recognition (OCR), 135
Optical memory, 245

Package programs, 184 – 188
  examples of, 185 – 188
Paging, 195 – 197
Paper tape, 134
Parallel test, 368
Parse, 175 – 176
Participation of users in design, 295 – 298,
    301 – 307, 391 – 392
PASCAL, 172 – 175
Patterns of processing, 146 – 150
Performance evaluation, 273 – 277
Physical record, 205 – 206
Planning for information systems, 89
  (See also Information services
      department, plan)
Planning language, 180 – 184
Plex structure, 224
PL/1, 172
Pointers, 217 – 221
Power:
  from computer systems, 482 – 483
  distribution of, 66 – 69
Precedence relationships in CPM, 379
Preliminary survey, 327 – 330
Primary memory, 114 – 119
  organization of, 115 – 116
  technology of, 116 – 119
Printers, 136
Privacy, 481 – 482
  legislation and, 488 – 489
Problem finding, 25
Problem solving, 25
Problem state, 193
Programmed decisions, 45
Programmer teams, 361
Programming goals, 360

Project management:
  uncertainties in, 376
  user responsibilities in, 376 – 377
Project scheduling, 377 – 381
  estimates, 380 – 381
Proposal evaluation for new computer
    systems, 279 – 281
Punched cards, 134 – 135

Query by Example, 254 – 255
Questionnaires and interviews, 307 – 310

Random access, 212 – 214
Reasonableness checks, 346, 471 – 472
Record:
  fixed-length, 206
  header and trailer, 207
  logical, 205 – 206
  physical, 205 – 206
  variable-length, 207
Record counts, 472
Refreshing in CRT terminals, 138
Registers:
  arithmetic, 120 – 121
  index, 121 – 122
  instruction, 120 – 121
Relational data structure, 224 – 227
Remote batch processing, 267 – 268
Report generator, 172
Rotational delay, 213
Reviews in programming, 364

SADT (Structured Analysis and
    Design Technique), 319 – 320
Satellite communications, 246 – 247
Secondary storage, 110, 129 – 133
Selection approach, 334 – 337
  committee, 332 – 334
  problems with, 333
  responsibilities of, 333
Semiconductor memory, 117 – 119
Semiconductors, 117 – 119
Sequential files, 208 – 212
  retrieval from, 212
  updating, 209 – 212
Service bureaus, 266 – 267

Services for computer processing, 266 – 267
Simon, H., 25, 45
Simon framework, 45
Simulation of computer systems, 274 – 275
Software, 156
Software vendors, 269 – 270
Sorting, 208 – 209
Source data collection, 343 – 344
Source language, 173
Special-purpose languages, 177 – 184
Spooling, 194
SPSS (Statistical Package for the Social Sciences), 177 – 179
Steering committee, 78, 93, 101
Storage address register, 120 – 121
Storage buffer register, 120 – 121
Strategic planning, 85 – 88
Structure of information services organization, 94 – 95
Structured Analysis and Design Technique (SADT), 319 – 320
Structured programming, 363 – 364
Supervisor of operating system, 188 – 198
Synchronous data transmission, 144
Syntax, 173 – 175
Synthetic modules, 275
System, definition of, 290 – 292
System specifications, 350
System use, 387 – 388
  mandatory, 388
  voluntary, 388
Systems analysis, 337 – 338
Systems analysts, 299, 301 – 302
Systems design, 338 – 341
  automatic approaches, 381
  considerations to ease user problems, 341 – 350
  creative, 392 – 398
  data collection for, 307 – 310
  examples of: AAS, 430 – 437
    Connoisseur Foods, 442 – 445
    Hardserve inventory system, 403 – 430
    portfolio management system, 445 – 449
    strategic planning system, 449 – 454
  input considerations, 343 – 345

Systems design (*Cont.*):
  output considerations, 341 – 343
  user-controlled, 393 – 394
  user-oriented, 301 – 307
Systems life cycle, 292 – 294
  resources, 293 – 294, 298 – 300
  responsibilities in, 295 – 298
Systems programmers, 299

Technical safeguards for computer misuse, 487 – 488
Telecommunications, 143 – 146
  analog, 143 – 144
  digital, 143 – 144
Terminals, 135, 137 – 138
Testing:
  of manual procedures, 366 – 368
  of programs, 365 – 366
    combined modules, 365 – 366
    units, 365
Throughput, 194
Time sharing, 191, 195 – 197, 267, 269
Top-down design, 291 – 292
Top-down programming, 364
Tradeoffs, 340 – 341
Training, 368
Transactions processing, 49
Translator, 163 – 165, 173 – 177
Trends:
  applications, 256 – 260
  communications, 245 – 248
  hardware, 241 – 243
  I/O devices, 248 – 251
  memory, 243 – 245
  software, 251 – 256
Turnaround document, 344
Turnkey systems, 269 – 270

Unbundling, 270
Uncertainty, 8, 20
Underdeveloped countries and computers, 486
Use of information systems (*see* System use)
User:
  attitudes, 74 – 76

User (*Cont.*):
  participation in design, 295 – 298,
    301 – 307, 391 – 392
  representatives, 79

Variable-length record, 207
Verification, 345
Very large-scale integration (VLSI),
  138 – 139, 242

Virtual machine, 195 – 197
Virtual memory, 129, 195 – 197
VLSI (very large-scale integration),
  138 – 139, 242
Voice input, 135, 250 – 251
Voice output, 136, 250 – 251

Word, 156 – 157